TODAY'S BEST
NONFICTION

TODAY'S BEST NONFICTION

THE READER'S DIGEST ASSOCIATION, INC.
PLEASANTVILLE, NEW YORK

The condensations in this volume have been created by The Reader's Digest
Association, Inc., by special arrangement with the publishers, authors,
or other holders of copyrights. Letters, documents, court
testimony, etc. may have been edited for space.

The original editions of the books in this volume
are published and copyrighted as follows:

A Reporter's Life, published at $26.95 by Alfred A. Knopf, Inc.
© 1996 by M and SA, Inc.

A Slender Thread, published at $24.00 by Random House, Inc.
© 1997 by Diane Ackerman

The Run of His Life: The People v. O. J. Simpson, published at $25.00 by Random House, Inc.
© 1996 by Jeffrey Toobin

Final Rounds: A Father, a Son, the Golf Journey of a Lifetime, published at $21.95 by
Bantam Books, a division of Bantam Doubleday Dell Publishing Group, Inc.
© 1996 by James Dodson

CONTENTS

7

A REPORTER'S LIFE

by Walter Cronkite

167

A SLENDER THREAD

by Diane Ackerman

289

THE RUN OF HIS LIFE

The People v. O. J. Simpson

by Jeffrey Toobin

459

FINAL ROUNDS

A Father, a Son, the Golf Journey of a Lifetime

by James Dodson

574

ABOUT THE AUTHORS

Walter Cronkite

A
REPORTER'S
LIFE

. . . I watched the gunships attacking suspected Vietcong concentrations. I flew into Hue, where marines were fighting house to house. I spent an evening at headquarters [and heard] the extent of the damage in casualties, materials, and morale.

There was no way that this war could be justified any longer. So I flew home and did a report on the Tet offensive. I ended, "It is increasingly clear to this reporter that the only rational way out will be to negotiate."

The President was actually stunned by the broadcast. "The President flipped off the set," Bill Moyers recalled, "and said, 'If I've lost Cronkite, I've lost Middle America.' "

—A Reporter's Life

Chapter 1—Youth

IF, AS they say, the threat of the hangman's noose has a powerful way of focusing one's attention, the same can be said of pregnancy.

This truth came to me on an early March day in 1948. Through the frost that fogged the windows of our Moscow apartment, I could just make out that snow had fallen during the night. It reflected a bright sun with blinding intensity. The grime of Moscow's air had not yet darkened its glory.

Betsy had awakened earlier and gone off to her job at the American embassy's United States Information Agency. Although my United Press salary wasn't exactly munificent, it wasn't the extra income that had attracted her to this job. It was more a matter of necessity to keep us fed.

The Soviet food ration was desperately small. Elsie, our elderly Finnish maid-cook, provided little supplementary food from the so-called free market. Goodness knows, the poor old lady tried. In winter she braved the deepest cold and the worst blizzards. Wrapped in her sweaters and coats and layers of shawls and wearing her rubber-soled felt boots, she shuffled out of the apartment before dawn every day.

She joined the other babushkas (grandmothers) in a half-dozen lines before she trudged home just before noon, bearing the day's treasures in her little crocheted shopping bag: perhaps one or two potatoes, probably spoiled; maybe a hunk of gristle that was meant to pass for edible meat; with real luck an egg or two.

Each month our government shipped into Moscow plentiful rations for the 110 or so Americans in the embassy. The only other Americans living in Moscow were the eight news correspondents and the wives of one or two of them, but the State Department, in its bureaucratic wisdom, determined that it would somehow violate its sacred rules to include enough rations to take care of us as well.

So Betsy worked at the embassy to get one American ration, which provided our daily minimum of calories, potassium, protein, and all those other things listed on cereal boxes.

On this snow-brightened morning she called from her office to find out if I was staying in our apartment-office for lunch.

"I'll be there, and I've got a surprise," she said.

She was pregnant with our first child. Her joyful announcement did indeed focus my attention. The peripatetic life of a foreign correspondent no longer seemed appropriate.

The first order of priority, however, was to have the baby, and there was no question in our minds that as much of Betsy's pregnancy as desirable would take place in the States, and that meant her hometown of Kansas City. Betsy cabled her parents that she was en route home, pregnant, but the brevity of the message, coupled with our well-known problems with Soviet censorship and the fact that we had not conceived in eight years of married life, convinced the good folks in Kansas City that this intelligence must be a code for some other dire incident. They were thus totally unprepared for her arrival home some weeks later.

By the time Betsy left Moscow, she was three months pregnant. It would be four months before I was able to join her in Kansas City. At last I raced halfway around the world to be present at the accouchement, only to find that my services were not really required.

Nancy arrived, as babies seem to have a penchant for doing, in the immediate predawn hours of November 8, 1948. Delivery, I thought, was notably easy—a very short wait in the "Fathers' Room," barely enough time to tamp down the tobacco in my pipe.

Betsy, too, had had a comparatively easy delivery, and the baby had the requisite number of limbs and digital extremities. I think the doctor even ventured an opinion that it was a beautiful baby, but he underestimated by at least half. She was gorgeous.

I left St. Luke's Hospital sometime in the early morning of that sparkling bright day. It was, to me, a day unlike any other. The revelation had come, the unveiling of the mystery of man's perpetual renewal. I looked back at the hospital and realized that there in swaddling clothes up on the fourth floor was the reason for Betsy's and my being on earth.

Such self-oriented, navel-examining profundities do not come often to me, but apparently such is the effect of the birth of one's first child. As a matter of fact, I wondered that morning whether similar thoughts had occupied my father upon my arrival at Dr. Grey's Lying-In Hospital in St. Joseph, Missouri, thirty-two years before. What, I wondered, was in the mind of that rather handsome young dentist who crunched through the fallen acorns to Dr. Grey's modest two-story clapboard medical establishment?

As he entered, a bell sedately tinkled notice of his arrival, and he announced his intentions to the nurse.

"I'd like to see Mrs. Cronkite."

"Of course, Doctor. And your little boy is adorable."

As my father greeted my mother on that auspicious day just a year after their marriage, he must have remarked upon her appearance. With her light brown, curly hair, her hazel eyes, and a beguiling smile, she was indeed beautiful.

We might also assume that as my father gazed down at his newborn son, he stroked his blond mustache. Neatly trimmed, it didn't require stroking to put it in order, but he did that all his life when he was admiring something—a piece of art, a passage of poetry, or a set of teeth he'd just finished fitting. He'd stroke first the right side of his mustache three times, then the left side, and at the end of the third stroke on the left, his finger would pause at the corner of his mouth and stay there for another thoughtful minute or two.

Twenty years later I would grow a mustache just like that. The purpose: to look older. Long after it had outgrown its usefulness, fifty-five years later, I would still have it.

It is unlikely that my parents pictured me with a mustache at that exultant moment at Dr. Grey's. Much more likely they were thinking of the immediate bliss ahead as, now a threesome, they began a new life together. But world events weren't going to let them enjoy that life very long.

On baby Cronkite's third day Dr. Cronkite stopped at the fire station on Frederick Boulevard and identified himself to the polling clerks to pick up his ballot. It took him only a moment to put an *x* in the box next to the name of Woodrow Wilson. It may have been the first Democratic vote ever cast by a Cronkite, but the young dentist liked Wilson's pledge to "keep us out of war."

That day's St. Joseph *Gazette* was still on the stoop of their bungalow when Dad got home. Its front page reported the frightful slaughter on the western front in the Battle of the Somme. There were alarmists who thought this Great War in France might suck the United States into its terrible maw, and there were powerful voices in the heavily German Middle West warning against American involvement. In the ethnic passions of the moment, there was the potential for a split in the household of young Dr. Cronkite.

The Cronkites were of pioneer Dutch stock. Old Hercks Seiboutzen Krankheidt, in fact, was one of the New Amsterdam colony's first bridegrooms, long before New Amsterdam became New York. He married Wyntje Theunis on November 16, 1642.

Mother's grandparents on both sides had come from Bavaria in the great German immigration of the mid-nineteenth century. Grosspapa Fritsche had the first hotel in Leavenworth, Kansas; Grosspapa Renz believed that his cigar factory there was the first west of the Mississippi, and it might have been.

This World War I threat that inherited nationalistic loyalties might impinge on Cronkite family tranquillity never would materialize. It was the greater cataclysm that shattered the bliss of the Cronkite household. Just five months after his "no war" election Woodrow Wilson took America into the conflict, and young Dr. Cronkite was among the first to march off to training camp. Mother, with baby at breast, trailed along and took up residence in Sapulpa, Oklahoma, until the 36th Division shipped out to France, with one young lieutenant as its dental surgeon and another commanding an artillery battery. The other fellow's name was Harry Truman.

To his credit Dad never claimed a close battlefield relationship with the thirty-third President of the United States, although, with a modesty probably meant to be becoming, he acknowledged having known the chap. Years later Truman, with probably more kindliness than honesty, acknowledged that he had known Dad.

No suggestion should be made that history, so early in life, was brushing my cheek. But who is to say that this coincidence didn't leave some sort of impression that inspired a future passion for current events, history in the making, the stuff of journalism?

I THINK I was seven when I got my first job in what later would become known as the media. I became a salesman of *Liberty*, a late coming rival of *The Saturday Evening Post* in the weekly magazine field. It sold for a nickel. I got to keep a penny from each sale—but even more important, for every five copies sold, I got a green coupon, and with enough coupons I could get a pony. My mother wasn't too enthusiastic about my going out alone around our Kansas City neighborhood with my *Liberty* sack over my shoulder, but I assume she thought that there were some lessons in self-reliance here—and besides, there was no hope that I ever would amass enough coupons for a pony to appear at our door.

Later, at the age of nine, I went into the newspaper business. I took the streetcar down to the Kansas City *Star* every Saturday night and, carrying as many papers as I could, caught the streetcar back to the end of the line and peddled my papers there. I could carry about ten Sunday papers, and I netted, after streetcar fares, ten cents. But it was a beginning.

There were other entrepreneurial excursions in my early life, although the earliest ones had a certain nepotistic coloring. By the mid-'20s Grandfather Fritsche had a drugstore on what was known in Kansas City as Hospital Hill. There were two hospitals above the Union Station and the railway freight yards—the city's big General Hospital and Research Hospital, a fine private hospital. The sprawling two-story plant of the Kansas City *Journal-Post* was also up

there. A sweeping lawn descended from the hospitals and surrounded the newspaper. From the hill I could watch through its
windows with rapture as the big presses rolled.

When World Series time came, the *Journal-Post* lawn was packed
with baseball fans. In their straw boaters, their ties undone, and
jackets hung over their shoulders, they came trooping up the hill,
refugees from whatever commerce they were supposed to be pur-
suing. Public-school truants augmented their ranks.

The attraction was a great display that covered the side of the
building. On it was depicted a baseball diamond. Along the base
paths and in the field appropriately placed lightbulbs could be ac-
tivated to give a graphic picture of each play of the game. Inside
the newspaper plant a recruit from the sports department translated the telegraphed play-by-play for the electrical circuitry. And
mingling among the assorted multitude was me—a sweating
young lad in knickers, hawking soda pop from a galvanized pail
sloshing with water and the remnants of ice that once had cooled
it. The pail was heavy, its handle cut my hands, and each trip back
and forth along the two blocks to Fritsche's Holmes Street Phar-
macy was roughly equivalent to Hannibal's trip across the Alps.
The money was much better, however, than the *Liberty* route.

When Graham McNamee took to the microphone at Forbes
Field, Pittsburgh, on October 7, 1925, to broadcast by radio the
meeting of the Pittsburgh Pirates and the Washington Senators for
the baseball championship, the *Journal-Post* World Series Score-
board was doomed. Barely a decade later that soda pop kid would
himself be broadcasting sports from a Kansas City radio station.

MY FOLKS were doting parents with their only child, but they
were typical of that live-it-up postwar generation. They doted, but
they did drink and they did party. Our house seemed something of
a hangout for their crowd, which, I suspect, enjoyed their hospitality and a frequent command performance by a towheaded tyke
in pajamas being ever so cute as he directed the orchestra music
emerging from the old console stand-up Victrola.

The happy years for them ended too early, when alcohol got the better of Dad. The dark days began after we moved to Houston, when I was ten. Dad never failed to appear at his office on time, and he always completed a long day's work, but before Mother picked him up in the car, he had begun to secretly tipple. He became a solitary drinker and withdrew from social associations.

It was strange. He maintained an appearance of total sobriety. Only his conversation, fed by a runaway imagination, gave away his drunkenness. There were tough nights at the dinner table, some of which live in my memory.

Lord Halifax, the British foreign secretary, was visiting Houston on one occasion, and at the table that night my father suddenly put down his knife and fork.

"Helen," he said, "how long has Lord Halifax been in town?"

"I don't know, Walter," she replied as both of us held our breaths for whatever diatribe this was the prelude to.

"He's been here two days, Helen. Have you done anything? Have you invited him to dinner?"

Well, while we weren't exactly lower class, we certainly weren't in the social circle of Lord Halifax's hosts. But Dad's tongue-lashing of Mother went on and on, with a long dissertation on her failure to promote the family socially—a matter that I feel confident never crossed his mind in his sober hours.

They divorced the year I went away to university. Dad had a very tough time, but he found a fine woman who straightened him out in his later years. He was sober for the last decade of his life, and we established a loving relationship. Silently but clearly we told each other how much we regretted the years of lost companionship that alcohol had denied us.

Mother soon married an old beau, but it didn't last. She enjoyed an active social life in Washington, D.C., until her death at a hundred and two. From her young days as the belle of the ball at the U.S. Army's Fort Leavenworth Staff and Command School, she had many friends living in the Washington area—mostly retired generals. With her almost perpetual youth and vitality, her only complaint was that her contemporaries were "so old."

"Why, Walter," she told me on one occasion, "General Gempel

took me to the theater the other night, and I had to slap his face."

"Gosh, Mom, General Gempel made a pass at you?"

"No, no, Walter. I thought he was dead!"

We danced at her hundredth birthday party, but when I took her back to her table, she was a little breathless and said, "Walter, I think I need my medicine."

Alarmed, I scurried for her nurse sitting outside. The nurse rushed to her side, and it took me a minute longer to get back through the crowd. Mother was at the table, glaring at a pill in her hand.

"Walter," she greeted me, "who said I needed that?"

"You did, Mother. You said you needed your medicine."

And she replied, "I meant my martini!"

OUR first week in Houston I discovered the world of racial discrimination. I am sure it existed in Kansas City as well—but there we saw few blacks, and they seemed to move more freely in our white society. The discovery, then, came with brutal force.

Dad had been lured to Houston to teach at the dental college and share an office with a wealthy dentist, a leader of the community. I shall call him Dr. Smith. We had been in Houston only a few days when we were invited to Dr. Smith's for dinner. He lived in River Oaks, Houston's first exclusive residential development. After dinner we retired to the front porch for what to a ten-year-old was a welcome relief—ice cream and cake. Home freezers were still a few years away, and ice cream was ordered from the drugstore for immediate consumption.

It was pleasant out there on Dr. Smith's wide veranda, rocking gently in the wicker chairs, the air heavy with the aroma of fresh-cut grass and early spring flowers. Then the pop, pop of a motorcycle broke the calm of the deserted lane. The black delivery boy shone his flashlight toward the sides of the house. Not finding an obvious path to the kitchen door and seeing us on the porch, he came up the walk from the street.

Dr. Smith stopped his monologue about the wonders of Houston. He stopped rocking too. With each step the delivery boy took

Above: I arrived at Dr. Grey's Lying-In Hospital in St. Joseph, Missouri, in 1916. Left: Dad shipped out to France in World War I as a dental surgeon. Below: At fourteen, I'm sitting between Grandmother and Grandfather Fritsche. Mother and Dad are standing.

Galveston, Texas
September 27 – 1930

up the walk, he leaned an inch farther forward in his chair. Now the tension was palpable. If this scene was being played in a film drama today, we would go to slow motion: The delivery boy reaches the first porch step—holding out the brown sack and its carton of ice cream. Dr. Smith charges out of his chair, a huge fist extended before him like a battering ram. The fist meets the boy's face, square at the tip of his nose. The boy goes flying backward to the lawn. The bag tumbles to the steps. And Dr. Smith shouts, "That'll teach you, nigger, to put your foot on a white man's front porch!"

Never before or after did I see my father in such a seething rage. As the bloodied delivery boy scrambled back to his motorcycle, Dad said, "Helen, Walter, we're going now," and he escorted us down the front steps, followed by Dr. Smith's mystified entreaties.

Dad ignored Dr. Smith's offer of a ride. We walked. And we walked. We walked in the dark of this strange town until we came upon a busy street and a passing car that stopped for Dad's hail.

I did not fully understand then the import of the offense or of Dad's courageous response to it. Although fully dependent upon Dr. Smith to launch a new practice, he broke off the relationship and struck out on his own. I couldn't have had a more searing example of racial injustice than this, my first brush with it.

The culture shock for us middle westerners newly arrived in the South was augmented my first day in the fifth grade at Woodrow Wilson Elementary School. In Kansas City, aside from my propensity in the first weeks of first grade to slip away and go home, I had had a spotless record for conning my teachers into believing that I was a perfect angel. Thus when I raised my hand and answered my first question in Houston—something as simple as two times two—I was more than startled to hear Miss Jung say, "That is not the answer. What is the answer?"

I was certain I was right. "Four," I repeated.

"Come stand here in the front of the class until you think of the answer," Miss Jung hissed. There I was, facing snickering classmates I hadn't even met yet, trying to will away the welling tears.

I dared not even look at Miss Jung, although in an hour her features had been fixed in my memory for a lifetime. Medium height, reddish brown hair worn in a boyish bob, and teeth scarred by drastic periodontal surgery. At last the bell rang for recess. And Miss Jung said in a tone as unkindly as only she could muster, "Now then, have you thought of the answer?" When I confessed that I had not, she enlightened me.

"The answer is, 'Four, ma'am.' "

That night Dad's indignation burned furiously again. "You may say, 'Yes, Miss Jung' and 'No, Miss Jung,' but you won't say, 'ma'am.' You go back and tell her that no son of mine will yield to this sectional ignorance."

That was easy for him to say. It was more difficult for me, and I was sent home at recess. Dad complained to the school board, and the case was compromised in his favor—but it was fortunate I had only two more months to endure the wrath of Miss Jung, who probably thought she was doing her part to maintain a fading southern gentility.

Or perhaps she just hated Yankees.

I was learning early the ways of the South, although they probably were different from those of the North only in their ingenuousness. My lessons on racial discrimination had a lifelong impact, but at the time, of course, they were only incidental to the process of growing up in the South.

The usual boyhood–early teen activities kept me busy: the Boy Scouts and DeMolay (the junior Masonic order), roller hockey and bicycle polo, tennis and golf, and swimming excursions to the beaches at Galveston. My constructive hobbies included building a telegraph system connecting friends' houses around the neighborhood. We were getting pretty good at Morse code when it all ended abruptly. The telephone company took what we considered to be unnecessary umbrage at our use of their poles to string our wires.

There was something I learned about myself in those years, but the lesson didn't sink in until later: I have an aversion to the slightest hint of regimentation, although I carry an antigen of distaste for challenging authority or conspicuous nonconformity.

The first trait was evident when I resigned within days of joining a high school ROTC unit, and later, although perhaps subconsciously, when I steadfastly marched north while the rest of the fellows reversed smartly and marched south, thus costing our De-Molay drill team a state championship.

On the other hand, I was a promising member of the track squad, where individual effort was more important than team co-ordination. I've often wondered since if it isn't this burning neces-sity for independence that leads a lot of people into journalism, where regimentation and conformity are dirty words. Although the formal educational process was not my forte, I was a voracious reader. My mother sold *The World Book Encyclopedia,* and as a small child, I spent hours poring through it. I was always curious, seek-ing new information, but I found most classroom routine and homework boring. Since I wasn't exactly a dunce, I blame unin-spired teachers for that.

Most depressing was the way history was taught. I was not lucky enough in either high school or college to have a teacher who seemed able to portray the conflict of fascinating personalities that underlies nearly all the critical moments of human experience. Re-ducing this great drama to the rote of names, dates, and places ought to be treated as a punishable crime. History must share with reading, writing, and arithmetic first rank as the most important subjects in the curriculum. Understanding the issues on which cit-izens of a republic are expected to vote is impossible without an understanding of the past.

And another thing—geography! Surely this knowledge is fun-damental to understanding our place on this planet, philosophi-cally as well as physically. When I travel, I am desperately unhappy if I can't refer almost constantly to a map, and I've always prided myself on some innate ability to sort out directions, a sort of built-in gyroscope.

This is not a trait of my wife's. In the early years after World War II our first two transatlantic flights took us over the northern route, with a refueling stop at Shannon, Ireland. On our third trip our flight followed the southern route and the refueling stop was in the Azores. We were chased out of the plane at first light and herded across the tarmac toward a white building with a green roof where we were expected to have coffee and buy souvenirs. It was just like the Shannon experience—the same beastly time of day, the same building, even the same fresh breeze from a nearby ocean.

"Where are we?" asked Betsy.

"The Azores."

"Who owns the Azores?"

"Portugal."

"Golly," she commented, "I remember when the Irish had it and called it Shannon."

Shortly after John Glenn made America's first orbital space-flight, I made a trip to our missile tracking stations all the way out on Ascension Island, that little pimple of volcanic rock in the middle of the South Atlantic, next to St. Helena, where Napoleon was exiled.

I was traveling so extensively in those days that Betsy barely listened as I described my destination. With her attention focused on bringing up three children, the question uppermost in her mind was how long I would be gone. So perhaps it did come as something of a surprise when our executive producer at CBS called her to say, "Betsy, Walter is in Ascension and he is all right."

"That's wonderful," she replied. "How many times has he been around?" Geography lessons might not have helped in that case.

LIFE is affected by many circumstances, some beneficial, some considerably less so. I am inclined to think in these terms when I think of meeting Fred Birney, a rather slight man who, despite his glasses, always wore a frown, as if he were looking for something beyond the range of his sight. He was an inspired teacher, who directed the course of my life. He wasn't even a professional teacher, but he had the gift.

Fred Birney was a newspaperman who thought that high schools ought to have courses in journalism. As an unpaid volunteer, he spent a couple of days each week circulating among Houston's five high schools preaching the fundamentals of a craft he loved.

His arrival at San Jacinto High School was timed as if decreed in heaven. That same year, suffering disabling shinsplints that kept me off the track team, I had wangled the job of sports editor of the *Campus Cub*, our semioccasional school paper. I was a sitting duck for Fred Birney, missionary from the fourth estate. I was enthralled as this wiry bundle of energy sat on the edge of the classroom desk spinning tales from the world of print. I devoured not only every book he assigned but every one on journalism that I could find in the library. This turned out to stand me in good stead.

That year he entered me in the newswriting competition of the Texas Interscholastic Press Association. We finalists sat at typewriters as a set of facts was printed on the blackboard. From them we were to write our one-thousand-word stories. The facts that were presented were from the notorious Leopold-Loeb murder case, in which two brilliant young scions of Chicago's wealthiest, most socially prominent families kidnapped and murdered fourteen-year-old Bobby Franks, another boy from their set.

The Chicago *Daily News* report on the case had become an entry in the 1924 edition of an annual compilation of the year's best news stories. Purely by happenstance I had just read that very story the night before. My competition didn't have a chance as I loaded my entry with descriptive matter that must have amazed the judges. Always a fast typist, I ripped the last page out of my machine and delivered the completed story to the front of the room while the others were struggling with their leads. I won.

We were a small group, we student journalists, and maybe that was the secret of Birney's success. He led us through our copy, showing us how to tighten here, explain more here, use adjectives and adverbs with caution lest they imply editorial opinion. He suggested questions we might have asked our interview subjects, noted facts we might have developed to improve our report. And every criticism, every suggestion, made clear that there was a sacred covenant between newspaper people and their readers. We journalists had to be right and we had to be fair.

Birney encouraged us to seek summer jobs at the local newspapers, of which Houston had three at the time. I was lucky enough to get on as a copyboy at the morning Houston *Post*. Actually, I was allowed to be more of a cub reporter than a copyboy. They let me cover luncheon clubs and civic affairs for which they could not spare, or which did not warrant sending, a staff reporter.

The luncheons were the only payment they gave me, but I required nothing more. The occasional paragraphs that I got in the paper were worth more than any gold. Just the chance to hang around the newsroom was payment enough.

I suppose that those dedicated to most crafts take pleasure in the sights and sounds and smells peculiar to them, but I can't imagine any being as exciting as the heavy odor of printer's ink and pulp paper and melting lead, the unique clanking of the old Linotype machines, and the building-shaking rumble of the big presses.

Of course, most of that is gone now. Photocopying has done away with the Linotypes, and there isn't much rumble to offset printing. The newsroom used to be a wonderfully noisy, dirty place of partially organized chaos. Toward edition time its floor was almost invisible underneath a layer of crumpled drafts of that day's history. Deafening was the din of clacking news-service printers and a score of typewriters, of rewrite men shouting into telephones, of reporters calling for copyboys, and of editors calling for reporters. God, how I loved it!

DESPITE my commitment to journalism, there was one occupational temptation in those days of uncertain youth that would not go away—radio. It had intrigued me since the early '20s, when Dad got the newest miracle of the moment, a crystal set. Wearing earphones, you maneuvered a small whiskerlike needle over a crystal about the size of a shirt button. When you made contact with a certain spot on the crystal, you "brought in" a particular station.

Radio listening in the crystal days had something of a cult quality to it. One could tell a wireless faddist. He or she was the one whose eyes were rimmed with dark circles from having stayed up all night, when reception was the best.

Then, around the mid-'20s, there came along something called the superheterodyne. It was a radio set with an array of tubes and a built-in amplifier. It was still a long way from today's printed-circuit miniatures, but it opened the way for the radio revolution that would change the world's social patterns. Families began staying home together to enjoy the best in entertainment.

The best in entertainment—but a long way from the best in information dissemination. The early newscasters were selected more for their entertainment qualities than their news abilities. Their information was taken mostly from newspapers, and their scripts were heavy with feature stories and personal opinion.

During my high school years Dad bought a fancy console radio with record player that had a primitive recording device on it. On aluminum discs one could record a scratchy sound track.

I interviewed most of my schoolmates, and when alone, I imitated the announcers I admired. Hand cupped to my ear to catch my own resonance, just as they did, I mimicked those fellows who did the dance-band remotes that filled the night airwaves.

It is strange, but I don't remember pretending to do news broadcasts. However, despite the shortcomings of mid-'30s radio news, I was destined to bounce between it and print journalism for the next several years.

My first appearance before a microphone was during my University of Texas years in Austin. A major local station was KNOW, and I persuaded the program manager to take this total neophyte and put him on the air with a daily report on sports scores.

The only problem was that the station had no press-service facilities to supply such information. My expedient was to tap the resources of a smoke shop just a block from the studio. It was a somewhat rough establishment with a clientele of overalls-clad, sombrero-topped men of no identifiable profession, who sat around playing dominoes and drinking what passed during Prohibition for beer. The place had a Western Union sports ticker. Like the old-fashioned stock tickers, under its glass dome a printer typed out on tape the day's sports results. Occasionally the bartender chalked up on a big blackboard the story the tape was telling.

Every day I dropped into the smoke shop, bought some pipe tobacco and a beer, and sat there at a table pretending to read the afternoon Austin *American-Statesman*. What I really was doing was memorizing those blackboard scores.

Five minutes before broadcast I got up to leave with all the casualness I could muster. Then, once out of sight of the smoke shop, I ran back to the studio and typed out my daily sports intelligence before it fled my memory. I had an inkling that what I was doing might be illegal and that the bartender might throw me out of the joint if I took notes from his blackboard.

This concern about legality has always plagued me. My mother and father drilled honesty into me until I became a wimp when confronted by authority. I carry such a guilt complex for things I've never done that a cop approaching to sell a ticket for the policemen's ball paralyzes me with fear.

It is a wonder, then, that my sports reporting stint at KNOW led to another brief occupation. Just as the KNOW job was ending with the baseball season, I was approached by a sharp-faced man in a checkered suit the likes of which was seldom seen in Austin. He didn't talk like a Texan either—a fast monotone out of the side of his mouth was his style. His name was Fox, he said, and he was opening a sports club—that's what he called it—and he wanted to know if I'd be interested in reading the sports results to his members every afternoon.

The job sounded a little peculiar, and so did the money—$75 a week, equivalent to $872 in 1996.

When I told other, more worldly members of my set about my great fortune, they reinforced my growing suspicion that Mr. Fox's "club" undoubtedly was a bookie joint.

Suspicions as to the nature of the enterprise were confirmed when I went to work the following Monday. It was as illegal as they got. It was on the second floor of a run-down office building, and to gain entrance one was identified through a sliding panel in the door. My job was to sit in front of a Teletype machine over which came information from the horse racetracks around the country. I was to relay this information by public-address system into the smoke-filled hall where my rough-looking colleagues would post the odds, results, and payoffs on a blackboard.

I lasted just $150 worth of ill-gotten gain. I spent a sleepless two weeks imagining the inevitable raid, the handcuffs, Mr. Fox and the rest of us being led to the paddy wagon, the probable death of my parents from acute mortification. I didn't tell Mr. Fox I was quitting. I just didn't show up. I was terrified that he'd shoot me on the spot to keep me from squealing. For weeks I lived in dread that he or his evil cohorts would hunt me down.

After my brief experience on the other side of the law, I went legit. I was fascinated by politics and spent hours in the galleries of the state legislature listening to the debates. I was fortunate to be introduced to a large courtly gentleman named Vann Kennedy. He was a sterling example of a type of journalistic entrepreneur to be found in most state capitols. Where a buck could be made in journalistic enterprise, there Vann was likely to be.

He had wangled some space amid the rafters of the capitol dome. There he published a political monthly, wrote speeches for politicians, and advised them on policy and election strategy. His empire expanded as he cajoled Hearst's International News Service into establishing a bureau in Austin. This required a modest increase in staff, and I was it—office boy and cub reporter.

Vann knew state politics inside out, and he knew how to report. And he patiently shared the knowledge with me.

The Vann Kennedy job may have been one of the best breaks of my life. But it was also the end of my college education, a matter I have regretted ever since. At the time, though, I found the Texas legislature and the newspaper business far more fascinating and educational than anything I was learning at U.T.

I slowly dropped classes to pursue full-time journalism and sort of slipped out of school. Oddly, no one, including my parents, made much of a protest. It may have been that, in the throes of the Great Depression, nearly everyone valued a job in the hand more highly than an education in the bush.

The Depression still held the nation in its grip when Vann lost me to a full-time job with the Houston *Press,* represented by the two-man Scripps-Howard bureau in the capitol. The two "men" were husband and wife Dick and Eleanor Vaughan, and they were wonderful tutors. They taught me everything, including how to keep one's mouth shut when harboring a professional secret.

When Governor Jimmy Allred had the audacity to nominate a woman for a state court judgeship, the more conservative legislators rebelled. The fight for confirmation became the year's biggest political battle. On such nominations the senators protected their political futures with a secret ballot.

The press was locked out, but Dick and Eleanor got the results, and the Scripps-Howard papers printed the way each legislator voted. The storm that broke over their heads threatened to wash the Vaughans right out of the pressroom.

Dick was brought before the bar of the senate on contempt charges. No threats were drastic enough to get him to yield his source. His spirited defense of the public's right to know overwhelmed the senators' wrath. A weak warning was his only punishment. I never found out the Vaughans' source although I, like others, suspected a senate clerk.

The woman was confirmed and went on to a highly successful career on the bench. Her name was Sarah Hughes, and it was she who, after President Kennedy's assassination, administered the presidential oath of office to Lyndon Johnson on the plane at Dallas.

The Houston *Press* recruited me from the Austin bureau to come to work for it in Houston. I had a feeling that I had reached the pinnacle of journalistic success. I had a desk in the city room, and I was dragging down $15 a week.

I got the usual freshman assignments. I did obituaries and wrote the weekly church page—a feature and the digest of a couple of sermons. And I was privileged to review the lesser movies to which our theater editor chose not to go.

The year on the *Press* was a learning time. Perhaps my first lesson came at the end of my first week, when I put in an expense account for a dollar or two. Carefully itemized were several phone calls at a nickel each.

"What are these doing on here?" city editor Roy Roussel demanded as he waved the account under my nose. "Don't you know how to make a phone call? Harold, show the kid how to make a phone call!"

So Harold took me downstairs to the lobby pay phone and

showed me. He had two straight pins and stuck one pin into one of the pair of twisted wires leading into the phone box and one into the other. Holding them together, he made the connection. The telephone company got wise to this a short time later and, always the spoilsports, put all the wires in impenetrable cables. It must have nearly broken Scripps-Howard.

I learned, too, the serious lessons of daily journalism. The need for accuracy, for instance. We competed in the afternoon with the Houston *Chronicle,* and at press time each paper had a copyboy standing by the loading dock of the opposition to grab several copies literally hot off the press. He then ran to breathlessly drop copies on the desks of his paper's key editors.

Roy Roussel spread the *Chronicle* out on his desk and stood over it, flipping the pages, exclaiming when he thought we had bested them, frowning when the shoe was on the other foot.

Then, if there was hope of catching up in the next edition, he'd get the reporter in for a hurried conference. The cry from the city desk had a different tenor, though, when Roussel found what he thought might be an error. The call penetrated the city room.

"Cronkite!"

The barely-innocent-until-proved-guilty hastened to the dock.

"The *Chronicle* spells this guy's name S-m-*y*-t-h. We've got it *i*-t-h. Which is it?"

He was a stickler for that kind of accuracy, but most editors were in those days. They understood a fundamental truth about newspapers and how the public perceived them. One mistake—*y* or *i*—standing alone didn't make that much difference perhaps. But for each such mistake, there were readers who recognized the error and whose trust in the paper was diminished thereby.

There was a frightening day when Roussel called me to his desk. His concern was the previous day's bank clearings, for which I was responsible. We carried a two-line item on the front page of each day's edition under a standard head, BANK CLEARINGS. The item said, "Today's Houston bank clearings were $3,726,359.27."

"You had the bank clearings wrong yesterday," the city editor said. He was frowning; his strong jaw was clenched. "You said twenty-seven cents. It was seventeen—seventeen! What happened?"

A ten-cent mistake on a multimillion-dollar number? Surely he was kidding. His countenance warned me that I had that assumption wrong too. I returned to my desk in a blue funk.

My mood was not alleviated by the older reporters' comments.

"Kid, you're in the soup now."

"How are you going to fix this one, kid?"

"Have you thought about getting out of town?"

The whole thing bore heavily on me as I dropped into the Press Lunch for the end-of-the-day beer. Paul Hochuli, clever writer and local columnist, greeted me.

"Where's your bodyguard, kid?"

My frustration—and my innocence—burst forth.

"What's this all about? A ten-cent error on a three-million-dollar number! What's the big deal?"

Paul and the others around him looked at me in amazement.

"Kid, don't you know why we print those bank clearings? The numbers racket pays off on the last five numbers of that figure. They paid off yesterday on a bad number—and they don't like the idea that somebody might be tampering with their numbers."

The next few weeks were a fear-filled time. Every car that paused alongside my jalopy at a stoplight was filled with hoods casing me for the hit. Kid Cronkite was about to die at an even earlier age than Billy the Kid.

THERE was one genuine brush with the underworld in Houston. Our ace police reporter was Harry McCormack. Harry looked a little like Bogart, a ruggedly good-looking guy. The felt hat was cocked back on his head whether he was outside or inside, its band showing signs of wear where he jammed in his press card when out on a story. A cigarette frequently dangled from the corner of his mouth.

I was the "second man" at police headquarters, when needed, so I did my best to imitate the great Harry McCormack. I mastered the art of picking up one of the then standard upright telephones. To show that you were a member of the press, you grabbed it from the desk in a sweeping motion that catapulted the earpiece from its cradle. With the left hand you casually snatched the hurtling earpiece from midair and proclaimed, "McCormack." (This was not terribly effective if your name was Cronkite.)

Mac was helpful to his cub protégé, but he didn't have much time for the social conventions. So I was mightily flattered the afternoon he suggested a beer after I got off. I imagined I would be with my hero at the best table in the police headquarters' hangout, Ed's Good Eats Grill. But it was not to be.

"I'll pick you up in front at five thirty," Mac advised.

In his car we started on a route away from downtown.

"We're going to a little speak I know out by the Ship Channel," Mac said. "Now listen, kid, and listen real careful. I'm going to meet somebody out there. I want you to not say a word no matter what. Just sit there and listen and enjoy yourself. Got that?"

So ours was a business date—news business or monkey business. On a back street behind the channel we pulled up at a small frame building and went in a back door. Four linoleum-covered tables, two of them occupied by some laboring types in overalls. A hefty woman greeted Mac as we pulled up a couple of old kitchen chairs. She put a couple of drinks in front of us. Rotgut—genuine, straight-from-the-bathtub rotgut. Mac contained his enthusiasm, just touching his drink to his lips.

I was pleased to perform my monkey see, monkey do act. We sat there a long time, perhaps a half hour. Very little conversation, Mac frequently checking his watch. And then a fellow walked through the door. He had on a felt hat and the blue overalls that were virtually a uniform in this part of the world.

Mac waved a greeting, and the newcomer pulled up a chair. Mac and he exchanged a few words—a brief discussion of the weather— and the guy left. We followed within a few minutes.

"Well, how about Ray there?" Mac asked.

"Ray who?" I asked.

"You didn't recognize Ray Hamilton?"

Mac's voice was rising. A hint of apoplexy maybe.

Well let's put this in context. The year was 1935. One of the biggest stories gripping the nation had been the depredations of a trio of desperadoes, Clyde Barrow and Bonnie Parker, and their sidekick, Ray Hamilton. They roamed the Southwest robbing banks, murdering lawmen, and thumbing their nose at the authorities, who seemed hopelessly inept in tracking them down.

But on a May day in 1934, in the bayou country of Louisiana, a police ambush caught Bonnie and Clyde. They were shot in a fusillade of fire worthy of Gettysburg. Hamilton was not with them, and the hunt for him over the next months narrowed to a small corner of southeastern Texas and Louisiana.

From out of those headlines Ray Hamilton had stopped in to see Harry McCormack in a sleepy Ship Channel speakeasy. And I hadn't even recognized the fugitive whose picture was in every paper in the land almost every day. McCormack was incredulous.

"All right, kid. But here's what you've got to do: You don't ever ever mention that you saw me with Hamilton here tonight. Ever! It'll go hard on both of us if you do. We've been consorting with a criminal. We could be in real trouble. So you don't ever say a word. Unless I need you to say that I met with Hamilton tonight. I'll tell you if I do. But otherwise, not a damn word!"

Naïveté played only a small part in my bewilderment. Nero Wolfe couldn't have imagined the deep plot that McCormack of the *Press* was spinning.

It began to unfold a few days later. Mac told the desk he was leaving headquarters to meet some anonymous informant. Shortly thereafter the desk got a call from the police saying they had received an alarm that a man who looked like McCormack had apparently been forced into a car at gunpoint.

Mac was missing for twenty-four hours until a farmer a few miles outside Houston found a car in his fields. In it was Mac, bound hand and foot, his mouth taped. As the farmer untaped him, Mac's first words were, "Don't touch the windshield."

When the sheriff's deputies arrived, Mac told them he had been kidnapped by Ray Hamilton and, to prove his story, pointed out that Hamilton had left his fingerprints on the windshield. Mac's tale was that Hamilton had kidnapped him because he wanted somebody to record his true story. The story was spread across the front pages of the Houston *Press* for several days thereafter. It was, of course, a sensation.

Mac stuck with the fiction that he had had no part in framing his "abduction." But clearly my role was to be his witness should the need arise to establish that he had a relationship with Hamilton. Mac was probably better prepared in his own mind to admit to consorting with a criminal than to having his story doubted. It never came to that, and my testimony, thank goodness, was not needed. Only weeks after Mac's coup Hamilton was caught and executed.

The newspaper competition was hot, heavy, and healthy in Houston, and in our daily effort to beat each other, we resorted to all the dirty tricks ever devised in the game.

There was the day that screaming sirens brought Bill Collyer, my *Chronicle* opposition, and me to the open window of the police pressroom. We watched as two ambulances approaching on different streets met in a horrendous collision. From the back of one the gurney, with a patient aboard, flew out and went rolling halfway down the block. One of the ambulances smashed into a storefront. The other turned over. It was a dandy wreck.

As Collyer and I grabbed phones to our offices, he said, "Hey, don't say you saw this thing. If you do, you'll end up in court as a witness the rest of your life."

The advice seemed well taken, and I took it. My story was strictly a routine third-person report. Collyer's first-person, eyewitness report was spread all over the *Chronicle*'s front page.

Newspaper competition led to a little practice called picture snatching. The idea was to get a picture of the victim by whatever wiles one could employ. Families were frequently reluctant to lend out photographs of loved ones at their time of bereavement, and perhaps having given a photograph to one paper, they weren't inclined to let their last picture out of the house.

I was honored to get the picture-snatching assignment from time to time. I assumed this was in recognition of my resourcefulness, but upon reflection I'm afraid that the attributes from which my city editor was profiting were youthful innocence and a willingness to engage in larceny in the splendid cause of the people's right to know.

I was remarkably successful, partly because I reached the home of the victim faster than the opposition man from the *Chronicle*. This was achieved through breakneck driving that would rival the kind seen in *any* of today's television films.

But sometimes other methods were called for, and it was an imaginative use of these that caused my downfall. A young lady had died in an automobile crash with a prominent married citizen whose wife she did not happen to be. Upon arrival at her home, I found no one there, but the door was unlocked. Through the screen door I could see on the mantel a picture of a young woman. If I left it there, the man from the *Chronicle* would surely filch it. Defensive journalism was called for. So I filched it, and a delighted city desk splashed it on the front page.

There was just one little hitch. I had gone to the wrong address. The picture was of a next-door neighbor. Surprisingly, I was not arrested nor fired for the incident. I deserved both.

Chapter 2—Kansas City

I SURVIVED at the *Press* long enough to take my first paid vacation. I collected my two weeks' pay, all $30 of it, and was on my way.

I visited my grandparents in Kansas City. It was a fateful trip. The first day there, sitting in the swing on the Fritsche front porch, I read in the Kansas City *Star* that a new radio station was coming on the air. Opportunity beckoned. I appeared the next morning at the spartan offices of KCMO and presented myself as a likely candidate for their news staff. I was received by the station manager, August Schlicker, who hired me not as a member of the news staff but *as* the news staff.

The station was as small as a radio station could be—100 watts' split time, which meant that it was licensed to operate only between 6:00 and 9:00 a.m., noon and 3:00 p.m., and 6:00 and 9:00 p.m. My grandparents lived less than a mile from the transmitter, and they had difficulty picking it up—if they could remember when it was on.

But Schlicker paid me a grandiose $25 a week, and I was in

what, compared with the Houston of 1936, was a metropolis. The wild, wide-open gateway to the Southwest had the aura of a big city. It was thoroughly corrupt, run by one of that era's big-city bosses, Tom Pendergast. Maybe the casinos weren't exactly wide-open, but if you stood outside certain bars-and-grills, you could hear the rattle of the chips and even the riffle of the cards.

It was the sort of town that practiced the political-machine custom of voting right and voting often. KCMO was owned by a friend of Boss Pendergast's and his handpicked Senator, Harry Truman. During my year there, I was at my desk on election day when two policemen walked up. "You haven't voted yet, have you?" one asked.

I hadn't lived in Kansas City long enough to vote, and besides, I wasn't old enough. I had lied about my age to get the job. I wasn't about to admit that, so I simply said that, yes, I had voted.

"No, we don't think so," the cop said.

"No, really I have. Really."

"I don't think you understand us," the cop said. "You haven't voted, and we're ready to take you down now to do it."

They escorted me to the police car and affably chatted as we drove toward the north end. Just before we got to the polling place, one of them handed me a piece of paper and said, "That's who you are. We'll take you back when you're through."

I went in to the desk. A nice little lady and gentleman looked up.

"Your name?" they asked.

I read it from the paper, "Anthony Lombardo."

They found the name on the register and handed me a ballot.

"All right, Anthony," they said with perfectly straight faces.

I cast my vote, and the police drove me back to the radio station. They would come back late in the day and, this time, simply note that my vote was needed. No pretense now of suggesting that I hadn't voted before.

The voting laws and democracy itself had been grossly violated, of course, but if any small drop of legality could be found in the process, it was that the police did not tell me *how* to vote. Since I worked for KCMO, they assumed that I knew that my civic duty lay with the Pendergast interests.

While the city's wide-open reputation attracted conventions and enhanced tourism, it also brought embarrassment to the righteous portion of the citizenry. They eventually prevailed. Boss Pendergast was indicted for income tax evasion, his machine collapsed, and a reform government was voted in.

Kansas City was a good newspaper town. The Kansas City *Star* and its morning edition, the Kansas City *Times,* dominated, but it had lively competition from the afternoon *Journal-Post.* Radio wasn't yet a really major news source, but two network stations and a couple of independents did a pretty fair job.

It was not unusual in those days for radio news staffs to simply rewrite the local newspaper, and at KCMO that's what I did. I made as much of a stab at doing some original reporting as a one-man news operation could: Occasionally I'd try to amplify a newspaper story by calling the source.

As proud as I was of my effort, with our limited power, there weren't many listeners paying attention. Few people had heard of Walter Wilcox. That was the name Schlicker had given me. There was a conceit at radio stations then that their talent might skip to another station. To prevent them from taking their fame with them, the station "owned" their name.

As Walter Wilcox, I was also the sports department. Here we did make something of a splash locally. We subscribed to a quite remarkable service provided by Western Union. Any radio station could purchase virtually any college football game that the networks weren't broadcasting. Western Union sent a lone telegraph operator to the game's press box, and from there he tapped out in Morse code a running report on the game.

The operators sent in their play-by-play reports in a tightly abbreviated form. In the radio studio at the receiving end another Western Union operator translated the Morse code and typed out the cryptic message. It might read something like "Brown 3 LT Smith." We announcers then let our imaginations run. My report on this play would go something like "So the ball's on the Trojans' forty-three, second and eight. Notre Dame's back in the huddle. They break. It's a shift to the left. A handoff to Brown, who hits a solid wall there. He didn't make much on that attempt. Maybe a yard or two. They're coming out of that pileup. It looks like Eddie Smith made the tackle. Notre Dame picked up three yards on the play. So Notre Dame's on Southern Cal's forty—third and five."

The announcer's skill at doing this and the phony excitement he could generate on demand were the keys to success. I was aided by a brilliant but slightly screwball announcer, Moreland Murphy, and some extensive research with which we backed up our broadcasts.

We took every Notre Dame game that wasn't on the nets. Kansas City had a big Catholic population, and a fair number of local fans made the trek to South Bend for major games. We checked on who was going and found out from their wives what they were wearing. We got in advance the description of the colleges' half-time shows and what the bands would be playing. At halftime I described Kansas Cityites in the stands and all of the halftime color while Moreland, at the studio console, played the bands' recordings.

The Western Union service was nearly flawless, except on those occasions when the wire would go down. These were rare and of short duration—a couple of minutes, tops. I filled in by simply calling a time-out. Who, I figured, was counting? When the wire came back, the sending operator quickly filled us in on anything that had happened on the field. No problem. Except one day—and it was the all-important Notre Dame–Southern Cal game.

The wire went down. Two minutes passed. Four minutes passed. The wire stayed down. I decided there was nothing to do but resume the game. The Irish had the ball when the wire went down. So I moved them down the field in gentle increments.

Now they were getting near the Southern Cal twenty-yard line, and I knew I couldn't get them inside the twenty. *That* would make the papers the next day and expose my fictional game. So I kept the two teams moving back and forth as near midfield as I could, and with absolutely nothing of interest happening.

That wire was down almost a half hour. It was the longest and dullest quarter in the history of organized football.

About the same time I was doing football at KCMO, there was a fellow doing telegraph baseball reports in Des Moines. His name was Ronald Reagan. Many years later President Reagan and I were exchanging stories and I told him of my long game.

A year or so after that I was chatting with some group about that Trojan-Irish broadcast and one of my listeners said, "Hey, you know President Reagan tells a story just like that about having to fill in when the wire went down during a baseball broadcast."

I won't say the President stole my story but . . .

THAT summer I met Betsy Maxwell. This gorgeous redhead came to KCMO straight out of the University of Missouri School of Journalism, hired as an advertising writer. That first couple of days after her arrival I was so stricken that I was afflicted with a shyness that is hardly my hallmark.

In those early days of radio, stations wrote and performed commercials. When it came time to broadcast a commercial that required more than one voice, Robert Simmons, KCMO's program manager, simply grabbed any employees within sight, pushed them in front of the microphone, and handed them the copy to read.

The third day after the arrival of the redhead I still had not managed to meet her, but this would be the fateful day. Simmons grabbed me for a commercial. At the studio's mike there stood the redhead and Moreland Murphy. Simmons passed out the scripts.

"You, Wilcox, are Boy. She's Girl. Morph's the announcer. Here you go."

We're on the air.

> ANNOUNCER: A scene at Twelfth and Walnut. Boy meets girl.
> BOY: Hello, angel, what heaven did you drop from?
> GIRL: I'm no angel.
> BOY: Well, you look like an angel.
> GIRL: That's because I use Richard Hudnut.
> ANNOUNCER: Richard Hudnut, the cosmetic that [blah, blah] . . .

Betsy and I went from the studio to lunch, and from lunch to dinner. And from KCMO through life together.

Our love-at-first-sight relationship almost produced a marriage at first sight. Within a couple of months we were seriously considering the idea. Betsy thought her folks wouldn't approve, and we decided on a secret marriage. We could accomplish that, we thought, by getting married in Independence, the county seat—a twenty-minute drive. So we took a lunch-hour break. We figured twenty minutes each way would leave us twenty minutes to get the license and get hitched by the county judge. By the time we got to the Jackson County Court Building, we were beginning to have doubts. For twenty minutes we sat immersed in searching debate, until we finally reached agreement—that we had to get back to work. Our courtship would last another four years before I finally got Betsy to the altar in 1940.

My KCMO job ended rather precipitously in a few weeks.

Simmons, the program manager, rushed to my desk shouting, "Flash it, flash it! The new city hall's on fire. Three people have jumped. They're dead. Get it on the air! My wife just called me. We live across the street. Get it on the air."

I reached for the telephone.

"What are you doing?" Simmons queried. "Get on the air."

I was calling the fire department to confirm the story, I replied.

"You don't need to confirm it. My wife's watching the whole thing."

I went ahead with my phone call. Simmons left, and a moment later, just as I'm getting the fire dispatcher on the line, I hear him broadcasting a bulletin with his wife's version of the fire. Even as he's blabbing away, the fire dispatcher is telling me that it isn't much of a fire. Some scaffolding on the new building had caught fire, it was just about out, and, no, there hadn't been any injuries.

The little contretemps that followed ended in my being fired. It wasn't putting an erroneous story on the air that bothered the bosses. My sin was daring to question management's authority.

My unemployment lasted a couple of months, long enough for me to have been inoculated with a lifelong appreciation of that terrible state. My minuscule savings were soon exhausted, and I was ashamedly bumming most of my meals at my grandparents'.

The KCMO experience had cooled any thought I had that radio

might be an interesting medium in which to practice journalism, and I limited my job search to the newspapers and the press services. I landed at the United Press.

The United Press and its larger rival, the Associated Press, were nearly identical in their operations. State wires connected the newspapers and press-service offices in a given state. Items selected for their regional interest were then condensed and filed on regional wires. Stories from these wires, selected for their broader interest, made it onto national wires, one for the eastern United States, one for the West. These two national wires fed into Kansas City, and so did regional wires from the midland and southwestern states. Large staffs of us reedited and sometimes rewrote the stories for the other sections of the country. Banks of Teletype machines clattered twenty-four hours a day, an insatiable maw demanding sixty words of copy every minute.

Our competition across the street, the AP, was doing the same thing. Our job was to write better than they and get our copy to the newspapers first. It was a blistering, relentless battle.

Unlike our brethren on the newspapers, we didn't have the luxury of only one deadline a day. We wrote fast, and because our client newspapers always compared our stories with the opposition's fact by fact, we had a powerful incentive to be right.

At one point I was sent to Dallas to temporarily relieve a personnel shortage. I had been there only a couple of days when the New London school in east Texas blew up. I was the editor of the state wire, and it was just coming upon three o'clock, when the wire was to be closed down for the night. Three bells rang on the machine, and a coded message came across from Houston: "Don't close this wire!" The reason became obvious within a minute or two.

Houston filed the first bulletin reporting an explosion in the consolidated school at New London and requesting all the ambulances the area could send. The Dallas bureau manager and I took off immediately for New London, a good four hours away.

There weren't car radios then. We had no idea how bad the explosion had been until we reached Tyler, thirty miles from New London. There was a funeral home on the main road, and for blocks around it there were ambulances and hearses and pickup trucks, all unloading bodies.

We reached New London just at dusk. Huge floodlights illuminated a great pile of rubble at which men and women tore with their bare hands, searching desperately for children still buried. Before they were through, they would bring 294 shattered bodies out of what had once been considered one of the most up-to-date school structures in Texas.

The architect had reinforced the building with vertical rows of tiles. The building was heated with residual gas from the oil fields, gas so volatile that it is usually burned off in the flares we see around most oil fields. The gas is odorless and invisible. It leaked in the sub-basement of the building and filled those columns of tiles. The school was a bomb waiting to explode. Two minutes before classes were to be dismissed for the weekend, a student in the basement woodworking shop switched off a band saw. The spark did its work.

A news reporter's duty can sometimes be difficult. It is not easy to approach someone in distress to seek answers to the questions that need asking, but stories change with each retelling. Even a person really trying for the most faithful recital of events is almost invariably susceptible to slight modifications with each recital. Accuracy of a story is in direct relation to how soon after the event it is recorded and how frequently the story has been retold.

Thus, I talked to the superintendent. I didn't know about the school's use of the highly dangerous residual gas. But he told me about it. He wept as he told how he and the school board had decided to tap into those gas lines. The use of the gas was illegal, but nearly everybody in the small towns adjoining the oil fields did it.

The world press poured into the little town of New London. The United Press sent down Delos Smith from New York, one of our fastest and best writers and editors, to head up our staff, and to handle the feature stories, Henry McLemore, our top sportswriter.

After I had been on the job for some forty-eight uninterrupted hours, Delos suggested I get some sleep. It was midnight when he sent me off to the Overton Hotel, a one-story structure with a single hall, off which were the rooms.

"You won't need a key," Delos said. "Our room is the first one past the men's room on the right. McLemore's there right now. He brought shaving stuff and toothbrushes. There are a couple of extra shirts in his bag."

So I stumbled down to the Overton, located the room, and fell into the twin bed opposite McLemore. Delos had sent me off at midnight, noting that he would have someone wake me up at six.

I was awakened by the sun forcing its way through the cracks in a window shade. It was eight o'clock. I was grateful to Delos for giving me a little bonus. Mac was up and out. I found a toothbrush, borrowed the razor, and stumbled to the shower. Upon my return I realized that Mac was even more of an eccentric than legend had it. He had arrived directly from the baseball spring training camps, but to come to a three-day assignment like this and decorate the room with framed pictures of baseball players? Wild. And when I went into his bag for that clean shirt, there were baseballs there.

In my clean shirt I appeared back at our headquarters. Delos looked up and without any notable cheerfulness, said, "Well, that's a young buck for you. You don't sleep for two nights, you get a few hours off, and you go shack up with some broad somewhere."

I was stunned. I protested.

"Cronkite," said Delos, "don't give me that. I sent for you at six o'clock, and you weren't in the room. I sent down there at seven, and you still weren't there."

He was right. I hadn't been in the UP room. I had ended up sharing the room of the manager of the area's semipro baseball team. I never met him. I still don't know who he thought it was sleeping in his other bed that night or if he missed the shirt.

THE UP sent me to El Paso to organize a new United Press bureau. I had been there only a week or two when a phone call came from Oklahoma City. The man on the other end talked so fast that I had to ask for frequent repeats. There scarcely had been the formality of a hello when he plunged in. "Gayle Grubb, WKY. Hear you're a great football announcer. We've just signed the University of Oklahoma to the first exclusive radio contract for all their

The Houston *Press* recruited me from its Austin bureau to work in Houston. That's me (left) in the background behind city editor Roy Roussel. Right: WKY offered me a job as a football commentator in Oklahoma City.

TODAY – 2:15 p. m.

KICKOFF AT 2:30 P. M.

FOOTBALL

DIRECT FROM SKELLY
STADIUM IN TULSA!

O.U. vs. TULSA

Play - by - Play Description Brought
to You by Kellogg Cereals

A four-star WKY team will be in the middle of every O. U.-Tulsa play Saturday, bringing you a vivid description of the color—the tension—the battle spirit. From the sidelines, Tom Churchill, standout O. U. athlete of all time, will maintain direct-phone contact with Wray Dudley in the radio box above the crowd on the 50-yard line. Dudley, operating the new WKY electric signal system from Churchill's messages, will double-check Walter Cronkite, ace WKY football commentator, as he describes every play—every plunge—every pass—every detail of this thrilling contest. Completing the broadcast team, WKY Chief Announcer Perry Ward will alternate at the microphone to bring you the color and sidelights.

WALTER CRONKITE
ACE FOOTBALL COMMENTATOR

WKY
SKIRVIN TOWER HOTEL

My gorgeous bride—forty-five minutes late for our wedding.

Here is Betsy, with Kathy in her arms, beside Nancy and Grandmother Maxwell. Below: The civilian war correspondents—the Writing Sixty-ninth—putting on flying clothes. I'm third from the right.

games—home and away. I want you to come here for an audition."

I wasn't that interested in getting back into radio, and I didn't know whether I could do a live football broadcast. On the other hand, I had been battling a sense of loneliness. El Paso was the farthest west I had ever been. And I feared it was far too far to keep the romance with Betsy alive.

So I got a weekend off to take the train as far as Dallas, where Mr. Grubb and his commercial manager, Matt Bonebrake, would audition me. In a bare studio they stood me in front of a microphone and directed, "Okay, broadcast a football game."

Well, that little order was right down my alley. I gave them an imaginary five minutes of an imaginary game. They came out and asked how much I wanted and when could I start.

Not wanting a job very much does wonders for one's bargaining ability. So I tripled my UP salary and asked for a big $75 a week. I was dumbfounded when they agreed.

WKY was a first-class operation. It was an affiliate of NBC and did a lot of fine local programming. There were still a couple of months to the football season, and they suggested I live on the university campus at Norman to get familiar with the team.

And, they asked, what assistance did I feel I'd need for the broadcasts? I suggested an electric board that would have little lights for each of the positions as the teams lined up for play. I would have a spotter for each team, and they would press buttons to light the bulbs that would indicate who carried the ball and who made the tackle. It would be no more difficult, I reasoned, than those telegraphed reports.

The first game was the traditional opener against Tulsa. There was a big party the night before—the broadcast executives and the University of Oklahoma officials. It was really a shame we couldn't have adjourned right then and there.

The broadcast was a disaster. My spotters weren't worth a darn, and the electric board was worthless. I was trying to get the numbers off the jerseys as the plays progressed, refer to the program, and finally deliver some sort of report of the play, which by then had unfolded some minutes before. I was hopelessly behind.

When the game came to its merciful end, Grubb invited—no, commanded—me to sit next to him outside the radio booth. We sat there for some time in silence. Finally he said, "All right. I'll see you in the office Monday morning." And he just got up and left, a man who clearly thought that his presumably bright career, along with mine, had ended up there in that Tulsa radio booth.

I was not quite dressed yet Monday morning when the phone rang. "Grubb," said the voice. "Mr. Gaylord wants us in his office at eight thirty. I'll meet you downstairs."

Mr. Gaylord was the big boss of the entire Oklahoman empire. That he wanted to see me at all, but particularly with Grubb, was as ominous a signal as a funnel-shaped cloud on the horizon.

A huge shadow of trepidation accompanied Grubb and me into Gaylord's office. I had never met him before. He could have stepped out of a *New Yorker* cartoon: the epitome of the big boss— a little on the heavy side, wire-framed glasses, balding, a frown that creased most of his forehead. He motioned us to chairs.

"Well, I thought you fellows did pretty good." He nodded. "I liked it. A few little things I know you're going to fix up, but I just wanted you to know that we liked it around here."

He practically had to invite us to leave. Relief had frozen Grubb and me in our chairs.

Needless to say, we fixed up the "little things." I had learned a lesson that would prove highly valuable. Never again would I be caught without having done whatever research was possible for whatever it was I was going to cover. For the football games, I learned the name and number and position, height, and weight of every member of each squad of every game we broadcast.

That next game was vastly different from Tulsa. Just by watching the game, if I could see the players' numbers, I knew who they were and all about them. We had a wonderfully successful season.

When it was over, I was assigned to the WKY news staff. The station had a widely held reputation as a superior news operation, but the lack of original reporting still left me feeling incomplete as a journalist. My heart was still with print.

So I was ready to move on and anxious to return to newspapering. I landed back at the United Press in Kansas City as the news reports from overseas were filled with the prewar clichés: "War clouds gathered over Europe today," "Lights burned late in the chancelleries of Europe tonight." As Hitler swallowed Austria, only the most irrationally hopeful felt that war could be avoided.

At the UP I was back in the world in which I felt I belonged. The days were filled with eminently satisfying work and heady prospects.

WITH my future settled, I convinced Betsy that our long courtship might indeed be ripe for marriage.

Betsy was beautiful as she walked down the aisle of Grace and Holy Trinity Episcopal Church on March 30, 1940. Frankly, she would have looked pretty good to me if she had shown up in overalls. Until she made her appearance, I wasn't sure I was ever going to see her again.

It was a big wedding. My best man and ushers were mostly up from Houston, old school chums and fraternity brothers. We were gathered in the sanctuary, self-conscious in our rented cutaways. The church filled, and at the appointed hour the organist played, at our request, "I Love You Truly."

At that point there arrived a runner from out front. Betsy, it seemed, had not arrived.

The minister was reassuring. "I've seen them as much as five, even ten minutes, late. Don't worry, Walter."

His allotted five minutes, and ten minutes, passed. Now the minister was more nervous than I. Meanwhile the organist, to whom my contribution had apparently been adequate for only one song, kept punching away at "I Love You Truly." The audience was stirring, none of its number more than my Uncle Ed, who, I learned later, had to go to the bathroom during most of the wait.

That wait lasted forty-five minutes, or approximately twenty-one renderings of "I Love You Truly." When Betsy finally appeared, our relatives were relieved. The minister was pale and shaken but bravely carried on. I was writhing somewhere between relief and disgust, like a parent whose lost child has reappeared.

It turned out that Betsy's brother, Allen, had burned up her new lingerie along with the gift wrappings, and she would not hear of a substitute. He had to go downtown to fetch the exact replacement.

But we did the "for better for worse, in sickness and in health" thing, Betsy agreed with me that I would never have to hear "I Love You Truly" again, and we have made it work—ecstatically some of the time, pleasantly most of the time—for fifty-six years.

I attribute the longevity of our marriage to Betsy's extraordinarily keen sense of humor and her tolerance for the uncertain schedule and wanderings of a newsman.

We didn't know as we left the church that we had less than two years before World War II would sweep us into that long separation so many of our generation would endure.

Chapter 3—World War II

I WAS on the desk at the UP bureau the night when the bells on the Teletype machines rang out the signal for a flash: GERMANY INVADES POLAND.

The war was on. In a few weeks I would be summoned to the foreign desk in New York.

The great conflagration that engulfed planet Earth in the fourth decade of the twentieth century is popularly known as World War II. Actually, it was the War of Failure. The most extensive and costliest war was the result of "civilized" man's failure once again to resolve differences without resorting to violence. As long as nations cannot learn to live cooperatively, there must be conflict. As long as there are aggressors, there will be resisters.

On September 1, 1939, Hitler unleashed his tanks and his Stuka dive-bombers against the horse-mounted Polish cavalry. For eight months nothing much transpired on the western front while Germans and Russians carved up Poland. Then Hitler's forces crashed across northern and western Europe, and the real war was on.

America tut-tutted with increasing alarm as the British became the last bastion of democracy across the Atlantic. We listened with horror as Ed Murrow described the bombing of London and Canterbury and other places dear to our Anglo-American heritage. Voices were heard for American intervention—but others renewed the old philosophy of American isolationism.

Japan's war machine ended all that on a bright December Sunday, the first Sunday in December, 1941—a date President Roosevelt said would "live in infamy." We were at war, and the personal aspect began coming home to the American people as the draft was accelerated and khaki became the uniform of the day.

After Pearl Harbor my United Press bosses sent me to navy headquarters in New York for credentials to go to sea with the North Atlantic convoys—at that time the nation's only combat role. By September I was en route with a sizable fleet from Norfolk to attack Morocco as part of the North African invasion. Our small task force, led by the pre–World War I battleship *Texas,* was to take the small port town of Port Lyautey and the Vichy French arsenal there.

There may be nothing more amusing than the army afloat, except perhaps the navy ashore. The army put aboard the *Texas* a team of reservists to operate something they called Clandestine Radio Maroc. Their sole function was to broadcast propaganda intended to persuade the army of France's puppet government to desert Hitler and come over to the Allied side. Their most important broadcast would be President Roosevelt's announcement of the invasion and his appeal for the colonials in West Africa to honor their French patriotism and join the Allied cause.

The navy assigned the radio team to bunks in the forecastle, just forward of the officers wardroom. Perhaps dictated by interservice rivalry or possibly accidentally, the hatch above their quarters was left open as the *Texas* reached the open sea beyond Hampton Roads. The first big wave poured down the hatch. The midnight watch had just changed, and the wardroom was full as the army contingent, their fancy civilian pajamas dripping with a goodly part of the Atlantic, came charging out of the forecastle. The men were halfway across the wardroom on the way to the boats when they skidded to a stop upon realizing that all was normal, with no indication that the *Texas* was soon to sink.

If that was a result of interservice rivalry, there was to be a more serious example as we hit the beaches of Morocco. A team of army communications technicians had been put aboard the *Texas* to install radio transmission equipment. The proud army types, possibly acting under orders of extreme secrecy, turned down the offer of the *Texas's* communications officer to help with the installation.

When, on that African D-day, the *Texas* fired off her big fourteen-inch guns for the first time in anger, even the ship herself suffered the repercussions. It was as if instead of disgorging the shells, she had been hit by them. She shuddered, she shook, she staggered. Ceramic bathroom fixtures shattered, and some pipes burst.

And just as it was getting warmed up with President Roosevelt's message, Radio Maroc was blown right off the air by the concussion.

"If they had asked, we could have told them how to prevent that," shrugged a navy communications officer.

The firing of those big naval rifles is awesome and, to the uninitiated, frightening. The great belch of flame threatens to engulf the ship herself, and the blast of heat sears the freshman war correspondent on the bridge. Whatever has been loose on deck is sent skyward, sucked into the vacuum the explosion has left behind.

As I stood there trembling from wonder, playing cards began raining from the heavens. One dropped on the back of my hand that was gripping the rail. It was the ace of spades.

WHEN Port Lyautey was secured, I went ashore with the *Texas's* gunnery officer, who was anxious to assess the accuracy of their fire. The *Texas's* big guns had spent the better part of two days pounding the French arsenal out behind the hills beyond the town, or so we thought. Our spotter planes were reporting that the shells appeared to be landing right on target, but through our binoculars we weren't seeing the sort of explosions that should have followed such marksmanship.

As our jeep approached the arsenal, the road became almost impassable. It was pitted with shell holes. The last shell hole was right on the edge of the arsenal. It had blown down the gate, and we passed through, to be hailed by an elderly French soldier. He introduced himself as the arsenal superintendent.

"Ah, gentlemen," he said in quite good English. "I see you are from the navy. From the battleship, perhaps? I am an artilleryman. Two world wars now. And, gentlemen, let me congratulate you. Never have I seen such shooting. You cut every road leading to the arsenal—and not one shell inside to do any damage. You have left it intact for yourselves. Splendid shooting, splendid."

Our lieutenant returned his salute and, with something less than satisfaction, ordered the jeep back to the beach.

The landing at Port Lyautey had not gone well. French resistance was heavy, the port we had hoped to use for unloading heavy equipment was blocked by scuttled ships, and the sea conditions were not conducive to landing the stuff by small boat. I heard that the *Texas* was going to take its remaining unloaded ships down to Casablanca, so I hitched a ride. But it turned out the *Texas* was bound for home, back to the States.

It seemed that my career as a war correspondent had crashed shortly after takeoff. While we navy correspondents had sworn that we would stay with our ship and not try to join the army ashore, any red-blooded war correspondent was going to jump ship and stay where the action was. That had been my intention.

Now, however, I was on the way back to Norfolk, like it or not. I saw only one silver lining, as gossamer thin as it was: At least I would be the first correspondent *back* from the North African invasion. Perhaps I would be able to write some stories that might have been censored from the thirteen I had sent from the *Texas*. That was my only hope of getting back into the UP's good graces.

Admiral Monroe Kelly, who had always been kind to me, sympathized. He was almost as sad as I when he called me to his cabin to report that the *Massachusetts*, the fastest of our battleships, was also on the way home, to Boston. He knew that aboard was one of my competitors, International News Service's John Henry.

The *Massachusetts* had spearheaded the action at Casablanca, helping to pummel the French fleet. John would have some great stories to tell, and there wasn't much doubt that the *Massachusetts* would beat us back home by days.

My despondency was shared by the crew until one of the navy

pilots, Bob Dally, came up with a brilliant suggestion. "If you get the old man's approval," he said, "I could fly you into Norfolk and save a couple of days. Maybe you could still beat the *Massachusetts*."

The admiral did approve, and the minute we were within range of Norfolk, Dally and I climbed into the open cockpit of a little OS2U observation plane. Almost midgets, these aircraft were biplanes fitted with pontoons to land and special gear for takeoff.

They nuzzled against a large catapult atop a short railway that ran across the battleship. The catapult was fired with one of the battleship's big fourteen-inch shells. This was as close to being shot out of a cannon as one could arrange without joining the circus. Dally revved up the engine, the cannon fired, my neck snapped, and the plane shot off the rail. I was on my way to Norfolk.

The flight was uneventful until shortly before the mainland came into view. At that point Dally noted that our gas was low. His attempt at reassurance wasn't as comforting as he meant it to be. "I think it's okay," he said. "I think we'll make it."

We did, sputtering up to the dock on the tank's last drops. Security threw up all sorts of roadblocks to making telephone calls from the air base, but there was a navy plane leaving immediately for New York. I skipped the phone call and hopped aboard.

At Floyd Bennett Field in Brooklyn, the same situation. A truck was on its way into New York City, so I skipped the phone call. Thus, I walked into the United Press office in the Daily News building unannounced. The Teletypes kept pounding, but the rest of the normal background noise went dead. The typewriters stopped. All faces were turned toward me. Mert Akers, as tough and as good an editor as they came, grabbed me in an embrace that may have been a first for him.

"My God, Cronkite, you're safe!" he exclaimed. The words scarcely having cleared his lips, he pushed me from him and added, "And where in hell have you been?"

It turned out I had been missing ever since sailing from Norfolk—almost six weeks. None of my dispatches had gotten through from the *Texas*. The ship had radioed them to the British navy's communications center on Gibraltar as instructed, but the British there had failed to relay any of them to our office in London.

My first question to Akers determined that my INS competition, John Henry, had not yet been heard from. Apparently we had beaten the *Massachusetts* back after all.

After emotional telephone calls to Betsy and my mother in Kansas City, I sat down to rewrite my previous stories. They hit the wires with an editor's note saying that I was the first correspondent back from North Africa and these were the first uncensored stories from that historic landing.

The note was only half right. They certainly were the first un-censored stories, but I wasn't the first correspondent back. The *Massachusetts* had arrived a couple of days earlier, but Henry, con-fident that I had stayed back in Africa as planned, had gone home for a couple of days' rest before filing.

My rest at home was fairly brief. Shortly I was off to England for, it turned out, the duration. I shipped over on an old Dutch pas-senger ship. The British Isles and London took some getting used to. England was damp and cold, and relief was nowhere to be found.

The London blackout was total. At times it was accentuated by the fog off the Thames, thickened by the heavy coal smoke that hung over the city. As we males walked along Picadilly in such darkness, we could hear the click of heels announce the arrival of a lady of the night. Wearing cheap perfume, she would run her hand along our pant legs. To the neophyte this might have seemed to be an opening to a street corner mating dance.

Wrong! This was economic foreplay. By feeling the pants' cloth, the ladies could tell whether the male was in the American or British army and was an officer or an enlisted man. On that de-termination hung the price at which she would open the bidding.

This was the environment into which the cream of American youth was plunged. Too many assumed that what they experienced was typical of England, just as the English assumed that the behav-ior of tens of thousands of young men barely out of adolescence was typical of American manhood.

Sometimes the contrasts and conflicts grated. The English,

struggling with the rationing of food and fuel, looked with barely concealed distaste on the apparently profligate American military, which shipped abundant food to their forces; stocked their post exchanges with tobacco, candies, and cosmetics; and paid their soldiers far better than their British allies.

And, of course, this comparative wealth proved a powerful attraction to the British girls. This led to the popular saying of the day: "The trouble with the Americans is that they are overpaid, overfed, oversexed, and over here."

It is too bad that thousands of GIs, restricted most of the time to their Americanized bases, had little opportunity to observe the strength of the remarkable British people. Britain stood against the Germans not because of its military, which was ill prepared, ill supplied, and too often ill led, but because of the unyielding strength of the British civilians. They suffered with unbelievable stoicism the Luftwaffe's terrible bombing. They gathered their children and went uncomplaining into the dank subway stations and other air-raid shelters. They came forth to find their cities and villages in ruins, but they picked up the pieces and carried on.

I WAS lucky enough to be assigned to cover the American and British air forces. The air war was the only war in Europe during that long year of 1943 and those months of 1944 before the landings in Normandy.

Sizable numbers of British bombers had been carrying the war to the German homeland. British fighters had wrested control of the air over England from the Luftwaffe, and the bombing raids on London were far less frequent and less effective.

By the end of 1942 the American Eighth Air Force, with its Boeing Flying Fortresses and the Consolidated Aircraft Liberators, was still testing its strength against targets in nearby France. They were testing, too, their daytime strategy, which was based on a belief that well-armed aircraft flying in formation could spread across the sky a field of fire that would defy attacking fighters.

This proved to be wishful thinking. Luftwaffe Messerschmitt and Focke-Wulf fighters were taking a heavy toll.

Our coverage of the air war consisted mostly of interviewing the bomber crews as they returned from their missions. We watched them coming home from battle, most with at least some damage— a cannon hole here or there or the almost delicate lacework of holes left by a trail of machine-gun bullets.

Sometimes the damage was so great that the headquarters staff gasped in disbelief that the plane had made it back at all. Engines would be missing, tail surfaces almost shot away, wingtips crumpled. And too often, out from the radio operator's window would fly a red flare. Wounded aboard!

I watched one day as an aircraft flown by a friend came gliding down to its landing. It appeared undamaged, but the red flare burst over it. An ambulance was there at the end of the runway and then departed, apparently for the hospital. The open truck that ferried the aircrews around the base came rolling back toward the debriefing shack, and all the crew seemed to be aboard. They drew closer and the scene changed drastically. There were only nine of them. There should have been ten. And to a man—or make that to a boy—they were crying uncontrollably.

Their captain was one of the most popular men of the 303rd Heavy Bombardment Group. He was twenty-six and had a beguiling smile for everyone and a hearty greeting for all. He planned to marry an air force nurse he had met in London. We had spent many evenings together at various London pubs.

His plane was hit by a single machine-gun bullet. It pierced the windshield—and his heart.

With my heart heavy I wrote the story. I called it "Nine Crying Boys and a Flying Fort." Nine crying boys and a war correspondent who thought he was too tough to cry.

THE air forces had plenty of heroes. The war in the sky had plenty of glamour. And for a number of reasons, not least the maintenance of home-front morale, there were the inescapable public relations campaigns.

The famed director William Wyler brought over Clark Gable to do a movie on the 8th Bomber Command. They were in the air force, and it was considered good public relations to get Gable an Air Medal. This required five combat missions. So they picked five milk runs to the nearby coast of France, and he was decorated with all the hoopla that air force public relations could muster.

Gable was a good guy. I saw him often during those days, and I thought he was just a little self-conscious about that Air Medal. He had good reason to be, but he was living the role assigned to him and doing it as graciously as possible.

In sharp contrast was Jimmy Stewart. Stewart had enlisted and gone through flight training to become leader of a squadron of Liberators, among the first in England. He led more than twenty combat missions, always the toughest ones. And he eschewed any publicity whatsoever. He even put his squadron off-limits to the press until we explained that he was denying recognition to his crews. He relented enough to let us do the hometown stories about them, but he himself remained unavailable.

SEVERAL of us war correspondents had been appealing for months for the right to accompany the bombers over Europe. The air force finally relented and sent eight of us to something called a Combat Crew Replacement Center. It became apparent that the air force intended to train us as fully qualified gun crews. Before we left CCRC 11, we were reasonably adept at taking apart and reassembling a machine gun—blindfolded.

We considered ourselves a pretty exalted group. An air force public relations man dubbed us the Writing Sixty-ninth, a parody of World War I's heroes, the Fighting Sixty-ninth. My Writing Sixty-ninth comrades included Andy Rooney of the army newspaper, *The Stars and Stripes.*

Our first mission was the Americans' second raid on Germany. The target: the submarine base at Wilhelmshaven.

It was a tough raid. Our fighter escort left us just before the coast of Holland, and over the Frisian Islands, off the coast, we watched the Luftwaffe fighters taking off to intercept us. We were under attack for two and a half hours until we came back under our fighter protection, and the antiaircraft fire was intense. Golden bursts of explosives all around us, dissolving into great puffs of black smoke.

I was assigned to a gun in the bombardier and navigator's plastic nose. I fired at every German fighter that came into the neighborhood. I don't think I hit any, but I'd like to think I scared a couple of those German pilots. I could hardly get out of the plane when we got back—I was up to my hips in spent .50-caliber shells.

Of the sixty-six planes that winged out that morning, thirteen didn't return.

DURING wartime, secrecy is a weapon. It was drilled into the troops. Mail was censored. Everything that even hinted at troop locations, movement, equipment was cut out.

For us war correspondents the secrecy rules were a heavy burden, and tension with the authorities was a constant. For most of the war, while England was still under threat of invasion, we had to write our stories in the physical presence of the censors in a large pressroom set up at the Ministry of Information.

The key question was whether or not the Germans could reasonably be expected to have knowledge of the situation about which the reporter was writing. If the answer was yes and the censors persisted in killing the story, the assumption was that either the censor was stupid or he was covering up a purely political decision.

I got embroiled in a controversy about daylight bombing. At the Casablanca Conference a courageous General Ira Eaker, commander of the Eighth Air Force, defying Winston Churchill, sought to persuade President Roosevelt to continue our daylight bombing. The British felt we would be more effective if we abandoned our attempt at high-precision bombing of military targets and adopted their nighttime tactic of area bombing. The pressure was intense. A lot of our missions had had to be aborted when the target area was covered by cloud, denying our bombardiers a clear look below. Of equal importance, our bombers penetrating Germany in bright daylight were taking a terrible beating from the German defenses.

The British bombed by the pathfinder technique. They sent a few daring bombers in at low levels under the clouds. They dropped the first bombs to light the target and sent up flares to help the following waves of bombers locate the area.

One of our UP reporters, Collie Small, found out that General Eaker had been training a squadron in the pathfinder technique. This was a big story, and Collie and I set up a watch for the break. It came with a raid on Emden, Germany. The Eighth Air Force for the first time bombed through the clouds using the RAF's pathfinder technique.

I wrote the story expecting censor trouble. It came. The story was killed. I appealed to the chief U.S. censor, an exceptionally bright colonel. I pointed out that the Germans at Emden sure as the devil knew that there was complete cloud cover through which those bombs tumbled. Their antiaircraft had fired through it. Who were we kidding?

The colonel agreed and cleared the story. When it led the British press and *The Stars and Stripes* the next day, it looked for a while as though it might be my last story from the European theater. Multimillionaire Jock Whitney, an air force colonel, was head of Eighth Air Force public relations. He phoned early that morning to say that we had both been summoned to Eaker's headquarters.

When we met, the usually unflappable Jock Whitney was near flapping. Eaker was angry, very angry, he said.

As Whitney and I crossed the parquet floor into the general's office, our footsteps bore an unsettling resemblance to those of a condemned man approaching the execution chamber.

Eaker was more than angry. He was apoplectic with rage. I had violated security. I had ruined the Allied air strategy, possibly lost the war to the Germans. I was to be sent home in disgrace.

Of course, all of this was politically inspired. The Germans knew exactly what we had done at Emden. My premature revelation scuttled air force plans to withhold the story from the American public and political leaders until after photoreconnaissance justified the new strategy. I've always believed that Eaker could have been so upset only if he'd thought that Roosevelt himself had not been told—Roosevelt, whom he had persuaded at Casablanca to stand up to Churchill in defense of daylight precision bombing.

Perhaps Washington wasn't as upset as Eaker expected. At any rate, calmer heads prevailed, and I was not thrown out.

MY FINAL wartime adventure with powered flight would come on D-day. My assignment was to stay in London and help write the lead story. I hated missing the experience of accompanying the troops, but on the other hand, landing on a beach in the face of the massed German armies could prove somewhat unpleasant.

The whole world knew that the invasion was imminent. The secret being guarded to the very death was exactly when and where.

I had just turned in when a knock came at my apartment door. Hal Leyshon, an air force major in public relations and a good friend, stood there in full uniform, dignified, official as all get-out.

He demanded to know if anybody else was there. He confirmed that there wasn't by personally poking his nose into all the rooms and closets. Finally he said, "Cronkite, you've drawn the straw to represent the Allied press on a very important mission. It will be dangerous. No guarantee you'll get back. But if you do, you'll have a great story. And security is on—you can't tell your office."

I dressed. I knew it had to be D-day. I figured if I made it, the UP would forgive me.

One squadron of bombers had been ordered at the last moment to bomb a heavy artillery emplacement that commanded Omaha Beach. It would go in just as the troops were landing, and to ensure accuracy, it would attack at low level—a maneuver made difficult by its normal tight formation and one it had never practiced.

The weather was lousy, but through the broken clouds I had a good look at the unbelievable armada of Allied ships. There didn't seem to be room in the Channel for another vessel. And then, just as we approached the beach, blackout. The cloud cover was total.

Our bomb bay doors were opened; our bombs were armed to go off on contact. But we couldn't see the target. And we couldn't see our own planes flying in close formation on either side. Any collision would probably set off a chain explosion, wiping out the squadron. Normally bombs would be jettisoned over enemy country, but our orders forbade this. We returned home with those bombs still armed. Now, *that* was a hairy landing.

I remained available for the airborne missions, and over the next couple of months there must have been eight or ten of them planned, only to be scrubbed when our speedy ground advance overran the drop zone before we could get under way. The war came to me in London, however. Shortly after D-day the Germans unleashed their V-1s on the city. These were bombs to which they had attached wings, a gyroscopic piloting device, and a little one-cycle engine. They were devilish weapons.

I saw the first one arrive in Bloomsbury as I left the nearby Ministry of Information one night. The air-raid sirens had sounded, but in the absence of any obvious action I was outside looking for a cab when I heard this lone aircraft just clearing the housetops, with flames pouring from its tail area. It crashed with a terrible explosion a few blocks away.

The government announced the next morning that the explosion had been the result of a gas leak. A couple of days later the euphoria that Londoners had felt with the invasion of the Continent was shattered with the announcement that the desperate Germans had turned a new weapon against them.

Hundreds of the so-called flying bombs were aimed at London from launching sites on the Channel coast. Air-raid sirens were screaming again day and night. The bombs exploded on impact and spread their death and destruction over wide areas.

It was the second week of the new attacks that I got mine. It was a Sunday morning, and I had just rung for our building's ancient servant, George, to order breakfast.

The air-raid sirens went off, followed a moment later by the unmistakable roar of a flying bomb overhead. I ducked back from the window just as the bomb hit a few hundred yards away.

Our old apartment building didn't fare too well. The hall door with its glass pane blew off its hinges, the plumbing broke, and dust formed a blinding, choking cloud. An eerie silence was shattered by someone crunching through the splintered glass that covered the hall's tile floor. There was a knock on the torn doorframe. There stood George, holding a towel over a bleeding eye. And, so help me, he said, "Did you ring, sir?" By God, and thank God, there will always be an England.

THE airborne call that counted came that fall. The operation was called Market Garden. The mission was to land three divisions of airborne troops to grab a road north through the Netherlands to the bridge over the Rhine at Arnhem. The main body of the British army under Montgomery would then roll across the bridge and turn east to invade the German homeland.

I was assigned to the U.S. 101st Airborne, ordered to land just outside Eindhoven to take the southern extremities of the road. I had no knowledge of any of this when the telephone call came on that morning in September '44, with the prearranged code to come along on "that picnic we'd been talking about."

I went to press headquarters at 20 Grosvenor Square decked out in full combat regalia. To my surprise, there was Stanley Woodward, star sports reporter of the New York *Herald Tribune*. He had just arrived in London, the *Trib* having finally yielded to his pleas for an overseas assignment. The man the paper had designated for the airborne mission, Ned Russell, was in Paris. When a message was left on the *Trib* desk for Russell instructing him to show up at 20 Grosvenor, the dutiful Woodward appointed himself Russell's substitute without having any idea of the nature of the story.

Stanley was a little overage for combat duty—overage and somewhat overweight. His eyesight was extremely poor. He showed up at 20 Grosvenor in his dress uniform—khaki jacket, pink trousers, oxford shoes—and with a demand to know what this was all about. I suggested to the baffled Woodward that he accompany me to our assigned base. Once in the car, I whispered that this was an airborne mission, that we would be parachuting behind German lines. He stared at me through his bottle-thick glasses.

At 101st headquarters we found the officers mess in a fit of a mission-eve adrenaline rush—aided and abetted by a considerable infusion of alcohol. We were embraced, toasted, and regaled with horror stories of the 101st's hairy landing in Normandy. Sometime midevening we were invited to General Maxwell Taylor's quarters for a private briefing. At this point Woodward could not be found. I had last seen him at the bar, the center of attention as he spun sports stories for an enthralled audience. I guessed that the 101st had discouraged him from attempting the landing.

Taylor's deputy gave me the bad news. I wasn't going by parachute. I was assigned to a glider. I knew the fate of the gliders in Normandy—impaled on the stakes the Germans had planted, splintered to kindling by midair crashes. I would have refused the assignment if I thought I could have faced my colleagues ever again. At least, I rationalized, it ought to be a nice, quiet way to die—no roaring engine, just a nice, silent glide into eternity.

I was wrong. Those gliders were built of aluminum tubing with canvas skins. The canvas cover beat against the aluminum, and it was like being inside the drum at a Grateful Dead concert.

Over the drop zone, the second surprise: The tow rope was dropped and down we went. No glide—a plunge almost straight down. The technique was to dive, right up until the point just before the g force would snap the wings off the plane—a mad dive to evade enemy ground fire.

For the same reason, our pilot didn't let us roll long once we were on the ground. As soon as the ground was soft enough, he nosed the glider in, totally oblivious to the danger. The plane did a half flip; the dirt came pouring in; our helmets went flying off.

I was with a headquarters company of about fourteen men. We dug ourselves out of the dirt. I grabbed a helmet and slapped it on my head. There was some enemy fire. I crouched and ran toward what I thought was our rendezvous point—a drainage ditch at one side of the landing zone. I glanced behind me, and there, apparently following me, were several men. One of them shouted, "Hey, Lieutenant, are you sure we're going in the right direction?"

I shouted back that I wasn't a lieutenant; I was a war correspondent. With a full GI vocabulary of unrepeatable words he advised me that I was wearing a helmet with an officer's big white stripe down its back. It was the only chance I had to lead troops in the whole war. I didn't do badly. The drainage ditch was that way.

I got to that drainage ditch and was working my way toward the copse at the end. In that little woods was supposed to be the head-quarters company and the radio transmitter that would get my story out. I stumbled on a heavyset fellow perched uncomfortably, implausibly, on the edge of the ditch. His helmet was pushed back on his head, which he held in his hands in obvious anguish.

"Stan?" I asked. "Is that you, Stan?"

Woodward looked up through bloodshot eyes, the picture of a man with a raging hangover.

"Nobody told me," he mumbled, "it was going to be like this."

Soldiers in combat are scarcely paragons of fashion, but Stan's habiliment was ridiculous. It seems that he had passed out at the bar and the fun-loving officers, certain that he wanted to go along, had dressed him and placed him aboard the glider. Find-ing combat clothing for his outsize frame had presented a chal-lenge. The pants were at least four sizes too small. They wouldn't close at the fly and were held together at the beltline by a piece of rope. He had already split the jacket at the shoulders.

Stan turned out to be a good sport and one terrific correspon-dent in the few days he was at the front. Our greatest difficulty was at night, when he could not see at all, and our greatest challenge was navigating down the slick sides of the Zon Canal onto a tiny raft made of empty fuel tins, and up the other side.

The Zon bridge was our first objective upon landing, but the Germans blew it up before we got there. A good part of the 101st had crossed the Zon on those rafts. The Germans had pulled back from Eindhoven, the city was undamaged, and the celebrating populace was out in force.

When the British arrived, they had to wait for a temporary bridge to be flung across the Zon. One smaller bridge had been intact on a country road just outside the town. The 101st had left it alone, hoping the Germans would not destroy it before the British arrived.

The first patrol from the slowly approaching British reached Eindhoven. The 101st artillery commander, General Higgins, rushed to meet the convoy of three armored vehicles. He greeted a cheery young lieutenant perched in the turret of the lead vehicle. Higgins pointed toward the bridge and told the lieutenant to rush it from this side while Higgins ordered a coordinated attack by the 101st from the far side.

"I say, General," responded the lieutenant, "you know my chaps have been going since dawn, and we haven't had our tea yet."

Higgins was reaching for the huge wrench, the tank tool, on the side of the vehicle. At that moment the Germans blew up the bridge. They saved the lieutenant from a probably fatal beating.

Now the bumper-to-bumper parade of British vehicles, brought to a full stop, jammed the highway. At dusk the Luftwaffe hit this choice target. The fuel trucks burned. The ammunition trucks turned all of Eindhoven into a display of deadly fireworks.

An old UP friend, Bill Downs, long since with CBS, had arrived with the British. I had joined him in his jeep, and when the bombers came, we were on the edge of the huge Phillips Park. We abandoned the jeep and leaped over a fence into the park. We huddled under the fallen trees, but somehow we became separated.

When the bombing was over and the sky was lit by the fires and the exploding ammunition, I began calling for Downs and conducting a somewhat tentative search for him.

Eventually I gave up and found his jeep where we had parked it, now covered with dirt and tree limbs. In the back was his recording machine, a cumbersome device like a large record player. I didn't know how to operate it, but I dusted it off, pressed a button or two until the record spun, and then delivered a eulogy to Downs. I left it there in the hope that someone might find it and recover the recording. I never heard of it again.

I visited nearby bomb shelters looking for Downs among the frightened men and women and crying children. No luck. Downhearted and beginning to compose in my mind my letter to his family, I hitched a ride to Brussels and its wire facilities.

I checked into the Metropole Hotel and, before going to my room, dropped into the bar. There stood Downs, immaculate in a clean dress uniform. My emotions seesawed from delight at his survival to anger.

"Damn, Bill, I spent all that time at risk of life and limb looking for you, and you just up and left me there."

He found his feeble excuse in the fact that the name Cronkite sounds like the German word for sickness. "Walter," he said, "I figured the Germans were going to follow up that bombing with a ground attack, and I'll be damned if I'm going to wander through that park calling out, 'Cronkite, Cronkite.' They would have figured I was sick and hustled me off to a hospital in Berlin."

Downs and I returned to Holland, and a few days later we were a little in front of our troops. We ran into some heavy small-arms fire, scrambled from the jeep, and took refuge in a ditch. We had been there a while when Downs, lying behind me, began tugging at my leg. I figured he had some scheme for getting us out of there, and I twisted around to look back at him. He was yelling to me, "Hey, just remember, Cronkite. These are the good old days."

I WAS in Brussels covering Montgomery's Twenty-first Army Group when the sky fell in. On December 16, 1944, Hitler took his last big gamble. He unleashed Field Marshal Gerd von Rundstedt, who sent a quarter of a million men crashing through the Forest of Ardennes in Luxembourg. He hoped to advance through Belgium, to split the Allied armies, and perhaps to win enough time for the Wehrmacht to organize the defense of the Third Reich.

The offensive caught the sixty thousand men of four American divisions by surprise. The attack sent them into headlong retreat, a new experience for U.S. forces in the European theater. Nineteen thousand Americans and forty thousand Germans would die in the ten-day Battle of the Bulge.

I was asleep in my Brussels apartment when I was awakened by the UP's First Army correspondent, Jack Fleischer. He was dirty, obviously tired, and considerably shaken. He had reached Brussels after being caught in the maelstrom of men and vehicles fleeing the front. He wrote a dispatch to me to try to get through the censors and remounted his jeep to return to the front. I filed the dispatch (it never went through) and sent an advisory to our Paris headquarters stating that I, too, was en route to the action.

Fleischer would die later when a stray bomb hit near the First Army press camp. I was luckier. Fighting my way through that oncoming chaos of trucks, guns, tanks, marching soldiers—a retreat that was close to panic—I finally reached the city of Luxembourg. The center of town was eerily calm, seemingly almost oblivious to the terror on the roads outside. I checked into the Cravatt Hotel.

For the rest of the Battle of the Bulge, several of us commuted from that fur-lined foxhole to the war each day, suffered through the snowstorms and the terrible cold that were bedeviling our troops, and returned each night to a hot bath and a warm bed. If Episcopalians are supposed to suffer guilt from such selfish indulgence, I'm afraid I missed that day at Sunday school.

Our troops had been regrouped, and the front was more or less stabilized by the second day. Then, like the cavalry of old, General George Patton's Third Army rode to the rescue.

Patton was tough, brilliant. He was highly respected for his talent—and feared for his temper. His career had barely survived a pair of incidents in Sicily when he had slapped hospitalized soldiers he thought were malingering.

He had earned his reprieve in the Ardennes. It was war in the worst of winter conditions. One of Patton's fixations was that windshields should be kept lowered on all vehicles so that the sun's reflection would not help enemy gunners. In the Battle of the Bulge that bordered on cruelty. The temperature was well below zero, and the windchill factor, even at the slow pace we made along the crowded roads, was almost insufferably bitter.

I joined the Third Army press camp that had set up in Luxembourg, and soon thereafter we were caught briefly in a firefight coming back from the front. My helmet bounced off and rolled into a field. The driver stopped, but in that field were signs in three languages left by a trio of armies. They all said DANGER. MINES. We resumed our trip with me helmetless.

One inviolable rule in Patton's army was, Helmets at all times, and trouble was on its way down that road. Here came Patton's little entourage behind us—his outriding jeep with a flashing red light and siren, the general himself and another escorting jeep behind. They stopped just in front of us, blocking the urgent traffic of war like cops at a minor highway accident. Out of the general's jeep bounced a full colonel, who came striding back to us.

"Okay, soldier," he shouted at me. "Where's your helmet?"

"My helmet," I said, "bounced off and is in that minefield."

That raised a look of utter disgust. But I bravely continued, "And I'm not a soldier; I'm a war correspondent."

Disgust changed to a sort of frantic disappointment.

"Stay as you are!" he ordered, and returned to Patton's side. We watched him gesticulate, raising his arms in the universal sign for "what can I do?" hopelessness. Whereupon Patton uttered a single word that might have been an expletive well known among the troops. The colonel climbed in, and they drove on.

VON Rundstedt got as far into Belgium as he did because of a break in the weather. The snow and fog that covered his attack hung on for eight days. It grounded the Allied air forces. I was lucky enough to be at a Ninth Air Force forward control point the day the pilots' discouraging helplessness ended. The weather gave promise of breaking, and U.S. P-47 Thunderbolts were patrolling above the clouds, the battleground shrouded somewhere below them. At control we were listening to the occasional radio chatter between them when there came the flight leader's electrifying words, "Blue flight, blue flight. I think I see an opening down there. Let's go. Follow me." And a moment later, "Jesus, there's the whole goddamn German army, boys. Okay, follow me. Wow-ee!"

The rest of the Ninth fighter force would be following him in short order as the weather continued to clear. The smoke from the burning tanks and trucks and guns they left behind was the funeral pyre of von Rundstedt's army and Hitler's dreams.

The war in Europe would end a few months later. Just before the general surrender at Reims, the Germans in western Holland surrendered to the Canadians. A Canadian correspondent and I disobeyed the press officers' orders to take a place far back in the column that would enter Amsterdam—we took a back road around the troops and entered Amsterdam first.

From our open command car we took the unrestrained adulation of the thousands of Dutch who jammed the streets. They pelted us with tulips until our car was hip-deep in them. The only blood I spilled in the war was that day—hit by a bunch of tulips tied together with a piece of wire.

That day of liberation I went around to where the UP office had been before the German occupation. And there, sitting on the front stoop, were three members of our rather large prewar staff—waiting for the UP correspondent they knew would be coming. Through their tears of joy they couldn't wait to tell me that they had a teleprinter available, that we could put the UP back in business. With incredible courage they had disassembled one of our Teletypes when the Germans entered Amsterdam. Each of them had taken a third of the parts to hide in their homes. If they had been caught, they would have faced certain execution.

The wire services' race to reestablish communications in Western Europe was on. The UP bypassed Amsterdam in favor of Brussels as our Low Countries headquarters, and there we won the race. Sam Hales, converted from a UP salesman to a war correspondent, gave us a head start by seizing as our personal reparations two Teletypes from the Siemens electric plant in Germany.

With one in Brussels and the other in Paris we were scheduled to open the first leased wire link between the two capitals and, by extension, Amsterdam. Although there had been delays, since wire was purchased from war-short suppliers, I was assured that the job would be completed in time for the scheduled opening day. Editors from the Brussels papers were on hand for the big moment. We were waiting for the first signal from Paris when the foreman of the crew that had been installing the wires appeared at the door. He wore a deeply troubled look. He reported that they were just thirty feet short of enough wire to finish the job. He shared my distress. But then he slapped his head and said, "I know where I can get the wire, but it is on the black market. It will cost."

I hated the black market, refused to deal with it, but this was an emergency. I produced in Belgian francs the sizable tribute demanded. The foreman disappeared—he could not have gone farther than the floor below—and reappeared with the requisite wire. The ceremonial greeting from Paris appeared on time.

Only days later we received our first bulletin from Paris. In French it reported that the Americans had dropped on Japan a bomb the equivalent of 20,000 tons of TNT. Clearly, I thought, those French operators have made a mistake. So I changed the figure to 20 tons before sending the story along to our Belgian clients. With further adds on the story my mistake came abundantly clear.

The war in Japan was over, but there was still some unfinished business in Europe. The Nazi leadership was being rounded up, as were their collaborators, who had helped rule the occupied nations. That fall the Allies put on trial in Nuremberg the top officials, civilian and military, of the Nazi regime.

There they sat in the dock before eight judges—two each from Britain, France, the Soviet Union, and the United States—twenty-one of the archvillains of our time or perhaps of any other time. I wanted to spit on them. It had never occurred to me to spit on anyone before, but this was what I wanted to do now.

I watched them as they watched films of the concentration camp victims. They buried their heads in their hands; they sobbed openly. And I couldn't help wondering whether they cried out of pity for the victims or out of fear of retribution.

Almost as shocking as those films were the tales from the witness stand, notably those of a very ordinary-looking man who calmly told of supervising the deaths of three million persons as if he were telling a farmer of having to put down a sick cow.

Rudolf Franz Ferdinand Hoess (no relation to defendant Rudolf Hess) was for three years the boss of Auschwitz. He unemotionally described in excruciating detail the operation of his gas chambers. "At least two and a half million victims were exterminated by gassing and burning," he recited almost in a monotone. "At least another half million succumbed to starvation and disease, making about three million."

Hoess was asked if he felt any remorse. He replied, "Don't you see, we SS [the elite Nazi security force] men were not supposed to think about these things. . . . It was something already taken for

The press at the Nuremberg trial was seated perhaps forty feet from the defendants. Below: A few years later, with Charlemagne on *The Morning Show.*

granted that the Jews were to blame for everything. . . . We were all so trained that the thought of disobeying an order would never have occurred to anybody."

Hoess was hanged in the Auschwitz compound next to the house where he had lived with his wife and five children.

The star witness was Hermann Göring, second only to Hitler from the beginning of the Nazis' rise to power. On trial for his life, he displayed on the stand all the arrogance with which he had once set out to rule the world.

Göring was on the stand for nine days. For the first three, under direct examination by his attorney, in effect he read into the trial proceedings a new testament of Nazism. With diabolical cunning, he calculated that the tribunal and subsequent historians would not tamper with the full transcript of the proceedings.

So he laid out in exquisite detail the Nazi philosophy and its program. He in no way apologized for any of it. Göring fell just short of stating flatly that Nazism should be restored. Most of the courtroom was not oblivious to what he was doing, but the chief American prosecutor, U.S. Supreme Court Associate Justice Robert Jackson, did not seem to catch on and registered no protests. Jackson had been brilliant in his four-hour opening statement, but he had virtually no experience in criminal law and totally lacked the bulldog tenacity of a skilled prosecutor. During three days of cross-examination Göring ran circles around him.

Several of the judges in subsequent memoirs were critical of Jackson's performance, none more than Britain's Sir Norman Birkett. In fact, he was critical of the Nuremberg proceedings as a whole. He was acidic in his complaints about the slowness of the trial, which he blamed partly on his fellow judges but primarily on what he considered the far too methodical German lawyers.

He had come to Nuremberg already famous in London courts for his sharp wit. He once offered a minor criminal his last words before the bench.

"As God is my judge," said the man, "I'm innocent."

"He isn't, I am, and you aren't," replied Birkett.

On many nights at the press-camp bar in Nuremberg and later

I argued for the legitimacy of the Nuremberg trial, defending it against those who contended it was built on the basis of law that did not exist when the crimes were committed. I always believed the trial was justified by the necessity of establishing judicial precedent even before the establishment of the international law that it was meant to support. This justification was built on the basic truth that the world is unlikely to survive a third world war, which would almost certainly bring universal nuclear devastation. If we are to avoid that catastrophe, a system of world order is mandatory.

When we finally come to our senses and establish a world executive and a parliament of nations, thanks to the Nuremberg precedent we will already have in place the fundamentals for the third branch of government, the judiciary. This, to my mind, was the meaning of—and the justification for—Nuremberg.

Chapter 4—Moscow

AFTER the war my next stop was the Soviet Union. But my United Press career almost ended on a dock in Helsinki harbor. Betsy and I came close to not making it to Moscow at all.

We took a ship from New York to Göteborg, Sweden, and the train on to Stockholm. We were alone in our train compartment as the Swedish customs inspector came through. The customs man inquired as to how much foreign currency we were carrying. I declared my puny UP allotment—only a couple of hundred dollars. Betsy made a totally ineffectual attempt to whisper. "Twelve hundred dollars," she said.

I was shocked. There was no way she could have saved that much money from my income. I'm embarrassed even now to recall the terrible suspicions with which I was briefly assaulted.

Her embarrassment may have been even greater as she confessed that the money had been given to her by her father. She explained, "Father always has given me enough money to get home from a date." She had the fare from Moscow almost literally pinned to her lingerie.

From Stockholm we took a Soviet ship, the *Sestoresk,* to Leningrad via Helsinki. Aboard with us was an acclaimed Swedish tenor, Jussi Björling, making his first postwar trip to Finland. Björling insisted that we have lunch ashore with him in Helinski. After we docked, we went to a charming little restaurant; his other guest was the chief of police, adorned in black leather from head to toe.

The mutual toasting was unrestrained. The clock crept toward our sailing hour, but the chief assured us he would get us to the boat in plenty of time. He miscalculated. Despite the flashing red lights and the screaming siren, we reached the dock to see the *Sestoresk* retreating from the harbor. The ship was the last means of entering the Soviet Union before our visas expired.

With a cavalier wave of the hand the chief insisted there was no problem. He ordered up a police boat. Now, with our flashing lights and siren waterborne, we overtook the ship.

The *Sestoresk* seemed to slow slightly and dropped a Jacob's ladder over the side. The deck seemed the height of the Matterhorn away. Betsy went first, and we climbed that swinging rope ladder straight up and up and up. It was the hard way to get to Moscow but perhaps no harder than the life we would find there.

The UP apartment in Moscow was in a five-story building, just off the Arbat Square, a fine location not far from the Kremlin and the American embassy. Its location was better than the structure. Its stucco exterior had peeled so badly it looked like a serious case of sunburn on the third day. Glass was missing from one of the front doors; the other hung by the thread of a hinge.

Our four rooms, bath, and kitchen were connected by a large foyer that gave the apartment a sense of spaciousness that was partly illusory. It was luxurious, however, compared with the building's other apartments, which were shared by a minimum of four families—five if the foyer was occupied, as in most cases, or six if the kitchen was inhabited.

Social life in Moscow was much more active than either of us had anticipated. The government extended only one privilege to foreign correspondents, but it was an important one. They gave us ambassadorial rank. This put us on the diplomatic list for invitations to all of the embassies' parties on the nights of their national holidays.

And the benefit of that was first, the food and second, the company. The embassies served elaborate buffets, but the problem was getting anything to eat. While cocktails were being served, the doors to the dining areas remained closed, and the guests—mostly the Russians and East Europeans—jockeyed for position in front of them. When the doors opened, it was the Oklahoma land rush. Men and women circled the buffet table, took their positions, and with elbows flailing to guard their space, ate whatever was within reach. If they were stuck by the radishes, radishes is what they had.

These occasions were just about the only opportunity we had to meet Russian government officials. They simply were not available to us at other times. At the parties we might exchange a word or two with members of the Politburo. Vyacheslav Molotov, the foreign minister, frequently was present; Stalin never.

When I wasn't in white tie and tails for "national days," I was in black tie for what in any place other than an outpost of empire would have been just another night out. Our hosts were members of the diplomatic colony, almost exclusively from the democracies of Western Europe and South America. They were our social set, since all relations with the Russian people were circumscribed. It was a little like attending a cocktail party every night with fellow occupants of a submarine.

There were no equivalent social associations with the Russians. The official propaganda line, warning the populace against friendship with foreigners, worked. Only two or three couples dared to invite us to their homes. These invitations took the form of chapters from a spy novel. They were notes always placed directly in our hands, usually in front of our apartment, by strangers to us but presumably trusted friends of our hosts. They instructed us to meet the messenger at a certain corner to be led to our hosts, usually by a circuitous route down narrow streets and narrower alleys.

In their apartment a phonograph played at full volume to thwart any devices intended to listen in on our conversation. The only silence was when records had to be changed, at which point the host put his finger to his lips.

Secrecy and fear were pervasive. They hung heavily over every transaction, every conversation in Moscow.

The UP office was in one small room of our apartment, crowded with my staff. Madame Tarasova was my secretary-translator, a woman whose tiny bones, pinched face, and sharp nose betrayed an upper-class heritage. A young college student, whose full round face and widely set eyes spoke of an Oriental background, was an assistant translator and messenger. The other messenger had stepped out of every painting of Russians at work—the small eyes and the button nose, a face capable of an astoundingly large range of emotions from hearty good humor to desperate sadness.

They drove me crazy. So few Russians did I get to know in my two years there that I cannot testify whether they were typical, although the experience of other non-Russians seemed to confirm my impressions. What I detested was the one trait they shared: They could not wait to try to prove their loyalty to me by citing the disloyalty of the others.

The moment one of them left the room, the others would shower me with allegations that their absent colleague had been seen going through my papers or making mysterious telephone calls. The planting of suspicion seemed to be their entire raison d'être.

I came to the conclusion that this uncivilized behavior was prompted by a history of one cruel dictatorship after another. A whole people had it drummed into them that the way to get along with authority was to establish one's own loyalty by impugning that of fellow workers, neighbors, or even family members.

And this, of course, was model behavior under Stalin.

The effect of the drumbeat of propaganda spread through a controlled press was brought home to me by my driver, Alexander, my principal source of the day's hottest rumor.

He had been a driver in the Soviet army, and during our first months together he spent most of our conversation time praising the American "zheep," as he called it. To his mind the jeep was the greatest technical achievement of the twentieth century, and the Americans, in developing it, had proved their technical superiority.

But Alexander was undergoing the brainwashing that the Kremlin propaganda masters had directed to wipe out such impressions left by American aid during the war. The propaganda was vicious and persistent. They claimed that Russians had invented every modern device from the telegraph to the airplane and reached the pinnacle of mendacity with the claim that they had invented baseball.

I thought surely that the people must find the official claims as ridiculous as I did. But I came to realize how effective lies can be when the truth is suppressed as I heard Alexander's tune change day by day. Within months he was asking me plaintively why we Americans claimed to have invented the "zheep," when we knew the Russians had.

It was this control that the communist authority had over the minds of the people that laced their propaganda with real danger. The morning that *Pravda* published a letter "exposing" our colleague Robert Magidoff as a spy, we all shuddered with apprehension. The letter allegedly had been sent by his secretary, a young lady of Finnish American background who seemed about as pro-American and anti-Soviet as one could be. Magidoff represented several U.S. business publications, and she cited letters from them asking about various financial and production matters in the Soviet Union. In any democratic nation these were the most routine news inquiries. *Pravda* turned them into "proof" that Magidoff was involved in industrial espionage, or worse.

Magidoff was of Russian heritage; his wife, Nila, was a Russian citizen. We trembled for their fate—and for ours, since this could be the opening of a campaign to drive all correspondents out of the country or jail us as examples of capitalist treachery.

Magidoff was expelled, but the Soviets showed a rare bit of humanity and permitted Nila to go with him. His secretary was never heard from again. The populace got the message regarding the sinister nature of foreign correspondents, and our jobs were made even more difficult in the months ahead.

Our reporting was almost entirely limited to interpreting the abstruse reports in the press and analyzing the order in which Politburo members stood and sat at public functions. First-person or descriptive stories not taken directly from the Soviet press were so heavily censored that they seldom made sense. The censorship was so complete and so inane that, when pneumonia laid me low, I could not advise my office that I was ill and out of action. For days they queried me on stories, with no response, until finally the embassy advised them of the problem.

In the long parade of depressing days in Moscow perhaps one of the worst was when the Pulitzer Prize was awarded to Eddy Gilmore of the Associated Press. It wasn't that Eddy wasn't a good reporter and a clever writer, but the dispatches cited by that supposedly learned awards committee had all passed through those Soviet censors. So the Pulitzer committee actually handed its award to Eddy Gilmore *and* the Russian censors. I lost a lot of respect for the Pulitzer after that.

An award should have gone to *The New York Times*'s Drew Middleton. Without any suggestion of their source, he sprinkled his articles with quotations from *Alice in Wonderland* that indicated that the Russian official "facts" he cited were as imaginative as Lewis Carroll could have made them. The censors never caught on.

Before I left Moscow I did a piece about the changes in the city since our arrival two years before. Making a series of parallels, I tried to report on the progress in that time. But the fool censors mangled that as well. At one point, for example, I had reported, "Two years ago, everybody was in the felt boots with rubber soles that they called *valenki*. Today one sees leather shoes on the people of Moscow."

That whole paragraph was reduced to "Today one sees shoes on the people of Moscow."

The secret police, notorious for their brutal tortures, imprisonment, and exile, could be devilishly ingenious as well. Travel within the Soviet Union was restricted even for the Russians. They needed internal visas to travel outside their places of residence. As for us foreigners it was rare that we could get such permission, but an undersecretary of our embassy by some subterfuge managed to get tickets for three couples to take the riverboat to Stalingrad—a nearly three-week voyage down the Volga.

Betsy and I accompanied the two embassy couples. We half expected to be stopped at the gangplank when we presented our tickets. Nothing was said, and we found the trip downriver fascinating. The boat stopped at small landings for women, children, traders, and farmers, packs on their backs and occasionally an animal at the end of a rope. At night they entertained themselves with accordion or balalaika music, a song, or a dance.

One of the entries in my list of most unforgettable characters was a gregarious older man who wore the tieless, buttoned-up shirt and leather-billed khaki hat of an old revolutionary. We played chess and talked to the limit of our restricted vocabularies.

On our last day out before Gorki, where he would be disembarking, we stood at the rail and he pointed to a distant smokestack. That, he said, was where he worked. And what did he do? I asked.

"Oh," he said, "I'm a member of the NKVD."

My dear new friend was a member of the dread secret police. It turned out, however, that he was in a nominally passive position as superintendent in a prison-camp shoe factory.

We, too, were disembarking at Gorki, where we were to change ships for the rest of the voyage to Stalingrad. As we docked, the ship at the wharf immediately ahead of us was identified as the one bound for Stalingrad. In a land without porters we managed to get our luggage to its gangplank. And there we were told that the vessel was oversold and our tickets could not be honored. In response to all our protests and inquiries we were told only that we could get the answers at the Intourist Hotel at the top of the hill.

Carrying all our luggage, we struggled upward to reach what must once have been a splendid hostelry of almost universally typical resort architecture—broad verandas that overlooked the river and the limitless plain beyond. There wasn't a soul outside, and we found there were no guests inside.

The lone receptionist sat behind a cashier's wicket. Her greeting carried a warning. "You should have told us you were coming. We could have prepared for your visit."

Our first question was about our boat passage to Stalingrad. She advised us that the next boat was full, as was the next one after that. In fact, there were no reservations left all summer.

We were beginning to get the drift. Could we perhaps get train reservations to Stalingrad? Not surprisingly, there were no train reservations available either. Then could we get train reservations back to Moscow? Unfortunately, none of those could be had.

"But," she said, "here are your airplane tickets back to Moscow. The plane leaves at six forty-five tomorrow morning."

If there was an airport at Gorki, that was not where we were taken the next morning. We were driven to a large field with no facilities. An old American twin-engine DC-3 sat at the end of our airfield. Standing at the foot of a ladder was a woman in military garb. Unsmiling, she helped us aboard and waved to the metal bench running down the plane's length.

The flight was not pleasant. Sitting in silence, each of us was highly apprehensive. We dared not voice our concern, certain that our conversation was monitored. It all seemed well within reason to conclude that we were being shipped off to a distant incarceration.

We put down at what was clearly a military airfield. But instead of taxiing to a reception building somewhere, the pilot stopped at the end of the runway. The hostess helped us and our luggage down, nodded a good-bye, and reboarded—and the plane was gone.

We hiked to a gate at the far end of the field expecting to learn our fate. A guard, his automatic weapon armed with a bayonet, saluted with a smile, and waved us through. Our embassy friends identified the landing field as a military base in suburban Moscow. Since no hostility was evident, they dared to ask the guard to borrow the phone, and they called the embassy for a car.

We couldn't believe we had escaped so easily. Yet we hadn't. We found our apartment ransacked. All of our clothes were gone. The jewelry boxes in which we had only memento stuff—fraternity and sorority pins—were gone. My files had also been gone through.

The police dusted the place for fingerprints. Of course, they came up with nothing. Their only response was to warn us that this sort of thing could happen when an apartment was left unoccupied. Or, in other words, we shouldn't have left town on an unauthorized trip.

OCCASIONAL OFFICIAL VISITORS briefly enlivened our endlessly dreary existence in Moscow. The censors severely restricted what we could report about distinguished visitors from other nations, but our contacts with them, limited as they were, provided important background for us.

Shortly after the Communists had seized power in Prague, when there was still the shadow of a coalition government, Jan Masaryk, the Czech foreign minister, visited Moscow. I had known him when he was part of the refugee government in London during the war. He was in Moscow only briefly, and there were no parties for him, no public meetings with him at all. The rumor was rampant that the Kremlin had proclaimed to him that Czechoslovakia was now a part of the Soviet sphere.

This was not certain when I learned that Masaryk was leaving on an early plane a couple of mornings after his arrival. Dawn comes very late on those long winter days in Moscow. The airport was in darkness as I took up a lonely vigil at the gate. No other correspondents had bothered to come out.

The official party arrived. Three Zis limousines stopped at the gate. Foreign Minister Molotov and Masaryk got out of one; the rest of the officials, Czech and Russian, tumbled out of the others.

Masaryk saw me and nodded a greeting. I took the signal as an invitation, and I approached him. I got a few steps before two plainclothesmen began moving toward me.

I waved a hasty good-bye and said, *"Au revoir."*

His reply was equally hasty as he was escorted away. "Oh, no, my friend," he said. "Farewell."

A few days after returning to Prague, on March 10, 1948, Jan Masaryk went out one of the windows of his apartment in the Foreign Ministry building. It was officially declared a suicide, although to this day there is deep suspicion that he was murdered by the Communists. I thought at the time of our farewell that Masaryk was simply confirming his gloomy awareness that the Iron Curtain was about to be lowered around Czechoslovakia, but I have wondered since whether his words bore a deeper significance.

Many times during the cold war I thought of Masaryk. And I

thought a lot about the fervent anti-Communists' slogan Better dead than Red. That sort of deeply patriotic sentiment, it seems to me, might have had some rationale in the days when wars had winners and losers. But does it stand up in the nuclear age, when a massive exchange of bombs would cause such great losses?

It does not seem to me unpatriotic to offer the possibility that it might be better to be Red than dead, under those nuclear circumstances. Even if the Red dictatorship had lasted with all of its horrors for a couple of centuries, would that not have been preferable to a world altered forever by nuclear poison?

I think I would rather be dead than Red, but I'm not at all sure that my personal preference, or even that of a whole generation, should be a basis for sound foreign policy.

One of those Red horrors, by the way, was the class inequality practiced by those master hypocrites. It was evident in a thousand ways, but perhaps none more so than those parades through Red Square in the waning years of the 1940s. As they passed Stalin's reviewing stand on Lenin's tomb, the open cars of the generals seemed barely able to sustain the weight of their passengers, resting their ballooning stomachs on the seats ahead of them.

The colonels marched behind them, their midriffs hinting of a miraculous pregnancy. And then the majors and the captains, almost as trim as those joggers that fill the paths around the Pentagon at lunch hour. Behind them the troops, so emaciated it was a wonder they made it the length of the parade route.

We watched those parades with awe at the heavy equipment, and we wondered about their nuclear capability. The Soviet inefficiency in all visible things made me doubt they had any.

When our apartment sink clogged up, we wrote the necessary letter to the proper authorities to get a plumber. Within a matter of weeks a child showed up at the front door and announced he was the plumber. He took a look at the situation, extracted half a hacksaw blade from his pocket, and proceeded to saw the drainpipe in two. He asked if we had a bucket. He placed the bucket under the top half so it would catch the drainage—and he presented the receipt for us to sign. Mission accomplished.

We didn't sign the receipt, but the authorities insisted until the day we left Moscow that the sink had been fixed and denied us further assistance.

When I returned to the United States, the UP sent me out on a lecture tour. I was speaking in Omaha one night and got the usual question about whether the Russians would get the nuclear bomb. Citing my plumber story, I said I believed that if they couldn't fix a stopped-up sink, they couldn't develop an atomic bomb.

I walked from the hall to see the headline in the next morning's Omaha *Bee:* RUSSIANS EXPLODE ATOMIC BOMB.

I had missed the obvious: All their experienced plumbers had been recruited to build the bomb; none were left for civilian duty.

That night in Omaha was an important one, a turn in the road.

Back in Moscow, Betsy and I had returned to our apartment one night to find a dollar sign painted on our door. This anti-American stigmata was the equivalent of the yellow star with which the Nazis branded the Jews.

Little did we know how that Russian graffiti artist would change our lives.

Chapter 5—Early TV

WHEN I got to New York from Moscow, en route to my pregnant wife in Kansas City, the UP made the most of me, a correspondent just returned from the Soviet Union, which, with its strict limitation on visitors and information was again proving to be, as Churchill put it, a riddle wrapped in a mystery inside an enigma.

They trotted me around to meet all the columnists who would garner an "inside story"—Walter Winchell and Leonard Lyons and a lesser known fellow named Ed Sullivan on the New York *Daily News.* And the UP sent me out to make speeches.

I returned to my hotel after that speech in Omaha to find a telegram from Earl Johnson, the UP's general manager in New York: EXPLAIN PLEASE LEONARD LYONS TODAY.

That was the full text. Its meaning was obscure. Of course, I knew Leonard Lyons, but explaining him? That might have been difficult even for Lyons.

Lennie was one of the nicest and hardest-working of the Broadway columnists. He eschewed gossip in favor of anecdotes about the famous. He had picked a strange occupation, considering that he was a law graduate and his sense of humor was greatly underdeveloped. As a consequence, he was noted for stepping all over the punch line of the stories that filled his column.

When we met in New York, the story of mine that had incited Lyons to attack his notebook concerned the anti-Americanism that Soviet propagandists were inspiring in 1948. As evidence, there was the day that Betsy and I had returned to our apartment to find that dollar sign scrawled on the door. I told Lyons, "When we saw it, Betsy said, 'If they had known we were newspaper people, they would have put a cents sign on the door.'"

Now, in Omaha with Johnson's cryptic telegram in my trembling hand, I rushed to my room, telephoned the UP desk in New York, and had them read me the Lyons column. Lennie's version of that last paragraph was, "If they had known I worked for the United Press instead of the Associated Press, they would have put a cents sign on the door."

The UP was always sensitive about its pay scale, which was somewhat lower than its principal competition. Johnson had a right to be offended. I wired back that I had been misquoted, which, in the case of a Lyons column, was a believable explanation.

It led to a discussion with Earl about the UP remuneration in general and mine in particular. I had believed my next assignment was to be general European news manager, based in London. This was to be a major step up the UP ladder, and it pleased me.

But that was not to be. When I asked Earl what raise I could anticipate in my new, exalted managerial role, he looked at me in amazement—feigned amazement, I suspect.

"Why, Walter, there's no raise in this. You already are getting more than any of our other foreign correspondents."

In the face of my clear disappointment, he grew avuncular. "How long have you been with the UP now—eleven years? Surely you must have learned how we operate. We take young men, train them, work them hard, don't pay them much, and when they get good enough to get more money elsewhere, we let them go."

This was indeed true. Until the mid-'70s there certainly were more former Unipressers serving on the nation's newspapers, magazines, and broadcast organizations than graduates of any other institution. We even had our own informal organization, called the Downhold Club in honor of the frequent instructions from New York to hold down expenses.

Earl's reminder was sobering, but unbeknownst to him or me, the wheel of fortune was already spinning toward a stop at TV.

Soon thereafter and still on leave back in Kansas City, I found myself lunching one day with a good friend, Karl Koerper, who was the second in command at one of the city's leading radio stations, KMBC, and who considered himself to be news-oriented.

These were the days when radio was enjoying its most successful period. The years of hectic growth were over; television wasn't yet a threat; the money was rolling in.

Karl asked how Kansas City looked to me after my years in Europe. I told him Kansas City didn't seem to be the lively gateway to the Southwest that it used to be. I said I thought it was because it had become a one-newspaper town, that something goes out of the spirit of a city when that happens.

Warming to my subject, I said it was radio's fault. "You guys have cut up the advertising dollar so many ways that only one newspaper can exist in a city," I charged. "And furthermore you haven't done a darned thing to take the place of the missing paper."

Karl wanted to know what I would do about it.

"The least you ought to do is put your own reporters out on the beats where the really important news is—city hall, the county courts, the state capitols, Washington."

One month and two meetings later I would be on my way to Washington, with a hefty salary, to open a bureau for KMBC and a consortium of other middle western stations.

I got there in time for the 1949 inauguration of Truman, a story of particular interest to his hometown, where his haberdashery

had failed and his county court judgeship had been undistin-
guished and where, therefore, there was considerable trepidation
when he first took office. By now, however, concern had been replaced by pride.

The Truman inaugural was the first and the last story of any
major significance during the life of our Middle West radio bureau.
I did six fifteen-minute commentaries a week—with surprisingly
little impact, considering that almost all of my ten stations were
leaders in their markets. It turned out that the news editor at only
one station had any idea how to use a Washington bureau. With
a Washington correspondent to answer their queries, these stations could have customized their news reports, but despite my
urging, only Jim Borman at WMT in Cedar Rapids, Iowa, had the
knowledge or interest to do so.

I suspected that some of this disinterest was a result of the kind
of show-business jealousy that plagues broadcast news. These local
broadcasters simply were unwilling to share any of their glory with
some Washington parvenu. There was not a great cry of rage,
therefore, when the service came to a precipitous end and I was
launched onto the network.

The Korean War did it. With the American commitment to the
fight and my World War II correspondent buddies already on the
way, I knew that was where I belonged—although Nancy was barely
a year and a half old and Kathy was on the way.

Ed Murrow had tried to hire me during World War II, when we
were both in London. I had accepted his offer and then reneged a
few days later when United Press gave me a raise. Now, hoping that
Ed had forgiven me, I rapped out a telegram to him saying that,
while I was one war late, I was ready to join CBS if they'd have me.

The answer was affirmative.

So I began getting my shots and attending the daily briefings at
the Pentagon preparatory to going to Korea. And I was substitut-
ing for various of our Washington correspondents on CBS Radio.

Eric Sevareid did one of our major broadcasts, the fifteen-
minute news and analysis at 11:00 p.m. He was taken ill, and the
manpower pool was so dry that they thrust me into the spot. Un-

fortunately, I had grown a little rusty on the techniques of fine-tuning a broadcast to the second, as demanded by the network.

The result was a shambles. I ran over by untold seconds—at least a half minute. Red lights were flashing in the studio, and bells clanging in the control room. No one in the Washington bureau had ever so violated the holy covenant of time.

So strapped was CBS for manpower that despite this start, one substitution job after another filled the days while I waited to go to Korea. The fighting wasn't going at all well, and I was beginning to doubt my sanity in volunteering for war correspondent duty. At just about that time, there were fateful developments on the Washington front. Much earlier than expected, the government suddenly granted CBS permission to buy an existing Washington television station. CBS changed its call letters from WOIC to WTOP-TV.

The network was anxious to put the stamp of CBS News on its outlet in the nation's capital. They needed somebody to deliver the news, but when they looked around the radio newsroom, the cupboard was bare. The regulars were in Korea or had a full schedule of sponsored radio programs that they were unwilling to drop for a medium whose opportunities were somewhere around the corner.

So I was asked to go out to WTOP-TV and do the six-o'clock newscast. They sent along a young radio producer who knew scarcely more than I did about television. With a cameraman who doubled as our graphics director, we were the WTOP-TV News staff in Washington.

We learned fast—with primitive equipment, no film except that which we shot locally, and a limited budget. Korea, of course, was the big story, and I covered that with a simple expedient.

We put up a large blackboard with an outline of Korea and, drawn across it, the thirty-eighth parallel, which was supposed to divide North and South Korea. I extemporized a chalk talk with a description of that day's action, slashing great arrows and crosses across the board to depict the movement of troops.

As new as television was and as little of it as I had seen (we didn't even own a television set yet), I had a gut feeling that television news delivery ought to be as informal as possible. I imagined

There has never been anything as exhilarating as driving at high speed in competition. Below: In 1950 CBS signed me to do the six-o'clock newscast at WTOP-TV in Washington, D.C.

The 1952 conventions were the only time the public would have such an opportunity to see our great political conclaves in pure, undiluted form.

President Kennedy helped us inaugurate network television's first
half-hour evening news broadcast in 1963. Below: "President
Kennedy died at one p.m. central standard time—a half hour
ago. . . ." The words stuck in my throat.

the newspaper editor running down a list of the day's big stories when asked at home, "What happened today?"

I had early training to do that. When I was on the night desk of the United Press in the early days of the war, our president, Hugh Baillie, used to call in from wherever he was to ask what was going on. He expected a seamless rundown of all the big stories on the wire. If he asked for more details, the deskman on the phone was expected to deliver them as if he had memorized them.

So the television ad-lib came easily to me, and I thought that this seemingly extemporaneous type of delivery fitted the concept of speaking to that single individual in front of his set in the intimacy of his own home, not to a gathering of thousands.

My "script" consisted of a list of the subjects on which I would report, proper names I would need to remember, and the occasional precise figure I might need. I crammed it all on a slip of paper I pasted behind the desk sign that identified the WTOP-TV News. We attempted some pretty dramatic effects, primitive though they were, to spice up the broadcast. As drought struck the Middle West, we went to an easel with a map of the United States. Behind the easel stood a studio assistant who pressed a hot studio light to the map behind Kansas, and lo and behold Kansas began to smolder and smoke and the "drought" spread to neighboring states. The effect was rather unique, as was the arrival of the fire department, summoned by the studio's smoke detectors.

We learned a lot in those early television days, not least that our new medium had a powerful impact. In 1953 the Netherlands suffered a devastating flood, and there were appeals from relief organizations for clothing and blankets. I had a brainstorm that veterans of the 101st and 82nd Airborne divisions who remembered with fondness the help of the Dutch in the war's Arnhem operation might spearhead an effort to repay those valiant people.

A good friend, Rex Smith, vice president for public relations of American Airlines, offered to use their ticket offices as collection points. American Airlines planes would fly the material to Amsterdam. An old friend from the 101st days, General Anthony McAuliffe, agreed to go on the air to mobilize the veterans.

Arthur Godfrey, whose CBS program was one of the nation's most watched, agreed to put McAuliffe on and said, "I'll switch you over to my writer for my lead-in," and he gave me to a gruff voice that barked, "Rooney. What have you got?"

It was my old World War II buddy Andy Rooney, who would go on to become a television personality in his own right.

The McAuliffe pitch went on Godfrey's show that very night. I was awakened the next morning by Rex Smith.

"What have you done to us?" he shouted. "Our ticket offices are inundated. There isn't going to be enough cargo room on our regular flights to move all this stuff. What are we going to do?"

What we did was get the association of American truckers to move the tons of material to a Hoboken pier from which we planned to ship it by sea to the Netherlands.

Smith's efficient American Airlines staff made all of these arrangements in the next few days while, I gather, Smith fought off American's other executives, who had a reasonable question as to how Rex had had the temerity to get the airline involved in such a massive venture without first clearing it with them.

The answer to that was, Rex and I agreed, simply that neither of us expected anything like the response of the public to McAuliffe's appeal. Despite the problems, Rex and I exulted in this new demonstration of the compassion for the unfortunate that is such a hallmark of our American people.

There was a lesson a day to be learned as we felt our way into the television age—about ourselves and our power to move people, and about the people we moved.

NETWORK television assignments began to fall my way, and one of the earliest may still hold the record as the most complicated in the medium's history. It was the coronation of Queen Elizabeth on June 2, 1953. The story had everything—a beautiful princess ascending an ancient throne with pageantry unmatched by any other event in the modern world. It was a grand opportunity for television to display its ability to bring the world into America's living rooms. The problem was that our abilities were still limited.

We were still in the age of film, which had to be developed—a time-consuming process. And most important, we didn't have satellites or any other means by which the pictures could be transmitted across the Atlantic. The challenge was to find a way to fly the film to New York and get it on the air the same day. The crown would be placed on Elizabeth's head in Westminster Abbey shortly after noon—7:00 a.m. New York time. The commercial piston planes of those days took fourteen hours, London to Boston. Given the five-hour time difference, CBS decided to go all out to beat the opposition with the first pictures on the network and, second, with the first full, instant documentary of the historic day. Furthermore, it was prepared to take a real gamble and promise that our first pictures would be seen at 4:00 p.m. eastern daylight time and the full documentary treatment would hit the air at 10:00. Separate task forces were set up. Don Hewitt would produce the documentary, with Ed Murrow as the commentator. CBS News president Sig Mickelson would produce the quick version, which I would report.

Hewitt's group chartered a BOAC Stratocruiser, among the fastest airliners at the time. They stripped out seats and installed facilities to develop and edit film. Desks and typewriters were provided for writers and researchers. They planned to have their program ready to go when the plane landed at Boston.

Our arrangements were even more complicated. Our film would hitchhike across the Atlantic on one of the first military jet aircraft, the Canadian Royal Air Force's speedy Canberra bombers. They could cross from London to Labrador in just five hours. We chartered a World War II P-51 Mustang fighter to fly our film from Labrador to Boston's Logan Airport, where we would set up transmission facilities just off the tarmac.

The best coverage of the coronation ceremony in Westminster Abbey certainly would be that of the British Broadcasting Corporation. We set up a studio and production center in an abandoned tower at the London airport. We had two rapid film developers that could take pictures off the television tube and deliver them in just fifty seconds. And we had a broadcast booth where, watching the BBC coverage, I could cut in at selected times to inject an

American angle to the story. A battery of film editors we had brought from the States stood by to cut the unwanted parts of the film and fit in my commentary filling the gap.

All seemed to be going well until about midmorning, when it was realized that our film editors were falling far behind; there simply weren't enough of them. Practically as the Canberra was warming up for takeoff, Mickelson made a command decision: The cans of still uncut film reels would be carefully labeled in sequence, and while they were on the way, we would dictate to the stateside editors just where, second by second, to make the cuts.

We got our film with the full Westminster ceremony onto that Canberra by the skin of our teeth. CBS News went on the air from Logan just as the Mustang appeared on the horizon. Our reporter was on the tarmac excitedly reporting the plane's progress as it taxied up to the ramp by our control center. The pilot handed down the film to our chief engineer. Whatever self-congratulations occurred to our Logan crew at that moment were instantly crushed. The film reels were not in the cans with the identifying numbers. There was no way to know the order in which to broadcast them.

The pilot later explained that he had had to take the reels out of their cans because otherwise he couldn't fit them all into the tiny cockpit of his plane. But we were lucky. The engineers reached into that grab bag of reels and selected one to slap on the air. It happened to be the reel of the coronation ceremony itself. As that reel ran, the staff at Logan got the rest of the reels in the proper order, with a lot of words of assistance shouted over a telephone line from London. Our viewers were told that now that they had seen the Queen crowned, we would take them back to the beginning of her day. It seemed as if we had actually planned it that way.

With daring coverage like that, television was growing up. The coronation broadcasts were a far cry from our first television remote—the return to Washington of General Douglas MacArthur from Korea in 1951. MacArthur, so incredibly arrogant, was openly questioning the White House direction of the war. Truman, on his part, had reason to question MacArthur's military leadership. He had pursued the North Koreans beyond the thirty-eighth parallel, up toward China's border on the Yalu River. His headlong chase after another great MacArthurian victory had brought the Chinese into the war. The winter on the Korean front was terrible; the enemy was fierce, and the casualties were high.

Truman, in his gutsy fashion, ordered home the great hero of World War II, General of the Army Douglas MacArthur. MacArthur's return to Washington was a major news event—loaded with emotion, controversy, and political significance.

We handled it from the top of a station wagon parked not far from the airplane steps. The public relations people were not yet concerned about staging such events for television. They did not keep the welcoming crowd at a distance great enough to give the cameras a clean look at the principal actor. As a matter of fact, I could barely make him out even from my elevated perch. I'm afraid that my description of MacArthur's historic arrival home was to a large degree imaginary. Actually, the great man didn't say much at the airport event anyway. He saved his oratory for an appearance before Congress.

He was a great public speaker, frighteningly good for a man with all his other accomplishments and attributes. He seemed to tower over men who were actually inches taller than his five feet eleven inches. He made no effort to hide his superior intelligence and sent every possible signal that he did not suffer fools.

His speech to the joint session was spellbinding. Watching from the House press gallery, I could feel the sense of enthrallment that gripped the chamber. I saw not a few lawmakers sneak a quick wipe of their cheeks as they rose to give him a rousing ovation after his closing sentence: "Old soldiers never die; they just fade away."

It was dramatic. It was also just oratorical hyperbole. He had no intention of fading away. Supporters were already pushing him as a Republican presidential contender in the 1952 campaign. They were confident that this hero would stampede the convention and then smother the Democrats.

Several things got in the way. Perhaps the greatest impediment to MacArthur's presidential ambitions was that the moderate Republicans had found their own war hero, one less controversial and far more personable than MacArthur—Dwight David Eisenhower.

I wasn't a great admirer of MacArthur's politics, but I'll admit I suffered a twinge of regret when he did actually fade away. You see, if my grandfather Fritsche hadn't been so darned protective, I might have been Douglas MacArthur, Jr.

When my mother was a teenager growing up in Leavenworth, Kansas, she was the belle of the ball at the Staff and Command School at Fort Leavenworth. One of her beaux was the young MacArthur—young, but apparently not young enough.

The family legend goes that MacArthur asked for Mother's hand in marriage. Grandfather accused the young captain of being a dirty old man, far too advanced in years for his daughter, and chased him off the front porch, one of MacArthur's few retreats.

Once, at a reception, I dared mention the matter to the general.

"Helen Fritsche," he repeated. I thought I detected a slight glint in his eyes. "Ah, yes. Yes."

And he turned to greet another guest.

POLITICS stuck its toe into the television age at the party conventions of 1948. Cameras were there, but the number of stations and sets were so few as to relegate that pioneering event to a historical footnote. By 1952, however, the nation was tuned in as politics entered the television age. For the first time, millions of Americans saw democracy in action—as it chose its presidential candidates. On television the public watched the critical battle for delegates, and they were taken to the keyholes of the smoke-filled rooms where decisions were being made.

Of course, the public didn't see everything that went on at the conventions, but it certainly got the flavor from television. The Republican nomination hung on the outcome of fights to be seated between opposing sets of delegates from seven states, in each case one slate supporting the conservative Senator Robert A. Taft of Ohio and the other supporting the national hero General Dwight David Eisenhower. The Republican National Committee decided that its debate and vote would take place behind closed doors. So we set up our cameras outside those locked mirrored doors of the Boulevard Room in Chicago's Conrad Hilton Hotel.

Standing outside with microphone in hand, I emphasized the secrecy of the deliberations going on behind what I referred to as the mirrored curtain. For one afternoon, however, I was broadcasting a fund of information about the goings-on inside. The source of those reports baffled both the Republicans and my broadcast opposition. My source was literally "on the inside."

Our chief technician had tapped into the microphones on the committee's podium inside the room. He ran a wire up the outside of the hotel and into a broom closet several floors above. There one of our newspeople listened to the proceedings through earphones and wrote notes that were rushed to me downstairs.

Unfortunately, this didn't last too long. Our man had to go to the rest room, and while he was gone, a reporter for a small out-of-town station became curious about that outside wire and traced it to the closet. He was just putting the earphones to his head when the Republican security people, also tracing the wire, broke in on him. We might never have had to admit that we were the perpetrators of the bugging except that, with good heart, we had to confess in order to get the inquisitive but innocent reporter off the hook.

The attempt to ban television coverage of the Taft-Eisenhower delegate fight brought thousands of protests pouring in from loyal Republicans across the nation demanding to know what the credentials committee was trying to hide. The committee saw the wisdom of opening its debate to television.

It voted to seat most of the Taft delegates, but the full convention overrode that decision and gave most of the disputed delegates to Eisenhower. This established Eisenhower as the nominee.

The television audience watched that fight, as it did the rest of the proceedings at Chicago's International Amphitheater, as first the Republicans, then the Democrats, met there. The TV viewers heard the open debate, and they watched skilled politicians maneuver as the Democrats' Speaker of the House Sam Rayburn and the Republicans' former and future Speaker Joseph Martin wielded their gavels with practiced and heavy hands.

With the informality of pretelevision days, there was virtually no decorum on the floor. Most of the delegates were men, and many of them were in shirtsleeves and suspenders. Frequently there were delegates sprawled across several of the folding chairs, napping away the previous night's indiscretions. Many read newspapers and tossed them onto the floor when they were through.

At the Democratic Convention, during one session that had gone on most of the night, the floor was calf-deep in paper. Somehow it caught fire, and flames immediately leaped from the floor.

Someone grabbed the microphone and was shouting in a voice tinged with panic, "Don't panic. Don't panic. It will soon be out. Don't panic." Delegates beat at the flames with their coats and stamped at the edges of the blaze. And without any professional help they did indeed get the fire out.

That was the convention that nominated the reluctant Governor Adlai Stevenson of Illinois. As we waited for him to arrive, an advance copy of his acceptance speech was given to the press. My colleague Eric Sevareid was sitting with me, and we both began poring over the speech. I was deeply impressed by the beauty of Stevenson's language. Eric and I finished reading, and as I looked toward him, that master essayist, expecting to hear a paean of appreciation, he tossed down the copy with a look of disgust. He said, "I'm not sure I'm going to enjoy covering a politician who writes better than I do."

Those 1952 conventions were not only the first but also the last time the American public would have such an opportunity to see our great political conclaves in undiluted form. By 1956 the parties had begun to sanitize their convention proceedings. In time platform and credentials hearings were moved farther from the convention, in part, it can be assumed, to discourage television coverage. The list of speakers was limited and carefully screened "to avoid confusion," we were informed; delegates were even told what they should wear and how to behave. In an effort to please the television cameras, chaos, to a large degree, was banished from the convention halls and so, to a large degree, was democracy. The conventions were reduced to marketing tools.

The photo bite was invented before the sound bite. The politicians learned fast and early on began trying to control their television appearances for maximum advantage. Of course, they ran headlong into broadcasters intent on transferring to television the journalistic ethics they had learned as newspaper reporters.

Early in that pioneering decade of the '50s the then majority leader of the Senate, Lyndon Baines Johnson, was persuaded to appear on our CBS Sunday morning panel broadcast, which we called *Capitol Cloak Room*. Shortly it would become *Face the Nation*. Johnson showed up at our studios on schedule for a prebroadcast briefing fifteen minutes before airtime. He sat down with the panel and handed a piece of paper to each of us and said, "Boys, here are the questions you'll ask me."

I explained to him that we didn't use prearranged questions.

"That's all right with me," he said, and took the papers and walked out the door. I caught him in the corridor and persuaded him to go on the broadcast, now minutes away, by agreeing that we would limit the questions roughly to the areas he had designated.

Bill Downs asked the first question—a tough fastball far afield from any of the Johnson-approved areas. The future President peered at Downs through squinting eyes and finally got his clenched jaws open far enough to say he wouldn't answer the question. The rest of the half hour went like that. Downs later chastised me for making the compromise with Johnson and pointed out that he had not violated the agreement to limit the questioning, since he hadn't agreed to it in the first place. It was not exactly television's finest half hour, but historically it may be significant as a harbinger of the relationship between politics and television—a standoff between an attempt to manipulate the medium and the medium's determination not to be manipulated.

The politicians' attempts to control television have led to some unfortunate confrontations. In the Wisconsin primary of 1960 the viability of a Catholic presidential candidate was still being tested. We persuaded John Kennedy to appear on our election night broadcast, and in the interview I naturally asked his opinion of how the Catholic and non-Catholic vote was going.

He was obviously upset by the question, and only later did I learn that his campaign manager, brother Bobby, claimed he had produced Jack for our broadcast on condition that the Catholic issue would not be raised. I was never informed of such a promise, if indeed one was made by our producers. Like Downs a few years earlier, I would not have agreed to it anyway.

Apparently Kennedy cooled down in his opinion of me, because a few months later he agreed, reluctantly, to appear on an interview program we had devised. I proposed a totally unrehearsed, unedited dialogue in which I would ask the candidates some probing personal questions—a formula so standard today that it is strange to think it could ever have been considered radical.

Kennedy turned me down at first but agreed to participate after Nixon accepted. Nixon even volunteered to be interviewed first, although the man who appeared in the second week would have the advantage of having gotten a taste of what was to come.

Early in the interview I asked Nixon, "Mr. Vice President, I know you must be aware . . . that there are some who would say, 'I don't know what it is, but I just don't like the man.' What is it that you think they don't like about you?"

Nixon answered that question as if it had been rehearsed. He thought it was three things: the strident nature of his campaign in California against Jerry Voorhis for the House and Helen Gahagan Douglas for the Senate, his active role in the House Un-American Activities Committee's Red hunt, and his physiognomy. He said he felt that his appearance was unfavorably affected by his rather low hairline and his heavy blue beard, which was obvious no matter how close he shaved.

Later, of course, it was his contention that the poor makeup job done to soften these features was what defeated him in his debate with Kennedy. The implication was that the CBS makeup woman had deliberately sabotaged him. The truth was that the Republicans had provided their own cosmetician. Unfortunately, the parents of our Frances Arvold, CBS's highly skilled makeup artist, were solidly loyal Republicans who almost disowned her when they read of the Nixon allegations.

In a private conversation at one point during the campaign New York governor Tom Dewey asked me what I really thought of Nixon.

I gave my standard answer about not rendering personal opinions on figures in the news.

"But," I added, "I can tell you what I believe a lot of people think. He reminds them of three of the archenemies of our time."

And I named the onetime German heavyweight champion, Max Schmeling, the Nazi leader Rudolf Hess, and the Red-baiting Senator from Wisconsin, Joe McCarthy—all with heavy dark beards and low hairlines.

Dewey grabbed my arm. "You know," he said, "I never thought of Schmeling!"

As for the rest of the Nixon performance on my interview show, he answered every question for the next half hour as if he were reading the answers from a TelePrompTer. The following week we did Kennedy in his Georgetown home. He seemed somewhat ungracious, a little annoyed by our presence.

The questions were not as tough as those I had asked Nixon— Kennedy didn't have the political record on which to base much— and the last question was the same: "What single quality do you think will be the most important that you take to the White House?"

It was such an obvious question that if he had seen our previous program with Nixon, he surely would have known it was coming. But he flubbed it badly. He stumbled around and finally stammered that his particular attribute was "a sense of history." The cameras off, he got up, said a perfunctory good-bye, and went upstairs.

I was out in the CBS truck parked in the street, when our producer came by to advise me that Kennedy was insisting on doing the program over. He maintained that because of the way we had positioned him on his divan, he appeared slumped over—but clearly it was his answers, not his posture, that bothered him.

The producer said that Kennedy had rejected all of his arguments as to why the interview should not be repeated, primarily that the Nixon program was unrehearsed and that, in fairness, we would have to issue a disclaimer stating that the Kennedy program had been redone at his request.

So I went up to Kennedy's bedroom to try my hand. The room looked like a college dormitory, down to the Harvard banner on the wall. Kennedy was lying on a bed, his shoes off, his collar undone, and his tie pulled down. "Ready to go?" he greeted me.

"No," I said, "I'm ready to argue some more." And I told him how unfair I thought it would be and, with the disclaimer, how unfair it would appear to others. But he was adamant, said he didn't care about that. At which point I vented my frustration.

"All right," I said, "but I think this is the lousiest bit of sportsmanship I've ever seen."

I was halfway to the door when he called me back.

"Okay," he said. "Let it go."

THE 1964 Republican Convention in San Francisco was a dandy. William Scranton, a former Congressman and governor of Pennsylvania, sought the presidential nomination that ultimately went to Arizona's Barry Goldwater. Betsy and I took our sixteen-year-old daughter, Nancy, along, with her promise that she would not get involved in any demonstrations or activities that could embarrass us, particularly any that could cast doubt on my impartiality.

Our caution was not unreasonable. We had been blessed with two lovely daughters—and cursed, in that they reached their teens in the terrible '60s. Nancy and her younger sister, Kathy, seemed to enlist in every ugly fad that, according to the standards of their parents, blighted their generation.

I'm sure that in their group I was classified as an old fuddy-duddy. I once told Nancy that, and she patted my head and said, "Yes, you are, but you also are a funny daddy."

I loved them despite my feelings about their general appearance most of the time. One Thanksgiving we persuaded them to dress for the family luncheon. Afterward friends joined them to go out, and Nancy disappeared upstairs. She came back down a moment later, out of her Thanksgiving dress and into some indescribable outfit that looked like it was from a remnants sale.

I dared a slight witticism. "Are you going to a costume party?"

Nancy shot back, "No, I've just been to one."

We parents were so frightfully ignorant that we thought that at least, thank goodness, they weren't into marijuana or worse.

Kathy's first book was about how children of famous parents coped with their parents' fame. In a clever tour de force she interviewed her sister. Their revelations of their teen years in New York threw their mother and me into a paroxysm of shock from which I'm not sure we have yet fully recovered.

We did have some hints during those dark days. On one occasion Kathy called us from school to say that her class was going to a concert and she needed an additional five-dollar allowance. How nice, we thought, conjuring up pictures of the Boston Pops at Tanglewood. That weekend we listened to radio reports of a wild gathering at a place called Woodstock. How terrible, we remarked when we heard accounts of drugs, alcohol, and nudity. And then an announcer referred to the affair as a "concert."

"Concert!" we shouted to each other as the truth burst upon us.

I later heard that Kathy had spent most of her time at Woodstock working in a makeshift first-aid center, nursing victims of narcotic overdoses. A barely perceptible silver lining in the cloud.

Our son, Chip, seven years younger than Kathy, didn't seem to offer as much raw material for serious concern. He reached teenhood just as the '60s faded. Youthful behavior patterns did seem to change then, or perhaps we parents and society at large were adjusting to life as it would be lived in the late twentieth century.

We still weren't halfway through the desperate decade, when the Cronkite family arrived in San Francisco in the summer of 1964 for the Republican Convention.

The first morning there, I was in the barbershop when a familiar voice came from under the towel covering the face of the fellow in the next chair. It was, unmistakably, Walter Winchell.

"Hey, Walter," he said, "that's the cutest little girl of yours. She was a sensation last night. She stood outside here, right in front of Goldwater's rally, pushing a big Scranton sign up right under his face. I'm leading my column with it."

The conservative leadership of the Republican Party came to San Francisco to play a tough game. Their speakers not only attacked Rockefeller and his supporters, they scarcely missed an opportunity to attack the press as well. Even Eisenhower joined in this game, including in his speech a paragraph sharply criticizing us: "Let us particularly scorn the divisive efforts of those outside our family, including sensation-seeking columnists and commentators, because, my friends, I assure you that these are people who couldn't care less about the good of our party."

As he read his statement, delegates rose and shook their fists toward our booths in the balcony.

The episode concerned me. I had never heard Eisenhower express such opinions before. So I went along to his suite at the St. Francis Hotel. He greeted me warmly, and we exchanged the usual niceties before I brought up the offensive paragraph. Ike seemed surprised, as if he hadn't heard those words before. He stumbled around in what seemed to me to be almost an apology. I got the distinct impression that the import of the words had not struck him as he rehearsed his speechwriters' work.

THE convention with perhaps the most far-reaching effect on American politics was the Democratic meeting in 1972. George Mc-Govern was nominated, and his forces made a revolutionary change in party rules. In an attempt to democratize the nominating process, they stripped most of the political Establishment of its privileges. Officeholders and state party officials no longer would automatically become delegates to the national convention. They would have to stand for election in either state conventions or primaries.

The first to take advantage of this revolutionary change was Georgia's governor Jimmy Carter. He realized that he did not have to gain anybody's approval to run for the party's presidential nomination. He raised the funds, and he beat the bushes, and he won in state conventions and primaries. The party would never be the same. And with the realization of their new importance states across the nation adopted the primary system.

The McGovern reforms had another effect: A new responsibility was loaded upon the press. Under the old system the party bosses selected candidates for offices from city councilman to President. They screened the would-be candidates, and while a noteworthy number of rascals got past them, the system was reasonably effective.

Deciding on a candidate, the party hacks in the smoke-filled room ran through the possibilities.

"How about Eddie Johnson?" one would suggest.

"Are you crazy?" might come a retort. "Eddie's a damned drunk."

"What about Henry Jones?"

"Come on. He's slept with every woman in the district. No way."

And thus went the screening process, a process virtually eliminated by the McGovern reform. So it fell to the press to examine the candidates' peccadilloes, which, if they could possibly affect their performance in office, would be revealed to the voting public.

FAME for me came suddenly—a bolt from the blue. The full impact of the career I had chosen began to hit me first with the political conventions of 1952, when fame engulfed all of us whose faces hung out there on the television tube.

There is a considerable upside and an almost inconsiderable downside to television fame. On the upside, of course, is the certainty of getting a good table in a crowded restaurant. A downside to celebrity is the autograph seeker who, getting your signature, turns to a companion and asks, "Who is he?"

But mostly it is up, not down. For instance, the benefits of wealth—let's make that "the benefits of being reasonably well off." Like the day I discovered that I could afford a sports car.

From an early age I had been fascinated by cars. In New York after the war I read of the new boom in British sports cars, but I didn't seriously think of buying one until I began noticing them in a used car lot under the elevated Red Bank, New Jersey, station, where the train stopped en route to the city. We were summering on the Jersey shore, and I was lounging on the beach when the postman brought a check for a lecture fee mistakenly sent directly to me instead of my agent. I suggested that day that Betsy take me all the way to the Red Bank station—so "we could spend a little more time together." That wasn't what I sneakily planned on spending.

As soon as she drove off, I ran under the tunnel to the used car lot. Clutching my check, I said to the salesman, "What sports car have you got for $1,767.50?"

The astonished salesman escorted me to the lot and showed me a dandy little Austin-Healey for $1,795.00.

"I'll take it," I said.

I hadn't driven a stick shift since the early '30s, and my departure from that lot was a little shaky—almost as shaky as my attempt to restart the machine after it stalled at the first tollbooth on the Jersey Turnpike. That couldn't discourage me. A few weeks later that tired four-cylinder Healey was traded in for the newest six-cylinder model.

I moved on to racing and got pretty good at it. The skill involved in driving a racecar intrigued me: shifting down and up for maximum speed around numerous curves; touching the toe to the accelerator even while braking with the heel and, with the other foot, depressing the clutch. So delicate was the touch that some of the best drivers wore ballet slippers.

I cut my racing teeth with the Austin-Healey and, with a codriver, won a ten-hour endurance race for economy cars in a Volvo. With my appetite whetted, I joined a group we called Club Lotus USA, for which we bought three used Lotus Club Eleven racing cars.

These extraordinary British racing machines were made of aluminum, so light you could almost lift them. The heaviest component in the car was the driver. Those devils had a top speed of 140 miles an hour and handled like the finest racecar built.

We were scheduled to race our Lotuses in the international twelve-hour race of endurance at Sebring, Florida. At the last moment, however, the Lotus builder withdrew our entry. Almost simultaneously Lancia, the Italian motor company, decided that Sebring would be the site of a test-drive for a new economy car they were about to introduce. They hired us to drive them.

It rained heavily the day before the race, and we had no time to adequately test the cars. They turned out to be incredibly slow. There we were, plodding along at barely over 100 miles an hour, sharing the course with the world champions going at nearly twice that speed. It was very sobering to be coming into a curve where passing was dangerous at best and finding in your rearview mirror the Ferrari or Maserati of Juan Fangio or Phil Hill.

It was the children who brought me back to earth and drew me away from racecars. As I spent more of my free weekends at the track, I realized that this wasn't exactly a family sport. I hadn't been under any pressure to quit. Betsy was stoic. So stoic, as a matter of fact, that I decided I must be overinsured. She later confessed that she threw up a lot. She did have one sneaky trick to slow me down. When she timed my practice runs, she told me I was doing better than I was so I wouldn't press too hard.

My emotional reaction to racing was strange. I wondered why I was doing it in the first place, and I came to the conclusion that a lot of us raced for the same reason that others do exhibitionist, dangerous stunts. It sets us apart from the average man; puts us, in our own minds, on a level just a little above the chap who doesn't race. For me there has never been anything as exhilarating as driving at speed in competition.

I HAD never been on a sailboat, but I decided that sailing was the family-oriented sport that I should substitute for racing.

The club where we summered outside Carmel, New York, had just begun racing the new Sunfish, a small, basically one-person sailing board. People had been urging me to try one, and now, with my new direction, I agreed. The instructions seemed simple enough: Pull on this string here, and it brings the sail in or out to control the speed—and this handle here moves the rudder to turn.

All that had just been explained to me when the time approached for the day's first race. They helped me into a boat, with instructions simply to follow their lead and do as they did and that we'd go down to that mark at the other end of the pond.

Well, for the first time and almost the last time, I was across the starting line first and was headed for the first mark. And I was pulling away from the rest of the fleet. Now what might have been a moderate problem became a first-class crisis. I didn't have the slightest idea how to make that ninety-degree turn around the mark. I did what came naturally. I capsized.

I later learned that the reason I had led the fleet to the first mark was that I was too dumb to know I was going too fast, right at the point of losing control. But I was hooked, and we transferred our sailing to Long Island Sound and began moving up in a succession of bigger and bigger boats. Betsy finally complained, "Doesn't anybody ever buy a smaller boat?"

The answer is, Not if they can help it.

Sailing for me has satisfied many urges. For one thing, it feeds the Walter Mitty in me, that inner heroism with which James Thurber endowed his unforgettable character. I never sail from harbor without either having a load of tea for Southampton or being under orders to pursue that villain Long John Silver and his rapacious crew. I love the challenge of the open sea.

There is nothing more satisfying than dropping anchor in an otherwise deserted cove just before sunset, pouring that evening libation, and, with a freshly roasted bowl of popcorn, lying back as the geese and ducks and loons make your acquaintance and the darkness slowly descends to complement the silence.

The cars, the boats—all made possible by the wages of fame.

On the other hand, the downside. Not the least of which involves the attention of the *National Enquirer.*

The *Enquirer* appeared one week with a big banner headline proclaiming the inside story of my encounters with unidentified flying objects. The story's lead was a description of my office and my posture as, feet on desk, I recited my experiences with UFOs.

The rest of the story was all in quotations—my first-person story of watching a dog being kidnapped from a Caribbean island by little people from a spaceship and other amazing adventures.

The story was a fabrication from beginning to end. The bylined writer who had concocted the fiction was Robin Leach, who would go on to fame and fortune with further television fables of the rich and famous. I hate to tempt them to try again, but the *Enquirer* didn't seem to seriously dent my credibility.

Hewing to my own personal standards honed by years of the United Press's total objectivity and now to the exceedingly strict CBS News standards, our *Evening News* broadcast won wide praise for its objectivity, and suddenly I, as its anchor, showed up on various polls—Elmo Roper's and the *U.S. News & World Report's* annual survey—as the nation's most trusted person. When asked to comment on this phenomenon, I could only suggest that they clearly hadn't polled my wife.

Of course, total objectivity doesn't please fringe fanatics. I could tell that we were in the middle of the road on controversial issues when complaints from the left and the right roughly balanced out. I felt that if we were being shot at from both sides, we must be in the middle of the road.

Among the ideologically committed who had not slipped into fringe lunacy, there was another interpretation of objectivity. Theirs was a simple construction: If you weren't against them, you must be for them. This is how I account for the numerous suggestions from both sides of the political spectrum that I run for public offices from city hall to the White House, and without exception—I repeat, without a single exception—not once did any of them ask where I stood on the issues of the day. I fear that these professionals figured that once I was in office, they could manipulate such an amateur and that it didn't really matter what my own views were.

One year a group at Vassar said they were starting a movement to draft me for the presidency. They claimed they had put a deposit on a storefront headquarters in Poughkeepsie but would like some assurance that I would run before they put up the full payment.

"I can go Sherman one step further," I wrote them. "Not only if nominated, I would not run, and if elected, I would not serve, but if perchance I did serve, I would be impeached."

Chapter 6—Presidents Who Have Known Me

THE first TV incursion into the White House was arranged with Harry Truman. He realized that the people should be permitted to see their leader's residence since its extensive remodeling—a four-year, $5,761,800 project. For the broadcast Truman would guide network correspondents on a tour of the house. The three networks would pool the coverage. I was the CBS man, and in our little lottery I drew the ground floor and basement. Frank Bourgholtzer of NBC took the second floor, and ABC's Bryson Rash the third floor.

My homework was thorough. By the day of the live broadcast I knew the story behind every room, every painting, and every stick of furniture on my two floors.

It turned out that I needed few of the facts with which I was loaded. And of the facts with which I dared to prompt the President, he either corrected me or topped me. I learned then of the kind of ego that grips a person who has been elected to probably the most powerful job in the world.

Examples:

As we entered the main-floor sitting room, I noted that this was the room Dolley Madison had taken such pride in redecorating after the British had played arson with the White House in 1814.

"Most of these decorations Bess has done," the President said, not about to let Dolley take anything away from his adored wife.

And again, as we entered a rather dungeonlike room with a vaulted ceiling in the basement, I remarked that this was the room from which Franklin Roosevelt had reached out to the people via radio in his effective fireside chats.

Naturally Truman put an asterisk to my note. "Yes, and I've done all my broadcasts from here."

Much of the broadcast went that way, and I thought of a cat, rubbing against the chair or its bowl, marking its possessions and its territory with the spoor nature had provided.

Truman was the third President I had a chance to know—although my acquaintance with one, Herbert Hoover, came when he was living in retirement at the Waldorf Towers sometime after his departure from the White House. He had been out of office twenty years and would die a decade later at the age of ninety. We spent an hour alone together, and I thought he was particularly lucid, if a little tendentious. I couldn't get him to discuss the past at any length, although I would have liked to hear him reminisce about his star-crossed presidency.

It was ironic, however, that Hoover, who had been brought down by his inability to stem the Great Depression, talked mostly about the current state of the economy under then President Truman. And he still referred to the "radical influences" in Washington, which he blamed for the policies that the Roosevelt administration called progressive.

A few years before, he had completed a monumental work commissioned by President Truman—a study of waste in government. The Hoover Commission's many-volume report contained hundreds of recommendations for trimming the vast government bureaucracy that Roosevelt's centralization had spawned. Hoover did not seem surprised that there had been no immediate attempt to implement any of the recommendations. He was too experienced in the ways of Washington to expect anything else. His guide as to how we might achieve fiscal responsibility might still be useful, but, forgotten, it gathers dust on the government shelves.

My acquaintance with Franklin Delano Roosevelt was not quite as limited as that with Hoover. I saw Roosevelt for the first time during the 1940 presidential campaign, when I joined the train on one of his swings through the Middle West.

What impressed me on that trip was the condition of the President. Although I had seen hundreds of feet of newsreel coverage of him, I had no idea of the extent of his disability as a result of poliomyelitis. The press clearly conspired, although I am certain without any formal agreement, to cover up the fact that our President could not walk or even stand without considerable assistance.

I don't believe this was a political decision, given the Republican orientation of most of the press at that time and the extreme distaste with which many publishers viewed the New Deal President. This was a rare show of delicacy on the part of the press.

I was to see President Roosevelt in slightly more intimate circumstances several times thereafter, when I was briefly in Washington and our White House man would take me along to Roosevelt's informal press conferences. In most of those years of the Roosevelt administration the White House press corps was but a handful of men—a very very rare woman, then—who had their desks in a small room in the West Wing of the White House, just around the corner from the President's office. When the President felt the urge, he'd send the word, and the dozen or so newsmen would pile into the Oval Office and stand in a semicircle around his desk.

The conversation was a free-for-all—questions and sometimes un-interrupted lengthy answers. Nothing could be attributed to the President unless he gave specific approval.

It was a wonderful system. It gave the press a far better sense of the background of the administration policies than is permitted by the present televised news conferences with their time limits and huge crowds.

Since Roosevelt, the President who handled the press best was probably John Kennedy. Some of Kennedy's closest friends were newspeople, noteworthy among them Ben Bradlee, who, when Kennedy was President, was *Newsweek*'s Washington bureau chief and later managing editor of the Washington *Post*.

Various alleged episodes of marital unfaithfulness have surfaced since Kennedy's death, perhaps none more shocking than a story recounted in a book by Joe Alsop. The columnist and author wrote that on the night of the inauguration, Kennedy forsook the White House and showed up alone at an informal open house Alsop found himself hosting at his Georgetown home. There, according to Alsop, the man who had been President a bare twelve hours enjoyed a bedroom tryst with a very attractive young actress.

The version I got years later from Jackie Kennedy Onassis—or at least the version I think I heard—was somewhat different. Occasionally we sail from our Martha's Vineyard summer home across Nantucket Sound to Hyannis. We drop anchor near the Kennedy compound, and almost always a vivacious Ethel Kennedy drops by in her sailboat. One day she said we had to come ashore and stay for dinner to help celebrate Jackie's birthday. Just four or five people, she said. Just the family.

It turned out to be so, and I was seated between Ethel and Jackie. It was a nice, intimate time, and Jackie was unusually loquacious, although with my bad hearing and her breathless whisper I was having trouble understanding everything she had to say.

I felt my ears were flapping when I heard her telling me of the fun she and Jack had had at the White House on inaugural night. Let me try to reconstruct her story as I heard it—or didn't hear it. "Oh, Walter, Jack was so funny. He insisted that we go into the

Lincoln bedroom first, and despite his back he wanted to carry me across the threshold like a bride. We got into the bedroom, and he dropped me on the bed and . . ." Her soft voice faded away.

"Oh, we laughed so, but then, Walter, we went over to our bedroom, and he picked me up and had trouble getting us both through the door. Then he went over to the bed again, and he . . ." It faded again.

I asked for a repeat at the critical points. I asked twice, and twice the whisper faded until there was nothing left but my imagination. If Jackie had just talked more and aspirated less, this story might have contributed something to the history of that night.

The revelations of later years about Kennedy's romantic escapades have posed justifiable questions about the integrity of the press. Surely newspeople covering the White House must have known of Kennedy's many liaisons? Why didn't they tell us?

Newsmen are usually quick to claim inside knowledge of almost any story in their bailiwick that comes up now or forever in the future. Yet none of the White House correspondents I know claimed at the time to have any evidence of John Kennedy's alleged bedroom escapades. Most will tell you today that they knew about the rumors but were never able to come up with enough evidence to go with the story. This alibi represents a denial of responsibility for a gross dereliction of the fourth estate's duty.

Certainly the Kennedy-era reporters were operating in a time almost as different from today as were the years of Lincoln or Washington. In the '60s, the media operated on a rule of thumb regarding the morals of our public men. As long as his outside activities, alcoholic or sexual, did not interfere with his public duties, a man was entitled to his privacy. This pardon was extended to the young President. In the light of later revelations that at least one of his lady friends had Mafia connections, this pardon was a mistake. If there were newspeople who knew about this and failed to report it, no wonder they are too embarrassed to confess now.

KENNEDY seemed as comfortable with the press as Nixon was uncomfortable. Even as Nixon's acolytes tried to manipulate an election by burglarizing the Democrats' Watergate headquarters and stealing their campaign secrets, Nixon engaged in an active conspiracy to destroy the press's credibility.

The Nixon administration policy was based on a simple formula: If it could bring down the press's credibility, it might improve its own. This was the Nixon who when defeated for the governorship of California told his concession news conference, "You won't have Dick Nixon to kick around anymore." My wife, Betsy, had a definitive observation on that. At lunch with some of her Republican lady friends the next day, she heard them say how affected they were as they watched Pat Nixon weeping copiously at her husband's side.

"I felt so sorry for Pat last night," one said.

"I feel sorry for her every night," Betsy declared.

Now, however, as the outstanding political phoenix of our time, Nixon sat in the White House and thought he had the power to get even. So he set his deputies on the job, and Vice President Spiro Agnew was named lead dog. Agnew opened the campaign in Des Moines, Iowa, with a speech written by White House wordsmith Pat Buchanan, who later would be overcome with delusions of presidential grandeur. He identified the network news organizations as the main target in a speech that dripped with vitriol.

The entire attack was predicated on a fundamental belief that there was a press conspiracy against the Nixon administration. Buchanan wrote and Agnew said, "A small group of men, numbering perhaps no more than a dozen anchormen, commentators and executive producers, settle upon the twenty minutes or so of film and commentary that is to reach the public. They decide what forty or fifty million Americans will learn of the day's events."

Buchanan even charged the network commentators with "instant analyses" after presidential speeches, although he had been present when White House aides briefed reporters and commentators before the speeches were delivered. Buchanan had been a newspaperman before joining Nixon's White House. He was joined in the antipress campaign by another former newsman serving on the Nixon writing staff, Bill Safire.

I like Bill Safire, and I don't have anything personal against

Buchanan. I think Safire is one of the best thinkers and writers in journalism today. But when serving Nixon, Safire and Buchanan lied.

They knew perfectly well that while it is true that a handful of people decided what would be on the three network news broadcasts each evening, there wasn't the slightest consultation among them. Indeed their intense rivalry prescribed just the opposite.

They knew, because they came from the business, that what goes onto a responsible network broadcast and how that news is played are determined, with rare exceptions, solely by the story's news value. That news value is put on a scale shared by all professional journalists. A story is newsworthy depending on how many people it affects and how deeply it affects them and/or how close it happens to home and/or how aberrational it is.

The Nixon antipress campaign was to get even nastier and more dangerous. At its height I testified at a congressional hearing that there was a White House conspiracy against the press. Some of my colleagues thought I had gone too far. They said I had no proof that the campaign was centrally directed and was in fact a conspiracy. I think I used the old duck theory: If it swims, walks, and quacks like a duck, it probably is a duck.

At any rate, when the Watergate tapes were released, there was the proof. Nixon's own marching orders read clear: "The press is the enemy."

Safire himself wrote years later:

> Was there a conspiracy, as Walter Cronkite of CBS once solemnly charged, on the part of the Nixon Administration to discredit and malign the press?
>
> Was this so-called "anti-media campaign" encouraged, directed, and urged on by the President himself? . . .
>
> The answer to those questions is, sadly, yes.

In an odd twist I got along rather well with Nixon. In fact, I was somewhat embarrassed that I did not make his news media "enemies list." He was quoted somewhere as saying that I was the best of a bad lot. I am not sure I would put that on my escutcheon.

MAKING COMPARATIVE RANKINGS of Presidents is an exercise fraught with contention but otherwise relatively harmless. And the results can be surprising. For instance, I think that of the Presidents I have known since Hoover, the best brain was possessed by Jimmy Carter.

I base this not on his political or administrative skills, which clearly were wanting, but on his incredible ability to read complicated material and file it in his memory so that it could be instantly recalled when needed. This orderliness of mind was evident in situations where he was speaking extemporaneously. Transcripts of his remarks read like a finely honed manuscript.

CBS and President Carter initiated what was to be a series of radio call-in programs in which citizens across the nation could address the President with their questions or their problems. I fielded the calls as Carter and I sat in a pair of wing chairs in the Oval Office of the White House. No questions were submitted in advance, and none was refused. I had given a lot of thought as to how I would handle what we expected to be long-winded questions and the callers who wanted to make speeches of their own. Surprisingly, that never arose during the entire hour of our broadcast. The problem, it turned out, was not with the public but with the President. No matter how far-out the question, he had in his head a textbook of knowledge about it.

One lady called in from Wisconsin to ask about milk price supports, and Carter delivered an excruciatingly long dissertation on every increase in milk prices since World War I.

Despite that, he and we thought the program a success. It had to be abandoned, however, because the telephone company said it jammed its facilities to a dangerous degree.

Carter was smart, but Nixon may have been the most ardent student to occupy the White House. He was diligent in his attempts to overcome the holes in his knowledge. His homework paid off, and he became exceedingly well informed on issues of the day, particularly in foreign affairs.

This stood him in good stead after he was forced from office. One of his first speeches as he embarked on a road he hoped would regain for him some measure of popular respect was deliv-

ered in a brave appearance at the hotbed of his disgrace, the National Press Club in Washington. It was a brilliant analysis of the
national and world situation, delivered without a note. It won a
standing ovation from a cynical audience.

To say that Nixon was the most complicated personality to occupy
the Oval Office is to barely touch the surface. At times he actually
seemed unbalanced. I was at a state dinner once when I noticed his
eyes fix on the molding at the edge of the ceiling. Then they began
following the molding across that side of the room, then across the
adjoining side, even to the side behind him. One would assume that
he was following an intrusive beastie, but I could see nothing there,
and a couple of other guests who also noticed this strange behavior likewise saw nothing to attract such presidential attention.

During his 1968 primary campaign one of his aides, Frank
Shakespeare, invited me to the candidate's hotel room at the end
of one of the strenuous days on the hustings.

Nixon was half reclining on the sofa, his stockinged feet on the
coffee table. As we sipped our drinks and talked, his language was
sprinkled with profanities. The whole scene was so contrary to the
formality, the stiffness I had always seen in the man that I decided
it was a setup to try to establish Nixon as one of the boys.

The Nixon revealed on the Watergate tapes, however, was the
Nixon of that campaign hotel room. It was the Nixon who had
embraced Senator Joseph McCarthy in the 1952 campaign. The
Wisconsin Senator's witch-hunt for Communists in government
was in full swing, and McCarthyism was a campaign issue.

Eisenhower had sullied his reputation by failing to stand up to
McCarthy. It can only be assumed that Eisenhower yielded to pressures from the party's conservative right wing—a problem that has
plagued every Republican administration since Hoover's, except
Reagan's, which was almost entirely right-wing anyway. Nixon himself was a product of the belief that the right wing needed constant
nursing. His selection as a running mate was suggested to Eisenhower to help assuage the right wing.

I never thought that Eisenhower cared much for Nixon. When
it was revealed during the closing days of the campaign that Nixon

had been involved in some shady fund-raising, it briefly appeared that Eisenhower might dump him from the ticket. Eisenhower let him twist in the wind until after the famous television address in which Nixon appealed to the public with a bathetic recital of his humble life. That was the broadcast that featured his wife's "good Republican cloth coat" and his love for his dog, Checkers.

He may have touched Ike's heart, but it is more likely that the party conservatives came to the rescue and convinced Ike and his advisers that Nixon had to stay.

I spent considerable time with Eisenhower after he left office. We made a trip to Normandy together in 1963 to film his reminiscences for the twentieth anniversary of D-day, and I spent a week at his Gettsyburg residence to record thirteen hours of interviews that were the basis for producer Fred Friendly's three-hour memoir of his presidency. And during all of that time I never succeeded in getting him to talk about Nixon except in the most perfunctory way. There was scarcely enough faint praise to constitute a damnation.

The Gettysburg interviews changed my opinion of Eisenhower as President. Until then I had joined in the common wisdom shared by most of my Washington colleagues: that Ike was a lazy President who excused himself from involvement in most of the decisions that emanated from the White House.

Gettysburg was a revelation. For three hours each morning we sat at the desk in his study with the cameras rolling. I had on my knee a pile of notes on the subjects I wanted to cover. Ike, who was seventy-one at the time, did not have a single sheet of paper in front of him. Yet for the entire five days of the interview I did not ask him about a single incident during his eight years in the White House of which he did not have intimate knowledge. Clearly the common knowledge of the White House press corps was not knowledge at all, but wrongful supposition.

The trip to England and Normandy with Ike was sheer delight. Ike had not had a chance since the war to tour the Normandy battlefields where Hitler's forces had suffered the defeat from which they would never recover. He had made two or three previous visits but always in an official capacity, surrounded by officials and

troops and thousands of spectators, circumstances hardly conducive to sight-seeing.

CBS owner Bill Paley, who had been a psychological-warfare
colonel on Ike's staff in London during the war, went along, as did
Mrs. Eisenhower, my Betsy, Fred Friendly, and his staff.

We took Ike back to all the scenes of his preparations in England
for D-day, including Winston Churchill's bomb shelter headquarters under the Admiralty buildings off Pall Mall and the briefing
room at Southampton, where he defied the terrible weather and
ordered the invasion to proceed.

On the beaches of Normandy we stood in the German bunkers
as he mused upon what the Wehrmacht lookouts must have
thought when, on June 6, 1944, they saw that great armada of bat-
tlewagons and landing craft emerging from the dawn's haze. At
one point Friendly planned to have me drive Eisenhower along
Omaha Beach as he pointed out some of the scenes of action
there, but then it occurred to Fred that it was Eisenhower who was
showing me the area and that he should be driving. Ike willingly
climbed behind the wheel. Watching this drama unfold were
Mamie Eisenhower and Betsy. Mamie gasped and reached over for
Betsy's hand. "Betsy, your Walter has never been in greater danger.
Ike hasn't driven in thirty years, and he wasn't any good at it then."

Incidentally, Ike was the subject of many rumors regarding his
affair with his British driver, Kay Summersby. She was always at his
side during the war, and their closeness was apparent to all. Shortly
after the war, as Ike's friends were becoming concerned that the
Summersby story might seriously tarnish the hero's reputation, I
was with a group of Ike's generals and his intimates—among them
dashing Rosie O'Donnell of the air force and Omar Bradley, the
universally admired commander of the First Army.

We were simply visiting and drinking when the matter of Summersby came up, and one of the generals delivered the wisdom of
Solomon as perceived by returning heroes. "Ike's a damned fool,"
he said. "He doesn't understand the first rule. When you get ready
to dump 'em, first get 'em a job."

The judgment was greeted with a chorus of approval, a chorus in which at this late date I would not swear that Rosie or Omar joined.

Generals and Presidents are not immune to the attractions of the opposite sex. We know at least some of the John Kennedy story. Franklin Roosevelt had his Lucy Mercer, and there were rumors about Lyndon Johnson, although I'm afraid I am quite unable to testify personally to any evidence in this regard.

In all the aspects in which I did see Johnson, however, he lived up to the most frequent of his many sobriquets. Indeed he was bigger than life. He strode through his political life from Congressman to President with confident bluster and with his left hand always cocked to snare an opponent's lapels and pull him nose to nose for a dose of some old-fashioned Johnson persuasion.

I made my first visit to the LBJ ranch west of Austin to do the campaign interview that was to be part of the series for which I had finally corralled Kennedy and Nixon. It wasn't much of an interview. Johnson was anything but forthcoming. Future interviews at the ranch would go far better, when they were at least partly at his own instigation.

We did a major interview on the future of the space program, a matter in which he had a keen interest. I was wearing a fine Rolex watch that the Swiss president of the company had given me. He had pointed out that this model was not available to the general public and that he had presented it only to heads of state. As Johnson and I sat under a spreading oak tree dripping with Spanish moss, I realized that his interest in space seemed to be waning as he stared at my lap. I was tentatively feeling to see if I was unzipped when he practically leaned into my face and demanded, "Where did you get that watch?"

When I told him that the watch was a gift from the Rolex president, he erupted. "That son of a gun told me that he only gave those watches to heads of state and such!"

I had a feeling that up to that moment he suspected me of having filched his.

There was later to be a minor impasse in a major CBS negotiation with the President. We contracted to do his memoirs, and I spent many hours over the course of several visits interviewing him

President Truman was the first President to open the White House to a television tour. Below: Eisenhower and me in Normandy filming his reminiscences for the twentieth anniversary of D-day.

Vietnam was a far different sort of war from what we senior correspondents had known in World War II.

Lyndon Johnson was quoted as saying, "If I've lost Cronkite, I've lost Middle America." Below: The meeting of Menachem Begin and Anwar Sadat was brought about by separate interviews with them on the *CBS Evening News*.

at the ranch. The Johnsons kindly put me up in one of their guest-houses. It was done in what might be called a desert brown, and my producer decided that I should wear a green suit. Not normally favoring green suits, I had to buy a couple from Brooks Brothers.

During the interview Johnson and I talked of the Kennedy assassination. At one point he said, "I can't honestly say that I've ever been completely relieved of the fact that there might have been international connections. I have not completely discounted it. Nonetheless, my conviction is that if there had been a conspiracy, some evidence would have emerged by now—secrets involving that many people aren't that easy to keep."

Try as I might, I could not get him to expand on this tantalizing but incomplete speculation.

When doing interviews with sitting or past Presidents, we extended a courtesy not offered others. Since Presidents were privy to so many state secrets, and we wanted them to not feel encumbered in speaking freely to us, we recorded audiotapes of the full interviews and then gave the Presidents a few days to review their words for security leaks. No questions would be asked if they requested that something be excised, but this privilege expired after a few days. This was to protect us from expensive reediting as an interview's exhibition date drew near.

A few weeks after the deadline expired on the Johnson tape, the President decided he wanted that assassination speculation removed. CBS at first refused, and the President and his lawyers grew more and more adamant until they were threatening to withdraw from the remaining interviews in the series. The deadlock continued for weeks—and my green suit hanging in the Johnson guest cottage became hostage to the negotiations. If Johnson sent the suit back to me, it would surely indicate that he was breaking off the negotiations. And if I sent for the suit, the Johnson forces could deduce that CBS intended to break off the negotiations.

CBS eventually agreed to cut the quotations, but LBJ's views emerged elsewhere later. I assumed that Johnson's suspicions of a conspiracy were based on the fact that he knew at that time what neither the public nor the Warren Commission knew—that the

CIA had plotted the assassination of Fidel Castro, thus providing the motivation for a Cuban plot against Kennedy.

The spread that was the LBJ ranch was an impressive one. LBJ was totally comfortable there, and he let you know it. On one of our interview visits the gracious Lady Bird invited our whole production crew to lunch. Johnson was out of the White House and was on a limited regime, taking frequent naps to rest his ailing heart. He showed up for the lunch with nothing but a robe thrown over his shorts. As he presided at the table with an entertaining fund of stories, his usual arm-waving gesticulations would spread the robe wide, revealing a less-than-attractive hairy torso. Mrs. Johnson was clearly embarrassed. Whenever she could catch her husband's attention, she would indicate that he might pull the robe together. He would peevishly tug on the robe, only to launch into another story for a repeat of the whole performance.

He was on a restricted diet, and we sympathized as he complained about it. With each course, and particularly the dessert, he kept a sharp eye on Lady Bird and, whenever her attention was directed elsewhere, without apology he would sneak a forkful of food from the guests' plates on either side of him.

ONE of our more affable Presidents was the President-by-accident, Gerald Ford—the only person who served as President without being elected either President or Vice President. Nixon had appointed Ford to fill the vacancy left by Spiro Agnew's resignation from the vice presidency. When Nixon resigned, Ford became President.

When Ford sought the nomination for reelection, Ronald Reagan made a run at him at the Kansas City convention and came close to unseating an incumbent, a rare apostasy in party politics. Jimmy Carter defeated Ford in the '76 election, but Ford was to play a bizarre role at the 1980 Republican convention in Detroit.

Reagan won the nomination, and the convention was awaiting his choice of a running mate when the hall was swept by an incredible rumor. Some party stalwarts were suggesting that Ford run for the vice presidency on Reagan's ticket. Negotiations were active between the Ford partisans and the Reagan headquarters.

I invited Ford to come to our convention anchor booth. He came and for the benefit of our CBS television audience said he was not seeking the nomination, but he was listening. However, he made clear that he would accept the offer only if Reagan would share with him some of the most important duties of the presidency.

"A sort of copresidency," I suggested, and Ford agreed. That cut it. Both at the Reagan and Ford suites the books were slammed shut. No presidential candidate could agree to such a deal. Our interview certainly made news; it probably shaped the course of events.

Throughout our interview, unbeknownst to Ford or me, a terrible rumpus had been going on outside our studio door. When Ford first appeared on our air, ABC had dispatched one of its fiercest and most successful correspondents to get him over to their booth. We had to call extra security guards as Barbara Walters literally fought to get inside our studio. They were barely keeping her at bay when the interview concluded and Ford emerged.

At a luncheon that both Barbara and I attended the next day, Ford told the group that he had a sore shoulder, suffered when Barbara twisted his arm to get him onto ABC.

The Fords were among the most friendly occupants of the White House, but Reagan won the affability contest hands down. I had trouble with his political philosophy, particularly his endorsement of laissez-faire trickle-down economics—the concept that if the people and industries at the top are successful, prosperity will somehow be visited on all the rest of us.

He was a strong President who lived up to his campaign promise to reverse Franklin Roosevelt's economic and social revolution. He did so by surrounding himself with the same advisers from the nation's top echelons of business and finance who had engineered his election, and then leaving them alone.

Almost every Oval Office visitor left impressed with the Reagan modus operandi. Before answering questions or introducing new topics, he slid his top desk drawer open enough to read from a set of cards presumably prepared by his staff.

He had one weakness that, while scarcely threatening the democracy, did plague his political opposition and the White

House correspondents who were assigned to put his comments into perspective. Reagan would read or hear of some incident that he felt demonstrated the rectitude of his policies or the fallacies of the opposition. His love of a good story frequently led him to stray far from the facts. The stories, often repeated, became part of the political lore, while the press and the Democrats found that their corrections never quite caught up. But, by golly, he was affable.

Chapter 7—Vietnam

IT IS too bad the Vietnam War gave itself such a bad name. It was its own worst enemy. When the United States got involved, the idea seemed rational enough. President Truman, in accordance with his 1947 doctrine to contain communism, poured millions into France's effort to hold on to its Indochinese colony, which was seething with the rebellion of independence-seeking natives. The French were driven out but salvaged something in Vietnam by a partition of the country—the Communists in the north and a regime sympathetic to capitalist-democratic principles in the south.

President Eisenhower bought into the emerging domino theory: that any further revolutionary successes among the old French Indochinese colonies would start a chain reaction, and they all would disappear behind the Iron Curtain. So he supported the new South Vietnamese government, not only with funds but also with military advisers to help train its new army.

At his inaugural President Kennedy pledged that this nation would "pay any price, bear any burden, meet any hardship, support any friend, oppose any foe to assure our survival and the success of liberty." With the depredations of the communist guerrillas growing more serious daily, by the fall of 1963 Kennedy had authorized 18,000 military advisers, up from 685 when he took office in 1961. This was a stretch of his inaugural pledge. It could hardly be said that Bao Dai and the successor we nominated, Ngo Dinh Diem, had established a democratic government. But they maintained that this was their intention, and that was taken by Washington as

grounds for hope that Vietnam might provide a toehold for democracy on a subcontinent that communism threatened to overrun.

While most of us knew little about Ho Chi Minh or the nature of
his North Vietnamese government, we realized that it was communist, and we agreed to defend democracy wherever the Red men-
ace threatened. The domino theory seemed reasonable and was
widely accepted. Thus, many of us supported President Kennedy's
decision to dispatch to Vietnam those military advisers to protect a
little plot of land where democracy might have a chance to grow.

The evidence was clear, and is frequently forgotten today, that
early on Kennedy was becoming disillusioned with the prospects of
political reform in Saigon and disenchanted therefore with his
own policy of support. And I have always believed that if he had
lived, he would have withdrawn those advisers from Vietnam.

Barely twelve weeks before he died in Dallas, I interviewed him
at his Hyannis, Massachusetts, home. In that interview he said:

> I don't think that unless a greater effort is made by the
> [Vietnam] government to win popular support that the war
> can be won out there. In the final analysis it is their war. They
> are the ones who have to win it or lose it. We can help them;
> we can give them equipment; we can send our men out there
> as advisers, but they have to win it, the people of Vietnam,
> against the Communists.
>
> We are prepared to continue to assist them, but I don't
> think that the war can be won unless the people support the
> effort, and in my opinion, in the last two months the govern-
> ment has gotten out of touch with the people.

That scarcely sounds like the statement of a President about to
commit more troops to the battle. It clearly was intended, however,
to send a powerful warning to Diem and his éminence grise, his
brother Ngo Dinh Nhu. Their nepotistic, pro-Catholic dictatorship
had led to serious troubles with the nation's influential Buddhists,
and discontent had even spread to some elements of the army.
The stability of an ally in whom two American administrations had
heavily invested was seriously threatened.

Unbeknownst to me and the American public, my interview with the President came as debate was raging within his administration as to what should be done with Diem. Just a week before the interview Kennedy's Vietnam brain trust had sent a message to our ambassador to Vietnam, Henry Cabot Lodge:

U.S GOVERNMENT CANNOT TOLERATE SITUATION IN WHICH POWER LIES IN NHU'S HANDS. DIEM MUST BE GIVEN CHANCE TO RID HIMSELF OF NHU AND HIS COTERIE AND REPLACE THEM WITH BEST MILITARY AND POLITICAL PERSONALITIES AVAILABLE. IF IN SPITE OF ALL OUR EF-FORTS, DIEM REMAINS OBDURATE AND REFUSES, THEN WE MUST FACE THE POSSIBILITY THAT DIEM HIMSELF CANNOT BE PRESERVED.

Actually, the brain trust, which included Undersecretary of State George Ball and Averell Harriman, drew up the message while three of its key players—Dean Rusk, Robert McNamara, and the President himself—were out of town. Rusk recalls that Ball telephoned the text to him and he approved, mistakenly thinking that the President already had. The cable went to Saigon.

When the senior trio returned to Washington, according to Rusk's memoirs, they tried to soften the instructions to Lodge, but in Lodge's hawkish view, their effort came too late. He cabled back:

WE ARE LAUNCHED ON A COURSE FROM WHICH THERE IS NO RE-SPECTABLE TURNING BACK, THE OVERTHROW OF THE DIEM GOVERN-MENT. THERE IS NO TURNING BACK BECAUSE U.S. PRESTIGE IS ALREADY COMMITTED TO THIS END IN LARGE MEASURE AND WILL BECOME MORE SO AS THE FACTS LEAK OUT.

What was clearly a warning in Kennedy's remarks to me actually might have been meant as more than that. The President, while using the broadcast to keep up the public pressure on Diem, at the same time might have been trying to disassociate himself from any future charges of American complicity in the coup that his administration's actions had already set in motion. That is speculative—but two months after the Kennedy statement Diem and his brother Ngo Dinh Nhu were assassinated in a military coup.

In his memoirs Rusk notes that as the coup got under way, he in-

Above: My best friend among the first astronauts was Wally Schirra. Left: I failed first-year physics. If my professor had heard me explaining orbital mechanics to an audience of trusting millions, I'm afraid he would have spun in his grave. Below: The back of a station wagon was broadcast center for our first manned space launch in 1961.

To say that Nixon was the most complicated personality to occupy the Oval Office is to barely touch the surface.

A raucous story at the White House with (left to right) President Reagan, Press Secretary Jim Brady (behind me), David Gergen, Attorney General Ed Meese, Vice President Bush, Chief of Staff Jim Baker, and (foreground) CBS producer Bud Benjamin. At left: Enjoying retirement at the wheel of the America's Cup twelve-meter *Courageous*.

structed Lodge to offer Diem arrangements to get him out of the country. "But in hopes of finding military units that would support him," Rusk wrote, "Diem rebuffed this offer, was captured and killed. Had we been as actively involved in the coup as others suggest, we could at least have prevented Diem's death." Note the former secretary's qualifying word "actively."

The inside story of that interview of mine adds another shadowy element to the story, with evidence buttressing my suspicions that the President hoped to use our broadcast to prepare a defense if, as Lodge so bluntly put it, "the facts leak out."

Kennedy had granted me the interview to help us inaugurate network television's first half-hour evening news broadcast. These daily showcases of broadcast journalism had all been fifteen minutes before then, in the pattern of the radio news programs. A quarter of an hour was adequate to tell the news of the day. But it had proved totally inadequate when pictures were added.

I had arrived in Hyannis to meet the following morning with the President. As I drove up to the motel where the White House press corps stayed, our veteran correspondent Robert Pierpoint was waiting at the steps. He lit into me in a show of daring disrespect for the anchorman.

"Listen," he practically shouted, "if you're going to break a big story, the least you could do is tell your White House man about it."

"What big story?" I asked.

"That the President is going to make a major statement on Vietnam on your broadcast tomorrow night. It's all over the AP."

This idea was offensive to me in several ways. In the first place, it indicated at the least that Kennedy intended to use my interview to plant a statement to suit his purposes, and no respectable newsperson wishes to be a conduit for official announcements, even ones by the President. It also suggested that Kennedy had been advised in advance of the questions I was going to ask. And further, I thought it was impossibly presumptuous of the President's press secretary, the affable Pierre Salinger, to leak to anybody something he hoped would come up in the next day's interview, and Salinger was almost certainly the source of the AP's story.

I was angry. I found Salinger at the bar and let him have it.

"And I promise you this, Pierre," I told him, jabbing an index finger into his chest. "I'm not going to even bring up Vietnam when I talk to the President tomorrow."

Salinger followed me to my room, arguing for the Vietnam question. I would be passing up a chance to really make news; if I didn't get into it, the President would make the statement elsewhere and I would look foolish for having passed it up.

Nothing would sway me. In the car on the way to the Kennedy compound the next morning Pierre spent the entire time arguing his case. I remained adamant.

But as I sat on the lawn of his Hyannis home with the President, I calmed down enough to realize that, since the interview would have to be edited for time anyway, nothing would be lost in asking the Vietnam question. If he indeed had something newsworthy to say, we could use it; if not, we could drop it. I did at least torment Pierre by not asking the question until deep into the interview.

That answer of his did make headlines. He effectively pulled the rug out from under Diem and changed the course of events in Vietnam. Naturally, the statement that I had said I had no interest in eliciting led our program and was an auspicious opening for the first network half-hour evening newscast.

Whatever Kennedy had in mind about the future of the Vietnam War, however, became moot in those terrible seconds in Dallas. His successor, Lyndon Johnson, was a superb politician and an effective administrator, but his weakness was foreign policy.

It was not a matter that had interested him, and so, in those first months of his presidency, he was at the mercy of his advisers from the State and Defense departments and the military buildup in Vietnam accelerated. The United States manipulated the makeup of the Vietnam government, and the war became ours. A reluctant Congress was brought along with Johnson's vast exaggeration of the Tonkin Gulf incident, the alleged attack by North Vietnamese vessels on two American destroyers.

Although by that time we were already deeply involved on the ground, with almost 20,000 troops in Vietnam, somehow this shad-

owy naval action was represented by Johnson as the step beyond
which the North Vietnamese could not go. And he persuaded
Congress to give him a virtual blank check to conduct a full-scale
war without ever declaring one. There were two basic mistakes in
the Johnson administration's handling of the war. The first was the
President's policy of trying to shield the American economy from
the consequences of the war. The people at home were not asked
to share in the costs of the war—there were no material shortages
or rationing, as in World War II, and taxes were not raised to pay
for it. This not only was disastrous economic policy, creating a debt
with which generations yet unborn will still be burdened, but it increased the frightful inequity of sacrifice: The lives of draftees were
sacrificed, or at least disrupted, while life on the home front was
scarcely disturbed.

The other administration mistake was far more insidious. Perhaps himself misled by a military either greatly overoptimistic or
incredibly duplicitous, Johnson never leveled with the American
people about the nature or likely extent of the war, although his
secret briefings with congressional leaders were fairly straight-
forward. Congress was suspicious and attempted to control the extent of our involvement, but under pressure from the military
experts it was apparently powerless to stop the escalation.

We were in the early stages of this buildup when I made my first
trip to Vietnam. Saigon still retained some of the old French colo-
nial charm that would disappear in the dust and smog of thousands
of military vehicles crowding its once lovely treelined boulevards.
The Caravelle Hotel, designated as press headquarters, was filling
with correspondents, but many of us still stayed at the less modern and hence more gracious Continental Hotel across the square.

The roof garden of the Caravelle provided a nightly box seat for
the war. We watched the bombing raids on the city's outskirts,
some nights more intense than others. One night, over to the
northwest, maybe seven miles away, was a brilliant display of flares,
lighting the countryside around. Tracers from unseen helicopters
poured fire below, accompanied by the occasional bump and concussion of 500-pound bombs. The next morning Armed Forces

Radio said that the U.S. command had reported there had been no important activity in Vietnam the night before.

A caste system that has always been applied to war correspondents to some degree has become more offensive with the growth of television. There are the grunts—the real battle reporters, who risk their lives alongside the soldiers in the foxholes. And then there are the anchorpeople, who spend a few days dipping their feet in the waters of war, but who never suffer total immersion.

The members of this latter caste are invited to dine with the generals and to have audiences with high officials in the host country. They are offered escorted tours of the war and hence see a somewhat different war than those sharing the foxholes.

I took advantage of the generals' dinners and the high-level political interviews, but I also made brief forays into what passed for the front lines in a war that had none. On that first visit I went out with the helicopter-borne 173rd Airborne Brigade, the first unit to be sent to Vietnam after the escalation from the military-observer stage. I rode with them into the jungle not far outside Saigon as they sought out the Vietcong. On subsequent visits I flew with the air-support helicopters as they swept low over the jungle's treetops, machine-gunning whatever was under that green canopy.

In the field and back in Saigon I heard the tales of the pacification officers who were working in the villages to win the hearts of the people. While they acknowledged that they were not encountering much enthusiasm for democracy, most of them had not yet sunk into the cynical pessimism that would come later.

I was still impressed with our effort—impressed enough to view with some embarrassment the performance of much of the press at the military's daily news briefing. While most of the older war correspondents appeared to be attempting in a rational way to extract the facts from the military, the younger reporters seemed to be engaged in a contest to determine who was the most cynical and confrontational in their rude challenges to the appointed spokesmen.

I was not yet prepared to grasp the fact that Vietnam was no ordinary war. This was no routine meeting of press and authority.

These hapless spokesmen were charged with explaining a war that had no explanation, and both they and the press knew this to be the awful truth. The press named the evening news briefing the five-o'clock follies. It could have been the name for the war.

Despite all this, I returned from that first trip to Vietnam with the feeling that the evidence in the field seemed to support the contention of Washington that we were making progress.

But then came the revelation of Cam Ranh Bay. That big open body of water was ringed by one of the most beautiful beaches in the world. It was so perfect that many of us cynics suggested that it would be the postwar site of a chain of hotels.

That would have been a kind fate compared with that which fortune dealt the bay. The United States built a huge naval base there, ruining the landscape and providing the first physical evidence that perhaps the military didn't themselves believe the optimistic reports they were giving the country.

The building of that base was ordered in April 1965, when the administration had led congressional leaders to believe that our ultimate commitment of troops would be no more than 200,000. Yet the base was designed to service the other end of a pipeline that could handle many times that many troops. With Cam Ranh Bay my disillusionment began. That and the increasing reports from the military and the political foxholes of Vietnam that neither the battle to subjugate the Vietcong nor that to win over the Vietnamese villagers was meeting with any tangible success.

Additionally, there was something distinctly uncomfortable about a war in which it was impossible to claim that we were liberating any sizable parts of the territory of South Vietnam. The criterion for success that our military adopted was the body count. The only way to measure victory, it seemed, was in terms of how many Vietcong we could kill. That was scarcely uplifting. It became increasingly difficult to justify the war as the terrible cost to ourselves in blood and material grew and the supply of Vietcong needing to be killed appeared inexhaustible.

My disillusionment was keeping pace with that of growing numbers of American people. And then came Tet.

The huge Vietcong offensive kicked off on the Asian New Year's Day in violation of a holiday truce. Within days it had swept through every important city in South Vietnam except the big marine base of Danang and Saigon itself. According to reports, in scores of villages that we had considered pacified, the peasants had turned back to the Vietcong.

All of this, even as we Americans were being told that the end of the Vietnam War was in sight. Polls showed that the number of Americans who no longer had faith in the administration or the military that served it had become the majority.

With the new uncertainties created by the Tet offensive, it seemed to me that perhaps we should put on the line that high level of trust the people had in our broadcast. Perhaps, I proposed to our news president, Dick Salant, I should return to Vietnam and try to present an assessment of the situation. Salant agreed, and that same night I was off for Asia.

Back on the roof of the Caravelle Hotel, I watched the helicopter gunships and bombers attacking suspected Vietcong concentrations on the city's outskirts and saw fires blossom on the docks downriver. I drove to the Chinese section, which the Vietcong had penetrated, and I stood in the smoldering ruins they had left behind.

I flew and trucked with GI reinforcements into the ancient city of Hue, where the marines were fighting house to house and where incoming artillery shook the command headquarters. It turned out to be harder to get out of Hue than to get in. Ambushes had closed the roads. We shared a helicopter out with the bags holding twelve marines whose war had ended that day at Hue. I thought about them as, back in Saigon, I was assured by our leaders that now we had the enemy just where we wanted him and with just 200,000 more troops we could finish the job.

Tell that to the marines on that helicopter, I thought.

As Tet wound down, I spent an evening at the Phu Bai headquarters of General Creighton W. Abrams, Jr., the military's number two man in Vietnam, whom I had last seen in the World War II Battle of the Bulge. He was remarkably candid in admitting the ex-

tent of the damage in casualties, materials, and morale. His officers joined us, and their conversation brought home the nature of
modern war as even the experience of battle itself had not. It was
a brutally technical discussion of firepower and kill ratios. How,
in effect, we could kill more Vietnamese. I wanted us to win the
war, but this emotionless professionalism was hard to take.

But most incredible was the claim from on high at our Saigon
headquarters that all we needed now was a few tens of thousands
more men and we could finish the job. As it was, after Tet, General
William Westmoreland asked Johnson for another 206,000 troops.
Johnson said no, in effect closing the book on Lyndon Johnson's
war. It would soon become Richard Nixon's war.

My decision was not difficult to reach. There was no way that
this war could be justified any longer.

So I flew home and did a special report on the Tet offensive. It
was as factual as we at CBS News could make it. But I ended it with
an editorial—a radical departure from our normal practice.

As we discussed the broadcast, Salant warned that I was placing
my reputation, as well as CBS's, on the line and that we might well
lose a substantial part of our audience. I had no problem making
my decision.

In the broadcast I made it clear that my subsequent words represented my own opinion. I said:

> "To say that we are closer to victory today is to believe, in the
> face of the evidence, the optimists who have been wrong in the
> past. To suggest we are on the edge of defeat is to yield to un-
> reasonable pessimism. To say that we are mired in stalemate
> seems the only realistic, yet unsatisfactory, conclusion. . . . It
> is increasingly clear to this reporter that the only rational way
> out, then, will be to negotiate, not as victors, but as an honor-
> able people who lived up to their pledge to defend democracy
> and did the best they could."

The reaction to the broadcast was not at all what we expected.
Although there were the usual letters of complaint from those who
disagreed, they were not in unusual numbers.

There was no reaction from the administration. I did not hear of, and I do not believe there were, any complaints from the White House to the CBS management, although in the past Lyndon Johnson had been quick to telephone me, and other anchorpeople, directly to complain of coverage to which he objected.

The explanation came months later, when we learned that the President was actually stunned by the broadcast. George Christian, the President's news secretary, and his assistant Bill Moyers, later to win fame on television, were present as the President watched the broadcast. "The President flipped off the set," Moyers recalled, "and said, 'If I've lost Cronkite, I've lost Middle America.' "

I think it is possible that the President shared my opinion, and that in effect I had confirmed it for him. He probably had as much difficulty as I had in accepting the military's continued optimism in the face of the Tet setback.

The broadcast, I believe, was just one more straw in the increasing burden of Vietnam, and as such it added that much more weight to the decision that was forming in Lyndon Johnson's mind not to risk defeat in the forthcoming election. It was just five weeks after the broadcast that he announced that he would not be a candidate for reelection.

Shortly after the post-Tet broadcast, Robert Kennedy invited me to lunch at his Senate office. It was just the two of us, and he wanted to explore my views on the conflict further. When he expressed his belief in the necessity of extricating ourselves from Vietnam, I suggested that he ought to take his argument to the people by entering the presidential primaries that spring. The press had been speculating that he might challenge Johnson.

"Give me three reasons why I should run," he countered, "and I'll give you three reasons why I shouldn't."

He saved me from having to play that game by continuing, "Let me ask you one. Where are you registered to vote—in Connecticut?"

No, New York, I told him.

"Then you aren't registered as a Democrat?" He had clearly been checking the rolls.

"I'm registered as an independent," I said.

"Well, that doesn't matter. We want you to run for the Senate this year."

He filled the void of my speechlessness by outlining the sort of support I could expect from the party. At the first pause I told him why I eschewed politics—namely, my concern that once a prominent network anchor ran for public office, the people might suspect all news anchors of doctoring the news to satisfy secret political ambitions. The subject was left at that.

When I got back to our Washington news office, the bureau manager, Bill Small, was eager to know what Kennedy had said about running for the presidency. I told him of our limited conversation on the subject.

"What did he tell you about the weekend meeting at Hickory Hill [his Virginia residence]?"

He hadn't mentioned it.

"Roger [Mudd] has the whole story. The old Kennedy brain trust is in town, and they are going to decide this weekend whether Bobby should run."

It was a top story from one of the best political reporters ever to work the capital scene. Obviously, it had to go on our air that night. But it presented me with a terrible problem. My lunch with Kennedy had been off the record. Now, when we put the Mudd story on the air, it would appear that I had used whatever he said to develop the story of the weekend meeting.

I called the Kennedy office to explain the situation to him. His press aide Frank Mankiewicz said Kennedy was on the Senate floor and couldn't be reached. Airtime was approaching, so I asked if Frank could take a message to the Senator.

I said, "Tell him that Roger has the story of the Hickory Hill meeting and that he got it entirely independent of our luncheon, and would the Senator please give me a quotation I could use about the meeting and his intentions to enter the race."

Mankiewicz called me back an hour or so later.

"The Senator gave me a message to read to you. He said you could use it only if you use it in full. I don't know what it means, but here it is: 'Senator Kennedy said that he was contemplating running for the presidency just as Walter Cronkite is contemplating running for the Senate from New York.' "

Bingo!

I MISSED the dramatic last days of the American stay in Vietnam—the terrible helicopter flights from the roof of the Saigon embassy. That is, I was not in Saigon. But I was determined not to miss the end of one of the biggest stories of my news career.

Of course, the story was far from over. Hanoi still held an uncounted number of our prisoners and finally agreed to release the first group. A small group of correspondents had gathered in Laos; then Hanoi arranged a plane and let us all in to North Vietnam. Hanoi had clearly taken a beating from our bombing. Hundreds of small individual shelters pockmarked the sidewalks. But the people seemed remarkably cheerful. They waved as our bus passed by.

We were taken to the infamous "Hanoi Hilton," from which this first batch of prisoners would be freed. The prisoners were standing outside small two-man cells that looked like horse stables. They were thin, but not emaciated, and wore a nondescript collection of loose clothing. It was immediately apparent that they did not know what was going on. In a final bit of cruelty their Vietnamese guards had not told them they were about to be released. Suddenly they were confronted with a busload of newspeople.

We were permitted to talk to them but were warned that we were not to discuss details of their release. Actually, we had no details except that they were being flown out that afternoon. We asked the usual questions about treatment, food, conditions of their capture, length of their imprisonment, and so on. Most of them were very cautious and, before answering the simplest question, would cast an apprehensive look at the guards.

I hit on a way to spread the word. Without addressing the prisoners, I said to my cameraman, "Say, we've got to move along. These men are supposed to be catching their plane home this afternoon."

Grins split their faces. But there was a telltale indication of the severity of punishment they had received in their prison. Not one of them let out a sound to celebrate the great news.

Chapter 8—Big Stories

IN TELEVISION news there are three categories of "biggest stories" that live in our memories. There are those major events that we all covered and in which we shared our experiences—wars, earthquakes, the conquest of space and disease. Then there are those stories that we developed ourselves and that proved to have some importance. And then there are the much rarer stories that we initiated but that developed a historic life of their own.

The assassination of John Fitzgerald Kennedy falls into the first category. Our invaluable *Evening News* editor, Ed Bliss, was standing over the United Press Teletype machine in our CBS newsroom when the first bulletin came from Dallas: THREE SHOTS WERE FIRED AT PRESIDENT KENNEDY'S MOTORCADE IN DOWNTOWN DALLAS.

Almost immediately another UPI lead said it appeared that President Kennedy had been "seriously" wounded and the motorcade seemed to be on the way to a hospital.

Ed shouted the flashes to me, and I shouted to the whole newsroom, "Kennedy's been shot. Let's get on the air."

But it turned out the cameras hadn't yet been put in place for our *Evening News* program, and it would take another twenty minutes to warm them up. I headed for a radio booth in the next room and from there broadcast the first television announcement of the assassination attempt. Our flash was heard over the CBS NEWS BULLETIN slide and interrupted the soap opera *As the World Turns*. We beat NBC onto the air by almost a minute.

As soon as the cameras were set up, I moved back to our newsdesk, where I would spend most of the next four days.

Our staff was quickly mobilized both in New York and Dallas. Dan Rather, our White House correspondent, who was on the scene at Parkland Hospital, kept us informed of developments.

For the first hour a shocked nation hung on to the sketchy details from the hospital. And then came the Rather report from outside the emergency room that they had learned the President was dead. We were still debating in New York whether we should put such a portentous but unofficial announcement on the air when, within minutes, the hospital issued a bulletin confirming the news. It fell to me to make the announcement.

It is an interesting thing about us newspeople. In the midst of tragedy our professional drive takes over and dominates our emotions. We move almost like automatons to get the job done. The time for an emotional reaction must wait.

I was doing fine in that department until it was necessary to pronounce the words, "From Dallas, Texas, the flash—apparently official. President Kennedy died at one p.m. central standard time—a half hour ago. . . ."

The words stuck in my throat. A sob wanted to replace them. A gulp or two quashed the sob, which metamorphosed into tears forming in the corners of my eyes. It was touch and go there for a few seconds before I could continue, "Vice President Johnson has left the hospital in Dallas, but we do not know to where he has proceeded. Presumably, he will be taking the oath of office shortly and become the thirty-sixth President of the United States."

I had been on the air for six hours when our producer, Don Hewitt, said Charles Collingwood was there to relieve me. I went into my office intending to call Betsy. I needed an intimate moment to share emotions. Millions of Americans were doing the same. All afternoon I had been reporting how telephone lines were jammed across the nation. I had not thought that this would create a problem for me, but on my desk all twelve of my incoming lines were lit.

As I stared, one of them blinked dark, and I grabbed it hoping to get an outside line. Instead there was somebody already there. And she was saying, "Hello, hello, hello. Is this CBS?"

I confirmed that it was.

"I want to complain," she complained, "of your having that Walter Cronkite on the air at a time like this, crying his crocodile tears when we all know he hated Jack Kennedy."

I was in no mood to listen to such distorted reasoning. I asked the lady's name, and it was something like Mrs. Constance Llewellyn-

Arbuthnot. She also threw in her Park Avenue address for full measure of her importance.

With all the outraged dignity I could muster, I told her, "Mrs. Llewellyn-Arbuthnot, you are speaking to Walter Cronkite, and you, madam, you are a damned idiot."

If she had a retort to that definitive statement, it is known only to herself and God. By the time she delivered it, my phone had long since been returned to its cradle.

The dramatic and emotional scenes over the next three days would wring us all dry. Every appearance of the young President's widow was a tearjerker, and none more than the picture of three-year-old John-John saluting his father's casket.

The drama soon faded into the long inquiry into the murder. President Johnson appointed Chief Justice Earl Warren to head a blue-ribbon panel to investigate the crime. It met for ten months and concluded that it could find no evidence of a conspiracy and that Lee Harvey Oswald was probably the lone gunman.

This opinion was not universally accepted. The larger conclusion depended on many minor conclusions based on what many felt was skimpy or downright doubtful evidence. At CBS News we set out to examine each of the questions of evidence that bothered us all. Producer Les Midgley spent the almost unheard-of sum of $1 million to test every possible thesis. We built a firing range duplicating the view Oswald had from the Texas School Book Depository window. From that position experts fired a rifle identical to the one Oswald had allegedly used and proved that it could indeed have been fired three times while Oswald had the President in his sights.

And on and on through the whole list of doubtful evidence until we had to announce our conclusion that the Warren Commission had delivered the only finding possible. As a news story this was a disappointment. We would have had a real world-smasher if we could have disproved the Warren Commission's finding.

What neither we nor the Warren Commission knew at that time was that there was a motive for a Cuban plot against the President, one of the conspiracy theories that had been proposed. The CIA did not reveal that it had plotted against Castro's life. What difference that information might have made to the Warren Commission can only be a matter of conjecture.

OF ALL man's achievements in the twentieth century, the one event that will dominate the history books a half a millennium from now will be his landing on the moon.

In books or on computer disks, or whatever people are using to record their past, the future residents of the universe will learn of the primitive but courageous voyage of a tiny spaceship called the *Eagle* to the surface of the moon and of man's first steps on a celestial body other than his own. They won't fully appreciate the trials and tribulations, the humor, and the drama that gripped the world as man first undertook flight in space.

At the conclusion of World War II the Russians and the Americans raced to capture the German rocket scientists who were the first to build long-range high-altitude rockets. They were based, for the most part, on the Baltic coast at Peenemünde. We got our share, including the Germans' brilliant leader Wernher von Braun.

The American test site was set up on a remote, snake-infested swamp called Cape Canaveral on the Florida coast east of Orlando. As the test site grew, so did the nearby villages of Cocoa, Cocoa Beach, and Titusville, until they replicated every boomtown in every bad movie ever made—cheap hotels, bars, girlie joints.

Those early days were marked by battles with the military for information. The program was being run by the air force, whose priority was to develop rockets as weapons. Naturally, it considered that top secret. We were not told when a launch was planned, nor were we given access to the Cape. The nearest public point from which our cameras could get at least a telephoto look at a launch was a jetty on the outskirts of Cocoa Beach.

Most of the launches were at night, and the bright searchlights that illuminated the launchpad were our tip-off. We equipped ourselves with food and drink and heavy coats against the night chill and fought for the more comfortable of the great granite rocks that formed the jetty.

The cameramen had it tough, as cameramen usually do. Once

set up, they had to keep their eyes pretty close to their viewfinders should the rocket suddenly blast off with that spectacular burst of fire. And they had to follow it closely, because, not infrequently, the rockets went off course and exploded with apocalyptic intensity.

Our problem was that, because of the air force secrecy and the fact that the searchlights usually stayed on, scrub or no, we had no way of knowing when a launch had been canceled. To our rescue rode a genial innkeeper named Henry Landwirth. When the bar at Henry's motel began filling up with the engineers back from the Cape, he sent a messenger to the jetty with the word that the mission had been scrubbed. He may have saved some of us from pneumonia. He saved all of us from death by boredom.

As with all trades, we had our little tricks to play on the neophytes who joined us for the first time on the jetty. Among the launching gantries on the Cape stood an ancient lighthouse. At night its lights could be mistaken for another launchpad. It was standard initiation procedure to direct a newcomer's attention not to the real launchpad, but to the lighthouse to await its launch.

When it was decided that the country should plan for manned flight, it was conceded that such an expensive program was going to need public support and that this would be hard to get in an atmosphere of secrecy. Hence the National Aeronautics and Space Administration was born and the program opened to the press.

Many of us were skeptical about NASA's plan to launch astronaut Alan Shepard on our first spaceflight. We knew it was a feeble attempt to catch up with the Soviets, who it seemed had won the space race by sending Yuri Gagarin into orbit around the earth. The United States wasn't ready for orbital flight, but NASA considered it essential to at least put a man into space, even if that flight would last only fifteen minutes. Shepard would ride the tiny one-man Mercury capsule on top of a Redstone rocket, a mere firecracker compared with the rockets that would follow. We had watched Redstones blow up on the pad or tumble wildly out of control, and we feared that Shepard's flight was premature and that NASA was taking a terrible risk. I watched that launch with greater trepidation than any of the many spaceflights I would see in the years to come.

My best friend among that first class of Mercury astronauts was
navy test pilot Wally Schirra, who had a great wit. After Wally's first
Mercury flight he made all the proper public relations statements
about having nothing to fear thanks to NASA's vigilant monitoring
and the safety features built into the craft.

Over a beer one night, I promised never to tell if, off the record,
he would level with me as to what he had really been thinking in
the last minutes before his rocket blasted off. And Wally said,
"Well, I was lying there looking up at all the dials and buttons and
toggle switches on the control panel, and I thought to myself,
Good God, this thing was built by the lowest bidder."

Some of the early drama of the space program was unnecessary.
There is a critical point in space travel when the vehicle plunges
back into the earth's atmosphere. The friction creates a temperature of up to 5000 degrees Fahrenheit. As the heat builds, all communications are blacked out. Until the spacecraft emerges from
this blackout three to five minutes later, ground control has no indication as to whether the flight has survived the reentry.

The drama of John Glenn's flight reached its pitch as, for the
first time in the American space experience, we awaited that fiery
return into the atmosphere. As he came out of the blackout, mission control piped his voice to us in the broadcast booths and a
nation cheered.

Scott Carpenter was the astronaut on the next orbiting mission
after Glenn's pioneer flight. As the seconds of blackout ticked
away, we heard nothing from him. What we heard was a clearly
strained voice from mission control trying to reestablish communication with the astronaut. All the indicators were ominous, but
in our broadcast we danced delicately around the possibilities.

This uncertainty went on for fifty-three minutes before mission
control announced that an unharmed astronaut had been picked
up by the rescue craft. The delay in the announcement of his recovery, it was explained, was because he had landed several miles
away from the planned point.

Later we learned that, right on schedule as the capsule emerged
from blackout, mission control had all the telemetry, the digital

messages, from the spacecraft indicating that everything was normal aboard. All that had failed was the voice link. But the public relations man neglected to give us that little detail and left us uninformed for most of an hour. It was inexcusable incompetency.

Sometimes the idiocy seemed to be on the part of the public.

The next phase of our spaceflights were the two-man trips in the larger Gemini capsules. On the Gemini 8 flight the controls locked and the ship began tumbling violently. It appeared that we were about to suffer our first space tragedy. We went on the air immediately, interrupting the program in progress. It was a dramatic broadcast as we listened in on the apparently doomed astronauts and mission control desperately fighting to solve the problem.

Meanwhile, however, telephone switchboards at CBS stations around the country lit up as angry viewers called in to complain that the program they had been watching had been interrupted. The program they had been watching? *Lost in Space.*

Astronauts Neil Armstrong and David Scott did beat the problem, and Gemini 8 made it safely home.

The first landing on the moon was the most extraordinary story of our time. To see Neil Armstrong as he took that giant step for mankind onto the moon's surface was a thrill beyond all thrills.

When Neil emerged from the *Eagle*, I had almost regained my composure, which I'd lost completely when the *Eagle* had settled gently on the moon's surface. I had just as long as NASA had to prepare for that moment, and yet when it came, I was speechless.

"Oh, boy! Whew! Boy!" These were my first words, profundity to be recorded for the ages. They were all I could utter.

I would cover all the remaining moon shots, but this was the apogee of my quarter of a century reporting the space adventure.

ONE of the biggest stories of our century was the engagement to gain civil rights for all Americans. From the moment on December 1, 1955, that Rosa Parks dared to sit down in the "whites only" front of a Montgomery, Alabama, bus, it was an unfolding story of a struggle for the soul of a country. The question was a simple one, horrid in its complexity: Could the people of the United States begin to live up to their credo that "all men are created equal" and establish that this was indeed "one nation indivisible"?

As managing editor of the *Evening News,* I felt heavily my responsibility to be sure that our stories, while reflecting the deep emotions of the conflict, were as calm, as factual, as impartial as good journalists can make them.

This may have been the most severe test of my own journalistic integrity since World War II. We were all on the same side then, and most of us newsmen abandoned any thought of impartiality as we reported on the heroism of our boys and the bestiality of the hated Nazis. This civil rights struggle that was tearing at our nation was of a vastly different order, an order of much greater magnitude in terms of the demands for neutrality in our reporting.

My natural sympathy was with the blacks. From the time I was ten until I went away to college, I heard my father rail almost nightly against some racial injustice he had witnessed that day. Dad's indignation in the evening clashed with my schoolboy life in the daytime. If anyone in Houston was daring to advocate integration, their words certainly weren't echoing in the halls of San Jacinto High School. There was no suggestion, either inside or outside the halls of academe, that there was anything wrong with the segregation we scrupulously observed in study and play, or that anything needed to be done about it.

My father had planted the seeds that would grow to full awareness of the fact that one class of Americans—a class to which we, by birth, belonged—were intent upon keeping in servitude another class—a class condemned by birth.

While this conviction was growing within me, I had no trouble bridging the gap between my views and the attitude held by my friends. While I found their opinions of blacks distasteful, I didn't have the courage to challenge this overwhelming majority.

I would not know socially a single black until well after World War II. There were no blacks in high school, none at the University of Texas, none in the Texas legislature or the Texas government, none in those parts of the military with which I was attached, none in the American embassy in Moscow.

We all know from our history lessons that the founding fathers, while proclaiming the right of equality for all, actually didn't intend to include blacks, Indians, or women. However, by the middle of the twentieth century the irony of segregating men called to die for their country so offended President Harry Truman that he integrated the military. Truman's daring edict strengthened the 1950s move toward civil rights. By the mid-1950s—after the Supreme Court's unanimous and historic decision outlawing segregation in public schools—Rosa Parks was encouraged to act. And I and a few hundred other reporters and editors were forced to put our journalistic ethics to the test against our own emotions.

I regret that the technological restrictions of the time—before it was routine for the anchor to travel—kept me off the streets to experience those historic moments of crisis: the sit-ins in Atlanta, the march at Selma, the rally at the Lincoln Memorial.

As aware as my southern boyhood had made me of the insults heaped upon the blacks, I thought that the principal cause of their unhappiness was economic, that it was bred in the rat-infested big-city ghettos. I missed at first what I now believe to be true—that the motivation that brings most blacks to the barricades is the desire to live in dignity. That ambition takes many forms, but it is clearly at the foundation of all fights for social justice.

Trying to tell the story of that quest in the 1960 battles put our reporters in considerable jeopardy. With few exceptions, wherever our reporter-camera teams appeared, they were surrounded by a crowd of angry whites who assaulted them with threats. Cameramen were frequently pelted with stones, and their cameras were pushed into their faces. Sometimes the police joined in the threats.

One of the more serious protests over our coverage came not in the streets but in the white-collar confines of our affiliate stations in the South. They complained that our reports were biased in favor of the blacks. Some of those station owners even threatened to withdraw their affiliation from CBS, an action that, if widely followed, could have shut down the network.

The critics of our coverage were not limited to the segregationists of the South. Many of those of the other persuasion across the nation, including the South, felt that television did not go far enough in exposing the inequities between the races.

Martin Luther King, Jr., had elevated the civil rights struggle from a mostly sectional concern to a national cause with his 1963 rally and oratory at the Lincoln Memorial. Two hundred thousand blacks and whites were there that day, and millions more heard on television his powerful "I have a dream" speech. He galvanized a nation—black and white, integrationist and segregationist—and moved the struggle for equality to a new plateau.

We did our evening broadcast from Washington on April 4, 1968, the night that King was slain. The bulletin came from Memphis when we were on the air, and we pumped out as many details as we had. That night I was awakened by the sirens and the red glow in my hotel room as, a few blocks away, Washington's black district was set afire. It turned out to be a herald of the many urban riots that would char our national conscience.

In those critical years the civil rights movement found an unexpected ally in Lyndon Johnson. As President of the United States he rose above the sectionalism he had served as a Senator from Texas and, with his legislative skills, pushed through the Civil Rights Act of 1964. Of all his achievements he may have been proudest of that one, and he should have been.

We have made huge strides in thirty years. Today we mingle easily in our offices and schools, and deep friendships are possible. But we have a long way to go.

THE Watergate scandal produced an example of a memorable story in which the journalistic perpetrator can take particular pride.

Ever since the burglars employed by Richard Nixon's reelection committee had been caught breaking into the Democratic election headquarters, the story had sporadically hit the front pages. It got a particularly big play in the early summer, when the Washington *Post*'s Bob Woodward and Carl Bernstein began digging up details that exposed it as a serious plot involving the White House.

Their first reports came in rather rapid succession, but then the revelations began coming more slowly. The stories appeared with less regularity in the papers across the country. With the newer developments growing more complex, the follow-up reports were getting harder to understand.

It occurred to me that it was time to try to pull this important story together in a cohesive review that would keep it from slipping into limbo—a simple ABC of the plot and the people involved. This we did in a detailed but easy-to-follow report.

What I did not know at the time was the amount of pressure that the White House was putting on the Washington *Post* to drop the story. It was threatening its advertisers and the *Post* itself with scarcely veiled reminders that the *Post*'s broadcasting empire was subject to government licensing.

Our broadcast revived public interest. Within minutes of the first installment of our scheduled two-part presentation, one of Nixon's factotums, Charles Colson, was on the phone with a forceful complaint to CBS owner Bill Paley. Paley was shaken enough to pass along his concern to CBS News president Dick Salant.

Salant did not pass Paley's concern along to us, but he represented as his idea that we had put undue emphasis on the story by the length of time we gave it. He suggested that we trim the next installment. Since Salant had not revealed that political pressure was involved, I saw no problem in acceding to his request. There was a lot of duplication in the second piece, and I felt we could shorten it without damage. This enabled Salant, without my knowledge, to go back to Paley and inform him that he could tell the White House that we were shortening the second story. This served to placate the Nixon people.

I did not find out for months that the White House had applied the pressure to which Salant responded. He took full responsibility, partly because he knew that if I thought he was responding to White House pressure, he might not be able to control the eruption.

As it was, I am sorry that it happened. Except for this single failure I have been able to claim that CBS management never brought any pressure on the *Evening News* to satisfy either political considerations or advertisers' demands.

Our contribution went widely unrecognized, except by the Washington *Post* management, but my colleagues and I can take a lot of credit for keeping that Watergate story alive until its dénouement in Nixon's resignation.

IN SHARP contrast I did not deserve the praise heaped upon me for bringing Egypt's President Anwar Sadat and Israel's Prime Minister Menachem Begin together and setting off the chain of events that would lead to the first formal peace between Israel and an Arab neighbor.

When the Egyptian dictator Gamal Abdel Nasser died, his political heir was Colonel Anwar Sadat. After several months in which Sadat was consolidating his power, I obtained the first interview granted to a Western correspondent. We sat and smoked our pipes under a vast spreading banyan tree at the President's country residence on the banks of the Nile. The interview was as tepid as the afternoon was hot. Sadat droned on about his hopes and plans for Egypt's future as I fought to stay awake. Suddenly he brought me bolt upright. I had heard him say he intended to go to Jerusalem.

Yes, he assured me, he would go to Jerusalem—just as soon as there was peace, a peace that would depend upon the Israelis meeting all of Egypt's conditions—for openers, the return of the Sinai to Egypt, the Golan Heights to Syria, and Jerusalem to Jordan. So his statement suggested that he was optimistic that peace would come in his lifetime and permit him to visit Jerusalem.

We didn't even use the quote in the brief report I was able to extract from that long, dull interview. In ensuing years I became an admiring friend of Sadat's, and on more than one occasion I heard him allude to his statement about going to Jerusalem.

The newswires from Tel Aviv on Friday night, November 11, 1977, reported a rumor that Sadat might visit Israel. Over Saturday and Sunday I waited for the rumor to be knocked down by Sadat. By Sunday night there was still no comment from Cairo, and the rumor was continuing its rounds.

As my *Evening News* producer and I discussed the next day's report, we agreed we should try to get Sadat on a satellite interview so that he could make his intentions clear.

So on Monday morning I had him on the satellite.

"Good morning, Walter, and how is Barbara?" was his greeting. He was fond of Barbara Walters, and somehow we were linked in his mind. He began every conversation with me by asking how Barbara was. Barbara is a friend of mine, but her health is not a burning issue with me.

After we got our Barbara preliminaries out of the way, I asked if he had any plans to go to Jerusalem. He would like to go very much, he said, and I asked what I knew would be the definitive question: What are your conditions for going? Whereupon he went into the usual litany of Egyptian demands on Israel—withdrawal from the Sinai and the Golan Heights, and on and on.

"And those are your conditions for going to Israel?" I asked, just to tie a ribbon around the denial.

"Oh, no, no, Walter," he replied. "Those are my conditions for peace. The only condition is that I want to discuss the whole situation with the hundred and twenty members of the Knesset."

Suddenly I was trying to put the ribbon around a much bigger story. What would he need to go? I asked. He said all he needed was an invitation. And how soon could he go?

"In the earliest time possible."

"That could be, say, within a week?" I suggested.

"You can say that, yes."

By the time I had told him good-bye, my producer was on the phone to Tel Aviv. Get Begin!

The bureau arranged to set up a temporary studio at the Tel Aviv Hilton, where Begin was scheduled to speak that night. He was clearly prepared. He took with considerable aplomb my report that Sadat was ready to come, that all he needed was an invitation.

"Tell him he's got an invitation," Begin said. I pressed him for details. He said he would make a statement to the Knesset the following day.

I had a feeling he didn't believe this was all for real. I think he envisioned that there was a great distance between this dialogue with an American correspondent and any possibility of Sadat's really coming. My report to him that Sadat said he would be prepared to appear within a week jarred him out of any such complacency.

"Very good news," he said. "Anyhow, anytime, any day he's prepared to come, I will receive him cordially at the airport, go together with him to Jerusalem, also present him to the Knesset, and let him make his speech to our parliament. I will follow him onto the platform, greet him, receive him."

The rest is history, as they say, except for a couple of sidebars.

Sadat flew to Israel four days later. The world press descended on Tel Aviv. On Thursday night at the TWA lounge at Kennedy Airport it seemed that all of our competitors were there. They were booked on a flight to Israel, and they assumed the same of me. But I was booked on a flight at about the same time to Cairo. I had arranged with Sadat to fly into Israel with him. My job was to protect that exclusive by letting our opposition board that Tel Aviv flight before they discovered my secret.

Fortunately, the Tel Aviv flight was called first, so I fell in with the others en route to the gate. Except I kept falling farther behind the crowd. I don't think they missed me until they were airborne.

It looked like a clean beat. But I hadn't figured on Barbara Walters—a serious mistake. She had taken an earlier plane to Tel Aviv. When ABC learned of our ploy, they got her a charter to Cairo the next morning.

Just as I was boarding Sadat's plane, along she came, running across the field with hand upraised like a substitute entering a sporting contest. Sadat invited her aboard, and her enterprise robbed us of our exclusive.

Sadat did invite me up to share his private quarters for much of the flight, and as we crossed into Israel, two fighters of the Israeli air force appeared off our wings as escorts. One of the pilots brought his plane so close that even through his visor we could see his broad grin as he waved a greeting to the Egyptian President.

It was later suggested that I had overstepped the bounds of journalistic propriety by trying to negotiate an Israeli-Egyptian détente. They did not know the full story—that my initial journalistic intention was to knock down the speculation over the visit.

ACCOMPANYING THE PRESIDENT of the United States on a trip abroad sounds glamorous, but it rarely is. It involves lengthy hours, torturous travel, a succession of public relations handouts, and a story that does not lend itself to much individual enterprise.

An airport reception upon arrival, a speeding trip through crowds of welcoming citizenry or shoulder-to-shoulder walls of troops. While the official party has a little downtime to rest, the reporter pounds out his copy or does a television piece posed in front of some national monument.

The reception and dinner that night: If you are lucky, they keep you outside, and you can lounge around awaiting the evening communiqué. You are there just in case anything untoward happens. If you are incredibly unlucky, you might be selected as the pool reporter, representing your colleagues lucky enough to be outside. You will get to sit through a boring dinner with boring speeches and, usually, a boring exhibition of the native dance.

Occasionally there are exceptions, and one was President Nixon's historic trip to China. Nixon, regardless of whatever other opinions people had of him, should be recognized for the move toward reconciliation with China that he initiated when most of the powerful members of the Republican Party hierarchy were deeply opposed. It was an act of great political courage.

When we flew to China, the country was just emerging from the so-called Cultural Revolution. It was the cruelest policy imposed on a regime's own people since Stalin's mass executions.

Beijing, as a matter of fact, reminded me in many details of Moscow after the war. The buildings were gray—darkened by the choking smog made up of equal parts coal smoke and grit blown in from China's distant western reaches. The people were gray, their quilted jackets and pants a perfect camouflage against the dull buildings past which they unsmilingly plodded.

Our convoy of limousines through Beijing's broad streets and the vast plaza of Tiananmen Square attracted little attention from the people despite the U.S. flags flying from the fenders. The regime had not promoted our visit. The canny Mao Tse-tung would see how things developed first.

They developed well indeed. Nixon, after the formal visits and interminable speechmaking, was able to announce a new relationship of better understanding between our countries.

The press wasn't there for Nixon's historic meeting with the ailing Mao, but we all went to the Great Wall. Forewarned about China's cold, I had purchased a pair of socks that could be warmed by a battery inserted at the top. As we left the bus at the wall, I dropped in the battery. I put it in wrong side up, and every time I took a step, my right foot got an electric shock.

I thought the little jig I performed before getting the sock off was worthy of a better reception than I got from the frozen-faced guards and my press companions, so intent on racing for the wall that they paid no heed to my distress. My separation from my press colleagues yielded a serendipitous dividend. As they were herded to the base of the wall to await Nixon's arrival, I wandered some distance up the wall, unimpeded by the guards.

From that point up that steep slope I saw the President's entourage arriving. I turned to hasten back to the press area. Now the guards closed ranks against my progress. I was stuck. But there, just ahead of me, was the President's aide H. R. Haldeman. He heeded my call for help and used his pass to escort me down. Because of the delay I now found myself on the other side of Nixon from the press assembled below. I made the rest of the wall tour almost at his elbow as my colleagues glared a lot.

Pat Nixon was off on her own sight-seeing tours each day. They were of no substance, but provided pretty pictures, and we always sent a cameraman along. One day Barbara Walters decided to accompany Mrs. Nixon's party. As they looked over some flower garden or such, she found the First Lady willing to talk.

Barbara frantically turned and called for a microphone. The ABC cameraman was somewhere else at the moment, but our man was standing near, so he handed her his microphone.

Later that day, close to airtime, Barbara returned to the ABC News hotel suite to ask what they were doing with her exclusive. They knew nothing of such an exclusive; they had seen no such tape. The puzzled ABC producer began calling the other networks. At CBS the interview, recorded by the wrong network, had provided an afternoon of jollity. Now our producer, Russ Bensley, drew out the joke just a little further by denying that we had the Walters tape. The fun ended soon after, as Bensley's sense of fairness overcame his sense of humor, and he surrendered the tape to ABC—just in time for their evening feed to New York.

We were kept under close escort at all times, always on the limited itinerary the Chinese had planned for us. A big deal was a three-block diversion from the approved route.

Although the trappings of the police state had worn heavy, I went to sleep our last night relieved that there had been no incidents. But in the middle of the night there was a brief pounding at the door before it was opened by the floor boy. In the light from the hall all I could see was army uniforms.

An officer and an aide stepped in. In the half-light he made what sounded like a most bellicose announcement. I got out of bed for what seemed like imminent incarceration. With that, his aide stepped back into the hall and returned with a huge box of candy. The officer saluted smartly and withdrew. It turned out that this odd ceremony had been repeated throughout the hotel. They may have meant well, but the Chinese water torture came to mind.

Chapter 9—TV News

I VISUALIZE the TV industry as a huge building dedicated to the business of entertainment. Journalism is in an attached annex next door. In that door between them is a huge vacuum that runs twenty-four hours a day threatening to suck anyone who comes too close inside the larger building.

The pressure has become more subtle but no less real in recent years. In the pioneer days it was blatant.

In 1954 CBS decided to produce *The Morning Show,* a two-hour variety presentation. The format had been introduced a year earlier by NBC with its *Today* show, featuring Dave Garroway. The news department produced the program, and I was to play host.

My role, it turned out, was to duplicate the Garroway performance, including the delivery of an occasional commercial. CBS, as it should have, strictly forbade any connection between news personnel and advertisers. For a newsman, doing commercials was considered the ultimate violation of journalistic principle.

But now CBS was making a grand exception for *The Morning Show*. It simply was accepted that I would improvise an occasional commercial, again imitating Garroway.

Our program would consist of now almost routine ingredients: We would have a news portion, a weather forecast, and a feature story. My role consisted of interviewing the newsworthy guests and mulling over the news of the day with a puppet lion, Charlemagne.

The first sponsor was the R. J. Reynolds Tobacco Company, which bought time to introduce a new cigarette, Winston. I spent some time in the ad agency's conference room being briefed on the selling points of the product.

The day for my first commercial came shortly after our show's debut. I lit up a Winston, grinned, and delivered the ad campaign's slogan: "Ah, Winston tastes good, as a cigarette should."

The program was barely over when I was hustled into a meeting with embarrassed CBS brass and unhappy tobacco company people. You would have thought that I had set off a nuclear weapon.

The slogan, they informed me, was "Winston tastes good *like* a cigarette should." I pointed out that this was not grammatical. There was a moment of silence that I erroneously interpreted as a sign of chagrin on the part of those who had perpetrated this faulty construction. As the reaction came crashing down around my head, I realized that the moment of silence was more like an advance memorial to my early departure as the Winston spokesman. CBS thereafter steered advertising accounts away from me, and the problem of my doing commercials didn't arise again.

Actually, we had a darned good show. Our producer was Paul Levitan, who had a keen imagination and a fearless willingness to attempt the innovative in television broadcasting. He managed to drag television cable to places it had never been, and he also improvised a combination of radio and long-lens photography.

Celebrities still traveled by luxury liners, and we regularly beat the opposition in getting the interviews with them. We took a tug alongside the incoming ships. From its deck our long-lens cameras photographed the celebrities while I interviewed them by radio.

Our *Morning Show* produced by the news department lived an uncomfortable life as the dominant entertainment department pleaded in the executive suites for the airtime to be returned to them. In our fifth month they executed their coup and I learned what it was like to be in the entertainment business.

I was at my host's position preparing for the morning broadcast when Charles Collingwood arrived at his newsdesk in the studio. He looked ill. To my worried inquiry he insisted he was able to go on the air but said he had something to tell me afterward.

When the show was over, he handed me a copy of a Broadway gossip column by Jack O'Brian. "CBS has finally gotten wise and is replacing Walter Cronkite on *The Morning Show* with that brilliant young West Coast comic, Jack Paar." By the time I got back to my office, my secretary was already amassing a list of calls from reporters and columnists seeking my response to O'Brian.

Not a single CBS executive, all so accessible the day before, was available to take my calls. To this day I think as a newsman, and I am unable to refuse to respond to legitimate inquiries by my press colleagues. But I had nothing to tell them except how ignorant I was of the situation, an answer that certainly would make CBS look bad.

I called the head of CBS publicity. I told him I was going to talk to the press at noon and tell them what I knew. If CBS wanted to give me some information, I would be glad to relay it. Within a few minutes one of the executives was on the phone with a lame explanation that the Paar deal was not wrapped up, that they had intended to tell me right away, ad nauseam.

It was clear that they had been caught unprepared by O'Brian's premature item. It turned out it was all true, but broadcast stations generally like to fire on-air personalities without giving them a chance to appear again on their programs. They fear that disgruntled performers will use their waning airtime to castigate their employers—not an unreasonable concern.

In this case, we dragged on for another week or so until Jack took the reins of *The Morning Show* and the office next to mine. Not many days after that transition I found among my fan mail a postcard from Indianapolis. It said, "Tell CBS that they have made a terrible mistake putting Jack Paar on instead of Walter Cronkite. Mr. Cronkite is the perfect personality for a morning broadcast. Jack's comedy would be better on a nighttime program."

The signature was that of Jack's mother, Lillian. I walked next door to Jack's office, only to discover that his sense of humor had certain limits. He didn't think the card was particularly amusing.

In those early days I had found that the fired in television are not infrequently the fall guys for the guilty. For instance, the 1964 political conventions. Our team had six conventions under our belt by the time preparations were under way to go to San Francisco for the Republican conclave that summer. We intended to set up our anchor studio, control room, and so on in the usual way, using a procedure we had perfected.

I flew out to San Francisco and was met by Fred Friendly, Ed Murrow's talented television producer who a few months before had been named the new president of CBS News. On the way to the hotel we stopped at the convention hall so he could show me our anchor setup. There had been a few "improvements." When he opened the door to my new booth, I was appalled. There were none of the facilities with which I was used to working.

The anchor desk sat in solitary splendor at one side of the room. There were virtually no communications to the desk at all. The anchor-desk assistant—who in the past always was within arm's reach to pass notes from our correspondents—would be across the room, with no means of reaching me except during commercials.

Any cues I needed, Friendly confidently explained, would be given through my headphones directly from the producer in the control room. We had learned in the previous conventions that cues through headphones invariably led to almost constant chatter from the control room. The babble blocked out the proceedings on the floor upon which I depended to guide our coverage.

Friendly presented all this change as a great advance in convention coverage. I was outraged that it had been set up without any consultation with me about my needs. Clearly it was meant to eliminate them. During the previous conventions it became obvious that I was the only person in the chain of command who had a sense of the running story from the convention floor.

It was not intended that way, and it wasn't my choice. The problem was the chaos in the control room. Producers were in constant shouting conferences with correspondents and cameramen on what stories were developing elsewhere, the movement of candidates, how much of a speech they should use. That created such confusion that no one in the control room had a coherent idea of the convention's running story. Sitting at the anchor desk, I did.

I believe that Friendly, in discarding the previous plans for anchor coverage, was essentially trying to regain control of the broadcast for the producer—himself—in the control room. By the time he sprang the new setup on me, it was too late to change it.

Our convention coverage was the shambles I expected it to be. I got the word that I was fired from the upcoming Democratic Convention while vacationing with my family at Disneyland. To a calliope background Friendly imparted the bad news in person.

The Democratic Convention was in Atlantic City. Friendly was surprised when I said I intended to broadcast the *Evening News* from there. He agreed, although his assumption had apparently been that I would stay in New York, quietly licking my wounds.

The first morning of the convention I found myself in my hotel elevator descending with Bob Kintner, the head of NBC News. By the time we reached the ground floor, we had hatched a scheme. The lobby was crowded with politicians and newspeople. We walked through the lobby with arms linked, willing to break our intense conversation only briefly to acknowledge our friends. Our conversation was gobbledygook, but by the time I reached the convention hall, Don Hewitt, our producer, ran out of the hall shouting, "What's this about your going to NBC?"

Kintner and I had planted a delicious rumor. By 1968, with Friendly gone, I was back in the convention anchor job to stay until my retirement from the *Evening News* in 1981.

MY DEPARTURE FROM THE *Evening News* has been widely misinterpreted to suggest that I was forced out by Dan Rather. An understandable interpretation, but simply not true.

I had told CBS two years in advance that I intended to step down from the *Evening News* when I turned sixty-five—in November 1981. They didn't hear me; they couldn't believe that any person would voluntarily leave a job of such international prominence.

Just before we entered the fateful year of 1981, I reminded our then CBS News president, Bill Leonard, of my intentions. I did not know that at that very moment Dan Rather's agent was playing a high-stakes game with ABC and CBS for his client's services. CBS, I gather, had to face the dilemma of figuring out how they could justify the huge salary Dan was demanding until the time I stepped down. Until Leonard remembered our conversation.

He called me in and wanted to know if I was serious. I told him I was. Whereupon he revealed that if negotiations were successful, Dan would be in the wings. By mutual agreement my retirement schedule was slightly accelerated to bridge my normal summer hiatus, and CBS was anxious to get started building up the new man. So I stepped down in March instead of November.

That summer hiatus, by the way, may have kept me from entering the history books as the first million-dollar anchorperson. With my remuneration already climbing to what I considered a nearly obscene number, I had entered our contract negotiations in 1973 with a single demand. I did not want a raise, but I wanted three months off a year. This was unprecedented, and the negotiations were long and arduous until we reached agreement.

The contract sent my friend Johnny Carson and me off on a jocund race to see how little work we could do and still hold our jobs. He won.

I WAS not happy about the course of events at CBS News after my departure from the *Evening News*. Within weeks the entire news division was reorganized. The president, Bill Leonard, was removed, and into his place went ambitious Van Gordon Sauter. He believed his job was to build Rather's reputation at whatever cost, and he seemed to be aiming to climb on Rather's back to the presidency of CBS Television.

At CBS News the new atmosphere was one of neon lights and whirling mirrors. Sauter was not satisfied with information. Infotainment was his game. There was nothing wrong with the formula, except that it wasn't right for CBS. Our viewers—and we had been the first in the ratings for years—expected us to be *The New York Times* of television news, not the *Daily Graphic*.

The *Evening News* would try to concentrate on a few stories that would be covered as often as possible with first-person recitations by the persons involved. If the few stories on which the program concentrated had been important ones, Sauter might have had something. I had long been concerned that our formula might be failing in its mission. We were essentially a headline service attempting to give our audience an overview of the day, hoping that we would inspire them to consult their newspapers for details. But the Sauter failing was that important stories were too often ignored for features with a light touch.

It is impossible to grasp how difficult it is to decide what should go into a news broadcast and what must be left out. The rule of thumb is that stories are assigned their importance on the basis of what affects the greatest number of one's viewers.

Of the thirty minutes of our broadcast, almost a third was eaten up by commercials and the necessary lead-ins and lead-outs—the opening of the broadcast, the good night, and the bridges into and out of the commercials. I'm afraid I added a full four seconds to that burden by my signature line: "And that's the way it is . . ." and the date. My line, depending on whether I recited it with humor or sadness or irony, became a six-word commentary on life's foibles.

Dick Salant hated the line. He argued that it arrogantly implied an accuracy of which we were not capable. Within days, however, the public seemed to have embraced the sign-off as they had Ed Murrow's "Good night and good luck." So I stuck with it.

After accounting for the commercials and lead-ins, we had to pack all the news of importance from around the world into about twenty-two minutes. It was a formidable job.

Our producer each morning checked with the CBS newsdesk to find out what stories had broken for the day's coverage. He talked with the bureaus that were working on already assigned stories. We also conferred with the news editor about anything on the press service wires that we had somehow missed.

Based on all this input, the producer did our lineup—the list of the items we expected to cover in their order of priority. As new stories broke, we had to decide whether they should assume a place in the lineup, displacing others.

In broadcasting the clock is the ever present evil. Perhaps I liked living dangerously, but I was inclined to crowd more into the day than the day could accommodate. I spent most of the time in my office, taking phone calls, placating affiliates, and researching future special events like spaceshots and political conventions. Additionally, there was constant network pressure to make a speech for an affiliate station or for a cause dear to a major sponsor.

Some days I wouldn't get out to the newsdesk until a bare hour before the broadcast. My three writers were excellent, but I frequently edited their copy to suit myself and occasionally rewrote their efforts. Their versions were probably better than mine most of the time, but my ego ruled. This last-minute effort meant that the whole news team was forced to operate in a state of high hysteria as they watched the clock.

I apologize now if I forced our staff to suffer unnecessary tension, but I think they were all proud that we put on one of the best newscasts ever. I can't believe that any news broadcasters today can possibly enjoy the work as much as we did. The smell of that excitement still permeated the newsroom, at least for a short while, after the Van Gordon Sauter bunch took it over.

CBS News under Sauter made no attempt to live up to their contract with me. I got a nice raise, but a promised thirteen-week annual series never came about. The existing successful *Walter Cronkite's Universe,* a summer replacement program, was canceled.

CBS had given me a lavish office and had put me on the corporate board. Meanwhile Sauter was treating me like a leper.

After finding that my concerns about the course of CBS News

had fallen on deaf ears among our executives, I began going public in the speeches I made to professional associations and university journalism groups.

Sauter called me to lunch and tried to silence my criticism by offering to let me do an occasional documentary program. But given the lack of management enthusiasm for it, there was simply no joy there, and we killed it after a few episodes.

At that lunch Sauter admitted that he was deliberately keeping me off the air because he felt that it would be easier to build up Dan's audience if I wasn't around as a distraction. As Dan became comfortable in the anchor chair, Sauter's successors thought it best not to tamper with the successful exclusionary formula.

Meanwhile the CBS board had become interesting. Larry Tisch, hotel operator, insurance mogul, and tobacco company owner, began acquiring CBS stock in large quantities. Within weeks he held more stock than Bill Paley. He was elected to the board and maneuvered himself into the chairman's seat. Tisch proceeded to dismantle the company in order to increase the cash equity for his stockholders and himself.

Tisch downsized and downgraded the remaining company. The news department staffs were reduced and bureaus closed, most disastrously overseas, where it is most important that American-trained correspondents keep an eye on our potential enemies and our supposed friends.

I protested these cuts to no avail. Sometimes I would get a faint "Hear, hear" from board members, but none stood up against Tisch.

By another of his adroit maneuvers Tisch managed to get rid of his three less enthusiastic board members in one move. It was agreed that board members should serve only until the age of seventy. That provided the plank for Roswell Gilpatric, Marietta Tree, and me to walk.

One of my major disappointments was that the CBS board, made up of some top-notch business, financial, and industrial leaders, was concerned only with the company's finances and paid no attention to its programming. We never discussed violence or children's programming or the suitability of commercials.

Each spring the entertainment executives would show a sampling of the next season's new programs. The board members frowned and grimaced at the sitcoms. They laughed, but only at what were supposed to be the serious dramas. As the lights came up, the members shook their heads, grinned embarrassed grins, and went about the business of the next financial report.

A CAREER can be called a success if one can look back and say, "I made a difference." I don't feel I can do that.

All of us in those early days of television felt that we were establishing a set of standards that would be observed by, or at least have an influence on, generations of news professionals to come. How easily these were dismissed by the Van Gordon Sauters and those who felt they had to imitate to compete.

The infotainment trend has been exacerbated by the network fight to hang on to a viable share of a shrinking pie. Cable and video recordings have reduced the total network audience to barely half of what it once was. Management now considers ratings more important than prestige.

Newspapers, under similar pressure of falling circulation, are also guilty today of trivializing the news. Much of the news is featurized, and a lot of it is condensed into "What Happened Today" columns. Basically the problem is, again, the bottom line.

The shame is that most of our newspapers have passed from the hands of individual publishers to large chains. These corporate behemoths are forced by their stockholders and the "get mine" mores of the '90s to seek constantly expanding profits.

Boards and their executives deny to their news managers enough funding to pay for the minimum coverage necessary to serve their consumers well. Good reporters, writers, and editors are spread so thin that they cannot spend the necessary time developing the stories that the public needs and deserves. A more responsible press depends not upon individual journalists, but upon more responsible owners. That is the real bottom line.

The big question is whether the major players in the new alignment—the entertainment and industrial giants—with no background in news and their focus primarily on profits, will be willing to underwrite the budget-bending business of serious news reporting. Will they continue even the level of reduced news and public affairs programming that their networks are providing today?

The problem is simply that television news is an inadequate substitute for a good newspaper. While television puts all other media in the shade in its ability to present in moving pictures the people and the places that make our news, it simultaneously fails in explaining the more complicated issues of our day.

The sheer volume of television news is ridiculously small. The number of words spoken in a half-hour broadcast barely equals the numbers of words on two thirds of a standard newspaper page. That is not enough to cover the day's major events.

The greatest victim in all this is our political process, and in my view this is one of the greatest blots on the recent record of television news. Studies have shown that in 1988 the average block of uninterrupted speech by a presidential candidate on the network newscasts was 9.8 seconds. Nine point eight seconds! The networks faithfully promised to do better in 1992. The average sound bite that year was just 8.2 seconds. The networks promised to do better in 1996. The average sound bite that year: 7.2 seconds.

The preservation of our liberties depends on an enlightened citizenry. As Thomas Jefferson said, the nation that expects to be ignorant and free expects what never can and never will be.

We must better educate our young people to become discriminating newspaper readers, television viewers, and computer users. We must teach them that to be fully informed one must go to good newspapers, weekly newsmagazines, opinion journals, books, and, increasingly, the Internet, as well as television.

By recognizing the advantages and limitations of each medium, this educated public would demand a better product. Thus, in a market-oriented economy, demand would raise the quality of both print and broadcast news.

TELEVISION will continue to play a major role in writing history. It has already had an impact on the tide of events. Once television signals from the West breached the Iron Curtain and showed to those locked behind it the benefits of a free society, public uprisings against the communist status quo were probably inevitable. The daily coverage of the Vietnamese battlefield helped convince the public that the carnage was not worth the candle.

As we approach the new century, we are living through a technological revolution potentially more profound in its impact—socially, politically, economically—than the industrial revolution of the last century. We have scarcely begun to identify its implications and adapt our institutions to change, although the first massive repercussions have already been felt with industrial downsizing. We are finding it as difficult to cope as a society as we are as individuals. We are all a little overwhelmed.

Flowing into that mainstream of technological change have been our generation's economic and political revolutions. They have been propelled by growth and rising expectations, but have frequently been blocked by finite resources and an inadequate educational system. Meeting these problems and satisfying the needs of the disadvantaged is the challenge of our time.

There is going to be social and political and economic evolution, which will explode with such suddenness as to have the character of revolution. The revolutionary forces are already at work today, and they have humankind's dreams on their side. We don't want to be on the other side. It is up to us to assume leadership of that revolution, to channel it in a direction that will ensure freedom's future.

I expect to watch all of this from a perch yet to be determined. I just hope that wherever that is, folks, as they do today, will still stop me and ask, "Didn't you used to be Walter Cronkite?"

Diane Ackerman

A SLENDER

. . . 10:48 p.m. The phone rings.
"Suicide Prevention and Crisis Service,"
I say in a welcoming voice, an achieved
voice. "May I help you?" For a few
seconds only silence answers. I think I
can hear the choked breath of someone
crying. A distraught woman.

In a voice half whisper, half sob, she
tells me—a stranger—the intimate and
horrifying details of her day.

"I'm so glad you phoned," I say,
trying to press my concern through the
slender thread of the phone wire. I want
it to be an invisible arm wrapping around
her. "You sound scared."

"Scared to death," she whispers.

—*A Slender Thread*

---------- **Preface** --

AT THE edge of the town I live in, a converted depot restaurant
called the Station reminds us of days when train cars shuffled in
a long conga line to Manhattan. A clock outside the restaurant
froze at 6:22, when the last iron fury left town, but the trains of cir-
cumstance have never stopped running.

Towns are like railroad stations, where at any moment hundreds
of lives converge. In time, everyone meets everyone, either by re-
pute or in person. When they are at their most frightened, desperate, or alone, they sometimes phone Suicide Prevention and
Crisis Service.

Its phone number can be easily found in the telephone directory or on posters strategically placed around town, but its whereabouts is a closely guarded secret. It's as if the people who work
there belong to a mysterious cult. Their names may not be spoken.
Their ages may not be given. Their professions may not be hinted
at. Because they touch the lives of desperate people, as well as
those of normal people in desperate moments, the address of the
building may not be revealed. Counselors enter and leave it discreetly, even furtively at times. Yet in that building the blood and
guts of human life, the minor sorrows and the bright catastrophes
play themselves out. It is an emotional landscape that alternately
expands and shrinks; one moment it may swell to the size of a re-

membered battle in Zaire, and the next it may huddle in the corner of a dorm room. The faces of the callers and counselors must be masked, but I can tell you about their struggles. The same is true of the building. I am not free to describe its façade, but I can tell you about its inner life.

Chapter 1

Borrowed Hearts

THE telephone room sits on the top floor of this rambling old house, whose wooden staircase creaks no matter where or how gently you step. The walls once were cream-colored, and the varnish on the stairs, windowsills, doors, and woodwork has aged into a deep resiny brown. There's something comforting and old-time about the creakiness, the drafty hallways, and twisting staircases. Downstairs are administrative offices and rooms where the counselors meet; upstairs, a kitchen, a bathroom with shower, the counselor room, and three more offices.

I climb the stairs one evening, shrugging the knapsack off my shoulders. The crisis lines are located in the counselor room, which has two simple polished oak plank desks arranged in an L shape. The walls are tan, mottled by hand with a feather duster dipped in green and white paint. Stare at them long enough and you will see a snowfall in a field of tall grass. A foldaway bed covered with a quilted green fitted cover serves as couch for day counselors and sleep spot for overnighters. I put my knapsack there and wave hello to Frieda, a slender woman in her sixties, one of the agency's new counselors, who is talking quietly with a caller.

In many ways it is an ordinary room. In one corner sits a small green velveteen armchair; in another, a golden-yellow hassock, torn at the seams and with the stuffing hanging out. Black steel filing cabinets contain the current monthly write-ups (brief reports on each call), referral information, emergency telephone numbers, clippings of interest. Two phones sit in the middle of each desk. Beside them a black gooseneck lamp offers a little extra light. Along the rear of the desks are more files and folders, a tan box of counselor communications cards (in case staff wishes to comment on some call a counselor has received). A well-thumbed green logbook lies ready for the next entry—all calls are noted according to date, time, and counselor. A red spring binder, the emergency resource book, steers counselors through everything from rescue procedures to the locations of local bridges. On an open-framed steel bookcase, back issues of the journal *Suicide and Life-Threatening Behavior* lie in stacks among various magazines and books. A gray school-model pencil sharpener is attached to a door-jamb, and near it, hanging on the door, is a large desk calendar on which counselors sign up for their shifts.

"Whew! That was exhausting," Frieda says, putting down the phone. She rubs her hand across her forehead and pushes her gray-blond bangs straight back, pulling the skin tight. "Mary Jo is having a tough day. We talked for about an hour. I'm out cold." Putting both palms on the desktop for support, she slowly stands. "I did the write-up as we were finishing." She tucks a sheet of paper into a folder, hoists a smile onto her face, and says in a weary drawl, "Bye-eye."

"Good-bye," I respond, and sit down at the desk. The chair is still warm as I settle into it.

Darkness has just begun to envelop the town. One tall window faces the driveway, and the other, behind one of the desks, looks out onto the yard next door. Cork bulletin boards on the east wall provide a guide to who is available for emergency after-hours— that is, who can be reached by beeper if a consultation is needed or an emergency unfolds. On the west wall a white poster offers a list of important places and their numbers: the Task Force for Battered Women, the emergency room at the hospital, the Poison Control Center, the Mental Health Clinic, Family and Children's Service, and so on. One of the most important filing cabinets, stationed between the two sets of phones, holds a laboriously gathered and researched library of special support groups, private organizations, and public agencies in the area. So it's possible to refer a caller to a support group for cross-dressers, or find help for a sexually abused child, or give a caller a list of places that will help him or her find a job, or a meal, or a safe house, or friends in similar circumstances. The business lines ring in the normal way, but the crisis lines ring with a sudden loud two-part jangle that's startling—the telephone equivalent of a fire alarm.

7:45 P.M. A single father phones about his sixteen-year-old daughter, who has become too wild for him to manage. She stays out late, even on school nights, drinking heavily with her friends and taking drugs. Though he's tried to talk with her about her addictions, she won't listen. Last night she returned home with a black eye and refuses to say how it happened. Seeing her physically hurt is more than he can bear. We speak for an hour or so, during which he unfolds his deep frustration and fear, then anger and guilt. When he feels calm enough to make plans, we discuss his joining a support group like Al-Anon, where he would find other people who have loved ones abusing alcohol or drugs. I cannot help his daughter, who did not call. The father is suffering; my job is to try to help *him*.

"Do you think it might give me a better relationship with my daughter?" he asks.

"I don't know," I answer. "But you would meet people in circumstances similar to yours, and they might be able to give you some ideas about what has worked for them—or not worked. At the very least you won't be facing this problem all alone."

"What's their number?" he says, his voice strong for the first time since the conversation began. I give it to him, and then I invite him to call back if the support group doesn't work out or if he just needs to talk. He thanks me, and we say good-bye.

Although I suggested an agency that could help him, I did little talking through the hour-long call. SP (Suicide Prevention) counselors are not therapists. Our job is not to search through psyches. We don't engage the caller in the usual give-and-take of a conversation or offer advice. What we do is listen. Sometimes it feels like auditory braille, and I can see the callers' faces in my mind's eye and read their expressions. Sometimes it works like echolocation: I send out small reconnoitering sounds—a leading question, perhaps—and wait to hear in what shape and from where it echoes back. There is an art to making listening noises.

We're not much distracted by personal thoughts, as one is in normal conversation—listening while thinking about what to say next, perhaps something about one's own related experiences. We listen actively, and it is physically exhausting.

Listening with one's whole attention, one hears the words, the sighs, the sniffling, the loud exhalations, the one-beat-longer-than-normal pause before a difficult or taboo word, the heavy tongue of drunkenness, the fumings of stifled rage, the bleak deadpan of the hopeless, the entrenched gloom of depression, the distant recesses of loneliness.

One hears the silences and the spaces between the words as well. They have a rhythm and shape all their own. And one hears ice tinkling in a glass, a cigarette being smoked, the television set on in a nearby room, the traffic outside the caller's window.

Just as doctors listen to the patient's chest down the line of a stethoscope, we press an ear to the warm receiver of the phone and listen for the heartbeat beneath the words.

8:47 p.m. A developmentally disabled woman calls, upset that some children teased her today. We talk for half an hour, and she decides it's time to go to bed.

9:22 p.m. The telephone rings, and I answer it briskly, only to find no one there. "Hang-up," I jot down in a logbook on the desk. Hang-ups are frequent—not everyone is ready to make contact, but they want to know someone is here for when they are ready.

In the lulls between calls I page through a notebook of press clippings and find the obituary of a young man, troubled by depression and loneliness, who called SP often over a period of three years. We could not save him. Perhaps we had for some while, for those three years when we were his lifeline. It reminds me of the time I was driving home from a shift at about eight o'clock on a Sunday morning. The streets were empty, but on one, near a bridge, I saw a group of ambulances. Sure enough, somebody had jumped. And I thought, Why didn't that person call us? We were there all night! The painful truth is that people irrevocably bent on suicide tend not to call. We are there for the people who still have some precarious, tenuous connection to life left. That's what we speak to when they call. We don't tell them not to kill themselves. Suicide is certainly one option open to them, but it's not the only option. Suicide is a permanent solution to a temporary problem, as we like to say. The part of them that clings to life called us, and so we explore what other options still remain.

9:15 p.m. A middle-aged woman calls. She is restless and on the edge. Her speech sounds a little slurred, perhaps from drinking. She has phoned often before, and I recognize her voice.

"This is Melissa. . . . Have I talked with you before?" she asks.

"Yes, Melissa. How are you feeling today?"

"Not so good."

The last time I talked with Melissa, two weeks ago, it was early morning and she was savagely depressed. I have been worried about her because she seems terribly fragile, and I'm afraid we may lose her. In her early forties, she is intelligent and articulate. She has two young children and is in a second marriage, this time to an alcoholic husband who sometimes becomes violent. Her life is riddled with stress, and it's only when something hits unbearable proportions that she phones.

By definition, a crisis is what impedes the normal flow of someone's life. When people call the hot line in crisis, I want to help them regain equilibrium. There was a time when extended families played this role, offering solace and understanding in times of trouble. Families expected crises to emerge from time to time, because crisis is a normal part of human life and cannot be wholly erased or relieved. In evolutionary terms it provides turning points; it allows necessary change. Habit is the great deadener, but habit also assures an organism that what worked before will work again. It is the best survival technique. "Eat the berries on that tree," it argues. "They didn't poison you before." Contented creatures don't feel driven to change their lives, as they often must to survive in a changing environment. So crises may be normal, and even liberating, but they are painful and frightening.

I cannot stop the crisis Melissa finds herself in when she calls. All I can offer her is a breather, a temporary safety zone in which to help explore her feelings and help review her resources and options. I can be with her in the long corridors of the night when troubles can take on monstrous proportions. I listen. At times I have urged her to call one of the agencies in town that provide support groups, legal advice, and ongoing help. On rare occasions, when I believed she was in physical danger from herself or someone else, I intervened and sent help. But my goal is not to intervene. My goal is to make intervention unnecessary because I've helped her reach a safer place—mentally or physically. My goal is for her to keep control of as much of her life as possible. I do not give advice.

"I don't know what to do," Melissa sobs tonight. Her husband came home drunk and beat her in front of her small children. She is terrified to stay with him and terrified he'll find her if she leaves. In any case, she has no money of her own, no full-time job, no way to feed the children. She is afraid he might even get custody if she runs off and isn't employed. "What should I do?" With all my heart I want to tell her, Leave him! Take the children and get out now! Now before he comes back home!

"I can't tell you what to do," I say, "but maybe together we can figure something out." Then we review several plans that have occurred to her and some that occur to me. In time, still frightened but a little more focused, she decides to talk to the Task Force for Battered Women, who have a safe house where she and her children can go while they help her put her life back together.

10:15 p.m. "Suicide Prevention and Crisis Service," I say. "Can I help you?"

"No." A male voice.

"What's on your mind this evening?"

Suddenly irate: "A bigoted society. Vicious, rotten, loveless, sucking-on-a-gun society. You're no good at all! Anyone who doesn't love me doesn't love God. Louis Armstrong said that. If I were evil,

I'd understand it, but I'm not. Anyone who hates me doesn't have the love of Jesus in them. You're all bigoted!" Caller hangs up.

10:17 p.m. Same caller: "Another thing. Women are the most vicious members of society."

"What do they do that's so vicious?"

Caller hangs up.

10:19 p.m. Same caller: "I've been the recipient long enough."

"The what?"

"The recipient." Long, loud scream like a lightning strike.

10:22 p.m. Same caller: "You're a monster. You're all monsters!"

"You sound like you're in so much pain." I say.

"Pain? Pain? You don't give a f___ about my pain! You're all monsters!" Caller hangs up.

10:25 p.m. Hang-up. Probably the same caller. He phones every now and then, insults a counselor for a shift, then doesn't call for days or weeks. Some of the counselors dread his calls and are rattled by them; some look forward to them as a challenge; one or two have managed to engage him in conversation long enough to discover a little of his bizarre story. Apparently he is a Vietnam veteran, suffering from Agent Orange exposure, who works as a night watchman at a factory. He lives in a cabin in a small farming community, has four children, and we're worried about all of them. He claims to have facial tattoos and a mechanical hand. We don't know his name, but one counselor labeled him Edward Scissorhands on a write-up, and the tag stuck. "Edward," I jot down in the logbook, and on the write-up sheet I note simply, "The usual."

10:30 p.m. I hear the front door open, the stairs begin creaking. Soon a woman with short red hair appears in the doorway to start the next shift. We say hello, and she goes into the kitchen to fix herself a cup of coffee. There are seventy-five counselors on active duty, and we take five-hour shifts—except for the overnight shift, which runs from 10:00 p.m. to 8:00 a.m. We have very little in common when it comes to background, education, family life, religious upbringing, personality, or income. Many of us have experienced great trauma or hardship, survived it, and want to help others. One might imagine that crisis-line counselors lead more stable, less troubled lives than the callers, but that isn't always true.

For example, a young man in my training class told how he had returned home one day to find his roommate lying dead in a pool of blood and a suicide note on the counter. He had loved his roommate dearly and knew he had been depressed, but not *that* depressed. How could he have missed the danger signs, been deaf to the appeals for help? In retrospect they seemed obvious. It took years for him to make peace with horror and guilt.

A mature woman in the same training class described a lifetime of coping with an alcoholic mother. Long after training was over, a gifted counselor confided that she has been struggling with depression for many years. One does not need to be stronger, fitter, morally better, or untroubled to come to the aid of people in crisis. One has to be able to put one's own problems on hold and listen heartfully, nonjudgmentally, and focus entirely on someone else's need.

Most counselors volunteer because the work makes them feel good. It's slightly different for everyone, but for me it's equal measures of compassion, accomplishment, a sense of myself as a good person, and a curious sleight of mind: the chance to renovate my past by helping others change the present.

My life includes joy, love, adventure, fulfillment, and discovery. No boredom. Never a dull torment. But I've seen enough of the dark side to identify with a wide range of callers. Their stories have been complex and fascinating. It's unbelievable what predicaments human beings get themselves into. So I find crisis work simultaneously heart-wrenching, frightening, stressful, and deeply rewarding.

AFTER talking with a friend who had been a counselor for nine years, I couldn't shake my curiosity about an agency that, according to my friend, performed quiet acts of mercy and heroism but also transformed the lives of volunteers. Who were these people? One fall morning I phoned SP to ask if they could use a laptop computer I didn't need. Marian van Soest, the director, proclaimed the call heaven-sent, since SP urgently needed another

computer, and she graciously accepted mine, adding, to my astonishment, that there was one condition: Since I was an author,
I would have to agree to speak at the annual meeting. Odd way to
accept a donation, I thought, but I agreed and gave a talk on al-
truism to a merry gathering of SP's counselors, staff, and govern-
ing board. They had a relaxed, somewhat macabre sense of
humor; they played hard, and they *felt* the world's troubles in an
unusually candid way. I liked their spirit. After that, one thing led
to another, until at last I found myself taking the training.

There are two or three training classes a year, and I trained in
the winter. For six weeks we met Tuesday and Thursday nights and
Saturday mornings in a conference room in which fifteen chairs
were arranged in a circle. My fellow trainees included an ex-
mortician, a social worker, a combat photographer from the Gulf
war, a musician, a premed student, an ex–radio announcer, a volunteer firefighter, a biogeneticist, a carpenter with a literature degree, an air-traffic controller, and a man who had delivered three
of his own children. They ran the gamut of ages and ethnic back-
grounds. The oldest was fifty-eight, the youngest twenty-two.

Much time was spent during the first weeks in explaining ourselves to one another, so that we were more than the name tag
worn at every session. Two of the trainees started dating. One
trainee (who couldn't bridle her strong opinions during calls) was
asked to leave. Three others dropped out. The rest of us practiced
following a six-step crisis model, which involves making contact
with the caller (by reflecting and identifying feelings), exploring
the current problem (through open-ended questions), summarizing the problem (and agreeing on a common understanding),
problem solving if possible, exploring resources (such as past coping techniques and agency referrals), and agreeing on a plan of action (or perhaps arranging a follow-up call).

At every session we received a short lecture, watched two experienced counselors—sitting back to back in the middle of the
circle—role-playing calls, and we practiced playing roles ourselves, with a counselor giving feedback. We learned about the
different parts of a call and practiced the opening moments as

well as the endings. We practiced talking with depressed callers, suicidal callers, addicted callers, battered callers, developmentally disabled callers, violent or abusive callers, obsessive callers, and a caravan of others. We discussed our own feelings and prejudices, the need for banishing them when we're on shift, and various ways of empathizing with the caller. We learned how to send rescue and where to find referrals and resources.

Stumbling and tongue-tied at first, sometimes disheartened and unsure, we discovered in time that techniques clicked into place. And yet, when training ended and we signed up for apprentice shifts, not one of us felt fully confident. How would we react when it wasn't practice, when lives were at stake? Each of us was riddled by self-doubt. Nonetheless I began counseling fifteen hours a month and sifting deeper and deeper into the soul of the agency.

10:48 P.M. The phone rings. "Suicide Prevention and Crisis Service," I say in a welcoming voice, an achieved voice. "May I help you?" For a few seconds only silence answers. Unconsciously I press my ear more tightly to the phone. I think I can hear the choked breath of someone crying.

A distraught woman says, "My husband just"—the voice hovers, searches for bearable words, then settles on—"hurt me."

"Your husband hurt you?" I repeat calmly. "Could you tell me about it?"

In a voice half whisper, half sob, she tells me—a stranger—the intimate and horrifying details of her day, how her husband came home drunk and brutal. A sarcastic remark made him erupt into a violent rage, during which he had torn off her robe and beaten her. Terrified, she ran out into the street and just kept running. She is in a phone booth in her nightgown. It is a clear March night, and there are frost warnings. She does not want an ambulance or the police. She does not want anyone to know. She feels humiliated and desperate. She refuses to say where she is. She is afraid her husband will come after her. Her voice trembles from cold, anger, and fright.

"I'm so glad you phoned," I say, trying to press my concern

through the slender thread of the phone wire. I want it to be an invisible arm wrapping around her. "You sound scared and upset."

"Scared to death," she whispers, adding, "I shouldn't have said what I did. It's my fault. I provoked him like I always do."

"No one deserves to be beaten," I say. "Look, I'm worried about you, and I'd really like to get somebody to come over and be with you."

"No. I can't face anyone. My life is such a mess," she says, crying. "I'm so confused. I don't know what to do."

"That's okay," I say. "I understand how frightened and confused you're feeling. How about if we just talk for a while. How would that be?"

Twenty minutes later, a little calmer, she agrees to let someone escort her to a safe place. When help arrives, they find her standing nearly naked in a phone booth.

Chapter 2

Squirrels and the Dark Night of the Soul

AWAKENING to a misty day, I fix myself a cup of Peruvian coffee that smells loamlike and bitter, and carry it into the garden room. I crank open a window and call the squirrels as usual, warbling to them in a melodic two-note that starts high and slides lower: "Squir-rels, squir-rels, squir-rels." Then I quickly scatter a mix of peanuts, hazelnuts, Brazil nuts, and almonds in a wide arc. The nuts are unsalted and still in their shells, just as squirrels would find them in nature—that is, if they happened to live simultaneously in Georgia, New York State, and the Amazon. Scufflings begin deep in the two acres of woods as squirrels leave the warmth of their leaf nests and rush down tree trunks, leap across brush and woodpiles, and run along telephone and electric wires toward the house, using their tails to balance tightrope walker–style.

I sit back and survey the dawn. There's nothing like the fecund beauty of spring in New York State. Separate raindrops lie along the twigs of a maple branch—round, brilliant globules—trembling without falling. All the light of the morning seems trapped in their small worlds. You can smell the mixing fragrances of spring, bud-luscious and full of growth. But it's a difficult time for animals. Spring means waking from the long coma of winter into a land of hardship and haste. Roused from their winter stupors, they find food scarce and little yet in bloom. Locating a mate becomes an urgent quest.

Humans suffer in this season, too. At the crisis center we receive more calls in spring than during any other time of year. No one is sure why. I think it may be the stark contrast between the blos-soming world outside and the perceived desert of the callers' lives.

A drumroll across the roof grows louder and then stops. I feel something watching me, look up, and see the Pleader—a large, muscular male gray squirrel—on the roof, examining me, the morning, and the sudden appearance of manna. Whiskers twitch-ing, he leans over the edge and fixes me with shiny dark eyes.

"Breakfast?" I ask.

He coils up fast, raises and lowers his head rapidly, springs off his haunches, leaps eight feet to a slender hickory, is down its trunk in four strides and at the window in two more. It's not that the strewn nuts aren't appealing; it's just that the Pleader prefers walnuts, and as he knows by now, I keep those indoors.

I hold a walnut lightly between thumb and forefinger and offer it to him, feeling the gentlest tug as he lifts it free. Twisting around fast, he takes a watchful position on a rock, turning the nut on the lathe of his teeth and paws until he finds the exact spot to drill a hole. This he does with his two chisel-shaped front teeth; then he carries the nut like a bowling ball as he runs to a large hickory and scampers up its shaggy trunk to the first branch. From that look-out post he can see a mob of squirrels arriving, grabbing nuts, squabbling over territories. He widens the hole in the walnut and attacks the meat, spitting out a plume of husks. He continues to watch me with a look of uneasy vigilance.

I call him the Pleader because of the way he always finds me in my study or in the living room. When he gets my attention, he runs to the glassed-in garden room, races up to the window, and stares. He stands up on his back feet, arms held at his chest, stretching to look in, face alert and expectant. Above all, the Pleader is daring—brave enough not to flee when I open the creaky window. Brave enough to take a large walnut from my hand. Brave enough to drive off competitors from his small pile of food. If I leave both the window and nut barrel open, he will climb right in, help himself, and dart outside to eat.

I'm halfway through a two-year research project for *National Geographic,* studying the secret life of gray squirrels, taking field notes, and trying my best to fathom their ways. I haven't exactly adopted the squirrels; it's just that I worry about their well-being during the hard winters, and I've become fascinated by their relationships, instinctive behaviors, and antics, especially the Pleader's.

In a flash the Pleader returns for a hazelnut and scampers back up the tree, barely disturbing the large gang of assembled squirrels. Busily feeding are Mr. Tatter Tail, a male whose tail falls in a scruffy shag; Narrow Nose, with his pliers-shaped schnoz; Black Chin, who reminds me of a helmeted British policeman; Red Tail, a female with a rusty stripe down her tail; Collops, one of my favorites, the largest female, who always seems to be pregnant (hence her nickname, which means "rolls of fat"); Snow White, who has a white scar across her nose; Topple, who stands up too tall when he eats and usually falls over backward as a result; and twenty or so unnamed others.

At the crisis center we have nicknames for many of the frequent callers whose real names we don't know. Not only Edward Scissorhands, but Prisoner, Endless Love, the Fall Guy, Don't Lie to Me, Ten Years, Garter Man, and dozens of others. We need a shorthand to be able to keep callers in mind as individuals when their names are unknown. Sometimes the nicknames we invent for SP callers are funny or ironic, sometimes sad, sometimes factual, but they do enable us to discuss a caller's problem or history when we need to with staff or other counselors. Giving callers names also forms them into a community in our minds. It cuts through the potential blur of voices and distresses and allows us to think of them as individuals with unique quirks, problems, fine qualities, and needs.

Mr. Tatter Tail and Collops shuffle a little, putting a few more inches between them as they eat. I always scatter nuts widely so that a few grays can eat side by side without feeling boxed in. Minimum separation seems to be three feet. At that distance squirrels will happily munch a pile of peanuts, but any closer they feel obliged to drive off the claim jumper.

Squirrels prefer to carry their food up a tree to a low, secure branch and scout the ground below as they dine. When they eat, they hold a nut with both paws together like mittens. Squirrels have three fingers and a thumb on each hand, but they don't flex or bend them to eat. Fastidious about skins, they carefully peel grapes and apples while eating. On the ground, squirrels face upwind when they eat so that their fur will be ironed shut by the wind, not ruffled up.

Today a dozen grays are dining. Males and females look the same color and size—fourteen to seventeen ounces of fur and appetite. Happy with about two pounds of nuts a week, they also enjoy mushrooms, buds, flower shoots, berries, apples, catkins, caterpillars, and other delicacies.

Four grays, bounding in from a neighbor's yard, pause to make a sudden detour. Squirrels don't like to head straight for anything. They move by innuendo, running past and sweeping around from the side. And that's just what one husky gray is doing, running a circle around the other squirrels to see if there's room enough to squeeze in behind. There isn't, so the only alternative is to challenge one of the others by running at it until it leaps straight up in the air, jumping right over the challenger, launched by the trampoline of its fear and aggression. Husky takes a position with nuts, and the others soon find new places. They're a little too close together, so they all eat with their tails folded into pompadours high over their heads. The purpose is to make themselves look taller, like big bad butch squirrels, and I guess it works.

Soon another intruder arrives—a medium-sized gray with a brown chin strap—and takes a spot close beside Collops. Her per-

sonal space threatened, Collops faces her foe and sits still, but
rapidly twitches her cheeks and, with them, her whiskers: a visual
growl. Even though her mouth is busily chewing almonds, she
makes small insistent harmonica-like noises that sound like a chug-
ging train. Too close! Too close! Too close! they warn. Chin Strap
doesn't retreat, and Collops cheek-twitches while bending her tail
right up and over her back and head into a warbonnet, growling
a terror whine that sounds like a swarm of insects. Still Chin Strap
won't budge, so there's nothing left but a tussle, and tussle they
do—first leaping high to kick box, then shrieking while nipping at
ears and flanks. The other squirrels watch and continue eating.
In a moment it is all over, and Chin Strap swiftly gives ground. Collops picks up a peanut, rips the husk off, and settles down to eat,
keeping a steady eye on Chin Strap, who circles around the crowd
and finds a less than ideal spot at the edge of the banquet.

While the squirrels continue feeding, I dress, pack a lunch, and
head down to the crisis center. The minute I sit down at the desk
and rest my feet on the hassock (which someone has repaired with
silver duct tape), the phone rings. A man's voice greets me. He
feels alone and troubled enough to call, but he must also feel
strong enough to seek help from others. "Only connect!" E. M.
Forster once wrote, reducing all of our human quests, hardships,
and fears to a basic need for contact with others.

"I don't know why I'm calling really . . ." he says.

"Would you like to tell me a little of what's on your mind today?"

Slowly he reveals that he's calling from his car phone. He is
parked at the edge of a scenic overlook outside of town. His wife
has left him and taken the two children with her. Laid off four
months ago, he hasn't been able to find a new job. And that's
meant living on welfare, which he feels ashamed of. Because he
can't make his car payments, he's going to forfeit his car, too. That
was the last straw. The car repossession notice arrived yesterday.
Something about losing the freedom a car represents has hit him
viscerally. Now he is planning to drive himself and his soon-to-be-
repossessed car over the cliff.

"Why shouldn't I?" he asks angrily.

"Tell me your story," I say, and then wait through the longest silence I can remember. To my amazement he starts to speak, slowly, beginning with his childhood. When we get to the here and now, we discuss a couple of agencies in town that could help him temporarily, with his legal and financial problems anyway. It's not much hope to salvage from the wreckage of his life, but it's something. After a while his voice changes from frantic to worn-out.

"How are you feeling now?" I ask.

"Exhausted."

"Maybe it's time to go home and get some sleep. Will you be all right driving home?" I picture him driving erratically on the highway.

"Yeah, I'll be okay."

"Would you like me to have someone call you tomorrow morning, just check in on you, see how you're doing, see if you need any advice with those calls?"

His voice chokes. "Yeah. That'd be good. I hate to be such a bother."

"It's no bother. That's why we're here," I say, trying not to sound dutiful or perfunctory. I want him to stay calm, but I also want him to feel comfortable about calling. As usual, I wish I had more control over my voice, wish I could sculpt its nuances so that regardless of the exact words I used, the tone would tell a caller like this one, "You're not alone. We're here to help you or, if help is impossible, at least to understand." I think it's possible to insinuate your emotions into your voice wholeheartedly like that, to speak sentences charged with pure emotion. I just can't figure out how best to do it.

"If you have trouble sleeping, call us. Someone's here all night. Okay?"

"Okay."

Something reticent in his voice worries me. "I'm concerned about you," I add. "How about if we make a contract that you won't do anything to hurt yourself without calling us first. Could you make me that promise?"

After a long silence he does.

It's a funny thing about promises. People tend to keep them. Even a promise they know will interfere with self-destructive plans. It is an ancient idea, to make a promise to another person, to oneself, or to one's God. Our species has survived partly because of our great skill at negotiating and working together. Most of our laws are based on contracts, the paper form of a promise. Because a promise foretells how one will act, it allows us the relief of knowing a small shred of the future, of relaxing some of our anxieties.

I think promising goes back to the unstated contract between a mother and child. It's no use her telling a child, "You must not go near the edge of the cliff, or touch fire, or wander off," unless the child agrees that it won't. If the child doesn't agree, then the mother must be more vigilant than is practical. What the child promises is to try to stay alive. What the mother promises, in return, is to love the child and try to keep it alive. That is the earliest contract humans make, or have ever made. So when we ask a caller to promise, we are touching an ancient nerve. The equation written in our cells, in our bones, is that keeping yourself safe will lead to love. It is the oldest and simplest promise.

Many people in our callers' lives have betrayed them in one way or another, the system has let them down, and life itself has broken its unspoken word. Their future no longer holds any hope. Yet callers trapped in that nightmare usually act honorably with us. If they make a contract not to kill themselves without calling first, they keep it. Sometimes a caller bent on suicide will say, "I promised to call first, and out of respect I'm calling, but I'm heading for the bridge now." That leaves just the narrowest chance for a counselor. A lifeline only a few minutes wide. Sometimes it's enough, sometimes not.

WANDERING into the kitchen, I microwave a frozen bagel and pour myself a cup of tea. When the phone rings, I hurry back into the counselor room, sit down, glance at the clock, jot the time down on a piece of paper, lift up the receiver.

"Suicide Prevention and Crisis Service. May I help you?"

No one speaks.

"This must be difficult for you," I say at last. "Take your time."

My heart starts to pound when I hear a tearful voice whisper, "I can't go on anymore." A small sob fills the blackness. "I've tried so hard," she says in a strained voice, a girlish voice that fragments into a whimper. "I've been holding on for so long. But nobody would want me to live in this pain, this pain that never goes away."

I recognize the voice as belonging to Louise, a fragile woman who has been calling the agency for a few years. Sometimes Louise introduces herself when she calls. Tonight she is beyond names. She is a substitute teacher who sings in an a cappella group, volunteers as a stagehand during the local theater's summer season, and sits on several boards serving the homeless, flood victims, handicapped children. Although she lives close to the poverty line, she somehow manages to raise a difficult teenage daughter on her own. Going about her public life, she appears confident, talented, attractive, smart, apparently on an even keel.

That seems incomprehensible. We hear from her only when she's in the quicksand of her depression, when she has laid pills out on the counter and is a hairbreadth away from taking them. In most of the write-ups after Louise's calls, the counselors predict that she won't be alive by morning. Although she calls every few weeks in a desperately suicidal state, it is not an act. We all agree: She is holding on by her fingernails. She has no money, no steady job, no boyfriend, a prickly relationship with her daughter, a long parade of antidepressants that haven't worked, and something organic—a depression that can appear suddenly in her day and stop her life cold. From time to time she has checked into psychiatric wards, but they never help much, just sedate her for a while. She fears that the stigma of her being a mental patient is keeping employers from hiring her, and she may be right.

Louise is special—caring, funny, sensible about most things, bighearted and decent with people. She's smart and sensitive, a real peach. How can I be uninvolved when she phones? Even in the densest thicket of her depression, her brave wonderful self shines through. I long to go knock on her door when she's feeling sad and drag her out shopping or biking or to a show. I long to insert myself into her life and heal her. But that is taboo, of course. All I can do is hope to be on shift when she calls. It would kill me to lose her.

"I'm so sorry you're suffering," I say. "What's made it tough today?"

"Everything, everything," she says. "My life is in ruins. I'm at work. In a phone booth. I keep going through the motions, but inside I'm dying. It's time to make the inside and outside match."

I sigh audibly, an exhalation of sorrow. "It must be horrible to feel so much pain that you want to die to make it stop."

"It is. It's so horrible." She sobs. "I picture myself at the bottom of the gorge, picture myself hitting the rocks, and I don't feel any pain. I just feel grateful that it's finally over."

Without meaning to, I also picture her lying broken on the rocks. I hate it when callers describe a horrible fantasy or event in their lives, because then it takes shape in my imagination, and sometimes it haunts me for quite a while. I always picture the callers in my mind's eye. The lines and rhythms of their voices paint living portraits of them, and I see them clearly, as if in a movie, see the emotion on their faces, how they're holding the telephone, when they smoke a cigarette, glance at their watches, fight their eyes from tearing up. I know what every caller looks like—not accurately, of course, but in an emotional landscape. To me Louise is an attractive woman of medium height, with curly shoulder-length brown hair parted on the left side and a delicate complexion that blushes easily. She's about thirty-five years old, needs glasses to read, and likes to wear skirts and sweaters. None of this may be true. It's fascinating how the sound of a voice obsessively expresses itself in vivid images. We are so visual a species.

Even though I don't know what the callers look like, they are not disembodied voices or crises. I only administer to one facet of a caller on one day, but I see him or her whole in my mind, and in my understanding I try to see each of them as more than their pain, more than this narrow self their depression has flattened them to. Often I recognize the voices; some of the callers are familiar, and each new call adds another chapter to a long narrative of struggle, survival, obsession, anxiety, and grief. I may feel comfortable asking Louise, "Has your daughter been much help with this?" even when she hasn't mentioned her daughter. The caller knows my voice, too, and replies with the ease of a confidante. We are intimate strangers.

Louise mentioned a bridge near where she works, and I think I know the one she means. Shouldn't I send the police? But if I do, will she lose her job, a job she desperately needs? If I don't, will she lose her life?

"Have you pictured loved ones finding you?" I ask gently.

"My daughter. I've thought about what it would do to her, and some days that's the only thing that's stood between me and the rocks."

"She needs her mother."

"It doesn't seem like that right now. We're always fighting."

"How old is she?"

"Fourteen."

The age of my goddaughter. "That can be a tough age for girls. What was she like as a child?"

"Oh, she was a wonderful little girl, so huggy. We were really close there for a while. We went everywhere together." Her voice brightens a little.

"Do you think it's possible this might be a stage she's going through, that it will pass?"

"It's possible."

"How do you think she would feel if you killed yourself?"

Her voice breaks into a soft whine as she says, "It would be really hard on her, but I think she would understand. She wouldn't want me to go on living in so much pain."

My cheeks fill with air, and I glance out the window as I slowly exhale. The sky couldn't be bluer, and an intricate thatch of clouds hovers over the lake.

"Are you standing outside?" I ask.

"Yes," she says.

"Look up."

A moment later she laughs a little, distracted from herself.

"That's amazing," she says. "It looks like someone has been writing up there, using clouds as ink. That's really neat."

All over town the trees are surging with buds, some of them folded into mysterious and beautiful shapes. She responded to the clouds; maybe she would respond to the trees. "You said there was a tree nearby. What kind is it?" I ask.

"It's a ginkgo. It has fan-shaped leaves."

For a few minutes we talk about how ancient the ginkgo is, how its leaves are brewed into a tea and drunk three times a day as a brain tonic beneficial for circulation and short-term memory. I didn't realize Louise was so knowledgeable about homeopathy, but apparently it's one of her hobbies. She gradually calms down a little, and we take some deep breaths together. Depression works like a lens, narrowing one's focus to a grim, painful obsession. All the irrelevant perceptions and idle thoughts that normally bustle through one's life seem to disappear. Reattaching a few can sometimes ease the sadness for a short while. Today that works for Louise, who, feeling a little better, decides to hang up and return to her office. But how about next time? For the rest of my shift I keep worrying when she will call again. Not this afternoon anyway, thanks to the clouds and the ginkgo tree.

We think of salvation as a large, heroic drama. But in depression one clings to life by such humble knots. I remember a day five winters ago when depression had been working on me all week, making me feel rejected and alone. It began as a sort of loose sadness; then by week's end I woke up crying and couldn't stop. All day I sank lower and lower. Despite that, in an effort to hold on, I kept my appointments; I told almost no one. But the next day the depression was so bad that I could barely move. My mind had begun mulling over grim ironies. As I knew from years before, when my dear friend Martin died in a plane crash—despite his dentist appointment, his dinner plans with me, and all the ropes and anchors we use to bind ourselves to life—death doesn't require you to keep a day free. People die even if they have appointments, even if they have newborns or unfinished business, even if it's the worst possible time for everyone they leave behind.

Tossing my cross-country skis into the car, I drove to the golf course and set out on the thin, wet, clumpy snow. It stuck to my skis, so that I couldn't glide, but I could snowshoe and shuffle. For half an hour I stomped toward the woods. It was then that I heard a sound. Geese honking. I closed my eyes. For a long moment I listened to the sound as a smile of wonder crept up my face. The honking grew louder, and I opened my eyes to see a large wedge of Canada geese low overhead, flapping, skiing through the air, and honking like mad. I savored the sound. It was a wonderful, crazy combination of trombone and kazoo.

Sometimes the smallest thing can be enough to glue you back to life: a salvation of geese, the snow polished by daylight, a signature of clouds above a budding ginkgo tree. But one doesn't know where or which or when or if.

Chapter 3

All the Bright Catastrophes

"HONEY, I'm home!" a basso voice calls from downstairs as Bob arrives to take the evening shift. Then two sets of doors rattle closed, and soon afterward size-thirteen feet start climbing the creaking stairs. I know it's Bob from the schedule posted in the counselor room. He is a sculptor who works exclusively with cement. He appears—a tall, thin man in his forties, with shoulder-length brown hair and the largest hands I've ever seen on a man—wearing jeans and a red-and-white T-shirt.

"Hi. How's it goin'?" he says.

"Busy day." I turn the logbook so that he can read the seven new entries. "Louise called. I don't think she'll phone back tonight, but I'm not sure. And there's a teenage girl named Jesse who may call. Her classmate phoned, worried because Jesse has been cutting herself." Both of us wince at the word teenage. The number of teen suicides has skyrocketed. There were four suicides in one local high school last year. After each tragedy SP sent in its postvention team to talk with the shell-shocked classmates, the grieving families and friends, the mystified school officials. Since then, more teenagers have phoned us for help, but the suicide rate continues to be alarmingly high. For every 660 depressed teens, one commits suicide. Researchers have found that over half of all teens think about killing themselves. Indeed, suicide is the third cause of teen death in the United States. Only accident and homicide claim more lives.

Our local teens find the world a frightening place. What with raging hormones, school pressures, family problems, world events, and such normal identity issues as who they are and what they should do with their lives, it's a miserably confusing and stressful time of life. Anorexia, bulimia, and self-mutilation are reaching epidemic proportions, and that's ironic, since these are often the afflictions of the educated, accomplished, "good" families, in which parents relentlessly demand excellence from themselves and their children.

"Cutters are tough," Bob says. "Had one the other day. He was this upright dude, a banker, who would sneak out to the bathroom at work to burn himself with his cigarette. Called here instead."

"At least he phoned first. That's a good step." I tell him about the woman caller I spoke with recently who had burned herself minutes before the call. She had a history of cutting but had only recently started burning herself, and she was afraid her problem was escalating, afraid of what her two young children would think. We talked about what she felt when she burned herself, how overpowering a compulsion it was, what might have precipitated it, if anything helps when she senses the urge coming on. Sometimes she would spend days thinking about hurting herself and go through curious rituals of preparation—stroking the area of the arm she meant to cut or burn, arranging the knives or razor blades or cigarettes in a tidy way. She was seeing a therapist, but progress was slow.

Self-mutilation is a stubborn addiction. It has something in common with eating disorders. People who suffer from one frequently suffer from the other. Cutters tend to be women who were sexually abused as children, people who can't complain about the torment in their family and can't fight back at their abuser. One theory about cutters holds that as children, they received nurturing only after they were badly injured, and thus as adults they injure themselves because subconsciously they associate harm with kindness, protection, love.

Or this strange affliction may be due to a physiological glitch. Cutters almost always report that they feel relief afterward, possibly because endorphins flow in response to the pain. They say that it makes them feel alive, in touch with reality, and that they otherwise feel dead inside and disconnected from life. Some analysts suggest that cutters may be consumed by an emotion like rage or resentment and are enacting the desire to symbolically punish their abuser by punishing themselves.

Whatever their motives, their actions are horrifying and leave me and other counselors feeling both helpless and sad. We know they rarely commit suicide, though sometimes they're so disgusted by their addiction that they do end their lives to end their misery. Ironically, when that happens, they choose an overdose or some other swift method unrelated to their condition.

I didn't know how to help my cutter, except to persuade her to flush her matches down the toilet, which she did while I waited. The next immediate problem was what to do to keep her hands busy. I gently asked the caller how she would feel about accomplishing something around the house. She said she'd put off cleaning her bathroom, and her kitchen was a mess, and yes, she might feel better about herself if she mopped and scrubbed them. After that she might take her sleeping three-year-old daughter out for a walk. By then it would be time to pick up her son from school and make dinner for the family. That was her plan of action when we hung up. I had asked her, begged her really, to call us *before* she hurt herself next time, but she confessed that at such times she entered a remote place mentally, far from help or self-control. That's probably why she responded so well to taking control of her life, if only for an afternoon. It's possible she may need us again tonight, which is what I tell Bob.

Alerting the next counselor to people who might call back

makes it possible to prepare a little, perhaps devise a strategy for dealing with them. Sometimes it feels as if we are all part of a slow-motion relay race, and the baton we pass to the next person is made not of matter but of energy. I envy those who can leave the callers behind when they go home. Some days I can, with a heartlessness that surprises me; today, as I head home, my shoulders feel as if I've been lifting boulders.

So, as evening falls, I sink into the Jacuzzi in my bathroom. Afterward a mug of decaffeinated hazelnut-spiked coffee adds a nutty-sweet scent to the atmosphere already fragrant from perfumed soap and a bowl of fresh raspberries. I have the day's mail, and I begin by opening a large manila envelope from a friend who is head of public relations at the National Zoo in Washington, D.C. What I find inside shocks me: a sheaf of xeroxed articles from the Washington newspapers regarding a bizarre, horrifying event. The clippings start on Sunday, March 5, and run through Monday, March 20, with each article disposing of more rumors and adding new, increasingly bizarre facts.

On Saturday, March 4, at 5:00 a.m., a woman went over a three-and-a-half-foot cement barrier at the National Zoo, crossed a four-foot-wide dirt buffer, lowered herself down a nine-foot wall into a moat, swam twenty-six feet through the water, and pulled herself out onto the large stone terraces of the lion enclosure. Two African lions watched her—a 300-pound female named Asha, and Tana, a 450-pound male. Then one or both of them attacked, ripping at her jugular, tearing back her scalp, and eating her arms clear up to the shoulders. A lion keeper found her at feeding time two hours later and called the police, who spent weeks trying to figure out what had happened. She had no remaining fingerprints they could check, and there were few leads. Who was this woman? Did she die in an accident, suicide, or slaying? Had she been killed first and then dumped in the lion enclosure? They discovered in her jacket pocket a bus pass issued in Little Rock, Arkansas.

Each day a new ghoulish fact appeared in print. The woman hadn't died immediately but lived for several minutes while being mauled. She was thirty-six. Police found a money order in her shoe and a business letter in her pocket. A tape recorder lay near her body. The bus pass was an "honored citizens pass"—a lifetime pass given to the elderly, infirm, or mentally ill. She was a twice-married, divorced mother of two, and one source said she had traveled to Washington to seek President Clinton's intervention in a child custody battle because, as she told a city clerk, "she couldn't get justice anywhere else." The clerk reported that she had tried to file a lawsuit to regain custody of her daughter but was confused about whom she wished to sue—possibly the President—and so she went away with paperwork to fill out. She said her child had been taken from her by Arkansas authorities because of her mental illness, but she seemed "focused," "attractive and well-spoken," and "calm."

At 3:00 a.m. on March 1 she checked into a cheap hotel; three days later she fed herself to the lions. A transient who lived in a veterans shelter, she had been diagnosed as a paranoid schizophrenic. Social workers in Little Rock reported that she was delusional and believed she was Jesus Christ's sister, talking to and receiving messages directly from God. She had been in and out of mental hospitals. In her hotel room there were some handwritten notes "of a religious nature." The coroner ruled her death a suicide. Her name was Margaret Davis King. Had she identified in some strange way with the *Lion King* movie? Did she imagine herself a latter-day Daniel walking into the lion's den, convinced that she would emerge unscathed? Or did she commit suicide in a most gruesome and public way?

And what of the traumatized zoo people who found her? Counseling was available to the staff, a zoo official reported, "but no one has used it."

Picking up the phone, I dial my friend at the zoo, thank him for the clips, and ask how he is doing. "You're the one who had to describe the scene over and over to the press and make sense of the mutilation—how are *you* feeling?"

"Okay," he says. "No problem really. . . . Well, now and then I get these flashes of that instant when she must have realized that she wasn't going to be saved, that she was going to be mauled and eaten. That single moment when the true terror of her situation dawned on her is what gets to me," he says. "But only now and then. Otherwise I'm okay."

I can't tell him that I'm a counselor at SP, but I can tell him about the organization here and its sister chapter in Washington, and ask if he thinks it might help him to talk with someone. He says possibly, and files the information.

When I hang up, I look once more at the clippings, the last of which includes notes that the lions seemed "high-strung and skittish" after the attack and that the keeper had trouble coaxing them back into their cages. Only the female was hungry enough to eat the prepared lion food, so presumably it was the male that attacked Margaret Davis King. These were lions born and raised in the zoo, fed a kind of dog-food mixture at each meal. That was the only food they knew. They had never stalked and downed wild animals, but when a prey animal in the form of a human entered their enclosure, pure instinct took over. If, afterward, they were agitated and ill at ease, perhaps it was because they had done something new, something exciting and savory but wrong. As any dog or cat owner knows, an animal knows if it has done something wrong.

Despite a public outcry, the zoo refused to kill the lions. After all, they were doing what was natural, what lions do. Should we punish them for their nature? And what of our own thinly controlled penchant for violence?

No lion behavior is more bloodcurdling than what soldiers can do, or gang members, or terrorists, or serial killers, or toxic parents. We're so addicted to violence that when we can't aim it at others, we unleash it on ourselves—gouge our skin, grow depressed, commit suicide.

What seems astonishing to me is that, despite our ferocious heritage, we so often act so well—as virtuosos of kindness, tenderness, peacefulness, generosity, cooperation, and spirituality. It's remarkable how we restrain and triumph over the dark side of our genes. We celebrate the world's beauty, sing songs of praise and forgiveness, help our kin and absolute strangers. We act nobly even when to do so may endanger us. It doesn't make sense that we should, but it is our nature.

Chapter 4

A Mass of Life

THE forsythia, daffodils, and squat, fragrant hyacinths all opened as if on cue yesterday afternoon. Only a piano flourish was missing. For a few moments I sit with my morning coffee and watch what looks like an Impressionist painting in motion—the cascade of yellows, purples, and pinks blurring as they rock in the morning breeze, a pale yellow sun welling right out of the earth, backlighting the forest of oaks and hickories, and the gray squirrels weaving among the flowers.

Two crows start violently mating on the grass. They flap together and peck, then dance and strut. A startling red cardinal, sitting on a bushy yew, seems to be wearing a Fu Manchu mustache. A closer look reveals that it's only a long, limp blade of dry grass hanging from his beak. With a slow-motion flutter of wings, he hovers for a moment, then dives inside the dense branches of the yew, where he and his missus are undoubtedly building a nest.

I finish my coffee, put on a few layers of biking clothes, and pack a picnic lunch. Most days I try to find time for a short ride through the countryside. An hour's outing may take me to the Plantations, a beautifully groomed arboretum with a lake full of ducks, or to Sapsucker Woods—the bird sanctuary—or perhaps to a village north or east of town. Whichever route I choose leads me beside forests and along farm fields, and I love watching the seasons blend into one another; the plants green, bud, blossom, spill seed, and dry; the animals change color, call, court, mate, feed, parent, migrate, and play.

As anyone setting out on a walk or bike ride knows, it's hard to empty your mind of worry and planning, analyzing and hurting, and that deadly armada of what-ifs. Your agitations seem to travel with you, and soon enough you conduct small theaters of the mind in which you play various roles and rehearse dreaded or hoped-for conversations in half a dozen ways. But if you can give yourself a mental vacation, leave at home all the usual worries and commotion of a life, then you can set off on a ride in which you are free just to enjoy the sensations of being alive. You can allow yourself the gift of being a photographic plate on which the world etches itself. The beauty of the light, the whisperings of the wind, the rustle of dry cornstalks, the squirrel calls, the birdcalls, the syrupy smell of lilac hedges, the pomander sweetness of apple trees. You can feel the wind and sun on your face, savor the air, which tastes different in every season. Even in a city you can sit down on a bench in the park and watch a pigeon or other bird for a while, watch it carefully, affectionately, watch how it struts like a petitioner, how it preens and puffs, bobs its head, cocks its neck, flashes its eye, pecks at food. Being completely absorbed by nature is a form of active meditation that I love.

Every weekend in less than bone-chilling weather I take a longer ride with my biking buddy, Cathy. Today we've decided to explore the narrow strip of land between Seneca and Cayuga lakes, and she arrives right on time at 9:30, with her teal mountain bike secured to a bike rack cantilevered off the back of her compact car. She's wearing black leggings, patterned with black roses, and a purple windbreaker, and she has tucked her shoulder-length brownish-blond hair behind a wide purple headband. We tether my purple bike to hers with a complex lashing of bungee cords, check our county road maps, and set off as the mist begins lifting and the sky clears to a radiant blue.

We drive north along the west side of Cayuga Lake, through villages and towns with Roman names. Occasionally the road curves to a hilltop vista, and we gasp at the postcard beauty of the lake, a deep Caribbean blue between plunging mountains. Along the tops of the trees, in the umbrella of branches exposed to bare sun, buds have begun to form and give the dense forests the soft pink glow I associate with spring. The weeping willow whips have already turned neon yellow. Wild daylilies have started to shoot up in the culverts. Homeowners have planted daffodils everywhere; half of them are in bloom. A flock of cedar waxwings invade a hedge of wild berries, hovering hummingbird-style and flashing their yellow tail tips.

I really love these weekend bike trips with Cathy, during which our friendship, tentative at first, has been steadily building to a close camaraderie. Cathy and I are the same age—we danced to the same rock-and-roll music as kids, wore the same felt skirts and saddle shoes, lived through the same history of spaceshots, Kennedy years, Vietnam War, and what was then called women's liberation. We're well matched athletically, which is paramount in an exercise partner. We crave lunch at the same time, and our energy flags at about the same point—three hours of steady pedaling.

For nearly a year Cathy and I have been taking these bike trips—most of them twenty to forty miles long, always with a lake or river in view. We pack a picnic lunch, choose a road with a shoulder wide enough for us to bike two abreast, and chat about the world and our lives as we drink in the sunlight, rejoice in the scenery, and get a thigh-quivering workout.

I'm fascinated by human behavior and so is she, so much so she decided to become a clinical social worker. A therapist in private practice, she has many clients—troubled children, couples, whole families in distress, college students, blue-collar workers—whom she ministers to in the course of a week. Although she has never been a crisis-line counselor, last year she served as president of SP's board of directors and thus knows many of my concerns.

"I'm worried about one of my clients," Cathy says as we bike. "She's just so fragile. But at the same time there's an enormous amount of rage she's trying to deal with. When she gets depressed, she can get very active and dissociative. Cut herself, threaten people—you name it."

"Wow. That must take your full attention." I can't imagine how I would deal with an unpredictable and aggressive client.

"No foolin'. And that's just *one* of my Tuesday clients. I've got two more who are completely chaotic thinkers. My job Tuesdays is to be a sort of mind sheriff—you know, help them round up their thoughts and impose some sort of order in the town. Not an easy role, I'll tell you, especially for me."

"Hard enough to tidy up one's own life, isn't it?"

"I'm worried about her in between visits," she says. "She's not sure she can keep from fraying. I suggested she call SP." Local therapists often refer their clients to SP; we help them cope after-hours, when their therapists aren't available.

"That's fine. I hope I'm on when she calls."

Turning left at Bayard Road, we climb west toward Seneca Falls as the land tightens and fights beneath us. We become more aware of the earth's muscle when we bike—its hard, steep shoulders and fistlike knolls but also its sensuality, its fertile fields, and long, languorous hills. Today the hawks, vultures, and other soaring birds are out in full force, spiraling up the thermals over the lake, and in envious appreciation we exclaim whenever we spot an especially fast and swervy one.

"I'm worried about one of my callers," I say after a while. "Well, worried about myself, too."

"Oh, yeah?" Cathy says in that inflection perfected by therapists—acknowledging and leading on at the same time.

I think of Louise, wondering how best to epitomize her. "She's an accomplished and savvy woman but also terribly fragile, prey to horrendous depressions, dangerous depressions."

"You sound really worried about her. Do you think she'll suicide?" Cathy asks. I've heard a lot of mental health people use suicide as a verb, referring to it frontally, not couching it in euphemisms, but I've never quite gotten used to the sound of the word. I find it jarring.

"Possibly. She's already doing that in small doses, sort of rehearsing the event."

"Rehearsing?"

"When she calls, I sometimes get the feeling she isn't simply struggling with a bad depression; I think she may be testing what it would be like—you know, what it would feel like, how it would affect loved ones—if she did kill herself."

"That must be scary for you, not knowing what she may do next. But you have other highly lethal callers. It sounds like she affects you differently."

"She's a sweet person—really well read and interesting and, even though I know this must sound odd in this context, very festive about life. She's just in so much pain, and she's trying so hard to keep herself alive. I admire her courage. We would probably be friends if we met in other circumstances."

"That does sound like a grueling situation. But you said you were also worried about yourself."

"Well, in one of her calls she mentioned that she goes to the Spiritualist services in Freeville on Friday nights during the summer, and I've been thinking that it would be nice just to go and see what she looks like—you know, see who she really is."

"Uh-oh," Cathy says. "Do I detect boundary problems here?"

Laughing lightly, I nod my head yes.

"What would that tell you? I wonder if it would make things easier or tougher for you. Would you be happy just seeing her? Or would you want to talk with her? Maybe even befriend her? Do you want to get that involved with a caller? I don't know. Having any outside contact with callers is frowned upon, isn't it?"

It would be regarded as a lapse in judgment. For a few minutes more we consider what would happen if I encountered Louise. The temptation is so great, though I sense it would be a mistake. Then we let the topic melt into the scenery, to be replaced by other issues, other events recalled.

After the sun sets, with a twenty-mile bike trip behind us, we drive back home, Cathy to cook a paella for her date, I to go on shift at the crisis center.

8:15 P.M. When I answer the phone, I hear a man whose voice I recognize as a frequent caller's; he recognizes mine, too. That makes it easier for me to ask what's been happening today and encourage him in what he knows I know has been a long struggle. He thinks it has been a struggle with life's harsher situations and people who don't want to accept and love him. I know it has been a struggle with mental illness and a personality disorder he may never be free from, which torments and depresses him and puts an impossible burden on whatever relationships he does make. He has a therapist; he has tried medications in the past. They cannot help him cure his terrible loneliness and longing for one truly loving soul to give him the all-consuming absolute love he craves. "Endless Love," I jot down on the ledger.

He tells me he has emotional pockets that will never be filled. As usual, he feels he has brought his suffering on himself, because he is a bad person. He once told me that he was a practicing Mormon. Tonight I try a new tactic and talk with him about Jesus' suffering. Jesus was a perfect person who suffered terribly, I observe—suffering doesn't only happen to bad people, nor should the caller feel diminished by suffering. That touches a nerve, and he talks animatedly about God's purpose and Satan's campaign for his own "dog-eared soul." In time he settles down into that chasm of hope-lined despair that he dwells in for much of his life. Just having another person believe in and empathize with his pain helps a little. But precious little. He does not know how he will survive until tomorrow. We concentrate on today, this afternoon, this hour.

The next call is from a tense man who's not sure if he should be calling us. I gently invite him to share his troubles with me.

"I don't open up to just anybody," he says defensively. I try to explain who and what we are in a way that leaves the door open for him to call back. When I hang up, I feel bad. There was a bludgeon of woe in his voice. What should I have said to make the connection easier for him?

A call comes in from an angry, sad woman who has been "depressed for a dozen years." Therapists label it this or that, but she knows she's not responsible for her upset—life has simply dealt her a lousy hand, and everyone is cruel to her. She tends to obsess about people, especially men, for long periods of time (years), is embroiled in various legal fracases—there's a restraining order against her by a chiropractor she had been seeing and was fixated on. She demands help and advice but will listen to neither. It's a tough call of pure anger, demand, and a sense of life's impossibility.

Endless Love calls back. He has moved out of his place and into a small trailer park beside a stream. He just phoned his girlfriend, but she won't come over. She won't inspect her motives and actions the way he wants her to, and she won't provide him with the "heartful, honest, truly loving support" that he needs. And where is his daughter? His ex-wife has tarnished the girl's "pure, beautiful spirit."

"It's soul murder. She should be here, helping me with her loving spirit and enjoying the spring with me," Endless Love laments.

Blossom Day. I had forgotten about Blossom Day. We usually celebrate it when my friend Annie's little girl, Alexandra, sees the first blossoms on the dogwood tree outside her window. Then Annie phones me, and the three of us "blossom sisters" gather beside the tree to perform our ritual of worshipping Mother Nature, praising the growing things of the earth, and pledging our loyalty to one another. We hold hands around the sapling, and each of us makes a little speech.

Some pagan rituals feel so right—baby showers, where women gather to welcome a forthcoming life into the tribe; birthday parties, when we celebrate a loved one's mere existence on the planet; and holidays that mark the procession of the seasons.

Once, at an artist's colony on a Florida estuary where I was leading a poetry workshop, thirty of us gathered outside to celebrate the summer solstice with song and ritual. We each wrote a wish on a small pennant of paper, then tossed the chits into the fire, where they burst into flames and danced on hot vapors into the night. Like fireflies, our unspoken hopes flashed toward heaven.

I'm sure each of us kindled an equally momentous hope of one sort or another. Looking from face to face, searching beneath the animation and jollity for a clue to the invisible realms they masked, it was impossible to read minds. Whole towns are like that sometimes, alive on several levels, with emotional riptides and currents that don't appear at first or twelfth glance. I didn't know then that I would become privy to some of my town's darker secrets, to the torments and dreams of so many of my neighbors. Seated at that solstice campfire, I watched each paper wish tremble into flame for a moment and kite higher and higher, until it joined the others in a bouquet of sparks, then mingled with the constellations and vanished into night.

Chapter 5

The Golden Apples of the Sun and
Silver Apples of the Moon

WHEN summer arrives, with its baggage of hot, humid days, I discover a serious change in the squirrels. They come for nuts and sunflower seeds as before, but they are much more aggressive, growling and leaping ninja-like at each other, flailing with claws and teeth. Most have bite marks and claw scars on their coats. One's left ear is split in three, and he is the fiercest. One squirrel has only half a tail and drags the stump behind him like a pirate with a wooden leg.

I haven't seen the Pleader for days, and I fear he may be dead, a victim of battle. Or perhaps he fell from a tree. This happens from time to time, especially if a squirrel is old or weak. Squirrels may live twenty years in captivity, and some of my well-fed yard squirrels are over three years old, but the average life span in the wild is only one year. The tattered ears on the remaining squirrels tell part of the story. When I feed them now, I'm careful to scatter the seeds over six or eight feet because they can't seem to resist warfare if they are within pouncing distance of one another. The squirrels have different personalities all of a sudden, but so do the other animals.

Expectant and rowdy, animals enter the green metropolis of summer all with noisy errands to run. They bustle about their business of courting, warring, and dining. Only humans fret over meaning and purpose. Animals have appointments to keep. Even the june bugs, those relatives of Egyptian scarabs clattering against the window screens—humming and buzzing, bumbling and banging—are on a mission of romance.

Spring meant scant food, faint light, and hardship. But summer is a realm of pure growth, the living larder of the year, full of sprouting and leafing, breeding and feasting, burgeoning and blooming, hatching and flying.

Countless birds seem to be auditioning. Large, glossy crows sound as if they're gagging on lengths of flannel. Blackbirds quibble nonstop from the telephone wires. Because every animal has its own vocal niche (so that lovesick frogs won't drown out the hoarse threats of a pheasant barking at a dog), summer days unfold as a symphony does, full of sprightly musical noise reassuring us that nature is on her inevitable way and all is right with the world.

Drawn by a familiar chirp, I look out my kitchen window to see a cardinal couple feasting together on sunflower seeds. Scarlet with a black mask, the male eats first, lifting a seed, rolling it to one side of his beak, where a built-in seed opener cracks the hull, then rolling it to the seed opener on the other side to finish the job. Meanwhile, the dusky female stands nearby and shivers. Puffing up her feathers and squeaking, she looks helpless and cold, but actually she's inviting her mate to court. Though acting like a hungry infant bird, she is perfectly able to feed herself, and will. This dramatic appeal is the time-honored way that female cardinals (and many other birds) play house. When the young are hatched, the parents must feed them nonstop, so she wants a mate who knows how to respond to the plaintive signs of infant need. Lifting a plump seed, the male cardinal pogo-hops over to her and places it carefully in her mouth.

Nearby, the lavender garden is a den of thieves as dozens of plump bees fumble the flowers. Skidding off shuddery petals, the bees manage to grab a little nectar but also get smeared with pollen as they career out of the blossoms. They hover for a moment, then dive headlong into the next flowers and spend the day in a feast of recovered falls. Flower petals are delicately balanced so that they will waver and flex suddenly without actually breaking off. The purpose of the design is to unsettle the bee. The bee is not supposed to be comfortable, secure, or happy—it's supposed to get smeared with pollen. Whether or not the bee suffers is irrelevant. So it goes with the evolution of anxiety, worry, grief, depression, and other states of emotional distress. Our brains evolved to solve such basic Stone Age problems as courting a mate, finding food, making kinship bonds, devising a language, cooperating with other members of the tribe, sharing food, braving the environment, and fighting to keep oneself and one's offspring alive. Problems vital to our survival. We've had to devise clever ways to deal with them: love and hate, a panoply of defenses, knacks of avoidance, gamesmanship, a taste for deceit, and many other basic strategies that produced the emotional weather systems we now are.

Evolution's single instruction—avoid what's harmful, desire what's helpful—we follow not by reason, but by instinct. When, through reason, religious teachings, or stark frantic need, we boldly override the governor on those instincts, we feel giddy, boundless, galloping with free will.

Anxiety, dread, panic, aversion, depression—a small demonology of our age. But they warn us of potential dangers so we can prepare. Indeed, our traits and tastes, as well as our negative behaviors, evolved at a time when humans lived in small bands of hunter-gatherer-scavengers.

Anxiety played a lifesaving role in our ancestors' lives by alerting them to potential threats so they could plan a response. A tiger may be in that grass, one instinctive train of thought might go. It looks like the sort of tall grass tigers hide out in. If a tiger is hiding there and attacks me, what would I do? Did I just see the grass move? Maybe not. On the other hand, maybe I better check again.

By attacking what we value most, chronic anxiety slowly brutalizes our sanity, burns up needed calories, interferes with work, and damages the body by flooding the tissues with cortisol, a stress hormone. Obsessive worry about nonexistent tigers may indeed lead to an infestation of stress-related illnesses, but overlooking only one hungry tiger can result in instant death. Evolution wagers risk against advantage. Better to agonize at every opportunity about a tiger than be wrong that one lethal time. Unfortunately, our penchant for anxiety doesn't sift out what's important. Every day is a feast day for anxiety. Doesn't matter if the occasion is relevant or irrelevant. Anxiety kicks in even when we don't need it, want it, or know how to stop it.

Anxiety about a relationship feels the worst of all. When you're faced with hunger, the elements, territory disputes, and wild animals, belonging to a loyal family group is your only hope. An aching need to belong becomes an instinct indisputable as rock. Not belonging is one of those things to dread and worry endlessly about. You keep checking to make sure you're wanted, won't be abandoned, won't be sacrificed if wild animals attack, won't be left to starve. And so we monitor relationships obsessively, fret about them when we don't need to, require too many gestures, promises, and reassurances, go to extremes to fit in, sadden when we feel isolated or alienated, worry ourselves senseless about attachments, sometimes worry ourselves to death.

Throughout the world 12.4 out of every 100,000 human beings will take their own lives. In affluent countries the rate rises to 20 out of each 100,000. Some suicides may be triggered by a real or imaginary belief that loved ones will profit (suicidal people often sound quite selfless, reasoning that their friends and family "would be better off without me"). Others may be the extreme outcome of a useful hereditary device—depression.

Faced with horrible adversity or nameless anxiety, the more vulnerable among us become depressed. In a sense, it's a form of temporary hibernation. Overloaded by stress, a person winds down to a low-energy state, speaks and moves very little. At night, when we sleep, we also conserve energy. Famine produces the same inert, energy-saving response. Depression also elicits concern and nurturing, and people tend to make allowances for the depressed person. I'm helpless as a child, the posture says. Protect me, exclude me from further stress, embrace me, tell the world that I'm not available for a while.

We still fear that isolation worse than anything. For much of our evolution, being an outsider was fatal. Small wonder loneliness frightens us as it does. Even though being excluded isn't deadly today, it still produces pain and fear, and conceals an ancient terror.

Our evolution is still under way, too slow to notice, as we sleep, play, lust, worry, learn, work, dream. We live on the cusp of two worlds—the fossil and the modern. No wonder we feel off-balance much of the time. I sometimes joke about this with my boyfriend,

Paul, as in, "I'm going gathering with the girls, dear. How about if you hunt down a wild peccary while I'm away?" "Wait a minute," he might reply. "We had peccary yesterday. How about a freshly scavenged carcass instead? But I'll tell you," he might say with a bogus gleam in his eye, "no one can cook rotting wildebeest the way my mother could."

COUNTDOWN, I think as I tap the latest number code into the door lock: 9876. For security reasons the numbers change regularly, and I devise a memory aid for each one. Before "countdown" (9876) it was "quartet" (4444) and before that "I ate two"(182).

Upstairs, Mikhail has already begun to pack up his notebooks, satchel, and lunch bag. A second-year veterinary student, he's wearing a Yankees baseball cap turned backward, a sloppy red sweatshirt, a pair of high-top black-and-white sneakers with a few holes in them, and a small gold hoop in his right earlobe.

"Like those sneakers," I say.

"My dad says they're more holy than righteous." He grins with mock pride. "Don't take any woodens." He starts down the creaky stairs.

I dump my gear on the daybed in the counselor room and sit down at the desk. Pulling a red notebook marked "Hot Sheet" from its tray, I open it to the first page. At the beginning of each shift a counselor reads the hot sheet and also the Friday letter, two notebooks in which the staff communicate directly with all the counselors. The Friday letter concerns agency gatherings, doings, or business, and the hot sheet alerts everyone to possibly suicidal callers who have been in touch during the preceding week. Today I find this note:

We have had a painful beginning to 1995. First we experienced the murder of Steve Starr and the suicide of the young man who shot him in Dryden. A few days later Fred Williams shot himself to death in Brooktondale. Last night we had news that a university student died while skiing on vacation. Many folks are hurting out there. We will most likely continue to get calls about these tragedies. Listen and reflect, reflect, reflect. Help callers to know that whatever they are experiencing is normal, whether it is recurring thoughts or images, guilt, sadness, sleeplessness, etc. It is hard to accept not knowing, not understanding the "why" of it all. Some call thinking they aren't entitled to their pain because they are too removed from the victim. Not so. Encourage all to continue to use SP to cope as often and for as long as they need. Healing can take months, years.

Wise words, from Kate most likely, the wonderful woman with platinum-blond hair who trains new counselors. Somehow she manages to combine ebullience and bigheartedness with seriousness, which makes her fun to be around. Under her note in the hot sheet someone has added a second entry:

Call from school principal at Pearson School. Suicide last week of a teacher. Wants postvention help.

Who was the teacher? I wonder. What subject did he or she teach, and, most important, what drove the teacher to suicide? Kate is right—it's hard to accept not knowing the why of it all.

The crisis line rings.

"Suicide Prevention and Crisis Service," I say as I jot down the time on a sheet of scrap paper. "Can I help you?"

"Hi. How you doing today?" a baritone voice asks. It's hard to decipher his age.

"Just fine. How are you doing?"

"Well, I can't be doing too well. I called you, right? What do you think?"

"What prompted you to call? Have you got something on your mind?"

"Yeah. . . . The wife seems to have . . . exited the premises."

"You're saying that your wife has left you?" He must feel awful.

"Yeah." The silence that follows doesn't last long, but it's heavy as a steel drum.

"And how are you feeling about that?"

"Well, confused, angry, feeling somewhat guilty," he says in a flat drawl. "I don't know. . . . We've been married a fairly long time. Things seemed to have been going well. I know she was unhappy about our financial situation, but . . ." A long silence.

"It sounds like this came as quite a surprise."

"Yeah. Why, I came home and . . . You know, we had an argument a couple of days ago, like we usually do, and she accused me of being silent and whatnot and not opening up and not talking about my feelings, et cetera, et cetera. She said she couldn't take it anymore as far as being with someone who didn't 'fight normally.' I mean, what the hell is that—'fight normally'?"

"What do you think she meant by that?"

"I guess in her head fighting normally means raising my voice, screaming, throwing things, quote unquote 'showing emotion,' as she puts it. But I figure there's no point in that. Why not just settle things rationally? There's no sense in letting things get out of hand."

"So you had this fight a couple of days ago, and then you discovered today that she had left?"

"Umm, hmm. I mean, I assume that she's left. She's not here. I don't see her purse or coat. I assume she's gone. I'm not sure."

"How long has she been gone?"

"Oh, the last time I saw her was yesterday noon. So it's been close to twenty-four hours. But I've been thinking about it. I just don't get it. Is it some sort of biological thing with women, that they just can't contain their emotions and fly off the handle? I mean, you're a woman. Tell me, what do *you* think?"

What I think about women won't help him deal with his marriage's unique problems. What was that line Tolstoy wrote in *Anna Karenina*? "Happy families are all alike, but every unhappy family is unhappy in its own way."

"Are you asking me that because you're wondering if I can help you understand why your wife would lose her temper and get into such a rage?" I ask.

"Well, it almost seems as if she would have *me* lose *my* temper."

"You're thinking perhaps that she provoked a fight? Why do you think she might do that?"

"Well, maybe to give her an excuse to leave, you know."

A disturbing element to this conversation is how numb the caller sounds. He must be bursting inside. "Let me ask you something. As we've been talking, your voice has been very calm, but what you've been telling me sounds pretty serious, and it seems to be deeply troubling you. I'm just wondering what you're feeling right now."

Voice cracking, the caller says, "I mean, what if she's really gone? What will I do without her?" A brief sniffling sound.

"You're feeling frightened."

"Yeah."

"It sounds pretty scary. It must be tough not to know what's happened, to be afraid she's left but not know for sure. What are your plans for today and tomorrow while you wait to see if she returns?"

"I'm not sure. Watch TV, I guess. Work this afternoon. See if she's here when I get home. But it'll be on my mind all the time."

"Do you have a friend you might spend a little time with?"

"I got a friend at work I sometimes hang out with."

"Do you think he might understand what you're going through?"

"I don't know. Maybe. How the hell could I tell him my wife left me! I couldn't do that."

"I bet he'd understand. Would you maybe like to rehearse it with me? What could you say to him to begin with?" For a few minutes the caller tests out ways to tell his friend. He decides to call his mother-in-law's house in case his wife went there. We discuss what he might do if and when his wife returns.

I like talking with this guy. Such callers can usually articulate their feelings; their circumstances, though awful, make sense, and they're open to problem solving. That makes the call rewarding for the counselor—you feel you've accomplished something— even if it isn't life-changing for the caller. Mind you, counselors all have their favorites. Some love to talk with retarded people because they're so childlike, and calming their worries or helping them with small tasks can mean so much.

Some counselors form almost family ties with repeat callers, who sometimes become chums. We all love Saxman, a jazz musician who is a manic-depressive diabetic with a grueling life of insulin in-

jections and other drugs, mood swings, recurrent bouts of blindness, unresolved distress about his older sister's suicide, and a host
of family, love, and bureaucracy problems. His main problem is
that he's sick to death of being sick all his life. Sarcastic and en-
gaging, with a slightly ghoulish sense of humor, even when he's angry or depressed, he has an indomitable spirit.

But many counselors, like me, prefer the sort of caller I just
spoke with—an intelligent person functioning at a high level who
is being ravaged by life—rather than someone with a thinking disorder. He seems all right at the moment, but he doesn't reveal his
deepest feelings. For all I know, there may be a tempest inside, bot-
tled up and ready to wreak havoc on the world. He may be the sort
of guy who lives quietly, then one day climbs a church tower and
fires a machine gun. I only hear his side of the story. He is my concern. I urge him to phone back if he needs support—anytime. But
for this moment, at least, I have stitched him back into his routine
for another few hours. That's really all we can do.

I think through how best to summarize the call, then fill out a
write-up sheet and file it. When the phone rings again, I hear a
familiar voice. The caller sounds like Joan, someone who has been
calling weekly for a couple of years. Usually callers seem to improve as their predicament improves or as they get used to their
lot. But Joan has been getting progressively worse.

Today she is tormented by her "longtime boyfriend," who has
been two-timing her with a disabled widow he met at a bar. Joan
doesn't talk sequentially. Information rains down all at once, and
the listener has to put it in the right order. Her boyfriend, Bill, is
seventy "but looks a lot younger." She slit her wrist the other night
because he had hurt her so badly she was simply "overwhelmed."
When he proposed on her birthday, she refused, saying she wasn't
ready to be engaged, especially since she's convinced he is running
around with other women. She didn't injure her wrist badly.

One day, in an excess of suspiciousness, she went through his wallet and found a woman's name—Charlene—and a phone number.
Bill was due to meet Joan late one night after work, and when he
didn't show up, she phoned Charlene's number and heard Bill's

distinctive voice answering the phone. That was enough for Joan to feel creased by rejection and want to hurt herself. Anyway, she snooped around his house and found suspicious letters from various women in one of his desk drawers. They sounded very lovey-dovey, but Bill said they were innocent letters from his nieces. Right. She can't trust him anymore, but she also cares for him. He's a real charmer. Handsome as the dickens. Works down at the Agway. She's confused about what to do. He tells her that her lack of trust is ruining their relationship. She sounds all in a tizzy, which eases only a little by the end of the call. I invite her to call back if she needs support at this confusing time, and she thanks me.

As I wait for the next call, I go through the logbook to see if Louise has called since I spoke with her a few weeks ago. It's something I always do on shift—check to see if Louise is still alive. Running my finger down the ledger, I backtrack through the shifts of the past week, and, sure enough, there's her name. Write-up number 104. A yellow lethality assessment has been stapled to it. Louise was depressed, drinking some, and highly suicidal that evening. The counselor on duty wrote down few details of the call, noting only that Louise's daughter had gone to visit her ex-husband, which meant Louise was home alone with gnawing memories. She was staring at a carefully arranged row of pills. For over an hour the counselor tried to explore what resources she might have left, but when the call ended, Louise sounded only fractionally less sad. "I feel awful," the counselor wrote. "I did everything I could think of, but nothing nothing nothing seemed to work! Very possible that this really is her 'last day on earth' as she fears it might be. She asked me to pray for her. I'm going to worry all night."

Oh, Louise. I sigh as I return the write-up to its folder. If she had killed herself, it would have been in the morning paper, so at least I know she somehow scaled the Everest of that night. It's Monday night. I remember she once said that she belongs to a women's a cappella group that meets Mondays at the church in Trumansburg. Good. Tonight she'll have friends and climbing harmonies; that should buoy her up a bit.

The phone rings again, and this time I hear an indignant

woman's voice shouting, "Do you know what that bastard did?"

"No," I answer. "What did he do?"

"He went up the chimney, and he didn't come down!"

"He's up the chimney?" I ask, honestly surprised.

"Drunk as a skunk!" the woman says. "It's the damn summer. He gets strange as all get-out and full of piss and vinegar." Stung by the summer. He and the rest of the world of nature, I think. She doesn't sound worried, just angry and annoyed.

Once before, he arrived at the chimney bottom in a heap of soot with a stupid grin on his face, the caller explains, "but this time the damn fool's gone and got himself stuck." Right side up, halfway down. I can hear her husband yelling or singing—I'm not sure which—from behind the brick. I try to get her to calm down enough to figure out what to do. She'll call his cousin Buck, she decides, because Buck is a big, strapping guy who knows how "rangy" her husband can get when he's been drinking. She'll call Buck; then she'll call me again, and we'll go from there.

Buck arrives but can't seem to get Joe unstuck. Joe insists he's never coming out. His wife gets scared when Joe suddenly goes very quiet; then the fire department is summoned. Joe starts scrapping with everyone, and all I can hear for minutes at a time is the combined uproar of events. I suggest the woman might like to call me back later, but she says she needs me right then and there, and I believe she does, so I stay with her. Finally the firemen succeed in pulling Joe out. When Joe starts to cry uncontrollably, his wife alternately yells at and consoles him, and then she decides to "see to Santa Claus" and call us back tomorrow.

"Bizarro," I say quietly as I begin the write-up.

"Bizarro?" a voice behind me echoes. "That sounds like an interesting call." I turn around and see Sharon, the next counselor on duty, sitting patiently on the daybed. Before I can explain, the crisis line rings. A fast glance at the clock—it's well past the end of my shift—and I hurry out of my chair.

"It's all yours," I say. "Have a good shift."

She answers the phone—"Suicide Prevention and Crisis Service. May I help you?"—and waves me a kiss with her free hand.

In the center's kitchen I make a cup of tea, just the thing for unwinding before I head home. Carrying the tea downstairs, I go out to the porch, pull up a wicker armchair, and watch the evening deepen in the field across the road. A gray squirrel gallops up the trunk of a large oak and disappears into a hole. Where on earth is the Pleader? I wonder yet again.

A promise of rain weighs down the air. When night starts seeping through glossy dark leaves, a whippoorwill cracks the long, three-stage whip of its voice, flaying the air alive. Love that sound. Whippoorwills belong to a family of birds whose Latin name, Caprimulgidae, means "goatsuckers," because they were often seen traveling with herds of goats and were thought to milk them dry during the night. Now we know that the birds, in fact, were hunting the goat-sucking insects. But the name stuck.

Fragrant steam rises over my face as I sip the tea, and I realize that it will soon be Midsummer Eve, June 23, which falls two days after the summer solstice. Solstice, from the Latin *solstitium,* "sun standing still." For a few days the sun will rise and set at almost the same spot on the horizon, a prelude to the longest day of the year, and then it will crawl south, through imperceptibly shorter days, toward a still unimaginable winter. But for the moment it is early, spine-tingling summer. Jasmine and pine leaden the scents of evening. Summer disavows any passion stronger than earth's in the sound of rain, in open field, as drizzle breaks into downpour.

Chapter 6

The Heart's Asylum

MY MORNING shift at the crisis center at an end this day, I feel the need to chew something over before I head home, and so I stop for lunch at Moosewood, a local vegetarian restaurant. My passion for vegetarian fare mystifies Paul, who fears he'll get nothing at that eatery but "twigs and leaves." In fact, he swears they once served him a bowl of sand. But I love its ingenious meals. I enjoy ginger-miso salad and a plate of hopping John (southern-style black-eyed peas on brown rice topped with cheddar cheese, tomatoes, and scallions) while I reconsider one of the morning's calls. Melissa again. At last she has found the courage to leave her violent husband and move into a safe house (provided by the Task Force for Battered Women) with her two small children, but she was feeling a kind of vertigo. After a few years even unhappy couples grow glued together at so many spots that it hurts brutally to rip themselves apart. It was as if she were watching someone else's life—the wrenching away from the marriage, the awkward half lies to the children, the barrage of legal and practical chores, the new faces, the alien neighborhood, the constant fear of retaliation. She filed a restraining order against her husband, but suppose he invaded her new island of safety? Suppose he killed her and left her babies motherless? Suppose he kidnapped the children? She pictured her children's faces on the backs of milk cartons, their rosy cheeks reduced to pools of black dots.

I knew the task force would help her if any of those nightmares bloomed into actuality. She was phoning SP in a philosophical mood, and that caught me off guard—before, we had only spoken when she was in acute distress—and I needed to slow up, calm down, and allow her to bask in memories, some of which were harsh. For the first time she shared with me details of a childhood scarred by violence and neglect, which she escaped by inventing a secret life.

"It was my only salvation," she explained. "I fled into another plane of existence, where no one could find me. As long as I believed I was a superhero whose value would be discovered in the fullness of time, I could ignore the horrible reality of my life."

In her fantasy life she was leader of a team of seven men and women who traveled the world righting wrongs, working against the forces of evil, helping the downtrodden, keeping the planet from self-destructing. Each member of her team had a specialty or two. She was superb at getting people out of places, and she was a brilliant field surgeon. In that imaginary world, where she became a combination soldier and saint, fighting like a man, finding love as a woman, and earning the respect and affection of all, she created an alternative to a homelife blighted by rejection and injustice. The hardest thing for her to admit to me was that even now, as a grown woman, she sometimes retreated into that same fantasy world. Abused children often invent secret worlds. Had she been less imaginative or weaker spirited, she would doubtless have crumbled in the ruins of her family. Instead, she built an escape route self by self, created a healthier reality, and that saved her. Without realizing it, she *had* triumphed over the forces of evil, *had* saved the innocents from injustice, *had* become heroic. But she perceived her fantasies as a shameful secret.

"This may sound like an adolescent thing to say," she said hesitantly, "but I really don't know who I am anymore. This morning I'm worried about what kind of mother I'll make, when I still feel guilty about things *I* did as a child, and heaven knows I feel bad about things I did as a wife." She laughed uncomfortably. "I wonder if we are ever guilty of all the sins we imagine."

Melissa's call touched me. So many selves make up a life, especially the early parts of one's life. Shouldn't there be a statute of limitations on guilt? "I am no longer responsible for acts committed by my previous selves" is a motto I sometimes wish we could live by.

ON THE way home I stop at a neighbor's to drop off a book I think he might enjoy postoperatively, a compendium of eccentrics that two quirky British researchers have spent a lifetime compiling. Just the thing to divert a healing mind. Leaving by way of his garden steps, I stumble, lurch forward, and twist my foot hard. Pain starts bleating along the right side of the foot. At home, I wrap it in an Ace bandage, ice it, and elevate it. By morning I discover that walking is impossible. To be safe I have the swollen foot x-rayed at a nearby clinic. There a doctor shows me a triptych of X rays and points out the awful truth: The fifth metatarsal is broken straight across. It's just my luck that the foot fractured in a fragile spot with little circulation. This means wearing a cast, and not a walking cast, mind you, but a non-weight-bearing one.

I'm doomed: eight weeks of immobility. No bike trips with Cathy. No sunshine walks with Persis, my neighbor. No mousing around quaint upstate towns with Paul. It's a nightmare.

Over the next few days I sink under the weight of the low D's—devastated, disheartened, demoralized, despondent. It's not just that I won't be able to get out to enjoy the summer, visit with friends, but handling the crisis line will surely be impossible, since there are SP's porch steps and two flights of stairs to scale. For an athletic and self-reliant person, what could be worse than suddenly becoming disabled? Imagine yourself sitting on a couch, growing chilly, and not being able to close the door, which is on the other side of the room. Imagine not being able to reach food or supplies, not being able to maneuver into the bathroom or take a bath.

Two days after the fall, trapped in a wheelchair on the living-room rug, whose pile is too deep for me to muscle my way across, I start to cry. All I want is to get to the screen door so that I can inhale the summer air and drink in a little sunlight, but I can't travel four yards. At last I know how desperate some handicapped callers must feel, how exempt from normal life, how impotent and alone. They say so, and I try to empathize, but now I know.

Suddenly a combination cook and bellhop, Paul runs the house errands, making dinner, washing up, and tending me. He bemoans adding my chores to his. I hate being an invalid, a passenger.

My dear friends gather around. Jeannie and Steve ferry me to and from the hospital. Cathy arrives Saturday afternoon, without her bike. She pushes me half a mile in my wheelchair to a deli, where we eat large, freshly baked mocha-chip cookies. Soon we're gabbing and laughing as usual, and I can't resist sharing with her a recent discovery—how many zoo animals are on Prozac.

"No!" she says, her mouth dropping open. "Which ones?"

"Well, there's Gus, the polar bear in the Central Park Zoo who was depressed—"

She interrupts, "How did they know the bear was depressed?"

"For one thing, he kept swimming all day long."

"Obsessive-compulsive behavior," she says, nodding in Freudian parody. "Go on."

"And then there was this weird trick he started playing on children," I explain. "Whenever he'd see kids pressing their faces to the window, he'd charge straight at them with claws out in a sudden, harrowing attack, which he'd stop right before he hit the glass."

"Unbelievable!" She laughs.

"When he wasn't compulsively swimming, he seemed listless, or he paced a lot or did other neurotic things like chew on his enclosure, bob his head, become overly sexual, hurt himself on purpose—you know, the same stuff severely troubled people do. So they gave him some Prozac."

"Didn't they try talk therapy first?" she asks wryly.

At the thought of a polar bear engaged in talk therapy—a huge white bear seated in a black leather Scandinavian chair, gesticulating with one paw as he talks about his cubdom—we both start laughing so hard that people turn to stare.

The principle, though, is a serious one. Captive animals often become neurotic, anxious, depressed. When bears that normally roam many square miles are jammed together like city dwellers or doomed to solitary confinement for years on end, should we wonder at their plunging spirits?

We can also lose our inner compass. The hardest thing about my injury is how it separates me from nature, whose moods fascinate me, whose rocks and birds help define my sense of belonging. Once knitted into nature, I feel myself slowly unraveling. I crave the outdoors. To heal I must rest, lie low, shelve things, restrict myself, be willing to sacrifice pleasure for recovery.

After a few days I decide to rent a walker and an electric scooter. One morning Persis and I go walking on our habitual route up and down the hill, past the Catholic church, and around a small, sweet woodland. Pushing me in my wheelchair, she doesn't seem burdened by the workout, and I'm relieved when she says buoyantly at the finish, "This was easy. Thank heavens we can take our summer walks." On our outing the following week I use the electric scooter, which makes it even easier. Sometimes I chug over to the grocery store, half a mile and twelve minutes away; the improved mobility, however slight, does much to lift my spirits.

Occasionally I "stroll" awhile in the sun, then park under a tree in the garden. Few things are as delicious on a sweltering summer day as dunking oneself in a pool of shade.

What would life be like without its small, cool, temporary asylums? The very word asylum fills one with a sense of relief and can make a lovely antidote to a stale metaphor. I like these, for instance: the asylum of your regard; love is the heart's asylum; how safe she felt in the asylum of his arms. And yet how ironic it is that some people still call psychiatric hospitals insane asylums. They do protect their residents from the weathers of the world, give them a kind of amnesty, allow them to retreat from life while they heal. But our prejudice about mental illness, and our fear of it, taints the word with horror. "You belong in an asylum!" a man might yell in anger. "They dragged him off to an asylum," a woman whispers to a friend. The word has lost its fundamental calm and dignity. Originally it meant a church or other sacred place that was inviolable, where one could not be seized by outsiders. And what have we replaced it with? Psychiatric institution? Mental ward? The euphemism we use with SP callers is hospital. "Do you think that you might feel safer in a hospital?" we might ask a suicidal caller. We could not say "asylum," or the caller would picture rat-infested cells where prisoners squirm in straitjackets. Asylum is a fine, rich word that even sounds protective, like a sanctuary with thick stone walls. If only people wouldn't attach "lunatic" or "insane" to it.

Chapter 7

The Darkness of Our Days

JULY days begin early, with a soft light that insinuates itself among the trees and ferns, picking out the pink of wild geraniums, the drooping jester hats of columbine. Life gallops through all living things, presses flowers up upon their roots, makes bellies swell. The long days of July feed our hunger for light and saturate the small pineal gland, located in the brain. We feel healthy and livelier than ever. Breed, the silent voice in the cell bids us. Do it now.

The clamor of an insane blacksmith has been filling the air for days, and the neighbors have been complaining to one another about some tactless early rising remodeler, so I track the sound to see what it's about. To my delight, right at the edge of the front yard I find a scarlet-headed, diamond-shaped woodpecker frantically using a metal stop sign as a sounding board for his mating songs. Two squirrels galloping loudly across the roof remind me to serve breakfast. Putting away my binoculars, I hobble into the garden room, open the window, and toss out peanuts and sunflower seeds. Ten squirrels appear and feed quietly side by side. A shudder of leaves and bushes catches my eye, and I see a battered, frightened squirrel staring tentatively at the nuts. A large patch of fur is missing from his back and head, where raw skin shows. My heart sinks and soars at the same time. It is the Pleader, woefully subdued, all the spirit knocked out of him. I open the window. He doesn't come. It is painful to see him so broken and ill.

At last the Pleader drags in, after most of the other squirrels have fed. I toss nuts out to him, and he eats a few slowly, in a kind of trance. His eyes are lusterless, not glossy and alert. The change in personality is startling. For a while there weren't enough nuts in the world to eat or store. He wanted all of them, endlessly, and could drive away any squirrel who bothered him. Now he seems lethargic, tentative, and frail, with little appetite. When other squirrels threaten him, he cringes. Slowly he climbs up a large hickory and lies down on a branch, looking tired and weak. A human in that condition we would call depressed.

I no sooner settle down in a chair than I hear the most godawful scream—a high-pitched, throbbing shriek. When I look out the kitchen window, I see a crow with some small furry creature in its claws. Suddenly the crow flies off to Persis's yard to dispatch its prey. Mouse? Its ears are longer. Maybe a kangaroo mouse? I return to the chair. But within minutes I hear the same bloodcurdling scream. Once again I hobble over to the kitchen window. To my utter amazement I see a baby rabbit with a chipmunk of equal size attached to its neck. A chipmunk trying to kill a baby rabbit!

By now the rabbit's screams are ear-piercing. Hobbling outside as fast as I can, I chase the chipmunk away and then approach the rabbit, which sits frozen like a statue, shocked and trembling.

"Run away," I gently urge it. But it remains stupefied. When I nudge it with the rubber tip of my crutch, it hops under the broad leaves of a caladium. Maybe it will wait out the day there, get its energy back, and have a brighter future tomorrow. I go back indoors.

Minutes later I hear the same death screams and know what carnage to expect. Sure enough, when I rush to the front door, I find the chipmunk has the bunny by the neck again. I scare the chipmunk away as I limp out after the rabbit. This time I try to chase the rabbit across the driveway and into the neighbor's yard, out of the chipmunk's territory, but the rabbit is too young to understand how to flee. It runs toward me instead of away from me, and when it encounters a wall, it swiftly grows confused. Limping back inside, I grab a large plastic bowl from the kitchen and head outside once more, where I find the bunny half exposed under the caladium leaves. I nudge it into the bowl with the tip of a crutch. Then I lay a crutch across the top of the bowl as a sort of grille and hobble toward the neighbor's yard just as young Cornelia comes running, her pigtails flapping.

"Don't chase the bunnies into the open!" she cries, her voice tense with worry. "The crows are eating them!"

Her eyes widen as I show her what I have in my hands: a bowlful of frightened bunny.

"I'm not chasing them," I explain, and tell her about the carnivorous chipmunk and the newborn bunny. "Could you take it across your lawn and turn it loose?"

"The crows will get it," she says, anguished. Then her face brightens. "I'll take it home," she says. "Maybe I can keep it."

"Good plan." I give her the bunny, a breathtakingly adorable quiver of grayish brown fur with small pointed ears. It is so new and alone, so confused and frightened. No wonder rabbits have many offspring; the attrition rate among bunnies must be colossal. But carnivorous chipmunks? I had no idea they were meat-eaters. Nor that they hunt down bunnies the way Serengeti lions do their prey, sinking sharp teeth into the animal's neck and dragging it down.

Again I return indoors. But soon Cornelia reappears, this time accompanied by two more neighbor girls. Cornelia's dad, who builds synchrotrons by day, has built a temporary cardboard house for the bunny, and her mom has given it some lettuce. Cornelia's plan is to call the SPCA tomorrow and ask if they'd like to place the bunny in a good home, or if there is a safe place to turn it loose. She promises to look after the bunny and to let me know its fate.

Even a bunny needs luck, I think as I go indoors. Those death screams resounded throughout the neighborhood. Sometimes at night I hear similar screams from the woods, and I've always assumed a raccoon was throttling a small mammal. Now I know it was the sound of a rabbit in its death throes. I suppose that nerve-shredding screech is intended to be the final sound the animal makes, a last-ditch effort to scare its attacker or to summon help. A desperate long shot. This time it worked in an unexpected way and brought compassionate humans running.

I DECIDE to spend a quiet afternoon on the patio behind the house, an aerodrome for moths and dragonflies, and am rewarded with visits from half a dozen hummingbirds. Manic and beautiful, the hummingbird is one of my favorite birds. Despite their joy and beauty, they lead secret lives of passionate danger. And there is one truth about hummingbirds that continues to astonish me.

A lot of hummingbirds die in their sleep. Like a small fury of iridescence, a hummingbird spends the day at high speed, darting and swiveling among thousands of nectar-rich blossoms. Hummingbirds have huge hearts and need colossal amounts of energy to fuel their flights, so they live in a perpetual mania to find food. They tend to prefer red trumpet-shaped flowers, from which nectar thickly oozes, and they must eat every fifteen minutes. Like a tiny drumroll, a hummingbird's heart beats at 500 times a minute. Frighten a hummingbird, and its heart will race to over 1200 beats a minute. Feasting and flying, courting and dueling, hummingbirds consume life at a fever pitch. No warm-blooded animal on earth uses more energy. But that puts them at great peril. By day's end, wrung out and exhausted, a hummingbird rests near collapse.

Then in the dark night of the hummingbird, as it sinks into a zombielike state of torpor, its breathing grows shallow, and its wild heart slows to only thirty-six beats a minute. When dawn breaks on the fuchsia and columbine, hummingbirds must jump-start their hearts, raise their body temperature, and fire up their flight muscles for another all-or-nothing day. That demands a colossal effort, which some can't manage. So a lot of hummingbirds die in their sleep.

While most birds are busy singing an operetta of who and what and where, hummingbirds are mute. If they can't serenade a mate or yell war cries at a rival, how can they perform the essential dramas of their lives? They dance. They spell out their intentions and moods just as bees or fireflies do. For hummingbirds that means elaborate aerial ballets in which males twirl, joust, sideswipe, and somersault. Brazen and fierce, they will take on large adversaries—even cats, dogs, or humans.

Last summer my friend Jeanne had an encounter with a female hummingbird. One day her cat dragged in something rare and shimmery—a struggling hummingbird. The feathers were ruffled, there was a bit of blood on the breast, but the bird still looked perky and alive. So Jeanne fashioned a nest for it out of a small wire basket lined in gauze and fed it sugar water from an eyedropper at regular intervals. To her amazement, as she watched, it miscarried a little pearl. Hummingbird eggs are the size of coffee beans, and females usually carry two. So Jeanne knew one might still be safe inside. After a quiet night the hummingbird seemed stronger, and when Jeanne set the basket outside at dawn, the tiny accident victim flew away.

It was a ruby-throated hummingbird that Jeanne nursed, the only one native to the East Coast. In the winter they migrate thousands of miles over mountains and open water to Mexico and South America. She may well have been visited by a species known to the Aztecs. Altogether there are sixteen species of humming-birds in North America, and many dozens in South America, especially near the equator, where they can feed on a buffet of blossoms. No hummingbirds live in the rest of the world. They are a New World phenomenon. So, too, is vanilla, and their stories are linked. When the early explorers returned home with the riches of the West, to their deep frustration they found it impossible to grow vanilla beans. It took ages before they discovered why—that hummingbirds were key pollinators of vanilla orchids—and devised beaklike splinters of bamboo to do the work of birds.

Now that summer has come at last, I spend lucky days watching the antics of hummingbirds. I find the best way to behold them is to stand with the light behind me so that the bird faces the sun. The trembling colors aren't true pigments but the result of light staggering through clear cells that act as prisms, or iridesce. Hummingbirds iridesce for the same reason soap bubbles do. Each feather contains tiny air bubbles separated by empty spaces. Light bounces off the air bubbles at different angles, and that makes blazing colors seem to swarm and leap. All is vanity in the end. The male's shimmer draws a female to mate. But that doesn't matter much to us gardeners, watching hummingbirds patrol the impatiens as if the northern lights had suddenly fallen to earth.

AFTER dinner I take a taxi downtown to the crisis center and, using my walker as a lever, maneuver up the porch stairs and then up the two interior flights, stopping to rest halfway. When at last I shoulder the door open and hobble into the counselor room, sweating and flushed, with my knapsack on my back, a heavyset man with glasses turns around in his chair and smiles—Jim, a kind-hearted, divorced, middle-aged lawyer. His body tenses to rise, and I think he plans somehow to stay on the phone while helping me sit down, so I pantomime that I'm okay. He nods and says into the phone, "Let me see if I understand this right. You've discovered that your ex-wife has been taping your phone calls and editing and retaping them to say something else? And she holds a mini tape recorder whenever she talks with you. . . . Uh-huh. . . . She can

splice them together that well? . . . What does she have you saying? . . . Oh, boy, I can see why you're worried. . . . I don't know
if it would hold up in family court. You'll need to ask a lawyer."

Sounds like an interesting call. Settling myself into a nearby
chair, I read the hot sheet and Friday letter and check the bulletin
board.

A postcard from Jamaica says, "At last a place I can sleep undis-
turbed. Tropical greetings to all, Jack." That would be Jack
Smythe, a counselor I've only heard about. One day a few years
ago Jack was on overnight shift despite a feverish flu, and when he
lay down to nap awhile, he tumbled into the world of cement
sleep. During the night a frequent caller, Hank, phoned and grew
concerned when no one answered. Possibly he had dialed the
wrong number. He phoned back. Still no answer. How could that
be at a twenty-four-hour hot line? Hank had been calling for years.
He regarded the SP counselors as friends, and as the night advanced, he grew more and more worried. At last, panicky, he no-
tified the police, who contacted Marian van Soest, who in turn
phoned SP and, when she got no answer, summoned the police
to meet her at SP. Racing upstairs, they found the door locked. No
amount of banging fetched a response. Rushing back downstairs,
the two policemen parked their car beneath a second-story window, climbed onto the car roof, and let themselves in through an
office window. Then they unlocked the upstairs door and let Marian in, and all three began shouting and banging on the locked
counselor-room door. Silence. Had the counselor had a heart attack? Rummaging through a desk drawer in one of the offices,
Marian found the key to the counselor room. Fearing the worst,
she and the policemen walked in to find Jack sound asleep on the
couch. When Marian lightly touched his leg, he snapped to attention and said automatically, "Suicide Prevention and Crisis Service.
May I help you?"

When Jim finishes his call, I stand up in my walker and inch forward. Jim helps me into position at the desk. "How on earth did
you do that?" he asks. For a moment I'm tempted to spin a good
yarn. Instead, I offer the bland truth—a few shallow stairs.

"Your stairs or someone else's?" he asks in a mock professional lawyer's tone.

"Forget it!"

He throws up his hands in a gesture of, Okay, I won't touch it with a ten-foot subpoena, and gives me a sympathetic pat on the shoulder as he leaves.

My first call of the evening comes from a twenty-year-old woman who wants to discuss her being a prostitute. Matter-of-fact and uninhibited, with a light Spanish accent, she explains that she's been divorced for less than a year from a thirty-four-year-old internist. In August she met a woman at a restaurant who recruited her into a call-girl service, and most of her johns are doctors. As her story unfolds—how the madam recruited her, the sort of men who hire her—I find my mouth hanging wide open in surprise. A call-girl service specializing in local doctors? I had no idea! She talks in some detail about how prostituting makes her feel more feminine, more whole. And then I realize that I haven't been paying close attention. Instead, I've been shocked and fascinated by the facts. The caller is what matters. At that point I slide back into step with her and try to understand why something many women would find degrading has the opposite effect on her. It's a puzzle.

My caller is scared to death her young son will find out, hates herself, and needs "to resolve the situation." We explore a few issues she might want to think about and pursue with a therapist. Is she trying to sabotage her future? Did she get married too young? Why does it make her feel "more feminine"? I urge her to call the Mental Health Association to find a counselor to work with, since she's keen to understand her motives and wants to change a behavior she's become addicted to. Ending the call, I encourage her to phone back to talk, and she thanks me, asking when I will next be on duty. Because I'm not allowed to tell her that, I assure her she'll find the other counselors equally concerned.

As I set the telephone receiver back in its cradle, it rings at once. A woman is worried about her medication, Paxil, which has worked well as an antidepressant for the past month but this week has prompted terrible migraines. Her psychiatrist works at the Mental Health Clinic, closed tonight, and she feels alone and frightened. I offer to find him—or someone knowledgeable—for her, try to calm her, reassure her that antidepressants can sometimes have frightening and confusing side effects that are not life-threatening. I call MHC but get a recording. Her doctor isn't listed in the phone book. So I phone an emergency after-hours consulting therapist, who advises me that Paxil can indeed produce migraines. She can stop taking it for today without harm, he advises, then call her doctor tomorrow. I phone her back, talk it through with her, and she sounds relieved.

Paxil, like Prozac and other relatives, is a drug that fights depression by increasing the amount of serotonin available in the brain. Many people believe that depression strikes most often when the brain's serotonin level drops. Indeed, researchers studying the brains of suicide victims discovered a much lower than normal level of serotonin. The question is, What comes first—the depression or the drop in serotonin? When something devastating happens, we may well become depressed. The event shocks our system, and the serotonin level drops, among other physiological changes. Or does a low serotonin level lead to our finding otherwise bearable situations devastating?

When I tried Prozac about five years ago, it lifted my mood as planned—if anything, it made me feel a little better than well—but the most extraordinary thing happened. To my surprise it temporarily altered how I think. For the first time in my life I became a linear thinker. I could arrange, structure, plan, analyze, explain, be practical and efficient to my heart's content. Had I been a linear thinker beforehand, this would have amplified my natural abilities and given my work a real boost. But I was born with a poet's sensibility, and Prozac made it impossible for me to do what comes naturally—think metaphorically, allusively, exploring the hidden connections between seemingly unrelated things. An iron cage fell over my imagination. This occurred in such a mechanical way that it didn't alarm me, because there was no question about what had happened. It felt as if someone had walked into the ballroom of the imagination in the middle of a festive party and turned the lights off.

On Prozac I could write straightforward sentences such as this one. But the minute I reached for the tongs of a metaphor to grasp a shadowy piece of life and drag it into view, nothing happened. So I stopped taking Prozac, and the minute I did, the ballroom came to life again as suddenly and mechanically as it had been stilled, and I was back in a familiar world.

Years later I was sharing this memory with a neuroscientist friend, who nodded knowingly and said, "I think I know why that might have happened. One of the things Prozac does is to raise the threshold for the neurotransmitter dopamine in the brain. For some creative people that could be an obstacle." Dopamine seems to be associated with processing novel information. As with all the neurotransmitters, too much of it is as bad as too little.

Some argue that schizophrenics seem to have too much and become flooded with more novel information than is useful. There are many schools of thought about what causes schizophrenia, a calamitous illness that afflicts 2.3 million people in the United States alone. Most researchers believe that an abnormality in fetal brain development is the main culprit. As the infant's brain is forming, important nerve cells migrate to the wrong place. Miswired, the brain then develops the altered reality of schizophrenia. But what causes neurons to move out of place? Some think the ultimate cause is genetic; others say it could be caused by a mother catching a virus during critical months of pregnancy.

Some scientists believe that too little dopamine may underlie what we regard as great eccentricity. According to this argument, eccentrics aren't able to process such basic information as how to function in society. Many eccentrics are happy and charming and beloved by appreciative friends, who cherish their uniqueness and sense of humor. But other eccentrics complain of feeling lonely and low—perpetual outsiders. When they're given amphetamines, which increase dopamine in the brain, they're better able to decipher the subtle rules of being personable, which allows them finally to fit in. Fascinating studies such as these imply volumes

A SLENDER THREAD

230

about personality and also show us how supple and trainable the mind is. In principle, depression, anxiety, paranoia, and other uncomfortable mental states could be eased by tampering with someone's neurotransmitters.

In a postmortem study of people who committed suicide, researchers discovered a host of biochemical abnormalities. As I said, they had much lower than normal levels of serotonin, a condition not only associated with depression but also with heightened impulsiveness. You feel dreadful, and you act on it. Equally intriguing, their brain cells controlling pleasure and pain were different. Lying on the surface of some brain cells, opioid receptors respond to opiumlike chemicals produced naturally by the body and play a vital role in our sense of pleasure, pain, or well-being.

But the brains of suicide victims, who presumably were horribly depressed, contained 100 to 800 percent more of one type of opioid receptor and only 50 percent of another opioid receptor. Because their brains were wired differently, life became a desert where thirst could swell to unbearable abstract proportions. "I can't stand the pain any longer," depressed people almost always lament, referring to a deep fracture of the spirit, a pain that seems to hurt all over the body but in no place they can point to. Many depressed people also suffer from chronic physical pain. (There's a link, for example, between depression and migraine or lower back pain.) Something going haywire in the opioid system, perhaps in people predisposed to it, may well trigger depression. I find it suspicious how often depressed people describe their suffering as pain. They feel helpless and hopeless, but they perceive this as raw pain. Why does it register that way in the brain?

That's just the sort of naïvely devastating question that led me to college in the first place. I remember the exact moment such thoughts began to tantalize me. I was sixteen, school was out for the summer, and I was sunbathing, reading the newspaper, when I stumbled on a brief report that schizophrenics' sweat smells different. Thunderstruck, I found the implications thrilling. Could all mental illness be a quirk of chemistry? Or perhaps a virus? How about creativity, belligerence, optimism, moodiness? Then what exactly is a self, and how does the brain become the mind?

When I was a freshman at Boston University, I intended to major in what was then called physiological psychology and look for answers to some of those intriguing questions. For various reasons in my sophomore year I transferred to Penn State, whose computer mistakenly placed me in English, and since I had been writing shyly but enthusiastically all my life, I considered it fate. But I've always kept my original fascination with human nature, a fascination often rewarded these days as biopsychologists turn up provocative hints and insights. For example, about eight percent of people who are hospitalized for psychiatric reasons, or who commit suicide, have a "Wolfram" gene that may predispose them to sadness. People with the gene (about one percent of the population—over a million people) are eight times more likely to need such hospitalization or to commit suicide. People with low cholesterol have twice the suicide rate of those whose cholesterol is higher. Scientists wonder if low cholesterol may slow down the transmission of serotonin. When people were connected to PET scans and asked to think sad thoughts, the orbital frontal cortex of the brain became active. In men, though, only the left side of the brain grew aroused; in women both sides of the brain participated. We know from experiments that women are better at recognizing sadness on the faces of both men and women. When some women complain that their men are insensitive to their feelings, they may be right, but not because the men don't care about them. Men, in general, are a little color-blind to expressions of sadness.

More women report being vulnerable to depression, and there are certainly good social reasons for it. Women have been helpless more often, had fewer opportunities, swallowed more injustice and inhumane treatment. But there may be biological reasons, too. Faced with stress, men, who were the hunters and fighters, had to be able to respond fast, in ways that led to action, even if it meant wasting energy in a fight with animal or man, and even if it meant risking death. As nurturers, women had to stay alive to bear and nurse the children, so when *they* were faced with stress, they would have profited more from energy-saving strate-

gies, ones that made them more sensitive to how others were feeling, so that they could avoid danger whenever possible.

As AN hour passes without calls, I idly wonder about the last
caller. I hope her migraines stop but especially that she makes
peace with her medication and that her fears subside. Who
wouldn't be frightened? We think of the body with fascination and
horror—fascination at its complex subtlety, and horror that our
consciousness hangs on to life by such coarse yet fragile threads.
Waiting for the phone to ring, I lean out the window and look up
at the sky. A cloud-strewn night.

The Pleiades, an open cluster of stars, sparkle in the constella-
tion Taurus. I locate them by looking for a group of flies on the
bull's rump. Viewable by eighty percent of the world's population,
the Pleiades have been worshipped, mythologized, or celebrated
by many cultures. Subaru, the ancient Japanese named the
Pleiades, and when six companies joined forces in 1953 to produce cars, they used a stylized star cluster as their logo. Among
Paul's collection of Hopi kachinas (the painted, decorated cot-
tonwood dolls the Hopi carve to teach their children about the
world) stands a black-and-white figure named Mastop. It is the
kachina of the sky, with a white handprint on its forehead to symbolize the human imprint on the universe. On one side of its face
eleven white speckles represent the Pleiades.

I love the night world, land of moonscapes and shadows, pa-
trolled by the flickering eyes of night creatures, overhung with a
bustier of stars. But I know I'm unusual in this. Most people associate the night with mischief or with the combination repair shop
and cinema known as sleep. In sleep the body seems calm, but all
the while the brain travels, tells tales, grows frantic, doodles with
strong emotions, wallows in the ghost-studded night.

By day our senses warn, charm, and guide us. But at night they
struggle, and we become vulnerable as prey. Things that live by
night live outside the realm of normal time, and so suggest living
outside the realm of good and evil. We come to associate night
dwellers with people up to no good, people who have the jump on

the rest of us and are defying nature, defying their circadian rhythms.

Severed from the sensory spill of daytime, with work done, no one to see, no place to go, people seem to grow most alone at night. They drink until they fill their minds with darkness or fantasize about becoming part of the darkness forever. People who call SP from the mansions of the night often sound as if they've strayed beyond time, lost their map and compass, and are wandering outside the huge pendulum of night and day. They have the predawn crazies. As F. Scott Fitzgerald wrote in *The Crack-up,* "In a real dark night of the soul it is always three o'clock in the morning." If they can just get through till daybreak, the gloom may lift a little, and familiar people and routines offer hope. Better if they could find a starlit path back home, but in the night world, crevasses lie everywhere.

Chapter 8

So Glory Descends

SHIFTS aren't always eventful, even night shifts. Unlike a big-city crisis center, which might receive hundreds of calls a day, at SP it's a bustling and busy day if thirty people call. And yet I've often been on shift when five or six people phoned per hour.

To pass the time, I read through past hot sheets, some of which have news clippings attached. Three events recently required SP's involvement—two suicides and a murder. The murder was also a self-destructive act, because a twenty-four-year-old killed the new boyfriend of his ex-girlfriend, dooming himself to a lifetime of imprisonment. One suicide, a sixteen-year-old boy, shot himself in a car. The married teenage father of a handicapped baby, he had felt unable to support his family and handle the sudden spate of responsibilities. This was the second suicide in his high school in the past year, and part of SP's ongoing job is to find ways to handle the subject in the school, which his brother still attends. We want the students aware enough that they can call SP, but not cause so much commotion that the surviving brother might be stigmatized. SP's postvention crew has gathered the family together and talked with them, because after a suicide, family members often blame themselves, get snagged at an "if only" stage, and can't get on with the necessary ordeal of grieving. On this occasion the family was in denial and couldn't fathom why the boy killed himself. But an investigation turned up clear motives: He was a teenager burdened by marriage and fatherhood, finishing school, trying to support his new family, and he was abusing alcohol and drugs. A psychological autopsy, it's called.

More clippings. A twenty-two-year-old woman shot herself after her boyfriend broke up with her. A few months before that, a thirty-year-old man had a fight with his girlfriend, went out to his truck, took a hunting rifle, and shot himself. She ran after him but got there too late. Finding the body horrified her, as it would anyone, and she needed considerable counseling.

Postvention counselors, working with the survivors, try to elicit memories of the physical facts rather than the emotions, draw out the sensory details that make an event unforgettable, because that's how traumatic memories are stored in the brain—evocatively. Incidental things may become obstacles. For example, if a woman cooking pasta received a call about her sister's suicide, making pasta might always tinge her with sadness, though she may not understand why. There's a technical term for this phenomenon—state dependency. If something is learned in a specific setting, then it will be remembered when a similar setting occurs. Especially trauma. If a similar state isn't encountered for a long while, the memory may lie dormant, an unexploded land mine.

Still the phone sits quietly on the desk. Ring, I command the telephone. Nothing mortal. Something solvable. Silence—yards and yards of silence.

From my knapsack I pull a yellowing, dog-eared copy of Walt Whitman's *Leaves of Grass* and browse among familiar passages.

In a town filled with artists, artisans, and performers, we often hear from creative people, and those callers sometimes pose special problems for me. I can't reveal how intimately I understand their struggles or how fascinating I might find their minds. When writers call, it's tempting to advise them, though of course I mustn't. For example, a college freshman phoned whose parents were hounding him to go into medicine, but he loved writing and wanted somehow to work in the arts and sciences simultaneously, but wasn't sure if that was even possible. A frustrating call, that. It was hard to resist guiding him. But he wasn't calling for my professional advice; he was calling because he felt dread, shame, and anxiety. He was calling to vent his frustrations, sadness, and fears, and so we talked about how it felt letting his parents down, and the best way to handle their upcoming visit and the inevitable confrontation. Although I did finally steer him gently toward an interdisciplinary department at his college, when we hung up, I felt thwarted.

I remember Nina Miller (first director of the agency and also a writer) advising counselors in training that "there are times when you talk to somebody, and the connection is so pure that it's hard not to feel, Oh, is this person lucky I happen to be on shift now, because look how we're connecting. I once was in the middle of that kind of call," she admitted, "with this very articulate, literary type, and he quoted a line of poetry, and before I could censor myself, I said, 'Oh, that's Keats.' And I lost the call. He stopped talking about what he called for, what he painfully needed to talk about, because of my own ego need. That's why you have to be very leery about sharing any kind of personal information. A caller is not calling to find out about the counselor."

It has taken me a long while to appreciate what Nina meant. A natural urge to connect, to prove that you understand, can tempt you to reveal experiences you've had that are similar to a caller's. Then the identity you've managed so successfully to shelve starts to slide off the shelf like the slippery fabric it is. Best to resist and keep your own life in the margins. But it's tough when you touch voices with a kindred spirit.

This is so hard to remember when someone calls in despair—that part of them may be indomitable, self-glorifying, pure acrobat. It's a therapist's job to help them come clean and integrate their bleak, agile, and dynamic sides. Our job, on the other hand, is far simpler, though it can feel elaborate. We strive to bind a caller to the present for a short while, a very short while—one more hour, one more day. It may seem a long, cool drink in the wilderness of their suffering or a breather only a few heartbeats long. "What will you do today?" I once asked Louise as we were ending an agonizing call. "It's not the days that worry me," she had said. "It's the hours."

The phone rings, and I'm so startled I flinch. My heart sprints a moment. I collect myself, clear my throat, answer on the third ring. "Suicide Prevention and Crisis Service," I say. "May I help you?" A loud click. Reaching for the logbook, I jot down, "Hang-up." "Rats," I say, and tap my fingers on the desk. Maybe they'll call back.

In the center's kitchen, I add water to a cup of corn chowder and pop it into the microwave. Someone has taped a panorama-shaped poster on the wall containing a list of names set in many elegant and stylish typefaces: Abraham Lincoln, Virginia Woolf, Eugene O'Neill, Ludwig van Beethoven, Robert Schumann, Leo Tolstoy, Vaslav Nijinsky, John Keats, Edgar Allan Poe, Vincent van Gogh, Isaac Newton, Ernest Hemingway, Sylvia Plath, Michelangelo, Winston Churchill, Vivien Leigh, Patty Duke, Michael Faraday.

Beneath that roll call runs a banner in red:

PEOPLE WITH MENTAL ILLNESS ENRICH OUR LIVES

Below that, a long red line, then a footnote:

THESE PEOPLE HAVE EXPERIENCED ONE OF THE MAJOR MENTAL ILL-NESSES OF SCHIZOPHRENIA AND/OR MANIC-DEPRESSIVE DISORDERS. FOR MORE INFORMATION: 1-800-950-FACT. ALLIANCE FOR THE MEN-TALLY ILL OF NEW YORK STATE.

An eye-catching poster, it's remarkable for all the equally af-flicted and brilliantly creative artists and scientists it doesn't in-clude: Hieronymus Bosch, Albrecht Dürer, Johannes Kepler,

Tycho Brahe, Hugo Wolf, Camille Saint-Saëns, August Strindberg, Charles Lamb, Guy de Maupassant, T. S. Eliot, Hart Crane, Robert Lowell, Anne Sexton, Jonathan Swift, Serge Rachmaninoff, Lewis Carroll (Charles Dodgson), William Blake, Martin Luther, Rod Steiger, Dick Cavett, Joni Mitchell, Beatrix Potter, Charles Baudelaire, Edvard Grieg, Arthur Schopenhauer, William Styron, Tennessee Williams, and Friedrich Nietzsche, to name only a few. Indeed, it's hard to think of many artists whose lives weren't troubled by alcoholism and/or mental illness. Can it be, as Aristotle insisted, that there is no great genius without a mixture of insanity?

Not all creative people struggle with depression, manic-depression, or psychosis. But studies of artists conducted in three countries show a much higher incidence of alcoholism, schizophrenia, and depression. Even so, the large majority of artists don't suffer from these ills.

On the other hand, artists are people who tend to have two or three jobs, face rejection and indifference, often live in poverty, don't keep the same hours or schedules most people do, don't fit into the norms of a workaday life, are more introspective than their neighbors, entertain unusual ideas or points of view for a living, feel deeply as a profession, and usually find little understanding or respect unless they become famous, in which case they're constantly being judged. That doesn't sound like an inherently stable lifestyle. Artists may require solitude to work, but where does solitude end and loneliness begin? Add to that the way artists sometimes romanticize extremes of consciousness. For some, creativity is a moody art, relying on a cynical outlook and many subtle rituals of despair.

I am convinced, though, that the part of the artist that becomes depressed, schizophrenic, addicted, or otherwise mentally ill is separate from the part that creates. It waits for a return to relative clarity and stability, a still point in which to create. William Faulkner wrote novels despite his alcoholism. As his drinking grew heavier and heavier, he was rarely able to write at all. The same is true for Eugene O'Neill, John Steinbeck, Dylan Thomas, Lillian

Hellman, Tennessee Williams, Ernest Hemingway, Victor Hugo, Malcolm Lowry, F. Scott Fitzgerald, Stephen Crane, Jack London, O. Henry, Truman Capote, and so many other alcoholic writers whose gifts didn't flow from the bottle but around it, and who would have written even more and better without it. Running away from the ghost of depression can also be a tonic. Frightened of being immobilized by despair, depressives often fling themselves into frantic activity. Hoping to keep gloom at bay, they work until they drop, seem to have inhuman stores of energy, and create art nonstop. They can't afford to stop. If they slow down, the missile of depression might catch up with them.

STIRRING the hot, thick, corn-sweet soup, I hobble back into the counselor room and carefully arrange myself at the desk, one foot on the hassock. Of all the names on that poster in the kitchen, Churchill's may be the biggest surprise. For most of his life he crumbled under the repeat blows of a depression so familiar, loud, and unshakable that he called it his Black Dog—I suppose because it hounded him. It had its own life and demands, was uncompromisingly brutal, and became a monstrous family member to be reckoned with. A small, feeble boy, bullied at school and neglected by his remote, glamorous, high-society parents, Churchill grew into a dynamo of a man packed with energy, assertiveness, bravery to the point of recklessness, a tough attitude, extreme ambition, plentiful ideas, willfulness, aggression alternating with compassion, artistic tastes, egomania, and a yen for daring adventures. The deprivation he felt as a child may well have fueled his ambitions, but having no innate sense of value, he was easy prey for the armies of depression that plagued him throughout his life.

Carrying a burden as heavy, unpredictable, and frightening as that, how on earth did Churchill raise children, rise in politics, paint beautifully, write with wit and confidence, and lead a nation through war? In his fascinating character study of Churchill, psychiatrist Anthony Storr argues that in 1940, when all the odds were against Britain, it took a bold conviction for Churchill to rally the

British people, but "it was because all his life, he had conducted a battle with his own despair that he could convey to others that despair can be overcome."

For the last five years of his long life Churchill sat in a chair staring at a fire, partly paralyzed by a stroke, wholly demoralized by depression. He stopped reading, rarely spoke. The Black Dog finally caught up with him and pounced, flattening him under its rough weight. But what a dynamo he had been—so inventive, so courageous, so resilient. A history-making, difficult life. Yes, I think, that's what we all lead, in smaller arenas perhaps, lives sometimes gleaming, sometimes difficult, that change history for many of the people with whom we come in contact. Isn't it odd that one big-brained animal can change the course of another's life, change what the other sees when it looks at its reflection in a mirror or in the mind's mirror? What sort of beings are we who set off on symbolic pilgrimages, pause at mental towns, encounter others who—sometimes without knowing it—can divert or redirect us for years? What unlikely and magical creatures. Who could know them in a lifetime? When I start thinking like this, wonder shoots its rivets into my bones, I feel lit by a sense of grace, and all my thoughts turn to praise.

Chapter 9

The Orators of August

AT THE Spiritualists' campground in Freeville, New York, wooden lodges nestle along meandering dirt roadways that lead down to a small chapel in front of a pond. Above the door to the white wooden church the words THE TEMPLE OF TRUTH appear in bold letters. Inside, fourteen wooden pews flank a center aisle. The chapel could hold about forty people, but the twenty present seem ample to fill the room with talk and laughter. I take a seat at the back, on the aisle, by the door. Two fans turn slowly overhead. On a small stage at the front of the room, next to the wooden pulpit, sits a low table with a glass vase full of carnations, baby's breath, and fern leaves. A large painting of Jesus oversees everything from the wall behind the stage. Wearing a pale green toga, He floats against a kingdom of golden clouds. The evening's director—a middle-aged blond woman—sits in one of two upholstered chairs, chatting with the visiting minister, Reverend Wilson, who leans toward her from the other chair. A white-haired man in his sixties, he has a kind, open face, a squarish jaw, and fair skin that's sunburned from the past week of hot, humid weather.

But where is Louise? I wonder as I quickly scout the room. I suspect the two young women up front are college students—something about their clothes and gestures. Too young to be Louise, who is in her mid-thirties. Next to them a chatty seventy-ish man and woman. Two middle-aged women friends, one of whom looks sad. Could that be Louise? I make a mental note and go on. A single woman, in her sixties I'd say, joking with an older man and woman. Two middle-aged women seated together, talking intimately about something. One has a round face; her braided hair ends in a white bow near the bottom of her neck, and her eyes flash urgently as she whispers to the other woman, who is auburn-haired with an angular face. Think hard—did Louise ever mention her hair color? I don't think so. It might be one of those women. I make another mental note and go on. An elderly woman wearing glasses. A woman with her middle-aged daughter. A woman in her twenties walks in and sits down beside a mother with a grown, handicapped daughter. At precisely seven o'clock, with twenty people in the pews, the doors close and the service begins. We stand and sing from the hymnal, *"He will take care of you, God will take care of you."*

Then the minister offers a benediction, inviting "loved ones in the spirit plane to come close to us, that they can bring us words of comfort and joy from their higher realms of existence." The Lord's Prayer follows. Next the director leads the congregation in a recitation of the Declaration of Principles, a pledge of allegiance to Spiritualist precepts. Number five states, "We affirm that communication with the so-called dead is a fact, scientifically proven by the phenomena of Spiritualism." When she sits down, the minister returns, asking us to bow our heads and close our eyes for his guided meditation. In a steady, comforting voice he says, "Slowly the unseen healing current will enter our systems, starting at the feet. Feel it flowing into the body, up the legs, along the arms and shoulders . . . and as we feel the spirit moving up through our neck and head, we know that we are being healed. We *are* being healed. We *are* being healed. We *are* being healed. And each of us has the ability to send forth this healing to others, knowing that *all* things are possible. Send it forth to the person who may need your healing this day. We send these healing forces forth, knowing that those people are being healed. They *are* being healed. They *are* being healed. And as this healing force gathers inside us, we feel it grow stronger, and we send it forth to those who are in institutions, on battlegrounds, in their homes—wherever their need takes us.

"And as I pause for a moment, each of you place into the ether the names of your loved ones who are in need of that healing touch . . ."

My mother is going in for a medical test on Tuesday. I place her name in the ether. And Paul, trying a new heart medication. And my counselor friend Ruth, who is getting a biopsy next week. As well as these dear ones, Louise and SP's callers.

"And as you send it forth, visualize them whole and well, knowing all things are possible. We know that they are being touched by the Holy Spirit and that they are being healed. They are being healed. They are being healed."

As each person flashes into my mind, I see the ill places on their bodies glowing red and picture a healing yellow light encircling them.

"And finally we send forth our healing throughout the country . . ."

My friends vanish like holograms.

"Especially to our own beloved United States of America, and as we reach all its individuals, they will be touched by this healing current, and the world will be led to peace in our time. And, dear spirit, we ask for a healing of mother earth, for we know that all things are possible, *all* things are possible.

"Now as the spirit slowly leaves our body again, flowing down the neck, down the shoulders and arms, down the legs and out the feet, we know that we've been truly touched by the divine force. And let each of us realize in the days to come, if we're in need of a healing touch, we but need to ask and we will receive, for we know that *all* things are possible. This is our healing prayer, in the name of Jesus, the Christ. Amen."

Scanning the room again, I still don't see anyone who might be Louise. While I was on shift this afternoon, she called, and at the sound of her voice the telephone began to get sweaty in my hand. She burned with an unbearable psychic pain, and there was no use problem solving. I just sat and held her suffering for a while, relieved to hear her voice, that she could still speak, still reach out. This afternoon she was grave and anguished, a tangle of depression and self-loathing.

Is she here tonight? Perhaps she didn't feel up to getting dressed, driving out, staging a public face. Sneaking glances around the room, I feel uncomfortable; I'd make a lousy spy. If I could just see Louise, examine the face that harbors the tormented voice, maybe then I could figure out how best to help her.

The balm of religion, the great soother of souls, how does it help Louise? I wonder. When depressed, she becomes afflicted with herself. Through guided meditation and prayer, can she achieve a temporary death of the self and some of the pain piercing it? Or is it the opposite—does she believe in the vividly imagined, personal healing Spiritualism promises? For that matter, how much support does Spiritualism provide Louise? Not enough, I think at first, and then correct myself. For all I know, it may be what stands between her and death. Or SP may be. Or her daughter may be. Or her work. Or her music. Or her garden. Or all of them. I keep forgetting there are no simple answers.

The congregation rises to sing "Count Your Blessings." Then Reverend Wilson begins his sermon. "We all have many blessings in our lives. . . ."

My eyes fall on a youngish woman wearing a black cloche hat in the fourth row. I missed her on the first scan of the congregation. If she turns her head, I'll have a better guess at her age. The minister grips the front of the pulpit with one hand as he talks, leaning forward as he speaks loudly but also intimately.

"Someone who knows me very well asked me one day, 'How can you say that life is a blessing?' Because people who know me know many tragedies in my life—a daughter who is in spirit; a young lady whom I loved very much who, two days before we were to be married, was killed in an accident. I know tragedy."

His fiancée died two days before the wedding? How awful.

"But out of tragedy I learned. As I have traveled on that road through life, I have found the biggest blessing of all has been my religion, my belief in the continuity of life."

Continuity. I say the word slowly in my mind, trying to understand what it must feel like to believe in a heaven where people wear clothes and use up-to-date turns of speech, to believe you are headed for that lifelike place from which you watch your descendants.

Who are Louise's spirits? I wonder. She rarely talks about relatives or friends, but I think both her parents are dead. She wishes her ex-husband were. No siblings. Does she heed the spirits? Does her common sense speak to her in that way, as advice she can attribute to others?

"Spiritualism teaches that healing is forever present. Why not sit down and meditate and ask for the healing touch to come to you. Take a few minutes each day to meditate. You'll be surprised how much better you'll feel."

Can't go wrong urging people to meditate. Anything that stills the nerves and quiets the radio station in the brain for a while.

"Look around yourself at the beauty of nature. Take time. Smell the flowers. Because nature, if you watch it closely, has so many answers."

With that, he steps back, to be replaced at the pulpit by the director, who says, "And now we give thanks to the minister." A man passes around a plate. The director leads us in "Sweetly Falls the

Spirit's Message," a hymn about those on the other side. Then the minister returns to the pulpit.

"Tonight we're going to use flowers for our message service," he says, gesturing to the vase of carnations.

The minister picks a multiflowered stem from the vase. "I want to go right here," he says, gesturing toward a woman with short curly white hair in the second row.

"God bless you," she says.

Caressing the flower, running his hand along its stem, he says, "I feel a lot of things. I want to go back a generation and bring a grandmother vibration to you. But I see her as a photograph. I don't think you knew her well on the earth plane. Do you understand that, please?"

"Yes," she says, nodding.

He continues stroking the flower. "And as I'm touching here, your spirit is showing me over on this other side here. See this little opening? I almost feel as though you've been going through a difficult time when things haven't been going along as easy as you'd like, if you understand that. There seems to be a little stumbling block. Do you understand that?"

"Yes, I do," she says, smiling.

"See, there's a new shoot here, and everything will be fine. You have a tendency to be negative. I want you to always look on the positive side. The spirit is there and wants to bring comfort and wants to bring change from the spirit side of life. The flowers here along the top are already starting to open up for you, which means to me that the cycle of your life is starting to change and you're moving into a much better direction."

"God bless you," she says as he hands the flower to a helper, who delivers it to her to keep.

Picking another flower stem from the vase, he considers it for a moment, then, without looking over the congregation, lifts his eyes suddenly and points with an open hand at the same time.

"I want to go all the way into the back," he says. "That lady there." Is he gesturing to me? He is.

"Good evening," I say cheerfully in a strong voice. Not the quiet, receptive voice with which I answer the phones.

"Yes," he says, running his hand over the single flower, "I'm very conscious that a gentleman is coming to us from the world of spirit—I have two—but the first gentleman I feel I want to be in a grandfatherly way here to you. And the other is a younger man I feel may have lost his life in some sort of mishap."

My heart pounds. I only know two people who have died—my grandfather and my friend Martin, a pilot who crashed when he was twenty-four. Thinking of Martin makes my eyes water.

"He sends you greetings from the spirit side of life and brings you love," the minister continues. "And he has a beautiful spiritual growth. He's growing well on the spirit side."

That's what we want, isn't it, to believe loved ones are still vital enough to grow? Growth is the opposite of decay. Hard as it is to think of our loved ones helplessly corrupted, becoming the earth, it's harder still to imagine our own crumbling end. "How can I die when I've collected all these beautiful things?" my mother once said wistfully when she was younger. It was horrifying to think of a lifetime spent collecting things—family, friends, wisdom, travel experiences, honors, money, a home, pastimes—all of which simply disappeared. If life just stopped, then what was the point of working so hard, worrying so much, *wanting, needing, wishing, hoping?* Such is the tragedy of our existence, we beings who crave life, cherish life, acquire life, spend life. We cling to life, and yet we die. Nothing can resolve that paradox. But if the dead are thriving in a parallel world, there's nothing to worry about, and nothing really changes, not even relationships. How much easier if the borders of life and death are blurred and an emissary in the form of a medium crosses them for you.

"There's a little new growth right here," he says, "and I feel that you are starting on a new venture. You understand that?"

"Yes," I say. There is the new venture of this book.

Turning, stroking, staring at the flower, he seems wholly entranced by it.

"Along in here I feel this little bend." He stops at something I can't see from my pew. "I feel that somebody here on the earth plane is having a little difficulty down through this area here." He gestures across his lower back, the location of the unbearable pain that I had only managed to stop recently by changing a lifelong habit of sleeping on my stomach.

"You know who it is. All right."

Reverend Wilson relaxes, as if he has finished, then swings into action again. "I see down here on the stem a blip. There seems to have been a little bit of a misunderstanding between you and someone else. Do you understand that? Sooner or later that fence will come down, and I can't say that the relationship will be the same, but it will be better than it is right now. And I think you should send a force out for healing in this particular area. And God bless you."

"Thank you," I say. His helper brings me the flower.

Picking another stem out of the vase, he looks immediately at a woman sitting in the third row and to his right. "Two women are coming to you from the spirit world," he says in a conversational trance. "Mom is one of them. But do you know a Lil or a Lilian?"

"Oh, yes. God bless you!" the woman says. She pushes her glasses up her nose with one finger, as if she might be able to see the spirits better that way.

The minister continues. "She says, 'I'm here, and I want to be recognized.' She wants to send you greetings from the spirit side of life. I have a gentleman who touches here with you, too, from the world of spirit. I don't know who he is, but I keep hearing 'Claude. Claude's here.' "

The woman smiles and shakes her head, much gladdened and moved.

"And he wants to send you greetings and say he loves you from the spirit side of life." Turning the flower stem around in his hand like a piece of crystal, he says, "Do you have a son living?"

"Yes, I do," she says in a concerned voice.

"I see here that there might be something that he wants to go ahead with, as far as work or business is concerned, because I want to say to you that the time isn't quite right here." His fingers travel up the main stem. "If I go up here a little farther, I see a very light shade of green up here, and it gets better, and I feel if he can just weather the storm, he'll be much more successful."

"All right," she says. "I'll tell him. Thank you." The helper gives her her flower.

Next he picks up a large stem, studies it for a moment, gestures to the woman in the black cloche hat, who says, "Yes. God bless you."

"I have a gentleman here whom I'm very conscious of, and I have to ask you a question. Did your father leave this world sort of quickly?"

"Yes," she says quietly, with a catch in her voice, "he did." A shiver runs across my neck. I know that voice. Moving a little to the left, I can see her more clearly—a pleasant face with brown eyes, straight bangs, strong nose, small mole to the left of her upper lip, and a look of tense belief.

"Okay, because this is the gentleman I have here. He left all of a sudden into the spirit world, and he wanted to talk to you. But, you know, as I look at this flower, I see a lot of things. There are a lot of things progressing down here in your vibration in a material sense, and I feel good about that, even though I feel right now you're closed to it. Do you understand that?"

"Yes, I do," she says. It is Louise—I'm sure of it. I'd know that soprano, slightly sandy voice anywhere. How did she rally enough to drive out here, walk in, be so composed?

"But over here there's a lot growth possible, and I want to say, Go for it! Because everything will be there when you need it. As I touch this stem here, this little bend in it, I feel as if you're going through a period of time right now when you're down, when you get a little bit depressed . . ."

A little bit?

"Because of the conditions around and about you. Do you understand?"

"Yes," she says.

"But I'm going up this stem, and there's all new growth here." He holds it up to her, as if she could see the green force that he sees. Does she? "Which assures me that the depression is going to be behind you. This bud here is tight, and even though you're feeling tight right now, I want to take a load off of your shoulders—do you understand that?—because the spirit is saying, 'Don't blame yourself.' So when you're looking at the bad, just look at things in a good, positive way, and that will build a positive future here for you."

See the bright side? Don't blame yourself? Heaven knows, people have tried that with Louise, and it didn't work. Does she listen differently to this minister than she does to SP's counselors or to her friends? If so, where does the difference lie?

"And I want to say that there's a lot of spirituality within you; you have a lot of good thoughts you want to send out to other individuals on this plane, which makes you a very spiritual being. God bless you."

"Thank you," she says, and receives her flower.

For the next hour the minister continues giving messages, until he has crisscrossed the room and spoken to everyone. At last he finishes, exhausted, which doesn't surprise me, since everyone in the congregation is exhausted just from listening so hard for so long. All the messages were healing, uplifting, encouraging, though he was a little tougher with the two men, admonishing one not to be so stubborn and the other to keep a better eye on his health.

The service closes with a benediction. The organist plays. As people leave the chapel, Louise passes close by me. She's a little shorter than I imagined, her hair darker and straight, her eyes brown not hazel, and her skin looks burnished. Perhaps from gardening. She often talks about how much pleasure she finds in gardening. I didn't expect her to look quite so intact, though she does seem distracted, trapped somewhere inside herself, as she walks out into the failing light. All right, I've seen her. Now what? I rise and follow. It would be easy enough to introduce myself as a neighbor, say we met at some other gathering. Then what? Befriend her? Offer her more intensive support? That wouldn't be fair to her. She has the right to make her own destiny, to call for a counselor's help when she needs to and on her own terms. She only seeks help from us when her mood becomes extreme, too extreme to impose on friends or to handle alone. At the moment she seems to be all right. When she doesn't feel that way, she'll phone. I hope.

Maybe I need to think about whose pain I'm really trying to ease. What right do I have to intrude in her life, just because her suffering is hard for *me* to bear? I hate leaving her. My instinct is to try everything when someone dear to me is suffering. Has she become that dear to me over the past years? I guess so, though I've never met her, seen her but once, and only ever heard her in the death grip of depression. Even within those limits you can get to know someone, respect them, cheer their triumphs, lament their hardships, hope for their success.

In the parking lot, I pass a white Dodge Spirit with a license plate that reads I4C. Below it a bumper sticker says PROTECTED BY ANGELS. Thank heavens someone has a sense of humor. A carnival of tree frogs, leopard frogs, pickerel frogs, toads, and crickets have been filling the air with plucks, snores, rattles, pops, rasps, and moans. Night is falling so fast it's hard to tell where ground ends and sky begins. As I drive away, I watch Louise grow smaller in the rearview mirror, then vanish suddenly as she steps between shadows.

Chapter 10

The World Unwound

WHILE drinking my morning tea, I watch the squirrels cavort in the yard, paying special attention to their best-known feature. Few things in nature are as marvelous as a squirrel's tail. Or as transformable. Almost half the squirrel's body length, it's an all-purpose appendage: a balance pole, a scarf on cold days, a semaphore flag. Squirrels can sit in their own shade. Indeed, the name squirrel comes from the Greek for "shadow tail." When marking its neighborhood, a squirrel flicks its tail in an arpeggio of twitches, then moves a few feet up the tree trunk or along the branch and marks again. It's amazing the way a squirrel can clasp itself on the back with its tail, embrace and comfort itself. Humans do that, too— hug themselves when they need nurturing and no one is around. When it rains, squirrels fold their tails up over their heads like um- brellas. As they sit and eat, they settle deep onto their haunches and throw their tails over their backs like scarves to keep them- selves warm. Tails are cozy as sweaters—the squirrels can wrap up in them when cold, or lay them aside when warm, or wrap them around small offspring.

It's a cool morning for biking, so I pull on a windbreaker over my sweater. For a change, I take my favorite bike route in reverse, starting with a long, gradual climb beside a cornfield where some- one has installed a dozen bluebird houses. As I approach Freese Road, I hear a clear *meep, meep, meep, meep, meep.* Hawk, my mind says. Again the call. Tracing the sound to the woods across the road, I see a large fawn-breasted red-tailed hawk sitting on a branch. Stretching its wings overhead, it tilts them like a parasol, then flaps away, helloing as it planes low over the cornfield, cir- cling once before it flies off. Two hawks return its call. It is migra- tion season, and the sky is full of red-tails.

Going downhill, I use all my high gears, and my speedometer reads 25 mph. I like that combination of speed and control. In high gear, you move fast but can still pedal and feel the bike se- curely in hand. The corn tassels, glistening tawny gold, shine against a blue sky and the encampment of clouds on the horizon. Some trees have begun to color, but most surge with the shadowy green one finds in Goya's paintings. Yellow butterflies barnstorm the meadows, now thick with goldenrod, ragweed, chicory, Queen Anne's lace, and other wildflowers. Even riding fast, I can smell woodsmoke, apples, and mown grass. It's warm in the sun but chilly whenever I enter a tunnel of tree shade—in short, a typical fall morning.

Today I pass a dead deer beside the road at the cornfield, a dead squirrel at the Varna bridge, a dead bird beside the

goldfinch woods. That visual litany of car-crushed animals produces a shiver. A thuglike fright slams through my mind at
intervals—what a sudden impact, as of a car hitting me, would
feel like. Quickly I chase the image out of my mind and rebuke
myself for such perverse and masochistic thoughts.

Funny how the mind teases and taunts and how ashamed we are
to let others know. Last night, though, embarrassing thoughts
spilled freely at my support group meeting. A mainstay of SP are its
four support groups, each led by a local therapist. No one is
obliged to attend, but it's strongly encouraged, and most counselors enjoy the chance to share problems and explore agency
matters. Thirteen people showed up for last night's meeting, held
at the office, where we sat around a conference table laden with
fresh grapes, apple cider, and cookies.

"Did anyone have any interesting calls this month?" Bea Goldman, a support group leader, had asked to get the ball rolling.
Joyce began by revealing how frustrating she found it to talk with
one frequent caller, a highly intelligent man who is impulsive and
manipulative and prey to large mood swings. Maggie chimed in
that she gave that caller time limits and politely but firmly ended
calls after fifteen minutes. Joyce confessed, in an exasperated tone,
that the last time she spoke with the caller, they ended up quar-
reling. As usual, the caller demanded that Joyce praise him by using certain quirky and colorful phrases, echo his ideas and
feelings, and swear to be his friend. When Joyce said she wasn't
comfortable saying such things, the caller became adversarial.

It's hard to know how best to handle a manipulative and angry
caller. Sharing techniques that have worked, or potential blind alleys, is always useful. But more important is the mutual wringing
of hands. It helps to know others are equally stymied. From that
caller we went on to several others, which led to mulling over the
role and limits of being a counselor. Three counselors—all of
them senior—confessed to a sinful secret. At one time or another,
in the midst of a marathon, rambling, circling call from a frequent caller who was monologuing, they were tempted to use a
free line to dial SP so that the caller would hear the second crisis

line ringing. Then, of course, it would be easier to insist, "I *have* to go now. Please call back another time." I was glad they revealed how tough it was, even after years of experience, always to be in control of a call. This was a good meeting because some of the counselors were able to voice dark feelings—anger, frustration, hostility—that sometimes arose.

You can end up dreading calls from certain people. You can wind up being critical of the very people you pledge to help. In training, counselors learn to be long-suffering, sympathetic, wholly nonjudgmental, able to picture themselves in the caller's shoes. Putting those ideals into practice isn't always easy.

Calls can sometimes last two or three hours and become very emotional. It's late at night, you haven't been to bed, and when you hang up, you're totally wrung out, drooping in the chair. The phone rings. You pick it up and you hear sobs, and you think, Oh, no! Here we go again! I'm not ready for this! New counselors start fired up, full of the warmth of human kindness, powerfully focused. But regardless of their goodwill, they can exhaust themselves. It has taken me years to understand that such feelings are normal in such a high-stress job, not signs of weakness or bad character but only too human.

A good support group session. We all let off steam, picked up some tips, socialized, and shared secret fears and misgivings. With any luck, these monthly meetings will help us avoid burnout. But it's hard to know. Although the turnover rate is high, with about two years being the average length of service, people leave for many reasons. New jobs take them away; school ends; they need to work full time; their families require more from them; illness saps their strength; personal problems begin to mortgage their spare time; their own struggles with mental illness intrude; they get bored; yes, they burn out.

At last I reach the Plantations and bike across the raised wooden boardwalk out to the pergola in the middle of a lily pad–thick lake. A hundred mallards rest and sleep onshore. I love watching animals fall asleep. A duck begins to breathe more deeply, its feet sprawl behind it like still paddleboat wheels, it nuzzles its bill into its breast feathers, its eyes close, its tail twitches and settles, and it becomes a feathered bellows as its whole body slips into a thick heavy breathing.

The lake looks oil-painting luminous today, reflecting the trees and sky, filled with lily pads and ducks with perfect white wakes trailing behind them in the green water. What stillness—the living mirror of the pond, the quiet broken only by a few duck calls and the occasional sparrow.

My odometer reads 320 miles. Not bad for one month. Most of those miles I've added on weekend bike trips with Cathy. Last Saturday we drove over to Watkins Glen, half an hour away. There we began at the state park and biked uphill along Seneca Lake until we entered the wineries country. Miles of grapevines were strung out on wires like martyrs. Still heavily hung with grapes—beautiful late fruiting Concords—they saturated the air with perfume. As we traveled through the vineyards, I was reminded how often beauty emerges from twisted, tortured-looking plants. True for grapevines and apple trees. For some reason I thought of Van Gogh at that moment, his gnarled mind and his life contorted by woe. That's what we talked about for a while as we pedaled past a dozen small waterfalls and endless scenic vistas—the beauty that can spring from troubled limbs.

We also talked about Cathy's work, and mine, and her childhood, and mine, and her relationships, and mine. For this trip she packed cheddar cheese, slices of sourdough bread, marzipan-filled croissants, leftover Halloween candy, carrot sticks, and two apples. I packed V8s, grapes, Cheshire cheese, *biscotti*, and hummus. So between us—as ever—we had a feast.

Thinking of food makes me hungry, and I head back home for a snack and shower before I go on shift.

STEPPING carefully, I climb slowly toward the counselor room. The creaking wood announces me, which is probably why I find Bob already packing up. Lifting a hand in greeting, he says, "Hey, babe, I bought a new dog yesterday." He pulls three Polaroids from his kit and hands them to me with all the zest of a new parent. Not only are the pictures out of focus, but the dog is hideous. Its head is square and blunt, its short legs too thin for the shape of its body, and it looks slightly porcine.

"Oh, what kind is it?" I ask cheerfully.

"It's a mongrel—part French poodle, part pit bull," he says, hoisting the knapsack onto his shoulder as he heads through the door. Then, poking his head back into the room, he adds, "Not much of a guard dog, but it's a *vicious* gossip."

With that, he jogs heavily down the creaking steps. On the hot sheet today a counselor offers advice about a recent caller who just needs a sympathetic ear, not efforts at problem solving. Her life is in such disarray that counselors sometimes are tempted to tell her what to do, what *they'd* do in her place. The hot sheet advises, "Make supportive little mewling sounds. In fact, anytime you are tempted to make a suggestion, make a supportive sound instead." Good advice, but hard to follow when you desperately want to wave a magic wand and fix things for someone, even if you can't know what will work in the caller's life and the caller isn't ready to take action anyway.

5:32 p.m. A thirteen-year-old boy calls to talk about how his father, drunk and out of work, has been beating him and his little sister. He keeps returning to how he must deserve the beatings, must be doing something terribly wrong. Victims of abuse so often feel guilty, as if somehow they provoked their harsh treatment. They grow up thinking there is something organically wrong with them, not that something is wrong with their abuser. As the boy talks, I focus hard on his predicament until I am sure he is safe, feels heard out, and has a plan of action.

"God, I hope he's all right," I say after we hang up.

6:00 p.m. An elderly man calls because he is feeling flustered about a social situation. A college student has sort of adopted him, has dinner with him every few weeks, and generally seems to be keeping an eye on him. Last year the student took him to the Syracuse Fair, which he enjoyed, and this year the student called to invite him there again. But he has a bruised hip and doesn't feel up to it. He's worried that the student may already have bought the ticket and will be out-of-pocket. He can't figure out what to say. I ask him to get out a pencil and paper, and I help him write down a little speech in his own words. It seems just right to him—concerned and grandfatherly—and he sounds clearly relieved. He says he is going to call right away.

6:23 p.m. A powerfully angry woman calls to tell of her frustration, disappointment, and sense of betrayal. One year ago she married a widower with a sixteen-year-old daughter. It was a second marriage for her as well, and she desperately wanted it to work. But soon after they moved in together, she discovered to her horror that father and daughter had rigid, well-established roles and there was no room for her in that equation. The daughter ruled the house and battled her new stepmother. When the daughter informed her that she intended to skip school for a few days to go to a rock festival in a nearby state, the caller told her that was out of the question. Volatile and disrespectful, the girl had a temper tantrum and hit her hard, then went crying to her father, who agreed to give her a note for school saying she was sick. When the caller complained to her husband about the girl's violence, he said the caller must have provoked it.

Constantly in trouble at school, the girl was known for her truancy, fistfights, and disrespect to teachers. Guidance counselors begged the parents to exercise discipline and also to enter family counseling with their daughter. But the girl swore she was innocent of all accusations, and her father took her side. Now she tyrannizes her stepmother whenever her father is at work. When the caller reports such events to her husband, he says she's making them up out of jealousy. Then he yells at her and threatens to divorce her if she doesn't stop "causing trouble." She wants the marriage to work, but she's also in a precarious position financially. They live in her house, paying off a large mortgage. Her husband doesn't make much, and he quickly depleted her savings. Uneducated and untrained, where is a woman in her fifties going to find a job? she asks fiercely.

In many ways this is a simple call. Until the inevitable divorce, the woman only needs a sympathetic listener. We even do some problem solving and come up with a few possible strategies she might use for bridling the daughter. When she offhandedly mentions suicide, I suggest we consider some other, less extreme options. We discuss divorce, agencies such as Displaced Homemakers, which could help and advise her, and various plans that, while they aren't wholly desirable, would at least give her some element of control.

The call, which lasts for over an hour, is a good one. The woman sounds a little calmer and less frantic when we hang up. But something curious happened. My empathy for her was so great that her rampaging anger, upset, and frustration transferred to me. I'm trembling with anger. For hours I stay tense and agitated from borrowed grief.

At last it occurs to me to try jogging in place. Maybe I can exhaust the anger, sweat it out. That does help a little, but not enough. Sitting on the couch, I try meditating. When the phone rings, my pulse jumps and my mind clears all at once.

9:02 p.m. "Crisis service," I say. "May I help you?"

"I'm just really confused," a man says.

"What are you confused about?"

In a whisper, as if to himself, he says, "This isn't any good. This is just not a good situation. I don't know what to do." The voice is young.

"You sound confused," I reflect. "What are you confused about?"

"I just don't know what to do. This is the last place I'm going to try. I don't know what else I can do now." His combination of frustration and despair worries me.

"You sound upset and frightened. What's happening?"

"What do you mean?" he asks, suddenly more formal. Maybe I've jumped to a wrong conclusion.

"Why have you called tonight?" I try again: "You sound very anxious."

This time the key fits the lock. He sighs. "There's no one else to turn to. Nobody listens to me. Everybody says, 'Oh, you can deal with it. Just deal with it!' I can't deal with it anymore, though. I was looking through the phone book; this seemed like a place to call."

"What is it that you're hoping to deal with?"

A longer sigh. "I don't know where to start. I'm just lost."

Casting around for a way to help him get started, I say, "Have you been feeling this way for long?"

"I don't know. Something feels like it just snapped." I don't like how weak his voice sounds, especially when he adds, "I'm just losing control here. I don't know what to do."

"Where are you now?" I ask in a quiet, even voice. Sometimes when I ask this of distraught callers, they get panicky.

But he responds easily. "I'm in my room."

"Are you there alone? Is anyone nearby?"

"He just left. That's why I can call you right now. I couldn't call if he were here."

Who is *he*—a roommate, a lover, a father?

"Do you feel safe?"

"Yeah, right now I am. I don't know when he'll be back, though. . . ." His words trail away, and I think he may be looking down a hallway or out a door.

"You're sounding pretty overwrought. May I ask you if you've been drinking something or taking something?"

"Me? Me drinking?" His voice strengthens with surprise. "No, no. It's not me. I wish I had been."

Back to square one. Talking softly—intimately, not seductively—I try to convey my concern. "What's making you so upset tonight?"

Suddenly the gates open, and he lets out a flood of words. "My roommate, *he's* been drinking—which he usually does—but tonight I think he snapped. He started to take it out on me, and then he left in a huff, babbling things, slamming the door."

"You say your roommate has been drinking, and he began taking it out on you—in what way?"

"He grabbed me by my sweatshirt and threw me across the room and right into the bookcase. Man, it freaked me out."

That does sound bad. "Are you hurt?"

"I'll probably be black-and-blue in the morning," he admits with a touch of embarrassment. "Nothing's broken."

"I see. Does this happen very often?"

In an urgent voice he says, "It's never been this bad before. He usually just goes nuts and runs out for a while and comes back and goes to bed. But this time he . . . I don't know when he's coming back. He could do anything."

"That sounds very frightening," I say. "Are you afraid that he might really hurt you when he returns?"

"If this continues the way it has been, I'm sure he's going to do something. To take it out on somebody."

"This is your roommate, you say. Are you living in an apartment or in college?"

"I'm in a dorm."

"In a dorm. What year are you?"

"Freshman."

Wow. First year away from home, and he gets a drunken and abusive roommate. "Is there someone, a counselor or resident adviser, you could talk to about this?"

"Well, I have talked to my RA, but he just sorta said, 'Well, if he doesn't do anything dangerous, it's okay. You'll just have to learn to live with him.' Only . . . This is the first time he's grabbed me. He usually just kicks a chair or pulls a drawer out or something. It's been scary, but he never hurt *me*."

"So it really seems to have gotten out of hand tonight?"

"Yeah. I'd say so. He's just working too hard. School is pushing him over the edge. It's been going on for four days now. He's started in on the No Doz thing, and he took one every four hours, and then he started one every hour, then every half hour. And now he's drinking on top of that."

"What do you think would happen if you went to the RA and explained that things had escalated a bit with your roommate, that he'd been drinking hard and taking a lot of pills, and coming after you, that you were concerned that he could get even more violent? How do you think the RA would respond?"

The caller isn't sure, and he also feels guilty about ratting on his roommate, guilty about not being able to help him cope.

I say, "We've been talking about a number of things over the past few minutes. One is your concern for your roommate. You've said you feel a sense of responsibility, and you want to help him. You sound frustrated about that. Another is the possibility that he could hurt you worse, since he's been so violent already."

"Yeah," he says with a shiver in his voice. "I'm his roommate and his friend—it's my job to help him. I should be able to deal with it, but I can't."

"You're very worried about him. You want to be a good friend and a good roommate, and you wonder how to help him."

"Yeah. Don't you want to help your friends?"

"You sound frustrated because it's so hard to help him all by yourself."

"I should be able to deal with him," he says again, defeated.

"I'm concerned about how difficult this is for you. It sounds like you're under a lot of pressure. And I'm concerned that you might be in danger when he returns."

Suddenly agitated, he says, "What am I going to do? This has got to stop!"

"What about going back to your RA and telling him how serious things have become since you last spoke with him?" I suggest again. "It could be helpful for you to have an ally."

"If *you* had a friend in trouble, wouldn't *you* want to help him, not report on him but help him? Wouldn't *you*?" the caller asks.

Of course I would, but we're encouraged not to personalize calls.

"You sound like a really good friend, a very concerned friend. It's tough to watch a friend in trouble. You've already made contact with your RA; he's not a stranger to you. Would you feel comfortable returning to him and talking with him?" I know I'm being directive, but I'm worried the roommate might return.

After a few moments the caller says, "I guess I could talk to my RA. He's a nice guy."

Thank heavens. "Is he there now? Could you go see him now?" I pray I don't sound as worried as I feel.

"I don't know. It's late. What if he's asleep? I don't want to wake him up." Unbelievable. The caller is concerned about everyone but himself. I'm sure he *is* a great friend. I just wish I could get him out of his room and someplace safe. He's got to do it for himself, though; otherwise he won't know what to do next time this happens.

"That's his job, to be on hand when people need him. That's why he lives in the dorm," I say.

"Yeah. That's right," the caller says.

"Why don't you go do that now, and if he's not there or if you're not comfortable after your conversation with him, call back and we'll talk a little more and see what else might be possible."

"Will you still be there?" the caller asks, and my heart breaks. For the first time he sounds little and afraid.

I wish I could assure my caller that I'll be here, but I don't know when he'll call. "It might not be me. But, if you like, someone here will know what the circumstances are. I'll make sure of that."

"Okay. You think I should go now?" He asks like someone just needing one more nudge.

"It might be a good idea to talk with your RA while your roommate is still out. What do you think?"

After a long pause he says, "Yeah, I think that might be a good idea. Before he comes back. I'll go see if the RA's there."

"Okay. Good-bye for now," I say, implying that we'll talk again soon. Sending him to his RA was good; he needs an ally. But what on earth will happen when the roommate returns drugged, drunk, and angry? I hope the RA will stash the caller somewhere else tonight, and tomorrow, when the roommate is sober, take whatever action is necessary. I'm worried about the roommate, too, but he's not the one who called.

At one point during the call, the caller had wanted me to tell him how to help his roommate. This is what we call a second-party call. He wanted help for someone else. We get such calls all the time—parents who seek advice for troubled children, spouses who want to help their partners with a problem, friends or teachers of people who are suicidal. The problem is, we don't know anything about those other people—who may not be real—we don't know their habits or personalities or strengths or resources or mental states. The caller is our client. Our job is to bring the conversation around to how the caller is feeling, how the caller is coping, what the caller can do to feel that he or she is acting responsibly.

In training, we practiced the protocol for handling second-party calls, which felt cumbersome at first. Actually, all of training felt strange, since it meant learning a new dialect of listening skills. I can still remember how nervous I was during the first half of training. I didn't know then the many octaves of hope and despair I would listen to. Even on my first shift I began learning an important lesson: the range of what's normal. The anatomy of each call is different, and every caller has a unique story to tell.

According to studies done by James Pennebaker at Southern Methodist University, confiding strengthens one's immune system. So by simply listening to the confidences of a caller, we perform a lifesaving act. Callers sometimes refer to us as their friends, who offer them genuine support and make them feel less alone. But there is also the benefit of venting one's troubles instead of stewing in them. When people clarify their troubles, turning them into a narrative and giving them just enough order to communicate to someone else, the fog lifts briefly and the world becomes a place that can be better understood, even if it isn't fully enjoyed. In Pennebaker's studies, people who didn't confide were more prone to disease and stress and early death. Much of their physical energy went into containing and hiding emotions, and that led to high blood pressure and a weaker immune system.

By telling stories we assimilate frightening or unexplained events and fit them into a world where action is possible. One becomes less helpless. Suddenly there are many options for escape or relief, many explanations for how an event that may have turned the world upside down can fit comfortably into one's life. The student who called this evening did not expect his roommate to be an alcoholic, pill-popping Goliath who could murder him in a rage. By making sense of the situation, telling the story repeatedly until it fit right, he could integrate that unexpected terror into his life, and we were able to discuss possible actions he could take. At that point his panic fled. But he will need to tell the story over and over—to authorities so that they can take action, to himself so that he can rehearse ways of coping, to others so that he can organize and revise the events in his mind. When he tells friends, he will also be communicating what sort of person he is—the sort who doesn't feel comfortable ratting on a roommate, who feels guilty about not being able to help his roommate, who allows himself to be victimized by a bully, but only up to a point, and so on.

The alternative is to worry, and he'll do that anyway, but it won't be as productive as confiding in others. To normalize the event, figure out what action to take, and feel good about how he handled it, or examine why he handled it poorly and what he could do differently next time, he'll need a listener. I think that's why many of our callers tell the same story over and over. Listening to their own stories, they understand parts of them better. As different counselors give them feedback, different parts of their stories take on importance or become clearer. The basic facts tend to stay the same, but the emotional relevance changes, depending on the caller's mood or new circumstances.

Chapter 11

Desperate Measures

IN THE icicled dreamtime of December in upstate New York, the fields deepen in opalescent snow and ice storms turn barbed wire fences into a string of stars. The streets look like bobsled runs. I love that sort of hard, gnawing winter. So, unlike many easterners, who feel imprisoned by winter and flee to hot spots with the mania of inmates out on parole, I never feel driven to leave home. Winter is an equation my body knows by heart. I love its snowy walls too thick to climb, its ice too sharp to handle, its cold painful as fire.

The afternoon shift begins quietly, with a request for a referral and two hang-ups. Then Saxman calls, very depressed, talking about suicide. Researching his medicines, he has discovered that overdosing on his insulin would do the trick neatly, with the least shock to his parents, who might assume it an accident. Last night held a cauldron of woes. A fight with a potential girlfriend, who got angry when he asked her to have an AIDS test, was followed by a canceled performance at a club. He also has a deadline looming. All week he procrastinated rehearsing for a concert at the marina tomorrow evening, and he feels completely unprepared. We talk about his diabetes—the flare-ups that produce temporary blindness, numbness in his hands, painful cracks in his foreskin and heels, and a grave fear of total blindness and loss of limbs. Diabetic since he was a teen, Saxman is understandably fed up with being sick all the time.

We talk about his suicide plans; the impending deadline; how worthless, witless, giftless he feels. I ask how he would feel if, by some miracle, he had already prepared tomorrow's concert, and when he allows that he would feel less stressed, we discuss triage. If he begins by rehearsing the easier tunes that could be transposed quickly, he could leave the tougher ones. At the very least, then, he'd have part of the concert prepared and not feel totally incompetent. And, who knows, if he did the easier ones first, he might actually get to some of the harder ones later. In his thinking-out-loud yet experienced voice, I can hear a mind fumbling and gauging a complex creative problem, testing it against the reality of what is possible in the remaining hours.

As he talks himself into the future and realizes that he can in fact master this one problem, his mood lifts a little. Toward the end of the call he seems stronger, but I might be wrong, so I ask him how he is feeling, and he replies that he thinks he'll be able to manage the day. We make a contract: He promises to phone if he feels driven to end his life. But he sounds precarious.

One good sign is that he started psychotherapy a few days ago; at least he's reaching out, creating a second lifeline. Apparently he interviewed four therapists and settled on a man who seemed insightful and sincere. Also a good sign. It takes energy and control to interview prospective therapists, as well as a belief that recovery is possible.

When we say good-bye, a thought dawns on me. I wasn't rattled by his talking directly about suicide. I stayed reasonably calm as I explored his degree of lethality. I didn't begin by assuming the call was an emergency. More important, perhaps, I allowed him to be suicidal. My job was to befriend him on this day, in this hour, give him comfort and concern, guide him to ways of coping if possible but, even if I couldn't do that, accept that he was headed for death sometime, somewhere. We all are.

Thinking about this new threshold, I write up the call. When the phone rings again, I hear the familiar voice of Endless Love. A quick glance at the logbook. He phoned three times in the night, four times the day before, twice the day before that. When I ask gently what's causing the pain, he explodes with anger. "I need you not to ask any questions," he says firmly, adding that he also needs me to praise his virtues according to a few set phrases, express my unconditional love for him, "testify to the injured innocence" he has experienced, swear I will "hearten and restore" him "with words of strong faith," and assure him that God has a loving purpose for him.

Ignoring his rigid rules, I listen for a few moments and unconsciously ask a small sympathetic question. This time he seethes with fury—didn't he tell me not to ask any questions! Don't I understand that my job is to do whatever he *needs me to!*

Anger whisks up inside my chest. Don't react, *observe*, I counsel myself. You're feeling anger; it's what he does to people. I explain calmly that I am not comfortable reciting his scripts. If he wishes to talk about his problems, I'm happy to listen, take his problems seriously, and give him whatever feedback he thinks useful, but like most people, I am extremely uncomfortable being told what to say. It's too much of a straitjacket.

I suggest we start over on a more relaxed footing, but he reads me the riot act. Splattering me with insults, he tells me that my job is to hear whatever he needs and to do whatever he needs. I politely explain that no, that isn't my job. If he needs to control me or yell abuse at me, the call really isn't going to work for either one of us.

How do I help this man? We've been shadow-dancing with Endless Love for years, and, if anything, he's getting worse. I think he may be phoning us because it's one of the few places—maybe the only place—where he can manipulate people and consistently get away with it. Are we making his predicament worse by encouraging that behavior?

Although he comes from a large family and works at a diner among many potential friends, he says they all avoid him. For years the central theme of his calls has been how people disappoint and abandon him, when he desperately needs only the simplest and most obvious thing in the world from them—"soul mates who will fill their hearts with joyous devotion and unconditional love," for he is "a purely loving heart whom everyone betrays." If he makes the same demands on his family and friends that he makes on us, it's small wonder he drives them away. I'd like to move the call around to discussing if I'm reacting to his demands the way his retreating friends do. But he hangs up in disgust before I have the chance.

5:25 p.m. Louise calls. At least I think it's Louise: a small female voice—not a child's, a woman's in extreme pain—a voice choking back tears while trying to breathe, cry, and talk at the same time.

"It sounds like you're having an awful day," I say quietly.

"I really am," she half whines, and then cries in a small staccato of pain. Some crying voices are ambiguous; there may yet be hidden strengths and resources to plumb. Some, like this voice, leave little doubt. I can hear the fast-fraying edges of hope in the way she gasps between cries. Her weak voice breaks up. Her mood is deadly. I think this is Louise. Her face flashes into my mind, but not the composed face I saw at the Spiritualist church. Tonight she is beyond their otherworldly healing. Do her suicide fantasies extend past death?

"I can hear how much pain you're in," I say in an intense, intimate voice. "What's made it so rough tonight?"

A long silence. Stay calm, I think. Don't lose her. Don't ask if she's all right. Don't speak just because the silence is uncomfortable. At first, when callers fell silent, I would nervously fill the gap with open-ended questions. But I've learned now to allow silence, which can be a positive part of a conversation. The silence around a thought can give it perspective and dignity.

"Are you still there?" I say at last.

She laughs a dangerous laugh. "For the moment," she says.

"Let's talk about the moment," I say, letting my voice fall into a conspiratorial whisper I hope will engage her and draw her nearer.

"All the heat is gone," she says. "It's so cold, so alone. Last night I saw a documentary on TV about penguins. They stand all alone at the edge of the world, like lonely, beautiful spirits, and stare out to sea."

I cannot tell her that I have seen penguins in the wild, and they were perfectly adapted to their environment. But in her mind they symbolize a powerful emotional climate, an icy wasteland where they endure the ravaging winds of daily life just as she weathers repeated brainstorms. In the Antarctica of her suffering, at the end of the known world, the vista looks bleak.

"It sounds like you're feeling as cold, isolated, and raw as those penguins."

"Raw," she echoes. "Like meat."

"With no protection from the elements."

"No. In a completely colorless world. I've been thinking about . . . the gorge. Then it would be over," she whispers. "The pain would finally be over. This long, sorry mistake of my life would be over."

The bridge again. The long fall. What is it about humans that makes us want to hurl ourselves from heights? Imagining the pain of those bone-shattering rocks below gives me a jolt. Even deep water feels hard as a steel door when you fall onto it from a great height.

Although I'm curious about what Louise meant by the "mistake" of her life, it isn't my role to ask. That's for therapy.

"You've been thinking of killing yourself in the gorge?"

She sighs. Often when a person is suicidal and you ask about it, you hear a sigh because no one else has believed them. They're relieved to discover that someone can listen to such awful thoughts.

Friends and family get scared and don't know what to say or do, so they ignore it or say, "Oh, you'll feel better." We take depression seriously and talk about it head-on.

"Yes," she says.

"How do you see it happening?"

"Flying. I would lean into nothingness, let go, and fly."

"Cold at the bottom," I remind her. Suicidal people get wedded to means. If you can disrupt the means, you can sometimes disrupt the plan. A very specific and available plan, like Louise's, signals high risk.

"Yes." She cries. Silence. I know she is picturing it.

I'm afraid of losing Louise. Saxman was very depressed, but within reach. With Louise, I'm not so sure. But if she truly wishes to die? We don't hear from her when she's not depressed. In more stable times I don't think she would choose death. But I respect her right to choose, and I tell her so.

"Look, you can always kill yourself. That's one option tonight. Why don't we put that up on the shelf for a moment and talk about what some other options might be."

Because she feels bereft of them, I want her to have choices. Choice is a signature of our species. We choose to live; sometimes we choose our own death. Most of the time we make choices just to prove choice is possible. But suicidal people have tunnel vision—no other choice seems possible. A counselor's job is to put windows and doors in that tunnel.

"Options?" The word probably seems tragically impersonal. "You mean like eating dinner?" she asks acidly.

"Have you had anything to eat today?"

A dry little laugh. "I bought some lamb chops but couldn't face cooking them. I can't eat something more nervous than I am."

I laugh. Her delivery was perfect. She laughs again. It is barely more than a chuckle.

"Cold . . ." She launches the word like a dark cloud, not attached to anything special, a nimbus of pure pain.

"How come so cold and lonely tonight?"

"I'm always lonely—lonelier than life," she says faintly; then, rallying a little, she explains, "When I worked at Montessori, I used to meet people there or, when my kids were little, through their activities. Now I don't meet anyone. Not at work in that pathetic office. My job is horrible. Not hard, you know, just boring and lonely, but it's the only one I could find. There's nothing out there for a middle-aged woman, and the minute they learn I've been hospitalized, they're afraid to hire me, like I'm going to napalm their filing cabinets or Krazy Glue their customers' thumbs to the counter or something."

"I understand. You hate your job, you don't make friends there, and it's hard to find a new one. Maybe we can figure out some other work."

"It's hopeless. I've tried everywhere. There's nothing."

Before I can reply, she swerves to, "And I haven't had a date in years, haven't been laid since I don't know when. And then there is my daughter. I mean, she's a teen, and suddenly Mom's a drag. We fight all the time. She doesn't want me to hug and kiss her anymore. I can understand that, but it hurts."

Breathless, she sounds like a child trying to tell a story faster than her tumbling words. I was rushing her. She wasn't finished with her lamentation. She still needs to be heard, so I sit quietly and listen, a borrowed heart.

"There's no point to my life. I'm not doing anything of value with it. No one would miss me. No one would care if I were gone. Well, that's not true. It might change how a couple of people feel—give my ex a few sleepless nights, send a message to my Neanderthal boss, make my daughter feel sorry about how cruel she can be."

Magical thinking—the belief that suicide will change a relationship with someone. One of the warning signs. "I'm lonelier than life," she says again. "How do I get out of this?" Then she says, "I just want the pain to end." A rustling noise. She is settling on a chair or a hallway step.

A mental inventory of her state alarms me. She's feeling unendurable pain. Her needs for love, friendship, achievement, and belonging aren't being met. She's feeling helpless and hopeless. She's so depressed that her thinking has shrunk to absolutes—life or death—and life has lost its tang. She openly talks about killing herself. Eighty percent of suicidal people give clear messages. Should I send the police? We have met at this crossroads before. The terrain is the same, the emotional whirlwind is the same, but is *she?* Is anything different?

"What a heavy burden that must be. I can hear how low you're feeling, how meaningless life seems, how bleak things look. I'm so sorry you're suffering like this."

"Promise you won't send the police," she says, reading my mood.

"How about if I promise that I won't and you promise not to give me reason to?"

She doesn't answer.

"Too much?" I ask.

"Yeah," she says. Kindly, not critically. Her tone says, We are in this together. "I just don't want to be alone right now . . . in these last minutes." I think she said minutes. Her voice dropped when she sniffled.

A hastily committed suicide, before all alternatives are exhausted, is the ultimate tragedy. I don't want Louise to miss the chance to recover and live happily.

"I'm worried about you," I say. "How about if I send someone over to be with you?" The tinkling of ice cubes against glass. I didn't realize she was drinking. She doesn't sound drunk, but the alcohol might give her the wrong kind of courage.

"I'm not at home," she says. "Anyway, it's too late for that. I put my coat on, but I don't need to, do I, to be warm when I fly?" She sounds wrung out, like she's giving up. "At least it won't hurt much."

"Won't hurt much?"

"I took a bunch of Tylenol."

My heart starts to pound, and with a huge effort at control I ask, "How much Tylenol did you take?"

"I don't know," she whines. "A bunch—enough."

It may not be much. She doesn't sound ill. The gorge is her

weapon, not the pills. But she may not know how dangerous an elixir Tylenol is—even a small overdose can do permanent damage to the liver, and a large one can be fatal. Taking them is one more preparatory act. That's it. I can't stand the risk any longer.

Without letting her hear, I notify the police to trace the call and accompany her to the hospital, where a doctor will give her yet another type of medication. She has tried eight different antidepressants over the past years, all mind-scrambling in their start-up phase, plagued with side effects, and, unfortunately, not effective in the landscape of her unique chemistry. But she has been willing to try them, God help her, and she has called tonight, with however faint a heart. The life-hungry part of her has phoned for help.

If she survives tonight, will she be afraid to call the next time? That may be a moot question. A trace can take hours and doesn't always work. She said she isn't home. On principle, to preserve a caller's anonymity, we don't have caller ID. Thus traces are laborious hit-or-miss events. We rarely initiate them.

"I'll stay with you." Which problem to focus on? Which section of the tunnel to drill windows in? Her job? Her family problems? Maybe her sense of isolation.

"You said no one would care if you died. But *I* would care."

"I bet you say that to all the callers," she says with coyness.

"Not so. You and I have had some good talks over the past few months."

"Yes," she says. "You've been swell. You've been my only friends. Well, not friends exactly. I mean, I'm just one of—"

"You'd be surprised how well you can get to know someone over the telephone. I bet you've gotten to know me a little, too, and the other counselors."

"Yes," she says, "I have, actually. *You* always sound so calm and even. You're a good person—patient, and kind, and strong."

"So are you. All those things."

"Strong? That's a good one. If you could see how weak I am . . ." Her voice trails away.

"Amazingly strong. Look how you've been fighting the torrents of depression—for years. That takes such courage. You've been working during that time, raising kids, surviving the nightmare of an ugly divorce. Okay, you've lost jobs, but you've picked yourself up and found new jobs. You've even found the time and energy and heart to do volunteer work and helped other people in trouble. You've been heroic. You're being strong tonight, calling us. Given how bad you're feeling, that takes real strength. I admire your courage."

"Admire?" she says, letting the word hover a long moment while she considers it. "You wouldn't want to live my life. It's only bad choices . . . except . . ." Sniffling.

"Death is always a possibility, but not the best."

"Do you know something about it I don't know?" she says with a morbid touch of sarcasm.

"Maybe so," I say gently. "It's hereditary, it's irreversible, and you don't need to keep a day free for it."

Silence. I can feel her thinking it over.

" 'Lonelier than life,' you said. Why don't we think of a few ways to help you solve that problem," I suggest.

"There aren't any."

"Sure there are." I list some ways for her to ease her loneliness— through classes, volunteer work, athletics, music, nature centers, city projects, and such. Not one appeals to her. I didn't think any would. Nonetheless I ask her to consider the list and arrange it in order of preference, "even though we'll agree that you're too tired and fed up to do any of them and they all sound bad anyway." Despite her strong resistance to each item, she goes through the motions of ranking them, and that distracts her a little. Arranging them in descending order, she objects to each one. But rummaging around in undesirable choices for the least undesirable opens a few tiny windows in her tunnel. And suicide is nowhere on the list.

"Will you hold on?" she asks abruptly. "There's someone at the door."

The police. That was fast—she must be at home after all. Maybe I didn't need to send them. And she'll be angry; she'll feel betrayed. She does. I hear her screaming at me, at the telephone, at the world. She calls me a liar, and she's right. The next voice I hear on the line is a policeman's, and I ask him about the Tylenol. He finds an empty bottle by the phone next to a glass redolent of alcohol. She's furious at me, but she does go with them to the hospital. Thank God for that.

Suppose the hospital releases her right away, and she heads straight for the gorge? Knowing and not knowing about callers, that's what gets to me. Maybe I could have calmed her and talked her round? Maybe someone else would have prevailed. Taking a large breath and letting it out slowly, I press my open palms against my face and laugh. Not a ha-ha laugh, a small sardonic one, the kind we save for the ridiculous, as I catch myself slipping into a familiar trap. I did fine. I did the best I could. Maybe the best anyone could tonight. Did I guess wrong about the extent of her lethality? Who's to say? Surely it's better to err on the side of caution. My next duty is to phone the hospital and alert a doctor to her imminent arrival, telling him of her emotional state, previous suicide attempts, and general psychiatric history. Not the details of our conversation or her life; she'll tell him those if she wishes.

She'll hate me, hate me, I think, as I get up stiffly and go to the kitchen for tea. Yes, but she'll be *alive* to hate me. Until the next time anyway, the next rock-bottom night when she longs to fly. Helping Louise survive is always an ordeal. Tonight she sounded even more determined and deathbound than usual. It was the right choice. I think.

Chapter 12

Before the Dawn

WITH three feet of snow on the ground, the streets look like a toboggan run. Seven snowstorms hit in a row this month, accompanied by sub-zero weather. Snow piles high on every roof, and huge waterfall-like icebergs cascade from the eaves. All over town the houses look tusked, part of a mammoth herd.

What a year it's been, I think as I sip a mug of tea. Each morning I've been studying the ways of squirrels, deer, birds, and other animals, whose struggles sometimes echo problems I find among humans at the crisis center later in the day. In both arenas I've tried to ease the suffering of the world a little, but I've also found a perspective on life that fascinates me.

At this crossroads it's possible to see the human world and the world of nature meet and become one. Observing the tumult, mysteries, grandeur of the seasons, the plight of animal families, and the crisis center emergencies, sometimes it feels as if I'm living in a novel, the setting of which is the sprawling, heavily haunted mansion of nature. Part of my mind lingers on the sometimes catastrophic phone calls I'm dealing with. Another part rejoices in the antics and struggles of the squirrels from day to day, from their aerial courtship and mating rituals to their warfare, from the schooling of their young to their frenetic and ingenious preparations for winter. Meanwhile, humans are gathering and preparing for winter, too, also schooling their young, courting and mating at considerable risk. What a marvel that these two realms of behavior exist at the same time in the same universe for essentially the same reasons. What a marvel that they differ in unique and prismatic ways.

I HURRY down to the crisis center, skidding along roads slick as silk. I tap the secret combination into the door lock, go in, and climb the stairs. Fred, the overnight counselor, is already awake, quietly doing write-ups at the desk. He looks scrunched up, sleepy-eyed, and boyish first thing in the morning. Fred and I chat amiably, and then he heads home to finish sleeping. The logbook reveals that it was a quiet night for him. Four hang-ups; one call from an anonymous female. The hang-ups came at regular intervals, just often enough to wake him every two or three hours throughout the night. Edward Scissorhands? Possibly.

As usual, I scan the bulletin board for notices, and a new postcard catches my eye. On one side is a reproduction of the Edward Hopper painting *Nighthawks,* in which three lonely souls sit drinking coffee in an overlit diner. Turning the card over, I find a neat, even handwriting, in blue ink, addressed to the agency: "I'm writing to thank whoever the counselor was I spoke with. . . ." Notes to SP frequently begin that way. But when the large open loops and rounded *d*'s mention the day and hour, my thoughts quicken. That was *my* shift. My eyes slide to the signature. It's from Louise, who has signed her real name.

Sitting down on the couch, I read the card carefully and learn that she went from the emergency room to a psychiatric hospital in Pennsylvania, where she spent three weeks "in palatial bedlam." When she returned to town, she met an acquaintance who volunteers for Displaced Homemakers; Louise discovered a genial group of people there and even took a paying job at the agency. A month later she's "finally in a good place," by which I know she means several terrains, including her job and her mood. She blesses the soul who "took my life in her hands that night," thanks us all for our good work, is just writing "to let you know what happened—I bet you don't hear very often." We don't.

Soon after 9:00 a.m. the phone rings. An older woman says, as if interrupted in midsentence, "Oh, I guess I'm just calling to hear a human voice." She sounds sad and tired. It's surprising how quickly a voice can reveal one's age. A low soprano, hers has thickened over the years and grown a little gravelly, but not wheezy or frail. She's in her early seventies, I'd guess.

"How are you feeling this morning?"

Voice breaking, she says, "Not so good. I've just had to pay the hospital bill. . . ." She struggles to hold her voice steady, even though she's crying.

In a softer voice I ask, "Hospital bill?"

Her voice catches a few times. "After my husband died," she says at last, "all these bills started arriving. He always paid them. I don't even know where the insurance coupons are, and then the bills arrive . . . the electric, the insurance, the car, the funeral home, the hospital, everything . . . and"—her voice dissolves into tears—"I remember so much."

"That must be painful. The bills are overwhelming in themselves, but worst of all, they keep reminding you of his death."

"Yes," she says, exhaling the word. "It was such a shock. He had a heart attack when we were out shopping at the mall. He just fell down dead. Collapsed. He fell so hard. The *sound.* I'll never forget that sound."

In the mall? I picture them walking hand in hand past the Hallmark card store, and her husband dropping like a big animal. "That must have been frightening for you."

"It was such a shock."

"When did he die?"

"Three months ago."

A fresh loss. "So there was the shock of his death, and now there are lots of aftershocks as the bills and paperwork come in?"

"Yes. I never learned how to do them." A familiar story. "It's so much. The car needs to be fixed. Dave always used to take care of that. I get his Social Security, but that's all, and it's been reduced now that he's gone."

"That's terrible. Your husband is gone, and they reduce your income?"

"It is terrible. I don't think there's enough to pay the telephone and electric this month. I've called them, and they've agreed to give me more time, but where will the money come from? And I'm so confused about things."

"Do you have family or close friends, perhaps, who can give you a hand getting through this tough time?"

"No. No one. My husband always said when we'd fight, 'You'll miss me when I'm gone!' And he was right. I do." She begins whimpering.

"It's really hard to have him gone, isn't it?"

"So hard."

"Is there a woman friend you can call to talk with a little?"

"Not really. He hated me to have people over. Dave wouldn't socialize at all. Now I don't have anyone." She sounds angry—angry at him but also angry at herself.

Another familiar pattern—men who keep visitors from the

house, discourage their wives from making friends, and leave behind widows with no community, no confidantes, nowhere to turn when they're feeling isolated and alone.

"Maybe this would be a good time to make some new friends," I suggest.

"Maybe."

"How would you feel about trying a support group of women who have also lost their husbands?"

"I called Displaced Homemakers," she says, "and they have a widows group meeting this Saturday. I was thinking about going but haven't made up my mind."

Good, she used her initiative. It's vital that I persuade her to go.

"A widows group—that sounds good. You'd meet other women there who understand what you're going through, and they might be able to give you some practical advice," I offer. "But it might also be a good place to meet some nice people, maybe make some new friends."

"Yeah. That sounds like a good idea. I'm going to go there."

Thank heavens for that. "There are a few days between now and then. What are you thinking of doing today?"

Quilting the days together with work, chores, decisions, appointments, phone calls, meals, hobbies, and family, we rarely worry how to make day become night. But for a number of our callers each day is a desert to be crossed inch by inch, and filling the gritty hours takes planning.

"I don't know," she says, crying, a small fright in her voice. "I have errands."

"Is there anything you can do to be good to yourself, anything comforting? Maybe stop for a cup of hot cocoa or tea somewhere?"

"I don't know if I can afford it. I know it's only pennies, but I just don't have anything right now. All these bills. I don't know how to cope."

"It sounds like it really feels overwhelming sometimes."

"It is. Sometimes—ha! all the time—it's just an avalanche. And I'm always thinking about Dave, about his just falling suddenly.

Everything reminds me. I can't seem to get on with my life. Or want to. I'm so confused, so worn out."

"I can hear what a tough time this is for you. It would be for anyone. What you're going through is normal. It takes time, and unfortunately, it really hurts."

"Is it normal to be this overwhelmed?"

That's what most people want to know when they're struck by grief. Is it normal to feel such extreme pain and despair, or am I just trapped in hell forever, with no way out and no control? Normalizing the pain reassures them a little.

"Yes, it is."

"That's good to hear. I thought I wasn't handling it very well."

"Everyone handles grief differently. There's no right way, no best way, no right amount of time. Eventually you'll find your own timetable."

"Calling you has been helping me get through," she says tearfully.

"It's tough going through a crisis like this alone," I say.

"It really is. You're never prepared. I don't know how to *be* anymore."

"To *be?*"

"Now that I'm on my own, without my husband."

I wonder if I can put what she's dreading into a more positive light. "Now that your life is changing and you have new responsibilities."

"Yes."

"It sounds like you've been handling quite a few of them."

"Oh, yes. That's kept me busy at least."

"And taught you new skills."

Laughing, she says, "And how! Never thought I'd be running the house, getting the car fixed—everything."

"How does it feel to know that you can do these things?"

"I'm surprised that I can. Hell, I'm amazed that I can. But it's just too much right now, all at once. And I still can't believe he's gone."

"It's still hard to believe, isn't it, a big shock, a big change in your life?"

"That's what it is." She sounds fearful.

"Have you got any tea you might make? Maybe listen to the radio for a minute or two? Or watch a movie? Maybe plan your trip to the support group on Saturday?"

"Yes, I could make some chamomile tea. I will go on Saturday. It's on Green Street. I'll park in the church lot."

"Would you like us to call you later, just to check in on you?"

"No," she says gratefully, "but thank you for offering. I'll be okay for a little while now, I think."

"Okay. Please do call back when you find you're having some trouble coping. This is hard to go through alone. We're here whenever you need to talk to someone."

After hanging up, I immediately call my mother and ask if she knows how to run the house, pay the bills, and so on. My father is eighty-six, and my mother has gradually allowed him to run the business of family life. He's very good at it and enjoys the responsibility, but she would be at sea if he were gone.

"Don't you think you should drive the car sometimes, just a little to keep in practice?" I suggest to her.

"Oh, your father drives everywhere. I don't need to, and the traffic down here scares me!"

The enclosed kingdom of their condo sits on a quiet street, at the end of which sprawls half a mile of shops. "How about just down to the mall at the end of the street, maybe to the grocery store and the drugstore? I mean, what if Dad were laid up sometime? You'd feel cut off, wouldn't you?"

Even though she understands my worry and agrees that it makes sense for her to learn how to run the house now while my father is alive to teach her, the possibility spooks her and she changes the subject. But at least I planted it in her thoughts.

10:06 a.m. A male caller stumbles awkwardly as he tries to convey his grave depression. Slowly I try to draw him out. He has lost his job of fifteen years and, with that, his income, his food, his self-esteem, and his reason for getting up each day. Little is left of his bedraggled sense of future. His work defined him, and now he feels no connection to society or life. For nearly an hour I concentrate on the man, his story, his pain.

When we hang up, a call comes in from the next counselor on shift, who has a crisis of her own—a chest pain she's convinced is nothing more than a hiatal hernia or a muscle spasm. But her daughter is going to drive her to the doctor for an EKG just to make sure. I agree to stay a little later.

12:05 p.m. A call comes from a frequent caller with an erotic obsession. He tries to trick counselors into saying the word prick as often as possible. A conversation might begin with his saying, "I feel like such a prick today."

"Why do you feel that way today?" I'll ask.

"What way?" he'll inquire, hoping I'll say back to him, "Like a prick." I never do, and that annoys him, so he continues trying to trap me, and when that fails, he angrily accuses me of being inhibited and prim, the source of all of society's troubles.

1:00 p.m. An Owego woman calls who says she's been drinking heavily and is probably drunk, but she doesn't sound it. She does sound convincingly suicidal, though, and I discover she has attempted suicide twice before and knows that she's right at the edge, close to the no-turning-back point. Her husband died three years ago in a mining accident. Her two children (ages four and six) were taken away from her after her last suicide attempt and put in the custody of their grandparents, with the understanding that she could regularly visit them. But her new husband won't allow her to see them. She says he wants her full attention and is jealous of the children. He also insists on always knowing her whereabouts, and he polices her. Before I ask, she says emphatically that he doesn't hit her, and the way she says it, defending him, sounds suspicious. But at the moment she is her own would-be assassin.

When I ask if she has a plan, she reveals that she's holding a bottle of Valium and means to swallow them all. They're what she OD'd on before. Even though she sounds sober, the alcohol is a wild card. I need her address, and it would be best if she gave it to me, but she's frightened of her husband's temper. He has threatened "to O.J." her. She is terrified of his rage if he finds out she phoned. So terrified that dying seems preferable.

For a while we tussle with words in a gentle tug-of-war as she insists she's in a quagmire and I keep suggesting ways to climb out of it. Her young children need her, she moans. They need their mother. But how can she leave her lover? A sip at something. She vacillates between swallowing the pills or accepting help. At last she agrees to go to the hospital. When I offer to send the police to escort her, she hesitates so long I'm afraid she may be taking the pills after all, but then she says all right and gives me her name—Marjorie—address, and phone number. Instantly she regrets it. Her husband will be furious.

Using the other phone, I call her local police, explaining telegraphically, "I'm a counselor at Suicide Prevention. I have a woman on the phone who has been drinking heavily and who is extremely suicidal. She needs to go to the hospital right away. Could you possibly transport her there?" They're eager to help. Then I keep talking with Marjorie. When the police car arrives, I wish her luck, say good-bye, and call the hospital to tell the emergency room and the mental health unit of her imminent arrival.

When the business line rings, an Officer Randal from Owego asks for me by the counselor number I gave his dispatcher. He was the officer who escorted Marjorie to the hospital. Because it's a small town, he knows a mutual friend who says her husband was beating her up—but he couldn't see any obvious signs of abuse. What do I think? I think it's likely, but she didn't confess abuse to me. The officer is still at the hospital, where the husband arrived mad and nasty. It's clear Randal wishes he could bust him.

Finding my voice familiar, the officer asks if we might have met at an After Suicide group. No, I answer, and ask what took him to that meeting. His mother-in-law attended for a while, he explains, and he drove her there, but he doesn't say why, and I decide not to pry. Owego . . . Owego . . . I search my memory for a suicide in Owego. After we hang up, I do remember, and it was a horrible death. A young woman, despondent when her boyfriend jilted her, shot herself in the head in her boyfriend's driveway. I read about it some months ago in the newspapers. Officer Randal was her brother-in-law.

Walking over to the window, I pull aside the blinds and look out. After a death, quiet is the greatest horror, the fact that the world doesn't stop, the sky doesn't split open. Instead, the world goes on its green, evitable way. But priorities arrange themselves automatically. The calendar begins filling in its own pages. I'm not surprised Officer Randal phoned us, unable to let the incident go or chalk it up as a simple police event on a snowy evening. The first time around, when the comet of desperation passed through his own family, he missed sight of it. But now he's only too aware of the trajectory Marjorie's life seems to be taking and wishes he could do something, somewhere, somehow, some way to help her change course. It won't bring back his wife's young sister, but long after a suicide, survivors continue to wage a war with their guilt, and sometimes with destiny.

4:00 p.m. The phone rings, and before I've finished saying, "Suicide Prevention and Crisis Service," a hysterical young woman gushes about a suicidal male friend who has been visiting her for the weekend.

"I don't know what to do!" she cries. "He's just run out of the house, and I think he's going to kill himself. I think he's going to jump off a bridge. What should I do?" she says, almost screaming.

"What happened?" I ask firmly.

She gives me a fast summary. For days he's been hideously depressed, crying and in a death trance, insisting that she alone can save him—not through talk or concern, but by allowing him somehow to attach his life to hers. Curled up in a corner of her dorm room, he would cry for hours on end, eat nothing, and sleep little. She hasn't slept a wink either. He kept insisting his life lay in her hands; his death would be her fault. But he wouldn't respond to entreaties, wouldn't let her take him to the hospital or to the Mental Health Clinic. He's a high school student from her hometown in Vermont, who drove in for the weekend, supposedly to check out the college. Although the boy sounds as if he's in horrible pain, I don't know him and can't reach him. The caller is my client. So I begin working with her as I would in any second-party call.

"I can hear what a nightmare this is for you. It's hard enough trying to cope with school without something like this happening."

He left a note, and she's frightened he may be heading for a bridge, but she's not sure, because she also thinks he may just be playing a mind game with her. I'm not sure either, and after all, she is my caller. Too agitated to hear, she waves aside my concern. She starts to repeat her story again, which isn't an unusual thing for a caller to do, but this time she includes one more small fact.

"He left a note, took off his watch and put it next to the note, and then he just ran out of the building. I read the note and ran after him, but I couldn't find him. What should I do?"

"He took off his watch? He left his watch?" I ask.

"Yes," she says.

The watch hits me like a sledgehammer. He intends to stop time. I believe the boy is going to kill himself right now. Everything changes.

"Okay. I want you to phone the police immediately and give them his description and tell them to go to all the bridges. Call them right now. Then call me back."

Will she call back? Will the boy survive? What will happen to *her* if he doesn't? I feel utterly helpless. Should I have called the police for her? No. I didn't know what the boy looks like or where he might have gone; and if this ends well, knowing that she took charge will help her recover. But if it doesn't end well? I collapse on the daybed. All I can do is wait.

There isn't enough air in the room. Walking over to the window again, I open it wide and stare out at the street, where snow glimmers like silk in moonlight, then over to the campus—a picture postcard of snowbanks, stone buildings, and slate roofs. Who would guess the invisible suffering of the visible world? Somewhere in that landscape a teenage boy is dissolving his life and a teenage girl is fighting to save him. He's so young. Last year over a million teens made suicide attempts. Reported ones, that is. Experts say the real figure may be three times that many. A million children in agony. Not all of them lucky enough to be found in time or accidentally live through it.

Twenty minutes of silence pass; then the phone rings with such a clang I jump. The girl, calling back as she promised. She contacted the police, who immediately dispatched a squad car and two officers, who found the boy! Although she has no details, she says they took him to a hospital for evaluation. The county hospital across the lake? She doesn't know. The police only told her that they'd found him and need her to stop by their office to fill in various details.

Thank heavens. We continue talking, this time about how traumatic the weekend has been for her, how frightening it was to watch her friend literally climbing the walls, continuously demanding from her but not being able to talk with her. He said that his parents hate him, ignore him for weeks on end, and wouldn't care if he lived or died. She is his only lifeline. Meanwhile, she has prelims tomorrow. She is only eighteen, a freshman. It is her first time away from home. School is demanding enough.

I suggest she talk with her professor about taking tomorrow's prelims later in the week. Now the toughest part. I need her to go to the Mental Health Clinic to see a therapist for her own distress. She refuses, says she'll be fine, doesn't need psychiatric help. I know that she won't be fine if she doesn't get help. A sly tactic is needed, so I propose that she talk to someone at the clinic about a strategy for dealing with her friend in the future. I'm not a therapist, I explain. I can't advise her on the best way to handle him if he does this again, and it would be helpful to have a plan. She agrees. Before she goes, I tell her how wonderfully she has handled this emergency, with great presence of mind, and she should be proud of herself. In a quiet voice she admits she did handle everything well. It surprises her. Does she have a confidante in her dorm? She does. I don't imagine she'll be calling us back, but if she relies on her friend and goes to the clinic for counseling, she'll probably be fine.

Even though the emergency is over, my heart keeps racing, my adrenaline keeps pounding, and my body can't seem to accept that peace has been declared and all is calm again. Strained hours pass without a call. When I look up, I'm startled to see a man with a crew cut wearing a state police uniform, a gun, and a badge. I didn't hear anyone walk in, and I didn't know we had a state trooper as a counselor. What he reveals stuns me.

"I was the one who found the fifteen-year-old," he says. "He's okay. In the hospital. His mother is flying in. But when we found him, man, was it tense! Two of us were in the squad car, and we could see a boy fitting his description climbing onto the bridge, but we were stuck at a light a block away. We were afraid that if we put our siren on, he'd jump. So we sat there for what seemed forever, and then we rushed across to him and jumped out of the car. But by that time he had one leg over the rail, and we had to drag him off of it. Man, did he fight us! He kept trying to jump. Thirty seconds more and he would have been gone. Great work!" He shakes my hand. "Great work!" He points to my chest at heart level and whispers, "You did it. *You* did it. Great work!"

One foot over the rail. Thirty seconds later, and he would have been gone. A fifteen-year-old. And only a few hours before, the woman in Owego. My eyes fill with tears of fright and fulfillment. What if I had known there was only a window of less than thirty seconds? A chill soaks through me. I would have been petrified. Yet two troubled, complicated, pained people now have a second chance. With any luck, both will turn their lives around. We rarely learn the outcome of our calls, but today, grace has delivered to me two officers with shining news.

The state trooper, Ben, goes on to say that when he had the coed come in to advise them about her friend's parents, background, and so on, he took the opportunity to counsel her for an hour. She didn't know he was an SP counselor. Then he called in a therapist who is also one of our support group leaders. The student will be taken care of; a support system has been put in place for her. When this officer took the boy to the hospital, talking during the drive over and while waiting in the emergency room, they bonded enough that the boy settled down some, said that he wanted to live, and thanked the officer for saving his life.

"They're only children," he says, his face tense and upset.

We both marvel that the system worked again, the training worked. We learn it piece by piece and are still amazed when all the pieces fit together and lives are saved.

"You did it," he says again as he stands up to leave, and shaking his hand firmly, joyously, I reply, "We both did."

With a wave of the hand he leaves for his evening rounds. I thought I knew most of the crew, but not Ben with his gun and badge, a secret counselor, a sorrow ranger.

"WANT something to eat?" a voice behind me asks. I hadn't realized that Barbara was sitting on the couch. So much for listening skills—I didn't hear her walk in. A glance at the clock. Ben left twenty minutes ago. I have no idea what I was thinking or doing since then. Time simply evaporated.

"How about moon on the half shell and a side order of stars?" I say wearily as I get up and crawl into an ankle-length down coat.

"I see," she says, laughing. "Another busy evening on planet Earth, huh?"

"Yes, indeed." When she reads my write-ups, she'll see.

Outside, I drink in long, strong drafts of cold air as if it were the rarest thing in the world. As I drive home through the tunnels of the night, my eyes keep tearing. The moment I walk in the door at home, the phone rings—one of the counselors heard what happened, asks if I need to talk. It's one of the strengths of the agency, how attuned people are to the trials of the job and counselors' needs. My support group meets next week; I'll pour out my emotions then. Or tonight over dinner with Paul, although I can't tell him the details. Or after dinner, when Cathy and I set out on our long-awaited sublunar trek.

AT 8:00 P.M. Cathy and I rendezvous at the golf course with our cross-country skis. The moon is full and blazing. Mars is up, too; nearby, the moon and also Venus. But the brightest spark in the sky is Sirius, a blue-white star loud as an outcry.

On the golf course the moonscape looks like a meringue hardened into craters. I've brought along a boom box and a tape of Beethoven's "Moonlight" sonata, and when we're all set to ski, I set the boom box on the hood of my car, turn the volume up high, and we glide away across the pastures of ice as the melodies rinse the cold air with lushness. The moon showers an eerie fluorescence over everything and casts long shadows. For some reason I've never noticed moon shadows before, but they're even more precise than sun shadows. Every turn I make, a shadow swivels and glides behind me. I cannot escape them, but I can influence their path.

After an hour or so, we grow too cold to ski and return to the car to find the boom box slurring sound, its batteries stricken. No matter. Climbing into Cathy's car, we turn the heat on, pop the tape into the tape deck, and continue our full-moon concert while drinking from thermoses of hot chocolate and eating chocolate cookies.

One of Cathy's clients checked himself into the hospital's psychiatric unit last night, and she's happy he took control of his life. I share my temporary relief about Louise and tell her of the afternoon's two rescues and how disturbed by them I still feel. Although our counselors have saved many people over the years, two rescues on one shift is rare. Something about those thirty seconds, so flimsy a tightrope, so narrow a filament of time, and yet life or death hangs by it. Barbara was right. It has been a busy day on planet Earth. A busy year. Almost everything dangerous or poignant that can happen to human beings has prompted a call to SP in the past year. I've encountered a pageant of human hopes, terrors, and predicaments. It's been like sitting in a chair in the middle of a war zone.

Over two hundred branches of SP receive calls from millions of people every year. Callers confide the most intimate details of their lives, the most desperate moments, the most shameful acts. And counselors listen to their stories, validate their pain, try to help them. Most of these events happen without the townspeople noticing, while babies are being born, gardens being planted, people cursing or blessing their bosses, and every family's Joan or John speaking a first word or packing for college. When we think of a town's personality, we focus on its gleaming, face-to-the-world demeanor and don't include its struggles, frustrations, darker facets, and hidden networks. But, as I now understand, many of the people I pass on the street work secretly with the center, have counseled there in the past, or use our crisis line and other services.

My arms ache, as if a year's worth of calls has accumulated in my bones. I feel shot through with every caliber of fatigue. But also satisfied. The planet is full of hurt people, angry people, lost people, confused people, people who have explored the vast cartography of trouble, and people stunned by a sudden grief. Someone has to help them, and so we become our brothers' allies, if not their keepers. We nourish them, and they inadvertently nourish us. The minute one imagines oneself in the victim's predicament and moves to save him or her, it becomes an act of self-love. Outside, the night is a coliseum of stars. For a few moments I sit and just behold those distant worlds—each one trembling, beautiful, and full of drama. Tonight they look closer than ever, and the darkness seems to burn with their small, urgent lights.

THE RUN

Jeffrey Toobin

OF HIS LIFE

The People
v.
O. J. Simpson

. . . "This morning," Gascon said, his voice unsteady, "detectives from the Los Angeles Police Department sought and obtained a warrant for the arrest of O. J. Simpson, charging him with the murders of Nicole Brown Simpson and Ronald Lyle Goldman.

"Mr. Simpson was scheduled to surrender this morning to the Los Angeles Police Department. Mr. Simpson has not appeared."

The room stirred.

"The Los Angeles Police Department right now is actively searching for Mr. Simpson."

An experienced group of reporters were gathered, yet none of them could recall having heard the sound they issued at that moment: a sort of collective gasp. And then one journalist, name lost to history, let out a long and very astonished whistle.

"Mr. Simpson is out there somewhere," Gascon said, "and we will find him."

—*The Run of His Life*

Prologue

ONE after another the Jaguars, the BMWs, and the odd Porsche pulled off the Avenue of the Stars and slipped into the nearly deserted underground parking garage. The owners of these cars, about two dozen of the top lawyers in West Los Angeles, greeted each other with slightly embarrassed smiles. All white, virtually all men, and mostly in their early fifties, they reflected the culture in which they had thrived, one where workaholism was no virtue and a weekend in the office anathema. Yet here they were on a glorious summer Saturday afternoon, June 25, 1994, forsaking golf and family for a meeting in a Century City tower. They came because everyone wanted a piece of this case—the defense of Orenthal James Simpson against charges that he had murdered his ex-wife Nicole and her friend Ronald Goldman.

Besides, they came because Robert Shapiro, Simpson's lead lawyer, had asked for their help. Many of these attorneys, who were among those closest to Shapiro, never knew precisely what to make of their friend. They could quickly catalogue his faults: his outsize ego, his self-obsession, his excessive comfort with the moral ambiguities of his profession. They chuckled at his endless socializing. But so, too, these lawyers knew another side of Shapiro, that of the generous friend. When the Internal Revenue Service had begun investigating scores of professional athletes for evading taxes on income made from appearing at autograph shows, many had come running to Shapiro for assistance. He in turn had referred much of this business to his friends. They remembered that. So they answered his call.

After the lawyers had settled around a large oval conference table, Shapiro began the proceedings with a question.

"So," he said, "how many of you think O.J. did it?"

Everyone froze. After a moment a few lawyers chuckled nervously and others rolled their eyes. In a flash Shapiro had brought home just how strange this meeting was. Defense lawyers talk to each other about their clients all the time, often with brutal candor—guilt is a given. But these cases are usually unknown to the public. Shapiro was talking about what was becoming the most sensational legal proceeding in American history. This was not the kind of question—or so it seemed—that an experienced defense attorney would want answered in a quasi-public setting. Shapiro, however, had no more illusions about this client than any other. The spotlight would never blind him to reality.

After his initial query brought only awkward silence, Shapiro moved quickly to introduce two of the guests—Skip Taft and Robert Kardashian. They were lawyers, too, but that wasn't the point. Taft was O. J. Simpson's business manager, the man who would decide, among other things, how much Shapiro would be paid. Kardashian had known Simpson for thirty years and had emerged as the defendant's closest friend and adviser. It was for them that Shapiro had assembled this show of legal strength.

Almost everyone else knew one another. There was Roger Cossack, who had pledged with Shapiro to the Zeta Beta Tau fraternity at U.C.L.A. in the early 1960s and who was to become CNN's local expert on the trial. Another of Shapiro's ZBT brothers, Mike Nasatir, was there, too, along with his longtime partner, Richard Hirsch. (About fifteen years earlier, the partners had employed a Southwestern University law student by the name of Marcia Kleks as an intern. She later married Gordon Clark and took his name.) When prosecutors began examining Kardashian's behavior in the aftermath of the murders, he hired one attendee, Alvin

Michaelson, as his attorney. When Shapiro was later sued for libel in connection with the Simpson case, he asked another attendee, Larry Feldman, to represent him. Johnnie Cochran, who was not part of Shapiro's social set, was not invited.

Though Shapiro was pleased to have collected all these fine lawyers together, he didn't listen much to what they had to say. Shapiro's confidence was astonishing: O. J. Simpson, he vowed, would go to trial and be acquitted. Shapiro was caught up short only once. Michael Baden, the medical examiner whom Shapiro had retained as an expert in the case, mentioned at the meeting that the autopsy results on the victims showed the possibility that more than one person had killed Nicole and Ron. Robert Shapiro paused to consider the implications. "So," he asked the group, "that means O.J. and who else did it?"

This remark, too, drew stunned silence, and the meeting soon broke up.

JOHNNIE L. Cochran, Jr., loved appearing on *Nightline*—as well as the *Today* show, the *CBS Evening News,* and the *NBC Nightly News.* In the days immediately after the murders in Brentwood he did them all, and the programs' producers were happy to have him, too. Cochran was a poised, accomplished, telegenic African American lawyer, the answer to a network booker's dreams. The *Today* show even made him a paid consultant.

As it happened, on the evening of June 17, 1994—the day Al Cowlings led the nation on the low-speed chase down the Los Angeles freeways—Cochran was booked to analyze the events of the day on *Nightline.* Though viewers never knew it, Cochran was a friend of O. J. Simpson's—not an intimate confidant, but certainly a long-term acquaintance. On the air Cochran was only mildly pro-defense. His comment was typical: "I think that the important thing for all Americans to understand is that this is a tragic, tragic case, but at this point he's still presumed to be innocent."

Off-camera, though, Cochran, like Shapiro, could afford to be more blunt. For example, during a break in that June 17 broadcast Cochran sized up the situation very differently. "O.J. is in massive denial," he told a friend. "He obviously did it. He should do a diminished-capacity plea, and he might have a chance to get out in a reasonable amount of time."

But in the days to come, Cochran learned that the defendant had no interest in pleading guilty. Simpson wanted to go to trial and win—and he wanted Cochran to represent him. The lawyer was torn. He enjoyed the broadcasting work, and the money wasn't bad, either. But how could he turn down what was shaping up to be the trial of the century? After the preliminary hearing ended on July 8 and Simpson was ordered to stand trial in sixty days, Cochran knew he had to make up his mind. The upside wasn't difficult to recognize. Any trial lawyer would relish the chance to perform in front of the biggest audience in American legal history. The downside, as Cochran explained to a colleague, was simple. "The case," said Cochran, "is a loser."

OF COURSE they knew.

Of course Robert Shapiro and Johnnie Cochran knew from the start what any reasonably attentive student of the murders of Nicole Brown Simpson and Ronald Lyle Goldman could see—that O. J. Simpson was guilty of killing them. Their dilemma, then, was the oldest, as well as the most common, quandary of the criminal defense attorney: what to do about a guilty client.

The answer, they decided, was race. Because of the overwhelming evidence of Simpson's guilt, his lawyers could not undertake a defense aimed at proving that some other person had committed the murders. Instead, in an astonishing act of legal bravado, they posited that Simpson was the victim of a wide-ranging conspiracy of racist law-enforcement officials who had fabricated and planted evidence in order to frame him for a crime he did not commit. It was also, of course, an obscene parody of an authentic civil rights struggle, for this one pitted a guilty "victim" against innocent "perpetrators."

These conclusions are the result of more than two years of reporting on the Simpson case. The week after the murders I was assigned to cover the story for *The New Yorker* magazine. In addition to attending Simpson's trial, I interviewed more than two hundred people, many of them repeatedly. I have had access to the full documentary record of the case—including internal memorandums of both the prosecution and the defense teams; advice provided by jury consultants to both the prosecution and the defense; the LAPD "murder book," with its summaries of all interviews with witnesses; the written summaries of all witness interviews by members of the defense team; heretofore secret grand jury testimony; and depositions from the then pending civil case against Simpson. I have also reviewed the enormous coverage of the case in the news media, an especially important task in the context of this case.

Indeed, the heart of the defense strategy featured an effort at shaping the news—the creation of a counternarrative based on the idea of a police conspiracy to frame Simpson. For this effort the defense needed a receptive audience, which it most definitely had in the African Americans who dominated the jury pool in downtown Los Angeles. The defense sought to identify the Simpson case as the latest in a series of racial abuses by the Los Angeles Police Department. As the events of the case unfolded, the LAPD more than lived up to its reputation as one of the worst big-city police departments in the United States, one that tolerated sloth, incompetence, and racism. As it happened, though, bad as the LAPD was, it did not frame O. J. Simpson.

It is ultimately unknowable whether a brilliant effort by prosecutors in the Simpson case could have produced a conviction in spite of the defense effort to make the case a racial referendum. There was, alas, no such splendid performance by the Los Angeles District Attorney's Office. The prosecutors were undone by the twin afflictions most common among government lawyers—arrogance (mostly Marcia Clark's) and ineptitude (largely Christopher Darden's)—and squandered what little chance they had for victory.

At its core the Simpson case was a horrific yet routine domestic-violence homicide. It metastasized into a national drama that exposed deep fissures in American society for one reason: The defendant's lawyers thought that using race would help their client win an acquittal. It did. That was all that mattered to them.

1

THE geographic spine of Brentwood—indeed, the spine of wealthy West Los Angeles—is legendary Sunset Boulevard. From the city's forlorn downtown it passes through the honky-tonk precincts of Hollywood and then moves, ever upscale, through Beverly Hills and on to Bel Air. When Sunset then crosses the San Diego Freeway, the air clears—literally. The next community is Brentwood, where ocean breezes scrub the pervasive smog from the sky. Big houses have always been the rule in Brentwood, though it is a less showy neighborhood than Hollywood Hills or Beverly Hills.

North of Sunset, sometimes called Brentwood Park, is better than south in real estate terms. On February 23, 1977, O. J. Simpson bought a house on a prime corner lot at 360 North Rockingham for $650,000 (the house was probably worth about $4 million in 1996): six thousand square feet in a timber-and-stone frame, with an adjoining pool and tennis court. A six-foot-tall brick wall protects the owner's privacy. Some of Simpson's monthly expenses, as revealed in his 1992 divorce from Nicole, give a sense of the scale of the place: $13,488 annually for utilities, $10,129 for gardening, and $4371 for "Pool–Tennis Court Services."

Nicole lived with O.J. in the Rockingham house for more than a decade, but when they separated in February 1992, there was never any doubt that the house was his. So Nicole and the two children moved to nearby 325 Gretna Green Way, on the southern side of Sunset.

As their divorce litigation went forward in 1992, it became clear that Nicole had many years earlier made herself a hostage to O.J.'s fortunes. "I spend my time caring for my two young children," she declared in an affidavit. Her attorneys wrote in a brief that as a teenager, around the time she met Simpson, Nicole "worked as a waitress for two months. Prior to that she worked as a salesclerk in a boutique for a total of two weeks. These two jobs are the sum total of her employment experience." In a court-ordered meeting

O. J. and Nicole Brown Simpson in 1989

with a vocational counselor, Nicole described herself as a "party animal" and said her personal goals were "to raise my kids as best I can; beyond that I haven't thought about me." She added, "I'm sure I will get a goal someday."

O.J. and Nicole's divorce was settled without a trial. On October 15, 1992, the parties agreed that O.J., whose after-tax income amounted to $55,000 monthly, would pay Nicole $10,000 a month in child support. Nicole kept title to a rent-producing condominium in San Francisco, and O.J. agreed to make a onetime payment to her of $433,750. "It is the intent of the parties," the settlement stated, "that a substantial portion of this sum shall be used by [Nicole] for the acquisition of a residence."

Nicole quickly developed a close friendship with real estate agent Jeane McKenna, who had been a broker in Brentwood since 1978. When the two women met in October 1993, McKenna learned that Nicole had been divorced for about a year. After a period of on-and-off reconciliations with O.J. she was finally ready to buy her own place, and as it turned out, McKenna had just what Nicole wanted.

Jeane McKenna used to refer to 875 South Bundy Drive as her "career listing"—the house she couldn't sell. Bundy is the main north-south artery of Brentwood, a noisy, traffic-filled thoroughfare. McKenna's property, the north side of a two-family condominium building, had had a FOR SALE sign in front of it for more than six months when she received a call from Nicole. The three-story condo did have its advantages. It was modern, built in 1991, and it had a two-story living room, skylights, and an assortment of high-end accoutrements, including a Jacuzzi. Nicole liked the condo, in part because of its location near a school. She wanted to be close to a playground because her children would no longer have a yard.

In January 1994 Nicole and her children moved into the Bundy condominium. Her relationship with O.J. oscillated between reconciliation and a final breach, and the financial tensions between them escalated until May 1994, when O.J. and Nicole's final attempt at a reconciliation ended. Nicole then called Jeane McKenna and said they would have to move out because O.J. was threatening to report her to the IRS.

Nicole had sold her rental property in San Francisco and invested the proceeds in the home on Bundy, but she apparently told the IRS that the new place was also a rental property. So she avoided tax on the initial sale. For tax purposes she kept Rockingham as her official residence. Around Memorial Day, O.J. told her that he would no longer permit her to use his address. "He's threatening to tell the IRS that I'm living in Bundy," Nicole told McKenna. Legally, O.J. seems to have had a point, but in the entry in her diary for June 3 Nicole quoted the exact words of O.J.'s threat: "You hang up on me last nite, you're gonna pay for this bitch, you're going to jail you f____ c___. You think you can do any f____ thing you want, you've got it comming—I've already talked to my lawyers about this bitch—they'll get you for tax evasion, bitch, I'll see to it. You're not going to have a dime left bitch etc."

On Monday, June 6, O.J. delivered on his threat in a formal letter that began, "Dear Nicole, On advice of legal counsel, and because of the change in our circumstances, I am compelled to put you on written notice that you do not have my permission to use my permanent home address at 360 North Rockingham as your residence or mailing address for any purpose." Not surprisingly, Nicole was horrified by the prospect of being forced to move out of Bundy less than six months after she had moved in. The next day she showed the letter to a friend. She also telephoned the Sojourn shelter for battered women in Santa Monica to report that she was being stalked by O.J.

On Thursday, June 9, on Nicole's instructions, McKenna officially put 875 South Bundy up for lease, asking $4800 a month. "Drop dead gorgeous 1991 townhome in the heart of Brentwood" was how McKenna described the property in the listing.

The following morning Nicole spoke with her friend Ron Hardy, a bartender and host at several Los Angeles nightspots. Nicole explained that she was just about to leave to go look at houses with McKenna. "She was happy," Hardy later recalled. "She said everything's great; she hadn't felt this good in a while. She felt that she had finally put O.J. behind her."

Nicole then spent the rest of the day with McKenna, seeking a place to lease. "We found a place for her in Malibu," McKenna later recalled, "a one-story contemporary with a pool and a view of the ocean, for five thousand a month. I remember walking up the hill there with her and she was saying, like she couldn't really believe it, 'I can really do this. I can lease the house and move.' "

Nicole called McKenna on Saturday night to ask when the FOR LEASE sign would go up in front of her condo. "She was anxious to have it up," McKenna said, "because she wanted to get on with her life, but also because she wanted O.J. to see it." As it turned out, McKenna was then in the process of switching real estate agencies, so she couldn't locate an appropriate sign until the following day, Sunday, June 12. She was going to a dinner party Sunday evening and figured she would put it up at Nicole's afterward. Later, as she was driving home, she had to decide which way she was going to turn on Bundy. "I lived north on Bundy, and she lived south," McKenna recalled. "I remember looking at the clock in my car when I hit the intersection of Bundy and San Vicente. It was ten fifteen. It would have taken me five minutes to get to her house. I said, 'Screw it. I'll do it tomorrow.' "

PABLO Fenjves, a screenwriter, and his wife, Jai, a costume designer, lived about sixty yards north of Nicole Simpson's condominium. Both Nicole's and Fenjves's back doors opened onto the same alley, though they had never met.

Sometime after 10:00 on the night of June 12 Pablo and Jai began to hear from their bedroom the sound of a dog barking. The actual time, Pablo later testified, was right around 10:15. Pablo walked downstairs to his study to fiddle with a script. Shortly before 11:00 he walked back up to the bedroom, and the barking had still not stopped. Fenjves remembered the sound because it was not the ordinary chatter of a neighborhood dog, but like "a plaintive wail," he later testified, "like a, you know, very unhappy animal."

Pablo Fenjves was not the only neighbor who heard Nicole's grief-stricken Akita in the moments after 10:15. Steven Schwab, who lived in an apartment on Montana Avenue, about three blocks from Nicole, was a man of extremely regular habits. He watched reruns of *The Dick Van Dyke Show* seven nights a week. On June 12, 1994, he set out with his dog, Sherry, shortly after his favorite program ended at 10:30 p.m.

Schwab walked his regular route around the neighborhood, a circuit that he designed to take about a half hour. At about 10:55, when he passed the alley behind Nicole's home, Schwab saw something unusual: a beautiful white Akita barking at a house. It paused to look at Schwab and then barked at the house again. Curious and a little worried about the animal, Schwab approached the dog, let it sniff him, and examined its collar. He noticed that the collar was expensive, but it did not give a name or address. As he studied the dog more carefully, Schwab noticed something else. There was blood on all four of the animal's paws.

Schwab couldn't figure out where the dog belonged, so he just headed home. The Akita followed him. Schwab made it home shortly after 11:00, just after *The Mary Tyler Moore Show* had begun.

While Schwab and his wife pondered what to do about the dog, which waited patiently outside their apartment, they gave it some water. At about 11:40 p.m. the Schwabs' neighbor Sukru Boztepe walked into the apartment complex. They chatted for a few minutes, and Boztepe agreed that he and his wife, Bettina Rasmussen, would keep the dog for the night. But when they took it inside, Boztepe later testified, the "dog was acting so nervous, we decided to take the dog for a walk." They let the Akita lead them, and the dog pulled them back toward Bundy Drive. "It was getting more nervous, and it was pulling me harder." Just after midnight the dog stopped in front of a gate on Bundy labeled 875. Boztepe remembered that the area was so dark that he never would have looked down the pathway behind the gate if the dog had not called his attention to it.

What did he see there? "I saw a lady laying down full of blood."

OFFICER Robert Riske of the Los Angeles Police Department was patrolling West Los Angeles in a squad car when his radio summoned him at 12:09 a.m. on June 13 to South Bundy, in Brentwood. Four minutes later Riske rolled up to the scene and found Boztepe and Rasmussen still tending to the Akita. Boztepe showed Riske the pathway to Number 875. The officer shone his flashlight on the corpse of Nicole Brown Simpson.

Nicole was lying at the base of four stairs that led up to a landing and the front door. The pool of blood around her was bigger than she was. Blood covered much of the walkway leading to the stairs. When Riske pointed his flashlight to the right, he saw another body. It was a muscular young man with his shirt pulled up over his head. The man, later identified as Ronald Goldman, was slumped against the metal fence that separated 875 from the property next door. Near Goldman's feet Riske identified three items: a black hat, a white envelope stained with blood, and a leather glove. Turning back to Nicole, Riske made out a single fresh heel print in the blood next to her body. Despite all the blood, there were no bloody shoe prints coming out the front gate.

Careful not to make tracks in the blood, Riske tiptoed past Nicole's body and up to the landing. From the landing he shone his flashlight on a walkway that stretched the entire northern length of the property. Along this corridor Riske saw a single set of bloody shoe prints. It appeared that the killer had gone out the back way to the alley that Nicole shared with Pablo Fenjves and

Ronald Goldman

other neighbors. On closer inspection Riske noticed fresh drops of blood to the left of those shoe prints. While leaving the scene, the killer might well have been bleeding from the left hand.

The front door to 875 South Bundy was open. Riske walked in to a scene of domestic calm. No signs of ransacking or theft. Candles flickered in the living room. The officer walked up the stairs. There were lighted candles in the master bedroom and bath, and the tub there was full of water. There were two other bedrooms, with a young girl asleep in one and a younger boy in the other.

Once Riske had identified the dead and closed off access to the scene, his only responsibility was to summon the investigators, who would begin looking for clues. As he prepared to call for assistance on his "rover," a portable walkie-talkie, he noticed a letter on the front hall table. The return address indicated that it was from O. J. Simpson. The former football star was also depicted in a poster on the wall, and Riske found photographs of Simpson among the family pictures scattered on tables.

Riske decided to call for help on the telephone. As he testified later, "I didn't want to broadcast over my rover that there was a possible double homicide involving a celebrity." Reporters monitored the police bands, and if he had used his rover, he said, "the media would beat my backup there."

So at 12:30 a.m. on June 13 Officer Riske telephoned his supervisor, David Rossi, the sergeant in charge of the West Los Angeles station at the time. Rossi promptly made a half-dozen phone calls around the LAPD chain of command, setting in motion the police response to the crimes. In an ordinary case, even a homicide, Rossi would probably have made only two calls—to the detective on duty, who would investigate the scene, and to his own commander. But Rossi's supervisor immediately told him to go higher in the command structure because of, as Rossi later put it, "the possible notoriety of this particular incident."

A steady stream of officers began converging on the murder scene. Sergeant Marty Coon was the first supervisor to arrive. Additional officers came to make sure no one passed through the yellow crime-scene tape. A squad car arrived to take the two children to the West L.A. station, and two more officers began walking through the alley, searching garbage pails for possible evidence and knocking on doors to find witnesses. By the time Rossi arrived at 1:30 a.m., the scene was quiet. On a quick tour Rossi saw the two bodies, the trail of blood heading toward the alley, the envelope, the hat, and the glove.

Before leaving the station for the crime scene, Rossi had reached Ron Phillips, the chief of the West L.A. detective-homicide unit that would be in charge of the investigation. It was Phillips's responsibility to visit the crime scene, talk with the uniformed officer who had discovered the bodies, and assign the case to one of the four homicide detectives who worked under him.

In the early morning hours of June 13 Phillips's on-call detective was Mark Fuhrman. The two arrived at the murder scene at about 2:10. According to the crime-scene log, Detective Mark Fuhrman was the seventeenth police officer to reach 875 South Bundy Drive.

Riske met Phillips and Fuhrman at the front of the house, on Bundy, and took them on a tour of the scene. Because the front pathway was so covered with blood, the three men decided not to try to tiptoe around it and up the stairs as Riske had done, but instead walked around the block to the back alley. They then entered the house through the garage and walked up a short flight of stairs. On the banister next to the stairs there was a partially eaten cup of

Ben & Jerry's ice cream—Chocolate Chip Cookie Dough in flavor.

Riske led the two detectives through the house, including the second floor, and then back to the landing. There Phillips and Fuhrman could see the two bodies in front and the bloody shoe prints on the walkway leading to the back alley. Riske shone his flashlight around the scene once more, pointing out the envelope as well as the hat and the glove, which were partially obscured by the foliage. They went back into the house and left through a door that opened onto the long walkway with the bloody shoe prints. The three men then went out the back gate, which was, Riske pointed out, also stained with blood, especially on the handle.

After they completed their tour, Phillips stayed outside while Fuhrman went and sat in the living room to make some preliminary notes of what he had seen, including the fact that the children had been taken to the police station. At 2:40 a.m. he was interrupted by Phillips, who told him that the West L.A. team was off the case. It was being turned over to Robbery-Homicide Division, which handles especially complex or high-profile cases. Mark Fuhrman's thirty-minute tenure as lead detective on this double homicide was over.

SHORTLY after arriving at Bundy, Ron Phillips had received a cellular phone call from Keith Bushey, the LAPD commander of operations for western Los Angeles. Since one of the victims was the ex-wife of O. J. Simpson, Bushey wanted Simpson personally informed of the murder. Phillips hadn't had a chance to act on this, because he had been inspecting the evidence with Fuhrman. Then, at about 2:30 a.m., Phillips's boss arrived, bearing the news that Phillips and his team were to withdraw from the case in deference to the Robbery-Homicide Division. In light of this change, Phillips decided that he would hold off on notifying Simpson as well. For the next hour and a half he and Fuhrman stood around and waited for the detectives who were going to replace them.

At 4:05 a.m. Philip Vannatter, a Robbery-Homicide detective, arrived. Phillips mentioned to Vannatter that Bushey had ordered him to tell O. J. Simpson in person about the deaths. What should he do? Vannatter brushed off the issue, saying he would worry about it after he had seen the crime scene. At 4:30 Vannatter's partner, Tom Lange, arrived. When the two senior detectives had completed their crime-scene walk-throughs, Phillips again raised the issue of Bushey's order for an in-person notification of Simpson. Vannatter said that since it was Simpson's ex-wife who had been murdered, he and Lange would need to interview him anyway. As Lange testified later, "I think it is very important to establish a rapport, especially with persons who are close to the victim, to get information." Also, Simpson, who was bound to be upset at the news of the murder, might well need some assistance in collecting the children from the police station. So Vannatter decided that all four detectives would make the trip to Simpson's home. Vannatter and Lange would introduce themselves to Simpson, assist in the notification, and then return promptly to begin their investigation of the crime scene, while the two junior detectives would help Simpson retrieve his children. But before they left, they had to settle one obvious question: Where did Simpson live?

Fuhrman knew. "I went up there a long time ago on a family dispute," he said. He didn't remember the exact address, but Riske, who had run the plates on the Jeep in Nicole's garage, told Fuhrman that the plates had come back to 360 North Rockingham. So at just about 5:00 a.m. Phillips and Fuhrman led Vannatter and Lange in a two-car caravan from Bundy to Rockingham. The two-mile trip took about five minutes.

Rockingham was empty—except for a single vehicle. Just before the detectives reached the intersection of Rockingham Avenue and Ashford Street, Vannatter noticed a white Ford Bronco by the curb in front of Number 360. It appeared that the vehicle was slightly askew, as if it had been hurriedly parked. The detectives turned right onto Ashford and parked their cars near an iron gate in the brick wall that surrounded O. J. Simpson's property.

A couple of lights were on in the house, and two cars were in the driveway. Vannatter rang the buzzer by the gate. No answer. He rang some more, and then Phillips and Lange rang for a while. Still no response. Phillips began calling Simpson's number on his cellular phone, but Simpson's answering machine took the call each time.

Fuhrman hung back while the other detectives tried to raise someone in the house. He was a level-two detective, while the others were at level three; it was therefore his place to defer. So with nothing to do, Fuhrman wandered around the corner, back to Rockingham, and over to the Bronco. He shone his flashlight into the back and saw papers addressed to O. J. Simpson. Fuhrman then noticed a small red stain just above the door handle. On the exposed portion of the doorsill he saw several more thin red stripes.

"I think I saw something on the Bronco," Fuhrman called to Vannatter.

The senior detective came by to study the vehicle more closely, and the two men agreed that the stains looked like blood. Vannatter directed Fuhrman to run the license plates and see who owned the car. The plates came back to the Hertz Corporation, whose products Simpson had long endorsed.

Vannatter and Lange decided to radio a request for a police criminalist to come and test the stain. More generally, they were growing concerned about what might have happened inside Simpson's property. Vannatter testified later, "After leaving a bloody murder scene, I believed something was wrong there. I made a determination that we needed to go over—to go into the property." Fuhrman—by far the youngest and fittest—hoisted himself over the wall, then manually opened the hydraulic gate.

Simpson's dog—a black chow—did not move as the detectives passed it on their way to the front door. Vannatter knocked. No answer. They knocked again and still heard no stirring inside. The four detectives decided to take a look around. Toward the rear of the house they saw a row of three guesthouses. Phillips peered into one.

"There's— I see someone inside," he said.

Phillips knocked. A disheveled man who obviously had just awoken answered the door. Shaking his mane of blond hair out of his eyes, Kato Kaelin stared at Phillips, who identified himself and asked, "Is O. J. Simpson home?"

The groggy Kaelin said he didn't know, but suggested the officers knock at the adjacent guesthouse, where Simpson's daughter Arnelle lived. The third guesthouse belonged to the housekeeper,

Gigi Guarin, and it was empty. Phillips, accompanied by Vannatter and Lange, then knocked on Arnelle's door. Fuhrman stayed behind and asked Kaelin if he could come in. Checking, among other things, the shoes in the closet for blood, the detective asked if anything unusual had happened the previous night.

As a matter of fact, something unusual *had* happened. At about 10:45 p.m., while he was talking on the telephone, Kaelin said, there were some loud thumps on his bedroom wall near the air conditioner. The jolts were so dramatic that a picture on the wall was jostled. He had thought there was going to be an earthquake.

The two men chatted a while longer; then Fuhrman walked with Kaelin into the main house, where the other three detectives were now speaking with Arnelle Simpson, who had used her key to let them in. Fuhrman decided to follow up on what Kaelin had told him. He walked back outside and saw that the south wall of Kaelin's bedroom—where Kaelin had heard the loud noises—faced a Cyclone fence at the edge of Simpson's property. There was a narrow passageway between the back of the guesthouses and the fence.

"I saw a long, dark path covered with leaves," Fuhrman testified later. When he had walked about twenty feet along the path, he saw a dark object on the ground, but it wasn't until he was practically upon it that he realized what it was: a glove.

It looked out of place. There were no leaves or twigs on it, and it looked moist or sticky, with some parts adhering to one another. Fuhrman didn't touch the glove, but he noticed something about it. "It looked similar to the glove on the Bundy scene."

ONCE they were inside the main house, Arnelle called Cathy Randa, her father's longtime secretary, who always knew O.J.'s whereabouts. Arnelle handed the phone to Phillips. Randa told him that O.J. had taken the red-eye flight to Chicago the previous night and was staying at the Chicago O'Hare Plaza hotel.

Phillips reached O.J. at the hotel at 6:05 a.m. He chose his words carefully. "This is Detective Phillips from the Los Angeles Police Department. I have some bad news for you. Your ex-wife, Nicole Simpson, has been killed."

Simpson was distraught. "Oh, my God, Nicole is killed? Oh, my God, she is dead?"

Phillips tried to calm him. "Mr. Simpson, please try to get ahold of yourself. I have your children at the West Los Angeles police station for safekeeping. I need to know what to do with them."

"Well, I'm going to be leaving out of Chicago on the first available flight," Simpson said. "I will come back to Los Angeles." Phillips then handed the phone to Arnelle, who agreed to ask Simpson's friend Al Cowlings to pick up the children.

Phillips never spoke to Simpson again. Later the detective found it worth noting that Simpson never asked how or when Nicole had been "killed." Phillips had not said (and Simpson did not ask) whether she had been killed in an accident or a murder.

Meanwhile, the drowsy children waited at the police station for someone to explain what had happened to them. At one point eight-year-old Sydney asked to call home. The answering machine picked up, and she left a message: "Mommy, please call me back. I want to know what happened last night. Why did we have to go to the police station? Please answer, Mommy. Please answer, Mommy. Please answer, Mommy. Please answer. Bye."

2

AFTER Phillips spoke to O. J. Simpson in Chicago, Tom Lange had the melancholy duty of notifying Nicole Brown Simpson's parents of her death. Lou and Juditha Brown lived in Orange County, about seventy-five miles away, and Lange suspected that if he didn't speak to them immediately, they would learn of their daughter's death from television news reports.

Lou Brown answered the telephone at 6:21 a.m. He took the news quietly. Lange did not know that Nicole's sister Denise, the oldest of the four Brown daughters, had picked up an extension.

Denise began screaming, "He killed her! He finally killed her!"

"Who?" asked Lange.

"O.J.!" said Denise.

Meanwhile, behind Simpson's house Fuhrman was quickly appreciating the significance of what he had found. The detective later recalled in testimony that "when I realized this glove was very close in description and color to the glove at the crime scene, my heart started pounding." One by one Fuhrman took the other detectives down the pathway to study the glove without touching it. They all agreed that it looked like a match. Vannatter sent Phillips and Fuhrman back to Bundy to make a closer comparison. Lange would go back, too, to begin examining the evidence there, while Vannatter would await the criminalist at Rockingham.

After the other three detectives left for Bundy, Vannatter decided to take a look around O. J. Simpson's property. The sun was coming up as he stepped onto the driveway, and Vannatter noticed what appeared to be a drop of blood on the ground. Then he found another . . . and another. The drops were all more or less in a row heading from the Rockingham gate to the front door. Vannatter opened that gate and took another look at the Bronco parked nearby. When he stared in from the passenger side, he noticed blood on the console between the two seats—and more blood on the inside of the driver's door. Vannatter went back to the house and found still more drops in the foyer. The trail of blood now led right into Simpson's home.

The criminalist, Dennis Fung, arrived at Rockingham at 7:10 a.m. and did a quick test of the red stain on the exterior of the Bronco. It was only a presumptive test, but it suggested the presence of human blood. A few moments later Fuhrman returned from Nicole's condominium. He said the glove at Bundy was for a left hand and told Vannatter that it did indeed look like a match for the right glove found behind Kaelin's room.

That's it, said Vannatter. We need to get a search warrant for this place. Vannatter left for the West Los Angeles station to write an affidavit for one. Once there he called Deputy District Attorney Marcia Clark at home. Vannatter and Clark had recently worked together on a murder case that focused on blood and other trace evidence, and the detective wanted a second opinion on the facts he had gathered so far in this case.

Clark listened to Vannatter dispassionately and was struck only by the fancy neighborhood where the murders had taken place.

"Marcia," Vannatter said, "it's O. J. Simpson."

"Who's that?" Clark replied.

"You know—the football player, actor, *Naked Gun*."

Marcia Clark was a workaholic who never followed sports and went to the movies only once in a while. "Sorry," she said. "Never heard of him."

On hearing the facts of the case, Clark thought there was more than enough evidence to get a search warrant. A magistrate signed the document in the late morning, and Vannatter returned to the Rockingham estate at just about noon on Monday, June 13, which was, as it happened, almost the same time O. J. Simpson arrived home from his abbreviated trip to Chicago.

SIMPSON'S friends often used the same expression to describe him: "He loved being O.J." That was, in many respects, his occupation—being O.J. By 1994 he was long retired from his days of football glory, but he still had modest visibility as a sports broadcaster and some minor success as an actor. He also judged beauty contests, shilled for Hertz, and pitched in an infomercial for an arthritis cure. His was a vaporous, peculiarly American kind of renown: He was famous for being O.J.

The event Simpson planned to attend in Chicago on Monday, June 13, was the annual Hertz Invitational golf tournament at the Mission Hills Country Club. When he first signed with Hertz in the 1970s, Simpson was still playing football and starring in some of the best-known television ads of the era. But a decade and a half later the company paid him about half a million dollars a year to be, as his friends put it, "the house golfer."

ORENTHAL James Simpson was born in San Francisco on July 7, 1947, the third of four children of James and Eunice Simpson. (His unusual first name, which O.J. loathed, was an aunt's suggestion of obscure origin.) His father was an intermittent presence in his life; in later life he came out as a homosexual, and he died of AIDS in 1985. His mother, who worked nights as an orderly and then a technician in the psychiatric ward of San Francisco General Hospital, supported the family as best she could.

In an authorized, highly laudatory biography published in 1974, when O.J. was twenty-seven, Larry Fox wrote of Simpson's childhood, "There was the throwing rocks at buses, the shoplifting, and, above all, the fights, the constant fights." Simpson himself admitted in an extensive *Playboy* interview in 1976, "If there wasn't no fight, there wasn't no weekend. . . . Sports was lucky for me. If I hadn't been on the high school football team, there's no question but that I would've been sent to jail."

When asked about his formative influences, Simpson repeated one story from his adolescence over and over again. In 1962 Simpson, a sophomore in high school, was in trouble. In some versions of the story he had been caught stealing from a liquor store; in others he had been arrested for a fight involving his gang, the Persian Warriors, in his Potrero Hill neighborhood. Knowing of O.J.'s troubles as well as of his athletic promise, a concerned adult arranged for Willie Mays, the legendary center fielder for the San Francisco Giants, to pay a call.

"Willie didn't give me no discipline rap; we drove over to his place and spent the afternoon talking sports," Simpson told *Playboy*. "He lived in a great big house over in Forest Hill and he was exactly the easygoing friendly guy I'd always pictured him to be. Mays always put out good vibes."

Getting a big house and putting out good vibes became the leitmotif of Simpson's professional life. After high school he spent two years playing football at the City College of San Francisco. He averaged more than ten yards per carry, so recruiters from the big four-year schools came calling in droves. But Simpson only had eyes for the University of Southern California. As a boy, he had admired the pageantry of U.S.C. football—the Trojan wearing a suit of armor seated atop a great white stallion—but as a prospective Trojan himself, he saw that U.S.C. delivered something more important: media exposure—and thus potentially lucrative contacts.

At U.S.C. in 1967, O. J. Simpson quickly established himself as the best running back in the school's history on what was perhaps the best team in U.S.C. history. As a senior, he won the Heisman trophy, awarded annually to the best player in the nation, in a landslide. The number of O.J.'s jersey—32—was retired at the end of

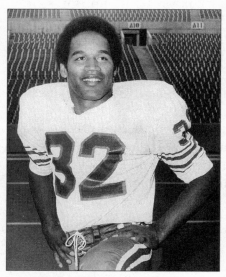

Heisman hero at U.S.C. in 1968

his career. To be sure, his success at U.S.C. was limited to the athletic arena. In those days, before the NCAA began to regulate the recruiting and schooling of college athletes, Simpson received virtually no education. Even today he can barely write a grammatical sentence.

Simpson was the first player selected in the 1969 professional draft and, in a characteristic gesture, parlayed that first year into a book deal as well as a lucrative contract with the Buffalo Bills. *OJ: The Education of a Rich Rookie,* cowritten by Pete Axthelm, is for the most part stupefyingly dull, but there are casually revealing moments as well. Simpson wrote, "I have been praised, kidded, and criticized about being image-conscious. And I plead guilty to the charge. I have always wanted to be liked and respected." In fact, his good looks and cheerful demeanor paid dividends as soon as he left college.

Before he had played a single professional game, Simpson won endorsement contracts with Chevrolet and Royal Crown Cola, and a broadcasting deal with ABC. "I'm enjoying the money, the big house, the cars; what ghetto kid wouldn't?" Simpson went on in that first book. "But I don't feel that I'm being selfish about it. In the long run, I feel that my advances will give pride and hope to a lot of young blacks. I believe I can do as much for my people in my own way as a Jim Brown or a Jackie Robinson may do in another way." Simpson had put his views on race more starkly in a

1968 interview with Robert Lipsyte of *The New York Times*. As some black athletes, like Robinson and Muhammad Ali, jeopardized their careers to participate in the civil rights movement, Simpson told Lipsyte, "I'm not black, I'm O.J."

O.J.'s professional football career started slowly. But then the team's owner, Ralph Wilson, reoriented the entire Bills operation around Simpson. Wilson brought in Lou Saban as coach and began building the group that would become famous as the Electric Company—because they "turn on the Juice." In 1972, the first season under Saban, Simpson ran for 1251 yards, the best in the league.

A 2000-yard season—something never before done in professional football—became his obsession. As he built his totals throughout the 1973 season, fans followed his race against Jim Brown's record 1863 yards and beyond. The hoped-for number had a magical quality.

To the public, Simpson was the anti-Brown, the smiling celebrity who never said a discouraging word before the cameras. In fact, this portrait amounted to little more than sportswriters' tinny conceits, but it affixed Simpson with a long-lasting glowing image. Simpson did, of course, break the magical barrier in 1973, finishing with 2003 yards as the nation's sports fans cheered.

In Simpson's years as a professional athlete and then afterward, his life amounted to a lesson on the manufacture and maintenance of an image—albeit one that bore little resemblance to reality. His charitable activities were minimal, and his marriage to his first wife, Marguerite—which took place shortly before Arnelle's birth, in 1968—was a sham. Simpson philandered compulsively, both before and after he met eighteen-year-old Nicole Brown in 1977. Nicole had already moved into the Rockingham house when the divorce from Marguerite became final two years later, the year that also marked the end of O.J.'s football career.

After that, Simpson drifted between golf games and long lunches, always surrounded by the sycophants who cluster around star athletes. From broadcasting, acting, and business investments he could count on about a million dollars a year in income in the late 1980s. He was charming and courteous to strangers and would sign autographs interminably without complaint. Ironically, in light of how his trial would unfold, Simpson always had a special fondness for police officers, and over the years many of them came by the house on Rockingham to use the pool or shoot the breeze. The cops turned out to be valuable friends, especially when it came to the events of January 1, 1989.

At 3:58 a.m. on that New Year's Day in Los Angeles the phone rang in front of 911 operator Sharyn Gilbert. At first she heard no one at the other end, but her console indicated that the call was coming from 360 North Rockingham. Then there were sounds—a woman screaming, then slaps. "I heard someone being hit," Gilbert later recalled. There was more screaming, and then the line was cut off. Gilbert rated the call a "code-two high," which meant that it required immediate police response.

Officer John Edwards and his partner, Patricia Milewski, went to the scene. Edwards pressed the buzzer at the Ashford gate to the property. After a few minutes a blond woman—Nicole Brown Simpson—staggered out from the heavy bushes behind the gate. She was wearing just a bra and a pair of dirty sweatpants.

Nicole collapsed against the inside of the gate and started yelling to the officers, "He's going to kill me! He's going to kill me!" She pounded on the button that opened the gate and then flung herself into Edwards's arms.

"Who's going to kill you?" Edwards asked.

"O.J."

"O.J. who?" he asked. "Do you mean O.J. the football player?"

"Yes," Nicole said. "O. J. Simpson the football player."

"Does he have any weapons?"

"Yeah," she replied, still breathless. "Lots of guns."

Edwards shone his flashlight on Nicole's face. Her lip was cut and bleeding. Her left eye was black-and-blue. Her forehead was bruised, and on her neck—unmistakably—was the imprint of a human hand. As Nicole calmed down, Edwards learned that O. J. Simpson had slapped her, hit her with his fist, and pulled her by the hair. She said with disgust, "You guys never do anything. You've been here eight times. And you never do anything about him." She then agreed to sign a crime report against her husband.

As Edwards turned to the house, he noticed O. J. Simpson, wearing a bathrobe, walking toward him. Simpson was screaming, "I don't want that woman in my bed anymore! I got two other women. I don't want that woman in my bed!"

Edwards explained that he was going to place Simpson under arrest for beating his wife.

"I didn't beat her," Simpson said, still furious. "I just pushed her out of bed." Edwards repeated he would have to take him in.

Simpson was incredulous. "You've been out here eight times before, and now you're going to arrest me? This is a family matter."

Edwards requested that Simpson go get dressed to be taken in to the station. When he returned, now dressed, Simpson began lecturing Edwards. "What makes you so special? Why are you doing this? No one has ever done anything like this before."

Edwards explained that the law required him to take Simpson in. When Edwards turned to brief a new set of officers who had arrived on the scene, the officers saw a blue Bentley roar out of the property's Rockingham gate.

Edwards and soon four other police cars chased after Simpson, but they couldn't catch up with him. Returning to Rockingham, Edwards asked Nicole what had prompted her husband's attack. She said she had complained because there were two other women staying in their home and O.J. had had sex with one of them that day.

With Nicole having signed a police report, the police were obliged to bring the case against O.J. at least to the next step. The case was assigned to Officer Mike Farrell, who reached O.J. by telephone on January 3. Simpson explained that they had had a verbal dispute that turned into "a mutual-type wrestling match. Nothing more than that." Nicole came into the police station the next day, and she, too, minimized the dispute. She said she didn't really want to go through with a full-fledged prosecution.

Still, under the law Farrell had to present the case to the city attorney's office, which would have the final say over whether Simpson would be prosecuted. The prosecutors told Farrell to determine whether there had been other incidents at the Simpson home. If there was a pattern, they would prosecute.

At first Farrell couldn't find a single cop who admitted to having gone previously to Rockingham. (O.J. had entertained about forty officers at his home at various times over the years, and with their silence the officers may have been repaying O.J.'s hospitality.) Eventually, out of all the cops who had handled calls at the Simpson home, one spoke up. Yes, this officer said, he had been out to the house on a domestic-violence incident.

In 1985, at 360 North Rockingham, Simpson had shattered the windshield of his Mercedes with a baseball bat. Upon responding to the incident, the officer observed a black male pacing on the driveway and a white female sitting on a car, crying. When the officer asked her if she would like to make a report, she stated, "No."

"It seems odd to remember such an event," he wrote in a January 18, 1989, memo, "but it is not everyday that you respond to a celebrity's home for a family dispute."

The author of the memo was Mark Fuhrman. Farrell passed it to the prosecutors, and on January 30 they decided to bring a case against O. J. Simpson.

As his lawyer, Simpson hired Howard Weitzman, an active U.S.C. alumnus who ran a well-publicized criminal and civil practice in Century City. Weitzman arranged for Simpson to plead no contest to the charge—which is legally identical to guilty but sounds better in the press. Simpson received in return a suspended sentence, twenty-four months of probation, and fines totaling $470. He was ordered to "perform 120 hours of community service through the Voluntary Action Bureau," to receive counseling twice a week, and to pay $500 as "restitution" to a battered-women's shelter in Santa Monica. This was the Sojourn Counseling Center, the same center that Nicole would call on June 7, 1994, five days before her death, to complain that O.J. was stalking her.

Simpson never reported to the Voluntary Action Bureau. Instead, he took it upon himself to select his own community service: organizing a fund-raiser for Camp Ronald McDonald, a children's cancer charity, at the Ritz-Carlton Hotel in Laguna Beach.

When Simpson went back to court on September 1, 1989, his form of community service was questioned by the judge. Simpson's response—indeed, his behavior at the hearing, where no journalists were present—was a mixture of indignation and self-pity.

"I moved my office to Laguna. I created this affair. I didn't just work for them. I created this affair. I talked everyone into it from Coca-Cola to— I flew to Atlanta. I flew to New York and met with Hertz. I flew to Boston to meet with sponsors like Reebok. We put on what I felt was the finest event they ever had in that area. At least that's what the press said."

The prosecutor complained that by organizing the fund-raiser, Simpson had merely engaged in business as usual.

The judge raised the prospect of Simpson doing a more conventional form of community service. Weitzman informed the judge that this would not be possible: Simpson was moving to New York to cohost NBC's pregame shows.

The judge asked, "What's going to happen with the counseling?"

"For whatever it's worth, Your Honor," Weitzman said, "I think the counselor did indicate that he believes whatever problem existed doesn't exist any longer."

Simpson's probation expired uneventfully, and he had no more formal contact with the criminal justice system until June 13, 1994, the day after his ex-wife's death, when he returned home and found that the police urgently wanted to speak with him.

SINCE Rockingham was now considered a crime scene—and since Vannatter now had a warrant to search the house and the Bronco—he did not want Simpson or anyone else allowed inside. If Simpson arrives, Vannatter instructed Donald Thompson, a uniformed patrol officer, detain him and let me know he's here. Vannatter's precise words later became a point of some controversy. Thompson remembered that Vannatter said, "Hook him up"— that is, handcuff him. Vannatter recalled that he simply said Simpson should be detained until detectives could speak with him.

Simpson arrived home at about 12:10 p.m. Curiously for a man who had been told only that his ex-wife had been killed—not necessarily murdered—Simpson had telephoned from Chicago to arrange for Howard Weitzman to meet him upon his return home. So Weitzman—as well as Simpson's secretary, Cathy Randa; his business lawyer, Skip Taft; and an old friend, Robert Kardashian— was waiting for Simpson on the sidewalk when he arrived at his house. Under the watchful eye of several news cameras Simpson left his bags with Kardashian and hurried up to the front door. At that point Weitzman, Randa, and Kardashian were not allowed on the property. Simpson was escorted to the front door by Detective Brad Roberts, Mark Fuhrman's partner.

According to Roberts's written report, Simpson pointed to the cops milling around his property and asked him, "What's all this?"

"It relates to the phone call you got earlier about the death of your ex-wife."

"Yeah, so?" Simpson replied.

"Well, I'm not the detective on the case," Roberts said, "but we came here because a blood trail led us here from the scene."

Simpson started hyperventilating. "Oh, man. Oh, man. Oh, man," he muttered to himself.

Acting according to his understanding of Vannatter's instructions, Officer Thompson placed a hand on Simpson as he approached the front door. He could have handcuffed him right there, but knowing that informal LAPD protocol for dealing with celebrities dictated that he refrain from making a show for the cameras, he instead guided Simpson over to a part of the yard out of the cameras' range. There Thompson shackled Simpson's hands behind his back.

Vannatter ambled over to Simpson and Thompson. He allowed Weitzman to join them, and the lawyer immediately asked that the cuffs be removed. Vannatter agreed and unlocked them himself. As he was working the key, the detective noticed a bandage on the middle finger of Simpson's left hand.

Vannatter told Simpson that they had some questions for him about the death of his ex-wife. Would he come down to police headquarters and talk? O.J. agreed without hesitation.

Simpson got into the back seat of Vannatter and Lange's car, and they made their way to Parker Center—the LAPD command center—in downtown Los Angeles. Weitzman and Taft followed.

Once everyone was reunited in the Robbery-Homicide Division reception area, Weitzman asked to speak to his client alone for a moment. The detectives gave Weitzman a conference room and told him to take as long as he wanted. He, Taft, and Simpson then conferred for about half an hour. When they emerged, Weitzman said that Simpson still wanted to talk to the officers but that he and Skip Taft did not want to be present. Weitzman's only request was that the detectives tape-record whatever went on.

Vannatter began by reading Simpson his constitutional rights in the form of a Miranda warning. "Okay, do you wish to give up your right to remain silent and talk to us?" Vannatter then asked.

"Ah, yes."

"Okay," Vannatter continued. "And you give up your right to have an attorney present while you talk?"

"Mmm-hmmm, yes," Simpson replied.

Vannatter began, "We're investigating, obviously, the death of your ex-wife and another man. Are you divorced from her now?"

Simpson said they had been divorced for about two years.

"What was your relationship with her?" Vannatter asked.

"Well, we tried to get back together, and it just didn't work."

Vannatter quickly changed the subject. "I understand that she made a couple of crime . . . crime reports or something?"

"Ah, we have a big fight about six years ago on New Year's, you know, she made a report." (Later in the interview Simpson explained the 1989 incident this way: "We had a fight, and she hit me. They never took my statement, they never wanted to hear my side. Nicole was drunk and she started tearing up my house. I didn't punch her or anything, but I . . . wrestled her, is what I did. I mean, Nicole's a strong girl. Since that period of time, she's hit me a few times, but I've never touched her after that.")

"So you weren't arrested?" Vannatter asked.

"No, I was never really arrested."

Vannatter asked, "When was the last time you saw Nicole?"

"We were leaving a dance recital. She took off and I was talking to her parents." O.J. and Nicole's daughter, Sydney, had performed on Sunday night at Paul Revere Middle School in Brentwood. "It ended at about six thirty, quarter to seven, something like that. . . . Her mother said something about me joining them for dinner, and I said no thanks." Simpson added that he left the scene in his Bentley, and Vannatter asked him where he went from there.

"Ah, home, home for a while, got my car for a while, tried to find my girlfriend for a while, came back to the house."

"So what time do you think you got back home?" Vannatter asked.

"Seven something. . . . Yeah, I'm trying to think, did I leave . . . I had to run and get my daughter some flowers. I came home, and then I called Paula [Barbieri, his girlfriend] as I was going to her house, and Paula wasn't home. . . . I mean . . . whatever time it took me to get to the recital and back, to get to the flower shop and back, I mean, that's the time I was out of the house."

This was an incomprehensible answer. Did Simpson buy flowers for Sydney before or after the recital? (She was holding flowers in a photograph taken at the recital.) Did he actually go to Paula's house? If not, where did he go? The officers could have tried to pin Simpson down, yet Vannatter's follow-up question was, "Were you scheduled to play golf this morning someplace?" Yes, Simpson said, in Chicago with Hertz clients. Vannatter then established that Simpson had taken the 11:45 p.m. flight to Chicago the previous night. He followed that with a question about Simpson's Bronco. When did Simpson park it on Rockingham?

"Eight something, seven . . . eight, nine o'clock, I don't know, right in that area." This was another meaningless answer, yet the detectives did not ask Simpson to estimate his arrival any more specifically. Rather, they established that Simpson had come home from the recital in his Bentley and then got into the Bronco.

" 'Cause my phone was in the Bronco," Simpson explained. "And because it's a Bronco. It's what I drive, you know. And, you know, as I was going over there, I called [Paula], and she wasn't there, and I left a message, and then I checked my messages, and there were no messages. She wasn't there, and she may have to leave town. Then I came back and ended up sitting with Kato."

"Okay," Lange now said. "What time was this again that you parked the Bronco?"

"Eight something, maybe. He hadn't done a Jacuzzi, we had . . . went and got a burger, and I'd come home and kind of leisurely got ready to go. I mean, we'd done a few things."

Neither detective asked anything about this trip for a burger. Instead, they pursued a new subject. "How did you get the injury on your hand?"

"I don't know," Simpson replied. "The first time, when I was in Chicago and all, but at the house I was just running around."

"How did you do it in Chicago?" Vannatter asked.

"I broke a glass. One of you guys had just called me, and I was in the bathroom, and I just kind of went bonkers for a little bit."

"Is that how you cut it?"

"Mmm, it was cut before, but I think I just opened it again."

Lange asked, "Do you recall bleeding at all in the Bronco?"

"I recall bleeding at my house, and then I went to the Bronco. The last thing I did before I left, when I was rushing, was went and got my phone out of the Bronco."

Lange asked where Simpson had gotten the Band-Aid he was wearing on his left middle finger. "Actually, I asked the girl this morning for it."

"And she got it?"

"Yeah," Simpson continued. " 'Cause last night with Kato, when I was leaving, he was saying something to me, and I was rushing to get my phone, and I put a little thing on it, and it stopped."

Again the detectives changed the topic. They established that O.J.'s maid, Gigi, had access to the Bronco, that he had not argued with Nicole at the recital, and that he had worn black pants and Reeboks the previous night. These clothes were never found.

Finally Vannatter said, "O.J., we've got sort of a problem."

"Mmm-hmm."

"We've got some blood on and in your car; we've got some blood at your house and sort of a problem."

"Well, take my blood test," Simpson volunteered.

"Well, we'd like to do that," Lange responded. "We've got, of course, the cut on your finger that you aren't real clear on. Do you recall having that cut the last time you were at Nicole's house?"

No, Simpson said. "It was last night. . . . Somewhere when I was rushing to get out of my house."

Vannatter, in effect, just threw up his hands and asked, "What do you think happened? Do you have any idea?"

"I have no idea, man. You guys haven't told me anything."

"Understand," Lange said a few moments later, "the reason we're talking to you is because you're the ex-husband."

"I know I'm the number one target, and now you tell me I've got blood all over the place."

"Well," Lange said, "there's blood at your house in the driveway, and we've got a search warrant. We found some in your house. Is that your blood that's there?"

"If it's dripped, it's what I dripped running around trying to leave. . . . You know, I was trying to get out of the house, I didn't even pay attention to it. . . . That was last night when I was . . . I don't know what I was. . . . I was getting my junk out of the car. I was in the house throwing stuff in my suitcase. I was doing my little crazy what I do. . . . I mean, I do it everywhere. Anybody who has ever picked me up say that O.J.'s a whirlwind."

After a few more desultory exchanges the interview drew to a close. At 2:07 p.m. Lange said, "We're ready to terminate this." LAPD investigators never had the opportunity to speak with Simpson again. The interview had lasted thirty-two minutes.

IT BECAME known almost immediately that Simpson had given a statement to the detectives, and the news media's legal "experts" (and that often included me) promptly excoriated Howard Weitzman for allowing his client to answer questions. In the months afterward, Weitzman often said in his own defense that he had tried and failed to stop Simpson from talking. It is true that such a decision is always the client's to make. And given Simpson's vast ego, he undoubtedly thought he could talk his way out of trouble. Similarly, he probably dreaded the humiliating prospect of the police leaking word to the public that O.J. had been afraid to talk.

But the debate over Weitzman's role missed the larger significance of the detectives' interview of Simpson. As in the 1989 abuse
incident, the police behavior suggested a fear of offending a
celebrity. Though Vannatter and Lange already had considerable
evidence that O. J. Simpson was likely a murderer, they treated him
with astonishing deference. Time after time, as Simpson gave vague
and even nonsensical answers, the detectives failed to follow up. Incredibly, they never even forced Simpson to account specifically for
his whereabouts between the end of Sydney's dance recital and his
departure for the airport. (This failure allowed Simpson's attorneys
to claim later, as they did at various times, that their client spent this
period sleeping, showering, and chipping golf balls in the dark.)

When the prosecutors heard the tape, they knew immediately
how dreadfully the detectives had botched this opportunity. Among
themselves the prosecutors called the interview "the fiasco."

3

OVER the course of June 13 the magnitude of the Simpson case
gradually dawned on Marcia Clark. Vannatter had asked her to
come out to the Rockingham house and monitor the situation
while detectives executed the search warrant, and it hadn't taken
long to size up the situation to her satisfaction. The following
morning, in her office downtown, a friend asked Clark whether
she thought O.J. had committed the murders.

Of course, Clark snapped. She was confident the tests on the
blood at Bundy and at his home would come back to implicate
Simpson. "He's evil," Clark said. "He beat his wife. He's evil."

It was a characteristic reaction. Quick-witted and quick to
judge, Clark was the paradigmatic "lifer"—the term prosecutors
use to describe those among them who cannot conceive of switching sides to criminal defense work. She saw her cases—and the
Simpson case in particular—as struggles between good and evil.
O.J. had killed Ron and Nicole; that was all that mattered to her.

Marcia Clark, in fact, belonged to the smallest and most intense subspecies of lifers—the trial addicts. She learned this about herself the hard way. By the spring of 1993, when she was almost forty, Clark had been trying cases in the D.A.'s office for twelve years, the last four of them in the special-trials unit, which handled the

county's most complex and sensitive investigations. Gil Garcetti, the district attorney, felt that Clark had earned a promotion. She became a supervisor. Most prosecutors are eager to escape the enormous burdens of trial work (and to get a raise). What happened to Marcia Clark's career as an administrator was unusual. "I hated it," Clark said not long after she took on the Simpson case. "I begged them to let me back in the courtroom." As it happened, she had returned to the special-trials unit just a few weeks before the murders on Bundy Drive.

Marcia Clark

From the moment Vannatter called her on that Monday morning Clark had thought there was enough evidence to arrest O. J. Simpson for the murders. Nevertheless, in what she regarded as an abundance of caution, she agreed to put off filing the case against Simpson until the initial blood tests were reviewed.

Shortly after seven the following morning, June 14, the criminalist Dennis Fung was hunched over a lab bench in the serology unit of the Scientific Investigation Division of the LAPD. Fung had gathered before him what he regarded as some of the best evidence he had collected the previous day—the gloves and various samples from the trail of blood that appeared to go from Bundy to Rockingham. He also had a blood sample from O. J. Simpson, which had been taken by a police nurse the previous afternoon at Parker

Center. Vannatter had traveled the twenty miles back to Rockingham in the late afternoon to give this blood sample to Fung.

At the lab bench Fung handed Simpson's blood and the rest of his samples to Collin Yamauchi, the LAPD criminalist who would perform the initial testing. As far as Yamauchi could tell from initial news reports, Simpson was in Chicago at the time of the murders: He had an "airtight alibi." So Yamauchi expected his tests would exclude Simpson as a possible source.

Yamauchi spent two days testing the samples. (He also was given blood from Nicole Brown Simpson and Ronald Goldman, obtained during their autopsies.) Because of the high stakes involved in the Simpson case—particularly the risk of making a very public mistake—Yamauchi used DNA typing on the blood samples instead of the conventional ABO typing. He conducted one of the simplest kind of DNA tests, one known as DQ-alpha, which places individuals into one of twenty-one categories.

The results surprised Yamauchi. The blood drops on the pathway at Bundy matched Simpson's type—a characteristic shared by only about 7 percent of the population. And the blood on the glove found behind Kato's room was consistent with a mixture of Simpson's and the two victims'. When the prosecutors learned of the results, Marcia Clark felt that they had enough pieces of the puzzle to arrest Simpson. Clark's supervisor, David Conn, agreed.

Bill Hodgman, the director of central operations, thought it over. Hodgman supervised most of the prosecutors in the Criminal Courts Building. Cautious, sober, methodical to the point of occasional dullness, he didn't want to rush into anything. Yet there was substantial evidence that Simpson was a murderer, and prosecutors arrest murderers—period. Clark and Conn were right. It was time to bring Simpson in.

Late Thursday, June 16, Hodgman planned logistics for the next day with Clark and Conn. Vannatter and Lange had already spoken briefly with Simpson's new lawyer, Robert Shapiro, who had replaced Howard Weitzman, and Shapiro vowed that he would arrange for Simpson to surrender at any time the detectives chose.

At 8:30 a.m. on Friday, June 17, the prosecutors agreed, Lange would telephone Shapiro, inform him of the charges, and demand that Simpson surrender at 11:00 a.m. Hodgman felt matters were so well in hand when he left for home on Thursday night that he decided to take the next day off.

At 8:30 A.M. on Friday, as planned, Lange reached Shapiro at home and told him that the police had an arrest warrant charging O. J. Simpson with the double homicide, with "special circumstances," of Nicole Brown Simpson and Ronald Goldman. Under California's special circumstances list of designated aggravating factors, the double homicide charge made Simpson eligible for the death penalty, and it did not allow for bail. So Shapiro knew immediately that O. J. Simpson was going to jail on June 17 and that he would remain there for the duration of his trial.

The conversation between the two men was polite. Lange told Shapiro that Simpson had two and a half hours to surrender—that is, until 11:00 a.m. Shapiro saw Lange's comments as more of a request than a command. The lawyer mentioned some concerns about his client's mental state—he might be suicidal—but said that he would do his best to bring Simpson in on time.

Shapiro had been Simpson's lawyer for less than seventy-two hours. When word that Simpson had given a statement to the police leaked out the evening of June 13, television executive Roger King, who knew Simpson from playing golf with him, was appalled that Howard Weitzman had allowed Simpson to be questioned. King called O.J. and recommended that he find a new lawyer. "I'll get you Bob Shapiro," King promised. He then tracked Shapiro down and asked him to take the case.

What makes this transaction curious is that none of the participants really knew one another. O.J. and Roger King saw each other rarely, but King, the chairman of King World, which syndicates *Oprah* among other shows, was the kind of man Simpson admired. More remarkably, King had never even spoken to Shapiro before, but he had some sense of Shapiro as a skilled defender of celebrities. For his part Shapiro did not hesitate before saying he wanted the case. And to Simpson, as always, image was everything: Robert

Shapiro became his lawyer because he fit the image of a smart lawyer in the eyes of a fellow who fit O.J.'s image of a smart guy.

Shapiro had a very busy first week. The first thing he did was arrange for Simpson to take a polygraph examination. Such tests are generally inadmissible in court, but criminal defense lawyers often use them to force their clients to come clean, face reality, and make the best deal they can.

Simpson took what is known as a zone of comparison polygraph, which measured heart rate, breathing, and the electrical sensitivity of his skin. According to the test, any score higher than plus 6 meant that Simpson was telling the truth; any number lower than minus 6 meant he was lying. A score between plus 6 and minus 6 would be ambiguous.

Simpson scored a minus 24—total failure. Some people tried to attribute it to Simpson's distressed emotional state at the time of the examination. The tester, however, regarded the polygraph as conclusive evidence of Simpson's guilt in the murders, and he reported that view to Shapiro.

Shapiro weighed his options, which included an insanity defense. To that end he called in Saul Faerstein on Wednesday, June 15. Faerstein, a respected Beverly Hills psychiatrist and expert forensic witness, went to Rockingham and joined Simpson on the couch in the living room. Simpson talked and talked—about himself. The press was out to get him; his image would never recover; it was all so unfair. What struck Faerstein most were the gaps in Simpson's narrative. There was no sadness for the loss of the mother of his children, no concern for his children's future. Simpson worried only about himself. His reactions were inconsistent with what Faerstein would expect from an unjustly accused man, yet Simpson was obviously not insane in any legal sense. Faerstein was convinced of Simpson's guilt.

On that same Wednesday, June 15, which was also the day of the viewing of Nicole's body at a funeral home, Shapiro asked an internist, Robert Huizenga, to give O.J. a detailed medical examination and to document with photographs any bruises or abrasions on Simpson's body. His lack of any major injuries would become part of his defense.

Detective Lange's call on Friday morning, June 17, presented Shapiro with a dilemma. What he should have done was simple: locate Simpson and take him in by the 11:00 a.m. deadline. But the situation was complicated. Simpson was not at home in Brentwood, as the police had assumed. On Thursday, June 16, following Nicole's funeral earlier in the day, Simpson had participated in an elaborate ruse to convince the vast media encampment outside his home that he had in fact returned. The person who was actually hustled into the Rockingham property with a jacket over his head was his old friend Al Cowlings. Simpson had been taken to his friend Robert Kardashian's home in Encino, in the San Fernando Valley north of Los Angeles.

At 9:30 a.m. Shapiro arrived at Kardashian's vast white villa, a garish affair resembling a Tehran bordello, all marble and mirrors. Simpson, who had been sedated, was still in the first-floor bedroom he was using during his stay, with his girlfriend Paula Barbieri. Shapiro and Kardashian woke O.J. and broke the news that they would be taking him to Parker Center to surrender. They explained that Drs. Huizenga and Faerstein were on their way to examine him before they had to leave for jail. Within moments the house was buzzing with people. First Faerstein arrived, followed by Huizenga and his assistants. Then Al Cowlings joined the group as Huizenga took more photographs to demonstrate that Simpson had no significant wounds. Granted the privilege of being allowed to surrender, Simpson was missing his deadline so that he could, in effect, conduct his defense.

As the deadline neared, Shapiro was on the phone every fifteen minutes to the LAPD, explaining that these things take time and that Simpson would be on his way shortly. After all, what difference did it make if he surrendered at 11:00 a.m. or 1:00 p.m.?

Vannatter and Lange grew fed up waiting for the lawyer to drive in the defendant. At around noon the detectives said they wanted to send a squad car to pick Simpson up. As always, the LAPD was concerned about the media: A news conference had been scheduled for noon, and now that had to be put off.

Shapiro finally provided Kardashian's address, but ever the negotiator, he secured an LAPD commander's promise that he and Faerstein could accompany Simpson on his trip downtown.

Moments later, at about 12:10 p.m., a squad car arrived at Kardashian's and a police helicopter began circling overhead. Even then, after all the delays, Shapiro had another request. He asked the officers if Faerstein, the psychiatrist, could break the news to O.J. that the police had arrived. (Simpson, who was in a back bedroom talking with Barbieri and Cowlings, had not been told that the police were coming.) The officers at that point had every right to barge in and take Simpson away, yet they agreed. Faerstein walked back to the bedroom and a moment later returned. "He must be somewhere else," Faerstein told the officers.

One at a time the people in the house fanned out. A few walked upstairs. With each passing second the pace of everyone's steps increased. O.J. wasn't upstairs. Chests constricted. There was no one in the garage. Panic. Then the realization dawned on them that no one had seen Barbieri or Cowlings, either.

As he had done when the officers came for him in 1989 for beating Nicole, so he did when they came for him in 1994 for killing her: O. J. Simpson disappeared.

AT 1:53 P.M. reporters at police headquarters got the two-minute warning: The Simpson briefing was about to begin.

With his neat black hair, obligatory mustache, and tightfitting uniform, Commander David Gascon cut a typical figure for the department he represented. He was also fairly relaxed and approachable, but when he stepped to the lectern that afternoon, he looked . . . different. He seemed shaken.

"This morning," Gascon said, his voice unsteady, "detectives from the Los Angeles Police Department, after an exhaustive investigation and analysis of the physical evidence, sought and obtained a warrant for the arrest of O. J. Simpson, charging him with the murders of Nicole Brown Simpson and Ronald Lyle Goldman.

"Mr. Simpson, in agreement with his attorney, was scheduled to surrender this morning to the Los Angeles Police Department. Mr. Simpson has not appeared."

The room stirred.

"The Los Angeles Police Department right now is actively searching for Mr. Simpson."

An experienced group of reporters were gathered in that room, yet none of them could recall having heard the sound they issued at that moment: a sort of collective gasp. And then one journalist, name lost to history, let out a long and very astonished whistle.

"Mr. Simpson is out there somewhere," Gascon said, "and we will find him."

Shortly after it became clear that Simpson and Cowlings were really gone, Kardashian materialized in the foyer of his house with an envelope that contained a letter. Shapiro and Faerstein read it, and they agreed that it seemed like a suicide note written by O.J. After Shapiro and Kardashian spoke to the officers on the scene, they left for Shapiro's office in Century City. (They also determined that Paula Barbieri had left the house shortly before O.J. and Cowlings, but not with them.) Though the letter was clearly important evidence, Kardashian took it with him.

Shapiro knew how furious the police and prosecutors were about Simpson's disappearance, and he knew they would hold him responsible. On the phone with D.A. Gil Garcetti, the defense attorney became nearly unhinged. "I didn't know he would run, Gil. You have to believe me." The two men were old acquaintances, but at this moment Garcetti addressed Shapiro with barely controlled rage. "Just get him in here, Bob. That's all we're thinking about now."

At 3:00 p.m., just after he got off the phone with Shapiro, Garcetti went to give his own press conference. Flanked by Marcia Clark and David Conn, a distraught-looking Garcetti went through more than a half hour of hostile questions.

Garcetti's press conference did nothing to ease Shapiro's anxiety, so Simpson's lawyer decided, in effect, to take his case to the public. He made a statement to reporters barely an hour after Garcetti's briefing. Shapiro spoke calmly, with no notes. He started with a plea. "For the sake of your children," he told O.J., "please surrender immediately. Surrender to any law-enforcement official at any police station, but please do it immediately." In retrospect his agenda at the press conference appears utterly transparent: Whatever else had happened that day, this mess was not going to drag him down with it. Shapiro began by summarizing the day's events up to the defendant's sudden disappearance. It was an extraordinary tale and highly incriminating of his client. Indeed, by some reckonings much of what had gone on that day may have been protected by the attorney-client privilege—a privilege that only Simpson had the right to waive. Yet Shapiro had hung his client out to dry in public in order to save himself.

Shapiro's statement was only the beginning of the proceedings. "Now," he continued, "I would like to introduce to you Mr. Robert Kardashian, who is one of Mr. Simpson's closest and dearest friends, who will read a letter that O. J. Simpson wrote in his handwriting today. Thank you."

HE BECAME one of the most familiar, if least known, figures in the Simpson saga: loyal friend Robert Kardashian, the one with the white stripe in his hair. Heir to a meatpacking fortune, Kardashian attended U.S.C. a couple of years before Simpson and served there as the student manager of the football team. He graduated from law school but quickly dropped practice for the business world. At the time of the murders he was running Movie Tunes, a company that played music in movie theaters between shows.

Robert Kardashian

From the moment Simpson was arrested, however, Kardashian suspended all other work, reactivated his law license, and toiled full-time on O.J.'s defense for over a year. His Rolls-Royce became a fixture at the county jail.

Head bowed, Kardashian followed Shapiro to the lectern and

began speaking into the nest of microphones. "This letter was written by O.J. today." (Actually, it was not. The letter was headed "6/15/94," two days earlier.) " 'To whom it may concern . . .' "

THERE is no way to tell for sure what O. J. Simpson truly intended to do when he composed the letter that Robert Kardashian read to the world on the afternoon of June 17, 1994. It is safe to say, however, that Simpson intended his letter to be understood as a suicide note—and as a public last will and testament. As such, it provides both intentional and unintentional clues to the nature of its author—and in particular to the banality, self-pity, and narcissism that are the touchstones of his character.

> First everyone understand nothing to do with Nicole's murder. I loved her, allways have and always will. If we had a promblem it's because I loved her so much. Recitly we came to the understanding that for now we were'nt right for each other at least for now. Dispite our love we were different and thats why we murtually agreed to go our spaerate ways.

Kardashian edited as he went along, first by omitting the date at the top of the letter and then quoting the letter as saying "First, everyone understand *I had* nothing to do with Nicole's murder." The text illustrates that Simpson in fact omitted these two important words. The note showed that Simpson was a terrible writer and speller, so it is difficult to draw any conclusions from his errors except about his near-illiteracy. However, it is tempting to infer some psychological significance from Simpson's failure to render correctly this most important sentence of his letter. (Most newspapers that printed excerpts of the letter cleaned up the grammar and spelling, thereby leaving the impression that Simpson was more literate than he was.)

> Like all long term relationships, we had a few downs + ups. I took the heat New Years 1989 because that what I was suppose to do I did not plea no contest for any other reason but to protect our privicy and was advise it would end the press hype.

Leaving aside the question of whether a criminal conviction for spousal abuse and Nicole's repeated pleas to 911 qualified as something more than "a few downs + ups," it is Simpson's self-obsession that is so striking here. He not only denies responsibility for beating Nicole but congratulates himself for accepting the blame for it. Ironically, there was in fact very little "press hype" about the 1989 incident. That O.J. should have been so wounded by what little there was again demonstrates his vast self-regard.

> I want to send my love and thanks to all my friend. I'm sorry
> I can't name every one of you.

O.J. then listed fifteen friends and golfing buddies. It is worth noting, given the way his case unfolded, that all of them except Cowlings are wealthy middle-aged white men.

When he turned to his fellow athletes, the style of the letter shifted to that of a high school yearbook.

> All my teammatte over the years. Reggie, you were the soul
> of my pro career. Ahmad I never stop being proud of you.

By the end, the letter came to resemble the speech Simpson gave on August 3, 1985, upon his induction to the Professional Football Hall of Fame. O.J. thanked many of the same people in much the same style. ("I wouldn't be here if it wasn't for Skip Taft and Cathy Randa . . .") Simpson seems to have composed his suicide note in the manner of the celebrity intent upon allowing a few friends to share in his reflected glory.

> I think of my life and feel I'v done most of the right things.
> so why do I end up like this. I can't go on, no matter what the
> outcome people will look and point. I can't take that. I can't
> subject my children to that. This way they can go on with thair
> lives. Please, if I'v done anything worthwhile, let my kids live in
> <u>peace</u> from you (press).

Simpson demonstrated a certain prescience here. Even though he was ultimately acquitted, he did become a pariah; people do look and point. But what is peculiar is how he converted his own inability to cope with unpopularity into a problem for his children. Sydney and Justin had lost their mother. A more rational and generous reaction might have been to hold them close and assure them that they were not going to lose their father, too. Nor did Simpson ask the police to locate the "real" killer of his ex-wife and her friend.

> Don't feel sorry for me. I'v had a great life made great friends. Please think of the real O.J. and not this lost person. Thank for making my life special I hope I help yours. Peace + Love O.J.

Inside the O in his name, Simpson scrawled a happy face—a flourish that is almost too perverse to contemplate.

THE LAPD had put out an all-points bulletin for Al Cowlings right around the time of Gascon's press conference, at 2:00 p.m. It wasn't until around 6:00 p.m., however, that the Los Angeles media confirmed the description of Cowlings's car: a 1993 white Ford Bronco with California license plate 3DHY503. Not surprisingly, perhaps, it was the broadcast announcement, not the law-enforcement effort, that produced almost immediate results.

Chris Thomas had been watching television when he learned Simpson was on the run. At 6:25 p.m. he and his girlfriend, Kathy Ferrigno, were heading north on Interstate 5, the Santa Ana Freeway. They had been joking about O.J.'s disappearance and studying in a halfhearted way the cars coming toward them, seeing if Simpson might be on his way to Mexico. After a few minutes of this Ferrigno looked into the passenger-side rearview mirror and started saying, "Oh my God!—Chris, Chris, Chris!" Thomas slowed down, and in a moment Ferrigno was face to face with Al Cowlings. When he noticed that she was staring at him, Cowlings glowered at her. Their location at that moment was about eighty miles south of Kardashian's house, about a five-minute drive from the gravesite of Nicole Brown Simpson. The Bronco was also heading north, back toward Los Angeles. Thomas pulled to the side of the freeway by a call box and phoned the California Highway Patrol.

As Simpson described it in his deposition in the civil case, he and Cowlings had intended to go to Nicole's grave, but they retreated when they saw that the cemetery was staked out by police. Just a few minutes after Thomas's telephone call Orange County sheriff's deputy Larry Pool spotted the Bronco returning to the northbound Santa Ana. "Ten-four, I'm behind it," he said into his radio, and with that, all air traffic on the police radio band receded into a stunned silence.

Al Cowlings

As the Bronco began to move on the freeway through the city of Santa Ana, the traffic grew heavier and then came to a standstill. Officer Pool and a colleague in another car, Jim Sewell, used the opportunity to advance by foot, with guns drawn, to the Bronco.

"Turn off your engine," the officers shouted to Cowlings.

Cowlings started screaming and pounding his left hand on the side of the door. "Put away your guns! He's in the back seat and he's got a gun to his head."

Fearing bloodshed, the officers watched Cowlings drive off as the traffic ahead of him cleared. Then they radioed for backup assistance and simply began following the Bronco. The chase was on.

Helicopter journalists picked up the chase a few moments later. It was, to be sure, an unusual moment in journalism, but not quite as rare as many people thought. The freeway chase, broadcast live by cameras mounted in helicopters, is a staple of television news in Los Angeles. For the national audience, however, it was another story. One after another the networks broke into their regular programming to pick up the chase live. Since the network anchors were far less familiar with these chases and with Los Angeles topography, their narratives reflected only bewilderment at the scene unfolding before them. On ABC, for example, Peter Jennings repeatedly confessed that he did not know where the Bronco was or where it was going. Somehow, though, the confusion made the chase even more hypnotizing. Approximately 95 million Americans watched some portion of the chase, a number that exceeded that year's Super Bowl audience by about 5 million.

The Bronco continued north on the Santa Ana, passing Disneyland in Anaheim, and then headed west on the Artesia Freeway. Cowlings turned off the Artesia, traveled less than a mile south on the Harbor Freeway, and then curved west and gently north on the San Diego Freeway.

O.J. and his helicopter entourage passed through white, middle-class Torrance without fanfare. In Inglewood and at the edge of Watts, the largely African American communities to the north, however, spectators were shouting encouragement. "Go, O.J.!" many screamed. "Save the Juice!"

Cowlings exited the freeway at Sunset Boulevard, then took a shortcut through Brentwood. With the helicopters still tracking him among the gated homes, Cowlings made a left onto Ashford, from which he could turn into O.J.'s driveway. There were so many television satellite trucks parked on tiny Ashford that he had to inch his way past them. With dusk fast approaching, Cowlings finally managed to pull into the driveway at 360 North Rockingham. It was shortly before 8:00 p.m.

AT ABOUT 7:15 p.m. Tom Lange had reached Cowlings on the cellular phone in the Bronco. Cowlings confirmed that he was heading to O.J.'s home and that Simpson remained suicidal. Lange did his best to calm the situation. Without telling Cowlings, Lange also arranged for the LAPD's SWAT team to go to the Rockingham house and prepare to arrest Simpson there. The team arrived about fifteen minutes before Cowlings did and immediately evicted everyone except Kardashian and O.J.'s twenty-four-year-old son, Jason.

As soon as the Bronco stopped in the driveway, Jason sprang from the front door and began yelling at Cowlings, who seemed to be equally hyped up. The 6-foot 5-inch Cowlings, a former defensive lineman for the Buffalo Bills, stuck his long arm out the driver's window and pushed Jason away. There was a considerable poignancy to the scene. Jason's relationship with his father had long vacillated between poor and nonexistent, and Cowlings's pokes made clear the status of the pudgy and unathletic son: He was not wanted in his father's moment of crisis. A pair of officers gingerly approached Jason and all but dragged him back into the house.

Lange had handed over negotiating duties to the SWAT team's Pete Weireter, who was posted in O.J.'s house. Weireter reached O.J. on the Bronco's cellular phone and attempted to talk him into surrendering. Minutes passed, and the world waited to see if O. J. Simpson would blow his brains out on live national TV.

The silence at the driveway standoff contrasted dramatically with a scene unfolding at the foot of Rockingham, on Sunset Boulevard. A raucous crowd several hundred strong had gathered there, drawn to the drama. The whites, a minority of the revelers, were curiosity seekers—"looky loos" in the LAPD phrase. The African Americans, on the other hand, had mostly come to show solidarity, and their chants and shouts made their feelings clear. "Free O.J.!" they repeated again and again.

Finally Simpson agreed to give up. He hesitantly put a foot out the door of the Bronco. It was 8:53 p.m., nearly an hour after Cowlings had arrived at Simpson's home. In his hands, O.J. held a couple of family pictures, which he had been clutching in the car. He staggered into the foyer and collapsed into the officers' arms. "I'm sorry, guys," Simpson kept repeating. "I'm sorry I put you through this." Simpson was allowed to use the bathroom and call his mother. Deferential even then, the officers finally asked whether he was ready to go. He nodded. The officers put handcuffs on him and led him out the front door to an unmarked cruiser.

With Simpson gone, members of the SWAT team examined Cowlings's Bronco. They found O.J.'s passport and a fully loaded Smith & Wesson .357 Magnum. It was registered to Lieutenant Earl Paysinger, one of Simpson's friends on the LAPD. About five years earlier, when Paysinger was providing security for O.J., the lieutenant had bought his client the gun.

An eighteen-car caravan escorted Simpson to his booking at Parker Center. He was then transported to the L.A. county jail for his first night in custody, which he spent on suicide watch. In his book *I Want to Tell You,* Simpson wrote, "The first week I was in jail I thought about Jesus being crucified."

4

SIMPSON was arraigned in municipal court on the following Monday, June 20. He was physically transformed from any O. J. Simpson the public had seen before. Looking dazed, he staggered from the holding pen to the defendant's table before Judge Patti Jo McKay. He wore a black suit and white shirt, but he was denied a tie, belt, and shoelaces for fear that he might turn them into instruments of suicide. Asked his name, he appeared confused, and Shapiro had to prompt his answer. Asked his plea, Simpson muttered quietly, "Not guilty." The proceeding was over in moments, and in the only real business transacted, Judge McKay scheduled the preliminary hearing for ten days hence, June 30.

Both sides held press conferences the same day. There was much to recommend silence. Shapiro had a client who had acted like a very guilty man the previous Friday. Garcetti's prosecutors, on the other hand, faced the prospect of convicting a popular celebrity. The worst thing they could do was appear unduly zealous, yet the adversaries could not resist an attempt to posture and spin.

Shapiro faced a bank of television cameras at his Century City office shortly after the arraignment. The lawyer was asked about the possibility of raising an insanity defense—that is, one based on the premise that Simpson had committed the murders. "Every possible defense has to be considered by any trial lawyer," Shapiro responded, "and I certainly would reserve all possibilities." His lawyerly words made Simpson look even more guilty.

Yet the prosecutors made even more trouble for themselves. Although it had been just two days since the arrest—and only eight days since the murders—at a June 20 press conference Marcia

Clark announced, "It was premeditated murder. That is precisely what he was charged with because that is what we will prove," thus writing off the possibility that Simpson had murdered his ex-wife in a fit of jealous passion. Of course, no responsible prosecutors would have filed charges against Simpson unless they felt he was guilty, but Clark heedlessly limited her options at trial by rushing into a single theory about how the crime had occurred. It was the public's first real view of her, and a revealing one at that.

Although Marcia Clark was an accomplished lawyer, she was far from an obvious choice to prosecute such an important case. In fact, she had simply taken Vannatter's call on Monday, June 13, and stayed with the case through the tumultuous first week. It is difficult to say whether Garcetti, given a real choice, would have picked her. Clark had prosecuted several murders, but other senior deputies had tried more, and more difficult, cases. In addition, the office's losing streak in big cases was well known. What was less known was that most of those cases had been lost by women prosecutors with pugnacious demeanors, among them Lael Rubin in the McMartin Preschool child abuse case and Pamela Bozanich in the first trial of the Menendez brothers, accused of killing their parents. Of course, it might have been just a coincidence that female prosecutors had failed in the high-profile cases, but the defense team regarded these perceptions as important, so they were delighted Clark had the case.

The events of the first week had been so public—and Clark such a visible part of them—that removing her would have caused a considerable stir, since a decision to remove her would have been seen as at least partially driven by her gender. Garcetti's base of liberal Democratic supporters would have rebelled, and the media would have rushed to the story. Besides, Garcetti gave little thought to replacing Clark that week because everything seemed to be going so well. With Simpson reeling, Garcetti and Clark's instincts told them to keep the pressure on.

THE California tradition of holding preliminary hearings is a relative anomaly in American criminal law. Prelims, as they are known, are essentially miniature trials held in front of a judge rather than a jury to determine, in a felony case, if there is probable cause that the defendant has committed the crime. Prosecutors almost never lose prelims. Still, they loathe them, since it forces them to offer up their witnesses for cross-examination by defense lawyers very early in the game.

By contrast, prosecutors love grand juries, whose deliberations are secret. Defense lawyers are not allowed even to attend the proceedings. Asked by a prosecutor to indict someone, grand juries invariably do—and they obviate the need for preliminary hearings. So in the Simpson case the prosecutors set out to have the grand jury issue an indictment before the preliminary hearing was to begin on June 30. That meant Clark had to move quickly. In fact, she had begun her presentation to the grand jury on Friday, June 17, even before Simpson was tracked down and arrested.

The grand jury met in the downtown Criminal Courts Building—a fact of considerable significance. Since the murders had occurred in Brentwood, prosecutors theoretically had the right to try the case in the Santa Monica branch of superior court—and thus to have access to that court's substantially white jury pool. Why, it has long been asked, did prosecutors choose to try a popular black celebrity in front of a heavily black jury pool?

Actually, the prosecutors made no such choice. A variety of factors made a trial in Santa Monica impossible from the outset. First, the courthouse there had sustained considerable damage in the Northridge earthquake just six months before the murders. Second, the county had set up metal detectors and other logistical accoutrements to lengthy, high-publicity cases on the ninth floor of the downtown courthouse; the judges insisted that all such cases be tried there. Finally, there was no grand jury room in Santa Monica, and cases indicted by the downtown grand jury usually stayed there for trial. In light of all this the prosecutors never even discussed any alternatives.

ON FRIDAY, June 17, the grand jury investigation of O. J. Simpson began with the sound of a telephone jarring Kato Kaelin awake at

6:00 a.m. An LAPD detective informed Kaelin, who had moved in temporarily with a friend, that he would be coming at 8:00 to escort him downtown for more interviews with the police. At the appointed hour a pair of detectives arrived with a grand jury subpoena demanding that Kaelin provide testimony that very afternoon.

This was a highly unusual and confrontational way to proceed—grand jury witnesses invariably receive more than a few hours' notice—but the prosecutors felt that they needed to lock in Kaelin's story under oath or it might change to help the defendant.

Escorted into Marcia Clark's office on the eighteenth floor late Friday morning, Kaelin stalled until his lawyer, Bill Genego, arrived to intervene.

"It's five to one," Clark told Genego. "You can have three minutes with your client before we take him down to the grand jury. He's going on at one o'clock."

"That's insane," Genego replied. "You don't subpoena someone for the same day he's going to testify."

"He's going in," Clark said. "That's that."

After Genego and Kaelin conferred briefly, the defense lawyer renewed his plea for a little time to talk the situation over. No deal, said Clark. Get in the elevator.

"Look," said Genego, "if you force him to go in there, I'll just tell him to take the Fifth and you won't get anything from him."

Clark was incensed. "If you try to interfere, I'll have you arrested for obstruction of justice."

Genego had never before been threatened this way by a prosecutor. Left no alternative, he scribbled out a page of instructions and handed them to Kaelin before Clark escorted him into the grand jury room. Clinging to his lawyer's script, Kaelin picked his way through the jurors, who were seated classroom-style in front of the witness stand, and flopped into the chair.

After he took the oath, Clark asked him, "Mr. Kaelin, were you acquainted with a woman by the name of Nicole Simpson?"

"On the advice of my attorney," Kaelin stated, "I must respectfully decline to answer and assert my constitutional right to remain silent."

"You seem to be reading from a piece of yellow paper, and there is some writing on that paper," the prosecutor said. As Clark would soon know only too well, Kaelin could never have uttered such a cogent sentence if left to his own devices. Kaelin admitted that he had been reading his answer.

Clark tried again, asking, "On the night of June 12, 1994, were you in the company of Mr. Orenthal James Simpson?" (Among prosecutors it would become sort of a trope to use Simpson's ungainly full name, no matter how stilted it made them sound.)

Kaelin repeated his refusal to answer questions.

Then, at Clark's direction, the foreperson of the grand jury read a stern message to Kaelin. "Mr. Kaelin, I advise you that your refusal, without legal cause, to answer questions before this grand jury does constitute contempt and will subject you to imprisonment pursuant to the laws of this state." When Kaelin still wouldn't answer, the foreperson officially found him in contempt and ordered the bewildered houseguest to the courtroom of Judge Stephen Czuleger.

Before Judge Czuleger, the prosecutors erupted in fury and indignation. Kaelin, they said, was not a suspect in the case but only a witness; therefore, he had no right to invoke the Fifth Amendment. Genego replied that Kaelin certainly had been treated like a suspect that morning. A thoughtful judge, Czuleger seemed put off by the prosecutors' strong-arm tactics. What was the harm, he asked, in giving Kaelin a weekend to talk to his lawyer, "putting aside he may flee the country and be in Brazil by morning." Everyone in the courtroom laughed at the ridiculous prospect of Kato Kaelin on the run.

The wisdom of Judge Czuleger's decision to put off the confrontation was proven on Monday morning when Kaelin agreed to testify without invoking his Fifth Amendment right. The weekend-long delay had defused the legal confrontation, but the rocky introduction set the tone for Kaelin's relationship with the D.A.'s office. He told the grand jury that on the night of the murders he and O.J. had gone to McDonald's for hamburgers shortly after 9:00 and returned at about 9:40 p.m. At about 10:45 p.m., while he was talking on the telephone in his room, he heard the three loud thumps on his wall. Shortly before 11:00 he had helped Simpson put his bags in the limousine for the trip to the airport.

It was, for the most part, an incriminating story. Most important, it established that Simpson's whereabouts were unaccounted for at the time the murders took place and that someone, possibly Simpson, had been rummaging around in the precise location where the bloody glove was found just a few hours later. Some details did favor Simpson. For one thing, as Kato described it, Simpson's demeanor during their trip to McDonald's hardly seemed that of a man who was moments away from slaughtering his ex-wife. Still, that kind of nuance might have evolved in the prosecution's favor if Kaelin had come to trust that the prosecutors would stand by him and, just as important, that he had nothing to fear from O.J. and his friends. But that kind of approach wasn't Clark's style. She relied far more on the stick than the carrot and succeeded only in alienating Kaelin.

Another grand jury witness was Jill Shively. If the glamour of O.J.'s and Nicole's lives represented one archetype of Los Angeles culture, the reality of Shively's represented another.

At the age of thirty-two Jill was working intermittent hours in a film-supply business and living in a tiny one-bedroom apartment, one mile and a world away from Nicole Brown Simpson's condominium on Bundy Drive.

On June 12 at around 10:45 p.m. Shively decided to drive to a favorite salad bar. Gunning her Volkswagen to beat the store's 11:00 closing time, she raced along San Vicente Boulevard, going east. As she approached the intersection where Bundy crosses San Vicente, Shively accelerated to make the light. A large white vehicle heading north on Bundy raced against the light, in front of her. Shively slammed on her brakes, as did the white car, which then ran up partially on San Vicente's raised center median. A third car, a gray Nissan heading west on San Vicente, also stopped suddenly, trying like Shively to avoid the white car.

Briefly the three cars were frozen next to one another. Then the driver of the white car began honking his horn and screaming,

"Move your damn car! Move it! Move it!" Shively noticed that the driver was black, and on second glance she thought she recognized him. It was O. J. Simpson.

The stunned driver of the gray Nissan was finally gathering his wits to move on. At last he did, and Simpson peeled off on Bundy.

Shively wrote off the incident and continued her search for salad. Her car lacked a radio, so when she went to work the next morning, she had no idea about the murders until her mother called her at her job. "Did you hear that Nicole Simpson was murdered last night?"

"That's weird," Jill said. "O.J. nearly ran me down last night."

Shively called the police, and on Saturday, June 18, a detective came to her home with a grand jury subpoena. By Sunday her name had leaked out as a witness, and reporters were banging on her apartment door. On Monday, Shively decided to give an interview. She went to the Paramount lot in Hollywood, found her way to the set of *Hard Copy*, and sat down to make a little money.

In the first public announcement of the murders Commander Gascon, the police spokesman, had issued a plea to the news media. "Over the next few days detectives will continue to interview possible witnesses and gather and analyze evidence," he said on June 13. "Detectives are requesting that the media not attempt to contact potential witnesses in this case, as those contacts may negatively impact the course of this investigation. I need to stress that. It's critically important."

If the tabloids had heard Gascon's plea, it didn't change their behavior. They offered cash to virtually every major participant (and many fringe figures) in the Simpson case. For the interview that she gave *Hard Copy* on June 20, Jill Shively got a relatively small amount—$5000. The following morning Marcia Clark led her through her testimony for the grand jury. Then that night *Hard Copy* ran the interview with Shively. Clark was apoplectic when she learned of it. Just before Shively had testified, Clark and David Conn had asked her if she had spoken to anyone about the subject matter of her testimony. Just her mother, Shively had replied. Now it was clear that she had spoken to *Hard Copy* as well.

The next day a terrified Shively tried to explain that she thought Clark and Conn had asked her who was the *first* person she told about the incident. That had been her mother. Shively said she didn't realize they wanted to know all of the people she had told. Clark ordered her to return on June 23 to explain herself before the grand jury.

After Shively's explanation on the twenty-third Marcia Clark asked for a moment to address the grand jury. "Because it is our duty as prosecutors to present only that evidence in which we are 110 percent confident as to its truthfulness and reliability, I must now ask you to completely disregard the statements given and the testimony given by Jill Shively in this case."

Prosecutors should never present evidence they find less than fully believable. But there was a kind of self-defeating sanctimony in Clark's posture as well. A simple request to disregard Shively's testimony would have more than satisfied Clark's ethical obligations. Instead, in a fit of pique Clark denounced Shively in terms that made her permanently useless to the government.

But Marcia Clark felt she could afford it. After all, the prosecution had plenty of witnesses.

IN THE first few days after the murders Robert Shapiro bought himself an enormous amount of high-priced help. He didn't know much about autopsies and crime scenes, so he called two of the nation's leading forensic experts—Henry Lee, the chief police scientist for the state of Connecticut, and Michael Baden, the former chief medical examiner of New York City. He knew nothing about DNA, so he recruited two lawyers from New York, Barry Scheck and Peter Neufeld. Shapiro had not gone to trial on many complex crimes—and he had never tried a murder—so he summoned his old friend F. Lee Bailey.

On Monday, June 20, 1994—the day the haggard Simpson mumbled his not-guilty plea in court—Alan Dershowitz, the famous Harvard Law School professor, appeared on public television's *Charlie Rose*. Dershowitz explained the thesis that "politically correct" sentiments often apply different criteria of culpability to people from disadvantaged groups. He speculated that the Simpson case "may end up in something like a hung jury. It may end up in a plea bargain, or it may end up with a Menendez- or Bobbitt-type verdict, which will send a message out, 'Gee, you can get away with this kind of stuff.' "

Dershowitz's comments irritated Shapiro. He told a friend, "How can we shut that guy up?" After a pause he said half jokingly, "I guess we'll have to hire him." And the day after Dershowitz appeared on *Charlie Rose,* Robert Shapiro invited him to join the defense team. Dershowitz dutifully informed Shapiro that he had made some less than supportive comments in the media. Shapiro didn't care. Alan, he said, we need you.

Alan Dershowitz

No law or even any ethical rule prevented Dershowitz from accepting the assignment. As Dershowitz himself cheerfully noted in his memoir *The Best Defense,* "Almost all of my own clients have been guilty."

Shapiro told Dershowitz that he had also hired Gerald Uelman, who was, like Dershowitz, a law school professor but was in many ways his opposite. Soft-spoken, with pale skin and white hair that seemed at times to render him nearly invisible, Uelman served as dean of Santa Clara University law school, in San Jose. The two professors shared, however, an aggressive criminal defense philosophy—that the defense had to stay on the offensive, endeavoring in every respect to create chaos in the prosecution camp.

Dershowitz and Uelman discovered their first opportunity to do this in the extraordinary onslaught of media attention to the Simpson case. They alleged that the pretrial publicity had poisoned the minds of the grand jurors. Moreover, on Wednesday, June 22, the Los Angeles City Attorney's Office, acting on media requests, had released the audiotape of Nicole Brown Simpson's heartrending telephone call to 911 on October 25, 1993. "Can you get someone over here now? He's back. Please," the trembling voice of Nicole said repeatedly on television and radio.

Uelman and Dershowitz put together a motion they called an Emergency Motion for Voir Dire of Grand Jurors and Determination of Prejudice from Improper Pretrial Publicity. The most they really hoped for was that a judge would agree to question the jurors and then determine the impact of the publicity on them. Almost as an afterthought they threw in the request that the grand jury be disbanded.

This motion had the intended effect of throwing the prosecutors off their stride at a time when the release of the 911 tapes had already complicated their task. D.A. Garcetti didn't want it to look as if he was treating Simpson unfairly, so he publicly criticized the city attorney's office for releasing the tapes in the middle of his office's investigation. Several people around the courthouse overheard some grand jurors talking about the tapes, although they had not been presented as evidence. The prosecutors realized they might have an ethical obligation to tell the judge, since going forward with a tainted grand jury could jeopardize a conviction on appeal. The prosecutors decided to join in the motion to disband the grand jury, which was followed by a terse ruling from the bench. There would be a preliminary hearing after all.

MARCIA Clark had only four days to put it together. During the truncated grand jury proceedings the prosecutors had learned that Simpson had recently bought a large knife at Ross Cutlery, a store in downtown Los Angeles. A preliminary comparison with the autopsy findings suggested that Simpson's recent purchase might be the murder weapon. So on Tuesday, June 28, Clark obtained a warrant to search Simpson's home for the knife. Cops turned the place upside down but came up empty-handed.

The next day, in the L.A. county jail, Gerald Uelman asked O. J. Simpson, "Where's the knife?"

After receiving instructions from Simpson, Uelman returned to

Rockingham and went upstairs to the master bedroom. Behind mirrored doors Uelman found, in a box, the knife that O. J. Simpson had purchased just a few weeks earlier. It appeared pristine—as Simpson had promised it would be.

Gerald Uelman had to decide what to do. If he were to touch the knife, he would immediately become a witness in the case, and in light of the cops' embarrassing failure to find the knife, they might accuse him of planting or hiding it. But the knife's pristine appearance seemed to reflect favorably on Simpson. Uelman kept his options open by simply closing the mirrored door. A night of feverish consultations among the defense lawyers yielded a plan.

The first thing the following morning, Thursday, June 30—also the first day of the preliminary hearing—Uelman and Shapiro went in secret to the chambers of Judge Lance Ito of the superior court. (Ito was, at that time, the judge who handled all miscellaneous criminal matters.) The lawyers asked Ito to appoint a neutral arbitrator to go to Simpson's house and remove the knife to the custody of the court. Ito agreed and sent retired superior court judge Delbert Wong, who brought it to Ito in a heavily taped envelope. No one—not the public and not the prosecutors—was any the wiser.

Uelman and Shapiro were delighted. From Ito's chambers they raced to the courtroom of Judge Kathleen Kennedy-Powell for the opening moments of the preliminary hearing.

The tense atmosphere there did not match Shapiro's cheery mood. Now, for the first time, all the principals in the case, including the families of the victims, were arrayed in one place under the scrutiny of a live national television audience: All three networks, as well as CNN and Court TV, had preempted regular programming to broadcast the hearing.

By this point David Conn, Marcia Clark's direct superior, had returned to his primary assignment of leading the retrial of the Menendez brothers. In his place Garcetti had named Bill Hodgman. Cool where Clark was hot, calm where she was excitable, Hodgman served as a good foil for Clark, in Garcetti's view. It was Hodgman who called the first witness to the stand.

Allen Wattenberg and his brother operated Ross Cutlery, nestled in a corner of the historic Bradbury Building, whose magnificent iron-and-glass interior courtyard has long served L.A.'s moviemakers. On May 3, 1994, the sidewalk in front of their store was the setting for a scene in a pilot for an NBC series, *Frogman*, starring O. J. Simpson. Allen Wattenberg testified that during a break in filming that day, Simpson had come into the store and bought a fifteen-inch folding lock-blade knife with a handle carved from deer antlers. Hodgman displayed an identical model on a board for the judge (and, of course, the television camera). In private, Shapiro and Uelman laughed.

The prosecutors got what they wanted—large and sinister photographs of the knife in virtually every newspaper in America. But there was another reason, besides high drama, that Hodgman and Clark wanted Wattenberg on the stand first. His employee José Camacho had testified in front of the grand jury the previous week. After he testified, Camacho had been approached by the *National Enquirer* and had accepted $12,500 for an interview, to be shared with the two Wattenberg brothers. Had the prosecutors known at the outset that Jill Shively was going to be only one of several witnesses paid by the tabloids, Clark might not have been so hasty to disown her in front of the grand jury. With Wattenberg and Camacho, who followed his boss to the witness stand, the prosecutors had figured that the mutually corroborating nature of their stories would trump the taint of tabloid money.

The saga of the Ross Cutlery knife had a bittersweet conclusion for the defense lawyers. Judge Lance Ito left on vacation and turned the package over to his boss, Cecil Mills, the chief superior court judge. Mills apparently failed to understand its secret nature and simply turned the envelope over to presiding judge Kennedy-Powell. She, too, had no idea of the story behind the envelope and brought it out on the bench with her when she received it. The media promptly dubbed it the "mystery envelope," but Clark and Hodgman had no trouble figuring out what was inside. Shapiro and Uelman were disappointed that they could never spring the surprise of the envelope's existence, but they did succeed in spooking the prosecutors; indeed, they would never attempt to identify a specific knife as the murder weapon. Eventually the defense obtained the court's permission to test the knife in the envelope. It was found to be in mint condition.

THE publicity-infected grand jury, the tabloid-tainted "knife witnesses"—they were merely a warm-up for the most important defense effort at the preliminary hearing. Simpson's lawyers wanted to establish that the detectives' first search of Simpson's home had violated the law and that in fact O. J. Simpson was yet another black victim of the LAPD.

Customarily police officers must obtain a search warrant before entering a suspect's property. But over the past two decades courts have established several exceptions. One of them holds that in an emergency the police can search without a warrant. The question for Judge Kennedy-Powell was whether there was any emergency that justified four detectives—Vannatter, Lange, Phillips, and Fuhrman—entering Simpson's property early on June 13.

Vannatter insisted that the detectives traveled from Bundy to Rockingham not because Simpson was a suspect but because they wanted to inform him of the murders and arrange for him to pick up his children. Once at O.J.'s home Vannatter decided to have Fuhrman vault the wall because the blood they found on the Bronco made him think that Simpson might also be injured.

Uelman argued, "We are told that four detectives all converged on the residence of Mr. Simpson simply for the purpose of informing him of the tragedy that had taken place at the Bundy location, a purpose that could just as easily have been accomplished by the placing of a telephone call." He pointed out that the drop of blood on the Bronco door "was just as consistent with a dripping taco or a driver with a hangnail." No, Uelman insisted, the detectives' purported concern for Simpson's welfare merely served as a pretext for their desire to tie him to the murders. Furthermore, one of the four, Mark Fuhrman, had been to the house before to investigate a domestic altercation; that history might certainly have made the officers view Simpson as a suspect.

The truth of the matter may well have been reflected in a third view—one that neither side would have wanted the judge or the public to believe. The defense never wanted to acknowledge that the police viewed O.J. with anything other than hostility and suspicion, while the police could not admit that instead of investigating the crime scene, they had preferred to coddle and hobnob with a celebrity. Vannatter's pretext for why they had gone there in the first place worked in the short term: Judge Kennedy-Powell decided not to suppress the evidence.

This prosecution victory came at a price, however. Public debate on the case shifted, at least in part, from whether O.J. was guilty to whether the police had acted appropriately. And although they failed to persuade the judge, the defense lawyers planted the idea with a pool of potential jurors that the police had a secret, nefarious agenda to get Simpson. That alone made the preliminary hearing worthwhile for the defense.

Simpson "lost" the prelim, of course. Judge Kennedy-Powell ruled on July 8 that Simpson had to stand trial. But all the legal action, as well as an unending stream of well-wishers visiting him in jail, considerably buoyed O.J.'s spirits. By the time he was arraigned in superior court he cut a dapper figure once more. He greeted his supports in the gallery with a wink and a thumbs-up, and when the judge asked him to repeat his plea to the charges of double murder, this time Simpson needed no prompting.

"Absolutely, 100 percent not guilty," he said.

5

FOR all the good that came out of the prelim, the hearing forced Shapiro to face reality. Clark had concluded her presentation with the first public airing of the government's blood evidence in the case. According to the tests, the blood drops to the left of the shoe prints at Bundy matched Simpson's—and that of only .43 percent of the population. In other words, 99.57 percent of the population could be excluded as sources of that blood.

It was devastating evidence. Even with the clever half steps he had taken so far, Shapiro could not win a simple jury referendum on whether his client had killed those two human beings. He knew, however, that he might win a referendum on a different subject—the racism of the Los Angeles Police Department.

THE revelation that tabloid outlets had paid several witnesses for interviews led, indirectly, to my own involvement in the Simpson case. Around the time of the murders I was completing a story for *The New Yorker* about "cash for trash," mostly on how the investigation of Michael Jackson for sexual abuse of minors had been compromised because so many potential prosecution witnesses had been paid by the tabloids. I had a chance to add a few details about the tabloids' role in the early days of the Simpson case—specifically, with regard to Jill Shively and the Ross Cutlery witnesses—and my story appeared on Tuesday, July 5, 1994.

Later that week, unbeknownst to me at the time, the editor in chief of *The New Yorker,* Tina Brown, sent the photographer Richard Avedon along with Susan Mercandetti, a *New Yorker* editor who often works with Avedon, to Los Angeles to take pictures of the defense and prosecution teams in the Simpson case.

On Monday, July 11, Tina told me that Shapiro had told Susan he might—*might*—agree to be interviewed by me about the case. She said I should make plans to go to Los Angeles the next morning. I doubted anything would come of it, but I went.

I did have one possible lead. While I was still in New York, I had had a brief phone conversation with Alan Dershowitz, who had by then joined Simpson's defense team. Ten years earlier I had taken Dershowitz's first-year criminal law class at Harvard Law School, and we had spoken occasionally in subsequent years. Dershowitz went on a lengthy tirade about one of the detectives involved in the case.

When I arrived in California late Tuesday, I found out there had been no progress in my getting an audience with Shapiro. So on Wednesday morning I decided to follow up on what I had heard from Dershowitz. If the detective really did have a bad record, there was bound to be an official file. The LAPD would not allow me to see anything in his records, but from my days as a prosecutor I knew that law-enforcement officials were often sued for violating the civil rights of people they encountered. Shortly after 10:00 I found the room at the Los Angeles County Courthouse where all cases are indexed on microform, and I sat down to see if this detective named Mark Fuhrman had ever been the subject of a lawsuit.

No—not exactly. But the file did indicate that on August 24, 1983, Fuhrman himself had filed a suit. And the defendant, curiously enough, was the City of Los Angeles Fire and Police Pension System. Since it was so old, the case file was in the closed archives across Hill Street. The clerk there handed me a file about two inches thick.

It amounted to a miniature autobiography of Mark Fuhrman: born February 5, 1952; grew up in Washington State; a brother died of leukemia before Mark was born; father a truck driver and carpenter; parents divorced when he was seven. In 1970 Fuhrman joined the marines, then served in Vietnam as a machine gunner. He thrived in the service until his last six months. Then, as Fuhrman later explained to a psychiatrist, he stopped enjoying his military service because "there were Mexicans and niggers." As a result of these problems, in 1975 Fuhrman left the marines and went to the Los Angeles Police Academy.

Fuhrman excelled at the academy, finishing second in his class. His early LAPD personnel ratings were high, but in 1977 Fuhrman's assignment was changed to the pursuit of street gangs in East L.A., and his evaluators began to show some reservations. One wrote, "After a while he began to dislike his work, especially the 'low-class' people he was dealing with. He bragged about violence he used in subduing suspects, including choke holds, and said he would break their hands or face or arms or legs if necessary."

While his job ratings remained high, Fuhrman reported that the strains of the job affected him, and in the early 1980s he sought to leave the force. His lawyers asserted that in the course of his work Fuhrman "sustained seriously disabling psychiatric symptomatology" and as a result should receive a disability pension from the city. In the city's answers, however, he was called a competent officer, albeit one involved in an elaborate ruse to win a pension. Fuhrman lost his case and, as a result, remained on the force.

As I studied the file, its implications were obvious. The Fuhrman disability case had the potential to thrust the specter of Rodney King into the middle of the Simpson case. The officer depicted in this battle over a pension seemed the archetype of the bigoted, bullying L.A. cop. If Simpson's lawyers chose to use this file—and I wondered at the time whether they even knew about it—it could transform the case, which to that point had been regarded as largely apolitical. Would that change? Having seen Fuhrman's file, I decided it was now all the more important that I speak to Shapiro.

As I had no appointment with him, I decided the best thing I could do was simply arrive at his office. I drove from downtown L.A. to Century City. In the lobby of Shapiro's office tower I consulted the directory and took the elevator up. As it happened, Shapiro was in his office. Susan Mercandetti had told me his secretary's name was Bonnie Barron.

"Hi, Bonnie!" I said with perhaps excessive enthusiasm to the middle-aged woman outside Shapiro's office. "I'm Jeff Toobin with *The New Yorker.*" I had put a copy of my cash-for-trash article in an envelope on the theory that I could say I was "delivering" it to Shapiro. I told Barron, "I have something for Bob, and I thought I might drop it off for him."

Shapiro looked out to see who was talking to his secretary. I saw my chance. I introduced myself and said, "I had a very interesting morning looking at Mark Fuhrman's employment records."

"You saw those?" Shapiro asked.

"Yeah, about how he hates blacks and all that."

"You're the only guy who's found those. Come in here and sit down." I did.

Shapiro was full of energy. Unshaven, he was wearing a work shirt and blue jeans. His messy office was distinguished only by his stunning desk, which appeared to be a genuine Napoleonic antique, full of inlaid woods and brass ornamentation.

I asked him what he made of the Fuhrman records. "There's worse stuff, too," he told me. "This is a guy who used to wake up every day and say to his ex-wife, 'I'm going to kill some niggers this morning.' "

Shapiro had learned of Fuhrman's disability-case file from a former LAPD detective named Bill Pavelic. Pavelic's career had stalled when he began speaking out against what he saw as the pervasive racism in the department. In 1992, after eighteen years on the force, he had quit and now hired himself out as a "consultant" to those with grievances against the LAPD. When Pavelic discovered Fuhrman's file, he mentioned it to his latest client, Robert Shapiro.

I asked Shapiro what he thought Mark Fuhrman meant for the Simpson defense effort. "Just picture it," he said, growing more animated as he spoke. "Here's a guy who's one of the cops coming on the scene early in the morning. They have the biggest case of their lives. But an hour later you're told you're not in charge of the case. How's that going to make that guy feel? So now he's one of four detectives heading over to O.J.'s house. Suppose he's actually found two gloves at the murder scene. He transports one of them over to the house and then 'finds' it back in that little alleyway where no one can see him." Discovering the glove would turn Fuhrman into "the hero of the case."

I was stunned. The thought that Fuhrman might have planted the glove at Rockingham had never occurred to me. But I immediately realized how clever the suggestion was as a defense tactic. This transformed the gloves from strong evidence of Simpson's guilt—who else but Simpson could have been at both Nicole's house and his own that night?—to evidence of a police conspiracy. I also realized that Shapiro's theory was also monstrous. The defense would attempt to persuade a jury, largely through innuendo, that a police officer, acting out of racial animus, had planted evidence to see an innocent man convicted of murder.

Trying to process all those thoughts, I briefly found myself at a loss for words. Shapiro, too, suddenly seemed to withdraw from the conversation. He picked up a stack of mail he had been looking at, and for a moment I watched him read.

We had never discussed ground rules for our interview, so I asked, "Can I quote you by name?"

"No," he said. "That's too much like an interview."

"So it's okay if I say 'a member of the defense team,' " I said.

"Something like that."*

And then, simple as that, our conversation was over. It had lasted no more than fifteen minutes. We said our good-byes, and Shapiro and I agreed to keep in touch.

I wrote up a draft of my article and faxed it to the editors in New York. The next day, Thursday, I spent conferring with other members of the defense team, polishing the story and filling in holes. That night I took the TWA red-eye home. (The in-flight movie was *Naked Gun 33 1/3*, starring, among others, O. J. Simpson.)

Friday morning, back in my office to close the piece, I realized this would be a very damaging story to write about someone. I had called the LAPD public affairs office and had been told that it would have no comment on the Simpson case. And no, I certainly could not interview Mark Fuhrman. That bothered me. I called around the LAPD to find a phone number for him. It didn't take more than five minutes. I dialed.

"Fuhrman," a man answered.

"Is this Mark Fuhrman?" I asked.

"Yes," he said.

I figured this conversation would not last long, so I identified myself and got right to the point. I explained that I was working on a story that said the defense was planning to charge him with planting the glove on Simpson's property. I asked him if he had.

Fuhrman paused, then said, "That's a ridiculous question."

I found that answer curious. So I asked Fuhrman again straight out if he planted the glove.

"Of course it didn't happen."

Fuhrman said he couldn't talk anymore and hung up.

---

*In a conversation many months later Shapiro gave me permission to recount that conversation in this book. Also, in his own book Shapiro disclosed that he was the source for my story.

MY STORY APPEARED ON MONDAY, July 18. All through the editing process the title had been "Playing the Race Card." But at the last moment someone at *The New Yorker* thought that was too similar to another headline in the issue, so mine was changed to "An Incendiary Defense." I wrote that in a series of conversations the previous week "leading members of Simpson's defense team floated [a] new and provocative theory." I summarized the defense hypothesis and explained its basis in the court records from Fuhrman's pension case, but I did not suggest that the theory was true—that is, that Fuhrman did indeed plant the glove. And, of course, I included Fuhrman's denial prominently.

In retrospect, what mattered most about my story, written just about a month after the murders, was that the issue of race was now out in the open. I wrote, "If race does become a significant factor in this case—if the case becomes transformed from a mere soap opera to a civil rights melodrama—then the stakes will change dramatically."

Robert Shapiro had a parochial, if accurate, reaction to my article. On the day it appeared, Shapiro called F. Lee Bailey in London and said, "It's over. I won the case."

IN THE eighth grade of his public school in Los Angeles, Robert Shapiro and his friend Joel Siegel—now the cheerful, lavishly mustached entertainment reporter for ABC's *Good Morning America*—had an experience they still talked about forty years later. A clique that called itself the Idols was having a meeting one day, and neither Shapiro nor Siegel was invited. The slight festered, and from that day forward Bob Shapiro, like an updated Scarlett O'Hara, made a vow: With God as his witness, he would never be unpopular again. And he never was.

Shapiro was born in Plainfield, New Jersey, in 1942, and the family moved to Los Angeles a year later—an advance guard in the great Jewish migration to West Los Angeles that followed World War II. His mother was a housewife. His father did a lot of things—drove a lunch wagon, worked in a factory—but Marty Shapiro's real passion was playing the piano in a small band that did gigs at bar mitzvahs and weddings. An only child much loved by his parents and his grandparents, Bob sought early on never to disappoint them, and he rarely has.

By the time he arrived at U.C.L.A. at the dawn of the '60s, Shapiro had a showman's moxie and a taste for action. He went on

to law school because, well, his fraternity, Zeta Beta Tau, practically went en masse. Shapiro thrived at Loyola Law School even though he went through a quick marriage and annulment while a student there.

Shapiro spent three years as a prosecutor—a successful if unremarkable tenure—before he caught the eye of the man who would change his life. The flamboyant Los Angeles criminal defense lawyer Harry Weiss had seen Robert Shapiro in action and found the young lawyer "presentable and charming," as

Robert Shapiro

he later recalled. But something a junior associate told Weiss about Shapiro really stuck in his mind. "You know, Shapiro is the only deputy D.A. I know who drives a Bentley." It was, to be sure, only a used Bentley, but it was all Weiss needed to hear. He hired Shapiro as a junior associate in 1972.

For fifteen years, the formative period of his professional life, Bob Shapiro was Harry Weiss's protégé. That fancy Napoleonic desk Shapiro sat behind in Century City? A gift from Harry. The '70s were the heyday of their association and boom years for their law practice. They shared a palatial penthouse suite at 8600 Sunset Boulevard that boasted a private swimming pool.

Mostly, Weiss and Shapiro cut deals for their clients. This was imperative, given the number of clients they serviced, but it also reflected the nature of their cases and the personalities of the lawyers. In the mid-1970s the police in L.A. still arrested large numbers of people for so-called victimless crimes—prostitution, drug usage, and some consensual-sex offenses. The firm specialized in the speedy and painless resolutions of such matters. Shapiro also became something like house counsel to ballplayers in trouble, a group that came to include José Canseco (gun possession), Darryl Strawberry (tax evasion), and Vince Coleman (throwing a firecracker at a group of fans).

There was a pattern to many of Shapiro's big cases: The facts were usually undisputed; the only issue was punishment—that is, how a bargain could be structured with the prosecutor and judge. Shapiro cut so many deals so successfully—the celebrities he represented almost never went to jail—that it contributed to an impression that he didn't know how to try a case.

It was true that Shapiro did not relish that side of the job. For example, he hated having to visit his clients in jail. In 1989 a client named George Guzman, who had been stopped in a car that contained cocaine, complained bitterly that Shapiro never came to see him. Guzman was even more offended that Shapiro had instructed him not to speak to him in court. Yet when the time came for summations in the trial, Shapiro became so swept away by the emotion of the moment that he embraced his client in front of the jury and shouted, "This man is innocent!" The prisoner recoiled so quickly that he threw out a muscle in his back. But he never complained; the jury acquitted him.

6

ONE of the enduring fictions of the Simpson case was the notion of the defendant himself as "involved" in his defense. O.J.'s attorneys manufactured this idea primarily as a gift to their client and as a way of remaining in his good graces. Moreover, treating Simpson as the equal of his lawyers fit nicely with the paternalistic approach many mainstream journalists take in writing about race. It also relieved them of confronting the obvious truth about him— that he was an uneducated, semiliterate ex-athlete who could barely understand much about the legal proceedings against him.

O.J. didn't even understand the nature of the defense strategy Shapiro had constructed. Shapiro was, for example, incredulous when Simpson wanted Gerry Spence as his trial lawyer. O.J. had seen Spence on TV for years and thought he was great. Shapiro had nothing against Spence, but the defense in this case would be race. What could a Wyoming attorney offer to—in Shapiro's preferred code words—"a downtown jury"?

In truth, Shapiro didn't really want any other high-profile lawyers added to the team. O.J.'s friends worried about Shapiro's reputation as a plea-bargainer, however, and his relative lack of trial experience. They wanted a high-powered trial attorney on the team, and Shapiro reluctantly agreed.

Shapiro mentioned Johnnie Cochran. Who else but the foremost black attorney in Los Angeles to conduct a defense based on race? Ultimately all of Simpson's friends agreed. For a time, only O.J. demurred. He liked Cochran, had even talked to him several times since the murders, but he wasn't sure if he wanted him as his lawyer. It is one of the richer and more revealing ironies of the case that only O. J. Simpson himself—"I'm not black. I'm O.J."—failed to understand the preeminent place of race in his own defense.

Shapiro and the others prevailed upon Simpson to put aside his infatuation with Spence, and Cochran was hired on Monday, July 18. Since the day of the murders Cochran had been commenting on the case almost daily for the *Today* show and other programs. In fact, he had been laying the groundwork all along for the role that he saw coming his way. As Cochran put it on *Today*, "I think this case is now clearly about the Fourth Amendment and whether or not it's alive and well in Los Angeles County."

Once Cochran signed onto the case, the question of whether Simpson had in fact murdered his ex-wife and her friend became immaterial. Cochran had a gift, and he knew it. Preeminently in his generation of lawyers, Johnnie Cochran had perfected the art of winning jury trials in downtown Los Angeles. Now he was going to do it for O. J. Simpson.

IN THE 1940S THE UNITED STATES witnessed one of the greatest internal migrations any country has ever seen: the black flight from the South during and after World War II. Kinship and custom dictated the destinations: Mississippians went to Chicago; North Carolinians headed to New York; and Texans and Louisianans, like Johnnie L. Cochran, Sr., went to California. Johnnie, who had sold insurance policies in Shreveport, found work as a shipfitter for Bethlehem Steel, building vast troopships in Alameda, next door to Oakland. He rented a three-bedroom apartment and sent word for his wife, Hattie, and the three kids to join him.

After long days at the docks Cochran senior took correspondence courses to hone the sales techniques that would serve him in peacetime. Within weeks of V-J Day the Golden State Mutual Life Insurance Company, the biggest of the black-owned companies on the West Coast, offered him a job. Promoted to manager in 1947, Johnnie was appointed to open a San Diego office in 1948 and then went on to a bigger job in Los Angeles the following year. There he bought a house for his family on a pleasant street in an integrated neighborhood called West Adams.

To a degree the Cochrans shared in the American dream, but no one (and especially not black Angelenos) confused their town with paradise. As one writer put it, "Life was still hard in L.A. and if you worked every day you still found yourself on the bottom."

Hattie Cochran was determined that her firstborn son was not going to wind up on the bottom. She made sure that Johnnie junior became one of about thirty black students out of the two thousand or so at Los Angeles High School, even though he didn't live in the district. For Hattie's son the experience among the children of doctors and lawyers would prove transforming. "If you were a person who integrated well, as I was, you got to go to people's houses and envision another life," Cochran said of those years. "I knew kids who had things I could only *dream* of. It made me get off my butt and say, 'Hey, I can do this!' " These slices of life among his largely Jewish peers were every bit as important to Cochran as an afternoon with Willie Mays had been to O. J. Simpson.

Cochran went to the city's great public university, U.C.L.A., and

THE RUN OF HIS LIFE

then graduated from Loyola Law School in 1962 (six years before Shapiro did). He spent his first three years as a prosecutor with the city attorney, building a reputation as a trial lawyer. Next he set up shop as a defense attorney, with one office near downtown and another in largely black Compton. When Watts exploded in the riots of 1965, Cochran basically sat out the controversy. And when the NAACP and other civil rights organizations launched efforts to integrate the fire department and local schools, Cochran left no mark on these struggles. Notwithstanding these absences, young Johnnie Cochran did find his way into the public eye in a case that reflected the city's painful racial dilemmas.

In May 1966 Leonard Deadwyler, who was stopped for speeding while rushing his pregnant wife to the hospital, was shot and killed by an LAPD officer. Self-defense, said the police. The Deadwyler family hired Cochran to represent them, and the resulting coroner's inquest was televised to a rapt citywide audience. According to the peculiar procedure of the inquest, Cochran had no right to address witnesses himself but instead had to ask the deputy district attorney to pose questions for him. The government lawyer's words as he relayed the questions—"Mr. Cochran wants to know"—became something of a mantra heard around the city. Cochran lost the family's civil suit against the city, but his career and his issue—police abuse—were launched.

COCHRAN's public relations triumph in the Deadwyler case contributed to a feeling of invincibility on his part, and this attitude extended to his personal life. In 1967 Cochran began living an extraordinary double life.

Over the course of that year his wife, Barbara, a schoolteacher Cochran had met at U.C.L.A., began to suspect that her husband was having an affair. Barbara hired a private detective, who reported that Johnnie was spending his evenings at the home of Patty Sikora, a blond legal secretary. When Barbara confronted Johnnie, she later wrote in a book, he turned violent, and he beat her on several occasions. She threw him out of the house they shared with their young daughter. Cochran, who has denied hitting Barbara,

Johnnie L. Cochran, Jr.

vowed to mend his ways, and she took him back after a separation.

The beatings stopped, but Cochran kept seeing Patty Sikora. As Barbara pieced it together years later, Johnnie would "stop over at Patty's after he left the office. He'd read, help April [Patty's daughter from a previous marriage] with her homework, or watch TV while Patty made dinner for the family. After April was in bed, they might have some intimate time together. Then John would leave and come home to our house." Barbara simply thought her husband worked late.

Incredibly, Cochran managed to juggle these two lives for ten years. Over the course of this period Patty had a son with Johnnie, and Barbara had another daughter with him. At last, in 1977, Barbara ceased playing the fool, and Johnnie faced a potentially expensive divorce settlement. He decided to make a career change. A crusading young liberal named John Van de Kamp had been elected the new district attorney that year, and Johnnie agreed to join him as the number three prosecutor in the office.

As always, Cochran's motives were mixed. Reducing his income at that moment allowed him to pare down his divorce settlement. But Cochran also brought unfeigned passion for racial justice to his new job, and as a top prosecutor, he had finally arrived in a position where he could take on the LAPD on nearly equal terms.

The three-year tour in the district attorney's office only added to Cochran's professional luster. By the 1980s he had returned to private practice, and his office became a regular port of call for victims of excessive police force. In little more than a decade he amassed more than $40 million in damages against the city—which meant that, according to legal-industry custom, Cochran netted about $15 million in fees from those cases alone. His personal life also settled down. He separated from Patty shortly after his divorce from Barbara and entered into a happy marriage with his current wife, marketing consultant Dale Cochran, in 1985.

Cochran's legend grew. Although he was little known in the broader white world, his reputation was matchless in black Los Angeles. Hiring him represented the logical next step in the race theory of Shapiro's defense, for Cochran gave this theory immeasurably more force than Shapiro or any other white lawyer ever could. It apparently mattered little that Cochran would be investing his vast credibility and reputation in service of a lie. He took the case with the goal of conveying a simple syllogism: Cochran stands for the cause of all African Americans; therefore Simpson does, too. Cochran started by casting aside his previous (if private) doubts about Simpson's innocence. As Cochran put it in an interview with Katie Couric on the *Today* show shortly after he was hired, "In the O. J. Simpson case, I think winning takes on the form of him being found not guilty, because this is one of those cases where, from the very beginning, he said, 'I'm innocent.' "

"And you believe him?" Couric asked.

"And I believe him," Cochran replied. "Absolutely."

"A hundred percent, in your heart, that he is not guilty?"

Cochran was adamant. "In my heart, I believe that, absolutely."

AT THE ARRAIGNMENT ON FRIDAY, July 22—when Simpson said he was "absolutely, 100 percent not guilty"—Judge Mills announced that he had assigned the case to Judge Lance A. Ito, of the superior court. Because Ito's wife, Margaret York, served as a captain in the LAPD and was one of the highest-ranking women there, Mills gave the defense the opportunity to have Ito removed from the case with no questions asked. But the defense team regarded Ito as about as good a choice as they could expect. Unlike many of his conservative colleagues, he had a reputation as a judge who would at least listen to the arguments of defense lawyers—especially these defense lawyers. Cochran and Shapiro knew him well. During his own stint in the D.A.'s office Cochran had supervised Ito. Shapiro, ever the networker, had also crossed paths with the judge any number of times over the years.

Ito was also known as an energetic judge, and this was important because speed remained the defense's objective: Both Shapiro and Cochran saw Simpson's popularity as a dwindling asset. The judge obliged their desire for an expeditious trial by scheduling jury selection to begin sixty days hence, on September 20. Each side promptly turned, in its own way, to the next and most important challenge on the horizon: how to identify and select the jury that would be the most receptive to its case.

As ever, Shapiro went for the best. He hired Jo-Ellan Dimitrius, a jury consultant based near Los Angeles, whose previous clients included the defendants in the McMartin Preschool case and the police officers accused of beating Rodney King.

The prosecutors, in contrast, followed a more tortuous route. Shortly before jury selection began, Garcetti's office announced it would not seek the death penalty. Death-qualified jurors, as they are known—that is, jurors who have stated that they are willing to consider imposing the death penalty—are well known for being more likely to convict as well. As a defendant without an extensive criminal past, Simpson was an unlikely candidate for the death penalty, but the prosecution did yield an important strategic advantage when it excluded even the possibility.

Prosecutors' offices almost never have the funds to hire jury consultants, so the lawyers generally rely on their experience and gut feelings to do the best they can. Marcia Clark's gut feelings told her that she had a special rapport with one group of jurors in particular: black women. In case after case she had won their smiles, their nods, their sympathy. She even had a fan club of sorts, a group of former jurors, all black women, who kept in touch well after their trials had ended. Clark felt that these women—*her* women—would understand the story she would tell of Nicole Brown Simpson's death. After all, African American women were disproportionately the victims of domestic violence. Clark didn't need any outsider to tell her what she felt in her trial lawyer's bones.

Yet a consultant did appear—and not just any jury consultant. Donald Vinson, a respected former marketing professor at U.S.C., had applied his work in the social sciences to the art of jury selection and had invented a new field. Using the most sophisticated research techniques—including focus groups, survey research, and even the hiring of "shadow jurors" who would sit in court and give lawyers day-by-day critiques of their efforts—Vinson transformed the way well-heeled trial lawyers prepare for court. His firm, DecisionQuest, was the industry leader. By the time of the Simpson trial Vinson employed two hundred people and had an itch for bigger challenges and a wider stage.

In January 1994, when the first trial of Lyle and Erik Menendez had ended in hung juries, Vinson had been appalled. He decided to volunteer DecisionQuest's services for the next Menendez trial. Garcetti and Conn immediately became boosters of Vinson's work, and they touted him to Clark. Vinson was game for another pro bono project, so Clark reluctantly agreed to see what he had to offer.

On July 23, 1994, DecisionQuest recruited ten "jurors" for a mock trial. Clark, Hodgman, and Garcetti watched from behind a one-way glass, and what they heard astonished them. Vinson had recruited a diverse panel—five men and five women, six whites and four blacks—and everyone expected some ethnic correlation to the results. But the racial divide, in this test at least, was stark and overwhelming: whites for conviction, blacks for acquittal. What was more, the partisans on both sides held their views passionately.

As an experiment, Vinson asked black panel members to change several assumptions about the facts of the case that practically directed a verdict of guilty. No matter. Three of the four blacks *still* said they would vote not guilty.

Vinson asked the black women on the panel to assume that Simpson had beaten Nicole and that he had threatened and stalked her. Their reactions were uniform: "In every relationship, there's always a little trouble." "People get slapped around. That just happens." "It doesn't mean he killed her."

Clark didn't buy it—not the process, not the answers, and not Vinson. She found the consultant a condescending snob. Clark's failure to separate the message from the messenger would have disastrous consequences for her case.

LANCE Ito forgot to turn on his microphone when he took the bench on Monday, September 26, 1994—a small sign that the usually meticulous judge had the jitters on the first day of jury selection. Ito had arranged for a huge pool of potential jurors—more than nine hundred—to be brought forward. They were roughly equal in men and women; 28.1 percent were African American and 37.9 percent Caucasian, with the remainder divided among Latinos, Asians, and others. Nearly three quarters of them had some college or were college graduates. It was a fair approximation of the overall jury pool in the downtown Los Angeles area.

The purpose of the first portion of jury selection, called the hardship phase, was to determine which jurors had irreconcilable personal conflicts with jury service and which ones would go on to the next round of inquiries. Ito was a soft touch: Anyone who wanted out got out. To his surprise, however, many jurors seemed downright anxious to serve on the case. After only four days the judge had 304 willing citizens from which the twelve jurors and twelve alternates would be selected.

Moving to the next phase, the lawyers on both sides spent the following ten days poring over the prospective jurors' answers to an elaborate questionnaire in which the judge had let both sides ask pretty much anything they wanted. This laissez-faire approach yielded a monstrosity—an eighty-page list of 294 questions to be answered in writing, many of them calling for essay-type responses. The questionnaire quickly descended into an absurd and insulting fishing expedition: "Have you ever asked a celebrity for an autograph?" "What do you think is the main cause of domestic violence?" "Have you ever dated a person of a different race?" "If not currently a fan, have you in the past ever been a fan of the U.S.C. Trojans football team?"

The answers revealed that the hardship process had acted like a vacuum cleaner for educated, white, and male jurors—all groups that had showed a predisposition in favor of the prosecution. In the group that remained in the process at the questionnaire stage, the number of African Americans jumped to about one half. And three quarters of the black prospective jurors were female—the most pro-Simpson group of all.

On October 12 individual questioning of prospective jurors—that is, voir dire—began. According to a law-and-order voter initiative passed in 1990, voir dire in criminal trials was supposed to be conducted principally by the judge, not the lawyers. But again Ito caved in and let the lawyers do the asking—and the puffing. Clark, for example, asked many jurors whether "the celebrity of the defendant would affect your ability to render a verdict."

One theme of the defense lawyers stood out. In question after question Shapiro and Cochran made sure that the jurors knew this was a case about race. On the first day Cochran asked a white candidate, "Now, with regard to the whole question of race, interracial marriage, you felt you had no problems with that?"

And so it went, day after day. Again to Ito's surprise, many jurors seemed to be auditioning, rather than shrinking from the prospect of service.

The case was making progress of sorts, as the parties had a chance to question a few jurors each day. Then forward momentum came to an abrupt halt and the case nearly collapsed altogether—thanks to the literary labors of Faye Resnick.

At the time of the trial Faye Resnick was thirty-seven years old, a native Californian with a trim build and orange hair. As the ex-wife of Paul Resnick, a wealthy Los Angeles businessman, she dabbled in charity projects, worked hard on her appearance, and worried about the effect of a dwindling divorce settlement on her expensive lifestyle. Faye needed the money a book deal could provide. The milieu in which she and Nicole lived is neatly summarized in her book: "Almost every woman I know has had breast implants."

Faye Resnick

Resnick and Nicole had become close friends after Faye separated from her husband in early 1991. Resnick became friendly with O.J., too, as he and Nicole pursued their on-again, off-again relationship in 1993 and 1994. Resnick implicitly blamed the stress of mediating between the two for the recurrence of her drug problem, and after the murder she became convinced that O.J. had killed Nicole.

Resnick had maintained a diary about what was going on between O.J. and Nicole, which ultimately became the book *Nicole Brown Simpson: The Private Diary of a Life Interrupted*. Resnick and her collaborator presented Nicole as a brainless, sex-obsessed young woman whose banality was exceeded only by that of her ex-husband. More significant as far as the trial was concerned, Resnick depicted Simpson as an insanely jealous former spouse who openly discussed his thoughts of murdering Nicole.

For maximum publicity the book was released in the middle of jury selection—on October 17. On the day it came out it actually rated rather modestly on the Simpson-news Richter scale, and Lance Ito's sensible course would probably have been to ignore it. Like every other sensation in the case, Resnick would have faded. But Tuesday morning, October 18—without even being asked by the parties—Ito suspended jury selection for forty-eight hours because of "the publication of a book that has caused the Court great concerns about the ability of Mr. Simpson to get a fair trial. I need to look into the ramifications." Ito's decision to stop jury selection predictably fueled intense curiosity about the book in the public, and the defense tried unsuccessfully to use the Resnick crisis to provoke Ito into abandoning the case entirely.

As he would so often, Ito backed away from the precipice. When he resumed jury selection on Thursday, he tinkered with the process only slightly. He stopped the questioning of jurors in front of one another, a change he hoped would encourage candor, and ordered the remaining candidates not to watch any television, read any newspapers or magazines, or set foot in any bookstore. Three jurors who admitted to watching television were eliminated, and with each winnowing, the pool grew ever more African American and female.

On December 8 the parties accepted a panel of twelve jurors and twelve alternates. Based on their answers to the question-naires, the twelve jurors who ultimately decided the case against O. J. Simpson had the following characteristics:

- All twelve were Democrats.
- Two were college graduates.
- Not one juror read a newspaper regularly.
- Nine lived in rented homes; three owned homes.
- Only two had management responsibilities at work.
- Five said they or a family member had personally en-dured a negative experience with law enforcement.
- Five thought it was acceptable to use force on a family member.
- Nine thought O. J. Simpson was less likely to have mur-dered his wife because he had excelled at football.

In a county that is just 11 percent black, the final twelve in-cluded eight African American women, one African American man, one Hispanic man, and two white women.

On the whole, Marcia Clark was pleased. She and Bill Hodgman didn't even exercise all twenty of their peremptory challenges.

7

FOR all his stormy and dissolute personal life, insatiable ego, and pervasive misanthropism, one fact stands out about Francis Lee Bailey: He invented the contemporary practice of criminal defense law. First, he understood the news media and how to manipulate the press for his ends. If Bailey did not invent the impromptu press conference on the courthouse steps, he made the practice his own. He recognized the general importance of appearance. His clothes were custom-made and so were his elevator shoes. Bailey also engaged in the kind of exhaustive preparation for cases that, before him, had been the practice of only the best lawyers in the biggest firms.

Bailey came of age in the 1960s, when the term superstar first came into vogue, and he was without question the first legal superstar. Before he was forty years old this Harvard-educated son of a struggling advertising man and a nursery-school teacher had an estate south of Boston and a helicopter for commuting to work, and he could boast that he had charged a client a million dollars.

Bailey's lust for the spotlight—and cash—led him astray in the years after his initial fame. In 1973 he was indicted in a federal mail fraud conspiracy case in Florida, along with a former client, Glenn Turner, whose motivational business turned out to be little more than a Ponzi scheme. Thanks to the efforts of his lawyer, Alan Dershowitz, Bailey managed to have the case against him dismissed. In 1982 Bailey was again charged with a crime, drunk driving, and his friend Robert Shapiro successfully represented him at his San Francisco trial.

For all his faults and traumas, though, Bailey continued to try cases throughout the 1980s and 1990s and, for the most part, try them very well. Indeed, of all the lawyers on either side of the Simpson case, Bailey had the most experience trying murder cases.

IMMEDIATELY after he was retained by O. J. Simpson, Shapiro called Bailey. He treated Bailey with a deference befitting the elder lawyer's exalted history as a defense attorney, but there were tensions from the outset. When Bailey appeared on the Simpson case's quasi-official forum, *Larry King Live,* on June 24 to announce that he had joined the defense team, King asked why Bailey had waited.

"Simply because with all the sniping that someone has been sponsoring, saying Bob Shapiro couldn't handle this case—which I think is silly—I thought it would be best to let the case proceed down the road a little bit, until it was firmly established that he had control. He has. He's handled it brilliantly."

In fact, there had been very little sniping about Shapiro's abilities until Bailey raised the issue on the air. As for the purported drama about when to make Bailey's announcement, Bailey invented that issue as well. By defending Shapiro, Bailey demeaned him.

Through the summer more tensions developed among the defense lawyers. When Johnnie Cochran had been hired, there was no question that he ranked behind Shapiro in the unspoken hierarchy of the defense team. But throughout the fall, Cochran spent increasing amounts of time at the jail with O.J., and Simpson became ever more enamored of him. Simpson had hired Cochran as a trial lawyer, and the trial was fast approaching. How could Cochran remain number two? The implications made Shapiro squirm, so he made a final effort to keep control of the case.

One afternoon late in the jury selection process, Bailey and Kardashian were talking with Simpson in the tiny lockup beside Judge Ito's courtroom. Shapiro joined them and said he had just spoken to the prosecutors. "The prosecutors think that you were mad at Nicole because she didn't invite you to dinner," Shapiro told Simpson. "They think you sat around your house getting pissed off, then went over to Nicole's. There was some sort of confrontation at the house, and you killed her. Then Goldman showed up."

They all listened to Shapiro's summary without comment.

"So," Shapiro went on, "that leaves room for manslaughter. And Bob [Kardashian] would have to account for the knife, but that's probably no more than five years for accessory after the fact."

There was stunned silence—incredulity that Shapiro would propose a plea bargain at this late date. But cutting deals was Shapiro's

F. Lee Bailey, Simpson, and Carl Douglas

specialty, and making one now was the only way for him to remain in charge of the case. Simpson did not reject the proposal so much as ignore it. The conversation simply moved on to other topics.

By proposing that Simpson agree to plead guilty to anything—at a time when O.J.'s outright acquittal was more likely than ever—Shapiro alienated his client beyond measure. Bailey saw that Shapiro had at this point no chance of remaining in charge. Indeed, Bailey had spent much of the fall cultivating Cochran so that he, Bailey, would be able to carve out a significant role at the trial. It would soon become clear that Shapiro had no allies left.

On January 4, 1995, a column by Mike McAlary of the New York *Daily News* was headlined VAIN SHAPIRO DESERVES HIS FATE. It began: "He has spent a year fooling the nation, this lawyer. He has made them all believers: that he is a heroic, hard-working lawyer in the hunt for a grand, fantastic verdict. Unfortunately, Robert Shapiro is your typical Hollywood invention—a character only tan-deep in makeup and significance." The column was filled with details known only to a handful of insiders.

Furious at the McAlary column, Shapiro asked private eye Bill Pavelic to conduct a secret investigation to see who had leaked the inside information. Pavelic reported back that it was John McNally, one of Bailey's investigators, who had quit because he couldn't abide Shapiro. Shapiro held Bailey responsible, and he decided to strike back in similar terms. He leaked word to *Newsweek*'s Mark Miller that he was no longer speaking to his old friend Bailey, and he told *New York Times* reporter David Margolick that he hoped Bailey would leave the defense team. "His presence before this particular jury adds nothing that can't be done by Johnnie and others on the team," the January 16 *Times* quoted Shapiro as saying.

Shapiro's public attack on a colleague was unprecedented. On the eve of opening statements, with his client's freedom for the rest of his life on the line, Shapiro shifted the focus to his own complaints—to O.J.'s clear detriment. Worse yet, Bailey himself was innocent of McNally's chicanery. In response Bailey took the high road. In a statement released through his office, he said only that he "declined to disparage Mr. Shapiro in any way. This case is not about Mr. Shapiro or Mr. Bailey. It is about O. J. Simpson."

The controversy ended the only way it could: Simpson demanded that all his attorneys meet him at the jailhouse and end all public feuding. "I played football with plenty of guys I didn't like," Simpson told them, "but it was a team and we got along. Your job is to get along."

On Wednesday, January 18, after court, the lawyers returned to the lobby for a news conference. Cochran—now clearly the leader of the team—stood between Bailey and Shapiro, and he beamed while announcing that "the Dream Team is never going to break up." Shapiro, looking pained, nodded dutifully. Asked about the controversy, Bailey said simply, "That's history." In the background, behind the first-string lawyers, Cochran's associate Shawn Chapman and Shapiro's colleague Sara Caplan started to laugh every time the lawyers told the reporters that the feud was over.

Shapiro sulked in court, and for the next nine months he and Bailey did not exchange a word. Outside the Criminal Courts Building, Shapiro's petulance took another form. Slowly but inexorably he began broadening the circle of people to whom he told his true feelings about his client. "Of course he did it," he would say. For his part, Bailey, who never worried too much about any client's guilt or innocence, just wanted to return to the big time.

THE decision—the last roadblock to opening statements in the Simpson trial—was the most important of Lance Ito's career. Would the prosecution be allowed to present to the jury evidence of Simpson's history of physical and emotional harassment of his former wife? On this and all issues raised in the Simpson case, Ito proceeded methodically. The judge came to work early, around seven every morning. The Criminal Courts Building was mostly empty when he slipped into his chambers on the ninth floor, just across a battered linoleum hallway from his courtroom, which was known as Department 103. Ito decorated his office in neo-workaholic style. Only two personal touches stood out from stacks of files and computer wires: a handsome photographic portrait of Ito and his wife, Margaret York, and a small stand of historic Japanese flags.

Shortly before nine Ito would stroll from his office to his bench and check to see if the day's paperwork was in order. He wouldn't be wearing his robe then, so a pocketful of pens—his nerd pack—would peek out from the breast pocket of his shirt. When dressed in full judicial regalia, Ito tended to hunch over; his robe would blend into his black beard, giving him a soft, pudgy look. This was misleading. The forty-four-year-old judge was trim, almost wiry, and the veteran of a pair of marathons.

In contrast to the adversaries before him, Judge Ito worked with very little assistance. A handful of students from local law schools rotated through his chambers over the course of the trial, but Ito did all the writing—and the deciding—alone. This meant long hours of work after court, either in his chambers or at his home, which was electronically linked to his office computer.

Ito, as much as anyone, understood the importance of the domestic-violence issue to the prosecution's case. He began working his way through the fifty-nine different "alleged significant events or incidents of misconduct by the defendant" one by one.

In order to avoid delaying the trial, Ito had to issue his decision by January 18. Up to that point he shared his conclusions with no one—or almost no one.

The judge did tell Larry King how he was going to rule.

Larry King Live was among the shows on which Faye Resnick had been scheduled to speak after the release of her book in October. King's show had canceled the interview at Ito's request, and Ito had written him a note of thanks and invited King to drop by his chambers. (It was a gracious gesture, but also one of a man who liked to have stars visit him.)

First-time visitors to Ito's courtroom who had previously seen it only on television always said the same thing: It's so small. The room was about the size of a tennis court, with only four rows of benches for spectators. That was it—about fifty people. It was the kind of place where newcomers were quickly noticed, and on January 14 there was no way to miss the arrival of Larry King.

During the midmorning break that day King, his senior executive producer, Wendy Walker Whitworth, and King's daughter, Chaia, were ushered into Ito's chambers. Ito was thrilled by King's presence and started rambling about the domestic-violence decision he had to make. "I know Nicole's call to the shelter is powerful evidence," Ito told his stunned guests, "but it's hearsay. I can't let it in." The talk meandered for about forty minutes until King finally asked, "Don't you have to get back to court?" The break had been scheduled for only fifteen minutes. Incredibly, King and his entourage followed Ito into the courtroom. O.J. rose in deference to the visiting celebrity and reached out to shake hands. The bailiffs, however, hustled the defendant back into his seat. Next King moved to Robert Shapiro, who gave him a bear hug. Then King shook hands with Lee Bailey. Suzanne Childs, Gil Garcetti's peripatetic director of communications (and a future romantic interest of King's), rushed from her seat and steered King over to the prosecutors. "I watch you all the time!" Marcia Clark told him.

At last King and his entourage, having worked the courtroom like the deck of a cruise ship, left through the spectators' door. Judge Ito had observed the whole scene with a serene smile.

LANCE ITO WAS A PARADOXICAL figure. Although he is a thoughtful jurist whose work reflects his earnest and rigorous approach, in the crucible of the Simpson trial a less appealing side of the man came increasingly to the fore. Frequently he behaved like just another celebrity-crazed resident of Los Angeles.

The contradictions between the serious judge and the ditsy Angeleno reflected Lance Ito's background. Of all the principals in the case he was the only one born in Los Angeles, and he had deep roots there. The judge's grandfather had helped found the first interracial Methodist church in the city. His father, James Ito, had graduated from college, started a truck

Lance Ito

farm on twenty-seven acres in West Covina, and even joined the California National Guard when World War II began. As it would for so many Japanese Americans, the war turned James Ito's life upside down. He was ordered to resign from the Guard, sell his assets, and report to a Wyoming internment camp—all within two weeks.

Lance was born in 1950, and his parents, who had met in the internment camp, eventually settled in the middle-class district of Silver Lake, near Dodger Stadium. The young Lance had an almost stereotypically all-American boyhood. He became president of the student body at the racially mixed John Marshall High School and excelled in the Boy Scouts, earning the coveted Eagle Scout badge.

At U.C.L.A. Ito did well in his studies, graduating cum laude in political science and earning admission to the University of California's eminent law school, Boalt Hall, in Berkeley. After graduating from Boalt in 1975, Ito spent two years at a law firm and then became a deputy district attorney in Los Angeles.

His experience as a prosecutor specializing in complex cases against violent Los Angeles gangs shaped Ito's judicial outlook. It was in 1983 and 1984, during the tenure of Robert Philibosian, one of the few Republicans to serve as Los Angeles district attorney in recent years, that Ito's career took off.

According to Philibosian, "Lance was a Democrat, and I was a Republican, but he was very sympathetic to the things we were trying to do in those days." One of the most important things Philibosian did after he left the D.A.'s office was to help launch a revolution aimed at toppling the liberal seven-member California Supreme Court. Ito's car back then bore a license-plate frame with the words CALIFORNIA'S SUPREME COURT; the young prosecutor's vanity plate read, in commentary, 7 BOZOS. In 1987 Philibosian recommended Ito to a fellow Republican, Governor George Deukmejian. The governor appointed Ito to the municipal court that year and to the superior court, where he remains, in 1989.

ONE of the most important buzzwords used in the attack on judicial liberals was "truth." Ito would also use it in one of his early written rulings in the Simpson case. The "truth school," as it is sometimes known, asserts that the paramount value is protecting innocent defendants from being wrongly convicted. But it is not at all troubled by guilty defendants who are convicted, even if the police may have violated some provisions of the Constitution in collecting evidence against them. That, of course, is the rub.

The judicial system's remedy for improper police work has been to exclude the evidence gathered by these means, and therefore sometimes the guilty go free. Truth-school adherents say that if the police violate someone's rights, it might be better if that person sued the cops in a civil lawsuit or if the offending officers were sanctioned for their violations. But in any criminal case, according to the truth school, the jury should be able to hear all reliable evidence against the defendant regardless of how the police behaved.

January 11, 1995, the day Lance Ito selected to hear argument on the admissibility of evidence about the domestic-violence incidents, was also the day he ordered the jury to report to a secret location—the Inter-Continental Hotel in downtown Los Angeles—for sequestration. This personal imposition on these citizens, as well as the accompanying financial burden on the county's tax-payers, gave a new urgency to Ito's desire to get the trial started. Before January 11 spectators were allowed in the courtroom on a more or less first-come, first-served basis. But on this day, for the first time, the bailiffs admitted only those with passes. A full complement of both victims' family members filled the available seats. No one could mistake that the crucial moment had drawn near.

The defendant showed the strain. O. J. Simpson has long been a compulsive talker. And no subject moved him to speak more than his relationship with Nicole. Visitors to Simpson in jail found him nearly obsessed by the subject. "Nicole wanted to get back together with *me*," O.J. would say over and over again. "I wanted to get away from her. How can they say I killed her because I wanted her back?" Simpson even talked a lot in the courtroom. Every judge allows lawyers and clients some leeway in communicating in court, but Simpson always seemed to intimidate Ito to a certain extent, and throughout the trial the judge gave this defendant nearly free rein to jabber. This was never more true than on January 11. As the lawyers dissected O.J. and Nicole's relationship, O.J. offered his own audible commentary as well.

The defense was represented by Gerald Uelman, the slow-talking professor from Los Angeles. The defense position on the domestic-violence evidence was well stated by Uelman at the outset. "By attaching that label, by saying this case is a domestic-violence case, they seek to transform these proceedings from an inquiry into who killed Nicole Brown Simpson and Ronald Goldman on June 12, 1994, into a general inquiry into the character of O. J. Simpson." The problem, Uelman said, quoting a well-known case, was that "it is fundamental to American jurisprudence that a defendant must be tried for what he did, not for who he is."

Uelman had his own "label" for this case. "None of the traditional earmarks of a domestic-violence homicide are present here," he said. "How many domestic-violence cases involve multiple victims? How many involve the use of a knife? How many involve stealth rather than being preceded by any sort of violent confrontation or argument? In fact, if we had to put a label on this case, the label we would put on it is that it bears all of the earmarks of a drug-related homicide."

As Uelman uttered the words "drug related," there was an audible intake of breath in the courtroom. The suggestion was (and remains) preposterous, even on Uelman's own terms. First, by any theory, Nicole was the real target of the crime. Ron Goldman just happened on the scene, and his murder was entirely consistent with jealous rage from Simpson. Second, drug dealers overwhelmingly prefer guns. Finally, most domestic-violence murders take place in or near homes, which means that frequently they are not overheard by others. Most important, neither Nicole nor Goldman had any ties to the drug world that would make them targets of a drug-related homicide. Uelman's suggestion—a real calumny on the graves of these two dead people—marked the beginning of a new phase in the defense strategy.

Uelman then proceeded to respond to the fifty-nine domestic-violence allegations one by one. He did so virtually in tandem with the defendant, who, seated between Shapiro and Cochran, provided a running commentary on each of the accusations against him.

The first incident was from 1977, when Simpson was alleged to have broken some picture frames during the course of a fight with Nicole. "*She* broke them," O.J. muttered to Cochran.

Uelman moved quickly to the fight at their home on January 1, 1989, after which O.J. pleaded no contest to battering Nicole. "With respect to this incident," Uelman told Judge Ito, "at the conclusion of a New Year's celebration in which both Mr. Simpson and Nicole Simpson had a lot to drink, they got into an argument in their bedroom. And the culmination of that argument was a physical assault in which Mr. Simpson admitted that he slapped and punched Nicole Brown Simpson."

Hearing this, O.J. nearly vaulted out of his chair. "I did not!" he told Cochran, who urged him to calm down.

The list of incidents went on. During the course of the argument a lawyer representing the Sojourn battered-women's shelter in Santa Monica appeared in Ito's court and handed a thin envelope to the prosecutors. At the end of the long day in court Lydia Bodin, one of the deputy district attorneys, disclosed the envelope's contents. "We have received information from Sojourn shelter that on the date of June the 7th, 1994, Nicole Brown Simpson made a contact with Sojourn. She complained that she was being stalked. She was afraid. She felt confused. She didn't know what to do, and she named the defendant as the person who was stalking her."

Again, many in the courtroom gasped: June 7 was just five days before the murder. Cochran and Shapiro looked stricken.

It was a sad moment. By any measure Nicole Brown Simpson was a wealthy woman, even after her divorce. Yet at her time of greatest fear, with her life literally on the line, she apparently felt unable to turn to the police, to her friends, or even to her family. She had nowhere to go except a public battered-women's shelter—the very charity that her husband was forced to contribute to after he beat her in 1989. And even Nicole's final appeal to Sojourn, the courtroom recognized at once, did not manage to save her life. For once, not even O. J. Simpson had anything to say.

UELMAN'S opposite number on the prosecution team was Hank Goldberg. Soft-spoken, with a paleness of skin and hair that seemed to render him nearly invisible at times, Goldberg gave the nearly perfect legal argument on the domestic-violence evidence—especially for a truth-school judge like Ito.

He began with a hypothetical question. "Let's imagine that we tried the case, Your Honor, without telling the jury that Nicole Brown Simpson was ever married to the defendant—was just a woman who was murdered," Goldberg said. "Ronald Goldman was just a man that was murdered, and we did not tell them of the existence of any relationship at all." The proposal, Goldberg said, was self-evidently absurd. "It is only when you understand the relationship, and you understand the jealousy, the possessiveness, that the killing of Nicole makes sense."

Ultimately, in a scholarly ten-page single-spaced opinion issued on January 18, 1995, Ito allowed the prosecution most, but not all, of the domestic-violence incidents it wanted to introduce, including the most powerful evidence—the 1989 beating and the 1993 call to 911. With some apparent regret Ito correctly excluded Nicole's call to Sojourn on June 7 as inadmissible hearsay.

Overall, Ito's ruling amounted to a paradigmatic and admirable example of his truth-oriented judicial philosophy in action—as well as a buoyant send-off to the prosecution's opening statement.

8

CHRISTOPHER Darden paced in front of the jury box. As he walked, he kept his eyes on the floor, and his double-breasted jacket flopped open in front of him.

"Now, we're here today obviously to resolve an issue, to settle a question, a question that has been on the minds of people throughout the country these last seven months. Did O. J. Simpson really kill Nicole Brown and Ronald Goldman?"

Darden was nervous, as any person would be in his position. On arriving at the courthouse this morning, January 24, the lawyers had run a gauntlet of twenty-six video cameras and twice as many photographers. Seven news helicopters had circled overhead.

There was an important new face among the spectators, too. Eunice Simpson, the defendant's mother—tall and regal even though racked by arthritis—appeared in her wheelchair in the courtroom's center aisle. As soon as Mrs. Simpson arrived, Juditha Brown—likewise a grandmother to Sydney and Justin Simpson—gave her a hug. Hands fluttering nervously on her lap just before Darden rose to begin his opening statement, Juditha Brown dropped her eyeglasses, and Kim Goldman casually leaned over from her nearby seat to pick them up. Retrieving Juditha's dropped glasses had cost Kim's brother his life.

That it was Chris Darden who began the case demonstrated how much the prosecution effort had evolved over the months leading up to the trial. As the scale of the trial had expanded, particularly in the scientific area, Clark and Hodgman realized they could not handle it all themselves. Clark, an old friend of Darden's, urged that he be invited to join the trial team. The racial tensions in the

Christopher Darden, Marcia Clark

case made the logic of adding Darden even more compelling. The case needed a black prosecutor. Clark and Hodgman had divided the labor so that Clark would handle testimony about the events of June 12, 1994, and Hodgman would focus on the scientific evidence. The ever expanding number of domestic-violence witnesses went to Darden. And since the prosecution lawyers had decided they would attempt to prove that O.J. and Nicole's relationship provided the motive for the murders, it made sense for Darden to begin the prosecution presentation to the jury.

In his opening Christopher Darden went right to the heart of the prosecution's theory. "The answer to the question is, Yes, O. J. Simpson murdered Nicole Brown and Ronald Goldman. And I'm sure you are wondering why right now. . . . Why would he do it? Not O. J. Simpson. Not the O. J. Simpson we think we know.

But that is another question. . . . Do you know O. J. Simpson?

"We watched him leap turnstiles in the Hertz commercials, and we watched him with a fifteen-inch Afro in *Naked Gun 33 1/3*. We've seen him time and time again, and we think that we know him.

"What we've been seeing, ladies and gentlemen, is the public face, the face of the athlete, the face of the actor. Like many public men they have a private face. And that is the face we will expose to you in this trial, the other side of O. J. Simpson, the side you never met before. And the evidence will show that the face you will see will be the face of a batterer, a wife beater, an abuser, a controller . . . the face of Ron's and Nicole's murderer."

Darden recited the litany of abuse in their relationship: "domestic abuse, domestic violence, stalking, intimidation, physical abuse, wife beating, public humiliation." And yet the list of incidents, on close analysis, was rather thin. In Simpson's trial the prosecution could point to only a single example of wife beating—the 1989 incident. There were no other proven examples of physical violence between them. Nicole had referred to several more incidents in her diary, but Ito had ruled (correctly) that that document was inadmissible hearsay evidence. Here the Simpson case illustrated one of the larger tragedies of domestic violence—that it usually takes place without witnesses.

Darden finished with the story of Sydney's dance recital on the night of June 12. The prosecutor had picked up confidence as he spoke, and he now addressed the jury instead of his shoes. O.J. arrived late at the recital, bearing flowers for Sydney, Darden said, and he greeted everyone in the Brown family—"except Nicole." Simpson moved a chair to the corner of the auditorium, and "he just sat there staring at Nicole. It was an angry stare, and it made everyone very uncomfortable."

The Brown family, Darden said, had decided to have dinner at the Mezzaluna restaurant, and "as they left, they made it clear to the defendant that he was not invited. And by not inviting him, it was a reaffirmation that it was over. He was no longer a part of the family. Nicole was getting on with her own life."

Darden's conclusion was almost elegant in its simplicity: "She left him. She was no longer in his control. He could not stand to lose her, and so he murdered her."

MARCIA Clark's style differed from her colleague's. Businesslike, almost chipper, she stood behind the lectern and moved only when she had somewhere to go—as opposed to Darden's nervous pacing. She employed a series of elegantly integrated photographs, slides, and charts in her presentation. This in itself was unusual. Most district attorney's offices cannot afford much more than a blackboard. But even though Clark had dismissed DecisionQuest from jury selection, the prosecution did accept the company's pro bono assistance in making charts and other visual aids, an effort that would have cost a paying client nearly $1 million.

Picking up the story on the evening of June 12, Clark introduced the jury to Kato Kaelin and told of his trip to McDonald's with Simpson, which ended with their parting around 9:40 p.m.

Her pace quickening, Clark turned to Nicole's movements in the hours before the murders. After dinner Nicole and her family had returned home, and then, also at 9:40 p.m., Juditha called her daughter to say she had dropped her glasses on the sidewalk outside the restaurant. "That was the last time Juditha ever spoke to her daughter Nicole," Clark said. Nicole called Mezzaluna and asked that her friend Ron Goldman, a waiter there, bring them to her house. He left for Nicole's at about 9:50 p.m.

It was a very specific opening statement, with a multitude of times and places identified for the jury. Clark's precision extended even to the animal world. "At approximately 10:15 p.m.," she said, "Pablo Fenjves, who lived diagonally across the alley behind Nicole's condominium, heard a dog begin to bark." Clark thus committed the prosecution to the theory that the murders took place shortly before 10:15 p.m., even though she knew that other credible evidence put the murders about fifteen minutes later. Leaving the time somewhat vague at that early stage in the case could have served the prosecution's purposes. But Clark's arrogance led her to an unwise commitment.

Speaking with few notes, Clark gracefully integrated the disparate strands of the story. O.J.'s whereabouts were unaccounted for after 9:40 p.m., when he and Kato parted, until Allan Park, the limousine driver, saw him at 10:55 p.m. hustling into the house. During that period Kato heard loud thumps outside, near the air conditioner, which was precisely where the bloody glove was later found. (Never in her opening did Clark mention Fuhrman.)

"Now I'm going to show you what Sukru Boztepe saw when Nicole's dog took him to 875 South Bundy," Clark said, and then she nodded toward the junior prosecutor controlling the video and slide projections on the large screen above the witness stand.

The photograph had been taken from the sidewalk. The young woman lay in a fetal position in a pool of blood. Clark had shown these photographs to the family members before so that they wouldn't have to see them for the first time in the courtroom. But Juditha and Lou Brown still shuddered.

Clark then described how Officer Riske crept up the walkway, trying not to disturb the trail of blood, "to a point where he was able to see that it was not just Nicole, but also Ron."

The photograph of Ronald Goldman came up on the screen. It was a far more gruesome image: his body wedged into the corner of the fence, his shirt pulled over his head, and his exposed muscular torso marred by knife wounds filled with congealed blood. Clark's words added to the horror: "He was literally backed into a cage where he had nowhere to run." A *cage*—the phrase was so awfully right for the place that Goldman had died.

Clark turned to the last and most powerful portion of her opening statement: the story of the blood. She offered a brief, homey introduction to the subject of DNA testing, and then the slides of the various blood spots went up, and Clark listed each match.

By the left door handle in O.J.'s Bronco: "Matches the defendant," said Clark. On the center console of the Bronco: "Consistent with a mixture of the defendant and Ron Goldman." The socks in Simpson's bedroom: "The blood on one spot matched the defendant. The blood on another spot matched Nicole." Each one of the blood drops to the left of the bloody size twelve shoe prints leaving the murder scene: "Matches the defendant."

"And the results of the analysis of that blood confirms what the rest of the evidence will show," Clark said, "that on June the 12th, 1994, after a violent relationship in which the defendant beat her, humiliated her, and controlled her, just as she tried to break free, Orenthal James Simpson took her very life in what amounted to his final and his ultimate act of control." She paused. "And in that final and terrible act, Ronald Goldman, an innocent bystander, was viciously and senselessly murdered."

THE following morning Ito called for Johnnie Cochran to begin his presentation for the defense. Cochran, wearing a periwinkle suit and a blue-and-white-striped shirt with a contrasting white collar, radiated a confidence that the prosecutors could not hope to equal.

The jurors, Cochran began, would hear a lot of talk about justice. "I guess Dr. Martin Luther King said it best when he said that injustice anywhere is a threat to justice everywhere, and so we are now embarked upon this search for justice." Cochran then paused to pay tribute to the jurors. "We are very, very pleased with the fact that you have agreed to serve as jurors, to leave your lives, to be sequestered as it were. Abraham Lincoln said it best when he said that the highest act of citizenship is jury service."

Having enlisted King and Lincoln in the cause, Cochran went on to charge that certain witnesses had been ignored by the police and prosecution, which all fit into a larger pattern. "This case is about a rush to judgment," Cochran asserted, "an obsession to win at any cost and by any means necessary." Invoking Malcolm X's most famous phrase, "by any means necessary," Cochran declared war on the LAPD. The case against O. J. Simpson, in other words, was really about the conspiracy to convict him.

It was about something else, too. In his opening, Cochran ran through a catalogue of Nicole Simpson's sexual exploits. Though nominally refuting the charge of stalking, he was just warming up for his main point about Nicole's sordid personal life—that the sinister figure of Faye Resnick was at the center of everything.

"Let me say this about Faye Resnick," Cochran said gravely. "On June 3, 1994, her boyfriend, Christian Reichardt, threw her out of their house because she was freebasing cocaine. She then moved over and lived with Nicole Brown Simpson." Cochran went on to say that Faye's drug problem got so bad that on June 8 her ex-boyfriend and ex-husband forced her to enter a drug treatment facility. Faye Resnick "called Miss Nicole Brown Simpson on the night of June 12, from this facility." After a pause, Cochran said darkly, "We will be talking about that and her role in this whole drama."

The remainder of Cochran's opening statement hewed predictably to the defense themes. He described O.J.'s "circle of benevolence"—a phrase the lawyer used to describe the defendant's financial contributions to charity (which in fact were minimal) and to Nicole's family (which were considerable). He disparaged the work of the LAPD employees who had collected and analyzed the evidence, and he offered a brief criticism of the DNA evidence. Finally he returned again to the witnesses who had been ignored, especially Rosa Lopez—the next-door maid who would testify that O.J.'s Bronco was parked on Rockingham at the time that the prosecution asserted the murders were taking place.

It was, on one level, a remarkable opening statement. If the defense lawyers could back up Cochran's claims, the prosecution's case would be shattered. But as it turned out, they couldn't; indeed, they didn't even try. By the end of the trial the defense would never call Faye Resnick. It would never even call Rosa Lopez (although she would indeed become a participant in the trial). There was nothing beneath Cochran's rhetoric.

But no matter. Cochran had planted the seeds: The LAPD was corrupt; O.J. was virtuous; Nicole deserved what she got.

COCHRAN's opening statement was also an unethical piece of lawyering. California discovery law obligated each side to turn over to the other all statements by witnesses it planned to call over the course of the trial. The prosecution had given the defense tens of thousands of pages of material, but the defense lawyers responded that they had nothing to share.

Then during Cochran's opening statement his majordomo, Carl Douglas, announced that he had found statements of twelve witnesses whom the defense was going to call. If Clark had known about them, she could have addressed them in her statement.

The next day Carl Douglas took responsibility for the discovery failures by the defense team. When the center of operations had shifted from Shapiro's office to Cochran's after the first of the year, it was Douglas's thankless task to untangle the files. Now he tried to explain that the withholding of the documents had just been an unfortunate mistake.

Ito, who had been studying the prosecution table as Douglas spoke, observed, "I have to say, Mr. Douglas, I've had long experience with Mr. Hodgman. I've known him as a colleague, as a trial lawyer, and I've never seen the expressions on his face that I've seen today." He turned to the usually stoic prosecutor and said, "Mr. Hodgman, why don't you take a few deep breaths, and we'll take a look at this."

Bill Hodgman supervised the discovery process for the prosecution. The disclosure about these twelve witness statements came on top of the defense's disclosure, one day earlier, that it had a list of thirty-four new witnesses it planned to call during the trial. These were appalling violations of the discovery laws, and Hodgman felt personally wounded by what he regarded as a dirty trick. As Ito observed, Hodgman now looked stricken.

When Hodgman rose to speak, Jo-Ellan Dimitrius whispered to Shapiro, "Bill doesn't look too good." Shapiro quipped, "Yeah, tomorrow they're going to take him out on a stretcher."

ITO broke for the day early on January 25 so that the prosecutors could decide what sanctions they would ask the judge to impose on the defense. As Hodgman and Clark were briefing Gil Garcetti, Hodgman noticed a strange tightening in his chest. At 6:20 p.m. an ambulance took him to the California Medical Center. He was, at the time, forty-one years old. Doctors found an irregular pattern in Hodgman's electrocardiogram and decided to keep him overnight. In the end, he was fine; his condition was temporary, seemingly the result of stress and overwork. Though he continued to supervise the case, Hodgman had to yield his courtroom role. Henceforth the case would be tried by Marcia Clark and Chris Darden.

Hodgman's absence deprived the prosecution of a voice of calm. He could tell the difference between an everyday dispute and a bona fide crisis. Clark and Darden, in contrast, tried cases in an atmosphere of perpetual turmoil, much of it self-generated.

The shift in mood was immediately apparent. Addressing Judge Ito about the discovery violations, Clark and Darden nearly became unhinged. True, the defense had engaged in rather cynical misconduct, but in the context of a long trial what should have mattered more to the prosecution was simply getting the case under way. Instead, for several hours Clark and Darden ranted.

A stronger, more self-confident judge would have stopped the debate and focused on the jury, which had been sitting in a hotel for two weeks and had not even heard all the opening statements. Ito, characteristically, said nothing during the lengthy harangues.

He did, however, reach a reasonable resolution: He agreed to put off Cochran's conclusion until Monday, January 30, to advise the jury that defense misconduct had caused the delay, and to allow Clark to make a brief reopening statement the following day.

9

IT WAS 10:05 a.m. on January 31 when Lance Ito asked, "Mr. Darden, who is your first witness?"

Prosecutors know they have a jury's full attention at the beginning of a trial, so they like to start out with a dramatic, powerful witness who cannot be effectively cross-examined. Darden and Clark chose well.

"Sharyn Gilbert, Your Honor."

Gilbert, a rotund and good-natured black woman, was the 911 operator who took Nicole's call January 1, 1989.

Darden played the tape. There were no words, just a rumbly silence, as if a phone had been left hanging limp from a table. Then a woman screamed . . . and screamed some more. Next, unmistakably, flesh collided with flesh—the sound of slapping. After about three minutes the line went dead.

Gilbert's computer had registered that the call came from 360 North Rockingham, so she urgently dispatched a police unit to the location. The assignment went to Officer John Edwards. Darden called him as his next witness. Edwards told of finding Nicole, her face battered, staggering around the bushes. He recalled her prophetic cries: "He's going to kill me! He's going to kill me!"

Cochran's cross-examination was more notable for what he didn't do than what he did. The lawyer never pointed out that John Edwards had been named one of forty-four officers identified as part of a "problem group" after the Rodney King beating. The reason for this uncharacteristic diffidence toward his testimony was not how hard Edwards had been on O. J. Simpson but how easy. Darden had asked him why he didn't arrest Simpson on the spot.

Edwards replied, "Because I knew that if I took O. J. Simpson, a person of that stature, to the station in his underwear that the media would show up and it would be blown out of proportion."

The true measure of Nicole's isolation came only with another witness, Ron Shipp, a former LAPD officer, who was a rather typical, if revealing, figure in Simpson's circle of hangers-on. Shipp had first met O.J. in the 1960s, when his brother played high school football against Simpson. But Simpson became a major figure in Shipp's life in the late '70s, when he was a patrol officer assigned to West Los Angeles. Shipp would often stop by O.J.'s house on Rockingham to use the tennis court or just shoot the breeze.

The prosecutors wanted to call on Shipp to testify about a late-night conversation with O.J. that allegedly took place on June 13, after Simpson had been interviewed by the detectives at Parker Center. "They asked me if I would take a lie detector test," Simpson had told Shipp, adding that he didn't want to take one. " 'Cause," Simpson added with a kind of a chuckle, "I have had some dreams of killing her." According to prosecutor Hank Goldberg, the statement would illustrate "the defendant's mental state and show his intention at the time of the murder." Ito decided to admit the dream testimony.

Simpson had absorbed the first few days of the trial impassively, but when Shipp walked to the witness stand, Simpson shook his head, muttered beneath his breath, and generally made his contempt unmistakable.

After he took the oath, Shipp tried to avoid Simpson's gaze. The former cop appeared a genuinely tortured figure—beholden to Simpson, still admiring of him in some ways, and yet conscience-stricken about what he knew.

Darden asked if he and Simpson remained friends.

"I still love the guy, but, um, I don't know. I mean, this is a weird situation I'm sitting here in."

Simpson was appalled that this hanger-on had turned on him. It upset the natural order of relationships he had lived with and ruled over for decades. Unfortunately for him, Simpson had to deputize the punishment of this lackey to Carl Douglas, who, since Cochran was distantly related to Shipp, was handling this witness for the defense. Douglas was almost certainly the weakest of the lawyers.

Instead of dismissing the dream comment, Douglas built it up. He asked a long series of questions to establish that the witness had not disclosed the dream conversation in a number of interviews—with the police, with defense investigators, with Douglas himself. Shipp essentially admitted all of this, but then Douglas made a cardinal error. He asked a "why" question, which allows a witness, in effect, to say anything he wants. Why didn't you tell these people about the "dream"?

Because, Shipp said, "I really did not want to be involved in this, and I didn't want to be going down as a person to nail O.J."

Suddenly the dream remark wasn't innocuous; it nailed O.J. Douglas shot back, "Well, you're not. So don't worry about that." Clark objected, and Ito scolded Douglas. "Counsel, you know better," the judge said. "The jury is to disregard counsel's remark."

Clark scribbled a note to Darden: "Thank you, Carl."

Carl Douglas set off on another series of questions aimed at proving Shipp had made up the dream story.

Shipp replied to them with quiet dignity. "Mr. Douglas," he said at one point, "I put all my faith in God and my conscience. Since

Nicole's been dead, I've felt nothing but guilt, my own personal guilt, that I didn't do as much as I probably should have."

Clark wrote it again: "Thank you, Carl."

Still Douglas continued to flog Shipp. He suggested that Simpson went to bed at 8:00 or 8:15 on the night of June 13 and said other family members would confirm the early bedtime.

Shipp did something extraordinary at that point. Instead of answering Douglas, he directed his testimony directly to the defendant. "Is that what they are going [to] testify to?" he implored his former patron. As Douglas pressed the issue, Shipp shook his head. He stared again at Simpson and said, "This is sad, O.J."

O.J. looked shaken, rubbing his hands nervously. Shapiro noticed this and put his arm around him, as if in protection.

Douglas moved to his big finish for the day. "Were you and he close friends?"

"I would say we were pretty good friends," Shipp said. "We never went out to dinner, like on a regular basis and stuff like that."

Douglas pointed out that Shipp and O.J. almost never ate meals together nor had they ever attended a football game together or gone on a double date. Shipp readily agreed. In contrast to Douglas's insinuations, Shipp was not trying to project any false intimacy with O.J. The power of his testimony came from the fact that Shipp knew what a toady he was. He knew he looked up to O.J., and he knew—ultimately—that O.J. couldn't have cared less about him.

WHEN Darden played the tape of Nicole's October 25, 1993, call to 911, the courtroom went absolutely still. Most people who listened to it on that day, including several jurors, had heard portions of the tape at one time or another, so many of Nicole's words had a familiar sound to them. Yet the playing of the tape in its entirety gave it a fresh meaning. Nicole could not have feigned the terror in her voice, the trembling.

"He's back. Please. . . . He's O. J. Simpson. I think you know his record. Could you just send somebody over here?" Weeping: "Could you please send somebody over?"

"Okay, just stay on the line," the dispatcher said.

"I don't want to stay on the line. He's going to beat the s___ out of me," Nicole said, then drew a long breath to try to calm herself.

It was almost impossible to make out most of what O.J. was saying on the tape, but his voice conveyed astonishing rage, in both the intensity of his tirade and its duration. For the full thirteen and a half minutes of the telephone call Simpson's screaming went on and on.

Nicole pleaded, "O.J., O.J. The kids. O.J., O.J., the kids are sleeping." O.J.'s response was one of the few times his words could be made out clearly: "You didn't give a s___ about the kids when you was sucking his d___ in the living room. They were here. Didn't care about the kids then." (The reference was to an incident in 1992, which O.J. had observed from his stalking post outside Nicole's front windows.)

Nicole: "Could you just please, O.J., O.J., O.J., O.J. Could you please leave? Please leave. Please leave."

"I'm leaving with my two fists is when I'm leaving."

THERE was one prosecution witness who had extensive firsthand exposure to O.J. and Nicole's relationship, including its darker sides. Since the moment Detective Tom Lange called her parents' home on the morning after the murders, Denise Brown was convinced that O.J. had murdered her sister. If anyone could explain how this had happened, it would be Nicole's older sister.

The four Brown sisters—Denise, Nicole, Dominique, and Tanya—all looked and sounded alike, and they reflected the values of their moneyed Orange County upbringing. All four had breast implants, but not one had a college degree. The two oldest sisters, Denise and Nicole, the brunette and the blonde, came closest to embodying a certain California ideal: lithe, athletic, out for a good time, each a high school homecoming princess. Denise graduated in 1975 and became, briefly, a New York model. Nicole graduated in 1977 and met O. J. Simpson three weeks later.

Denise circulated on the periphery of Nicole's life for many years, alternately competitive and supportive. She dated many of Simpson's friends, including Al Cowlings. Married briefly in 1984,

Denise had a child with another man several years later. In 1994 she and her son were living in her parents' home.

Though still beautiful, Denise Brown had an unmistakable hard edge. On February 3, taking the stand wearing a black pantsuit and a large gold cross, she obviously wanted this jury to convict.

Denise Brown

After answering a few introductory questions, Denise recalled a scene in 1987 at the Red Onion restaurant in Santa Ana. "At one point," Denise said, "O.J. grabbed Nicole's crotch and said, 'This is where babies come from and this belongs to me.' And Nicole just sort of wrote it off as if it was nothing, like—you know, like she was used to that kind of treatment and he was like— I thought it was really humiliating, if you ask me."

It was obvious that Denise was trying her best to bury O.J.— volunteering the additional (and inadmissible) details that Nicole was "used to" this treatment and that Denise found it "humiliating." Cochran objected, and Ito directed Darden to take better control of his witness.

Darden moved to another domestic-violence incident, a fight between O.J. and Nicole at the Rockingham house sometime in the mid-1980s. It started, Denise said, when she told O.J. he took Nicole for granted.

"He started yelling at me, 'I don't take her for granted. I do everything for her. I give her everything.' And he continued, and then a whole fight broke out, and pictures started flying off the walls, clothes started flying." Denise was on the verge of tears at this point. "He ran upstairs, got clothes, started flying down the stairs, and grabbed Nicole, told her to get out of his house, wanted us all out of his house, picked her up, threw her against the wall,

picked her up, threw her out of the house. She ended up on her—
she ended up falling. She ended up on her elbows and on her
butt. . . . We were all sitting there screaming and crying, and then
he grabbed me and threw me out of the house."

"Are you okay, Miss Brown?" Darden asked.

"Yeah," said Denise, pausing between tears. "It's just so hard. I'll
be fine."

Throughout the two days of Denise Brown's testimony Darden
tried to pile on misdeeds by O.J. in front of the jury. It was an am-
ateurish mistake. Properly prepared, Denise could have given the
jury some real understanding of Nicole and O.J.'s relationship, the
good times as well as the bad. An honest summary of their relationship would have given Denise that much more credibility when
she started describing O.J.'s bad acts. Instead, Darden tried to present O.J. as simply a domestic-violence machine, which was untrue
and, in any event, unlikely to be believed by a jury already sympathetic to him.

Perhaps Denise really did see O.J. this way. But the jurors, un-
moved by her tears, regarded Denise with cold, hard stares.

DENISE Brown's testimony essentially closed the domestic-
violence part of the prosecution's case. At this point Marcia Clark
set out to prove her murder case. She called a series of witnesses
who had testified at the preliminary hearing: the waiters at Mezzaluna who had served Nicole and her family on June 12; the bartender who took the call from Juditha Brown at about 9:40 p.m.
and then ran out to the sidewalk to locate her dropped glasses; the
dog-walkers who tended to Nicole's bereaved Akita and then located the bodies. The defense lawyers mostly gave these early witnesses a pass—until the police officers started taking the stand.

Cochran's entire demeanor changed when he rose to cross-
examine Robert Riske, the first officer on the crime scene at Bundy.
Riske had actually done very little. After briefly inspecting the bodies, he had walked through the house and called for reinforcements.

Two themes stood out in Cochran's cross-examination. First, he
spent several hours on the cup of Ben & Jerry's ice cream that

Riske had discovered on a back stairway. Riske had said the dessert was "melting," not "melted." To Cochran's way of thinking, that meant that the time of the murder must have been at 11:00 p.m. or even later; otherwise the ice cream would have been completely melted. The other theme was the coroner, who had not arrived on the scene to remove the bodies until 9:10 a.m. According to Cochran, if the coroner had arrived earlier, he might have been able to pinpoint the time of death.

As defense arguments, these two issues were absurd. The police had no way of knowing for sure how melted the ice cream was when it was first placed by the stairs, presumably by Nicole. Thus the ice cream would have yielded no relevant information. Likewise, even if the coroner had come to the murder scene within minutes of Riske's arrival, forensic pathology is simply not capable of narrowing down with such precision a time of death. However, by raising the questions over and over again, Cochran made it sound as if there had been some major police lapse at the crime scene. The focus thus shifted from O. J. Simpson to the deficiencies of the LAPD.

Early in his cross-examination of Detective Thomas Lange, Cochran asked about the detective's arrival at the murder scene. "And then you drove from your home in Simi Valley down to the location, is that right?"

"Yes."

The mention of white, conservative Simi Valley was anything but accidental. The place—even just the words "Simi Valley"—was anathema to black Angelenos because it was the site of the notorious acquittal of the police officers who beat Rodney King. Cochran wanted the jury to know that Lange lived there.

Cochran also wanted his Faye Resnick theory in front of the jury—the idea that the murders had been committed by drug dealers looking for Resnick. To this end he needed to establish that Resnick had lived with Nicole for a few days in the beginning of June, but he did not want to call Resnick as a defense witness. So he tried to get his desired sliver of the story in through questioning Lange.

"Did you find out that Faye Resnick moved in with Nicole Brown Simpson on or about June 3, 1994?" Cochran asked Lange.

Clark objected, but Ito let Lange answer, and the detective said he had heard that Resnick had moved in on that date.

When Cochran asked another question about Resnick, Judge Ito called the lawyers to the sidebar. He asked Clark if Resnick really had lived with Nicole: "Is this a disputed fact?" Clark was so angry she could barely speak. "It doesn't matter whether it is a disputed fact or not. We have all kinds of slop in the record now that has been thrown in front of this jury through counsel's method of cross-examination." Clark said Cochran should call a witness who could testify from firsthand knowledge.

Cochran decided to twit his adversaries. "I can choose the witness that I want," he said. "They haven't tried any cases in a long time, and obviously don't know how, but this is cross-examination."

Darden rose to Cochran's taunting, saying loudly, "Who is he talking about, doesn't know how to try the case?"

"Wait, Mr. Darden," Ito instructed. The judge had made a rule that only one lawyer per side could speak on any issue. This was Clark's issue.

But Darden kept on talking against the judge's orders. "Is he the only lawyer that knows how to try the case?" Darden blurted out.

Ito was appalled at Darden's direct violation of his order. "I'm going to hold you in contempt," the judge threatened.

Darden couldn't stop. "I should be held in contempt. I have sat here and listened to—"

"Mr. Darden," Ito continued, "I'm warning you right now."

"This cross-examination is out of order," Darden shot back.

Ito moved from the sidebar back to the bench. Sighing, he excused the jury. The brief pause should have given Darden a moment to compose himself.

It was so simple. All Ito wanted was an apology. Every lawyer knows that judges sometimes act irrationally, rule incorrectly, act impetuously. Here Ito had arguably made a mistake by letting in hearsay evidence, and Darden had exploded. His job, his obligation as a prosecutor, was to apologize and get on with the case.

But Darden would not apologize. He stood alone by the jury box, head down, arms crossed in front of him, agonizing.

CHRISTOPHER Darden was no fool. He knew he should have learned to ignore Johnnie Cochran. Yet he couldn't help himself.

In some respects Darden's family story bore an uncanny resemblance to Cochran's. Both families had arrived on the West Coast during World War II—the Cochrans from Louisiana, Chris Darden's father from outside Tyler, Texas. Johnnie Cochran, Sr., had found work building troopships for Bethlehem Steel; Eddie Darden welded submarines for the navy at Mare Island.

Despite these similarities, the two black families were separated by a gap that is no less real for being mostly invisible to white Americans, who tend to regard African Americans as a single struggling social unit. The difference between them was class. Johnnie Cochran, Sr., bolted the blue-collar world as soon as Japan surrendered. Eddie Darden, in contrast, had a blowtorch in his hand until the day he retired decades later. His son Chris, the third of eight children, had no family guide in the hunt for entrée into the professional world.

The Dardens and the Cochrans did have, however, similar attitudes about education, and here the Darden family was fortunate. John F. Kennedy High School opened within a few blocks of the Dardens' home in Richmond, a city next to Oakland. A modern building, with a pool and athletic fields and a fully integrated student body of about two thousand, Kennedy High drew the city's most motivated students. Edna, the oldest Darden child, served as student body president in 1972; Chris's beloved older brother, Michael, was a standout on the track team, though he later succumbed to a life of drug addiction.

A quiet kid, with a temper that heated and cooled quickly, Chris Darden worked hard in school, made a mark as both a student and an athlete, and held down a job in a liquor store besides. A National Honor Society student, he scraped together the money for junior college and then, a year later, for San Jose State.

The formative experience of Darden's college years came from his membership in Alpha Psi Alpha, the oldest and most prestigious black fraternity (Martin Luther King, Jr., and Thurgood Marshall were members). Alphas at San Jose State had an activist, even militant, cast. They devoted themselves to organizing such projects as a tutoring program for kids in the city's poorer neighborhoods.

His political consciousness growing, Darden applied to Hastings law school, in San Francisco. His passage was anything but smooth. As he later admitted, he shoplifted regularly through college, and he fathered a child out of wedlock while a student at Hastings. Darden graduated in 1980 and took a job with the National Labor Relations Board. A few months later he moved to Los Angeles and the district attorney's office.

Christopher Darden had come farther and overcome more than any of the principal lawyers in the Simpson trial and probably bore the best intentions as well. But he was not, alas, an especially talented or experienced trial lawyer.

In repartee at the sidebar Darden often revealed a lack of professionalism. More seriously, he wore his emotions on his sleeve, alternately mugging and scowling to telegraph his reactions to testimony. Sometimes he jangled his keys in irritation. Whatever the message Darden intended to send with these gestures, the jury only picked up on his nervousness and immaturity.

Of course the jury had been excused when Darden had his showdown with Ito on February 23. After several more agonizing moments of silence Darden broke down and offered grudging words of conciliation. "It appears that the Court is correct, that perhaps my comments may have been or are somewhat inappropriate. I apologize to the Court. I meant no disrespect."

Ito, in contrast, was far more gracious than Darden had any right to expect. "Mr. Darden," the judge said, "I accept your apology. I apologize to you for my reaction as well. I know that your response was out of character, and I'll note it as such."

Ito then invited the jury back to the courtroom, and Cochran resumed his cross-examination of Detective Lange. It didn't last long, however, because a new and even more bizarre crisis erupted. Rosa Lopez was threatening to return to El Salvador.

10

IN HER opening statement, Marcia Clark had surprised Johnnie Cochran by declaring so emphatically that the murders had occurred at precisely 10:15 p.m. Talking with his colleagues on the defense team, Cochran learned from investigator Bill Pavelic that he had a witness who said she saw Simpson's Bronco outside his house at 10:15 p.m. That was Rosa Lopez, the maid at 348 North Rockingham, next door to O.J.'s house. In his opening statement Cochran made the point repeatedly that if the murder took place at 10:15 and the Bronco was still at Rockingham at 10:15, O.J. could not have done it.

No one was more surprised to hear this than Rosa Lopez. What she had told friends and family was that she had seen the Bronco at around 10:00 p.m., not 10:15. As she well knew, a 10:00 sighting was incriminating for O.J. because the murder scene was only a five-minute drive from his house. Word began circulating in the neighborhood that Rosa was now lying or had been paid off or was otherwise in thrall to the defense camp. The reporters staking out her home, the rumors, the scolding looks from her friends and family—they all combined to turn her misery to panic. Lopez quit her job on February 10 and went into hiding in New Mexico. From there she called her lawyer, who, on Cochran's behalf, begged her to return. She agreed to fly back to L.A., but only, she said, for a single day, February 24. She vowed to leave for her native El Salvador the following morning.

When Ito called Lopez to the witness stand—to allow the judge to decide whether he was going to interrupt the prosecution's case and allow Lopez to testify—she revealed a quirky stage presence. Ito had called in a Spanish interpreter, but Lopez obviously understood all the English that was spoken around her.

"Why were you living in another state over the course of the last several days?" Cochran asked her during direct examination.

"Because the reporters won't leave me alone. I'm tired of looking at them." Lopez's style was cryptic, dismissive, and oddly grand. Lopez said she had reservations to fly to San Salvador on Saturday, but the prosecution discovered that this was not true.

"Miss Lopez," Darden said in cross-examination, "we have called the airline. They don't show a reservation for you. Can you explain to the Court why it is that you just told us you have a reservation?"

Lopez serenely adjusted her story. "Because I am going to reserve it, sir. As soon as I leave here, I will buy my ticket and I will leave. If you want to, the cameras can follow me."

And so it went—for hour after hour. Rosa Lopez remained unflappable even as her story crumbled around her. Even her supposed loathing for the press seemed questionable. Lopez had actually given several television interviews, including one with a Spanish-language station just a week earlier.

At the end of a long day of dubious testimony Ito conceded that Lopez had contradicted herself any number of times, but he thought she was sincere in her determination to leave the country.

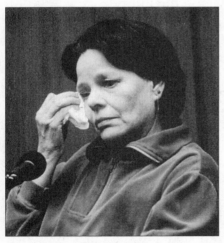
Rosa Lopez

Based on Cochran's representation that Lopez would say she saw the Bronco at 10:15 p.m., he thought she was important enough to delay the trial. It was already after 5:00 p.m., but Ito ordered the bailiffs to bring the jurors from their hotel to the courtroom.

At 5:49 p.m. Marcia Clark, her voice husky with emotion, made a request. "I have informed the Court that I cannot be present tonight because I do have to take care of my children, and I don't have anyone who can do that for me. And I do not want proceedings to go before a jury when I can't be here." She said she had thought that Ito was going to order Lopez's testimony for Monday.

Ito backed Clark and said he would put Lopez up in a hotel for the weekend. Lopez wailed, in English, "I don't want to be here any longer."

"Ms. Lopez," the judge continued solicitously, "the planes fly, as you know, to El Salvador on a regular basis. I will start your testimony in front of the jury the first thing Monday at 9:00."

Suddenly almost coquettish, Lopez said to the judge, "I will do it for you, Your Honor."

MARCIA Clark's problem was not so easily solved. She had been separated from her second husband, Gordon Clark, for a little more than a year. On June 9, 1994—just three days before the murders on Bundy Drive—she had filed for divorce. Clark's sudden celebrity, combined with the extraordinary demands on her time generated by the Simpson case, increased the tensions between them.

The events of February 24 were typical of their problems. Marcia and Gordon Clark had two boys, ages three and five at the time. According to the custody-sharing agreement they had worked out, Gordon would have the boys every other weekend, starting at seven o'clock Fridays. However, according to Marcia, the boys preferred for her to take them to Gordon's rather than for their father to pick them up. She had told Ito several times that day that she had to be home in time to take the kids to her husband's by 7:00.

Gordon Clark wasn't watching the trial on February 24—he made it a point never to watch—but when he found out what Marcia had said to Ito about her childcare obligations, he and his lawyers were aghast. Gordon could easily have picked up the kids himself. In their view Marcia was lying to the court to gain time to prepare for cross-examination of Rosa Lopez—and public sympathy for herself as a working mother. Thus did a private and, alas, fairly typical divorce become part of the communal narrative of the Simpson case.

The media took Marcia's side with a vengeance, and she became an overnight heroine of working women everywhere. There was some truth in this cardboard-cutout portrayal of the prosecutor. Real life, however, was considerably more complicated.

A TALL AND STRAPPING ISRAELI native, Abraham Kleks came of age with the young nation, serving as a seventeen-year-old lieutenant in the War for Independence. Shortly after that war was won in 1948, Abraham decided to see the world a little and followed some friends to the University of California at Berkeley. At the Jewish Community Center of San Francisco, Abraham met and fell in love with a girl from Brooklyn. Abraham and Roslyn married, settled in the United States, and a year later, on August 31, 1953, had their first child, Marcia.

Abraham was drafted into the U.S. Army for the Korean War. He had studied microbiology at Berkeley, and he pursued this interest at army medical laboratories in Texas and Washington State. From the army Abraham joined the Food and Drug Administration, where he moved up the ladder with jobs across the nation: five years in Los Angeles, four near San Francisco, one in Detroit, one near Washington, D.C., and two in New York City. Marcia completed her high school requirements in Staten Island. By this point she had a brother, Jonathan, six years her junior.

Marcia was a quick-minded, good-natured girl with an extraordinary talent for languages. She mastered Spanish and, after just two months in Israel one summer, gained a fluent command of Hebrew as well. Notwithstanding the frequent moves (or perhaps because of them), she became a great joiner of activities—cheerleading, school plays, and the like.

A rift between Marcia and her parents began when they moved from New York back to Los Angeles—their final relocation—in 1970. Marcia wanted badly to get out of the house, but the local high schools required a year's residency before they would give her a degree, even though she'd already fulfilled all her course requirements. She couldn't go to college without the degree. Amid the tension at home and frustration about school, Marcia developed bulimia, an affliction she would battle on and off for more than twenty years.

At last she escaped to U.C.L.A. She was still an undergraduate when she met her first husband, Gaby Horowitz, a dashing and handsome young man, like her father an immigrant from Israel.

The courtship was brief but intense, and they married shortly after she graduated, without even telling Marcia's parents first.

Gaby Horowitz made his living as a professional backgammon player while Marcia started law school. The late 1970s were boom years for the game, and for a while Horowitz thrived in the epicenter of the craze. He was, in fact, a controversial figure in that world. According to Danny Kleinman, who self-publishes books about backgammon and bridge in Los Angeles, "He was a very good player, but he used to cheat."

In 1979 Marcia told her parents she was divorcing Gaby. About a month later she announced she was marrying Gordon Clark. At twenty-two he was five years her junior and an administrator with the Church of Scientology in Los Angeles. She didn't invite her parents to that wedding either.

The years Marcia and Gordon Clark lived together were the time that Marcia came of age as a prosecutor. Gordon returned to college and became a modestly successful computer programmer. They had two sons.

At the end of 1993, a few months after her fortieth birthday, Marcia Clark made several dramatic changes in her life. She told Bill Hodgman that she wanted to return to the courtroom, and she told Gordon that she wanted a divorce. To both Gordon and her parents, she was cryptic about her reasons. "He's not for me," she told her father in Hebrew. And then about a month after she split with Gordon, Marcia told her parents that she never wanted to speak to them again, saying they had been icy and unsupportive.

The Kleks were thunderstruck, heartbroken. They had become very close to Marcia and Gordon's older child, who was four at the time his parents separated. They figured the crisis—whatever its mysterious origin—would blow over. It never did.

Gordon was shocked and bitter about the separation, and Marcia's sudden celebrity gave him the opportunity to take a very public form of revenge. On February 24, the same day Marcia said she had to leave court during Rosa Lopez's testimony, Gordon filed a motion to change their custody arrangements. The actual adjustment he sought was rather minor and reasonable: increased visi-

tation while Marcia was working late on the case. But in his accompanying affidavit Gordon portrayed her as a workaholic and
a neglectful parent. It was this affidavit that made Marcia's personal life a matter of public controversy.

Professionally powerful, Marcia was personally fragile. Gordon
Clark thought she drank too much. She smoked more than she
wanted to. The years of bulimia had also exacted a painful price.
Extreme tooth decay is a common side effect, and in her original
divorce petition with Gordon, Marcia said, "Within the last two
years I have suffered a medical/dental catastrophe for which I
initially borrowed $16,000.00. In addition, it was necessary to
withdraw $26,000 from my pension plan, in order to finish my
dental work." At the time of their separation Gordon's earnings
amounted to a little more than half of Marcia's $96,829 yearly
salary, so he could not be counted on for major support.

At times the compounded stresses of ending a long marriage,
trying the Simpson case, and enduring the indignities of unsought
celebrity nearly drove Clark to the breaking point. During Denise
Brown's testimony the *National Enquirer* published topless photographs of Clark from a vacation years earlier with Gaby. She was
so humiliated that one day she actually began sobbing quietly at
the counsel table. She scribbled a note to Scott Gordon, the prosecutor seated next to her. "I'm losing it," Clark wrote. Thinking fast,
the roly-poly Gordon jotted Clark a response: "The *Enquirer* was
going to run the same pictures of me, but Greenpeace wouldn't
let them do it." Clark smiled, and that crisis, at least, passed un-
noticed by the public.

When court convened on Monday, Marcia Clark opened with a
passionate appeal for Lopez's testimony to be taken on videotape,
not in front of the jury. The defense could play it later if it chose
to do so; that way defense evidence would not be deposited right
in the middle of the government's case. Ito agreed.

Rosa Lopez returned to the witness stand wearing a new purple
dress with a beaded collar and shiny black pumps, gifts from a
defense-team supporter, and Johnnie Cochran finally began walking her through the events of June 12, 1994. When she reached

the critical moment in her testimony—what she saw at around 10:00 that night—Lopez hedged. She said she took her dog for a walk and saw O.J.'s Bronco sometime after 10:00, but it could have been anywhere from two to fifteen minutes after the hour. What was clear from the outset, then, was that Rosa Lopez was simply not a very important witness. She didn't help or hurt either side very much. Yet because of her Ito had allowed the trial to come to a crashing halt.

In the end, Lopez stayed on the stand until Friday, and the jurors did not return to the courtroom until Monday, March 6—*nine days* after they had last heard testimony. The interlude amounted to another example of the prosecution's bad luck. If Lopez's testimony had been presented live to the jury, the jurors would have seen her implode on cross-examination. Ultimately, of course, the defense would decide not to play the tape.

Rosa Lopez did indeed return to her remote hometown of Sensuntepeque, El Salvador. She has never returned.

11

ON MARCH 9 the trial reached a critical juncture.

"The People call Detective Mark Fuhrman," said Marcia Clark.

Neither side made even a pretense of treating Fuhrman as just another witness. The D.A.'s office went to extraordinary lengths to insulate him from any unplanned encounters. Unlike any other witness in the case, Fuhrman came down from the district attorney's headquarters on the eighteenth floor on the freight elevator. And unlike other witnesses, he walked into court surrounded by a quartet of beefy bodyguards.

In the flesh Mark Fuhrman was an imposing figure, a muscular six foot three inches, the first man in the courtroom who appeared a physical match for the defendant. The room perked up when he walked in, and even O. J. Simpson looked a touch startled by the detective's commanding physical presence.

Marcia Clark stepped to the lectern, cocked her head to one

side, and asked her first question as if it had just popped into her head. (It was, in fact, carefully planned.)

"Detective Fuhrman, can you tell us how you feel about testifying today?"

"Nervous," Fuhrman said, not at all nervously.

"Okay," Clark prompted.

"Reluctant," Fuhrman continued.

"Can you tell us why?" she asked.

"I have seen a lot of the evidence ignored and a lot of personal issues come to the forefront. I think that is too bad."

"Okay," she said. "Heard a lot about yourself in the press, have you?"

"Daily," Fuhrman said gravely.

Under Clark's sympathetic questioning, Mark Fuhrman presented himself as an earnest civil servant who tried to do his job in the face of unwarranted and irrelevant personal attacks. Clark's message to the jury could not have been clearer: Here before you is a good man. But in light of what Clark knew at the time, her examination of Fuhrman stands as her biggest miscalculation of the trial.

As OFTEN happened in the Simpson case, a disclosure in the media had flushed out additional people with similar stories to tell. After my story in *The New Yorker* hit the newsstands on Monday, July 18, 1994, one person who saw a television report about it was Kathleen Bell. The report so startled her that she was moved to write a letter to Johnnie Cochran.

"I was quite shocked to see that Officer Ferman [*sic*] was a man that I had the misfortune of meeting," Bell wrote. "I remember him distinctly because of his height and build." She explained that she had worked as a real estate agent in Redondo Beach in 1985 and 1986, and her office was above a marine recruiting station where Fuhrman sometimes visited friends. Talking about his police work one day, "Officer Ferman [*sic*] said that when he sees a 'nigger' (as he called it) driving with a white woman, he would pull them over. I asked would if [*sic*] he didn't have a reason, and he said that he would find one. It became obvious to me that he was very serious. Officer Ferman went on to say that he would like nothing more than to see all 'niggers' gathered together and killed. He said something about burning them or bombing them. I was too shaken to remember the exact words he used." Her story surfaced in the news several months before the trial began.

Clearly, then, Marcia Clark must have known that there was not just smoke but fire in Mark Fuhrman's past. There were several ways she could have taken the middle ground with respect to Fuhrman. She could have introduced the glove found at Rockingham through Lange or Vannatter. That strategy would have prompted some mockery from the defense, but Simp-

Mark Fuhrman

son's attorneys could always have called Fuhrman themselves. Or she could have called Fuhrman but signaled the jury that the prosecution was not embracing the detective. A brief, chilly direct examination would have sufficed.

But it was not in Marcia Clark's nature to equivocate. It was, after all, her job to tell the good guys from the bad guys, and she had no doubts about her ability to do it.

She took Fuhrman briefly through his background and then had him tell the jury about the time he responded to a domestic-violence call at Simpson's home in 1985, when O.J. shattered a Mercedes-Benz window with a baseball bat. Then she moved to a new topic.

"Now, back in 1985 and 1986, sir, can you tell us whether you knew someone or met someone by the name of Kathleen Bell?"

"Yes, I can tell you," Fuhrman said evenly. "I did not."

Clark displayed Bell's original letter to Cochran on the overhead projector. The jurors had the opportunity to study the precise, awful words that Bell said Fuhrman had uttered. It was one thing for Fuhrman to issue a general denial, but Clark pushed these ugly sentiments right in the jurors' faces.

She continued, "Did the conversation Kathleen Bell describes in this letter occur?"

"No, it did not."

This entire exchange was little short of madness on Clark's part. Bell was a credible witness; indeed, on *Larry King Live,* Bell had told King she thought Simpson was guilty. More important, Clark knew that the defense could corroborate Bell's story.

The remainder of her direct examination was uneventful, underlining Fuhrman's minor role in the investigation. The idea was to show (correctly) that there never was a second glove at Bundy to move to Rockingham and, furthermore, that even if he had wanted to, Fuhrman never had the opportunity to move or plant any evidence.

Clark turned over Mark Fuhrman to F. Lee Bailey.

BAILEY was so hungry for the spotlight—and so embarrassed by his meager role to date in the trial—that he held a series of press conferences in the courthouse lobby to announce how much he was looking forward to cross-examining Mark Fuhrman.

In a display of brooding courtroom machismo Bailey had not objected a single time during Clark's direct examination, but when his turn came, he rushed to the lectern in a burst of manic energy. He was so pumped with adrenaline that he couldn't focus on any subject for more than a few moments. He talked about Fuhrman's education—he was a high school dropout who later received an equivalency degree—then jumped to the 1985 domestic-violence incident, returned to Fuhrman's activities on the night of the murder, and finally was off to the marine recruiting station that Kathleen Bell worked above. As Bailey meandered on, Fuhrman grew confident enough to make a little joke. "The name Bell does not ring a bell."

Bailey became frustrated and by the end of the day was ready for a desperate lunge. "Did you wipe a glove in the Bronco, Detective Fuhrman?"

This surprised the witness. It was preposterous enough to suggest that he would take a bloody glove to plant at Simpson's house, but the idea that Fuhrman, or anyone for that matter, would use the glove as a sort of paintbrush to spread incriminating evidence—well, it was actually kind of amusing. Yet there was an insidious cleverness to Bailey's conjecture. If Fuhrman had wiped the glove in the Bronco, it would explain how Goldman's blood wound up there. (In fact, after the trial several jurors mentioned this as a possibility.)

Fuhrman gave a small smile, a faint chuckle of perverse admiration. But all he said was, "No."

Through several fruitless days of cross-examination Bailey failed to budge Fuhrman on his story about his role in the investigation. In the end, Bailey's greatest achievement was to leave the sound of one word ringing in the ears of the jurors.

Bailey knew better than most lawyers the power that the word "nigger" could exert over a jury, especially one that included African Americans. When he had defended himself against fraud charges in Florida in 1973, the government's first witness in the trial was a man named Jimmie James. Though all of Bailey's fellow defendants were white, Bailey asked James during his cross-examination if he had ever said, "I hate niggers." James denied it.

Continuing, Bailey had asked, "You say that you did not. You do not use that word at all, do you?"

As Bailey explained in his book *For the Defense,* "I knew that if James denied using the word, I could put a witness on the stand to refute him, thereby impeaching that statement and casting doubt on the rest of his testimony as well."

On March 15 Bailey sought to re-create almost word for word his cross-examination of Jimmie James with Mark Fuhrman. "Do you use the word 'nigger' in describing people?"

"No, sir," said Fuhrman.

"Have you used that word in the past ten years?"

"Not that I recall, no."

Bailey was going to make sure he had Fuhrman's denial down cold. What followed was perhaps the most quoted exchange in the entire trial. "Are you therefore saying that you have not used that word in the past ten years, Detective Fuhrman?"

"Yes," Fuhrman said with just a touch of nervousness.

"And you say under oath that you have not addressed any black person as a nigger or spoken about black people as niggers in the past ten years, Detective Fuhrman?"

"That's what I'm saying, sir."

"So anyone who comes to this court and quotes you as using that word in dealing with African Americans would be a liar."

"Yes, they would."

"All of them, correct?"

"All of them."

"All right," said Bailey. "Thank you."

Bailey had closed every possible escape hatch.

Marcia Clark could have cried in frustration. She knew without being told that Fuhrman had probably said nigger in the past decade. At that point there was nothing she could do. After embracing Fuhrman during his direct testimony, there was no way she could distance herself from him at this point.

WITH the Fuhrman testimony behind them Shapiro and Bailey were free to return to their top priorities: themselves.

Bailey, who for many years had lived by the sword of public acclaim, was now dying by the sword of "expert" condemnation of his cross-examination of Fuhrman. Despite his public mask of bravado, the criticism wounded Bailey, and he set off on a rather desperate attempt to pump up his reputation, doing rounds of interviews to praise his own performance.

Shapiro had his own strategy for reputation overhaul. After Fuhrman left the stand on March 16, he denounced his colleague's cross-examination of the detective. "My preference," he told a flock of cameras, "was that race was not an issue in this case and should not be an issue in this case, and I'm sorry from my personal point of view that it has become an issue in this case." This was an especially shameless display, considering that Shapiro had launched the race-based defense in the first place.

He brought his petulance into the courtroom the following week when he cross-examined Philip Vannatter. Shapiro did a competent job, but the lawyer conducted the questioning while wearing a blue ribbon on his lapel. The chief of the LAPD, Willie Williams, had started a campaign for citizens to wear these lapel pins, explicitly stating that they stood for defending police officers against accusations leveled at them by O. J. Simpson's lawyers. Shapiro never made clear just why he had decided to wear one. (To mock Shapiro around Cochran's office, one investigator also took to wearing a blue pin—on the fly of his pants.)

Shapiro's blue pin gesture nearly drove his client over the top. Simpson gave Shapiro an ultimatum: One more stunt and you're off the team.

This would have been Shapiro's opportunity to flee—that is, if he had really wanted to get off the case. But in his heart Shapiro loved the attention—the winks from celebrities, the autograph seekers. He also knew that he wanted to write a book about the trial. He couldn't give it all up now.

BESET by the tabloids and a vengeful ex-husband, Marcia Clark was watching the Simpson case become more racial morality play than murder trial. Clark had a gift for surviving on very little sleep, but so, alas, did her two sons, and they did not always choose the same five hours as their mother. That, plus her incessant smoking, gave her a cold and a persistent cough that lasted for weeks.

And then she had to deal with Kato Kaelin. Kaelin's cuddly image obscured a darker personal history. He may have looked and acted like a teenage slacker, but he was a lot closer to forty than twenty, and his perpetual freeloading was viewed with scorn by his ex-wife, the mother of their daughter, whom Kaelin intermittently supported. For that and any number of other reasons Marcia Clark loathed him. But she needed him. Kaelin circumscribed O.J.'s alibi; the two men had arrived home from their famous trip to Mc-Donald's at about 9:40 p.m. on June 12. Kaelin had also heard the thumps near the air conditioner, which had prompted Fuhrman's expedition to the pathway behind the house.

When Kaelin took the stand—twitching, tieless, in black jeans and, of course, his unruly mop of greasy blond hair—everyone, in-. cluding the usually deadpan jury, had to smile at his bravura goofiness. On the night of the murders, the jury learned, Kaelin spent

from 7:45 to 8:30 p.m. in O.J.'s Jacuzzi—a marination of almost superhuman duration. Clark asked him about the clock in Simpson's Bentley, the vehicle they drove to McDonald's.

"Was this a digital clock?"

"No," Kaelin said, and he then began waving his arms in a sort of cretinous attempt to act out the hands of a watch. "It was a numbered clock. Well, I mean numerals." He stumbled along. "A digit would be that, too, but you know what I'm saying."

Ito finally ended the agony. "Analog," he said.

Kato Kaelin

Ultimately Clark did get the bare minimum she needed out of Kaelin, but her hostility, combined with his vapidity, made this witness ultimately a lost opportunity for the prosecution.

Not so Allan Park, who represented one of the rare occasions when fortune smiled on the prosecutors. Poised, intelligent, with a record of cellular telephone calls to corroborate his story about the night in question, the man who drove Simpson to the airport in a limousine proved a devastatingly incriminating witness.

Nervous about picking up a celebrity for the first time, Park had arrived about twenty minutes early. He drove up Rockingham at about 10:25 p.m., and—this was crucial—*Simpson's Bronco was not there.* He made a right onto Ashford and waited. He rang Simpson's bell at about 10:40 p.m. No answer. He went around the corner to the Rockingham gate. No signs of life—and still no Bronco. Park began to panic. He didn't want Simpson to miss his flight.

Using the limo's cell phone, Park called his boss. He also kept ringing the bell to the house. Peering through the gate, he saw that the house was dark except for a single light upstairs. At 10:52 p.m. Park's boss called him in the limo. A minute or two later Park caught sight of a six-foot, two-hundred-pound black person walking into the front door of the house. Park buzzed again. For the first time the lights went on downstairs, and O. J. Simpson answered the intercom, then opened the gate by remote control.

"I overslept," Simpson said. "I just got out of the shower, and I'll be down in a minute."

Simpson spent about five minutes rooting around in the now fully lit house and rushed downstairs with a few bags, Park said. Kaelin and Park helped him load them into the car, although Simpson insisted that only he touch a small black duffel bag. (Prosecutors argued that this bag held the clothes Simpson wore during the murders.) When Park drove down the driveway shortly after 11:00 and made a left onto Rockingham, he noticed that "something was obstructing my view" on the right—apparently the Bronco. In other words, O. J. Simpson's Bronco was *not* parked by his house at the time of the murders, but it was there after Simpson materialized back at his house. It was startling evidence of Simpson's guilt. Cochran made scarcely a whit of progress on cross-examination.

On that rare happy note for her in late March, Marcia Clark effectively disappeared from the case. She did not examine another witness for nearly three full months, until June 21. Preoccupied with her divorce, Clark rarely even made it to court on time. She would burst through the courtroom doors often at 9:30 a.m. or later. The jurors, who had to rise daily at 5:30 a.m. and had no choice about being on time, regarded her entrances with long, cold stares.

BARRY Scheck looked different and sounded different. His entire wardrobe of ill-fitting double-breasted suits probably cost less than just one of Cochran's or Shapiro's buttery ensembles. And Scheck spoke in a language that few in the courtroom understood. There was his accent for starters—a New York honk that never blended into the beige California soundscape—and there was also his vocabulary: the language of forensic DNA technology, with its "alleles," "autorads" and "daughter ions."

But the courtroom camera never caught the most important difference between Scheck and the other defense lawyers. Scheck worked. Cochran left the detail work to Carl Douglas. Shapiro enjoyed a nap after a day in court. When Scheck left Ito's courtroom, he would bend his pudgy frame over a table in Cochran's office suite and examine the scientific evidence against O. J. Simpson. Shapiro had hired him with the vague idea that Scheck and his partner, Peter Neufeld, would brief Shapiro on the admissibility of DNA evidence. At that point the idea that Barry Scheck would deliver one of the closing jury arguments would have been laughable. But by dint of the sheer quality and quantity of his effort, Scheck emerged, after Cochran, as the most important trial lawyer in the case—and, in terms of courtroom skills, the best trial lawyer as well.

What Scheck did in those endless sessions at the table in Cochran's office was construct a brilliant defense. The genius of it was that it merged perfectly with the cruder race-based strategy orchestrated from the beginning. Scheck's efforts had little to do with establishing that someone other than Simpson had murdered Ron and Nicole and everything to do with undermining the integrity and competence of the LAPD. His goal was to establish that the mountain of forensic evidence against his client meant nothing.

The most remarkable thing was that Scheck actually accomplished this goal. By the end of the case he had a plausible scientific basis for arguing away every piece of physical evidence against Simpson. To be sure, many of these explanations were fanciful, some were silly and, in part, contradictory, positing a police department that was both totally inept and brilliantly sinister. But Scheck's passion and skill made his theories real for the jury. And for that reason he as much as any other person in that courtroom was responsible for the verdict that came out of it.

WITH a shift of about a half-dozen years Barry Scheck might have been Marcia Clark (and she, him). Both came from upwardly mobile middle-class Jewish families that stressed education and liberal politics. Both were smart, verbal kids who did well in school. But Scheck, born in Queens, New York, in 1949, came of age at a time when the highest goal for a liberal lawyer was to fight the system—as a criminal defense lawyer at least, a legal aid lawyer at best. A few years later kids like him would become prosecutors.

When Scheck arrived at Yale in the 1960s, he wore ties and cast his lot with Yale's Young Democrats; by the time he graduated, he could only enter the Yale Club in New York through a side door because his political convictions demanded that he wear work shirts. Along the way Scheck presented his draft card to the famous Yale chaplain William Sloane Coffin for delivery to the Pentagon in protest of the Vietnam War. Scheck campaigned for Norman Mailer when he ran for mayor of New York City. He went to law school at Boalt Hall in Berkeley and after graduating, went to work for legal aid in the Bronx.

Scheck spent about five years in that combative, highly political office (where Neufeld also worked), until he took a job as a clinical law professor at a law school in lower Manhattan. The position allowed Scheck to teach and also to defend criminal cases, and in 1987 a fellow lawyer called him with a plea for help. The lawyer's client, Joseph Castro, had been charged with murder, and the case against him was based principally on the infant science known as DNA fingerprinting. Scheck and Neufeld agreed to help out.

What struck the two lawyers was the hypnotizing power of DNA technology. As they steeped themselves in this new science, they realized that the best way to attack it was through the evidence collection and preservation techniques of the police. Garbage in, garbage out—that was the theory. Scheck and Neufeld persuaded the judge to exclude the DNA evidence as unreliable. (It wasn't wrong, though. Castro himself ultimately pleaded guilty.)

The power of the technology pricked the two men's social consciences as well. They realized that DNA testing on blood or semen could free the unjustly convicted, and they began representing prisoners they believed were innocent. Calling their efforts the Innocence Project, Scheck and Neufeld helped more than fifteen convicted prison inmates go free.

At one level, though, these two lawyers weren't so different from their more cynical colleagues on the Simpson defense team. They trashed DNA when it implicated their clients and embraced it when it excluded them. The pair dealt with this contradiction by resolutely refusing to acknowledge it, asserting instead that DNA "matches" were simply less reliable than exclusions.

THE forensic-evidence portion of the Simpson case began with the testimony of Dennis Fung, the diminutive, soft-spoken thirty-four-year-old criminalist who had collected evidence on the morning after the murders. The prosecutor was Hank Goldberg, a skilled appellate advocate but a trial lawyer with the stage presence of a voice-mail attendant. Prodded by Goldberg, Fung told the story of how he had collected the various tiny drops and hairs into plastic bags for transportation back to police headquarters.

Scheck began cross-examination on the afternoon of April 4. A junior colleague of Fung's, Andrea Mazzola, had assisted the criminalist in processing both crime scenes. It was only Mazzola's third crime scene, and Scheck explored whether, in earlier testimony, Fung had exaggerated his own activities in order to play down the role of his novice accomplice.

"So you didn't tell the grand jury that Andrea Mazzola swatched that red stain off the handle of the Bronco, right?"

"At the time—" Fung stumbled.

"Did you tell them that?"

"No."

"You said *you* did it."

"Yes," said Fung.

Scheck thus began by establishing that Fung had made repeated misstatements about evidence. Scheck then went after Fung's competence. This went on for days—a medley of Fung's mistakes, some trivial, some not. Large purple blotches began to appear under Fung's eyes. First Fung said he was sure that he never collected evidence with his bare hands; then he wasn't sure. No, he hadn't seen any soil inside Simpson's home at Rockingham. Yes, he should have taken larger samples of blood from O.J.'s Bronco. At least some of

Barry Scheck

these flaws could be attributed to the LAPD's underfunding of its Scientific Investigative Division (and undertraining of its personnel), but whatever the reasons, the failures reflected on the prosecution's case against O. J. Simpson. It was a brilliant—and devastating—cross-examination.

These efforts served a larger goal than merely embarrassing Dennis Fung; Scheck used them to offer a comprehensive view of the evidence. His dissection of the blood evidence on the back gate at Bundy was a classic demonstration of the Scheck method. Through sheer intellectual calisthenics he not only neutralized some of the most powerful evidence in the case against Simpson but turned it into arguable proof of a police conspiracy.

Scheck noticed first that Fung had not collected the blood on the gate until July 3, 1994—three weeks after the killings. Fung had explained in his direct examination that he had simply missed this blood on the morning after the murders.

Scheck then noticed something curious in the test results. For many of the stains that Fung collected from the walkway outside Nicole's home, the DNA had substantially degraded and could only be subjected to the PCR type of DNA testing, which yields less precise results than the RFLP method. But the blood on the back gate was scarcely degraded at all. It was so rich in DNA that the police did do RFLP testing on it. Scheck found this paradoxical. Why would blood that had sat outside for three weeks be *less* degraded than blood that was collected within a few hours of the crime?

Scheck didn't stop there. He examined photographs of the crime scene. The only head-on pictures of the stain on the rear gate were taken when Fung finally did remove a sample on July 3, but Scheck found one photo from June 13 that revealed a distant view of the gate. Blown up many times, the photo was ambiguous. Scheck could argue that the blood was simply not there. He showed Fung the July 3 photo, where the blood is clearly visible, and then the earlier photo, where it is not.

"Where is it, Mr. Fung?" Scheck asked with a sneer in his voice. Fung couldn't say. This exchange ended the court day on April 11.

But Scheck wasn't finished. In the preliminary hearing Thano Peratis, the police nurse who took Simpson's blood sample on the afternoon of June 13 at Parker Center, had testified that he had taken about 8 milliliters—a standard amount. Scheck reviewed the records to see how much of Simpson's blood sample had been used up in all the subsequent testing. Again Scheck found something peculiar. The subsequent tests accounted for only about 6.5 milliliters of blood. Scheck also found an expert to say that the blood on the gate contained EDTA, a preservative used in the test tube where Simpson's blood sample had been stored.

Thus Scheck had the raw material for his counternarrative: On June 13 Fung did not collect the blood on the back gate because it wasn't there. Between June 13 and July 3 someone—probably Vannatter—planted O.J.'s blood on the back gate. (After all, Vannatter, curiously, had brought O.J.'s blood sample all the way back to Brentwood from downtown Los Angeles to hand to Fung.) The DNA of the blood left at the actual crime scene had degraded, but because the blood on the gate came from Simpson's fresh sample, it yielded definitive results. Someone had planted some of Simpson's "missing" blood on that back gate: Q.E.D.

The prosecution had a complicated response to this story, and it depended, in significant part, on the jurors' believing in the incompetence of the LAPD, which was not a message the government otherwise wanted the jury to accept. The prosecutors asserted that on the first morning Fung collected dozens of stains, and this one just fell through the cracks. The fact that many police officers saw the blood on the back gate established that it was not planted at some later date. As for the good quality of that blood, on June 13 Fung had stored the samples for several hours in an unair-conditioned truck. He shouldn't have done that, because heat and humidity degrade DNA. The blood on the gate, by contrast, spent three weeks resting on a clean, painted surface in the cool Brentwood air. Naturally the DNA in it did not degrade. The photographs proved nothing, establishing only that neither Fung nor the photographer had paid attention to the back gate stains on June 13. And in some of the most highly technical evidence in the case, an FBI expert said the blood from the gate contained no EDTA.

As for "missing" blood, that was a figment of Scheck's imagination. When it comes to such small differences as 1 or 2 milliliters, nurses generally pay little attention to the amount of blood they take, and Peratis confessed that he had been too categorical when he testified at the preliminary hearing that he took 8 milliliters from Simpson. It might have been as little as 6.5 milliliters. As for Vannatter's delivery of the blood to Fung, that took place at O.J.'s home on Rockingham. A news video showed Fung placing the vial in his truck outside O.J.'s house. Thus that blood couldn't have been planted at Nicole's condo on Bundy.

More fundamentally, though, the prosecutors wanted the jury to believe that the police did not plant blood on Nicole's back gate, because they would not do such a thing. Vannatter, Lange, Fung—they all gave their word that they did not do it. That, the prosecutors believed, should have counted for something. But with a jury predisposed toward sympathy for the defendant and hostility to the police, Scheck's counternarrative found a receptive audience.

THE PRESENTATION OF THE results of the DNA testing should have been the highlight of the prosecution's case. Garcetti had recruited two of the top DNA prosecutors in the state to present this portion of the evidence—Rockne Harmon from Oakland and Woody Clarke from San Diego. Attempting to be thorough, though, Woody Clarke made the subject boring and incomprehensible, especially to an uneducated jury.

Still, the results of the RFLP testing were striking. For one of the blood drops on the path at Bundy the odds were 1 in 170 million that it came from anyone other than Simpson. For the blood on the socks found in Simpson's bedroom the odds were 1 in 6.8 billion that they came from anyone other than Nicole Brown Simpson. (There are about 5 billion people on earth.) The results from the less exact PCR tests were less impressive only because of the overwhelming numbers from the RFLP testing.

In every one of several dozen tests the DNA results matched the prosecution's theory. In the case on which Marcia Clark and Phil Vannatter had first worked together, they had won a conviction based on a single drop of blood. But in the Simpson case the possibility of evidence planting cast a pall over all of these prosecution numbers, impressive as they were.

Whatever the jury may have thought, the DNA testimony had a shattering impact among O. J. Simpson's wealthy L.A. friends. At this stage of the trial his most prized supporters melted away— among them Allen Schwartz, a clothing wholesaler and probably O.J.'s closest friend in Brentwood, and boutique owner Alan Austin, O.J.'s most frequent golfing partner. Now they finally knew what they didn't want to know—that O.J. had killed Nicole.

It was perhaps because of this abandonment that O. J. Simpson, seemingly the only person in the courtroom to do so, took the DNA evidence so hard. As the experts gave their reports, Simpson greeted them with scowls of derision and nervous monologues to Cochran or Shapiro or whoever sat next to him. Though the jury had yet to speak, at this point Simpson knew with certainty that his former life was over. The friends, the hangers-on, the world of "being O.J.," was now, clearly, gone forever.

12

THEIR greatest humiliation, the jurors remembered later, came right before bed. At 11:00 every night one of the deputy sheriffs would walk around the fifth floor of the Inter-Continental Hotel, knock on the jurors' doors, and demand their room keys. This went on every night for months until finally someone worked up the nerve to ask why they had to surrender their keys.

"It's so you don't go into each other's rooms," the sheriff's spokesman replied.

That was that. The jurors were to be trusted to decide whether O. J. Simpson murdered two human beings but not to sleep with the keys to their own rooms. There was no protest, and the jurors continued to yield the keys until their last night in confinement. As with so many petty insults, the jurors lived with this one, too.

By summer they were struggling. With the exception of occasional weekend outings—a much enjoyed group ride on a blimp, a disastrous boat ride to Catalina Island, on which almost everyone got seasick—the world of the twelve jurors and twelve alternates was circumscribed by the courthouse and the Inter-Continental, about a mile away. Their rooms had no telephones or televisions. Deputy sheriffs dialed and monitored all telephone calls and screened newspapers for references to the case, clipping them out. Blockbuster supplied an unending stream of movies for a pair of "video rooms." On only one night a week, from 7:00 to midnight, were the jurors allowed unsupervised conjugal visits with their spouses or significant others.

Not surprisingly these arrangements produced lasting stresses. The strain showed itself in trivial ways. The jurors argued over video selections and, like prisoners everywhere, they complained about the food. There was also the Ross discount store shopping incident.

The aggrieved shopper was Jeanette Harris, a thirty-eight-year-old African American employment interviewer and a divisive force on the jury from the first day. In a secret session on February 7, just a few days into the taking of testimony, Harris told Ito and the lawyers that the jury was splintering along racial lines.

Harris had requested the meeting ostensibly to complain about the shopping incident and her difficulties with another juror. She said the deputies had intentionally given the white jurors an extra half hour to shop at Ross while hurrying the black jurors through the store. Harris also asserted, improbably enough, that she had been pushed by Catherine Murdoch, a white legal secretary and only the first of several jurors Harris would accuse of striking her. Shocked by the accusation, Murdoch denied any malign intent, and Ito believed her. Nevertheless, the very existence of the accusation put everyone on notice about just how fragile the jury was.

Murdoch was removed from the jury for an unrelated reason: Her arthritis doctor, who also treated Simpson, had been listed as a defense witness (though he never testified). Other jurors also left the case in the early weeks, one because she was found to have covered up a history of domestic violence, another because he worked for Hertz and had apparently met Simpson, another for failing to report that he had been arrested for kidnapping a former girlfriend, yet another because Ito believed he was keeping notes for a book.

Then in March the judge received an anonymous letter suggesting that Jeanette Harris had been a long-term victim of domestic violence. Sheriff's deputies followed up and learned that in 1988 Harris had sought a restraining order against her husband. The prosecutors wanted her off the jury, asserting that she had lied during the course of jury selection when she had specifically denied any personal involvement with domestic violence. The defense lawyers wanted her to remain, arguing that her answers amounted only to innocent mistakes. Through all the jury controversies the one constant was the prosecution wanting to shed black jurors, the defense seeking to evict whites. In any event, Ito dismissed Harris for her lack of candor about the domestic violence in her past—and she, in turn, promptly created an uproar.

On April 5, just hours after she was dismissed, Harris sat with Pat Harvey, an anchorwoman at KCAL, a local television station in Los Angeles, and shared her impressions of the trial.

"From day one I didn't see it as being a fair trial," she told Harvey. Prosecutors were "saying a whole lot of nothing," and she believed that Mark Fuhrman was "capable of probably anything," including planting evidence. As for the defendant himself, Harris was "quite impressed" with Simpson and his ability to handle his grief.

Even worse than her pro-defense interpretation of the evidence was Harris's suggestion that the racial tensions surrounding the case might influence jurors' votes. "There is maybe a person that—say one of the Caucasians—will say, 'I can't vote him not guilty because when I walk out of here, I want to walk back into a life,' " Harris told Harvey. "Or an African American might say, 'I can't say he's guilty because I want to walk out of here.' You know, those things cross your mind." In other words, jurors might vote to please their racial group. In addition, there was no doubt in Harris's mind that the sheriff's department was promoting racial divisions on the jury. Worst of all, as Harris told a reporter for KCAL off-camera, jurors were discussing the facts of the case among themselves—in clear violation of Judge Ito's orders.

This allegation raised the troubling prospect of additional misconduct by the jury and the removal of more jurors. With only six alternates remaining (and likely months of testimony to go), this was a disheartening possibility for the judge, to say the least. But Ito felt he had to follow up, so he decided to interview the remaining jurors one by one. For the lawyers this was an extraordinary opportunity to get a glimpse of the jurors and their state of mind in the middle of a trial.

The white jurors reacted to the racial issues with some hesitancy. Asked about racial tensions, Anise Aschenbach, a sixty-year-old white woman, said, "Well, nothing has been said that I could pinpoint where that really is a problem." And several black jurors detected no animosity from anyone.

The real news of these sessions was that several African American jurors were furious, especially the men. That the black men were suffering was hardly surprising. Though it was not well known outside of southern California, the Los Angeles sheriffs had a reputation for racism that matched that of the LAPD. Willie Cravin, one of the black jurors, told Ito simply that "some of the black jurors are treated like convicts."

But Ito completed his examination without finding reason to dismiss any more jurors. He did make one change as a result of his interviews, however. He transferred three of the deputies who had been guarding the jurors at the hotel.

The jurors noticed their absence on the night of April 20, and several jurors were outraged. They had formed attachments to some of the deputies and felt that the deputies had been treated unfairly. Thirteen jurors decided to write a letter of protest to Ito, and the following morning, Friday, April 21, all thirteen wore black outfits to court. The rest of the jurors defiantly wore bright colors in counterprotest. To a certain extent the protest crossed racial boundaries, but all of the counterprotesters were African Americans.

Ito explained that the deputies had been transferred, not fired, and gave everyone a weekend to cool off. The next week the judge eased tensions on the jury when he dismissed Tracy Hampton, a black twenty-five-year-old flight attendant. She had looked almost catatonic through the trial, rarely directing her glance away from her feet, and she had asked several times to be excused from the case. On May 1, without objection from either side, Ito agreed.

In late May, Ito also dismissed Francine Florio-Bunten, a thirty-eight-year-old white juror, for lying about a note passed to her by another juror. On June 5 Farron Chavarria, a twenty-nine-year-old Hispanic woman, was let go for being the author of that note, as was Willie Cravin because "the Court has received numerous reports of personal conflict between [him] and other jurors."

BOTH in the courtroom and in what passed for their private lives, several jurors showed signs of depression. One juror tried to kill himself after he was dismissed. Tracy Hampton was rushed to the hospital with an apparent anxiety attack on the day after she left. The jurors were further shaken when they learned that on July 19 one of the deputies who guarded them in the courtroom, Antranik Geuvjehizian, was murdered while trying to stop a burglary. The isolation, the endless waits as Ito listened to the lawyers haggle, and the mind-numbing testimony about arcane scientific matters all gave the jurors more than adequate reason to be miserable. Watching one after another of their colleagues summoned to Ito's chambers and then dismissed—without being allowed so much as a good-bye or an explanation—added to the strain. Denied access to alcohol by the sheriffs, several jurors took solace in food. Family members, struggling to find some common ground with their increasingly estranged loved ones, began bringing gargantuan feasts to the hotel during visits. The jurors gained weight at a fantastic pace, which only compounded their despair.

There were now twelve jurors and just two alternates. Next to appear in front of these fourteen survivors was Dr. Lakshmanan Sathyavagiswaran, the Los Angeles county coroner.

Dr. Lakshmanan, as he was addressed, believed a single killer with a single knife could have inflicted all the wounds on both victims. In his scenario Nicole was first knocked out by a blow to the back of the head. The killer then leaned over her unconscious body, pulled her hair back, and slit her throat. Prosecutor Brian Kelberg had Lakshmanan demonstrate the movement by standing behind Kelberg and using a ruler to simulate a knife. Jurors and spectators alike recoiled at the grisly spectacle.

Those with military experience recognized that the killing bore great similarity to the way U.S. Navy SEALs are trained to dispatch their adversaries. In the weeks before the murders Simpson had been filming an NBC pilot, *Frogman,* where several ex-SEALs had served as technical advisers. Had O.J. been trained to kill this way? The prosecutors made a halfhearted effort to make the connection, but the technical advisers weren't very cooperative, and the issue faded amid the press of other business.

IN A trial that showcased a good deal of shoddy detective work, the police investigators also scored some brilliant successes. One of them involved the famous pair of brown leather gloves. The detectives set out to learn where and when—and, if possible, by whom—the gloves had been purchased. Each glove bore a tag with the trade name Aris, the size (extra large), and the style number

(70263). A phone call to the Aris Isotoner company revealed that even though Aris was the biggest glove company in the world, this particular style constituted only a tiny part of its inventory. Even better, the style was sold only at one chain of stores in the United States: Bloomingdale's. Richard Rubin, who had been the general manager of the Aris Isotoner glove business in the early 1990s, told Vannatter, "You have no idea how rare those gloves are."

Vannatter and Lange carefully looked through Nicole Brown Simpson's old credit card bills to see if there might be a charge for a glove purchase at Bloomingdale's. To their astonishment and delight there was—right around Christmas 1990. The actual sales receipt showed that on December 18, 1990, Nicole had bought two pairs of Aris Lights at Bloomingdale's in New York.

Besides the DNA evidence, this sales receipt may have been the most incriminating evidence in the entire case—even if one accepted the theory that Fuhrman had planted one glove at Rockingham. Who else in Los Angeles except O. J. Simpson would have had access to these extremely rare gloves? Who else except O. J. Simpson would have used them to murder his ex-wife? It is therefore all the more astonishing that the day prosecutors presented this evidence to the jury turned out to be the single best day of the trial—for their adversaries.

ON THURSDAY, June 15, the defense lawyers spent much of the break examining—and goofing around with—the gloves. Just about every lawyer tried them on. Shapiro and Cochran noticed that the gloves, even though size extra large, were not very big— and Simpson's hands were. The gloves, they suddenly realized, might not fit.

Sometime earlier the prosecutors had examined the gloves and found just how tight they were. This snugness was intentional on the part of the maker: Made from extremely thin leather, Aris Lights were designed to fit closely, almost like racing gloves. At lunch Clark and Hodgman discussed whether they should put the evidence gloves on Simpson's hands. They decided it wasn't worth the risk. All the wear and tear might have made them shrink.

Worse, Simpson would have to wear latex gloves underneath. Mostly, though, they feared that Simpson himself would control the experiment. Clark passed the word to Darden just after lunch.

"Don't do it."

Darden nodded agreement. He called the glove expert Richard Rubin to the stand.

Rubin's direct testimony was brief. He testified solely to explain that Aris had delivered only about three hundred pairs of brown extra-large Aris Lights to Bloomingdale's in 1990. After a rather aimless cross-examination by Cochran, Rubin was about to be excused.

Just then, though, a paralegal arrived in the courtroom with a new pair of gloves from the prosecution headquarters. When Darden looked like he was going to ask Simpson to try them on, Cochran asked to approach the bench and then objected. Ito had an understandable reaction: "I think it would be more appropriate for him to try on the real gloves."

Clark responded, "He has to wear latex gloves underneath because they're a biohazard, and they're going to alter the fit."

Ito decided to excuse the jury for a moment to let Rubin examine the new gloves. As the jury was filing out, F. Lee Bailey sidled over to Darden. "You have the b____ of a stud field mouse," Bailey whispered to Darden. "If you don't have O.J. try them on, I will." Rubin said that the new pair was not the same model as the evidence gloves, so Ito disallowed their use. Flustered, Darden told Ito, "Before the jury returns, we would like to have Mr. Simpson try on the original evidence items."

But Ito was momentarily distracted, and he invited the jury back in before Darden could conduct the demonstration. Embarrassed by his own lack of preparation and goaded by Bailey, Darden barreled ahead—now in front of the jury.

"Your Honor," Darden said, "at this time the People would ask that Mr. Simpson step forward and try on the glove recovered at Bundy as well as the glove recovered at Rockingham." Seated beside Darden, Marcia Clark widened her eyes in astonishment.

For several agonizing minutes Simpson struggled, and plainly failed, to get the latex gloves on all the way. Thus even before Darden handed the evidence gloves to the defendant, it was clear that they could not fit over the latex.

Darden handed Simpson the left glove and asked him to walk toward him and the jury. As Simpson walked, he began trying to put on the left glove. At all times Simpson kept his thumb bent outward at a right angle to his wrist. That, too, made it impossible for the gloves to fit properly. O.J. grimaced and said more or less to Cochran, but really to the jury, "Too tight."

Simpson struggled with the other glove and then began pounding between his fingers as if he were trying to make the gloves fit. But the bunched latex limited how far the gloves could go, and Simpson never pushed between his bent thumb and forefinger.

Darden saw Simpson's cocked thumb and said, "Can we ask him to straighten his fingers as one normally might put a glove on?"

Ito said yes, but Cochran burst in, "Your Honor, object to this statement by counsel." Simpson simply ignored the request.

Recognizing the catastrophe he had wrought, Darden tried to salvage something. "Could we ask him to grasp an object in his hand, a marker perhaps?" Simpson took a marker and held it in his fist the way a baby would, his thumb still splayed out. Ito sent Simpson back to his seat. O.J. slipped the gloves off in a flash, which would not have been possible if they were really too tight.

Soon after, the judge called it a day. Back in his office, Darden— shell-shocked by the experience—sank into his chair. Hodgman sought him out and said, "C'mon, Chris, we're trial lawyers. There's a way out of this." Hodgman invited Rubin into Darden's office, and they began planning how to undo the mess.

Clark, however, did not speak to Darden. As she was driving home from the courthouse that day, she called a friend on her car phone. "Do you think this is it?" Clark asked, not really wanting an answer. "Do you think it's over now?"

ON MONDAY, Darden asked Rubin a series of questions, attempting to undo the harm. Rubin had brought an unworn pair of the precise make and model of the evidence gloves, and those—placed on Simpson's hand without a latex barrier—clearly did fit. The damage-

control operation succeeded mostly in underlining that the prosecutors themselves regarded the previous week's stunt as a disaster.

Once again the prosecution's distress overshadowed some highly
incriminating evidence that came next. Forensic expert William
Bodziak conducted a remarkably detailed analysis of the shoe
prints leading away from the murder scene. Bodziak said the prints
had been made by a size twelve Bruno Magli shoe that retailed for
about $160. Based on the lengths of the strides and the size of the
shoes, Bodziak said the individual who made the impressions was
probably a little more than six feet tall. (Simpson stood six feet two
inches and, like only 9 percent of the population, wore a size
twelve shoe.) What was more, Bodziak had found a slight impression of this Bruno Magli type of shoe on the rug of Simpson's
Bronco, the presumed getaway vehicle. And perhaps most important of all, Bodziak's analysis of the crime-scene photographs
showed only one set of shoe prints at the scene.

Finally, in the grisly conclusion of his testimony, Bodziak said
that impressions on Nicole's back and on her dress were also consistent with the size twelve Bruno Maglis. In other words, he suggested, Simpson had planted his foot on the unconscious Nicole's
back, grabbed her hair with his left hand, and cut her throat with
his right—an image of startling savagery.

Clark had just one more important witness to present to the
jury, Douglas Deedrick, an FBI hair and fiber expert. Deedrick
presented a stunning catalogue of the evidence tying Simpson to
the murders. Among his findings: Hair in the blue knit watch cap
found near Goldman's feet matched Simpson's hair. Hair found
on Ron Goldman's shirt matched Simpson's hair—which was likely
deposited by "direct contact," possibly when Simpson grabbed
Goldman by the throat from behind. Hair matching Nicole's was
found on the bloody right-hand glove at Rockingham—consistent
with the coroner's and Bodziak's testimony that Simpson had
yanked her by the hair before he slit her throat. Fibers from Goldman's shirt matched those found on each of the gloves. Carpet
fibers like those from Simpson's Bronco matched those found on
the knit hat and on the Rockingham glove.

In the end, the hair and fiber evidence seemed to have had virtually no impact on the exhausted jurors. It was not even mentioned during jury deliberations.

Deedrick completed his testimony on July 5, almost one year to the day after the end of the preliminary hearing before Judge Kennedy-Powell. And so on July 6, 1995, after 92 days of testimony, 58 witnesses, 488 exhibits, and 34,500 pages of transcript, Marcia Clark told Judge Ito and the jury, "The People rest."

13

FORCED for months to respond to whatever the prosecution threw at them, the defense lawyers hungered for the opportunity to make their own case to the jury. As always, their egos played a big part in their considerations. Each wanted his moment onstage.

But in responding to the needs of their own vanity, the defense forgot something very important: Their client was guilty. And so to the extent that it concerned the events of June 12, 1994, the evidence they presented made Simpson look more guilty, not less.

Cochran wisely played it safe to start. He called to the stand three Simpson women: O.J.'s daughter Arnelle, his sister Carmelita Durio, and most dramatically, his mother, Eunice. All poised, all dressed in yellow, and all conspicuously loyal to O.J., the three women served more as exhibits than witnesses, with nothing of substance to say about the evidence.

Cochran followed Simpson's relatives with a number of people who saw O.J. in the days before the murders: a fellow guest at a fund-raising dinner on June 11, an interior decorator who met with him on June 6, and a man who played golf with Simpson on June 8 at a Hertz event in Virginia. All of them testified that Simpson had behaved appropriately, in a friendly and cordial manner. One can scarcely imagine less provocative (or relevant) testimony.

Another defense witness was Robert Heidstra, a "car detailer" who lived up the block from Nicole. On direct examination he testified that he was walking his dogs on an alleyway parallel to Bundy at about 10:40 p.m. on June 12, 1994. At that time he heard a commotion in the area of Nicole Brown Simpson's condominium—two voices, one clear, saying, "Hey, hey, hey!" and the other indistinct. In this respect Heidstra bolstered the defense theory that the murders took place around 10:30. (In a sobering reminder that this case involved actual human beings, Patti Goldman, Ron Goldman's stepmother, told me at a break in Heidstra's testimony that she could tell this witness was indeed describing Ron's voice. "That's just what Ron would say if he came on a scene like this," Patti said. " 'Hey, *hey*, HEY!' ")

The prosecution had interviewed Heidstra several times and nearly decided to call him as a witness in their own case (dropping him only because he conflicted with Clark's desire to place the murders at 10:15). Indeed, as Darden began his cross-examination, it became clear that Heidstra had a good deal to say that helped the government's case. For starters he admitted that he usually walked his dogs at 10:00, which, if he had done so on the night of the murders, would have put the killings at precisely the time the prosecution claimed. Heidstra also said that he saw a white vehicle that could have been a Bronco leaving the scene—another fact that was consistent with the government's case. Twitching at the defense table, Cochran was losing his customary sang-froid. Darden asked Heidstra, "The second voice that you heard sounded like the voice of a black man, is that correct?"

Cochran nearly jumped out of his chair. "Objected to, Your Honor," he sputtered. He caused such a commotion that Judge Ito excused the jury and told Heidstra to step outside. Darden patiently recounted to the judge that an acquaintance of Heidstra's had told Detective Lange that Heidstra said "he heard the very angry screaming of an older man who sounded black." Thus, Darden explained to Ito, he had every right to ask the question.

But Cochran was not to be mollified. "I resent that statement," he thundered. "You can't tell by someone's voice when they're black. That's racist. I think it's totally improper in America, at this time in 1995, just to hear this and endure this."

Darden looked stricken. He replied evenly that he was simply questioning Heidstra about a statement the witness himself had allegedly made earlier. Then he addressed Cochran with quiet dignity. "That's created a lot of problems for my family and myself, statements that you make about me and race, Mr. Cochran." Ito called a recess, and tempers cooled.

Cochran's outrageous behavior revealed much about him. In the first place he was simply wrong. Many African Americans do have distinctive accents and speech patterns. But Cochran's cynicism ran deep. His outburst came just as one of his witnesses was blowing up in his face. How better to stop an effective cross-examination than by throwing a stink bomb of racial grievance into the middle? When the facts went against them, Simpson's lawyers turned, as they always did, to race.

SHAPIRO had not entirely disappeared from the case, and though he had little to do, he maintained his sullen vigil at the defense table to the end. When the former chief medical examiner of New York City, Michael Baden, testified, Barry Scheck made like a ventriloquist and fed Shapiro the questions he should ask. Shapiro spent time eliciting Baden's qualifications, which were considerable. But in the end Baden had little of substance to add to the Simpson case other than that he thought the coroner used too much guesswork in reconstructing the crime. As for the detectives' failure to call the coroner immediately after discovering the bodies, Baden had the integrity to admit under cross-examination that it would not have made any difference in determining the time of death.

The story was much the same several witnesses later with Connecticut forensic expert Henry Lee. Under Scheck's questioning, the centerpiece of Lee's testimony was his claim that the LAPD criminalists might have missed a possible single non–Bruno Magli shoe print at the murder scene. Thus, according to Scheck, there was a second killer at the scene. Yet there were more than a dozen shoe prints from the size twelve Bruno Magli shoes. Did the second killer hop into the murder scene, remain on one foot during the entire struggle, then hop away? The idea that this evidence truly suggested the involvement of a second killer was preposterous.

AT SHAPIRO'S REQUEST, ROBERT Huizenga, a Harvard-educated Beverly Hills internist, had examined Simpson on June 15, 1994, just three days after the murders. The defense's (and especially the defendant's) idea was for Huizenga to testify about Simpson's various ailments in an effort to persuade the jury that O.J. lacked the physical ability to commit the crimes. As even a layman could tell, such a claim was absurd. What Huizenga's testimony did demonstrate was the extraordinary extent of Simpson's self-pity, the same side of his character that drove him to complain of being a battered husband.

According to Huizenga, Simpson suffered from a "whole array of the typical post–NFL injury syndromes." He had a pair of bad knees, a bum right ankle, and a case of arthritis. Huizenga showed the jury the photographs of Simpson taken during the examination of June 17 (at Kardashian's house just before O.J. and Cowlings disappeared). His torso was massive and hugely muscled, but Shapiro pointed out that he had no abrasions to suggest he had just fought a life-or-death struggle less than a week earlier. In Shapiro's breezy way he asked whether the photographs didn't show "a man to be in pretty good shape."

Huizenga helpfully disagreed. "There are some very lucky people that looks can be deceiving and certainly in his case, although he looks like Tarzan, you know, he was walking more like Tarzan's grandfather."

Prosecutor Brian Kelberg, a former medical student, began his cross-examination by exploring the question of bias. Had the doctor viewed his role as "to start preparing a possible defense in the event Mr. Simpson was charged"?

Huizenga pouted and disagreed. "I took it to address his mental problems, insomnia, and difficulty handling this incredible stress that maybe no other human being, short of Job, has endured."

There was a pause in the courtroom.

Kelberg knew just how to follow up. "Is it your characterization that Mr. Simpson is in a situation which, to your knowledge, only Job has suffered more?"

"I think the pressure that was on him, for whatever reason, was a tremendous weight, the change in his life status that very few, if any, people have experienced in my opinion," Huizenga answered.

"And if he had murdered two human beings, Nicole Brown Simpson and her friend Ronald Goldman, would that be the kind of thing that would cause a great weight to be on a man's shoulders?"

Shapiro objected in vain, and Huizenga had to say, "If someone hypothetically killed someone, they certainly would have a great weight on their shoulders."

The prosecutor meticulously went over the photographs of Simpson's hands that were taken on June 17 and revealed to the jury that Simpson actually had *seven* abrasions on his left hand and three cuts. His right hand was unmarked. (This fit with the prosecution's theory that Simpson lost his left glove during the struggle at Bundy, cut his left hand, and did not lose his right glove until he returned to Rockingham.)

The climax of Kelberg's cross-examination came when he played raw footage from an exercise video that was later released as *O. J. Simpson Minimum Maintenance for Men*. Simpson had taped the routine—in which he looked fit and healthy in a T-shirt and Lycra shorts—at the end of May, 1994, just two weeks before the murders. Trading inane patter with the coach, Simpson stretched, marched, bent his knees, did push-ups and sit-ups. The tape alone scotched the notion that Simpson did not have the physical ability to murder his ex-wife and her friend.

The most remarkable part of the tape came so fast that it was possible to miss it the first time through. One of the routines involved the participants simulating a punching motion—right jab, left jab, right jab, left jab. As the coach on the videotape later testified, Simpson ad-libbed a narration to this exercise. "Get your space in if you're working out with the wife," Simpson said to the camera, punching at the air with his thick, muscled arms. Then he chuckled and added, "If you know what I mean, you can always blame it on workin' out." Meaning, if you punch your wife, you can always blame it on working out.

A convicted wife beater jokes about beating his wife. Could there have been a more chilling glimpse into O. J. Simpson's subconscious? (The jurors, it turned out, never paid any attention to this. Indeed, they said little about the defense case at all, they were so exhausted and numb. By this point, it appears, they had already made up their minds.)

ON JULY 7—the day after the prosecution rested its case—a secretary in Johnnie Cochran's office patched through a phone call to Pat McKenna, the lead private investigator for the defense. The caller sounded saner than most of the other tipsters who called with purported information about the case, and he offered unusually specific information. He said he was a lawyer from San Francisco and he had a client who had a friend named Laura. Laura had about a dozen audiotapes of Mark Fuhrman talking about his police work. As the caller talked, McKenna scribbled what the caller said Fuhrman had discussed on the tapes:

—Plant Evidence
—Get Niggers
—So. Africa—Niggers—Apartheid

The caller gave McKenna a phone number for Laura, with a 910 area code—North Carolina. McKenna dialed Laura.

"This is Laura Hart McKinny," she said.

"I'm a private investigator working for O. J. Simpson," McKenna told her, with an edge of nervous pleading in his voice. "We really believe our client is innocent, and we understand you have some tapes of Mark Fuhrman that we think could help us very much." Polite but noncommittal, McKinny told McKenna her lawyer would give him a call. Fifteen minutes later a lawyer named Matthew Schwartz, who was based in Los Angeles, rang McKenna. Schwartz confirmed that the tapes existed and that they were authentic. He thought if the defense subpoenaed the tapes, they could probably work out a way for them to be turned over.

IN THE struggle over the Fuhrman tapes, the last great drama of the Simpson trial, it was as if the id of the case had been unleashed. All the smoldering passion, anger, and resentment shot directly to the surface. The Fuhrman tapes controversy gave the defense something it never had in earlier battles: the truth. About Mark Fuhrman's character the defense was right and the prosecution wrong. Having had full warning about Fuhrman's twisted soul, Clark

Laura Hart McKinny

had embraced him nonetheless. With McKinny's tapes Clark and her colleagues paid the price.

Laura Hart McKinny had met Mark Fuhrman in February 1985 at an outdoor café in Westwood. McKinny was working on a screenplay about female police officers, and she immediately recognized Fuhrman as a potential resource—an insider who could give her the perspective of the hostile, sexist LAPD traditionalist. Ultimately they had twelve sessions together, yielding about twelve hours of interviews. According to a producer who knew her, "Laura really did her homework. There was just one problem: She didn't write a very good play." McKinny's work, like most screenplays, found no takers.

The early 1990s were a difficult period in her life. In 1993 McKinny and her cinematographer husband, Daniel, owed $80,000 in credit card bills and back taxes. They declared bankruptcy, pulled up stakes, and signed on as professors at the North Carolina School of the Arts.

When the trial heated up the spring of 1995, McKinny's agent told her she probably should get a lawyer. In late May she called Schwartz. Her fondest hope was that some company would finally produce her screenplay, but the lawyer recognized that the tapes were the more valuable commodity. He proposed—and McKinny agreed—that he "test the waters" to check out the cash-for-trash industry. Several publishers and media outlets expressed interest.

It was, in all likelihood, this proto-auction that prompted the call to Pat McKenna. When word of the tapes' existence spread around the defense team during the second week in July, there was outright jubilation. Cochran took an almost mystical joy in them.

On July 12, the day of Cochran's "sounds black" outburst, he and Shapiro went to Matthew Schwartz's office to try to get access to the tapes, but Schwartz put them off. A week passed, and Schwartz now said McKinny regarded herself as a "journalist" in her meetings with Fuhrman, and she did not wish to share the fruits of her reporting. Frustrated, Cochran sent his majordomo, Carl Douglas, to appear in secret before Judge Ito on July 20 and explain the situation. Ito agreed that the tapes were material to the Simpson case and signed a subpoena.

A week later Cochran and Bailey, armed with this subpoena and a brief prepared by Bailey's law partners in Boston, appeared before Judge William Z. Wood, Jr., in Forsyth County, North Carolina. Unaccountably, Wood ruled against Cochran and Bailey, asserting that the tapes were not material to the Simpson defense case. Bailey immediately set his law partners in Boston to work on an emergency appeal.

Cochran had, however, accomplished something important. When McKinny took the stand in front of the North Carolina judge (and the waiting press corps), Cochran managed to work a few quotes from the tapes into his questions. For example, he asked McKinny, "Did Detective Fuhrman say to you during this first interview, when you were getting his attitude—quote—that 'we've got females and dumb niggers and all your Mexicans that can't even write the name of the car they drive.' Did he say that to you?" McKinny said he did.

The public quickly became more interested in the Fuhrman tapes sideshow than in the trial itself. The North Carolina Court of Appeals overturned Judge Wood's plainly incorrect ruling on August 7, and the McKinny tapes arrived at last in Cochran's office on August 9. Cochran, however, couldn't trust that Ito wouldn't, like Judge Wood, thwart him at the last moment. He needed a public airing of the tapes—in other words, leaks to the press.

The prosecutors, for their part, could tell what Cochran was thinking, and they tried to limit public exposure of the tapes. On August 10 Ito directed that the tapes should "remain under seal."

In light of the protective order Cochran couldn't simply hand the transcripts over to a friendly reporter. Same with the other defense lawyers—the risk of exposure was too great. The question thus became, Who on the defense team wouldn't mind directly violating a court order? All signs pointed to one man: Larry Schiller.

Schiller, the co-author of Simpson's *I Want to Tell You,* had spent the entire trial ingratiating himself with reporters as well as gathering material from inside the defense camp. He loved being at the center of the action, so he was only too happy to share the McKinny largesse with his journalist friends, and they were likewise pleased with their scoops. For the next week or so Schiller leaked hate-filled tidbits to reporters. (Schiller denies doing this.) The ensuing outcry from the public against Fuhrman added immeasurably to the pressure on Ito to admit the tapes into evidence, just as Cochran knew it would.

Cochran kept the pressure on. As he had done for Michael Jackson in 1994, he orchestrated a news conference of black ministers on August 28, this time to call for Judge Ito to release the Fuhrman tapes to the public. The media event was spearheaded by Danny Bakewell, head of the Los Angeles civil rights organization known as Brotherhood Crusade. Bakewell predicted dire results if the tapes were not released. "This community is a powder keg," he said, "capable of repeating the actions of 1992"—that is, the riots that had followed the acquittal of the LAPD officers who beat Rodney King. Bakewell's rhetoric was pure racial extortion: Release the tapes—or else.

The political maelstrom left Ito little choice when the issue was finally posed to him the next day.

"I think that there is an overriding public interest in the nature of the offer that you are making," Ito told the defense in a hearing before the television cameras but outside the presence of the jury. The judge allowed the defense to play the portions of the tapes they wanted the jury to hear. All of the defense work—from Schiller's leaks to Bakewell's threats—had paid off.

The first few examples from the tapes were fairly straight-forward—brief sentence fragments of Fuhrman's familiar voice: "You do what you're told, understand, nigger?" Female officers, he said, "don't do anything. They don't go out there and initiate a contact with a six-foot-five nigger." And, "These niggers, they run like rabbits." These snippets were bad enough, but then, late in the morning session, Uelman began to play a tape of what appeared to be Fuhrman's recounting of an incident that had happened to him in the field.

> Two of my buddies were shot and ambushed, policemen. Both alive, and I was the first unit on the scene. Four suspects ran into a second story in an apartment project—apartment. We kicked the door down. We grabbed one of their girlfriends by the hair and stuck a gun to her head and used her as a barricade. Walked up and told them: "I've got this girl; I'll blow her f_____ brains out if you come out with a gun." Held her like this—threw the bitch down the stairs—deadbolted the door. "Let's play, boys."
> We basically tortured them. There was four policemen, four guys. We broke 'em. Numerous bones in each one of them. Their faces were just mush. There was blood all the way to the ceiling with finger marks like they were trying to crawl out of the room. These guys, they had to shave so much hair off, one guy they shaved it all off. Like seventy stitches in his head. You know, knees cracked, oh, it was just— We had 'em begging that they'd never be gang members again, begging us. I mean, you don't shoot a policeman. That's all there is to it. . . .

When this taped excerpt ended, Lance Ito's courtroom was as quiet as it had ever been over the previous year. Then there was a sound: Kim Goldman started to cry.

ON AUGUST 31 Ito ruled that he would allow only two brief excerpts of the Fuhrman tapes to be played before the jury: "We have no niggers where I grew up," and "That's where niggers live." In lieu of playing the tapes, he would allow McKinny to tell the jury that Fuhrman had said "nigger" forty-one times on the tapes. Ito found that everything else on the tapes was either irrelevant to the case or unduly prejudicial to the prosecution.

Cochran was distraught. He proceeded to an impromptu news conference on the ground floor of his office building on Wilshire Boulevard. Surrounded by nearly a dozen colleagues on the defense team (but not Shapiro), Cochran denounced Ito, calling his ruling "perhaps one of the cruelest, unfairest decisions ever rendered in a criminal court." He declared, "The cover-up continues. This inexplicable, indefensible ruling lends credence to all those who say the criminal justice system is corrupt." And in a lightly veiled reference to Bakewell's incendiary threats of earlier in the week, Cochran said, "So all of the citizens in Los Angeles, they should remain calm."

At long last, on September 6, the jury heard McKinny and the two short excerpts from the tapes. Ironically, after the trial most of the jurors said that the McKinny tapes had had little impact on their verdict. Even if one accepts this at face value, the tapes still had an enormous influence on the trial. The entire gestalt of the case was transformed. Because the tapes established definitively that Fuhrman had lied about using the word "nigger," the prosecution had to abandon its categorical defense of him. Fuhrman's damaged credibility, in turn, made it that much harder for the prosecution to argue that all the other LAPD officers were telling the truth.

The tapes also loom as an important historical artifact beyond the give-and-take of this trial. In the aftermath of the case the LAPD and the U.S. Attorney in Los Angeles launched investigations based on the tapes. Fuhrman's extraordinary account of the beating of suspects following the shooting of two police officers had fictional aspects, but it did appear to be loosely based on a real event that occurred in 1978. The tapes also pointed to a larger truth. Mark Fuhrman—and others like him—thrived in the LAPD. Ultimately, it is not surprising that black jurors decide to punish the police for its sorry past and that, alas, O. J. Simpson turned out to be the undeserving beneficiary of this ignoble tale.

14

ONE night toward the end of the Fuhrman tapes controversy, many leading figures of the African American community in Los Angeles filled the vast Santa Monica Civic Auditorium for the annual Soul Train Lady of Soul Awards. Gladys Knight hosted this annual salute to black women in show business, and at the climax of the nationally televised broadcast she said she had a special announcement. "To present the Lena Horne Award for outstanding career achievements," Knight said, "here is a man who has been a wonderful friend to all of us . . . a longtime supporter of everything good and positive that takes place in our community—Mr. Johnnie Cochran!"

Cochran appeared from behind a curtain, splendidly turned out in a perfect tuxedo and bright red cummerbund. The audience of three thousand burst into loud cheers, and a handful of spectators started a chant, which quickly spread to the entire crowd: "Free O.J.!" "Free O.J.!" "Free O.J.!"

In the last weeks of the trial, as each side called its final few witnesses, Johnnie Cochran was indeed taking every opportunity to promote the Simpson cause outside the courtroom. After court nearly every Friday he headed for the airport en route to speaking engagements around the country. In his remarks he invariably seized on the Simpson case as the paradigmatic civil rights issue of the day.

It is difficult to determine with precision what impact Cochran's speeches had on the trial. In interviews afterward jurors said they had been unaware of Cochran's public assertions. Yet by the end of the case all the jurors did know how contentious a national civil rights issue the trial had become.

FROM the day he was hired in the case Cochran teased the press with the possibility of Simpson testifying in his own defense, but his comments were just public relations. With the exception of Bailey, who thought with good reason that Simpson would have no chance of resuming anything like his former life unless he addressed the charges from the witness stand, no one on the defense team ever took the idea very seriously.

Still, as part of the formalities of ending the case, Ito had to ask Simpson on September 22 whether he waived his right to testify. Cochran, in turn, requested that Simpson be allowed to make "a brief statement" as part of his waiver. Even though the jury was not present, Clark objected. "This is a very obvious defense bid to get material admitted that is not admitted in court. . . . Please don't do this, Your Honor, I beg you."

Cochran replied with great indignation. "There seems to be this great fear of the truth in this case," he said. "This is still America. And we can talk. We can speak. Nobody can stop us." Ito caved, and Simpson rose to deliver a sound bite for the evening news.

"Good morning, Your Honor," he said. "As much as I would like to address some of the misrepresentations made about myself and Nicole concerning our life together, I'm mindful of the mood and the stamina of this jury. I have confidence, a lot more it seems than Ms. Clark has, of their integrity, and that they'll find—as the record stands now—that I did not, would not, and could not have committed this crime. I have four kids—two kids I haven't seen in a year. They asked me every week, 'Dad, how much longer?' "

This was more than even Ito could take, and he cut Simpson off with a curt, "All right."

Simpson said, "I want this trial over."

TUESDAY, September 26, 1995, the day that summations were to begin, broke chilly and drizzly. Jury selection had commenced 365 days earlier. The trial of O. J. Simpson had taken one year.

Even before she uttered her first words to the jury, Marcia Clark was exhausted, with large half-moons of purple under each eye. She looked emaciated beneath her simple beige jacket.

Clark thanked the jury, which was customary but not, for her, heartfelt. Over the course of the trial Clark had felt no warmth from this group, no sympathy for the victims, no core of emotional revulsion at the murders. Clark had come to see that these were fearful jurors, more concerned about the reaction to their verdict than about reaching the right one.

Clark's first words about the facts of the case were about Mark Fuhrman.

"Did he lie when he testified that he did not use racial epithets? Yes. Is he a racist? Yes. Is he the worst LAPD has to offer? Yes. Do we wish that this person was never hired by LAPD? Yes. In fact, do we wish there were no such person on the planet? Yes.

"But it would be a tragedy if, with such overwhelming evidence, ladies and gentlemen, as we have presented to you, you found the defendant not guilty, because of the racist attitudes of one police officer."

This categorical denunciation of Fuhrman was probably the best Clark could have done, but it also underlined how the racial issue paralyzed the prosecution. Clark was rushed over the next five hours as she attempted to pull together all the complex strands of evidence, but still she delivered an adequate, professional summation—and a persuasive one for a jury willing to listen.

Ito had decreed that there would be evening sessions during closing statements, so Darden rose to address the jury on the domestic-violence portion of the case at shortly after 7:00 p.m.

Television, of course, was sending the proceedings around the world, but this first nighttime session of the case gave the courtroom a curious intimacy. Chris Darden captured that mood and that moment. Just as he deserved the blame for his several failures in that courtroom, so too did Darden earn the credit for this triumph.

He used a perfect metaphor for the Simpson marriage: a burning fuse. He noted that the defense had argued that "just because" there was marital discord, "it doesn't mean anything. . . . Well, this isn't a 'just because' issue. This is a 'because' issue." Darden then took each of the domestic-violence incidents in chronological order and punctuated them with the phrase "And the fuse is burning." He played the pair of 911 calls—the wordless slaps from 1989, and the terrified "He's going to kill me!" from four years later.

Darden closed for the night by recalling one of the briefest witnesses in the trial—the district attorney's investigator who drilled open Nicole's safe-deposit box after her death. There wasn't much in there: her will, letters of apology from O.J. after his 1989 conviction, and the photographs of Nicole's beaten face from that incident. But Darden asserted that Nicole had a larger purpose for preserving those few items. "She put those things there for a reason," Darden said quietly. "She is leaving you a road map to let you know who it is who will eventually kill her. She knew in 1989. She knew it. And she wants you to know it."

WHEN Johnnie Cochran began his address to the jury on Wednesday, September 27, he started in a conventional way. He attacked the prosecutors' time line. He dwelled on the glove demonstration and used a catchy phrase that had been suggested to him by Gerry Uelman. "If it doesn't fit, you must acquit." Cochran continued to ignore or downplay domestic violence. "He is not proud of some of the things he did," the lawyer said, "but they don't add up to murder." Cochran even took a silly turn when he put a black knit cap on his head to suggest the absurdity of someone as famous as O. J. Simpson using a disguise. In fact, wearing a knit cap at night can be an effective disguise—one favored in particular by the navy SEALs who had been Simpson's tutors on the set of *Frogman*.

But Cochran was only warming up to the crux of his argument, which was about the LAPD. "If you can't trust the messengers, watch out for their messages: Vannatter, the man who carries the blood; Fuhrman, the man who finds the glove." He called the two men the "twins of deception" and then the "twin demons of deception" and finally "the twin *devils* of deception."

It was the classic Johnnie Cochran summation. The case was about the police, not his client. "Your verdict goes far beyond these doors of this courtroom," he advised. "That's not to put any pressure on you, just to tell you what is really happening out there." It was, one supposes, just a sort of courtesy to warn the jurors what their lives might be like if they happened to vote to convict this man.

So what was the jury to do? "Stop this cover-up. Stop this cover-up. If you don't stop it, then who? Who polices the police? You police the police. You police them by your verdict."

Barry Scheck followed for a brisk tour of the forensic issues in the case. It was, at times, extremely arcane, but Scheck did make clear the defense position that the police had cleverly planted the blood on the socks at Rockingham and on the rear gate at Bundy—though at the same time they had incompetently contaminated the blood on the walkway at Bundy.

That evening, the last night of the case, the prosecutors gathered on the eighteenth floor to plot strategy for a rebuttal. Bedeviled by excruciating dental pain, Clark made an emergency appointment with a dentist at 6:30 that evening, and it turned out she had an abscess. She was knocked out with general anesthesia, operated on, and sent back to the courthouse at around 10:00 p.m. She stayed until just before 4:00 in the morning.

Five hours later, on September 29, the prosecutors spoke for the last time. Frazzled and drained, Clark unwisely tried to respond to each of Scheck's assertions. The defense lawyers interrupted her more than forty times with objections. Ito overruled most of them, but they succeeded in preventing Clark from establishing any kind of rhythm. For once Clark lacked the energy to fight back.

There was one hint of what was to come. Bill Hodgman had spent much of the previous month working on an impressive chart entitled "Unrefuted Evidence," a summary of all the non-DNA, non-Fuhrman-related evidence in the case. It was a rather complicated graphic, and Clark did not discuss every point on it, so she offered the jurors an option. "If you would like to take notes on this," Clark said, "I can leave it up for a little while."

Not one juror wrote down a thing.

THE jurors selected a foreperson on the afternoon of Friday, September 29. The assignment went to juror number one, Armanda Cooley, a fifty-one-year-old black woman who worked as an administrative assistant for the city of Los Angeles. Cooley was obviously a levelheaded and friendly person, and she had steered clear of most of the jury tempests during the trial. After they selected the foreperson, Ito sent the jury back to the hotel; deliberations were set to begin on Monday morning.

At 9:16 a.m. on Monday, October 2, the jury settled into chairs in the deliberation room just across the back hallway from Ito's courtroom. Ito's clerk, Deirdre Robertson, wheeled in a cart piled with trial exhibits arrayed in black binders. Robertson closed the door and said the jurors could begin discussing the case.

It was agreed that Armanda Cooley would conduct a vote by secret ballot, just to get a sense of what everyone was thinking.

"Just write 'guilty' or 'not guilty' on a piece of paper and put it in the bowl," she said. After a moment or two Cooley passed around a glass bowl that Ito's clerks had kept full of candy over the previous months. Carrie Bess, like Cooley, a single black woman with grown children and a civil service job, volunteered to tabulate the responses on a blackboard. Cooley called out the votes, and Bess wrote them down: ten for acquittal, two for conviction.

Anise Aschenbach, a self-confident and poised sixty-year-old woman, was one of only two whites left on the panel. She had been stewing all weekend. Aschenbach had been so angry during Cochran's summation that she almost got up and told the lawyer to shut up. "I was so outraged at what he said," Aschenbach told her fellow jurors. "He wants us to send the LAPD a message. Does he think we're so stupid that we're going to send a message rather than decide based on what we heard in the case? I hope I was not the only one offended by his remarks."

Her fellow jurors responded with total silence.

Armanda Cooley distributed the exhibit binders. Jurors began leafing through them and offering comments about the evidence.

Why wasn't there more blood around the glove Fuhrman said he found at Rockingham?

Goldman had bruises on his knuckles. If they were from fighting back, why didn't O.J. have any bruises on his body? (The prosecution had argued that Goldman had injured his hand flailing against the fence behind him.) Dave Aldana, the Hispanic man in seat four, was a martial arts expert. He got up and demonstrated how to defend in tae kwon do. He thought Goldman had put up a good fight.

Aschenbach volunteered that she was one of the two votes for conviction. (The other never came forward.) Hearing this, Sheila Woods, a black female juror, flashed an angry look at her. "Why did they go after him as a suspect from the beginning?" Woods said to Aschenbach. "They insulted us with their testimony. They went after that man."

Someone mentioned the glove demonstration. Several jurors said they thought it didn't fit on Simpson's hand.

There was only one reference to DNA tests. Both Dave Aldana and Sheila Woods said they didn't think it was reliable when all of the DNA came from the back gate at Bundy. This was important to them. (It was, of course, completely wrong, too. Several other tests of blood at the murder scene tied it to Simpson.)

After about an hour of discussion the topic turned to the testimony of Allan Park, the limousine driver. Carrie Bess said Park didn't know how many cars had been in Simpson's driveway. Others were confused by the time that Park said various events occurred. The group decided that they would like another look at Park's testimony.

Shortly before noon Cooley sent out a note requesting Park's testimony. She thought the judge would simply send back a transcript the jury could examine, but the judge relayed that he would have the testimony read back by a court reporter in the courtroom at 1:00 p.m., following lunch.

AFTER seventy-five minutes of the read-back, Ito called a break to give the court reporter's voice a rest. Back in the jury room, Cooley took advantage of the break to ask if all the questions about Park's testimony had been answered. By consensus the answer was yes. Suddenly, it seemed, no one had anything more to say. Cooley sent a request to Ito for the verdict forms. Before they arrived, she conducted another secret ballot, and this time the vote was unanimous. Cooley filled out the forms and pushed the buzzer to the courtroom three times—the signal for a verdict.

It was shortly before 3:00 p.m. The jurors had discussed the merits of the case against O. J. Simpson for about two hours—less time than most other adults in America.

Cochran was giving a speech in San Francisco. Bailey was appearing at a snack food distributors' convention in Laguna Beach. Only Carl Douglas was by Simpson's side when Armanda Cooley presented the envelope containing the verdict forms to Ito.

"We will accept the verdict from you tomorrow morning at ten," Ito said. "See you tomorrow morning at ten o'clock."

No one had predicted so swift a verdict. The entire building seemed afflicted with vertigo. After all these months and all the debates over evidence, strategy, rulings, and rumors, only one question remained: What had the jurors done?

The jurors returned to the Inter-Continental for their two hundred and sixty-sixth, and final, night in residence. The hotel threw the jurors a champagne reception in the presidential suite on the nineteenth floor. Everyone had a few drinks, which loosened tongues. Reyko Butler, one of the two alternates, couldn't resist asking one of the deliberating jurors how it had all come out. The juror couldn't resist answering. "N," the juror said. Not guilty.

This curiosity extended to the sheriff's deputies as well, who had the same question and received the same answer.

Cochran arrived too late to make it to the jail, but Bailey, Kardashian, and Skip Taft gathered in a final vigil with Simpson. As it turned out, Simpson was in good spirits. "All the deputies here are asking for my autograph," he told his lawyers. "They hear from their boys over with the jury that it's going to be the last chance for them to get one."

It was the last leak in the case—from the sheriff's deputies guarding the jury to their colleagues guarding Simpson: O.J. was going to walk.

THE scene at the courthouse on the morning of Tuesday, October 3, resembled some sinister carnival. The police shut off all traffic in the immediate vicinity of the courthouse, and crowds of people milled about in the empty streets. Except for the trial, all business in downtown Los Angeles seemed to come to a halt.

People jammed the hallway outside Ito's courtroom. Bookers for talk shows had taken up more or less permanent residence in that hallway for weeks, and on this day several stars of the shows joined in the vigil. NBC had forty camera crews ready to roll for reaction to the verdict. ABC had assigned four producers to each juror.

At 9:49 Darden walked into the courtroom alone. Three minutes later Clark arrived with a retinue of four police bodyguards. At 9:55 Johnnie Cochran, Simpson's sisters, and their Nation of Islam volunteer escorts completed the cast in the courtroom.

At one minute before 10:00 the deputies escorted Simpson from his lockup, and he nodded to his family just as he had every day.

For perhaps the first time in the entire trial Ito appeared and started the proceedings precisely on schedule. "Counsel," he said to the lawyers, "is there anything else we need to take up before we invite the jurors to join us?"

For once the answer was no.

The jurors filed in in their usual order, expressionless as always. Ito directed Deirdre Robertson to hand the envelope containing the verdict forms to a sheriff's deputy, who walked it over to Armanda Cooley to check their condition.

Ito cautioned the audience that "if there is any disruption during the reading of the verdicts, the bailiffs will have the obligation to remove any persons disrupting these proceedings."

The judge paused. "Mr. Simpson," he instructed, "would you please stand and face the jury." Unbidden, Cochran and the rest of the defense team rose with him. "Mrs. Robertson," Ito cued.

The judge's clerk stumbled as she read the title of the case, then steadied herself as she came to the verdict.

"We the jury in the above-entitled action find the defendant, Orenthal James Simpson, not guilty of the crime of murder in violation of Penal Code Section 187A, a felony, upon Nicole Brown Simpson, a human being, as charged in count one of the information."

At the words "not guilty," Simpson exhaled and gave a sort of half smile. He looked as if he was going to cry, but didn't. Cochran, standing behind him as they faced the jury, pumped his fist quickly, then grabbed Simpson by the shoulder and in a startlingly intimate gesture placed his cheek on the back of O.J.'s shoulder.

The moment of verdict

Robert Shapiro looked stricken, crushed. His alienation from his colleagues and client was never more visible than at that moment.

Robertson then proceeded to read the second verdict, that in the murder of Ronald Lyle Goldman. At the second utterance of the words "not guilty," Kim Goldman let out a trembling howl. She grabbed her hair, then buried her head in her father's shoulder.

I was sitting behind Kim, in the second row. Numb with shock, I stared at Simpson and had a single thought: He's going home. There is no red tape after an acquittal. The handcuffs come off, and you're on your way.

As Robertson finished the formalities and Ito polled the jury, asking them all whether this was their verdict, noise from the audience grew louder. Everyone in all of the families was crying— for joy, for sorrow, at their release from this extraordinary tension.

"The defendant, having been acquitted of both charges," Ito said evenly, "is ordered released forthwith."

The jurors filed out in their usual silence. Lon Cryer, a black male, had the longest walk to the door. He kept his head down most of the way, then turned to the defense table and raised his fist in a black power salute. Then he, too, left the courtroom.

Most of the jurors dissolved into tears when they arrived back in the deliberation room. They hugged and wept and clung to one another for support. After a few minutes a pair of deputies came to escort them up to the lounge on the eleventh floor where they had done most of their waiting over the course of the trial. There the tears mostly stopped, and the jurors sat in shell-shocked silence. Finally Carrie Bess said something to no one in particular.

"We've got to protect our own."

Epilogue

WITHIN an hour of the verdict, Simpson was driven in a van from downtown to his home in Brentwood. He was accompanied by Robert Kardashian, author Larry Schiller, and Schiller's camera.

Exclusive photographs of the victory party would command a hefty price, and in the weeks before the verdict Schiller had arranged to sell first rights to the photos to the supermarket tabloid *Star*. Simpson and Schiller split the six-figure proceeds. All during the evening Schiller snapped dozens of photos, hurriedly developed them in a makeshift lab in Simpson's garage, then transmitted them by satellite to the *Star*.

It was a rather quiet celebration that evening. The small, dedicated group who had stood by Simpson throughout the long trial all paid their respects. There was his family, of course, presided over by his mother and two sisters, as well as his older children, Jason and Arnelle. Al Cowlings was there, as was Skip Taft. Most striking were the absences—the golfing buddies, Nicole's friends, the dozens of pals who used to attend Simpson's annual Fourth of July bash. They had all chosen the other side in this case. Simpson mostly stayed in his bedroom, receiving guests in small groups. Only one person stayed by Simpson's side the entire evening. That was Peter Burt, a reporter for the *Star*, whose presence was part of Schiller's deal with the magazine.

On October 6, three days after the verdict, Schiller's literary agent faxed a letter to book publishers offering a sequel to *I Want to Tell You*. This next book, to be entitled *Now I Can Tell You*, would be "O. J. Simpson's first person account of the trial from his arrest to the not-guilty verdict and his reunion with his family." There would be an additional bonus: Schiller's "original and unique" photographs of Simpson's reunion with Sydney and Justin Simpson, which took place on October 4.

All through the summer of 1995 Skip Taft and Larry King had engaged in negotiations about a pay-per-view special following the verdict, featuring King interviewing Simpson live, as well as phone calls from viewers. Turner Broadcasting would buy the rights from Simpson for $25 million. In lieu of a fee for himself, King would arrange for about $1 million of the money to go to his favorite charity, the Cardiac Foundation. Simpson would receive about $4 million personally. The balance of the money—more than $15 million after expenses—would go to establish a network of O. J. Simpson Boys Clubs in cities across America.

The photographs of the victory party ran as scheduled in the *Star*, but none of the other schemes came to fruition. There has been no sequel to *I Want to Tell You*. As soon as word leaked out to the public that Larry King was even considering participating in a pay-per-view interview with Simpson, executives at CNN's parent company announced that no such project would take place. Cable-system operators across the country said they would refuse to distribute any broadcast that would enrich the former defendant. The darkly comic notion of O. J. Simpson Boys Clubs never materialized.

All of these projects fell victim to the enormous backlash against the verdict in mainstream—that is, white—America. Because of television, the announcement of the verdict became a nationally shared experience—one on par, incredibly, with the assassination of John F. Kennedy. In the days immediately after the end of the case in court, televised images of the verdict itself yielded to images of people watching the verdict. The pictures revealed many scenes of African Americans cheering the verdict. White viewers, by contrast, watched in stunned, generally appalled, silence. Reaction to the verdict was replaced by reaction to the reaction, and so on—as Henry Louis Gates, Jr., observed, "black indignation at white anger at black jubilation at Simpson's acquittal." The passing months did not so much heal the wounds in race relations as witness the growth of an ugly scar.

In assessing the "meaning" of the Simpson case, it is necessary to return to the underlying events—that is, to what happened outside Nicole Brown Simpson's condominium on the night of June 12, 1994. The Simpson case was never some free-floating set of ideas ripe for any number of equally valid interpretations. The case emerged from a set of facts, and those facts matter.

As to the central fact in the case, it is my view that Simpson murdered his ex-wife and her friend on June 12. Any rational analysis leads to that conclusion. This is true whether one considers evidence not presented to the jury—such as the results of Simpson's polygraph examination and his flight with Al Cowlings on June 17—or just the evidence established in court. The case against Simpson was overwhelming.

It is theoretically possible, of course, that Simpson was guilty *and* framed by the police, but I am convinced that did not happen. In their summations Cochran and Scheck suggested that the police, in their effort to frame Simpson, planted at least the following items: (1) Simpson's blood on the rear gate at Bundy, (2) Goldman's blood in Simpson's Bronco, (3) Nicole's blood on the sock found in his bedroom, (4) Simpson's blood on the same sock, and (5) the infamous glove at Rockingham. The defense never spelled out how all this nefarious activity took place, but pulling it off would have required more or less the following. Not only would Fuhrman have had to transport the glove with its residue of the crime scene to the defendant's home, but he would also have had to find some of Simpson's blood (from sources unknown) to deposit upon it and then wipe the glove on the inside of Simpson's locked car (by means unknown)—all the while not knowing whether Simpson had an ironclad alibi for the time of the murders. To me this possibility is simply not believable, even taking into consideration Fuhrman's repugnant racial views.

The other police conspirators (conspicuously unnamed by the defense) would have had to be equally adept and even more determined. Someone would have had to wipe off the blood on the back gate and apply Simpson's. The autopsies, where blood samples were taken from the victims, were not performed until June 14, more than a full day after the murders. Someone would have had to take some of Goldman's blood and put it in the Bronco, which was then in police custody. And someone would have had to take some of Nicole's blood and dab it on the sock, which was then in a police evidence lab. All of these illegal actions by the police would have had to take place at a time when everyone involved in the case was under relentless media scrutiny—and all for the benefit of an unknown killer who, like only 9 percent of the population, happened to share Simpson's shoe size, twelve.

After the trial the jurors gamely tried to defend their verdict, insisting that it was based on the evidence, not mere racial solidarity. Several of them believed that the glove demonstration doomed the government's case. Sheila Woods decried the sloppy lab procedures of the LAPD. Lon Cryer was concerned about evidence contamination and rejected Allan Park's testimony because he was mistaken about the number of cars in the driveway. The three jurors who wrote a joint book about the case—Armanda Cooley, Carrie Bess, and Marsha Rubin-Jackson—attributed the decision to a combination of these factors. Anise Aschenbach, the white juror who initially voted for a conviction, asserted with some sadness that she might have fought on if she had felt any possibility of support from her colleagues. In any event, Aschenbach was deeply troubled by the testimony of Mark Fuhrman and the evidence of his racial views.

All the black jurors denied that race played any role at all in their deliberations or their decision. To me this is implausible. The perfunctory review of nine months' worth of evidence, the focus on tangential, if not actually irrelevant, parts of that evidence, and the constant focus on racial issues both inside and outside the courtroom, lead me to conclude that race played a far larger role in the verdict than the jurors conceded. As Carrie Bess indicated in her unguarded words after the verdict, they were protecting their own. This is not especially unusual. For better or worse, American jurors have a long and still flourishing tradition of both taking race into account in making their decisions and denying that they are doing any such thing. The ten whites, one Asian, and one Latino in Simi Valley who in 1992 acquitted the LAPD officers in the Rodney King case denied that race factored into their decisions. Nor is this phenomenon limited to celebrated cases. In the borough of the Bronx in New York City, where juries are more than 80 percent black and Hispanic, black defendants are acquitted in felony cases 47.6 percent of the time, which is about three times the national acquittal rate of 17 percent for defendants of all races.

That race continues to count for so much with African American jurors should come as no great surprise. Racism in law enforcement has persisted through many decades of American life, and black citizens, and thus black jurors, have stored too many insults for too long. But the genuine grievances that have led to a tradition of black hostility to officialdom have, in turn, fostered a mode of conspiratorial thinking that outstrips reality. An Emory University study of a thousand black churchgoers in five major cities in 1990 found that more than a third believed that HIV was a form of genocide propagated by white scientists, a theory shared by 40 percent of African American college students in Washington, D.C. Understanding the roots of these beliefs should not mean endorsing them. To do so is merely patronizing, a condescending pat on the head to those incapable of recognizing reality. Better, rather, to hold everyone to the same standards, and better, likewise, to speak the truth: Whites didn't concoct HIV—and O. J. Simpson wasn't innocent.

FINAL ROUNDS

A Father, a Son, the Golf Journey of a Lifetime

by JAMES DODSON

. . . Golf became much more than a game between my old man and me. It became our playground and refuge, the place where we sorted things out or escaped them altogether, debated without rancor, found common ground, discovered joy, suspended grief, competed like crazy, and took each other's pocket change. We played through rain, wind, heat, birth, death—so many rounds in so many places, I couldn't possibly remember them all.

I loved those times and never even knew it.

—Final Rounds

Prologue
A Father's Voice

Toward the end of the afternoon world golf Hall of Famer Tom Watson sits in his office talking to a golf writer. The golf season has just ended. The golf writer is me. We have been talking for almost two hours. There is a thin skin of ice on the pond in the park across the street. Traffic is a muted sigh in the winter shadows of Kansas City. Christmas presents for his children are stacked neatly in a shopping bag at his feet. Watson's wariness of the press is famous, but he has been relaxed and generous, talking about his life, career, heroes—even making self-deprecating jokes about his well-publicized putting woes. This confirms my best hopes. Watson is forty-three, five years my senior, the best golfer of my generation, now a lion in winter. In my former life as a political journalist it would have been deemed grossly unprofessional to admit I am my subject's fan. But golf, unlike politics, as Alister Mackenizie is supposed to have said, is at least an honest game. I am Watson's fan because he played with such honesty and heart during his golden days and because of how he conducts himself now that the glory has faded.

What Watson reveals in our conversation is both thought-provoking and surprising. I ask if he can identify the worst moment of his career, and he tells me about once rushing out of the locker room at the World Series of Golf, brushing off a boy seeking his autograph. The boy's father followed Watson and tapped him on the back.

"He looked me straight in the eye and said, 'I just want to tell you, Mr. Watson, my son was really a fan of yours.' " Watson shakes his head. "I couldn't believe it—how badly I felt, I mean." He falls silent, pursing his lower lip. Somewhere outside I can hear Christmas music playing. For a second or two Watson stares at the running tape recorder, then shakes his head again. "I still feel bad about it," he says simply.

The thing is, I believe him. Watson could not believe what he says he believes—namely, that golf represents the most honorable of games—and feel otherwise. So I flip the coin—best to part on a cheerful note—and ask him for the best moment.

"It's funny," he says, pausing again. "The greatest thrill I had may have been the day my father invited me to join him and a couple of his regular golf buddies at his club. I was so excited, really aching to show him what I could do. I guess I was maybe eleven or twelve." Watson, the former Stanford psychology student, studies me with those eyes that always look as if he's been out walking in a linksland wind. "Even now I think about that. It was a very powerful moment. My father means so much to me. I can always hear his voice in my head, telling me to keep my head still or make a good swing. I don't know if I ever felt that way again, you know?" He smiles somewhat wistfully, revealing the boyish gaps in his teeth. Turning off the tape recorder, I admit that I know what he means because I hear my father's voice, too.

Almost every day of my life.

1
Opti the Mystic

THAT Christmas I sent my father a new set of golf clubs.

I was sure he'd love them. After all, they were the latest thing in "super senior" equipment technology. My father's Wilson Staffs were almost as old as me—heavy blades meant for a man half his age and twice his strength.

He sent them back two weeks later, with a pleasant note addressed to Bo, his nickname for me. "Thanks for your thoughtful gesture, Bo. These are mighty handsome clubs, but I don't think they're for me. I have a good idea, though. Since these are so light and easy to swing, why not keep them for Maggie and Jack to use? I'd be honored to buy them their first clubs. I've enclosed a check. Love, Dad."

The check was for a thousand dollars. He'd clearly missed the point of my thoughtful gesture. I called my mother to see if perhaps her husband had recently been beaned on the golf course or simply forgotten that his grandchildren were only three and four, more interested in making music with a purple dinosaur than divots in the yard. She laughed and said, "Well, sweetie, bear with him. I think your father may be a little down in the dumps. Although with him, as you know, it's never easy to tell."

She was right. My old man was the original silver-lining guy. As a teenager, I dubbed him—not entirely kindly—Opti the Mystic because of his relentless good cheer, his imperturbable knack of seeing any problem or crisis as "an opportunity for growth," and his embarrassing habits of kissing strange babies in grocery stores, always smiling at strangers, and quoting somebody like Aristotle or Emerson when you least expected it, usually in the presence of my impressionable high school dates.

Opti almost went out of his way to expose his crazy optimism to strangers. One time he picked me up from a guitar lesson with a startling occupant in his car: a drunk in a Santa suit. He'd found the man wandering aimlessly around the parking lot of his office building with a bottle of wine under a wing, muttering about shooting himself for the holidays.

Only Opti would have rescued a suicidal Santa and attempted to cheer him up. Dad bought him a hot meal, and we heard his tale of woe: He was dead broke, and his wife thought he was a bum, and his girlfriend was pregnant again. But after he sobered up, he appeared to feel slightly better for having gotten his problems off his chest. We dropped him off in front of his dingy cracker-box house, and Dad discreetly slipped him a fifty-dollar bill and asked him to buy something nice for his wife.

Perhaps it was a foolish gesture, a hopeless charity. Maybe the guy was just going to go buy more wine and shoot himself after all. But as he left our car, the man looked at me with his bloodshot eyes. "Your father's a real southern gentleman, kid," he growled. "I hope you *know* that. Merry Christmas."

I knew Opti was a southern gentleman, because people told me this my whole life—school chums, girlfriends, parents who needlessly reminded me how lucky I was to have a dad like that. In Mrs. Moon's English class I couldn't read Geoff Chaucer's line about the gentle, parfit knight en route to Canterbury with the other pilgrims or hear the voice of Dickens's old Fezziwig exhorting his employees and neighbors to come join the Christmas dance without thinking of Opti, my sappy old man. It sometimes annoyed me to have people think I had such a saint for a dad, a human Hallmark card for a father.

If Opti was now "in the dumps" even a little bit, this qualified as big news. My first thought was that it must be his health. After all, his advertising business was thriving, his golf handicap was holding steady at 22. Dad liked to say he would indeed someday consider retiring when and if he finally got old. But even he had to accept that he couldn't live forever.

It was easy to forget that Dad was pushing eighty and facing, medically speaking, a situation that would have wilted the spirits of a man half his age: a daily injection of insulin and the unpleasant aftereffects of a radical colostomy, as well as a poorly done trim job on his prostate that left him wearing a pair of unwieldy collection bags strapped to his thighs. He also suffered from a cataract in his left eye, his knees were weak, and his hearing was going. Typically, if we mentioned these problems, he merely laughed off our concerns.

"So what's wrong?" I asked my mother.

"He lost his golf group."

I thought about that. "You must be joking," I finally replied.

"I wish."

This explained a lot. Dad dearly loved his longtime Saturday morning golf group. They fussed and squabbled, but they were clearly addicted to each other's intimate sporting companionship in the best way available to fully grown, heterosexual, registered Republican southern males.

It turned out that Bill Mims, Dad's best friend and primary golf nemesis, had developed a heart condition and Alex the Scotsman had retired and moved to the south of France. Richard had somehow just "lost interest in playing" when the others gave up the game, which left only Dad.

"He's taken to playing with younger men," Mom reported. "But I honestly don't think he *likes* it."

"*Of course* he doesn't like it!" I shouted back at her, thinking of how desolate I'd feel if my own regular group of buddies vanished from my life. "That's why these clubs I sent him are so important. They'll help subdue those dangerous young turks."

"In that case, maybe you should send them again," she suggested.

I mailed the high-tech super-senior wonder clubs to North Carolina the next morning, along with the check; he sent the clubs back to Maine the next week. The only people prospering from this long-distance minuet were the boys from United Parcel Service.

"Dear Bo: Again, many thanks. I just don't think these clubs are right for me. Maybe I'm just too sentimentally attached to my old Wilsons. After all, we've been down a lot of fairways together. (Ha ha.) I do appreciate you thinking about me, though. When's your next research trip? Any chance you'll be coming this way? I'd enjoy a chance to pin your ears back on the course. Love, Dad."

Opti the Mystic had spoken. Ha ha.

I donated the clubs to the church's summer auction committee, hoping somebody could find use for them.

THE poet Ovid said we give gifts to try and seduce men and the gods.

Seduction was obviously my game. With those clubs I wanted to seduce my father into believing he could still compete in the most difficult and fulfilling game of all. And I wanted the golf gods to grant us a bit more time on the links together.

We had been golf pals for thirty years, ever since he put the club

in my hand at about age ten and introduced me to the complicated splendors of the game he loved most. Like Tom Watson, I
can remember as if it were yesterday the day my father invited me
to play with him at his club. I was thirteen, the age of manhood
in most cultures. My father helped me become a man, and golf
showed me the way. But it wasn't easy. I threw a lot of tantrums in
those days. I threw a lot of clubs, too. I don't know how my father
tolerated these volcanic outbursts. He would sometimes place a
hand on my shoulder and urge me to "relax and enjoy the round.
The game ends far too soon, Bo."

I didn't have a clue what he really meant. He was given to pro-
nouncements like that, an adman with a poet's heart.

Watching me flail at the game, he once observed, "The peculiar
thing about this game—any game, really, but this game far more
than most—is, the more you fight it, the more it eludes you. Everything contains its opposite. By trying to make something magical
happen, you create the opposite effect: You drive the magic away.
When you worry about finding the way, you lose the path. Someone said the way to heaven is heaven. A little less is a lot more."

He sounded so damn sure about this I almost hated him for it.
It is the fashion these days to speak of golf as a kind of religious
experience, a doorway to the spiritual side of man, an egress to the
eternal. My father was a man of faith, but I don't think he viewed
the golf course as a path to God. He thought golf was a way to celebrate the divinity of life, the here and now, and simply the best
way to *play*. He loved healthy competition and was playful to the
core. During the Depression he'd played semipro baseball and
helped guide his high school football team to the state finals. Ironically, he'd made money as a caddie in those days but couldn't
afford to take up the game seriously until he went away to war and
discovered the great golf links of England and Scotland.

For thirty years my father, Braxton Dodson, had been the senior
southern ad rep for the world's largest industrial publishing firm.
He'd transformed a sleepy advertising backwater into a thriving
multimillion-dollar territory, becoming one of his company's leg-
ends in the process. To Opti hard work was a form of play because

work involved solving problems, a life view that fit the philosophy of his favorite game like a glove. Golf was the ultimate playful exercise in problem solving. The real joy of playing, he said more than once, was bound up in the mental process required to create solutions to the riddle of any particular golf shot—an unfair break, a horrendous lie in the rough, and so forth. Golf was the greatest challenge because no two golf shots were ever the same. Every situation was unique, every moment "new and pregnant with possibilities"—another of his favorite phrases. The best players could see the problem, create the solution, and seize the pleasure of the moment.

To him golf was also a character builder that could teach you valuable lessons about yourself, others, and the wide world around you. For that reason he was a stickler for the rules, a gentle but firm rule-book Elijah. You marked your ball properly; you fixed dents in the green; you putted in turn; you offered to tend the pin; you congratulated an opponent on a good shot.

One day I missed a short putt and slammed my putter into the lush surface of the fifteenth green at Green Valley Golf Club in North Carolina, my father's club. He grew silent, then calmly insisted that I leave the golf course. To add insult to injury, he made me walk straight into the clubhouse, report my crime, and apologize to the head pro.

Eventually, when I calmed down and grew up, golf became much more than a game between my old man and me. It acted as my personal entry hatch to my father's morally advanced cosmos—a means of seeing who this funky, funny, oddball philosopher really was and who I needed to become. I know no other game that would have permitted us the opportunity to compete so thoroughly, so joyfully, for so long. The golf course—any golf course, anywhere—became our playground and refuge, the place where we sorted things out or escaped them altogether, debated without rancor, found common ground, discovered joy, suspended grief, competed like crazy, and took each other's pocket change.

We played the day Neil Armstrong walked on the moon. We played the day before I got married and the day after my son, Jack, was born. We played through rain, wind, heat, birth, death. We

played on holidays, birthdays, to celebrate nothing and everything—
so many rounds in so many places, I couldn't possibly remember
them all. We played some of the best courses in America and some
of the worst cow pastures and goat tracks, too. We discovered that
in good company there is no such thing as a bad golf course.

We preferred to play late in the day, following our shadows in
the last of the light, the fairway ahead of us robed in hues of red
and gold and very often deserted. You could feel the coolness of
approaching night, perhaps witness a sliver of moon rising. Our
routine almost never varied. My father would leave work early; I
would ride my bike to the club with my bag swaying on my back.
Sometimes we would grab dinner on the way home. A couple
times we stayed out on the golf course to look at stars. I loved
those times and never even knew it.

This pattern of play, this communion of being, carried us
straight through my college years and into my first reporter's job
at the same newspaper where he'd begun as a copy runner in the
early 1930s. For years we would meet at a golf course somewhere
on the East Coast, in big cities and small towns. We found this a
great time to talk. No topic was out of bounds: sex, women, God,
career, money. We argued intensely about Nixon, TV evangelists,
the fate of the modern novel. We had epic putting duels on darkened greens, in motel rooms, in the lobbies of his business clients.

Jung said children dream their fathers' dreams. In those private
moments of play, something ordained my future and sealed my
fate. As a boy, I dreamed of being either an actor or a classical gui-
tarist; I grew up instead to become a political journalist, a job I
worked hard at for a while before having the good fortune to
become a golf writer. More important, at several particularly difficult moments in my life when I drifted away from the game and
even seemed to lose sight of my life's purpose, my old man was always there to shepherd me back to golf, and myself.

Out of the blue he would call up, make a joke, challenge me to
a round. He always said he was going to pin my ears back, though
he seldom did. He wasn't just my best golf pal but my best friend.

That's really something. I see that now. As a father of small children myself, I perhaps know some of what he knew, felt, and understood way back then: that we really get only a few precious moments to connect before the magic vanishes. Not surprisingly, I read my children the same storybooks my father read me. Their overwhelming favorite, as it was mine, is about a boy who lives to duel a notorious pirate in Neverland, a lad who refuses to grow up because life outside that magical realm, where no one visibly ages, is clearly no fun. Only when Peter Pan fails to believe in happy thoughts does he fail to fly.

The truth is, when my father sent back the new golf clubs, I couldn't bear to think he and I had played our final rounds together. That's why I'd tried to bribe both him and the golf gods. At forty I was *still* my father's child, and I told myself we had unfinished business in Neverland—somewhere out on the golf course. If we believed that, we could still *fly*.

IT WAS not until the next October—far too long to suit my tastes—that we played again. I'd been working hard, traveling a lot. Two of my colleagues at *Golf* magazine invited me to join them for a round at Pinehurst Number 2, where Opti and I had played many rounds over the years. The course was one of his favorites. I invited my father to join us, and he agreed.

The day was raw, wet, and cold, and everyone's game was off, but my father's was really desolate. He topped balls and missed putts he could once have made with his eyes shut. At one point I was passing a steep fairway bunker when I heard him sheepishly call my name. I turned and saw him asking me for a hand up. I reached and took his hand. It was trembling ever so slightly. My heart almost broke on the spot.

On the drive home we rode awhile in silence. He seemed as down as I'd ever seen him. Then an idea came to me.

"Let's take a trip," I said.

"What trip?"

"The trip we always talked about. The one we never took. Don't you remember?"

"Of course. But you go there all the time."

"I go there all the time by myself," I corrected him. "I've never been there with you. We've got some unfinished business."

"I suppose so." He managed to conceal his enthusiasm for the idea. I hoped his rotten day on the course accounted for this.

In any event, that's where it really began, the first step in our final golf journey—a trip to the places where he learned to play golf as a sergeant in the 8th Army Air Corps during the war. "There" was St. Andrews in Scotland, the birthplace of the game. Thousands of golfers went there every year. But we hadn't. It was now or never, and almost that simple.

But nothing is really that simple. I knew not to push my father on the subject. Things were changing fast in his life. I sensed a powerful urgency in him to tie up loose ends, to finish whatever needed finishing at home and in his life and work. We didn't speak of it again for months. I got on with my own life, telling myself I'd planted a proper seed. I hoped—I even prayed—it would grow.

STORIES about the fiftieth anniversary of the Allied invasion of France began to crop up on the news. Reunions were about to happen. Clinton went to Normandy.

Then one day in early July the phone rang. It was Opti. We made our usual lighthearted banter about the state of the world; then he said, "Okay. You set the whole thing up, and we'll go. Let's shoot for late summer, after all the D-day hoopla has settled down."

"Great," I said, knowing exactly what he was talking about, trying not to sound *too* pleased. "I'll give you seven strokes a side. Please don't ask for more. You're getting the senior citizen discount."

"Who's asking? I'll take six and pin your ears back, insolent pup."

By early August everything was set. I'd made plane and hotel reservations, reserved the rental car, and contacted several club secretaries. It read like a grand tour of the British golf Establishment: Royal Lytham, Turnberry, Carnoustie, possibly Muirfield, and, of course, St. Andrews. I'd been to most of these places on my own but couldn't wait to go back with my old man.

Two weeks before the trip he called again. The cancer of a decade ago had come back, he said, spreading radically throughout his pelvic region. It had moved into his back, had even invaded his stomach and intestines.

I asked for the official prognosis and will never forget what he told me: a month, two at most.

Then he laughed. Only Opti would have laughed at such a verdict. He said he would call back when he knew more.

I went through the next few days in a trance. Then my father called back.

"Well, the options are not good," Opti said, sounding eerily like his old self. "They can pump me full of poisons and maybe hook me up to some machines and buy a few more weeks. Who the hell needs that?" He said he planned to let nature take its course.

I told him I admired his courage.

He told me to save my lung power for the golf course.

"I'm planning to whip your tail at Lytham and St. Andrews," he said. "Here are my terms. No complaints. No long faces. We go to have laughs, hit a few balls, maybe take a bit of the Queen's currency from each other's pockets. But when I say it's time to go home, I go home. No questions asked. I've got plenty of stuff to do. But I do want to pin your ears back for old times' sake so you'll at least remember me."

I sort of laughed, then agreed.

"Good. See you at the airport," he barked happily, banging down the phone.

Opti the Mystic had spoken again.

2
The Road Hole

AS OUR plane bored through the darkness five miles above the Atlantic, Dad put aside his *Wall Street Journal* and turned to me, smiled, and said, "Know what I'm anxious to see? How you'll take the corner when the pressure's on."

I knew exactly what he meant—the dogleg corner of the seventeenth hole on the Old Course at St. Andrews, sometimes called the Road Hole, regarded by many as the toughest par-four hole in the world. It is 475 yards of celebrated Scottish madness that offers the player the difficult choice of firing his ball dangerously over a set of old railway sheds or the opportunity to play "safe" and face a tough shot to a slightly elevated green bordered by an infamous pebble road and wall in back—to say nothing of the murderous bunker that lurks in front and has buried the hopes of more ordinary mortals and great players than probably any single patch of sand on earth.

"Same as always," I assured him, sipping my Scotch. "Grip it and rip it over the shed to the heart of the fairway. A neat five- or six-iron to the green, followed by two putts. No problem."

"You seem to have it figured out nicely. You've played it that way, have you?"

"Only in my dreams, I'm afraid."

I knew exactly how my father would play the Road Hole, though. His usual short fade off the tee, two more irons to the green, and one good putt for par. That was the ideal approach and how he basically approached every par-four hole—pretty much how he approached life in general, come to think of it, a patient player who accepted the physical limitations of his game and waited for his moments to score. Never gifted with length off the tee, his salvation was his short-iron game and his putter.

"How many times did you play the hole?" I asked him.

"Only twice. I took the train to Scotland once in late '43 and again in '44, just before D-day. Then they sent me off to France."

"So how'd you do on it?"

"I double-bogeyed it the first time." Two over par.

"And the second?" I asked.

"I almost hate to say."

"C'mon, I won't tell. A snowman?" An eight.

"No. A birdie, I think." One under par!

I stared at him. "You *think* you birdied it?"

"Actually, I know I did"—he smiled again, remembering—"because the little gentleman I was playing with was so ecstatic about it he insisted on buying me supper to celebrate. I have to say, it was one of those crazy shots you couldn't do again if your life depended on it. I chipped in from off the green."

"From where, exactly?" I shouldn't really have been too surprised. Over the years I'd seen him chip the ball into the cup dozens of times, from the worst kind of lies—out of sand, rough, hardpan dirt. Still, a *bird* at the Road Hole! I couldn't think of anyone I knew who'd done it. Most professionals never even came close.

Dad was obviously in no rush to reveal anything more. He sipped his Scotch, settled back, and smiled. "Why don't I show you when we get there?"

For me the reason for, if not the soul of, this trip was almost entirely bound up in the memory of hearing about St. Andrews and the Road Hole for the first time.

It was a balmy evening in the 1960s, and my father and I were headed up the eighteenth fairway at Green Valley. A small plane flew overhead. "Look at that," Dad said with obvious pleasure. "An old J-3 trainer. I flew one just like that before the war."

As we watched, the plane's engine suddenly stopped; the ship seemed to hover dangerously on the evening's air currents, and then the engine refired. "He's practicing stalls at sunset. I used to do the same thing. It's amazing how well you can see everything from up there at this hour. Saint-Exupéry said the airplane revealed the true face of the earth to man."

I looked at him. "You flew an airplane?"

"Sure. Didn't I tell you?"

No, he hadn't. I'd never heard of a saint called Exupéry, either.

That evening a box of old letters and photos came down from the attic, from my parents' life before my brother Dickie and I were born. Dad and Mom lived in Cumberland, Maryland. Dad wrote an aviation column for the paper, sold advertising space, and flew on weekends. He loved to fly his old Cessna low along river valleys, following the seams of the earth. My mother drew the line when he volunteered to fly a plane through a flaming wall at a

Jaycee air show. "I told your father it was that plane or me," she said, sliding him a meaningful look. "For a while," he added with a wink, "it was a toss-up."

Not really, of course. In these black-and-white photos they were both so young, carefree, aping for the camera. My mother thought Dad looked like the movie actor Alan Ladd in his tech sergeant's uniform. There were pictures of him posing with a bunch of grinning GIs outside a Quonset hut in England; sitting astride a white horse at the edge of a forest in France; taking a swing with a golf club on a barren piece of ground, with the broken rooflines and church spires of an almost medieval-looking town rising up in the distance. The town turned out to be St. Andrews. The picture went into a frame that sat on my bedroom dresser for years. I used to lie on my bed and gaze at it and think, I'm going there someday.

For me everything seemed to happen that year. The Beatles came to America, and I got my first guitar, a Silvertone from Sears. I also got a new set of Northwestern golf clubs for Christmas and a book called *Education of a Golfer* by Sam Snead.

In April 1965 we all went out to the Sedgefield Country Club to the Greater Greensboro Open. I wanted to see Sam Snead because he was my father's golf hero. I also wanted to get him to autograph my copy of *Education of a Golfer.* On Saturday afternoon my father and I followed Snead in the third round. Two months shy of fifty-three, the Slammer was on or near the lead. I hugged my book and waited for my chance.

At the eighteenth hole the crowds grew very large. I remember laying the book down on a concession table to climb up on a radio broadcast tower to try and see better. My father and I had gotten separated. When I climbed back down, the book was gone. I couldn't believe it. I watched Snead head off, and then I walked back down the fairway, furious with myself and blinking back tears.

The next morning another copy of the book was lying on the breakfast table. "Try and hold on to this one for a while, will you, Bo?" was all my father had to say about the matter, glancing at me over the Sunday funnies.

We drove out to Sedgefield again and watched Snead make history. By winning Greensboro, he became the oldest man in history to capture a regular PGA title. The problem was, his triumph made even getting close impossible. My father told me we would get the autograph "next year."

NOT long afterward I told a girl named Kristin Cress that Sam Snead had autographed my book. It was a daring lie, and I don't know why I did it except I desperately wanted her to like me. She was two inches taller and a year ahead of me in school, but we sang in the same youth choir at church. She was very popular and very pretty, with big brown eyes, shiny black hair, and an unusually fine singing voice. She was a junior high school cheerleader and the star in school plays.

Kristin didn't seem impressed by my Sam Snead story, and it was another two years before she even seemed to notice me.

By then I'd invented a secret golf game involving Kristin Cress, which I sometimes played on the putting green at Green Valley. If I could putt my way completely around the nine-hole putting green in fourteen strokes or less (Kristin was fourteen), it meant Kristin Cress would fall in love with me. I could envision the whole thing. We would marry, have children, maybe move into a big house on a golf course. I played this game over and over for most of my thirteenth summer, trying to make the magic happen. But it never did.

Then one day in autumn, when I was just rapping putts for the heck of it, I realized that all I needed to do to complete the Kristin Cress love grail was to finish the ninth hole in one putt.

The putt was a twenty-footer. I took a deep breath, made a solid stroke, and watched the ball roll beautifully and drop into the cup. She was *mine*.

It took a while for Kristin to realize this. Four more years, in fact. So I admired her from afar, practiced my game, and helpfully grew several inches. Then one day, as she and I were walking out of the senior high choir-practice room, Kristin turned and asked me for a ride home.

As we sat in her parents' driveway, she explained that she'd just broken up with her college boyfriend and, out of the blue, asked me if I wanted to go with her to the homecoming dance.

I never told her about the cosmic putting match, because she thought golf was kind of silly. Her love was drama. Still, after we began dating, she agreed to walk along and watch me play. She picked flowers, wrote in her journal, and studied her lines for *Long Day's Journey into Night*. One afternoon near Christmas I almost aced the Valley's par-three fifth hole, a steep downhill shot. My ball bounced on the front apron of the green, kicked right, and followed the contour of the putting surface right up to the pin. One more half rotation and it would have dropped. Kristin missed the brilliant shot entirely. I was incensed. We quarreled, and she left me to finish the round alone. That night I called her to apologize and explained that a hole in one was every golfer's dream. It was the *perfect* shot in golf.

"If it's supposed to happen," she replied, "it'll happen."

We dated until the beginning of my senior year, at which point Kristin went to a college in the mountains to study drama. I had a new girlfriend and a new gold Camaro. I played golf matches with my father or my best friend, Pat McDaid, sang in the school madrigals, and won the city's short-story contest. I gave Kristin Cress no more than a passing thought. At Christmas she sent me a card. "Have you scored that hole-in-one yet? If not, keep the faith. Everything happens when it should. Miss you, K." I never wrote back. A year later I heard she was getting married.

DAD was snoozing. I took the Scotch glass out of his hand and turned off his overhead light.

Kristin had been on my mind a lot lately—a bittersweet apparition that always seemed to come calling around the middle part of autumn. As passengers around me settled down under blankets to sleep, I tugged my father's blanket up to his chin and sat there wondering why the past is such a maze we never seem to escape.

At college I'd almost finished my English degree and decided to take extra semesters of religion and drama classes to kill time and figure out what I was supposed to do with my life. I'd been offered a reporter's job at the Greensboro *Daily News*. A drama professor had urged me to seriously consider graduate studies in theater up north, while somewhere in the back of my mind I even thought of going to a music conservatory to study classical guitar.

Predictably, my father was as elusive as fairway fog on the subject. When I asked his parental advice, he merely smiled and came back with one of his maddeningly Socratic evasions: "What do *you* really want to do, Bo?" Finally one afternoon, when decision deadlines were looming and we were playing together at Green Valley, the subject came up again, and I snapped at him that all I *really* wanted to do was talk to Kristin Cress.

"Why don't you call her up?" he said, as if that were all there was to it.

"Yeah, right, Dad. In case you forgot, she's married."

"So? Doesn't mean she won't be pleased to hear from you."

I called her. Kristin's marriage had ended, and she was living in a small house on the outskirts of Hickory, a town in the Smoky Mountains, working as a social worker and part-time steakhouse hostess and acting with a highly respected Equity rep company at a mountain playhouse. She invited me up to visit.

We stayed up all night that first night, talking and catching up. In the morning we went out to watch the sun come up over a quarry lake. There was a high rock where Kristin went on Sunday mornings. She called it Sabbath Rock because she no longer believed in any one church. Her interest was in the religions of the East—Buddhism and Hinduism, mainly. I learned she'd done a play off-Broadway and was saving money for a long trip to India.

Kristin, the only vegetarian steakhouse hostess in America, had to work, so I practiced sand-wedge shots over her gorgeous rose beds. It was a balmy evening in late September, and I was suddenly incalculably, almost unbelievably happy.

I went back to see her four weekends in a row, a five-hour haul each way, falling more under the spell of my first love, I believed, each time. I gave her my spare classical guitar and taught her beginner chords. We sat on Sabbath Rock and read books or sometimes said nothing until I couldn't stand the meaningful silence any longer and started cracking jokes. She told me I should learn to meditate. I told her she should learn to play golf because reaching a par-five in two was a religious experience. She said golf and music might be my *yanas*—rafts to enlightened consciousness. I wondered if you had to pay green fees when you got to heaven.

"The great spiritual teachers of almost every tradition say that heaven is right here and now, all around us every second. We only have to wake up to that fact in order to see it," she said.

I asked why she was so hot to go to India, and she said spiritual journeys always revealed things—not always pleasant, but true realities. I said this might explain why I'd wanted to go visit St. Andrews since I was a kid. Every man has his India.

She looked at me and, smiling, shook her head. She said I would probably never grow up. Her remark gave me the perfect opening to ask her what she thought I should do with my life.

Like my father, Kristin maddeningly resisted giving a straight answer. She said I would find my dharma—life's purpose—when I quit searching for it. I told her she sounded like my old man.

"Your dad's always been very cool," she said, "for a Republican and a golfer."

Two days later Kristin was dead.

My father drove down to school to break the news to me. On the Tuesday after we'd parted, she'd gone to work at the steakhouse, and three young men had strolled in to clean out the cash register. One of them put a gun to the pretty hostess's head, and terrified patrons later recounted that they heard her speaking consolingly to the guy, reassuring him. He pulled the trigger anyway. The killer had just turned seventeen.

I drove home to Greensboro with my father, numb to the bone. I told him I couldn't bear to see Kristin's family or face any of my friends or even attend the funeral. He said he understood these feelings but thought I should make myself go anyway. Addled with grief, seething with anger, I said nothing.

"I have an idea," said my old man. "Let's play a straight-up match. If you win, you choose whether to go or not. If I win, you go whether you want to or not. And I'll go with you."

I searched his pale gray eyes for the reason he was pushing me on this. It was so unlike Opti. Didn't he understand what the hell I was going through? Hadn't he ever felt so miserable all he wanted to do was find a hole to crawl in and hide? Public grieving, I said emphatically, wasn't my style. It wouldn't bring Kristin back.

"No," he agreed, "but a long time ago I learned it may help you go on."

I looked at him. "What are you talking about?"

He shrugged. "Something that happened long before you were born, sport. A little girl I knew died. I probably should have gone to her funeral, but I didn't. I regretted it later. It's what stays with you." He fell silent. Then, "Shall we get our spikes?"

"You don't have a chance," I snorted. My handicap was probably nine strokes better than his.

"We'll see."

He had me by the seventeenth hole.

"You knew you'd win," I said to him as we climbed the eighteenth fairway toward our second shots. The hike had done me good. My mind felt clearer, my troubled soul a bit more at ease. At least the entire world was no longer lining up against me.

"No," he replied. "But I knew you'd go."

I sent roses and a small note to Kristin's parents that said, "She gave to all and showed us how to give." I don't know why I wrote those words. I also didn't know until many years later—because I never went back to her grave—that Abe and Alice Cress had those words engraved on their youngest daughter's headstone.

All I knew for sure at that moment was that Kristin had given me something powerful and nurturing and some kid with a handgun had taken it away from me forever.

The church was packed—her old cheerleader pals, kids we'd known from choir, lots of her professors and acting mates from college. I sat through the service without uttering a peep, my father's hand resting helpfully on my left shoulder throughout.

3
A Sunday in London

I settled into one of the Hotel Berkeley's overstuffed reading chairs. Dad was in the suite's spacious bathroom, preparing to shower. The venerable Berkeley, one of London's première society hotels, had been specifically chosen by me as our starting point because fifty years ago my father's first night on English soil had been spent hunkering under a military poncho in the November rain.

I turned on the telly, hoping to get the weather for Royal Lytham, our first stop the next morning, but there was no weather report. I switched off the TV and looked at my watch. It was now approaching early Sunday afternoon. Dad was bushed, and all my fabulous plans—a round at Sunningdale, perhaps a motor-carriage tour through the city—seemed to be trickling hopelessly down the tubes with the bathwater.

Restlessly I stared out the window at the street below, where a young man and a pretty, dark-haired woman of about twenty had just emerged from a taxi. They were laughing and holding hands.

Suddenly my autumn ghosts had returned, and I found myself thinking, Good Lord, I've been here before.

The two years following Kristin's murder were difficult for me. I'd lost interest in playing the classical guitar, and little by little I could feel even my desire to play golf leaking away, too. Every time I went to Green Valley, my game seemed to get worse. People kept telling me how well I was "handling" Kristin's death, but beneath the skin I felt so angry I wanted to beat somebody to a pulp. But whom? A seventeen-year-old kid? I honestly wondered if this might not be the early stages of madness.

I accepted the reporter's job at the Greensboro *Daily News*. My father, after all, had begun there as a copy runner. It seemed to be a family tradition and the work I was destined, if not happily determined, to do. Three months into the job, though, haunted by something I couldn't quite place a name to, I walked into the editor's office and resigned, saying I had to go to Scotland. She asked me what was so all-important in Scotland.

"I don't know," I said, then added, "Golf courses."

Nobody except my father believed it was the right thing to do. Dad drove me to the airport and gave me an extra thousand dollars. "Emergency money," he called it. We embraced, and I went off to Europe. It was almost two years to the day since Kristin died.

I roamed around the Continent for nearly three weeks—Luxembourg, Germany, the south of France, Paris—ludicrously dragging my unused golf bag with me the whole time. I slept in cheap hotels and sometimes went to museums or just hung out in cafés drinking strong black coffee and reading Graham Greene novels on rainy days. My rough idea was to make St. Andrews the grand finale of this strangely rudderless pilgrimage, but on a train my golf bag got swiped, and I found myself arriving in London short of funds and golf clubs. I caught the *Flying Scotsman* to Edinburgh, where I rented a car and drove to St. Andrews.

It was raining lightly, but the Old Grey Toon, as St. Andrews is called, looked pretty much like my old man's picture of it— dark, windswept, oddly majestic. I stood on a knoll beside the Road Hole and watched several groups of golfers play through, the October sea wind penetrating my skin. I remember thinking how strange it was that I'd finally reached the birthplace of golf but felt none of the magic I'd grown up believing was there. To me it looked just like any other golf course in the rain, and I felt no real desire even to play it. What was the big deal? My little pilgrimage, I decided, was a bust because I was still as sad as the day I'd left home. I remember wanting to weep, but I couldn't even be bothered to do that.

It felt like my childhood was over.

I SAT by the window of the Berkeley, watching London traffic pass through the late sunny afternoon, alternately wishing we were playing golf and wondering if I hadn't made an enormous mistake dragging my dying father to Britain.

On that first pilgrimage twenty years ago, I'd set off to Europe with my old Hogan golf clubs, my dad's "emergency money," and a lot of impossibly high expectations that a journey to the birthplace of golf would somehow clarify my thinking and rekindle my zest for the game of my youth. In the process, it would repair whatever was deeply broken in me, cure cancer, and bring about lasting world peace. Was that too much to ask for one four-week trip abroad?

Apparently so. The Old Course had been a dud, and just the opposite had happened: I returned home and abandoned golf. Was this trip now simply an eerie shadow play of that former failed odyssey? Was there still something missing I hoped to find or reclaim or perhaps simply exhume by dint of another trip to the sacred turf of St. Andrews? If so, what? I'd been to the Old Course many times and grown to love it; I knew people in the town and even counted a couple local players as golf buddies.

That first trip was simply a bad memory, I told myself. *This* trip had a different set of dynamics, problems, and challenges, not least of which was the fact that my mother was sitting at home six thousand miles away worrying her brains out about what calamity might befall her husband.

Days before we left, she called me to say my father had just bought a new rain suit because, he had informed her, we would be walking several golf courses in Britain, as few places had motorized golf carts. She said this surprised and worried her. I explained that it was merely one of the timeless charms of British golf—you *had* to walk, and as a result, you could play in just about any kind of weather. "That may be," she observed feistily, "but I don't think your father's legs are up to walking *any* golf courses, especially in the rain. He won't tell you that, but I will."

She gave me her list of worries about the trip, ending with us driving along all those "scary little roads where people drive on the wrong side." I told her most of the roads in Scotland were so narrow it didn't matter which side you drove on. I assured her we would be fine. I wouldn't take any chances.

"I hope so, darling. Your itinerary sounds ambitious."

The itinerary I'd finally settled upon *was* a bit ambitious: The day after we arrived in London, we would drive three hours due west to Royal Lytham, then dip south to Royal Birkdale before heading up the west coast of Scotland to Turnberry, Muirfield, Carnoustie, and St. Andrews. If Dad's strength was holding up after that, we might grab a flight to Paris and drive out to Compiègne, where Dad ran a prisoner-of-war camp briefly after the liberation of France. In the beech forest next to Napoleon's old summer palace at Compiègne, my father had carved his and my mother's initials in a tree. I had this crazy idea we might search for the tree, assuming a shopping mall hadn't been built on the spot.

"Call me an old romantic," I'd said after explaining the whole thing to my mother.

"I'll call you a lot worse than that if anything happens to your father," she said.

Now, while my father napped, I sat by the window in the deeply upholstered silence of the Berkeley, feeling the first genuine pangs of worry creep in. Once again I was traveling with a golf bag full of hope. But hope for whom? This trip was my dream, but was it my father's as well? I knew in my heart there were things I wanted to say to Opti, but I couldn't think what they were. There were things I also hoped to hear from him, though I couldn't at that moment imagine what.

I suddenly realized why we were there. We were *there*, by God—and maybe even by the grace of God—to play golf. To have a few laughs, to see some old familiar sights in each other's company, to take each other's pocket change. That had been Opti's own list of terms. And whatever unexpected difficulties faced us, that was good enough for me.

I got up and walked to the bedroom, paused, and peeked in at my father. He was lying perfectly still on his back, his face a serene pale mask, with his hands perfectly crossed over his chest like a Westminster poet laureate in repose.

For a second or two I thought I'd already lost him.

Then he cracked open an eye and smiled up at me.

"How about a nice little putting match?" he proposed, already beginning to rise. "Loser buys supper."

THE unshaven attendant at Hyde Park looked up from his book. He was a good-looking kid of about twenty, with a lime-colored streak of green running through his hair and one perfect small gold earring piercing the flange of his left nostril—a heartthrob yob. He was reading a book called *How We Die*.

"That seems to be a pretty popular book," said my ever cheerful *père*. "I've seen it around a lot of places. How do you like it?"

The kid offered an indifferent shrug. "Kinda technical and dull, like, to be honest."

Dad smiled. "Dull? Death? Wasn't it Saint-Exupéry who said death is a thing of grandeur because it rearranges the world?"

"Please don't give away the ending," I insisted. "I always like to wait for the movie version myself."

The clerk stared at us as if we were a pair of escaped lunatics, two Yanks armed with putters. When faced with potentially dangerous foreigners, his employment manual perhaps read, "Always *humor* the rotters."

"Right, gents. One pound fifty. Each."

We paid our fee and walked out to the first tee. It wasn't much of a putting course—a woefully neglected collection of putting greens set down by some cricket fields. I reminded my father that people no longer read Antoine de Saint-Exupéry, the author of *The Little Prince* and the best books ever written on flying.

"I know. That's too bad," he said. "I carried *Wind, Sand and Stars* all over Europe with me when I was here. I think that book was one reason I was so anxious to become a flier. I even gave it to my mother one Christmas. She kept it right beside her Bible for a long time. She was crazy about flying."

"How'd she get the flying bug?" I asked.

"One year, when I was about twelve or thirteen, Amelia Earhart came through Greensboro doing exhibition flights. I believe she might have had a Ford Trimotor plane. At any rate, your grandmother won some kind of drawing and got to go up with her for a short spin. Amelia Earhart was just about the most famous woman in the world at the time. I think that was the beginning of it, really."

"What a great story," I said, pleased that the trip had already yielded one juicy morsel of unknown family history. "I just saw a documentary on public TV that said Amelia Earhart was a terrible flier who never bothered to learn Morse code."

"Really?" Dad thoughtfully wiped a speck of mud from his putter face with his thumb and shrugged. "Well, she was a hell of a heroine to your grandmother. Frankly, I don't know why people are so anxious now to tear down historical figures like Amelia Earhart. The people who complain the loudest that kids don't have role models anymore seem to be the worst offenders."

I agreed with him, saying at least we had Arnold Palmer.

We flipped a coin, and Dad won. He always seemed to win our coin tosses. For that matter, he always seemed to win our putting matches, too.

He dropped his ball and putted. Watching his ball scamper along the sparse turf, my eyes were drawn to a man and two small children ahead of us on the putting course. The children—a boy and a girl—were about my own children's ages.

It pleased me to think that nothing about my father's putting stroke really ever changed. He was a deadly putter, wasted precious little time over the ball, and used the kind of gently stabbing wristy style that modern instruction gurus deplore.

Over the years I'd seen him make some awesome putts, but the one that still stood out in my mind he made just a few years before, during a small Atlantic gale on the Ocean Course at Kiawah Island. As partners, we were playing a par-five on the closing nine against an assistant pro and my old pal-nemesis Patrick McDaid. Pat had just wedged up a shot within five feet of the hole. The pro was in decent range of a birdie that would seal the match in their favor. Dad had limped his *fourth* shot to the front of the green but faced an impossible eighty-footer uphill for par. As near as I could figure, his ball would have to pass through several small swales and break at least three different directions.

"C'mon, Brax," Pat needled him. "Let's see you make one of those patented giant killers of yours."

"You really want me to?" Dad calmly gave it back to him.

Pat smiled. "Sure. Otherwise you guys are dead. We need to keep this match interesting."

"Very well, then." Dad stepped up to the ball, looked at the hole, and popped it with his wristy stroke. The ball seemed to take forever rising and crossing the green. It turned left, then right, and then seemed to gather speed as it came off the slope and raced toward the hole. The ball thumped the back of the cup and dropped in. After everybody stopped laughing, both Pat and the pro missed their putts and we went to the eighteenth still one hole down and there lost the hole and the match, but Dad's brilliant putting had once again made it *interesting*. Now in Hyde Park, though, his putt was poor. He would have called it a Little Mildred. It bounced weakly along the dense turf and plunked into a sand trap fifteen feet short of the hole.

"Tough break."

"I'm just getting warmed up, sport."

I lined up my ball. Putting is the weakest aspect of my game. Basically I am a long-ball striker who can slug the ball to the next zip code, occasionally even the correct one. I grew up admiring the social grace of Arnold Palmer but copying the playing style of Jack Nicklaus. The main difference between me and Jack Nicklaus, I sometimes tell myself—aside from the fact that he is (a) rich, (b) famous, and (c) the most successful golfer who ever lived—is the fact that, unlike me, the Golden Bruin can really putt.

This time my ball rolled past my father's ball and dropped into the hole, proving golf really is a riddle wrapped in a conundrum.

I announced, "I think maybe we'll go to Rules, for bitter and steak with onions."

"Don't order your steak and kidney pie just yet, sonny boy."

After just nine holes I was already two down—our usual depressing pattern. It was yet to be determined if my father could walk an entire golf course, but he undoubtedly could still *putt* one. In a few minutes we caught up to the father and his two children.

Tom Neek was an actor, with a face like a pugilist beneath a flat wool cap—a natural Iago. He was reading a newspaper as his children, Sarah and Andrew, took turns slugging balls at the cup.

"Daddy," complained Sarah in her shiny yellow rain slicker, "Andy keeps knocking my ball away. Tell him it's not fair, please." I liked the way she said Daddy: *Dod-day*.

"Andrew, that's not fair. Let your sister putt unhindered, please."

Andrew said, "She's a sack of hammers."

"Daddy, please tell Andrew not to call me a sack of hammers." *Dod-day*.

"Andrew, please don't call your sister a sack of hammers."

Tom glanced at us. "Rather a silly little game, don't you think? Knocking little balls in holes and such."

"True," agreed Dad. "But that's why we love it so much."

I saw my father smiling goofily at Sarah. He sometimes went goofy around small children, especially little girls. Perhaps this was the result of having had two sons. When my daughter, Maggie, was born, he insisted on calling her Magic, and I never heard a recitation of Mark—the bit where Jesus says, *"Suffer the little children to come unto me, for of such is the kingdom of God"*—without thinking of my father's goofiness around small children.

Tom and his children allowed us to play through. "You remind me of my granddaughter," Dad said to Sarah, mussing her hair gently as we passed. I saw Sarah slide Andrew a look and roll her eyes. *What a sack of hammers, eh, Andy?*

By the end of our first eighteen I'd managed to climb back to within one hole of squaring the match. Dad suggested another circuit, so we started again.

I reminded him that my first golf lesson had been on a putting green. I couldn't remember where, but I could recall some of what he had told me because he told me the same thing for a year. "First get your balance, because golf is a game of balance. Then try and keep your head still. Lead with your left hand, and PLK."

"What?"

"PLK. That stands for Putt Like a Kid. That's what you told me. 'Remember,' you'd say, 'lead with the left hand and putt like a kid.' "

He smiled. "I think I remember saying something like that. God knows where I picked it up."

"Actually, I think you were onto something. I never knew what you meant, but I think I do now."

"What do you think I meant?"

"Kids are fearless putters. Just watch 'em. They set up, aim, and pull the trigger without a lot of second-guessing and body tension." I told him my daughter, Maggie, displayed signs of becoming a putting prodigy. She seemed to think the object was to move the hole back a foot or two. "She's not the least bit shy about it. Loves to bang it at the hole. Leads with the left, putts like a kid. Wish I could putt half as well as her," I admitted.

"Interesting theory. I wasn't aware you're afraid of putting."

"Utterly terrified," I said, lining up a three-footer.

"Hold it right there," Dad said. "Step back."

I stopped, looking up at him. "What?"

"Let's see you set up again, and this time"—a smile crept across his face—"let's see you lead with your left and putt like Maggie."

I shrugged and took a deep breath. I walked away from the ball and came back, got my balance, took one last look at the hole. I putted with the wristy old style of my childhood. The ball clattered into the cup.

"How 'bout that," Dad said with a grin.

"Even I get lucky."

He shut me out at the thirty-second hole, five up with four to play, the usual rout. "Well, you won," I said. "I'm buying dinner. Where shall we go?"

"How about Rules? I haven't been there in at least half a century."

I WAS glad he chose Rules. Rules of Covent Garden, London's oldest restaurant, had significance to us both. On leave during the war, my father thought he saw novelist Graham Greene dining with friends at Rules and almost asked him for his autograph.

He told me this story again as we settled over beers at the bar. We were early, the only dinner customers in the place as yet.

"Thank God I didn't go over and disturb the man. I wasn't even certain it was Graham Greene. Someone only said that it was him because he always ate at Rules."

"Why didn't you go find out?"

"My group was—how shall I put it?—a bit rambunctious."

"Drunken?" I helped him.

"And a bit disorderly. That's what happens, I'm afraid, when you give five American sergeants real English folding money and a week's leave and point them in the direction of a large city."

"How'd you pick Rules? Had you read Graham Greene?"

"Nope. I wasn't that literary, I'm afraid. Some fella selling newspapers at Victoria Station told us the classy, good-looking girls went to Rules."

I had memories of Rules, too. By the time I arrived in London on my strange nongolfing golf pilgrimage after Kristin's death, I'd read every book Graham Greene had written. His romantically sad protagonists—drunken priests, lonely foreign diplomats, businessmen reluctantly made spies in service to Queen and country—and his theme of redemptive loss greatly interested me. I didn't want to know Graham Greene so much as *be* him.

On one of my first nights in London I set out to try and find him. I knew, thanks to my father, that the writer was a habitué of Rules. Fortunately for Graham Greene, he wasn't there that night. But I certainly wouldn't have hesitated to ask him for his autograph, finishing what my father had started thirty years before.

I told my father this story as we had our beers, and he made me feel better by smiling. "I don't think you were really looking for Graham Greene," he said. "I think you were really looking for yourself." He paused, then added, "That was a pretty difficult time you were going through."

I turned my pint slowly on the cardboard coaster, noting how the condensation made a perfect circle on it.

"Did you know it's been twenty years since Kristin died?" I said.

"Good heavens. That long? I had no idea." He fell silent.

"The strange thing is, it doesn't feel that long ago. It feels like it happened . . . I don't know . . ."

"She was a marvelous girl," he said.

"Funny how we never talked about it afterward."

"I thought if you wanted to talk, we would talk."

"I wouldn't have known what I wanted to say."

"Do you now?"

I looked at my father and smiled slightly. "I don't know. I guess life doesn't seem to make any more sense than a Graham Greene novel. Life is probably much tougher than art."

"It certainly separates us—life, I mean."

"The way I separated you from a thousand dollars."

"How's that?"

"That was the emergency money you gave me at the airport," I reminded him. "I used it to come over here and mope my way through the glorious capitals of Europe. Talk about a waste."

"With all due respect, sport, I don't think it was a waste at all. On the contrary, I think you learned something very valuable."

"Right. I learned I wasn't Graham Greene."

Dad ignored me. "Grief is powerful stuff. Especially when you don't let it go. I forget who said the dead are the lucky ones because they don't have to grieve. It may even have been your friend Mr. Greene."

Before I could say more about this, a waiter led us in to dinner, seating us at a table by the window. We ordered fresh beers and game hens, and my father excused himself to go phone my mother to remind her, he said, that tomorrow was garbage-collection day.

My parents had been married fifty-three years and were obviously devoted to each other. My father took care of most of the external duties of domestic life. He earned the money, paid the bills, saw to the house and yard maintenance, even did the lion's share of the grocery shopping and some cooking. My mother handled the social duties and the decorating, kept up on neighborhood gossip and both their complicated medical routines, and volunteered at the church soup kitchen.

I knew he worried about her a great deal. She suffered from a painful lung condition that caused her to be hooked up to a lung-medicating device for an hour or so each day. I sometimes wondered how she would possibly cope when my father was gone. I knew he had recently been teaching her how to properly keep up with the checkbook, pay bills, and replace blown fuses. Other seminars were apparently scheduled soon to follow.

My father came back with a little smile on his face.

"Everything okay back at Camp Jan?"

"Fine." He took a seat, tucking his napkin over his knees.

I asked him to finish what he'd started to say at the bar, about my learning something important from that trip twenty years ago.

I could see him thinking this over. Perhaps he was thinking that his answer was important because our first time discussing the subject would also probably be our last.

"You learned your mother and I loved you enough to let you go and enough to welcome you back. That's something even more powerful than grief. Everyone needs second chances, new starts, whatever you want to call them. I sometimes think that's why we like golf so much—every round is like a second chance to finally get it right."

"I must have been driving you and Mom nuts," I said.

He laid aside his silverware. "As you're discovering, the hardest job on earth is being a parent. Every child has to grow up. You'll have to let Maggie and Jack go, and trust them to do what is right. That's the hard part. I think Francis Bacon said a parent's joys and sorrows are secret—they won't speak of one; they can't speak of the other."

Our dinner conversation reminded me of one last little-known Graham Greene story. It involved the great man's brief encounter with golf. The end of that affair came quickly.

"Greene, you know, tried to play golf at Balliol College," I explained to my dad. "He beaned his caddie on the first swing, and that was all it took. His companion shot his ball through the open window of a passing bus and nearly killed the driver. They threw their clubs down and ran like hell."

"I've had days just like that," Dad said with a robust laugh. "Unfortunately, not all of them were on the golf course."

motorway early the next morning, angling toward the Lancashire
coast, dodging lorries and motor coaches. A sign to Preston
appeared, and we veered off and began twisting through a series
of turns that led to a stretch of potholed road. We finally crossed
a small bridge, and my father cheerfully piped up, "That's the
river Ribble. We're getting close."

A few minutes later we were driving along a better dual car-
riageway, and even the inky sky was brightening above us, allowing glimpses of a widening river estuary through trees to the left.

"I used to ride a bicycle along this road," my father mused, looking for landmarks. "All the way from Freckleton to Preston."

"To meet girls?"

"No, wise mouth. To go to the movies. Come to think of it, there
were always these English girls waiting around the movie house
looking for an American date. They'd spot your uniform and stroll
up and say, 'Hello, Yank. Care to have some fun tonight?' "

"Ever manage to see any movies?"

"A few," he said, looking out the window with a smile.

Between November 1943 and December 1944 my father served
as one of four chief parachute inspectors at Warton Base Army
Depot Number 2, the sprawling 8th Army Air Corps maintenance
facility on the outskirts of a village called Freckleton, where 10,000
Americans lived and worked, primarily repairing, testing, and
building B-24s and other Allied aircraft. Freckleton during those
years was called Little America, and it was my father's home for
thirteen months prior to being sent to northern France.

A few miles north lay Royal Lytham and St. Annes Golf Club,
sometimes simply called Royal Lytham, where Bobby Jones captured the British Open in 1926. More important to me, it was

where my father used to play golf on his days off fifty years ago. The first round of our last trip was going to be here.

I slowed the Omega as we rolled into Freckleton's picturesque center, past a collection of tidy shops and a large brick Anglican church where the standard read HARVEST FESTIVAL THIS SUNDAY. EVERYONE WELCOME. I saw my father staring at the church; then his eyes shifted to a group of schoolkids in dark blazers fooling around on the corner. Watching them, my father smiled and said, "We had kids just like that hanging around the base. A lot of them were evacuees from London and Birmingham. We'd give 'em candy and magazines."

"You could get twenty years for that today," I said.

He ignored my joke. "One of my jobs was to put together the daily information briefing for the base colonel. I carried around an old Hasselblad camera and took photos of a lot of the kids from Freckleton. We had one wall at the PX covered with nothing but snapshots of local kids."

We drove straight through Lytham's bustling town center and on into the outskirts of adjoining St. Anne's. The golf club was several blocks off the main drag, and amazingly, my father remembered the way. We found Eddie Birchenough, Royal Lytham's popular head professional, sitting in his cozy office in the small white pro shop. He shook my father's hand vigorously and welcomed him back on behalf of the club. We collected our bags and deposited them on pull carts—what the Brits call trolleys. A few minutes later we were standing on the first tee.

Dad's eyes roved slowly across Royal Lytham's flat green landscape, taking in the course, the ivy-wreathed Victorian red brick clubhouse, the prim-roofed town beyond. The sun was welcomingly bobbing in and out, but the light breeze had a chilly bite.

"So how does the place look to you?" I asked.

"Very nice indeed. What's Auden's line about being unable to repeat the past but also leave it behind?"

I admitted I didn't know the quote. Only my old man would have been thinking about Auden at such a moment. I asked him how many times he'd played Lytham when he was here.

"Hard to say. Quite a lot. I used to ride my bike up here at least one afternoon a week. What I liked was they always welcomed American servicemen and you could always scrounge up a match. The British love to play matches. We Americans spend all our time worrying who has the lowest score."

"Who do you think is right?"

"Oh, I think the soul of golf resides in a golf match," he said without hesitation. "The joy of going with a fellow and playing him head to head, regardless of the score at the end—that's special. Let the pros keep medal play if they want."

Some say Royal Lytham lacks the physical charm and visual majesty of the other great British linkslands because its contours are fairly subtle and the course is hemmed in by a coastal road and suburban neighborhoods on all sides. It doesn't have the eccentric double greens of St. Andrews or the soulful ocean vistas of Turnberry. What it has, though, is extraordinary grass and a glorious history of beating up the world's best golfers. Did I mention the 190 lethal sand bunkers?

The first hole is a little brute—a 206-yard par-three guarded by a series of sand traps. I watched my father tee up his Top-Flite, then send his ball scampering along the beautiful turf, throwing up a fantail of water. He'd topped his Top-Flite.

"Take a mulligan purely for old times' sake," I suggested.

A brisk shake of the head. "No, thanks. I'll play that." A free shot here perhaps would have been a sacrilege to him. He'd suddenly grown reflective. The old golfing sergeant had come home.

We played the hole in silence, recording double bogeys.

Our second tee shots were much better. The limp I'd noticed in my father's gait on the first hole began to disappear as we walked. He lofted a beautiful three-iron shot to the front of the second green, and before I knew it, he was toddling off down memory lane again.

"I remember there was this friendly pro here in those days named Furman or something like that. Real nice fella. A club maker. That's how pros in those days made their money. He always wanted to make me a custom set of clubs. I was never in any hurry, because I used the clubs of a member who was away in the war."

"Did you take any lessons?"

He smiled. "No. But I had some help with my swing from an unusual source—the pro's daughter. Her name was Nickie. She was about seventeen and really knew her stuff. She liked to caddie for me. She used to tell me to keep my head down and get my bum into the shot. 'Head down and bum into the shot, love.' " He laughed. "I haven't thought about that in years."

"So you're telling me my golf swing is descended from a girl?"

"Something like that. A sturdy redhead. Very lively lass."

We played two more holes, more or less with our bums down and no chatter. By the end of the fourth hole, alas, I'd already toured three of Lytham's famous bunkers. On the plus side, Dad showed no indication of fatigue whatsoever. There was even a discernible lilt in his step. At the frighteningly bunkered par-three fifth we both parred. The day was getting better in several respects.

"Did you wear your uniform when you played?" I asked him as we walked off toward six.

"Of course. Every time. We all did. It was wartime."

I could picture him swinging in his staff sergeant's uniform, all necktie and peaked cap.

"How many matches did you win?"

"None that I remember. I wasn't very good."

"Probably forgot to keep your bum down, you bum."

I managed to birdie the par-five seventh hole, and Dad was nearly up to his old magic at eight, just missing a chip-in from the fringe. Soon we were standing on the ninth tee, which ends the course's outward march toward the sea. The ninth is the shortest hole on the course, a tidy par-three of just 164 yards.

The wind was diagonally in our faces from right to left. There appeared to be half a million little bunkers around the ninth green, each one whispering my name like a sea siren.

I said, "I've never had a hole in one. Wouldn't this be a perfect spot?"

"Anyplace would be a perfect spot for a hole in one," he said.

"Here goes," I announced, then proceeded to fire my ball into the depths of the huge yawning bunker in front. "What I meant was, this would be the perfect spot to make two from the bunker." Dad looped his five-iron shot to the grass just in front of the green, chipped on, missed the putt, and made bogey. I made double, saving my ace for another day.

We sat down to rest on the grass at the tenth tee.

"Our scores are awful," I said, adding up the damage.

"Ah, well. No matter." He yawned. "This is so delightful. Look at those birds."

Several white seabirds were darting over the peaked red rooftops of St. Anne's. The sun was now sprinkling late September warmth over the sea, and the moment really was delightful, proving—as someone who probably never broke 80 once said—that golf is mostly about whom you choose to play with.

"People were very decent to soldiers here," my father observed. I noticed him massaging his left leg, reminding me what an effort this hike really was. Thank God, I thought, for Lytham's gentle, old terrain. "We were basically a bunch of smart-aleck kids a long way from home, and they made us feel welcome. That may strike you as just an old soldier's sentimental memory," he said to me, "but there was such civility in the way we were treated here. You don't forget kindness like that. The world could use some civility like that."

Watching the birds soar and plunge to earth, I agreed.

THE back nine at Royal Lytham is loaded with danger and history. Bobby Jones played heroically down this stretch to capture the first of his three Open championships in 1926—the first year that fans actually paid admission. Ten thousand spectators paid half a crown for the privilege of watching the two best players in the world compete. Both were Americans but might have hailed from different galaxies: Walter Hagen and Bobby Jones.

Jones and Hagen were symbols of golf's past and future, playing the game for entirely different reasons. Jones was the ultimate amateur in an age when amateur meant something good. In his relatively short career he won four U.S. Opens and three British

Opens. At twenty-eight in 1930, a mere stripling by today's standards, he hung up his clubs and called it quits "to avoid getting myself into a position where I would have to keep on playing." He noted that he intended to "keep golf in perspective" by using it as "a means of obtaining recreation and enjoyment."

Hagen was something quite different: Brash, flamboyant, money-loving, he took the golf world by storm and became the game's first touring professional and slickest "mental" player. The British press ripped him for his cheeky off-course extravagance, which only endeared him to the masses. He chartered airplanes to fly to tournament sites and dined on Champagne and lobster in clubhouse parking lots. His golf philosophy was, "Never hurry and don't worry." Pursued by ex-wives and creditors, consorting with British royalty and Gatsby rogues, Sir Walter became the game's first true glamour boy.

By the third round of the 1926 Open at Lytham, neither Jones nor Hagen was on the lead. That belonged to a Detroit club pro named Al Watrous, who held a two-stroke lead at 215.

Dad and I talked about Jones and how his love of sportsmanship really set golf apart from every other sport. As we played the next four holes, I noticed Dad was limping slightly again. Oh, well, I thought. Never hurry and don't worry.

Lytham's hole fourteen begins a final stretch of long par-fours that can wipe out anybody's score. During the final round of the Open in 1926 Jones came alive at Lytham's daunting fifteenth, a 463-yard par-four some say is rivaled in difficulty only by St. Andrews's Road Hole. He birdied it to catch Watrous. The players were still even at the seventeenth, a 462-yard par-four that bends slightly to the left and where a player's drive must be played to the right so he can have an open approach to the green. In Jones's day a frightful sand-waste area stretched down the left side of the fairway, and that was unfortunately where he pulled his tee shot. Unable to see the green and with Watrous's ball already on the putting surface, Jones fired one of the most miraculous shots in golf, ripping a flawless four-iron over the dunes. His ball came to rest on the green closer to the flagstick than Watrous's ball.

Shaken, Al Watrous three-putted to oblivion. Jones got down in two.

Fittingly, there was really only one man left on the course with a chance to catch Bobby Jones. That was Sir Walter, the showman. Hagen came to the final hole at Lytham two strokes behind Jones, needing to hole out from the fairway to tie. It was an impossible shot. But gifted entertainer that he was, Hagen slowly walked to the green and asked his caddie to please hold the pin. Sir Walter's theory on performing for the masses was to make the hard shots look easy and the easy shots look hard. He walked back to his ball and took aim. His pitch nearly struck the pin before trickling off the back side of the green.

Jones had his first Open championship. But Sir Walter once again sent the masses home smiling.

MY FATHER soldiered along Lytham's rugged back nine with his usual collection of bogeys and doubles and only one triple, but my game came seriously unglued. I made the hard shots look hard and the easy shots look *harder.* After the eighteenth his 102 was respectable enough, considering his age and the fact that he hadn't walked an entire golf course in over a decade. My 92 was one of the worst golf scores I could just about remember. I don't know which of us looked more exhausted.

At the clubhouse, Tony Nickson, a former club captain, was waiting for us. Nickson was a dapper seventy-six-year-old in a blue blazer and club tie who had recently authored the club's comprehensive history, *The Lytham Century.* He gave us a delightful walking tour of the large Victorian clubhouse, which is one of those great, drafty places that seem to be all ancient paneling, cut-glass doors, and wide, quiet corridors.

Nickson showed us pictures of Lytham's distinguished line of Open champs. He emphasized, though, that one name transcends the rest—Bobby Jones. In the empty club room, with its high ceiling and vast polished wooden floor, he showed us what amounted to a shrine to Bobby Jones: various memorabilia, including copies of his original cards for all four rounds in 1926 and the club he used to strike his famous shot from the sand at seventeen.

We had a drink in the men's bar, and in this great place where I'd never been but felt such warmth and kinship, I once again found myself marveling that my father and I were finally here. All this talk of Bobby Jones had opened up a host of my own memories. Bobby Jones had brought me here, in a sense. But it wasn't the Bobby Jones my father and Tony Nickson were chatting about.

It was the female version of the greatest player who ever lived.

ONE day in 1983, after years of hard work as a political reporter and no golf, I called my father. "I think I don't want to be a reporter anymore," I told him flat out.

"Really?" He sounded surprised. "Maybe you're just tired. When was the last time you played golf?"

"Let's put it this way. Carter's polls were still good."

He suggested that I meet him in Raleigh. He picked me up there the next morning, and we drove to Pinehurst. Dad played his usual game and finished in the respectable mid-80s. My drives, on the other hand, kept screaming off into the surrounding pinewood.

Afterward Dad and I sat drinking iced teas beneath a slowly turning ceiling fan in the club's grillroom.

"So why are you tired of being a reporter?" he asked.

I shrugged. "I don't know. Journalism is supposed to make democracy work. Mostly it's making me feel creepy." Politicians and their assorted handlers, regardless of party stripe, were all beginning to sound eerily the same to me.

"Maybe you're just writing about the wrong subject. What would you *like* to write about?"

I sighed and glanced around at the photos on the walls of several great golfers in their prime. Nicklaus. Snead. Hogan. Nelson. Palmer. Floyd. They'd all been through Pinehurst.

"In a perfect world?"

" 'Fraid there's no such thing, Bo."

"I dunno. You'll laugh."

"Try me."

"Golf, maybe."

My father didn't laugh. He took a thoughtful sip of his tea.

"In that case, maybe you should become a golf writer."

I laughed at his suggestion, pointing out that I didn't know a soul in the golf world, didn't even belong to a club, and couldn't keep my balls out of the woods, in any case. It would be easier, I said, to start a career as an astronaut.

"If you believe that, it probably won't happen. On the other hand, I've found that anytime I followed my heart, good things almost always happened. It may not be what you think will happen, or even what you think *should* happen. But the heart can open doors. I really believe that. Thing is, you'll have to walk through them on your own. You may be surprised at the possibilities."

I smiled at him, choosing not to think too much about what he'd just told me. So often his words took time to sink in.

"Thanks, Opti."

That's how we left it, as simple and direct as always. I remember looking out the window at a golf course as my plane lifted into the sky and thinking that at least I could finally play golf again. It was almost as if some kind of permission had been given from on high. I still had a life's direction to figure out, but I felt a lot better.

A short while later I took a job at an old, established New England magazine called *Yankee*. I moved to a small solar house on a river in Vermont, got a retriever pup, took up fly-fishing, and chiseled down my golf handicap to a respectable double digit at an old club where Rudyard Kipling was supposed to have once chased the pill while finishing *Jungle Book*.

One day Tim Clark, the magazine's managing editor, who knew of my revived ardor for golf, came to me and asked if I'd ever heard of someone named Glenna Collett Vare. "Sure," I said. "She was called the female Bobby Jones. Won something like five or six national championships. Died several years ago."

"Somebody evidently forgot to tell her," he deadpanned. Glenna Vare was about to play in her sixty-second Point Judith Invitational. Tim wondered if there was a nice little story in that.

I drove down to the town of Narragansett, Rhode Island, on a sunny morning and walked across an immaculate lawn to a huge shingled ark of a house. No one appeared to be about, but I heard a strange thumping sound. I knocked on the screen door and was commanded by a stern voice within to enter. I eventually discovered up on the second floor a stocky, heavily suntanned, and wrinkled elderly woman up a stepladder, giving the ceiling sturdy cracks with an ancient brassie club.

"Have you ever had raccoon piddle on your ceiling?" she demanded.

I admitted I hadn't.

"I've got a whole family of raccoons vacationing in my rafters," she explained. "I'm trying to urge them to leave before I have to call some dreary man who will come with a gun." She came down from the ladder, and we shook hands. At eighty-one Glenna Vare still had a grip.

"So what is it you want, young man?" she asked testily. "I was about to make some soup."

I explained that I'd come to talk with her about winning six U.S. Women's National Amateur Opens. The Ladies Professional Golf Association's Vare Trophy, handed out annually to the player with the lowest scoring average, bore Glenna's name.

"Oh, nuts. Nobody cares about that," she said, dismissing me with a wave of her hand, marching down the stairs and tossing her brassie into an umbrella stand. She rambled toward her kitchen with her small dog, Jimmy, frowning at me from her heels and snapped over her shoulder that nobody had written about her "in at least twenty years."

I followed her into the huge sunny kitchen and tried to explain the point of doing a story on her. She instructed me to "pipe down" and chop some carrots. I chopped carrots and then onions. She poured me a glass of sherry while the soup cooked, then told me that since I'd helped make the soup, I'd better eat a bowl.

We ate soup at a small table on Glenna's big porch overlooking Narragansett Bay, and I asked if she would permit me to caddie for her at Point Judith. "Absolutely *not*," she replied quickly. "Nobody should watch an old bird like me play golf now if they don't have to." My penance for making this ludicrous request was not terribly severe: She made me get on the stepladder and whack the ceiling with the golf club while she went to change into her "driving shoes." She invited me to ride with her into town to "start the mail delivery," which I did, holding Jimmy on my lap as she gunned her Cadillac through the thickening tourist traffic.

We talked about contract bridge, her grown children Ned and Glenny, the nuisance of summer tourists (she was one, too, though I didn't point that out), Gene Sarazen's shoes ("that man always had the spiffiest shoes"), shooting skeet (Glenna was a former champ back in Philly), and the new generation of LPGA stars ("some most attractive young women, though some of them could do with a bit of makeup"). When she let me off beside my car, she smiled sweetly and said, "You're a nice young man. You should get married. Come back sometime, and we'll have soup again."

The next day I sneaked out and watched her play from a safe distance in Point Judith's thick yew bushes, and I was gratified by what I witnessed. Her driving touch turned out to be as solid as her grip. I went back to have lunch with Glenna every spring for the next four or five years, until her death in 1989. We became friends, but she never agreed to let me watch her play golf. She said her golf game was "dead." She was happy to learn I was getting married. "It's about time you did that," she said. "Who's the lovely but unfortunate victim?"

I explained her name was Alison. She was an editorial assistant at *Yankee*. Her parents were real Scots. She'd gone to Harvard. She looked like the actress Ali McGraw.

"Does she play golf?" Glenna demanded.

"No."

"Probably just as well. Too much in common, you know, can kill a marriage. Always leave some mystery."

The story I wrote for *Yankee*, about making soup with Glenna, was read by the editor of the United States Golf Association's *Golf Journal*, who purchased it for his magazine. One of Britain's top golf editors read it there and mentioned it to an editor at *Golf* magazine, who called me up exactly eight months after I'd met

Glenna. He asked if I would care to write a profile of a promising young player named Davis Love III.

Just like that the door my father had talked about that day at Pinehurst had unexpectedly opened. I effectively stepped through to a brand-new world, a place I felt comfortably at home.

5
Lady Sunshine

THE next morning, while Dad rested his legs, I took another shot at Royal Lytham. I wore my best khaki pants, a white polo shirt, and just to be on the safe side, I carried my lucky Pebble Beach ball in my left rear pocket.

I tell myself I'm not really superstitious on the golf course. But most golfers really are. Were it not for the indisputable fact that I always play better when I wear my lucky khakis and a white polo, use an odd-numbered Titleist balata ball, make sure I have only white golf tees in my left pocket, wear my lucky Foot-Joy teaching shoes, eat a Granny Smith apple on the way to the golf course, and carry my lucky Pebble Beach golf ball (a time-ravaged Spalding Dot, circa 1950, that I plucked from a hedge on Pebble's fifth tee shortly before miraculously going par-birdie-birdie-par)—if it were not for these field-*proven* aids to scoring, I would probably be the first to tell anybody who is *genuinely* superstitious on a golf course that they have, à la Glenna Vare, raccoons in their rafters.

Playing alone on a somewhat raw and windy morning gave me time to work out my swing flaws and reflect on events of the preceding afternoon. Our golf scores hadn't been pretty, but everything else had worked out so beautifully, and it was possible to take the suddenly improved mood of the trip as a sign of good things to come. Dad had thoroughly enjoyed his roast beef and Yorkshire pudding feast at a local pub afterward and was sleeping like a babe by ten that night. All in all, a perfect reunion.

I reached Lytham's intriguing short ninth, the par-three where I'd brazenly predicted my first hole in one but taken five. Perhaps since that day on the seventh tee at Green Valley with Kristin, I quietly obsessed about making golf's perfect score, no doubt in part because everybody I knew seemed to have at least one ace. The elderly mother of one of my best friends, for Pete's sake, had *four* of them! Sometimes I comforted myself with the knowledge that Ben Hogan, maybe the best ball-striker who ever lived, scored only one ace in his competitive career.

Every now and then I toyed with the idea of starting up a grass-roots organization for ace-challenged golfers like me. I would call it the Hole-in-None Society, and we would share horror stories of lipped-out seven-irons or balls that traitorously struck the hole in flight and popped out. Any member of the society who was caught making a hole in one would immediately be required to tender his membership card and forfeit all society benefits.

For the second day in a row I failed to score an ace at Lytham's ninth. (Surprised, huh?) My ball flew toward the pin but landed on the front of the green and stayed there, leaving me fifteen yards shy of expulsion from my own society.

MY FATHER and I rendezvoused at the Taps, a low-beamed tavern on the small street just behind the Clifton Arms Hotel. I found him in the midst of a lively group of locals enjoying an afternoon snog a few steps from a crackling fire. He waved me over, ordered me a bitter, and asked if twice proved a charm at Royal Lytham. I showed him my much improved card—a respectable 82.

"Stick around," he said, "and you may get to like the place."

"I already do."

Dad was in excellent spirits. He'd risen late, soaked in the tub, phoned home to check up on things, taken a leisurely breakfast, then gone for a walk around the town. He'd bought my niece Rebecca a little silver bracelet and gone to the library to read *The Times.* While having lunch at the Ship and Royal, a pub up on the main drag, he'd met a couple of retired local school-teachers who spent an hour filling him in on some of the town's changes over the decades. The cars had gotten too big, the gist of their narrative went, while the streets remained too small; kids didn't respect their mums and dads; and nobody in Lytham was really as neighborly as they used to be. The pubs were full, the churches empty.

A man named Jeff inquired if Dad and I were planning to stay in the area awhile, and his wife, Rachel, wanted to know if we had attended the recent D-day reunion at the former Freckleton base. I said we had missed the reunion and were unfortunately only planning to stay in the area a day or two because we had to meet my Scottish mother-in-law for lunch in Glasgow.

"Lots of Americans came to the reunion," Rachel said. "And there was apparently quite a memorial service up at the church, you know, because of the bomber."

"What bomber?" I said.

"Why, the bomber that crashed," Rachel replied. She glanced from me to my father and then back at me. "It was such a heartbreaking thing, wasn't it? All those lovely babies gone. People round here never quite got over it."

Dad was staring at Rachel. He said nothing.

I shrugged and admitted, "I don't know anything about a bomber crash." I looked at my father again. "Do you know the bomber they're talking about?"

He nodded almost imperceptibly. His high spirits were gone. His complexion had turned pale. "Yes." His voice was scarcely more than a whisper. "It was . . . very bad."

I could see ripples of tension coursing through his jawline, indicating this was a discussion he wanted no part of. His eyes shifted to the burning fire. Rachel apparently saw the same thing and gently touched my arm.

My mind was groping to find an explanation for my father's sudden mood shift. I'd never seen anything like it. What did the crash of a bomber have to do with him? I knew most of my old man's war stories, and there was nothing in them about a plane crash. His sudden, stricken withdrawal made me queasy. I leaned over and asked him if he was all right.

"No," he said, looking at me with a startling intensity. He took a final sip of his beer, then pushed it aside and got up. "Come with me," he said. "There's something I have to show you."

DESPITE all the stories I knew, there were things about my father's war years I didn't understand. In late 1942, married to my mother and working in the ad department of the Cumberland *News,* he'd enlisted in the army air corps and been offered a chance to go to officer candidate school, where he hoped to become a combat or glider pilot. Simultaneously, though, his draft board had mailed him a draft notice assigning him to the technical training school at Chanute Field, Chicago, so he went there instead. At Chanute he scored in the top five percent of his class and was offered a second opportunity to attend OCS, this time with the personal recommendation of General Hap Arnold.

He declined the recommendation and stayed at Chanute for six months as a life-raft and parachute inspector. In early '43 he was shipped off to San Antonio, where he was made a staff sergeant but once again turned down OCS. In November of that year he was sent to the war in Europe to fill a chief-inspector slot at Warton Air Base in Freckleton. There he was assigned to a "casual" pool, which granted him an unusual amount of freedom of movement—hence his two golf trips to Scotland. Twice more the top brass recommended him for OCS, and twice more he declined.

Why was this?

On our first night in Lytham, in the afterglow of our great day at Royal Lytham, I'd put the question directly to him. His quietly rendered answer had taken me by surprise.

"When I joined the army, I was a pretty cocky young guy. I had a beautiful wife, a good civilian job, and a zippy comeback for everything—not unlike you, come to think of it. I suppose part of that was an intellectual arrogance. I'd read a lot of books, been a few places. I thought I knew more than most other guys, including the colonels and generals. That somehow made me different, maybe even a bit better than them. Coming here taught me otherwise."

I asked how so.

"Oh," he answered vaguely, "just something that happened. I'd really rather not go into it. The point is, smart guys like me grow up thinking we've got it all figured out. We think we're fully in control of everything that happens. The truth is, the control we think we have is really an illusion. Shadows. The only thing life really promises us is pain. It's up to us to create the joy."

I asked what happened to change his thinking in this way.

He looked at me and said two words: "The war."

WE DROVE in the fading light, after leaving the Taps, toward the tranquil village of Freckleton. I now knew that the answer to my question the evening before had something to do with a bomber that crashed. But that's all I knew, because Dad was stone-silent as we went along.

A few schoolkids were still straggling home in their plaid jumpers and navy blazers. A little yellow-haired girl walking with a chubby black-haired companion reminded me of my daughter and her best friend, Eileen. The larger girl was dragging her overcoat on the pavement behind them.

"Stop the car here," Dad suddenly said.

We were in the center of Freckleton, just off the Preston Road. There was a post office, a small market, a fish-and-chips parlor, and the handsome red brick Trinity Church. Pansies were still blooming in window boxes.

He opened his door and got out. I followed him in silence across the street toward Holy Trinity. Without speaking a word, he walked purposefully toward a small pedestrian lane that ran between the residential close next door and a small button shop.

The lane led to an iron-gated burying ground at the rear of the church. On the far side of the graveyard was a public park with a rose garden. Dad opened the gate and proceeded along the stone pathways of the graveyard, eyeing the headstones. I followed him to a large polished granite cross. It was a common grave. Wreaths and wildflowers had recently been placed there, but the chill nights had turned the bundles of asters and poppies and chrysanthemums rusty. I read some of the names inscribed on the stone border: GILLIAN AND JUNE PARKINSON. GEORGE PRESTON. MICHAEL PROBERT. KENNETH BOOCOCK. LILLIAN WAITE. SILVIA WHYBROW. JUDITH GARNER. ANNIE HARRINGTON. . . .

The names went on, thirty-eight in all. A mass grave.

"How did these folks die?" I asked.

"They weren't folks," he replied softly. "They were children."

The words didn't sink in at first. "Children?" I repeated finally.

He nodded. "Four- and five-year-olds. Maggie's and Jack's ages. They went to the infants school here at the church. One of our bombers crashed into the school. The airfield was just over there." He lifted his head solemnly to indicate where.

I didn't have a clue what to say. I'd never heard of anything so awful. So for a change, I said nothing.

We stood in silence for a few minutes more before he spoke again. He shut his eyes and opened them. I wondered if he was praying or just reliving scenes I couldn't begin to imagine.

He spoke evenly. "It was about ten in the morning. A large thunderstorm had just come up. We had our parachute crews working double shifts because this was six or seven weeks after D-day. I'd just stretched out on my cot to steal some shut-eye when I heard a big roar overhead followed by an explosion. The whole hut just shook. I knew it was one of our birds. The hut I was in was probably the closest one to the school here. One of the other guys ran out, and I ran after him. It was raining like hell, but I saw fire down at the school and started running. We were all running."

Dad cleared his throat. I placed my hand on his arm.

"I guess I was one of the first to reach the school, though others got there quickly. God, what a sight. The plane had gone right through the school and struck a café where lots of our guys and RAF personnel used to hang out. It set half the town on fire. Burning fuel was running down the street. I just remember starting to pull away pieces of things—pieces of the plane, you know, also bricks and mortar—and all these precious little kids inside, buried alive or killed by the explosion. I remember the sound of a child weeping. I couldn't seem to find her. We pulled out several of the children. They were dead or badly injured. You didn't have time to think. You just kept digging."

His voice stopped. I saw tears gathering in his eyes for only the second time in my life. The first time had been when we buried my nephew Richard, one summer day in 1987. Richard, his first grandchild, had been gamely battling a rare nervous-system disorder when he died in his sleep. Richard was nine.

I slipped my arm around my father.

We stood that way for several more minutes. He cleared his throat again and said in a stronger voice, "I knew a lot of these kids, Jim. As I told you, they were always hanging around the base. The guys loved them. We each had our favorites. There was one little girl in particular I loved. She was always laughing, like your Maggie. I called her Lady Sunshine. I used to tell her I hoped I had a daughter like her someday. She was one of those killed."

Good Lord, I thought.

"A week or so after the crash, after the funeral and all of that, I found a note attached to the bulletin board from that little girl's parents. They wondered if anybody had taken a photograph of their daughter. Can you imagine? They didn't even have a picture of their only daughter. I took them all I had. They were so grateful. We sat there in their little front parlor and just cried. I don't think I ever experienced anything quite so sad."

"Were you okay?"

My father gave me an anguished look. Dumb question, I realized.

"Hell, no!" he snapped. "How could anybody be okay after something like that?"

"I'm sorry. I guess I meant physically. Were you injured?"

"Yes . . . no. . . . My hands were burned a bit. Wore bandages for a while. No big deal. I was fine, but I didn't feel up to going to the funeral. They brought Bing Crosby in to sing to the people of Freckleton. I couldn't even stand to go hear him sing. I think I went somewhere and tried to play golf. Burned hands and all. I just wanted to be alone."

"Do you remember the little girl's name?"

Dad, better now, considered the names on the grave.

"Harrington. Maybe it was Annie Harrington." He took out a handkerchief and blew his nose. "Lady Sunshine," he murmured.

I took my father's arm, and we left the burying ground, slowly closing the iron gate behind us. The air was cold. The moon was already out. It was going to be a beautiful night.

"I'm surprised you never told me this story," I said when we reached the car.

He paused and looked back at the church.

"The war ended for me right here," he said. "I promised myself I would never speak about it again."

SOMETIME in the early morning hours at the Clifton Arms Hotel I woke to the sound of my father's voice barking angrily from the twin bed just beside me.

"I want you men to get back. Get back now! We need help here. Can't you see that? Get going now. On the double."

He was having a bad dream.

"Dad?" I said quietly, reaching over to touch his arm. He was rigid as a board. "You okay?"

There was silence; then he calmly answered, "Yes, Jim. I was just . . . Go to sleep now, son."

I waited till his breathing told me he was asleep again. He slept peacefully, but I lay there for a long time, trying to decide if I felt better or worse about having exhumed this devastating event from my father's past. My father's world had forever changed one rainy summer morning fifty years ago, and in thinking about this unspeakable sadness, I suddenly fully understood why my father had been so adamant about me attending Kristin's funeral—willing to wager everything on the outcome of a silly golf match.

It wasn't a gesture intended to simply honor Kristin's memory and lend support to her family. It was a way of prying open a door to liberate something deep in me. In the years that followed Freckleton, he'd obviously learned the importance of surrendering everything to grief, even though his strongest impulse after the bomber crash had been the same as mine: to run away.

Had the cocky young sergeant died in the wreckage at Freckleton and Opti the Mystic been born right then and there? That would explain so much—why he seemingly never let life knock him off stride and went about afterward spreading good cheer like some self-appointed Appleseed of joy. "The only thing life really promises us is pain," he'd said the night before. "It's up to us to create the joy." Bill Mims, Opti's oldest golf pal, once said to me, "No matter what he shoots, your old man never seems to have a bad day on the golf course." Perhaps a bad day period—after Freckleton.

I thought about these complicated things for a while, watching the moon spilling its light over the tranquil Irish Sea. I thought about my own young children, somewhere on the other side of that light, preparing to go to bed about now. They were growing up in a world full of shadows, a place where children like Lady Sunshine vanished too soon and for no acceptable reason. My own Christian tradition held that God's greatest gift was hope. As I lay there, I told myself it was enough for me to *hope* that my own children would someday find God—whoever and wherever God was—or that God at least would simply somehow find them.

I hoped they'd never know the kind of pain my father had known at Freckleton and I'd known with Kristin—or maybe, if they must, that the pain would simply serve to pry open their hearts and wake them up to become Appleseeds of joy. My own prayer was simple: Please make them little Optis.

I don't even remember falling asleep.

6
Return of the Slammer

A FEW years ago I spent a day with Sam Snead. We met at the Greenbrier in West Virginia, where he'd just returned to serve as pro emeritus. We teed off to do a playing interview on the Old White Course, where he'd once given Dwight Eisenhower golf lessons.

In his inimitable fashion Snead regaled me with tales about playing golf with hacker movie stars and pigeon millionaires and
Presidents he'd known (and in Richard Nixon's case, caught
cheating—moving his ball in the rough). Somewhere in this mov-
able jamboree of memories I asked Snead if he fully compre-
hended what he'd done for golf—not only won more tournaments
than anybody else (81 by the PGA Tour's count; 86 by the Slammer's own) but also been the first true media "star" of the postwar generation that produced the biggest popular golf boom in
the history of the game.

"Yeah, I've thought about that from time to time," Sam admitted, giving me a sly granddaddy-catfish smile. "That's not bad, I
reckon, for an ole country boy who taught himself to play with a
stick in a cow pasture."

I suggested we set up a match to see who won the most holes,
but Snead declined, explaining that he never wagered on a match
"until I see a man play." At eighty, Snead's butter-smooth swing was
still a marvel to behold. Snead went out in 35, while I managed 38.
On the tenth tee he spotted a problem with my setup and gave me
the same advice he'd once given Ike. "Stand up straighter, and
stick your butt out more." He noted how that would promote a
better shoulder turn and a straighter shot.

I asked the Slammer how the commander in chief had responded
to being told to stick his butt out more.

"He kind of laughed. I reckon he wasn't used to people talkin'
to him that way. Nice fella, though. Wanted like hell to be good.
Ike's real handicap, you know, was a state secret," Snead explained.
"They didn't want the public to know, because if he was bad, they
might wonder why he was bad, and if he was good, they might
think all he did was play golf all day."

This begged the logical question from an old political dog like
me: How good was Ike?

"Not that bad—'bout a ten or twelve handicap, I reckon, at his
best. Never seen a fella more crazy about a game, though."

We arrived at Old White's eighteenth dead-even on the home
nine. "How 'bout a little match?" my host said, grinning again

like a granddaddy catfish. "Let's say the winner buys lunch."

From the rear tees the eighteenth, an unusual finishing par-three hole, played just 165 yards. My host invited me to shoot first. I made a decent swing with my six-iron and landed my ball fifteen feet to the right of the pin, certainly within range for a birdie. Snead's ball landed a foot above the hole and spun back a bit.

I conceded the putt to Snead. He watched me take my position over the ball, a smile playing faintly at his lips. My nerves were taut, and the resulting stroke was poor. The ball leaked two feet left of the hole.

"Let's go have lunch," Snead declared, picking up my ball and tossing it underhand to me.

In the Greenbrier's clubhouse grill, Snead ordered a chocolate ice cream and a whiskey and asked me with a suspicious squint for the second time that day if I was sure old Linwood Dodson wasn't my "deddy." "That ole boy used to hustle the pants off me," he remembered.

I assured him there was no connection. I said my father was an adman from Greensboro.

"Greensboro was always special to me," Snead said with a genuine smile. "It's where I won my last regular tour event."

I said I knew that, because I was there.

I explained how my father had taken me to the Greensboro Open in 1965, the year I was twelve, and how I'd carried around a copy of Snead's memoir, *Education of a Golfer*, for the entire weekend, hoping to get his autograph.

"Did I sign it?" he wanted to know, shoveling a spoonful of ice cream into his mouth.

"No. I lost the book. By the time I got another, you were busy making history. I couldn't get close."

Snead found this story amusing. I pulled out my beaten-up copy of *Education of a Golfer*, which I'd brought with me in anticipation of this meeting, and asked him to autograph it. He wrote, "To my good friend, Jim. Always, Sam Snead." He handed it back with a lopsided grin.

Dad and I drove down the coast from Lytham to Southport the next morning, hoping to play Royal Birkdale, the course where Arnold Palmer won the British Open during a week of tumultuous winds and rains in 1961, establishing himself as the dominant player of his day. Birkdale, with its rugged high dunes and penal bunkers, came late to the ranks of Open championships in 1954, but in the past thirty years no British club has hosted more major events. The pros like it because its fairways are essentially flat valleys between high dunes, producing fewer of the quirky bounces than at most seaside courses. With roughs that can be freakishly difficult due to thick native grasses—buckthorn and willow scrub—Birkdale rewards the straight driver.

Unfortunately, as our Omega rolled into town, the rains that had kindly held off at Lytham roared back with a gusty vengeance in Southport, which calls itself Sunny Southport. With a forecast calling for even heavier weather by midafternoon, we decided our best hope for playing was to make a beeline straight to the course and save checking into the hotel for later.

I drove slowly along Lord Street, Southport's main drag, allowing Dad the opportunity to reacquaint himself with a town where fifty years ago he had come to play golf and to listen to live big-band orchestras in the famous seaside hotel ballrooms.

"Good thing you bought that new rain suit," I commented. The temperatures were supposed to reach only the high fifties at best. "Sure you're up to a hike in this mess?"

"I am if you are," he replied as we approached Birkdale's stark white art-deco clubhouse, sitting dramatically among the sandhills.

At the pro shop the young assistant pro on duty collected our fifty-pound green fees and explained that another group of Americans had just gone off ahead of us. Dad deposited his bag on a trolley, and I slung mine on my back, and sure enough, we found a trio of Americans who'd brought their own caddies—their teenage sons. "We've come this far," a paint contractor from Pennsylvania assured us with a stoic grin. "Damned if we're going to let a little liquid sunshine ruin it for us." He explained that tomorrow the roles would be reversed: Fathers would be caddies.

Left: My parents, a very good-looking couple.
Below: I'm on the right, with Opti the Mystic as cheerful as always.
Bottom: The Old Course at St. Andrews.

We wished them luck and watched them make their way down the dune-bordered fairway into the gloom. As we stood there waiting to hit, getting colder and wetter by the minute, I asked my father what his father had thought of him caddying at Sedgefield when he was thirteen.

"He thought golf was a game for rich playboys. But basically he didn't object too much. The Depression had just hit. The money in caddying was pretty good. My regular customer, old man Sapp, paid me thirty cents a round plus a dime tip—that's what John D. Rockefeller regularly tipped on the golf course." It was Sapp, a prominent Greensboro attorney, who gave my father his first iron, a hickory-shafted seven-iron.

I knew my grandfather only as a kind old man in paint-flecked rumpled pants who smoked King Edward cigars and seldom spoke much except to comment about the weather or what chicanery the Republicans were up to in Washington. He'd had no more than a rudimentary education and had done odd jobs most of his life, including tobacco sharecropping, driving a milk truck, and working on crews that raised the first steel electric towers across the South. His name was Walter, which was my middle name.

I forget who told me my father's father lacked "gumption"— possibly my crazy maiden aunt Lily, Walter's older sister. By gumption she meant ambition. When I asked my father if this was true, he smiled and explained that if his father lacked ambition, it was a trait he'd inherited honestly from his own father, a prominent Orange County landowner who prided himself, as Dad put it, "on never letting work interfere with the pleasures of life."

My great-grandfather kept a north pasture full of cows and a south pasture full of horses. A family story held that during "the War for Southern Independence" he creatively sold horses to the invading Yankees and then had them stolen back at night. He was a dapper rogue who wore a white handlebar mustache and a blue felt bowler. A tintype photograph of him on his seventy-seventh birthday, looking as pleased as if he'd just swiped a few Yankee horses, sits on a shelf in my house in Maine. He was, I knew, a revered figure to my father. Dad spent most of his childhood summers at his farm near Chapel Hill.

Thinking of these things as we stood in the dreary rain on Birkdale's first tee, I asked what my great-grandfather thought of golf. He seemed to have had the perfect disposition for the auld game.

"To tell the truth, I don't know that he'd ever heard of golf. He was pretty much a man of the last century. But what a delightful old codger," Dad remembered, smiling. "He thought of himself as something of a backwoods philosopher, and he used to say to me, 'Braxton, remember, it's always better to laugh than to cry. You just remember that, son, next time you feel like cryin'.' You know what? I did, too."

It seemed like useful advice—especially for Birkdale in the rain.

"We came here for some laughs," I said, staring impatiently at the group ahead of us. They seemed to be playing in slow motion. I didn't see another soul anywhere out in those famous dunes and fairways. "Come on," I said, consulting a damp course-routing card. I picked up my bag and grabbed his trolley.

We crossed through some heavily grassed dunes, then came out near Birkdale's fifteenth tee. A pair of four- and five-pars constituted Birkdale's homestretch, where almost all the history of the place was made, much of it by Americans.

As I hoped, the fairway ahead was empty. "Let's play a four-hole match," I proposed. "I'll give you two strokes a hole due to the regrettable playing conditions."

"Don't dig yourself too deep a hole, laddie. You're feeling your oats this morning."

"Must be all the porridge we've been eating."

Dad teed up and swatted a little fading drive that was boosted by the wind, which was beating over our right shoulders more or less in the direction of the green. I made a swing that was much too quick, producing one of my patented power fades that usually finishes with the sound of breaking glass and a voice shouting in alarm. I saw my ball vanish far into the dunes on the right. I managed a double bogey, just tying Dad.

We went to sixteen, a par-four that doglegged slightly to the right. The rain was hammering us now. "I think we'd better forget this," I said.

"We'll play in fast," Dad said, teeing up his ball. He struck a nice little drive. I put mine in play, too, and we walked off the tee with our hoods lowered, keeping to ourselves.

Considering the awful weather, we played Birkdale's sixteenth pretty well. With the strokes I'd given him factored in, Dad was now two up with two left. Unfortunately, we were now hitting directly into the teeth of the gale. The seventeenth hole is a long par-five, which played monstrously long in the wind.

"Are we laughing or crying?" I said to Dad, having to remove my glasses because water was trickling down my cheeks.

"I think laughing," Dad said, wiping his own face. He smiled at me. "I hope so, at any rate." He teed up and drove his ball about a hundred yards.

"At this pace I should get there about Thursday," he quipped.

I teed up and set my Big Bertha driver behind the ball. A gust rocked me gently, and my club nudged the ball off the peg.

"That's one," Dad said cheekily. "I always heard you were straight but short off the tee."

"Very funny. Please leave the low humor to a professional," I urged him.

I reteed and hit a nice drive that flew about as far as I normally hit my seven-iron. We resumed our silent march to the clubhouse.

MY FATHER had the sweet disposition of his father—and his father's father—but he also had plenty of gumption, a gift no doubt from his mother's side of the ledger, the Taylors. The Taylors were from north of Raleigh, an ambitious tribe of good-natured Baptists. My grandmother Beatrice Taylor, a native of west Texas and a distant relation of Zachary Taylor's, was a firm believer in the powers of Holy Scripture, good biscuit making, and book education.

Her advice to my father was that the Lord liked a boy who wore clean underwear, worked hard, and steadily improved his mind—

an injunction he clearly took to heart. At fifteen he played semi-pro baseball and sold the Greensboro *Daily News* on street corners and worked as a copy runner and stringer for the nighttime sports editor. At seventeen, while still in high school, he went to work at a department store in Greensboro, writing ad copy for the newspaper and dressing window displays at night. During his senior year at Greensboro High (my alma mater) he played second-team halfback on the football team, which went to the state finals in Durham, where his team lost (Dad knocked himself out cold by running into the goalpost). But a businessman who saw him play and admired his hustle offered him a job at a Durham department store and a chance to attend the university in his spare time.

He stayed at Chapel Hill for one year. He thought he might want to be a political columnist or the next Ring Lardner. Instead, he met an airplane mechanic who agreed to teach him how to fly, and soon after that, someone recommended him for a job at a department store in Washington. He caught the train north, arriving on the streets of the nation's capital with fifteen bucks in his pocket. The job didn't pan out, and he was down to his last dime when he won a blueberry pie in a raffle. "I was walking out of the store eating the pie," he once told me, "trying to figure out where I would go next when I physically ran into your great-aunt Edna." Edna was Walter Dodson's other older sister (the non-crazy one, as I liked to think of her), a government secretary.

Aunt Edna took my father home to Bethesda, Maryland, and a week later he found a job selling advertising for the Washington *Post*. That job led to a bigger job, at the Cumberland *News*. One day in 1940 he strolled into McCrory's Five and Ten to purchase a pocket comb and spotted Janet Virginia Kessell, who was twenty years old, the youngest of eleven kids, and who had recently won the Miss Western Maryland Beauty Pageant. She had won an all-expense-paid trip to the 1939 World's Fair, the theme of which was the World of Tomorrow.

Now she was back home selling big-band records and wondering if she should marry a local boy named Earl. Though he didn't own a record player, my father bought a Benny Goodman disc. He went back a few days later and bought an Artie Shaw record and asked the beautiful salesclerk out. She told him she was engaged.

My father proved his gumption by going back to McCrory's until she agreed to go out with him. They went to a place called the Crystal Palace to hear Kay Kyser and his orchestra. After their second date my mother broke off her engagement to Earl. Earl moved to Baltimore. My parents got married less than a year later.

AFTER Birkdale we drove back to Southport to check into the Prince of Wales Hotel, maybe England's most famous golf hotel. There were lots of elderly people scattered about in the Prince's lobby, most taking naps in chairs. I gave the clerk our name and asked specifically for Arnold and Winnie Palmer's regular room. The clerk disappeared briefly into a back room and reappeared with a large key that looked as if it could open a Spanish galleon chest.

In our dim tower room on the second floor, the ceiling was high enough to permit pole vaulting and the air was warm enough to bake bread. I tried to open a window, but it was painted shut. The radiator clanked like Marley's ghost.

How could this be the most famous golf hotel in England? The answer, of course, was that the Prince had once been a superb hotel—maybe even a great one, as its dim elegance suggested—but was clearly now feeding off its own fame.

After our showers Dad suggested we amble across the street for a predinner drink at the Scarisbrick Hotel, which looked to be in an even more advanced state of decay than the Prince of Wales.

"That used to be a swell place to go on a Friday night," he remembered fondly as we walked down the Prince's wide staircase to the main lobby. "That was a real air force hangout in those days, with lots of good-looking local girls and great swing music."

At the Scarisbrick, we found a dark wood bar where a number of elderly men sat alone in booths staring moodily at their beers. Dad slipped into a booth, and I went to the bar and ordered us beers. "How about this?" I said, handing him a pint of Old Speckled Hen. "A funeral home with a bar."

He sipped his beer and said, "Now, now. Your turn is coming, dear boy. Someone said that to an old man any place that's warm is a homeland. Especially after playing Birkdale on a day like today."

He told me how he'd first come to the Scarisbrick, with the daughter of a local man named A. H. Tarbuck, whom he'd met on the train. "A charming Jewish gentleman. He'd owned jewelry stores all over Europe before Hitler took over. He invited me here for a drink. He was an older gentleman, with a wife and a married daughter whose husband was in North Africa. He invited me home for dinner. Tarbuck belonged to the Conservative Club and knew Churchill. He once showed me a bag filled with South African diamonds."

"What was the married daughter like?"

"She was attractive. Very attractive. Her name was Miriam. She and I used to go out for a drink sometimes at night. We'd come in here. This place, as I say, really got swinging."

"You seemed to spend a lot of time during the war going to the movies or dancing with attractive English women. Did Mom know?"

"I suppose, though I never mentioned it. She went to USO shows all the time back in the States. There was an admiral at Annapolis who was nuts about her. Good thing I wasn't in the navy."

"Did you ever have a wartime romance?"

My father looked at me. It was the kind of brazen question he probably never expected me to ask. He didn't seem either surprised or bothered.

"Are you asking me if I ever fell for a woman I met over here? The answer is no. Absolutely not. I was married to your mother, and I loved her."

That, of course, was not what I'd asked him. I'd asked him if he'd ever had an *affair,* a wartime dalliance. Women were always attracted to my father's breezy charm, even at eighty.

"I'm not going to pretend to you that I was a saint over here," he said quietly, fingering the rim of his pint. "The war was on, and we were a long way from home. That's no moral justification for anything except, perhaps, to say I believe I honored my vows to your mother. I knew she was the woman for me."

"Was there anybody in Paris?"

He gave a vague smile. "As a matter of fact, yes. I used to hang out with a Canadian nurse named Helen. We went to some plays, saw the sights. She helped me buy a couple hundred dollars' worth of perfume for your mother the week before I shipped home. It was all pretty innocent. I'm sure you can't even imagine it."

Having said this, he drank his beer silently. He was right. I couldn't. Or maybe I could. At any rate, I believed what he said. He and my mom had been married almost fifty-four years and still liked to put on big-band records—well, CDs now—and dance in the kitchen, like in the old days at the Crystal Palace. That's when it suddenly came to me how we could have a little more fun.

I DROPPED a Titleist on the thick hall carpet of the Prince of Wales. I picked up a water glass, walked to the other end of the corridor, and placed it upside down on the carpet. Then I strolled back.

"The object," I said, "is to see how many chips and putts it takes you to hit the glass. We'll play nine holes. Best of nine wins the match and buys dinner."

My father looked wary. "I don't think this is such a good idea. People could be trying to rest."

"Dad, this place makes the city morgue seem busy."

I took aim with my pitching wedge, drew the club back, and made (if I say so myself) an excellent chipping swing. The ball ricocheted off the hallway's ornate wallpaper just below a Constable reproduction and struck the leg of a small table halfway down the corridor, coming to a stop twenty yards from the glass.

"Good grief," muttered my father, "you're destroying the place."

"You're right. I probably should have used a longer iron."

He dropped his Top-Flite and took a quick jabbing chip as if he expected an enraged floor manager to come wheeling through the staircase door at any moment. None came. His ball rolled neatly down the corridor and stopped four feet from the water glass. The man could have chipped on the hood of a Buick.

I made him putt it out anyway. We walked back to the end of the corridor. He was one up, with eight to play. He duplicated the chip and left his next shot only about three feet from the glass. My turn, I decided to putt rather than chip, and smacked my ball hard enough to send it bouncing off the baseboard at the far end of the corridor, a resounding crack that made my father wince.

"Finesse doesn't seem to be your long suit today," he said. "Something chewing at you?"

I shook my head, then admitted I was annoyed that our room was so disappointing.

"Forget it," Dad said. "We've both stayed in worse. Why waste time worrying about it? Let's play."

Opti was right, of course. We played another "hole," this time halving, and walked to the end of the corridor again. I said I'd enjoyed our strange, abbreviated round at Birkdale. My father nodded.

"You held up really well," I said. "Mom will be pleased."

"I doubt that. She wasn't thrilled about this trip. Let's keep the details of our adventures a little vague, shall we?"

I agreed; then I told him I'd spent a lot of the round thinking about my grandfather and great-grandfather and how much he now seemed to be like them.

"I'm flattered you think so. They were good men. Pop could barely write his name, but he was the most civil man I ever knew. He never turned anybody away from our door during the Depression—black or white. His father was quite a charming old gent. I never heard him raise his voice."

We chipped again. As we approached our putts, I said, "I remember when Pop died. You said you had to go to Florida to take care of him for a few days. The next thing I knew, Mom said he had died. I couldn't believe it."

"Well, you were only eleven or twelve. Death doesn't seem possible at that age."

"You're right. It's funny what goes through a kid's head. I recall being fascinated by the idea of death. I always wanted to ask you what it was like being with him when he passed away."

"He died with a lot of dignity, just sort of ebbed away. His kidneys were failing, but he was pretty clearheaded right up to the end. We sat and talked a lot. The last thing he asked me to do for him was give him a shave. I tried to find a barber, but no one would come to the house, so I did it myself. I lathered up his face and used his old straight razor."

The hallway doors opened, and a young man in a dark suit approached us with a strained smile on his face. Uh-oh, I thought, the management cometh.

"Good evening, gentlemen," the man said, clearing his throat. "I'm Weeks, the hotel floor manager. Seems we've had a bit of a noise complaint about your . . . golfing."

"Really?" I said, the picture of innocence abroad.

"I'm very sorry," said my father, blushing. "We'll stop right away." He padded off dutifully to retrieve the water glass and our balls, and Weeks smiled after him like the pleased headmaster who's caught the boy scribbling dirty words in the hymnals.

"Are you a golfer, Weeks?" I asked him.

"Actually, I am not, sorry to say." He sounded as if I'd asked him if he enjoyed beheading small animals.

"So you don't know who that is?" I indicated the elderly figure scurrying to please him. Weeks looked at my father with slightly less disdain.

"Actually, no. As a matter of fact, I haven't a clue."

"Ever heard of Sam Snead? They called him the Slammer. Winningest golfer who ever lived. Won more than a hundred tournaments worldwide, including your Open at St. Andrews in 1946. Called the place a cow pasture and never came back again." I waited for this critical information to penetrate his bony Anglo brow. "You see, Weeks, we got rained out over at Birkdale this morning. Dad just felt like chipping a bit, for old times' sake. You've got champions' names written all over that mirrored wall downstairs. This guy was the best of the bunch."

"*Really?*" he murmured. "I had no idea."

"That's okay. Please don't make a fuss over him." Dad was headed back now. "He hates for people to make a fuss over him."

"I understand." Weeks switched on a five-star smile for my father. "Sir, if it would be of interest to you, we could perhaps make one of our larger reception rooms available for your practicing."

"That won't be necessary," Dad said contritely. "Our little game is done. I'm sorry for any trouble we may have made."

"No bother whatsoever," Weeks assured him. "And if there's anything further you require, Mr. Snead, please don't hesitate to call me personally." He bowed and left us.

My father handed me the balls and glass and frowned.

"Mr. Snead?" he said.

I gave him the same defiant grin my son sometimes gives me when he's been caught clobbering the dog or bashing a lamp. "I guess something I might have said made him think you were Sam Snead," I said, patting him gently on the back. "Isn't that funny?"

"Not really. Next thing you know, they'll be asking me to sign that ridiculous mirror downstairs." An entire wall in the hotel's pub was covered with signatures of the world's most famous players—everybody from Ray Floyd to Nick Faldo. I was pretty sure a kid named Bruno from the kitchen really painted them.

I said dinner was on me because he'd whipped my tail at Birkdale. "When we reach Scotland tomorrow," I promised him, "I'll take me revenge."

"Dream on," he said.

7
The Game Within Us

A WINDING road from Dumfries, Scotland, took us to Southerness, a marvelous short-links course overlooking the Solway Firth, where we met up with a retired vet named Dr. Jupp and his wife, Freddie, for a late Saturday afternoon round. Our first day in Scotland was rain free, the sun gloriously warm on our shoulders.

"We've been to America quite a number of times," Dr. Jupp pronounced loudly. He was a tall, thin man, with a wisp of duck fluff waving from the crown of his bald head. "Got some foreign friends in St. Louis."

He was frowning at me, though I quickly realized frowning was Dr. Jupp's natural expression. His scowl fell somewhere between that of a disapproving owl and a constipated eagle. We watched Freddie tee up and crack her ball a hundred yards down the fairway with a big, loping swing.

"Get your arse lower to the ground, Freddie," Dr. Jupp shouted helpfully at his wife. "Arse to the ground, that's the ticket."

"Fizz off," Freddie said.

I smiled at my father, wondering what it was about Brits and their arses. He seemed to be thinking the same thing. Was getting your arse to the ground anything like getting your bum into the shot?

Southerness is considered a "plain" course by some devotees of Scottish linkslands, a seaside creation over relatively flat pastures and hayfields. There is an unhurried grace about it—evidenced by the fact that upon a golfing barman's strong recommendation, we'd simply dialed up from a local pub where we were having lunch and been politely invited to drop in.

Southerness was a bonus. It was supposed to be an "off day" for Dad to rest his wheels, but the hot lunch and cold beer seemed to give him renewed enthusiasm for the game, and a lively round with the Jupps ensued.

A stiff breeze was whipping off the Solway, but snuggled under my checked wool cap and swinging a club much better than I had all week, I'd run off a string of pars almost before I realized it. The unhurried pace and flat terrain seemed to suit my father, too. He fired off some excellent approach shots, making his usual share of ten-foot putts.

IT WAS nice to be in Scotland finally with my father. My son was already talking of the day I would take him there. At the moment, Jack was more interested in bagpipes than golf bags, but I could happily picture the day we would hack around the land of half his ancestors. The great links by day, the great bagpipe bars by night.

Dad and I drove to the village of Kirkoswald the next morning—
a cool, cloudy Sabbath—and attended services at the little stone
kirk where Eisenhower had supposedly worshipped. The minister,
a potato-shaped man with wild gray eyebrows, gave a cracking sermon about the evils of permissive living that had something
vaguely to do with telecommunication satellites running amok
overhead and polluting impressionable Scottish minds with German porn. Twice he halted the proceedings dead in their tracks
and ordered us to sing hymns louder.

After church, as the clouds peeled back and the sun came out,
we drove a few miles up the coast road to Turnberry. It was a
bonny afternoon, with abundant warmth and virtually no breeze.
The Turnberry Hotel, when it finally appeared, resembled a wedding cake sitting on a green hill.

An hour later we teed off. We even had caddies. Dad's was
named John, a scrawny older man with a filterless cigarette dan-
gling from his lips. John mumbled "hallo" and scarcely said another word for the next two hours. Mine was named Mike. Mike
was almost mahogany from a fortnight's vacation on Cyprus. "Why
would you want to go to Cyprus when the weather here is so lovely
and the gorse in bloom?" I asked Mike.

"Because it's not Scotland, mate," he replied.

The start of our match was highly inauspicious. I hooked my
opening drive fifty yards into the hayfieldlike rough on the left.
Dad topped his drive and trickled his ball maybe fifty yards off the
tee. I required three attempts to return my ball to the short grass.
Dad topped his second shot and sent his ball scampering another
hundred yards. My caddie, Mike, perhaps daydreaming of Cyprus,
was looking at me with genuine sympathy—though for me or him
it was difficult to tell. I was reminded of the old joke where the
American golfer, mentally unglued after a round in which everything has gone wrong, finally lashes out at his Scottish caddie,
"Angus, by golly, you're the worst damn caddie this game has ever
seen!" Angus thinks for a moment, shakes his head, and calmly
replies, "Oh no, sir. That would be too much of a coincidence."

After the third hole I whispered to Dad that my game was about to get on track. The fourth hole is an aptly named par-three called Woe-betide, a fairly short 160 yards to a slightly elevated "pulpit" green.

I'd been to kirk that morning. I'd said my prayers. If God is a just God, I thought, *here's* where I'll finally make a hole in one.

Dad's shot hit the apron just in front of the green. I made a smooth pass with my six. The ball drifted up into the air currents, rising from the cliffs to the left, and then dropped on the green.

It wasn't in the hole—inches short again. My life story. Charter member of the HIN Society. I tapped in. Mike handed me my ball, and we slapped hands.

Dad's legs, I could see, were already giving out. That was too bad. I was sure I was finding my game.

After the fifth hole Dad admitted he didn't feel like playing anymore.

"Are you okay? Shall we just head in?"

"Relax, Bo," he said. "I just want to walk and watch you play."

Mike reminded me that the halfway house was up ahead at the ninth, a good spot to rest and have some refreshment. I thanked him and said I would prefer to carry my own bag from that point on and would settle up with him and John later. "No problem, mate," Mike said. Breaking his silence, John said he would make sure Dad's clubs got cleaned and taken back to the hotel.

On the way to the halfway house I played the next four holes pretty well. Once there, we ordered beers and sat on a bench overlooking the remains of Robert Bruce's castle. Families were picking whelks off the rock below, and people were out walking their dogs in the balmy evening light.

Dad said, "Doesn't feel like the end of September, does it?"

"Not September in Maine, mate."

"How's your house?"

"Almost finished."

He smiled drowsily. "I've heard that one before."

My house in Maine was an ongoing saga and something of a complicated subject between us. Nine years before, my wife and I fled from Boston, moving a hundred miles up the Atlantic coast.

We purchased five acres on a forested hill. When I informed my father that I planned to build our period-correct post-and-beam house with my own hands, he reminded me that the rough theory behind attending college and finding a good job was that you could earn enough money to pay someone who knew what he was doing to build your dream house. He urged me to seek serious professional help—either a real carpenter or a shrink.

I laughed and told him I'd heard him say many times that he would dearly love to build his own house with his own hands.

"That's true," he agreed. "I meant a log cabin somewhere in the Smokies, though. I used to say I wanted a little farm, too. That doesn't mean I'm going to start raising pigs in the backyard."

I Sheetrocked the walls, laid the pine plank floors, finished the windows, hung the doors, made the cabinets, laid the tile, varnished everything in sight, and hammered and sawed and power-glued myself into a period-correct state of exhaustion.

Now the house was finished, and I was cultivating the estate. There was no truth whatsoever to the silly rumor circulating in town that I had plans to create my own little nine-hole executive golf course up in the forest. *One* hole was all I really needed.

Before I could steer the subject safely away from my house and back to the golf in Ayrshire, though, Dad changed it for me.

"You know who would love this place?" he said as we loitered on the sunny Turnberry bench. "Bill and Bob." He meant his old golf pals. "We could really go at each other in a place like this."

He closed his eyes, lifting his face to the breeze.

In a year Dad would be gone. In five years someone else might own my dream house. This moment, though, however imperfect, would never come again. That larger point was finally beginning to sink into my head. Opti had a gift for always returning me to the importance of the moment. I made a note to tell Bill and Bob how my father had mentioned them one glorious evening on a bench at Turnberry.

FROM where we sat, I could see that the fifteenth tee was open. I suggested we skip holes ten through fourteen and play in from the fifteenth. Dad seemed a bit reluctant, but being a seasoned hole skipper, I prevailed on him.

On Turnberry's seventeenth I missed an easy putt for par. I'd neglected to putt like a kid.

"I'm putting like the old Tom Watson," I said, "not the young and fearless one."

"It happens to us all," Dad commiserated, replacing the flagstick.

"Hasn't happened to you," I accused him, causing him to smile.

We stood on the green, and he reminded me of Nick Price's recent magnificent fifty-five-footer that had crossed the green as if it had eyes, and rattled the cup during the final round of the Open in 1994. That brilliant eagle fulfilled Price's childhood dream of winning the British Open.

I told my father Price had recently told me that his father had died when he was ten. They'd been able to play only two rounds of golf together. If you asked Price to name his ideal four-ball group, he would tell you Bobby Jones, Byron Nelson, and his father.

"That's lovely," my father said. "What would yours be?"

"That's tough. Probably Snead, Nelson, and you, or Palmer, Watson, and Price. You'd unfortunately have to watch. You?"

"Jones, Julius Boros, and Sam Snead."

"Some nice swings there."

"Save one of your own for eighteen."

As we walked off toward Turnberry's home hole, I thanked Dad for playing when I was sure he'd rather be resting. He said the pleasure was all his. We went back to our room, and he showered and quickly fell asleep on the bed. I then hopped into a steamy shower myself. When I got out, I heard the magical skirl of a bagpipe being played. A piper strolls the grounds at the Turnberry Hotel each evening at dusk. I picked up the telephone and quickly dialed home. When my son got on, I held the receiver out the window so he could hear it.

THE next day we drove up the Ayrshire coast for brief visits at Prestwick and Royal Troon. Then we pushed on to Bridge of Wier, where we hooked up with Kate Bennie—my Scottish mother-in-law—and her longtime friends Tom and Elizabeth for lunch at a place called the Fox and Hounds. Kate was making her annual pilgrimage home to Glasgow, and she asked my father if I was behaving properly. "Depends on what your definition of proper is," he replied. "He's made the staff at every hotel deliriously happy at the sight of our departure."

"The boy can be a devil boy," she said. I wondered if she was still holding a grudge about my brilliant sand-wedge shot, fired through the window of her two-hundred-year-old farmhouse from 180 yards across the pond in front. Mum had been reading a book in her favorite chair when the ball crashed through the glass and came miraculously to rest on the table next to her tea. As I'd told her, I'd never come close to hitting a sand wedge *that* well.

Mum ordered haggis, neeps, and tatties, so I ordered them, too. Despite what you hear in Scotland, nobody on earth really likes haggis—a dish made from sheep guts, dishrags, and old Glasgow daily papers.

The neeps and tatties—turnips and potatoes—were excellent, but the haggis was dry and tasteless, which may have been a culinary break. "The only way to fix a bad haggis," my mother-in-law said, rising brilliantly to the moment, "is to order a nice extra sauce made of Drambuie. You drink the sauce and throw out the haggis." Mum was in lively spirits, and I asked Tom and Elizabeth if she was behaving properly.

"Well," said Elizabeth, "she seems to have grown a wee bit more *American* with each passing year."

I assured them Mum's full assimilation was utterly impossible. For one thing, she'd been on American shores for thirty-five years and stubbornly refused to eat peanut butter or charcoal-grilled steak or to drink Pepsi. She had never watched a Super Bowl or voted for a Republican. She was to true American citizenship, I pointed out, what a tropical heat wave is to Olympic bobsledding.

THE next day, while Dad poked around Glasgow, I played Ranfurley Castle with a man named Big Jim Patterson through a driving mist storm, which Patterson insisted on calling "a nice Scotch mist."

We went on to Cameron House, by the southern shore of Loch Lomond, to have dinner with Douglas Dagleish and his son Colin. Douglas was president of the Scottish Golf Union and Colin a former Scottish amateur champ.

The Dagleishes gave us a list of their favorite hidden gems of Scottish golf, places off the beaten path where Americans seldom ventured—Boat o'Garten, Bridge of Allan, Golspie, Tain, Brora, Oban. It was good information to have. Douglas described them aptly as "lovely wee places you truly ought to see."

"So where's your next stop?" he wanted to know.

"Carnoustie."

"Ah, *Carnoustie.*" The name rolled solemnly off Douglas's tongue as if it were an oath. His smile broadened again.

"We're all sons of Carnoustie, you know."

FIVE British Opens have been decided at Carnoustie, a fairly gray and nondescript village by the Firth of Tay that has probably done more to foster the growth of golf outside of Scotland's borders than even St. Andrews, its principal rival an hour to the south. However, there had been no Open championship held at Carnoustie (the sternest test in all of Britain, some feel) for two decades.

Such decisions, made by the longbeards of the Royal and Ancient Golf Club, based at St. Andrews, flew in the face of Carnoustie's evangelical pedigree. Around the turn of the century a couple hundred of Carnoustie's sons left their native land to teach golf to the world, effectively becoming the Johnny Appleseeds of the game. A proportionately high number of them settled in America.

Theories abounded why the all-wise Royal and Ancient had bumped sweet Carnoustie off the Open rotation like a rough but favorite uncle being kicked out of a wedding. There was a man I hoped would give me the real lowdown and maybe a proper lesson on how to execute the famous "Carnoustie run-up shot" to boot.

His name was Tony Gilbert, one of Carnoustie's best-known teaching pros, and he was waiting for Dad and me.

In Carnoustie's putting-green area I found a trim, lean-faced man with youthful blue eyes and the kind of complexion that comes only from strolling for years in the sea wind. He was dressed in a red windbreaker and wearing a striped necktie, industriously rapping ten-foot putts into a hole with depressing repetition. I asked Tony straightaway about the Open controversy as we set off down the fairway from the first tee.

"For one thing," he explained, "there has always been a heady competitive spirit between the golfers of Carnoustie and St. Andrews, Scotland's two leading municipal layouts. These things are fairly cloaked in mystery, but I have a sneaking suspicion that the decision came down purely to personalities. Golf is a character-builder, they say, and the burghers of St. Andrews perhaps simply think they've got the superior character."

The way he chuckled I could tell he found this notion simply laughable. "Our Carnoustie golfers regularly beat their St. Andrews counterparts in regular competitions," he added.

Tony stopped in his tracks and gave me a quizzical look, as if we'd forgotten something.

"Say, aren't you supposed to have your father with you, laddie?"

I explained, somewhat uncomfortably, that my father had run into some "unexpected difficulties" and would possibly join us later. Tony left it at that.

I was trying not to let my concern show. My nerves were frayed from an incident back at the Glencoe Hotel. When I'd barged excitedly into my father's room, babbling on about my eagerness to play Carnoustie finally, I'd been horrified to discover him stripped naked, red-faced, with a stomach that appeared to be, well, *exploding.*

He'd shouted at me to either "invite the whole world inside or please shut the door," and I swiftly obeyed, unable to take my eyes off the huge bulge on his abdomen and the angry red welt. "Good God, what's going on? Should I call a doctor?" I stammered.

"Calm down," he snapped at me. "I've just blown the gasket that holds the flange to the stoma bag in place. No big deal, except I seem to have left my spare at home."

"But what's that—that big thing on your stomach? And that red *thing?*"

"This?" He patted the bulge and smiled ruefully. "This, dear son, is what's called a colostomy. And this red thing is my intestines. Please forgive me for being a little *indelicate,* but when you conduct your bowel movements into a little bag, it's important to have a bag that properly works. That, in a nutshell, is my big problem at the moment."

I was momentarily dumbstruck. It was just the kind of unexpected development my mother had forecast and that I, somewhere in the back of my mind, feared might scuttle our trip. As he cleaned his stomach with a damp bath towel, I told him I would go phone Tony Gilbert and cancel our round.

"Don't be ridiculous," Dad said sharply. "You go on and play. I'll take care of things here." He explained that he'd already spoken with the hotel manager, who was phoning up a chemist.

"Go, go, *go!*" he snapped at me, and I involuntarily began to back up. I bumped into the door, paused, turned to look at him once again, and then left him with a sinking feeling in my own gut.

TONY and I made a par and a double bogey, respectively, on the first hole. We walked to the second tee, nestled in crumpled dunes and hummocks of sea grass. The hole, a long par-four aptly called Gulley, was a narrow doglegged corridor that cut left to right. "Position A would be just to the right of that large bunker in the middle left. That's called Braid's bunker," said Tony, and proceeded to slug his ball there as if he simply did it every morning before eating his porridge. I teed up my ball and buried it under the lip of Braid's bunker, or position F. Tony watched my darkening mood as I slammed the sand and advanced the ball a meter or two into the fairway.

"You're workin' mooch too hard on that shot, laddie," he said calmly. With that, he climbed down into the trap and dropped a ball and showed me how to strike it smoothly out of the sand, using mostly my arms. His ball soared, leaving only the smallest indentation in the firm sand.

"You have a loovely swing, Jimmy," he said soothingly. "Stay back on your heels now, relax, and let the shot coome oot." I dropped a ball and stroked a decent shot out of the bunker, though nowhere near as fine as his. "You're a good teacher," I said.

He smiled, extended me a hand up from the trap, and said, "You're a good pupil. Tell me now, where did you learn that big nice strong swing of yours? Your father, I expect?"

I shook my head and explained that my father had introduced me to the game but refused to give me lessons, insisting that I learn from a real teaching professional.

Tony smiled. "Aye, your dad's approach was a wise one. He let you come to the game, and the game come oot of you. There's a good game within us all, laddie. I try and do the same thing with my wee ones—encourage the game to come oot of its own accord."

"You teach kids?" I'd assumed he worked with older and more skilled players. Somebody had told me Tony Gilbert was the best teacher in Carnoustie.

"Aye. That's who I teach, in the main. The little ones, the wee ones. I march 'em down to the beach to learn the sand game, and we have a nice day of it. They're usually fearless in the sand after a day at the beach with old Tony. Some of my older lads are doing quite well up in the ranks, I'm proud to say."

The day was becoming sunny and mild, and my father's situation slipped momentarily from my mind. Tony and I chatted amicably and played. As we started on Carnoustie's infamous back nine, probably the roughest home walk in golf, especially if the wind is up, Tony asked where Dad and I were headed next. I decided not to say, "Probably Edinburgh Airport." So I replied, "Muirfield. A man named Archie Baird is getting us a game there."

Tony nodded. "Aye. I know of old Archie. Good man."

I played horribly on Carnoustie's difficult back nine, but picking Tony's brain about when and how to teach my own wee ones was a pleasure. He showed me the Carnoustie run-up shot—a shot in which, by adjusting your stance and keeping your hands firm, the club face of a lower-lofted club is kept low and the ball scampers forth with a low trajectory and a beautiful overspin. I was bending over a twenty-foot birdie putt at eighteen, concentrating hard, when Tony commented mildly, "There's a man who seems to be waving at us. Could that be your dad?"

I turned around and saw my father standing on Carnoustie's acre-size practice putting green. He was wearing a fresh change of clothes, his old Ping putter was in hand, and his soiled green St. Andrews cap was jauntily cocked.

"That's him."

I made the putt, and we shook hands and walked over. I introduced Tony. "It's too bad you could not join us, Brax," Tony said, "but I would love for you to come by the house to meet my wife, Julie. We'll have a drink and a proper visit if you like."

We agreed to come at seven.

After Tony left us, Dad and I conducted another putting examination on Carnoustie's empty putting green—two spins around the eighteen holes. We finished in darkness, and he beat me yet again, winning by three holes. "I trust you're feeling better," I said as we started across the street to the Glencoe. "Much better," he said. "Thanks."

"I gather our next stop isn't the departures lounge in Edinburgh, then?"

"Be kind of a shame to miss Muirfield and the Old Course, wouldn't it?"

I knew no further questions were required or desired.

Tony Gilbert's house was on Kinloch Street in Carnoustie. We'd planned to stay twenty minutes but lingered three hours. Tony urged us to come back for the Open championship in a few years.

"We'd love to," Dad said without hesitation.

"Excellent," said Tony. "It's settled, then."

"Maybe I'll even bring my wee ones," I said, "for the Carnoustie run-up and a lesson on the beach."

"Even better."

8
Mystery of the Hole

"RIGHT. Here we go."

Archie Baird took a deep breath.

"We'll begin at the beginning. The first stick-and-ball game we know about was a Roman game called paganica, which came up through Europe, into Holland, where the Dutch made the most of it, playing a game they called *kolf*. We have evidence the Dutch played *kolf* going back to 1300. There is no evidence of golf in Scotland before 1450. *Kolf,* a game played on ice in winter and fields in summer, died out completely around 1700. It was probably Scottish wool merchants who brought the game back here. On the east coast of Scotland, with an abundance of land, we transformed the game from playing to a stake on ice to playing on natural land to a rabbit scrape—a *hole*. I truly believe the game as we know it today would never have evolved without rabbits. The rabbits, you see, would gather in the hollows and nibble the grass down smooth and prevent scrub vegetation like buckthorn from overrunning the linksland. In the middle of the scrape the buck rabbit would create a hole and urinate in it to mark his territory, and the early golfers played from one hollow to the next. The hole was usually marked with a gull feather. It was very simple golf."

Baird peered at us somewhat skeptically. "I can go on for hours and hours about this stuff. Are you sure you're up for it?"

I nodded. "Fascinating," said my father.

Archie Baird, former RAF fighter pilot, retired fourth-generation small-animal vet, golf collector par excellence, and Muirfield's redoubtable archivist, gave us a small proprietary grin. I'd heard about Archie and his dog, Niblick, for years. Baird operated the best private golf museum in the world.

Archie was a ruggedly fit seventy-year-old, with rawly barbered hair and a brisk no-nonsense manner. Niblick was a small, wiry-haired Border terrier whose face uncannily resembled Clement Attlee's, the former Prime Minister. We were standing in Archie's little museum—a small, damp, chilly room of artifacts housed in a former cart shed near the pro shop of Gullane Golf Club—in the sleepy East Lothian village of the same name.

"Very well." Archie resumed his museum spiel. "A word or two, then, on historical golf equipment. We must mention the featherie ball. It took one man an entire day and two top hats full of feathers to make just two featherie golf balls. The ball would fly about one hundred and fifty yards. It cost more to produce than a club. The first club heads, by the way, were made of apple, beech, and blackthorn, with a bit of lead in the back. The first iron clubs were made by blacksmiths. This was how the game was played for more than three hundred years. Obviously it was not a poor man's game. In 1850 there were still only fifteen golf courses in the world—all but one of them in Scotland. That year the gutta-percha ball was introduced. Gutta balls were cheap and durable, as opposed to the fragile and expensive featherie balls. For that reason alone, golf suddenly exploded in popularity. By 1900 there were more than two thousand golf courses in the world. Next came the Haskell rubber-core ball, invented by a clever American in the early part of the century, but frankly a bit bouncy and erratic, so they started marking the face of clubs to put a bit of helpful spin on the ball. Control became a central part of the game. Club makers replaced blacksmiths. The so-called modern game was born."

Archie showed us a practice ball with a parachute, a metal-headed driver dating from 1900, a pitching iron with a hole cut into the face ("meant for playing out of the water—didn't work, I'm sorry to say, which explains why they're so rare"), and a "flicker book"—a flip-action instruction manual that animated the swing of Bobby Jones, a sort of crude portable home golf video.

"What a place," said my father. "You must get lots of tourists in here."

Archie shook his head. "That's not the case, Brax. I'm not so brokenhearted if only a few people come by asking for a tour each year. That means they're really interested. There's so much blessed mystery surrounding this game. Take, for instance, the mystery of the hole."

"The hole?" we both said in unison.

"Right. What you Americans sometimes unfortunately call a cup. We know the hole was invented by a Scot. The rabbits were critical to the process, but somewhere along the line someone had to come up with an actual hole. We just don't know who that clever individual was." Archie gave us a slow, solemn look and then shook his head. Niblick sighed and leaned against my leg.

"It remains one of golf's greatest mysteries—lost forever, I'm afraid, to the mists of time."

FOURTEEN British Opens have been contested at Muirfield, home of the Honourable Company of Edinburgh Golfers. Descended from the Gentlemen Golfers, who had played at Leith Links in Edinburgh since the fifteenth century, the Honourable Company's rules of golf were adopted almost word for word in 1754 by the society destined to become the Royal and Ancient Golf Club of St. Andrews—rule makers of the modern game.

Jack Nicklaus made his Walker Cup debut at Muirfield at age nineteen in 1959 and captured his British Open here seven years later. History-steeped Muirfield sits well above the sea and features beautiful turf. There are no forced carries, no water hazards, no ruinous outcroppings of prickly gorse to speak of. "The good shot is consistently rewarded," writer Jim Finegan says. "The indifferent shot is just as consistently chastised."

The primary challenge at Muirfield lies in the ever daunting sea winds, a bearded rough that can resemble the wheat fields of Kansas before harvest, and far too many exquisitely constructed sod bunkers. My first drive hooked badly out-of-bounds left, prompting Archie Baird to recall fondly that the great James Braid of Elie also miserably hooked his opening drive over the wall on the left the year he won the first of his two Open championships at Muirfield, in 1901. He seemed to be telling me there was always hope. I staggered off the hole with a triple bogey.

Archie made par, Dad a surprisingly easy bogey.

"You seem to be off to a poor start," said Archie as they headed for the riding cart Archie had thoughtfully arranged for Dad.

"Jim always starts late," my father chipped in, smiling at me. A day's rest had done him good. I heard a lilt in his voice and saw renewed vigor in his swing. "Takes him a while to figure it out, but once he gets his head on straight, he can post fine numbers."

This was nice of my father to say. Unfortunately, it didn't turn out to be the case. I was keyed up and worrying again about the outcome of the trip. We'd been away thirteen days. Something told me Dad wasn't planning to go much farther.

As the East Lothian sun shone down, my mind slipped back a few weeks to a useful lesson I had learned on another dramatic far-away coast, in the company of a friend named Laird Small. Laird is the head professional at Spyglass Hill Golf Club, Pebble Beach's famous sister course among the tall, coastal pines of the Monterey peninsula. He is responsible for fine-tuning the games of several promising young tour players.

I also started miserably at Spyglass that day. As we climbed the hill to the third tee, I was almost ready to head back to the club-house. Laird suggested we sit on the grass of the third tee for a few moments and talk. I apologized and admitted I was kind of rattled. This was mere days after my father had called to tell me he was dying of cancer. I'd hoped a memorable round at Spyglass would take my mind off my problems. Laird smiled and said he under-stood. That's why many folks played golf. Unfortunately, their mind usually *was* the problem.

As we sat looking at a glorious panorama of the Pacific Ocean, he proposed a little experiment. He asked me for the scorecard, and I handed it over. He tore it up and said, "Let's see if we can get you into NATO."

"NATO?"

"That stands for Not Attached to Outcome."

He said the idea wasn't original with him—a blind golfer pal had thought of it—but that every good teacher knew that the more you pushed against the game of golf, the more the game tended to elude you.

I told him he sounded like my own father, with his talk of "everything contains its opposite" and how trying to create the magic makes it vanish.

"There're really no new ideas, are there?" Laird suggested that we play merely for the simple pleasure of each other's company and the opportunity to be out on such a fine morning, unburdened by scores and trying to determine the outcome.

A memorable round did indeed follow. I recall us stopping to watch seabirds and listen to the way the wind soughed through the famous Monterey pines. Deer crossed our paths, pausing to wiggle their noses at us. I vaguely recall in the midst of all this a string of pars and even a couple birdies happening. It may have been the finest round of my life, but I'll never know for sure.

It was an exercise worthy of Opti the Mystic. I'd come to Spyglass tense and worried, hoping to bury my sadness by beating a great golf course into submission. Instead, I'd submitted and left relaxed and reminded once again of things I'd known since I was a boy at my father's golf club.

AT MUIRFIELD's tenth hole—one of Nicklaus's all-time favorite holes, a mammoth 475-yard par-four—I unleashed my best drive of the day: a three-hundred-yarder that Archie Baird said compared favorably to anything the Golden Bear had done on the hole.

He and Dad rolled down the fairway in their sputtering cart, with Niblick trotting importantly just ahead and slightly to starboard. Golf didn't seem to be the particular aim of either man. The weather was mild and sunny, the tall rough leaning beautifully in the slight breeze off Aberlady Bay.

I took out my scorecard and tore it up, immediately feeling better. I looked at Dad. He was laughing and obviously having a good time. In the honorable company of Archie Baird, a voluble host and a fellow veteran of the air war, sharing stories and reminiscences that had little or nothing to do with golf, my father seemed thoroughly in his element at last. In Archie he'd met a Scottish version of himself.

My father finished with a 93, which made him visibly happy. I finished with . . . who can say? I was happy, too.

BUOYED by our bonny trip around Muirfield, Archie drove us through the village and explained a bit more about the history of East Lothian, then whizzed us up a residential lane in his little Ford Fiesta, very nearly to the crown of Gullane Hill. Writer Jim Finegan says this is one of the half-dozen "most enthralling spots in all the world of golf," a spectacular rise from where you can see fourteen counties on a clear day, distant Edinburgh, the Forth Bridge, the Kingdom of Fife across the gray waters of the Forth, and the green fairways of Muirfield, nestling against the village less than a mile away.

We parted with a drink at the Old Club House Pub, which over-looked the children's links, where several future club champions were out shooting at red flags. Archie wanted to know where we were putting up that night.

I mentioned we had a couple rooms at Greywalls, the fine coaching inn right next door to the tenth hole, where I drove a ball like the Golden Bear.

"Oh, splendid," Archie said. "If there's a good moon tonight, be sure and look out at the golf course. It can be quite an extra-ordinary sight."

My father thanked him for his hospitality. I added my Hear! Hear!

We touched our glasses, drinking to the eternal mystery of the hole, whoever invented it.

"That's why we love this game," said Archie. "The bittersweet mystery of it all. The uncertainty of what we shall discover."

"It's new every time you go out," agreed my father. "Wasn't it de Vicenzo who said golf is like love—one day you feel too old, the next you want to do it again?"

"Right you are, Brax." Baird felt his own familiar quotation com-ing on. " 'A tolerable day, a tolerable green, and a tolerable oppo-nent supply, or ought to supply, all that any reasonably constituted human being can expect in the way of entertainment,' " Archie recited. "That's Lord Balfour. The rest of the quote goes thus:

'With a clear course and fine sea view the golfer may be excused if he imagines that golf, even though it be indifferent golf, is the ultimate end of man's existence.' " He looked at me and said, "He was thinking of Gullane Hill when he said that."

Several hours later I had a clear view of the course and the sea beyond from my room at Greywalls. The moon and sea made me think of a Zen belief that enlightenment is like the moon reflected on water: The moon does not get wet nor the water broken; the light is wide, but a whole sky can be reflected in a single drop.

True to Archie's word, I could see a great deal of the linksland, washed blue by the moon and stars. I flipped on the TV. The late news was on. Former President George Bush was visiting St. Andrews to attend the annual autumn meetings of the Royal and Ancient and play a little golf.

My father wasn't in his room. I strolled downstairs and found him in the library playing old war records on an old windup record player sitting on the piano.

"Look at this," he said as I entered. "Great stuff here."

He showed me several 78-rpm records from the war years and reminded me for the umpteenth time how he'd met my mother in the record department of McCrory's. Then he told me a story I'd never heard—that my mother made a recording of "I'll Walk Alone" and had it sent to him overseas. During the war he used to take the record to village libraries and play it on their record players.

He handed me one of the records. "Look. Tony Martin singing 'To Each His Own.' "

"Who's Tony Martin?"

"Big Hollywood star in the '30s and '40s."

We played the Tony Martin record. Tony Martin had a superb voice. I pictured slinky women with cigarette holders and eyelashes that could wound.

"So how was Mom?" I knew he had vanished to his room after dinner to call my mother.

"Your mom is fine," Dad said. "She's having a man come and waterproof the wooden fence in back." He held another record up to the light and squinted at the title. "I guess she's learning she doesn't need me around quite as much as she first thought."

I started to say something but couldn't think what to say. So I said I was going to walk out and stand on Muirfield's tenth tee in the moonlight. He said he might join me in a minute. As I left him, Tony Martin was crooning that he'd found his one and only love.

I walked out back and stood on the little stone wall above the tee, thinking about the mystery of the hole. The hole was critical to golf, yet a hole was really nothing more than ten ounces of air, a divine nothingness. The object of the game was to reach this place of nothingness as economically as possible, to pass through nature with as much grace and dignity as we could muster. Even if golf wasn't the ultimate end of man's existence, it struck me that a small, ever shifting, mysterious nothingness was precisely what gave the game its essential allure, a power that was simultaneously as visible and elusive as moonlight on the water.

I decided to step down onto the grass and, stepping forward off the wall, kept going, falling about four feet. I landed directly on my back and lay there, the wind knocked out of me, on a pillowy pad of fragrant grass, feeling really dumb but far more startled than injured, staring up at the moon.

So much, I thought, for Buddhist woolgathering. After a few minutes I got up, rubbed my backside, climbed back over the wall, and went inside. My father was just heading up the stairs.

"How was the golf course?" he asked mildly.

"Very comfortable."

He slipped his hand through my arm to give his knees a bit of support as we slowly climbed the steep stairs together. I started to say something about my mother being brave under the circumstances, but he seemed to read my mind.

"Your mother will be all right," he said as we neared the top. "Change is difficult for her, but she's a surprisingly tough lady."

The corners of his mouth turned up slyly.

"You know, it's only been the past five years I've gotten her to sleep in the nude. You sleep much better in the nude. I've told her that for years. I think she's finally beginning to believe me."

9
Haunted Ground

ON OUR first full day in St. Andrews my father and I strolled down to the first tee of the Old Course to watch 20-handicapper George Bush tee off.

It was a cool, overcast morning, and a large crowd had gathered in anticipation of seeing the former President. Standing in the crowd near the front steps of the Royal and Ancient's famous sandstone clubhouse, I heard snatches of several languages—French, Japanese, and someone who was clearly from Brooklyn. Bush, with his entourage of fellow Royal and Ancient members, finally appeared and waved to the crowd.

Bush, whose father was a U.S.G.A. president and whose maternal grandfather, George Herbert Walker, gave the prize cup to the international amateur matches that bear his name, teed up quickly and slapped a respectable little drive to the right side of the generous opening fairway. The crowd cheered.

After Bush and company were gone, Dad and I walked over to the little white starter's house to see if our names had made it through the Old Course daily ballot, but the results wouldn't be known until later that afternoon. We had several hours to fill up.

About 42,000 rounds a year are played on the Old Course, almost half of them reserved for the citizens of St. Andrews, an inalienable right they've enjoyed since Archbishop John Hamilton signed a decree in 1552 granting them unhindered access to the town's linksland—in effect, creating the world's first municipal golf course.

The balance of Old Course tee times are made available to visitors, but demand grew so fierce that Links Trust Management, which operates the town's six golf courses, was forced to institute a daily ballot drawing. Pilgrims who find they've made it through the daily ballot feel as if they've been granted a special dispensation from the gods. In the five or six times I'd played the Old Course, I'd never encountered the slightest difficulty getting a tee time. That's because I usually appeared alone and was penciled in to fill out some other group's foursome.

Officially, you're supposed to have a 28 handicap or better to get on the Old Course, evidenced by some kind of official documentation—a U.S.G.A. certificate, say, or a letter from one's home club pro—but visitors work diligently to subvert this essentially fair-minded system, producing letters from nonexistent pros back home or, in the case of some overzealous guests, submitting Scottish-sounding names in the doomed hope it will somehow improve their chances of acquiring a desired tee time.

My own method of subverting the system, if it came to that, was a caddie I knew named Bruce, who said he could make sure I got on the Old Course anytime I wanted. Bruce had carried the bags of lots of tour pros and famous folk. His office was a barstool at the pub beside the Old Course Hotel, and when Dad and I arrived there after watching George Bush tee off, Bruce was still out on the course with a client. I left a message for him to call me later at the Scores Hotel.

We took our pints out to the pub's little courtyard and stood overlooking the knoll where I'd first come and stared out at the Road Hole in the rain, twenty years ago. Dad sipped his beer and seemed pleased to be looking once again at this venerable, embattled turf. Then he turned to me and said, "Why is it so important for you to hook up with your friend Bruce?"

I explained that regardless of how we fared in the daily ballot, Bruce could probably make sure we got on the Old Course. He knew the right people and had proved helpful in the past.

"Why would you want to do that?" my father said, puzzled.

"That should be rather obvious. We didn't come all this way not to play the Old Course, did we?"

He thought for a moment. "Do you think it's fair if we ignore the rules and get to play the Old Course, while someone who follows them doesn't?"

"That's not the issue, Dad. The issue is, half those people don't really care about *playing* the Old Course. To them it's just a trophy, something to boast about back home." I felt like I was twelve years old, trying to explain that I'd only *glanced* at that week's spelling list, which Donnie Alberson had "somehow" gotten his hands on and passed around on the school bus.

"So why do you want to play it? You've played it plenty of times."

We looked at each other. It was me who finally blinked. I looked away, shrugged, and shook my head. I didn't agree with him, but he had a point. I had played it many times. Why was it so all-important now? Of course, I knew why. We both did. I was certain my father was going to say he had to go home after St. Andrews. It was possible, even likely, that any round on the Old Course would be our final round of golf together. It would be a fitting way to finish, but a finish is a finish, and that's what I feared most.

"If that's how you want it," I said. "We'll put all our hopes on the ballot."

"That's the only way I want it, and you would, too, if you'd just think about it."

We emptied our pint glasses and walked into the adjoining pro shop at the Old Course Hotel. The shop was full of American and Japanese customers who seemed to be clearing the shelves of any item bearing the St. Andrews logo. I purchased an Old Course ball cap for my son, and my father bought my mother a pin with the Saint Andrew's cross (a symbol later adopted by the Confederate States of America for use on their battle flag).

To kill more time, I suggested we take a stroll down to the Himalayas, the eccentric public putting course situated between the Old Course and the wide sand beach where filmmakers had shot the opening scenes of *Chariots of Fire*.

Dad walked a few paces and asked, "How's your beautiful wife doing these days?"

It was a gently loaded question. I knew he worried about my modern marriage, as he called it—the long hours and frequent travels and busy professional schedules Alison and I both kept, attempting to strike the proper balance between careers we loved and the full demands of parenthood. This was not an area of my life I was in any rush to open up for general floor discussion with my father, because I knew he didn't think unions where the partners poured as much of themselves into their work as their family life stood much hope of making it over the long haul.

In some respects my ten-year marriage to Alison seemed almost too perfect. She was beautiful, smart, funny, a great wife and mother. The ten years had whizzed past, and I could count the number of serious arguments we'd had on just one hand. Friends often commented how strong our relationship seemed. Lately, though, something had grown a bit fuzzy between us. We were both to blame. Alison was working more hours than ever, and I was feeling neglected and resentful. It had been many years since our last family vacation. My resentment, on the other hand, made her feel unloved and stretched even thinner. All we knew was that we loved each other and adored our kids.

But I didn't want to dump this complicated stuff on my father—especially now that his time was so limited.

So I kept to safe generalities. "She's fine. Working far too hard. But it seems to be what she wants right now." I explained that she'd just been made associate vice president of the college where she worked and that executive recruiters seemed to phone the house almost as frequently as telemarketing operators.

"I wish I could somehow slow you both down," he said, slipping into Opti mode. "Ambition is a kind of siren song. Especially in a job like yours. The danger of great ambition is that you'll work so hard you may someday wake up and find that the things you really wanted were the things you had all along."

As usual, he'd just put his finger on one of my biggest fears—the nagging worry that our thriving careers were gently wedging us apart. I said nothing.

"Well, in any case," he said, "give her a big kiss for me. You can never kiss your wife enough."

"I will," I assured him.

At the Himalayas, we played another thirty-six-hole match that I once again lost. Losing putting matches to my father next to the great golf courses of England and Scotland appeared to be my real dharma.

On the way back to the Scores we paused once again at the little white starter's shed to see the results of the ballot. Our names weren't on the list.

THAT evening I took my dad to a place I knew in the hills just east of town for dinner. The restaurant had a lovely view of the town and the sea. Its beams were low, the fire blazing. The barman brought two expensive French brandies (Churchill's favorite breakfast tipple) to the table. We considered how the world had changed since Dad's last visit to St. Andrews.

"The world has doubled twice in population, but polio and smallpox have been eliminated. That's real progress," Dad said.

"South Carolina built three hundred golf courses, posted legal speed limits, and outlawed marrying your sister," I volunteered. "That may be even greater progress."

"A glass of really good French brandy now goes for twenty bucks."

"How much was it in your day?"

"I don't know. Only Churchill could afford to drink the stuff."

My father grew quiet, scanning the menu. We both settled on Angus steaks.

"I'll tell you another way things have changed since I was over here," Dad said.

"How's that?"

"Back when I was a soldier over here, I used to wonder what it would be like to be a father." He was looking out the window at the roofs of the town. He turned his head to me and smiled. "Now I spend my days trying to remember."

Our dinners arrived, and the conversation shifted back to the war, to the months he spent running a small prisoner-of-war camp in Compiègne after the liberation of Paris. The camp was on the outskirts of the town where Joan of Arc's military career came to an end in 1430, and German prisoners were used to sort and pack up weapons, uniforms, and other materials the German army had

abandoned as it fled France in 1944. The camp, my father explained, had no fences to speak of, because the German soldiers
were weary of war and were receiving two hot meals a day. Out of
the sixty or so prisoners, there was only one card-carrying Nazi,
an unapologetic sergeant named Krauss.

"Krauss was a problem. He was Bavarian, a bully, and a real bel-
ligerent son of a bitch. We had to watch him pretty closely. The
captain who was really in charge of the camp was never around—
he had a girlfriend over in Soissons, the next village—so I made
most of the decisions. Krauss didn't like me very much, and I
didn't like him. You probably know that Compiègne was where
the Germans surrendered to end World War One. The first thing
Hitler did when he occupied France was order the railcar where
Germany had signed the Armistice in the forest of Compiègne to
be dismantled.

"You may not know, though, that the little rail station in Compiègne was used by the Nazis as the embarkation point for sending
French Jews to concentration camps. That's why there were so
many reprisal killings after the liberation. The Free French wanted
revenge on some of their own for collaborating with the Germans."

"How many people are we talking about?" I asked.

"I heard it was well over fifty thousand people. Men, women,
and children. Many of them came through Compiègne. A lot of
them were gassed. It was still fairly unknown what had happened.
But once locals started coming around to the camp, the story got
out pretty quick."

"Why'd locals come? To mock their German captives?"

"Goodness, no. They were starving and freezing to death. It was
almost winter. A lot of them were farmers who'd lost everything. I
remember one man who showed up with his little girl one morning in late November. He was barefoot, if you can imagine. I gave
him some German army boots and some sweaters and jackets. I
may have even given him a rifle and ammunition to hunt rabbits
with in the forest. He was so grateful. A few days later he showed
up with another child—a boy, slightly older. I gave him more boots
and clothes. I wish I could remember his name."

Dad thought for a moment. "He came back several times. He had six children. One day he brought me a giant mushroom he'd grown beneath his house. I remember how proud he was of it—how much he wanted me to have it. I had a cook named Walter slice it up and fry it. It was delicious. Our cooks had been German army cooks. Walter was just eighteen. Said he wanted to be a chef at the Paris Ritz someday. Had a wallet full of family pictures. His favorite thing was to read palms. He used to read my palm and tell me the same thing. He told me I would someday be very wealthy."

Dad smiled at the memory. "Fortunately, he cooked better than he read palms."

"Wasn't that against military regulations, giving boots and stuff away to civilians?" I asked.

"Sure it was. They could court-martial you for that. Nobody really cared, though. Everybody wanted the war to be over—everybody except maybe Krauss."

"What happened to him?"

Dad sighed. "I gave him to the Belgians."

"*Really?* Why?"

"As I said, Krauss and I had this thing going. He tried to get my goat by saying that Americans were weak people—too sentimental for our own good. That would be America's downfall. He never put a cork in it and always gave the Nazi salute. I finally told him if he gave me another Nazi salute, he would have to do it with his feet because his arms would be in plaster casts. His real gripe, though, was with the kid Walter. One day Krauss used a forklift to crush Walter to death against a wall. He thought nobody saw him do it. But his own soldiers turned him in. I personally marched the bastard to the town jail with a machine gun at his back. If he'd said anything, I might well have shot him right there. It just so happened that we had some Belgian underground fighters passing through on the way back to their country. I gave Krauss to them."

"A death sentence?"

"Probably."

"Did you regret it?"

"I've spent years wondering."

A large, cheerful waitress brought our steaks. She had a moun-tain of red hair piled on her head and gaps between her teeth, a Scottish Wife of Bath. "You two must be Americans," she insisted. "Americans always order the steak."

When she was gone, I said, "Something's just occurred to me. I'll bet you got your palm-reading thing from Walter."

One of Opti's oldest party tricks was to read palms.

Dad set his fork aside and sipped his Cognac. He nodded. "You may be right. I never really thought about it until now."

"I'll tell you something else you never thought about. You never read my fortune," I said. "Wrong gender, I guess."

"I guess." He ate some steak, then said, "Give me your hand."

I stuck out my hand, palm up.

He was always adept at reading the palms of attractive women. He told them outrageously positive things: "You are deeply admired for your loving intuition." "I see an extraordinary career in public service, perhaps an ambassadorship or the United States Senate." "I don't believe I've ever seen a more intriguing lifeline. Have you ever been to Khartoum during the rainy season?"

He studied my palm, continuing to nip at his Cognac.

"Am I going to be rich?" I asked. "Please don't tell me I should run for the Senate."

He shook his head. "This is very interesting."

"Interesting good or interesting bad?"

"Good and bad. You're already rich but may not realize it. I see other things."

"A hole in one? A new Chevy Blazer?"

He shook his head. "Those aren't important. I see some inter-esting changes coming in your life, some important connections of the heart you will finally make, things you will pass along to your children. Your children are your real job, you know."

"Right, right," I said impatiently. I saw the Wife of Bath closing fast from three o'clock.

"He's telling my fortune," I explained to her.

"Get on," she said smartly. "I thought he was proposing. Is he any good at it—the fortune-telling bit?"

"He predicted the end of the '80s and the demise of the leisure suit," I assured her. "Even before they happened."

"Brilliant. Would you care to do mine, love?"

"Delighted," Opti said, releasing my hand like a stone.

Her name was Beth. He told Beth of Bath she was going to have a long life, several gorgeous children, and a nice house by the sea and possibly would win some kind of big contest involving Border collies. "Good heavens, I *have* two Border collies," Beth shrieked deliriously, and went away to fetch our dessert puddings as if she'd just won the Scottish National Dog Trials.

"You sure know how to warm a big bonny lassie's heart," I said.

"That's my job," Opti said with a wink.

THE next morning we drove over to the nearby village of Elie and played the short but cunning links there, a gently elevated seaside course laid out in 1895. In my view the course is distinguished for two reasons. First, the links at Elie has never been closed in its entire history. Second, because the first hole is a blind tee shot over a steep hill, play cannot proceed from the first tee until a little man pops out of a shed that features a submarine periscope on top and announces, "Please play away, gentlemen." The periscope is used to make sure the forward grouping is safely out of cannon range.

The day was kind to us at Elie. The sea air heated up nicely, and Dad limped around to a highly respectable 91, while I managed 78 and seemed to be finding a respectable game.

We drove back to the Scores, and I phoned up the Links Trust and learned that our names had once again failed to make the Old Course tee-time list for the next day. There was a message from Bruce the caddie, though, and a phone number.

"This is ridiculous," I murmured, looking at Bruce's number, wondering if I shouldn't just call him and hope my father didn't find out. I wadded up the paper and tossed it into the wastebasket.

Dad came out of the bathroom, where he was running a tub of water for a bath. He was holding a Bible and the little leather notebook where he jotted down thoughts for his weekly men's Bible class. He'd been moderator of the class for fifteen years. I broke the news to him that we hadn't made the ballot once again.

"Well," he said, not particularly dismayed, "let's give it another day and see what happens."

He picked up his fountain pen and headed back to the bath.

"And then what?" I said, perhaps a bit sharper than necessary.

He paused and looked at me. "Well, I think after that, if we don't have any luck, Bo, it may be time for us to move along."

I said evenly, "You mean go home."

"Correct. I've got some things to do. We've had a great time. Let's give it one more day and keep our fingers crossed."

He disappeared into the bath, and I went out for a walk, and after a hike up to the remains of the town's old cathedral, I found myself standing above the stone steps leading down to the first tee at the Old Course, enviously watching the two final players of the day tee off. Darkness was perhaps only an hour or so away. The sleeves of my windbreaker flapped sharply in the wind. I stood there feeling more than a little sorry for myself, sulking the way I used to do when I was thirteen. We'd come all this way, I told myself, for naught.

Just then a voice behind me remarked, "I'm told golf has been played out there for almost five hundred years and that by law anyone is basically entitled to walk these public grounds."

My father was standing behind me, his windbreaker zipped to the chin and his St. Andrews cap tilted jauntily.

"That's the story they feed the public," I said. "The truth is, they remove any violators who haven't paid a proper green fee."

He gazed out at the old linksland. "Want to risk it? I thought I would at least take a stroll around the Old Course, just to see if the place has held up without me."

"I guess so. Sure."

By the time we reached the first hole, where the two players had just finished, the winds had slackened off a bit and the clouds had peeled back to permit a few rays of sun to spill across bay and linksland. Ahead of us I saw holes where nobody was playing—the wind or the cold had driven them off.

It's said you can really only see the glories of the Old Course at sunset, when shadows reveal the character of a piece of ground that has influenced the thinking of more golf-course architects than any other place on earth. The Old Course was built by no man, only shaped a bit, and it therefore abounds in eccentricity: massive double greens, crisscrossing fairways, target lines that seem to shift with the ever shifting sea winds or that don't exist at all. You aim for distant church steeples, nubs of fairway, eruptions of gorse. The dangers are mostly hidden from view. The Old Course has 112 bunkers, many of which are so well disguised and lethal that they have ominous monikers—Principal's Nose, Coffin, Grave, Hell. As a result of these factors and the ever present wind, you proceed cautiously and *learn* to play the Old Course perhaps more than any course on earth, your respect deepening with each circuit. "You have to study it," Bobby Jones advised. "And the more you study, the more you learn. The more you learn, the more you study."

We walked slowly all the way out to the Eden estuary, careful to keep well shy of greens and fairways where players were engaged, and eventually came to the eleventh green: the 172-yard par-three called High Hole, one of the most dangerous holes in all of golf. As a young man during his first Open in 1921, Jones finished the eleventh with a triple bogey, ripped up his card, and stalked off the course. The incident, though, had a transformative effect on Jones. He was so thoroughly ashamed of himself for quitting, he vowed to set the highest standard of sportsmanship for the rest of his career.

Since nobody was near the hole, my father and I stepped up to the tee. I explained that the Strath bunker had caught my ball several times and the green looked indecently puny with the Eden estuary spreading out behind it. Moreover, the wind usually came straight off the water, knocking anywhere from two to three lengths off your club. I'd tried everything from a six-iron to a two-iron at High Hole and almost always came away feeling low.

"Try it now," Dad said. "The wind is down."

I smiled at him. "I don't have a club."

"By all means," he replied, "use one of mine." He handed me an imaginary golf club.

It was another of Opti's little exercises.

"What is it?" I asked.

"What do you think you'll need?"

I looked at the hole. "Four-iron flush."

"It's a four, then. Hit it flush."

I took my stance and made a swing, finishing with my hands held high, as Jones used to do in his prime.

"That's the way," Dad said soothingly. "Think that little darling has a chance to go in the hole?"

"Not a chance," I said, and explained about my Hole-in-None Society plans.

"Oh, well," he replied mildly, "that makes two of us."

He motioned me to vacate the tee. A trio of fast-moving players who looked like local teenagers were closing from the tenth green. We walked off the tee and started to cut across the empty twelfth.

"I never knew you never scored an ace," I said. "Considering how well you play your irons, I guess I naturally assumed you had an ace—probably several."

He said, "Oh, I came close a few times. It just never seemed to be my moment. After a while I just quit worrying about it and accepted what the game gave me. That's the key to a good round of golf, you know—let it happen. Besides, if you don't have an ace, you always have something to look forward to."

On the way down the side of the twelfth fairway I told him about Laird Small and Spyglass Hill and the importance of learning to stay in NATO.

"That's a wonderful story," he said. "Someday you can pass it along to your kids."

"Was that what you meant last night when you cut short my palm reading? You said I would pass something important along."

"I wasn't talking about passing along your old Blazer, sport."

A plane flew low overhead, an old-fashioned biplane. It reminded me of the day all those years ago when a plane had flown over us at Green Valley, prompting Dad to mention Saint-Exupéry and opening a brand-new world to me.

"Tell me something," I said. "Why did you give up flying?"

This was something else I'd never thought to ask my father. He smiled and shoved his hands into his windbreaker.

"It's a funny story. Or maybe it's not so funny. I almost killed myself and your brother."

"You're joking." It seemed to be an evening for revelations.

"Unfortunately not."

He told me the tale. One day in the early spring, when my brother was about a year old, my father decided to introduce his firstborn to the joys of flying. He strapped him into the seat of a Cessna plane and took off to visit an old friend at an airfield near Chapel Hill.

"I wanted to show him my brand-new son," Dad said, "and I thought Dickie would get a thrill out of the ride. The thrill was a bit more than I anticipated."

After taking off for the forty-mile return trip to Greensboro, the plane suffered a sudden power loss and began to lose altitude. Dad sensed a fuel-line blockage and began desperately trying to fix the problem but couldn't.

"We were barely flying over the tops of the trees," he remembered. "I was looking everywhere for a place to put her down, but there wasn't a field or road that looked right. I couldn't figure out what the hell was wrong."

"Did you think you were going to die?"

"Sure. That goes through your head. Mostly I was thinking about your brother. How damned unfair it was if we crashed and he died."

"What'd you do?"

"Flew along trying to avoid treetops and plowed-up fields. A freshly plowed field in the spring, you see, gives off cold air. Old-time aviators were terrified of freshly plowed fields. They can knock you right out of the air. I followed roads and fallow fields. We zigzagged all over the place."

"But you made it back."

"Yep. That's when I found the problem. I'd forgotten to switch on the heater that keeps the carburetor from freezing up. It was a beginner's mistake. But if I was making mistakes like that—risking my own son's life—I told myself it was time to quit. I thanked the good Lord for getting us back in one piece, took your brother home to his mother, and never flew again."

"That's quite a story," I said. "Did you ever miss flying?"

"Not really." We walked a few paces, and he added, "Well, yes, I did. But life goes forward, doesn't it? You trade this for that." He smiled. "I did fantasize, though, about taking your mother up in a hot-air balloon sometime. I pictured us floating around up there with a good bottle of French Champagne, smooching a bit, singing old love songs from the war." He fell silent, then said, "Well, well. Look here, Bo."

We were standing on the seventeenth tee of the Old Course. The Road Hole. The sun was gone, the air was cold, a few stars were visible above the clouds, and there were lights on in the Old Grey Toon.

"This is where I wish we had our *real* clubs," I said.

"Aw, who needs 'em?" Dad said. "Let's play anyway."

"You're right," I agreed. "We could play air golf with the ghosts of St. Andrews the way I played air guitar with the Beatles. Please play away, Mr. Dodson."

Dad teed up his air Top-Flite, took his stance, and swung. "There," he said. "Right over the sheds. Just like fifty years ago."

I teed up my air Titleist and asked, "How fast did that fifty years go by?"

"Stick around. You won't believe it."

I struck my shot and outdrove him, as usual, by at least a hundred yards.

We walked down the darkened fairway side by side. For a change, I wasn't really thinking about all the greats who had walked this way to immortality: Jones and Snead, Nicklaus and Lema, Ballesteros and Faldo. I was thinking, instead, how simply fine and proper it was that my old man and I were finally playing the Road Hole together. Now came Opti and son.

From the heart of the fairway Dad used an air three-wood to lay up short of the infamous Road Hole bunker. From the left rough I swatted a beautiful air four-iron to the lower half of the green. We were playing our own games, if I may say so, magnificently.

He walked up to his air ball, just shy of the bunker, and announced he was using his air sand wedge, then lofted his ball sweetly to the green, stopping it within a few feet of the cup.

"Very nice," I said. "Before we putt out, though, tell me about your birdie."

He looked at me, then nodded solemnly at the bunker.

It took a few seconds for me to realize what he was telling me. He'd somehow made birdie from the Road Hole bunker!

"That's unbelievable," I said, shaking my head. "I've never heard of anybody doing that."

"It came as a major shock to me, too."

I demanded that he describe in detail this miraculous little feat. He said the details were kind of foggy, but he seemed to think the hole was considerably different then. "For one thing, the bunker was shallower than it is now. The sod wall was nowhere near as high as it is here. You could escape pretty easily with a decent shot." He stepped closer, sizing up the wall, which was higher than a man's head. "I don't see how anybody could come out of this thing." He added that the pin he'd shot at fifty years ago was on the lower half of the green. The greens were thicker grass in those days, before modern lawn mowers.

"You still made a hell of a shot," I said to him. "And it wasn't an air ball."

"No," he said a little wistfully, "it wasn't. Sometimes, though, it takes on the quality of a dream. Perhaps I simply imagined it."

"No," I said, "not a chance."

We putted out quickly. I made an uncharacteristically fine air lag from the lower part of the green and tapped in for four—a brilliant air par. Dad sank a clutch five-footer to halve the hole.

"Two air pars on the hardest hole in golf," I said as we shook hands.

We walked to the eighteenth tee, struck fine drives into the

darkness, then moseyed down the fairway of the most famous
finishing hole in golf, crossing the little arched stone bridge. For
weeks I'd been so fearful of this moment, anticipating how
awful I would feel when it finally arrived. But strangely, I wasn't
the least bit sad now. I was *cold* as blazes but almost unnaturally
happy to be finishing a round of golf that only I would ever
remember. No card would ever show the score. Our match would
vanish into the air.

"Call me sentimental if you like," my father said, taking my arm
as we approached the Valley of Sin, the dangerous swale that
guards the front of the eighteenth green. "I think it's been a hell
of a journey."

"You're just being sentimental," I replied. "The showers were
much worse than expected."

"You're talking about the trip," he said. "I'm talking about the
journey."

THE next morning I drove my father to the airport in Edinburgh for a dawn commuter flight to London. We decided to
leave St. Andrews before finding out if we'd made it through the
Old Course ballot that third day. Nothing could have topped the
round of air golf we'd played the evening before.

On the way to the airport my father proposed to me that I finish our golf trip alone, push on to France to see what I could find.
I told him that was pointless without him, but by the time we'd
crossed the Forth Road Bridge, he'd persuaded me to change my
mind. I agreed to go on for another week or so.

At the airport, a boisterous group of Scottish teenagers was
headed for Texas, whooping it up excitedly, while moist-eyed parents were desperately attempting to check bags, collect hugs, and
issue brilliant nuggets of travel wisdom. It vaguely reminded me
of the day my father drove me to the airport to fly to Europe for
the first time.

I kissed my father on the cheek, and he kissed me. We hugged,
and then he was walking away, leaving a whiff of his Aramis after-
shave, falling in step with a gawky fifteen-year-old girl carrying a

Pearl Jam backpack and a small black boom box. I saw him speak to her and saw her turn her head to a friend—a shorter girl, on her right. Both girls giggled, and then the shorter girl skipped around to my father's unaccompanied side and took his arm. I half expected to see her stick out her palm.

Opti was up to his old tricks.

10
La Forêt de l'Amour

Six weeks later my father suffered a stroke.

I was seated beside him at the Thanksgiving table in Greensboro when food suddenly started tumbling out of his mouth. I remember looking at Alison; she looked so sad.

By the time we got him to the emergency room at the hospital, his blood pressure was two hundred over sixty, a runaway train. They placed us in a curtained alcove.

"What are we doing here?" Dad quietly asked me.

I took his hand. It was unusually cold. "Waiting for a guy to come check out your heart," I said.

"Oh." He added calmly, "Where's your mother?"

I explained she was out in the emergency-room lobby harassing the hospital staff, trying to separate the heart specialist from his Thanksgiving dinner.

"Is it Thanksgiving?" he asked.

"Yep." I explained I knew it was Thanksgiving because we'd played golf that morning at Sedgefield. On the nation's turkey day some American males traditionally watch football; we play golf. I was pleased our actual final round hadn't been at St. Andrews but at Sedgefield, where he'd first walked onto a golf course as a caddie seventy years ago. We'd finished where he'd begun the game.

"How'd we do?"

I said we did okay. The course had been deserted. I shot 79. He'd played every other hole—made some nice putts, as usual.

He asked me where I'd been traveling. I explained that I'd just come from Fort Worth, where I'd spent a nice afternoon talking with Byron Nelson for a piece I was writing for *Golf.*

"You have a job men would die for," he whispered.

"Are you trying to get my job?"

He managed a dim smile. "Funny boy. Keep that sense of humor. You'll need it." He closed his eyes and then opened them again.

"Tell me about France," he said.

I hadn't brought up the trip to him while we were playing that day. I pulled up a chair and sat down, still holding his hand.

In France, I said, I rented a car and drove to Compiègne, checked into a small hotel next to the medieval city's main bridge and the train station where the Germans, I soon learned, deported close to 80,000 French Jews to concentration camps during the war. On my second day in town I visited Napoleon's sprawling summer palace and went searching in the vast adjoining royal forest for the beech tree where Dad had once carved my mother's initials.

"Did you find the tree?" Dad asked.

"I think so."

I explained that I'd found a broad lane vanishing into the yellow forest, but thousands of lovers' initials were carved into the skins of the ancient beeches, decades of declared amour. It had seemed fairly hopeless. After an hour or so of searching, though, I'd come upon what appeared to be "JKD" and another set of illegible initials, encased by a crude heart and the date 1945, halfway up a large, leaning beech. I decided this must be it—even if it wasn't. I opened my Swiss army knife and carved my own and my wife's initials and the date below them.

As I worked, an elderly man in a wool topcoat came shuffling down the gravel path. He stopped, leaned on his cane, and watched me finish the carving. He was shabbily elegant: brown felt bowler, cashmere wool scarf. He made a comment in French. I explained to him that my French was very poor. He nodded and smiled with brown, broken teeth. *"C'est la forêt de l'amour,"* he declared, waving his arm expansively. The Forest of Love.

After that, pleased by my discovery, I'd strolled farther into the beautiful forest till I came to a small creek, a pretty wooden bridge, and a row of bushy poplar trees. I saw a patch of green beyond the trees, and white rail fences. I pushed through the limbs and stepped out onto the grass just as I heard a solid metallic thwack and someone shouting angrily in French. I turned and saw two men thirty yards away, gesturing furiously at me. They were holding golf clubs. One of them had just fired his tee shot a few yards over my head. I'd stumbled out of the Forest of Love onto the Golf Club of Compiègne.

I apologized as best I could and hurried toward a white stucco beamed structure that I assumed was the clubhouse. I found an attractive middle-aged lady who hadn't a clue what I was saying.

"You see Dick," she said.

"Dick?"

"Yes, Dick." She bustled away. I went into the bar and ordered a Coke. Soon a robust-looking gray-haired man rambled in with an attractive woman by his side. "I hear we've been invaded by the Americans again," he said, offering a brisk handshake. Dick Di Salle, the club's *président sportif,* introduced me to his wife, Rolande. We found a table and ordered venison sausage for lunch. I learned Dick and Rolande had met just after the liberation when Dick, a first lieutenant from Colorado who arrived in France three months after D-day, helped set up a hospital in nearby Soissons.

I explained that he'd arrived about the same time as my father. "I remember the camp," Dick said. Rolande talked about the horrors of the German occupation, and Dick explained how he'd met the love of his life and decided to build a life in France. I asked them about the handsome golf course outside. "It was here during the war," Dick said. "You just couldn't see it. The Germans parked their trucks on it, and the Allies later bombed it." He said a bunker on the eleventh hole (near the spot where I'd barged onto the course) was in fact the remains of an old American bomb crater.

It was an unexpectedly bountiful day. As I left, the Di Salles urged me to come back again someday with my father or my wife or my children.

I drove on to Paris and checked into a small hotel behind the Opéra and walked around the City of Light for a day, thinking about my father and his great affection for the French and their famous river city. On my last night in Paris, clear and cold and starry, I sat on a set of wooden bleachers by the Arc de Triomphe and watched a parade of World War II veterans from Britain, France, and America pass in review beneath the arch, elderly men with too tight uniforms and forgotten medals pinned to their chests, shuffling down the Champs-Elysées.

The next morning I flew home.

MY FATHER was sleeping now, taking very shallow breaths, still holding my hand. I wasn't sure how much of this he'd even heard.

He did not die, though I had honestly expected him to.

Instead, he pulled off another small resurrection feat. Two weeks later, after a brief restless rest, he went back to work with only a faint slur in his speech, cracking jokes about tippling on the job.

For Christmas he took my mother to the Grove Park Inn, F. Scott Fitzgerald's old Smoky Mountains haunt. Our evening phone call once caught them breathless. They'd been hoofing to Benny Goodman in the den while Molly, the dog, chaperoned from Dad's favorite armchair. They behaved like two people caught up in the first blush of courtship.

My father went to Florida for his annual winter sales meeting. His territory, as usual, was one of the top earners in the country. He was already a sales legend in his company but had plans to expire in harness.

Two days later he came home and went straight into the hospital. I flew south to be with him.

Steve Blieveneick, my father's longtime friend and a brilliant cancer specialist, asked me to step out of the hospital room. "I've almost never seen anyone with cancer so pervasive," he said. "It's everywhere. His pelvis. Intestines. Liver. His back. I don't have a clue how he's gone on this long. The man should have been dead months ago. Your father astounds me."

He looked me straight in the eyes.

"We're in God's realm now. The medical Establishment is basically helpless at this point. Your dad's a racehorse. When he decides it's time to go, I have a hunch he'll go the way he lived—no complaints, no questions. I'd like you to be there."

I assured him a stable of racehorses couldn't drag me away.

"Good."

An ambulance brought Dad home from the hospital. We set him up in a special bed in my old room and learned to take care of him. Together my brother Dick and I became his late-night companions. With Dad we became couch potatoes and watched the NCAA basketball season drawing to a close. The U.N.C. Tarheels were playing tough. Dad, turning grayer by the day, was pleased.

I drove out of town to do a bit of work. Four hours to the east, in Wilmington, I sat down with Ike Grainger, the famous U.S.G.A. rules official. Grainger had just turned one hundred years old, and my piece on him—a man who had made some of the most critical rulings in many of the biggest matches in the history of the game—was for the centennial edition program of the U.S. Open, which was to be held at Shinnecock Hills in June.

That night, as Dad and I sat watching basketball, I told him some of what Grainger and I had discussed—how the rule of equity is the heart and soul of golf, how whenever there's no formal rule to cover a situation or dispute, you must try and do what's most fair. I said how much Grainger's love of the game had reminded me of his. I also told my father I wished he could accompany me to Shinnecock.

"Maybe I'll get out of this contraption and we'll go," he said quietly, thumping the arm of the wheelchair. I said I'd be pleased to arrange the passes.

"I'm sorry for so much trouble," he added, coughing dryly, shifting uneasily in his chair.

"It's no trouble, Dad."

"You'll just never know how much I loved you all."

"We love you, too." My mother had quietly appeared in the kitchen doorway, dressed in her quilted bathrobe, the overhead light shining behind her, fingers to her throat. She was helpless to do anything but wait. My father didn't see her. She was crying. She turned and went back to bed.

A little while later Dad said, "You know what I'd really like, Jim? I'd like to crawl in bed with your mother."

"You got it."

I woke up my mother and carried my father to their bed. Switching off the light, I heard my mother planting soft kisses on her husband's face. Her voice had a girlish cant. "You scoot over here, hon, and let's snuggle, just you and me. *There* now. Warm enough?" His reply possessed more strength than I had heard or seen for days. "Yes. Thanks. Delighted to be in bed with you."

"My goodness, sweetie, you need a shave."

The next day he asked me to give him a shave.

I shaved my father with his own safety razor, slipping glances at his eyes. His pale gray eyes were even paler, further away. They made me think of Gorky's description of the dying Tolstoy: "He listens attentively as though recalling something which he has forgotten, or as though for something new and unknown."

BUDDHISTS and Native American people believe the way a person dies tells the story of how he lived. To them, dying is a living art, the beginning of further passage to something new and unknown.

For a change I tried not to think too much about the future—what was going to happen to my mother after my father was gone, how our lives would change, how I would feel. I simply could not imagine a world without my father in it. As long as your father is alive, someone said, you will always be a son.

The lonely overnight cable vigils with my father and brother continued. We watched an old Jeff Chandler western together, followed by an infomercial for Hollywood psychics. By then Dick was asleep. I knew this was hitting him very hard. He had just gone through a difficult divorce and was working to keep my father's business together.

My father finally dozed off, too. I carried him to bed, and he opened his eyes. "What are you doing here?" he asked, surprised.

"Putting you in your bed."

"I don't want to be in this bed."

"I know. But you need to rest, and I'm supposed to make sure you get some."

He asked me why I was being so mean to him.

"I'm not being mean," I said. "I love you."

"Why don't you go paint the house," he suggested.

"Okay. What color shall I paint it?"

"Carolina blue."

I smiled. "Are you sure?"

"Yes." A loyal Tarheel to the end. I sat on the edge of the bed until he was asleep, mulling it over.

The next day, a Friday, his mind was already somewhere new and unknown. Certain mystics believe that a calm, meditative state as death approaches is the closest a human being can get to true enlightenment. When my father asked me where we were, I explained we were still inside our house on Dogwood Drive.

"No," he said with great conviction. "There's grandfather's gate." He was smiling at the wall but seeing a gate in his grandfather's pasture.

I looked at the wall and said, "Oh, yeah. How 'bout that." He asked me for some water, and I brought it. Taking a sip, he said, "That's good spring water. We have an excellent well, don't we?"

"The best," I agreed.

That night the heavy rain turned to sleet, glass shards bouncing off the mullioned windows. Around midnight Dad sat up. "Did you paint the house yet?" he asked.

I noticed his lips were making little pursing movements. "What are you doing?" I asked, not really expecting an answer. He replied with a peaceful whisper, "Kissing the babies."

Bill Mims and Bob Tilden, Dad's oldest golf pals, dropped by.

They seemed pleased to hear that Dad had thought of them one day at Turnberry.

That night, a rain-swept Sunday, Dad opened his eyes and looked at me. I was surprised by his sudden alertness.

"Hey, Opti," I said.

"I was just thinking about something. You should take Jack and Maggie to Shinnecock instead of me. They would love that."

"We'll see."

"Good." He nodded, closed his eyes, and then opened them again as if he'd remembered something. "Is that rain?" he said.

"Yes."

"Don't worry. It'll be fine in the morning. Go kiss your wife."

I assured him I wasn't worried. I said I would kiss my wife. These were the last words I heard my father say.

LIFE separates us too soon. That's what my father had said on the road to Scotland.

In the days following Opti's funeral, as I got back to the busy routines of my own work and family life, I thought perhaps my father and I had luckily escaped this fate. Perhaps we hadn't been separated too soon. After all, we'd had forty years to be together, two and a half decades to play as golf pals, and the golf trip of a lifetime to finish up the day. As far back as I could remember, there wasn't a moment when I doubted my father's love, a moment when he failed to express his love or help me when I asked for it.

This was far more than most men get, I told myself. We'd gone the full distance, finished the round, and said what needed saying. After a life rich with memories, my father had died a peaceful death at the same age as Buddha, seeing in the afterlife, perhaps, a beloved pasture from his childhood or—who knows?—a beautiful golf course waiting with an open first tee.

For a while these things sustained me and gave me strength. Life got back to normal. In many respects it even got better. For our tenth anniversary my wife gave me a beautiful concert-quality classical guitar. For that same anniversary I sent my overworked working wife to one of the most exclusive health spas in the world to be fed gerbil-size portions of inedible vegetarian goo and force-marched into the hills by an aerobics lunatic. It was her idea of heaven.

The spring that tentatively showed itself in Carolina finally crept north to Maine. I went out with my regular pals and shot 75 in my very first outing. I had a new putter like the one I'd used as a kid, and I was also trying once again to lead with the left hand and putt like a kid. It seemed to be making more balls mysteriously roll into the hole. My scores began to inch down scarily. Had I found some missing element of my game?

I was still trying to figure that out on Masters Sunday, when my daughter and son surprised me by asking to go play golf. I wanted to stay home and watch the Masters finish because (a) it's my job, and (b) two players I greatly admire, Davis Love and Ben Crenshaw, were neck and neck coming down the stretch.

Instead, I took my kids to the golf course. Jack saw the gas carts sitting by the clubhouse and begged to take one, and Maggie quickly joined the beggar's chorus. They politely endured my Sophoclean lecture on the Virtues of Walking in Golf, then pleaded shamelessly again for a riding cart. The assistant pro agreed to let us take one but demanded we stick to the back nine, which was drier.

We drove to the tenth tee. I love the back nine at my club, the original nine of the club. I struck a decent drive off ten and agreed to let Jack drive the cart for the first hole. He popped onto the seat, jammed down the accelerator, and nearly tossed both his sister and me out onto the ground. We careened wildly for a moment or two until I could get a hand clamped safely onto the steering wheel. Jack grinned at me. "I love golf," he declared. And then a few yards farther along he added, "When does hockey begin again, Dad?"

For years I'd hoped I might raise the next Tom Watson. Perhaps the next Bobby Orr was really more like it.

If only to humor his old man, though, Jack took his club up onto the tenth green and putted out the first hole, then picked up his ball and scampered back to preserve his driver's rights behind the wheel. Maggie made a nice little chip shot from off the fringe that rolled to within ten feet of the cup. I congratulated her. She picked up her putter and walked over to her ball, looked once at the hole, then rapped a ball that nearly went into the cup. I congratulated her again. We high-fived and went to the next hole.

As we played, a couple things kept crowding into my head, distracting me from the pleasure of the moment. I was naturally wondering about the Masters and only hoped my video recorder was running properly.

I was also troubled by a dream I'd just had. In it, I'd forgotten the sound of my own father's voice. I woke up in a fierce sweat and realized I'd been weeping. Unable to go back to sleep, I sat in a chair by the window, struck by the powerful reality that I would never again be able simply to pick up the phone and call my father and hear him laugh and say he was going to pin my ears back. I remember sitting in that chair thinking I was no longer a *son*.

It was grief pouring forth, though it took me a while to fully recognize and accept that. Sometime after the dream, at the suggestion of a friend, I actually went and sat in a quiet upstairs room with a friendly family sociologist named Herman. We talked for several weeks about childhood, marriage, and fathers, about how mothers give us life and fathers help define us. He helped me see that a man is never finished being a son—and he never leaves the influence of his father's life behind.

During our last session he said, "Your father gave you something very useful, but you may not even be aware of it yet."

"What's that?"

"A gift for letting go. He showed you the value of accepting life and the importance of letting it go. When it's time, you'll do it. You'll hear his voice again."

We stood and shook hands. Herman suggested I think of making some final act of closure that Opti would have appreciated.

I thanked Herman for his help. I still couldn't hear my father's voice, but I walked out feeling better.

NONE OF THIS WAS APPARENT TO me on that unnaturally warm Masters Sunday with my kids, though. The pain of the dream was still too fresh. And yet something happened that had Opti's invisible hands all over it.

We played a couple holes and skipped a couple holes. Jack seemed to be confusing golf with formula car racing. Maggie, on the other hand, dropped several lengthy putts that had her glowing and me beaming. I told her she reminded me of her grandfather.

Something about the fine afternoon and being away from the world with my kids began to soothe me. Maybe it was the angle of the light or the general emptiness of the course that seemed to recall that wonderful day at Muirfield with my father and Archie Baird.

Something amazing, at any rate, happened when Maggie and I walked off the sixteenth green to where Jack the chauffeur sat impatiently. We climbed aboard, and he nudged me gently in the ribs. He smiled up at me and suggested that I scoot over. I asked him why, thinking maybe I was cramping his driving style.

"For Granddaddy," he answered matter-of-factly.

I looked at him.

"What?"

"For Granddaddy," he repeated calmly. "He's riding with us."

I stared at my five-year-old son, unable to speak. Then his sister let out one of her infectious belly laughs, and I laughed, too.

"Jack's such a goof," she said.

"Do you believe Granddaddy's riding with us?" I asked her.

She looked at Jack and then at me and then grinned. A child's belief is so strong you can almost feel it. She was missing four teeth.

"Sure," she replied, as if that much should be obvious even to a dolt like me. "And you know what else?"

"What?"

"You sound like Granddaddy. Especially when you sneeze."

"*Really?*" I said.

"Uh-huh."

Slipping my arms around both my children, I felt a powerful

stinging in my eyes. I couldn't yet hear my father's voice, but I could hear his words. Long ago, on a golf course that was no longer there, he'd told me to open my eyes and see the glory of the world. The way to heaven, he said, is heaven.

At that same moment, about 1200 miles away, Ben Crenshaw had won his second Masters. I confess I wasn't thinking about events in Georgia, though. I was thinking about . . . well, finally, nothing but *this*. It felt wonderful.

"Okay, pal," I said. "Let 'er rip."

And with that, we careered wildly down the fairway.

LIFE, Thoreau said, is a great circle sailing.

Three months after my father's death I found myself once again hurrying down from the Scores to the Old Course with my golf bag slung on my back. I was back in the Old Grey Toon to gather material for an essay about the upcoming Open championship.

I decided to go out late so I could loiter on the course, and the starter was kind enough to match me up with the final group of the day, an unlikely trio of lively Australians. One of them was dressed like Crocodile Dundee, complete with rolled-up jeans and working boots. Another was a budding golf writer named Paul. The third was a physician on vacation.

We played an amusingly erratic round, firing shots all over the place. Paul the golf writer played best, going out to the Eden estuary in 41 before blistering the home march with a succession of brilliant birdies and pars. I settled in to play my usual humdrum Old Course game—a par here, a triple bogey there—trying not to think too much about what was coming up.

As we approached the Road Hole bunker on the seventeenth hole, I pulled a small blue velvet satchel out of my golf bag and began undoing the silken cords. The others watched solemnly. I'd warned them what was coming—my real reason for playing in the final group of the day. "You guys look like the three other horsemen of the Apocalypse," I said to them. "Please show a little proper disrespect." I told them my old man had said golf is a game that made you smile. "So please smile, damn it."

As they smiled, I slowly scattered my father's cremated ashes around the Road Hole bunker and dumped some into the sand itself. A circle in my life had finally been completed and perhaps, as I felt that day with my kids on Masters Sunday, another larger one had begun.

My new Aussie mates and I finished the Road Hole with bogeys and walked to the eighteenth tee. I don't remember a lot of talking. The darkness had caught up to us. We teed up and finished the hole and shook hands. I can't for the life of me remember what I scored on the hole. I was definitely in NATO.

I walked slowly up to my hotel, with a mind that was remarkably at ease for the first time in a very long time. Then I decided to walk back and just look at the Old Course in the darkness.

Halfway down the hill a boy passed, headed the other way—a fellow late-finisher. He was maybe eleven or twelve, hurrying home to dinner with his head bent and his bag on his back. He looked up as we passed, his clubs softly clicking. I thought of myself headed home from Green Valley. I thought of Jack maybe someday playing here with his old man.

"Did you shoot a good one?" I asked.

"Not so good, sir," he admitted. "Me driver's a wee bit off."

"That's okay," I said. "Enjoy it. The game ends too soon, you know."

"Right. Thanks."

He walked on, and I walked, and then I stopped. That's when I realized I'd heard it—my father's voice.

I smiled. Opti was back.

About the Authors

WALTER CRONKITE is still trying to get a handle on what he calls "this so-called retirement business." He continues to accept speaking dates and writing assignments that, he says, "tie me up and keep me from having a totally carefree life." Splitting his time between homes in New York City and Martha's Vineyard, Cronkite also tries to squeeze in time to pursue his love of sailing. And he is considering writing a sequel to *A Reporter's Life*. So chances are the carefree days of retirement are still in the future for this reporter.

Poet, essayist, and naturalist **DIANE ACKERMAN** may be familiar to television viewers as host of *Mystery of the Senses*, a PBS series based on her best-selling book, *A Natural History of the Senses*. Her nature writing has appeared in *National Geographic*, *The New York Times*, and *Parade*, and she has received numerous literary prizes and awards. She is presently at work on a series of nature books for children. She has earmarked a portion of her royalties from *A Slender Thread* to go to the crisis center where she volunteers.

JEFFREY TOOBIN has long combined his talents for law and writing. At Harvard Law School, where he graduated magna cum laude in 1986, he was an editor of the *Harvard Law Review*. He later served as a staff prosecutor in the Iran-contra hearings, which led to his 1991 behind-the-scenes book, *Opening Arguments: A Young Lawyer's First Case—United States v. Oliver North*. He also served as an assistant U.S. attorney in Brooklyn, New York, before joining *The New Yorker* in 1993 as a staff writer specializing in legal issues. Toobin lives in Manhattan with his wife and two children.

JAMES DODSON, a contributing editor of *Golf* magazine, won the Golf Writers of America Award for his columns in 1995. His work has appeared in many national publications, including *Reader's Digest, Outside, Travel & Leisure,* and *Yankee*. He is working on his next book, *Faithful Travelers,* which recounts the six-week summer trip he made last year with his daughter, Maggie— a cross-country camping and fishing adventure that took the two of them from their home in Maine to Old Faithful in Yellowstone National Park.

Today's Best Nonfiction is issued every two to three months. The typical volume contains four outstanding books in condensed form. Any reader may receive this service by writing The Reader's Digest Association, Inc., Pleasantville, N.Y. 10570 or by calling 800-234-9000.

Visit our Web site at http://www.readersdigest.com